971

EX-LIBRIS
Robert L. Reiner

H.U.C. J.I.R. N.Y.
WITHDRAWN FROM COLLECTION

Rabbinic Essays
BY
JACOB Z. LAUTERBACH

This volume is a publication of the Alumni Association of the Hebrew Union College-Jewish Institute of Religion. It is made possible through the quinquennial fund of the Association.

Rabbinic Essays
BY
JACOB Z. LAUTERBACH

HEBREW UNION COLLEGE PRESS

CINCINNATI ◊ 1951

Copyright, 1951, by
Hebrew Union College Press.

PRINTED IN THE UNITED STATES OF AMERICA
PRESS OF Maurice Jacobs INC.
224 N. 15th ST., PHILADELPHIA 2, PENNA.

Table of Contents

	PAGE
Foreword	vii
Julian Morgenstern	
A Note on the Editing of the Essays..................	xi
Lou H. Silberman	
Jacob Zallel Lauterbach — An Appreciation............	xiii
Solomon B. Freehof	
Bibliography of the Writings of Jacob Z. Lauterbach.....	3
Walter E. Rothman	
The Sadducees and Pharisees (1913).................	23
A Significant Controversy between the Sadducees and the Pharisees (1927)................................	51
The Pharisees and their Teachings (1929).............	87
Midrash and Mishnah (1915)........................	163
The Ethics of the Halakah (1913)....................	259
Tashlik (1936)....................................	299
The Sabbath (MS).................................	437
Jesus in the Talmud (MS)..........................	473

Foreword

ACCORDING to Pirķe Abot, 1.1 the "Men of the Great Assembly" were wont to guide their professional conduct by a self-imposed, tripartite charge: "Be cautious in rendering judicial decisions, raise up many disciples, and erect a fence for the Torah." It would seem that Jacob Z. Lauterbach, a worthy, spiritual disciple of these "Men of the Great Assembly," guided his entire professional life and service by these same three consecrating principles.

He was always exceedingly cautious and reserved in formulating and announcing scientific conclusions. He would test his evidence and chain of argument again and again. He delighted to discuss his theses with a few chosen friends, in whose scholarly ability and integrity he reposed confidence. And just as he gave unselfishly of his own vast store of knowledge, so he welcomed eagerly and weighed receptively information and suggestions which might have import for his own studies. He was truly an open-minded and responsible scholar, who stamped the impress of his scholarship and of his friendly lovable, personality deeply and beneficently upon his generation.

For thirty-one years, 1911-1942, he was Professor of Talmud at the Hebrew Union College. True, he retired from active teaching, formally and at his own request, in 1934; but it was perhaps during the eight years of his retirement, the last six of which he spent in living quietly and happily in the College Dormitory, that he exerted the most potent influence of his entire College career in shaping the thinking, habits and professional destinies of the students. During this period they came, literally, to idolize him. His straightforwardness, his humanness, his profound devotion to Judaism and the Jewish people, and his enthusiasm for his beloved Talmud were contagious. Many appreciative and grateful students he inducted into the seeming mystery of Talmudic lore. And in truth he raised up many disciples, five in particular, at least two of whom he was privileged in time to have as his associates upon the Faculty of the College. What truer testimony than this to the inherent greatness of a creative scholar and teacher!

And to the exalted task of erecting a fence for the Torah his entire scholarly life of over forty years was dedicated, dedicated with unsurpassed fidelity and joy. He could hardly be considered a prolific writer. The caution and reserve of his scholarship forbade that. But almost every one of his published studies was momentous, illumined some important and perplexing problem of Jewish belief, practice or tradition. By the resultant clarification of the historic unfolding of Judaism's basic institutions, ceremonies, sects, ritual and literature he integrated Judaism's proud past with its hopeful future, deepened Jewish faith and loyalties, stimulated Jewish scholarship, and awakened enthusiasm for reverent, intelligent and progressive Jewish life in the modern world. He was an ardent lover of Torah; and for the countless disciples of his teaching and his spirit he made the Torah a veritable "tree of life."

Among his effects, after his death, were found two manuscripts, almost ready for publication, one dealing with the weighty theme, "The Sabbath in Jewish Ritual and Folk-Lore," and the other with the no less timely question, "Jesus in the Talmud." Also copies of various of his published studies were discovered, carefully annotated by himself, and with their scientific value considerably enhanced thereby. These two manuscripts and the most important of the published studies with his annotations are collected in this volume.

The editing of these manuscripts and annotated studies has been a work of love and devotion by three of his closest disciples, Rev. Dr. Solomon B. Freehof (H. U. C. 1915), Rev. Dr. Bernard J. Bamberger (H. U. C. 1926), and Rev. Dr. Lou H. Silberman (H. U. C. 1941). It was a responsible and by no means easy task. It is not surprising that nine years should have been needed for its completion. In all their labors the editors have been animated by a constant affection for and loyalty to the memory of their teacher. Now, with the preparation of this

FOREWORD ix

volume, they have, with almost filial piety, erected a worthy monument of dignity and honor to a noble man and a distinguished Jewish scholar.

The Hebrew Union College Press rejoices in the privilege of publishing this volume as a memorial of one who played no small role in its establishment some thirty or more years ago, and whose name and spirit will abide firmly in the minds and hearts of his colleagues of the Faculty and of his many pupils for blessing and inspiration.

JULIAN MORGENSTERN, *President Emeritus*

April 25, 1951.

A Note on the Editing of the Essays

OF THE eight essays included in this volume, six have been published previously and two are here presented for the first time. The six that have already appeared have their date of publication noted so that the reader may discover the place and occasion of their appearance as well as other pertinent data by referring to the Bibliography. Except for the insertion of a number of notes which the author himself had made on the margins of the author's copies of these papers, a task undertaken by Dr. Solomon B. Freehof who was able to cope with the intricacies of Dr. Lauterbach's cursive Hebrew style, all that was required was the uniform styling of the essays.

The two unpublished manuscripts, however, required somewhat different handling. The essay entitled "The Sabbath in Jewish Ritual and Folklore" was undated. It was, however, the matrix from which "The Origin and Development of Two Sabbath Ceremonies," published in 1940, was created and so antedated that work by some years. Although Dr. Lauterbach had made a number of revisions both in the text and in the notes, the paper was left in an unfinished state and required some further revision, particularly in joining together the torn edges left by removal of the material on the two Sabbath ceremonies. On the whole, however, the paper remains very much as it was when the author turned away from it.

On the other hand the essay "Jesus in the Talmud," dated November 1938, was plainly marked "First draft. To be carefully revised." It had its origin in a summary of class notes prepared by Dr. Lauterbach for a group of students who had studied this subject with him the previous academic year. Dr. Lauterbach began a revision of these notes and made some verbal changes and a few excisions but was not able to do the general revision he felt was necessary. He was anxious that the paper be readied for publication and left specific instructions that this be done. This entailed the checking of all references as far as possible, the removal of all references and citations from the body of the text to the footnotes, and in many instances the revision of whole sentences and paragraphs as well as the deletion of some few obscure passages. On the basis of five years experience as Dr. Lauterbach's secretary, I feel that all of this has been without any distortion of his meaning. In fact, despite the changes of language and style, the basic text and of course the material and argument are none other than those of the author.

The manuscripts in their original form were read by Dr. Julian Morgenstern, Dr. Solomon B. Freehof and Dr. Bernard J. Bamberger who made many valuable suggestions but who are in no way responsible for whatever inadequacies and deficiencies may be found in the editing of the two previously unpublished essays.

This volume contains only a small portion of Dr. Lauterbach's creative contributions to the field of Jewish learning. The Bibliography, prepared by Dr. Walter Rothman, reveals the extent and scope of his endeavors and suggests that eventually all of his major papers should be made available in collected form. There are in addition several other manuscripts in various stages of completion that may yet see the light of day.

I wish to express my deepest thanks to Mr. Harold Hahn of the Hebrew Union College for his invaluable assistance in reading the proof on this volume. Likewise my gratitude is extended to Dr. Maurice Jacobs and his splendid staff whose courteous assistance and never-failing help have carried me over many difficulties and prevented many errors.

Lou H. Silberman, Editor

Jacob Z. Lauterbach: An Appreciation

JACOB ZALLEL LAUTERBACH was the complete Jewish scholar. He embodied almost every important phase of European Jewish learning. The old traditional learning, extending over the centuries, spanning oceans and continents, beginning with the Soferim, continuing through to the latest Novella and Responsa the unbroken chain of Talmudic learning, was maintained in its pristine strength in his native Galicia. He grew up to intellectual manhood under its influence.

The critical historical and textual studies fostered in the German universities, the modern scientific re-evaluation of the historic Hebrew sources were added to him during his student years in Germany; and he was able to harmonize the old world which he inherited and the new one which he had acquired. All through his life he remained loyal to the traditional lore while cultivating the critical scientific method. Both co-existed in him in perfect harmony, yet each was distinguishable, neither being submerged by the other. He would make use of all the exact critical methodology in establishing the text of a passage in the Mekilta yet would delight in recording the folklore current among the old-fashioned people of his native Galician town.

Jacob Lauterbach was primarily a Talmudist. Although he was at home in many departments of modern Jewish learning, he was by basic training and by preference devoted to the Talmud. To him the Talmud was everything that it traditionally was in Jewish life plus a great deal more which modern interests have added to it. It was to him first of all the basic discipline of study, the theme of his thoughts and meditations, and the moulder of his mind. Then it was for him, as it classically came to be, the prime source of legal decision. As was the proud practice of the greater Respondants in the *Sheelot u Teshuvot*, legal decisions were to be based not upon the Codes such as the Shulchan Aruch and its commentators but first of all in the Talmud itself. If one studies his Responsa for the C. C. A. R., one will discover at once that his decisions begin with the Talmud in true classical style. Thus, except for the fact that his decisions are liberal, giving contemporary needs greater weight than an old fashioned *Moreh Hora'ah* might give, he is, in method at least, in line with the historic tradition of legal interpretation and decision.

Added to all this was the influence of modern scholarship. Perhaps the outstanding characteristic of modern study of classic writings is the desire to establish a correct text. Dr. Lauterbach was at home in all the methodologies used in such work: the deciphering of manuscripts, the mutual comparison of various manuscripts and editions, the discovery of lost parts of certain works embodied erroneously in other works, the suggestion of emendations in existing texts. All these procedures are used skillfully in the various texts he has edited and especially in his monumental edition of the Mekilta.

As in modern Biblical studies, the "Lower Criticism" developed into the "Higher Criticism," that is, the establishing of what is considered to be a correct text, led to a reinterpretation of the history of Israel, so in his Talmudic studies Jacob Lauterbach moved on from textual work to an interpretation of history: the history of the Talmud itself, the history of Scribes, Pharisees, and Sadducees. Then as modern interests have shifted from history and philosophy to sociology and psychology, so in his later years he turned to the social psychology to be found in the Talmud, in its observances and its folklore.

A scholar working in the field of original research rarely has the satisfaction of seeing any practical good come from his work. He cannot foretell when or whether some other scholar may study his work and base his own, perhaps more practical, discoveries upon it. "Pure science" requires complete and unselfish devotion to the task in hand. Research is generally a lonely occupation. This is especially true of research in the field of Jewish studies. The scholar must wonder occasionally what good may ever come out of his labors. There are, moreover, so few scientific scholars devoted to Jewish studies that the number engaged in any one of the various specialities is very small. A book produced after many years of careful research will be read by only a handful. The faculties of the few modern Jewish theological schools left in the world are composed of small groups of scholars each of whom works in his own separate field. The Jewish scholar is a solitary worker.

Dr. Lauterbach was perhaps more fortunate than many another Jewish scholar in that he had the satisfaction of seeing some tangible human benefit emerge from his studies, and moreover he always had the joy of constant and varied companionship. His studies on the Sadducees and the Pharisees had a far-reaching effect in the world of everyday living. Part of the popular scientific foundation of the modern "goodwill" movement certainly was derived from his investigations. There can be no question of the fact that the expanding movement toward cooperation between Jews and Christians in the English-speaking world would have been slower to develop had not recent scholarship broken down some of the prejudice growing out of the New Testament denunciation of our Pharisaic Judaism. R. Travers Herford, the English scholar who popularized the true appreciation of Pharisaism among Christian scholars, based his work largely upon the researches of Dr. Lauterbach. He made gracious and generous acknowledgment of his debt. In the Introduction to his widely read book "The Pharisees" Herford says:

> "Of the many writers whose work has helped me in my studies of Pharisaism, I would mention two to whom I am especially indebted — Professor J. Z. Lauterbach, of Cincinnati, and Dr. Leo Baeck, of Berlin. Of the former I have written in the introductory chapter, and will here say only that without the help of his theory I could not have written the present book at all."

And again on page 16:

> "Lauterbach . . . has spoken the master-word on the subject, and all future treatment of Pharisaism must take account of it. In the following pages I have fully accepted and made use of Lauterbach's theory, and I would here express my deep obligation to him and my grateful acknowledgment of the help that I have derived from his writings."

A Jewish scholar working in a specialized field thus had the satisfaction of knowing that his studies resulted in the increase of comradeship and mutual understanding among thousands of people whom he had never met.

As for his less technical articles, scores of them are to be found in "The Jewish Encyclopedia" where they will be read by students for many years to come.

He was on the Faculty of the Hebrew Union College for many years and lived at the College long after his retirement. He influenced a whole generation of rabbis. His companionable temperament, his insatiable interest in all manner of people built for him a constantly renewing circle of disciples and comrades. He found great joy in his studies but greater joy "in the souls he had acquired."

The Alumni Association of the Hebrew Union College-Jewish Institute of Religion, half of whose membership had been his pupils, has cooperated with the Hebrew Union College Press in publishing this volume of Dr. Lauterbach's essays. The first six of these essays had been previously published and the last two essays are published now for the first time from his manuscript. Thanks are hereby given to the Hebrew Union College Annual, to the Jewish Quarterly Review, and the Central Conference of American Rabbis for permission to republish the essays which had appeared in their respective publications. All these essays had been provided with addtitional notes by Dr. Lauterbach. They are published here from the enlarged and annotated texts.

At a time when Central and Eastern European Jewry has suffered such cruel blows at the hand of an oppressor, its colleges and yeshivoth closed, its libraries destroyed and its scholars scattered, we find comfort in the task of putting into permanent form some of the best work of a great European scholar who brought his learning and ability with him to this New World and taught and guided us for many years.

SOLOMON B. FREEHOF, *Editor*

A Bibliography of the Writings of Jacob Z. Lauterbach

A Bibliography of the Writings of Jacob Z. Lauterbach

Walter E. Rothman

THE material of the bibliography is arranged chronologically; the works, articles and reviews under each date are arranged alphabetically. Reprints follow the entry irrespective of date, and the title is not repeated unless there is a change. The reprints are provided with subnumerals and are not counted as separate items. A list of the articles appearing in various encyclopedias is appended to the main bibliography.

The following abbreviations may be noted here:

    C. C. A. R.   Central Conference of American Rabbis.
    H. U. C. A.   Hebrew Union College Annual (Cincinnati).
    J. Q. R.   Jewish Quarterly Review (new series, Philadelphia).

1903

1. Saadja Al-fajjumi's arabische Psalmenübersetzung und Commentar (Psalm 107–124). Inaugural-Dissertation ...der... Universität zu Göttingen. *Berlin: H. Itzkowski*, 1903. 67(1), xxv p. 8.

1a. Saadja Al-fajjumi's arabische Psalmenübersetzung und Commentar (Psalm 107–124). Nach einer Münchener und einer Berliner Handschrift herausgegeben, übersetzt und mit Anmerkungen versehen. *Berlin: M. Poppelauer*, 1903. 67, xxv p. 8.

1911

2. The ancient Jewish allegorists in Talmud and Midrash. (*J. Q. R.* n. s., v. 1, 1910–11, p. 291–333, 503–531.)
2a. ——— n. t.-p. [*Philadelphia*, 1911.] p. 291–333, 503–531. 8.
3. The Talmud and Reform Judaism. (*American Israelite.* Cincinnati, 1911–12. v. 58, no. 18, p. 1.)
    Address delivered on the occasion of his installation as Professor of Talmud at the Hebrew Union College, Saturday Oct. 21, 1911.

1913

4. The Ethics of the Halakah. (*C. C. A. R. Yearbook*, v. 23, [cop. 1914], p. 249–287.)
4a. ——— n. p., 1913. 40 p. 8.
5. The Sadducees and Pharisees. A study of their respective attitudes towards the Law. (*In*: Studies in Jewish literature; issued in honor of K. Kohler... *Berlin*, 1913. p. 176–198. 8.)
    "This essay is a part of a larger work on the Sadducees and Pharisees which the writer has in preparation."
5a. ——— [*Berlin: G. Reimer*, 1913.] 24 p. 8.

1915

6. Midrash and Mishnah. A study in the early history of the Halakah. I–IV. (*J. Q. R.* n. s., v. 5, 1914–15, p. 503–527; v. 6, 1915–16, p. 23–95, 303–323.)
6a. ——— n. t.-p. [*Philadelphia*, 1915.] p. 503–527, 23–95, 303–323. 8.
6b. ——— *New York: Bloch Pub. Co.*, 1916. 2 p. L., 119 p. 8.

1917

7. Bacher, Wilhelm. Tradition und Tradenten in den Schulen Palästinas und Babyloniens... *Leipzig*, 1914. [Review of.] (*J. Q. R.* n. s., v. 8, 1917–18, p. 101–112.)

1918

8. Joseph E. Sales; an appreciation. (*Hebrew Union College Monthly.* Cincinnati, 1918–19. v. 5, no. 1, p. 4–5.)
9. The three books found in the temple at Jerusalem. (*J. Q. R.* n. s., v. 8, 1917–18, p. 385–423.)
9a. ——— *New York: Bloch Pub. Co.*, 1918. 2 p. L., 39 p. 8.
    With dedication: To the memory of Edward L. Heinsheimer, President of the Board of Governors of the Hebrew Union College.

1919

10. Tschernowitz, Ch[ajim]. Die Entstehung des Schulchan-Aruch... *Bern*, 1915. [Review of.] (*J. Q. R.* n. s., v. 9, 1918–19, p. 489–496.)

1920

11. The name of the Mekilta. (*J. Q. R.* n. s., v. 11, 1920-21, p. 169–196.)
    "The plan of the Jewish Classics for which series I am preparing a new critical edition of the Mekilta provides but limited space for Introductions. I am, therefore, publishing here part of what should be an introduction to my new edition of the Mekilta. The next article will deal with the arrangement and the divisions of the Mekilta.
    "The views as to the meaning of the name Mekilta, expressed by me in the *Jewish Encyclopedia*, vol. VIII, p. 444 f., are hereby abandoned."
11b. ——— n. t.-p. [*Philadelphia*, 1920.] p. 169–196. 8.

1921

12. The attitude of the Jew towards the non-Jew. (*C. C. A. R. Yearbook.* v. 31, [1921], p. 186-233.)
12b. ——— n. p., 1921. 50 p. 8.

1922

13. Report of Committee on Responsa. I. Celebration of marriage between New Year and Atonement. II. Removal of the dead. (*C. C. A. R. Yearbook.* v. 32, [1922], p. 41–42.)
14. Responsum on question of women rabbis. n. t.-p. n. p., [1922]. f.

    A broadside issued previous to its publication in the C. C. A. R. Yearbook, from which it varies in title and in the omission of all Hebrew quotations. It has the following heading: "Dear Colleague: This subject will be taken up for debate at the coming Conference. This responsum is merely offered in its present form to aid discussion."
14a. Responsum on question, "Shall women be ordained rabbis?" (*C. C. A. R. Yearbook.* v. 32, [1922], p. 156–162.)

1923

15. Report of Committee on Responsa. (*C. C. A. R. Yearbook.* v. 33, [1923], p. 57–63.)

    Contains various responsa; two of the responsa written in collaboration with Martin A. Meyer and Henry Berkowitz.
16. Strack, Hermann L[eberecht]. Einleitung in Talmud und Midraš. *München*, 1921. [Review of.] (*American journal of Semitic languages and literatures.* Chicago, 1922–23. v. 39, p. 226–228.)

1924

17. The arrangement and the division of the Mekilta. (*H. U. C. A.* v. 1, 1924, p. 427–466.)

1925

18. The ceremony of breaking a glass at weddings. (*H. U. C. A.* v. 2, 1925, p. 351–380.)
18a. —— n. t.-p. [*Cincinnati*, 1925.] p. 351–380. 8.

19. An introduction to the Talmud. (General survey.) *Cincinnati*: Hebrew Union College, 1925. 1 p. L., 47 p. 8.
Preliminary issue printed but not published.
20. The Jewish attitude toward autopsy. [A responsum.] (*C. C. A. R. Yearbook.* v. 35, [1925], p. 130–134.)
20a. Report of Committee on Responsa. [The Jewish attitude toward autopsy.] n. p., [1925.] 4 L. 8.
21. The name of the rabbinical schools and assemblies in Babylon. (*In*: Hebrew Union College jubilee volume. *Cincinnati*, 1925. p. 211–222. 8.)
21a. ——— *Cincinnati*, 1925. 1 p. L., p. 211–222. 8.
The title of reprint reads: The names ...
22. Shall person called to the Torah recite only the benediction? [A responsum.] (*C. C. A. R. Yearbook.* v. 34, [cop. 1925], p. 70–74.)
23. הצופה (שבירת עצם בפסח). Budapest, 1925. v. 9, p. 235–241.)
23a. ——— [*Budapest: Katzburg Brothers*, 1925.] 8 p. 8.

1926

24. The Jewish home. (*In*: B'nai B'rith manual. Edited by Samuel S. Cohon. *Cincinnati*, 1926. p. 24–36. 24.)
Editor's note: "From a chapter of a work, in preparation by the author, which he kindly placed in the hands of the editor, to utilize the material in accordance with the plan of the Manual." This work was never completed.

1927

25. Is it permissible to let a non-Jewish contractor, building a synagog, work on the building on the Sabbath? [A responsum.] (*C. C. A. R. Yearbook.* v. 37, [1927], p. 202–206.)
26. Scheftelowitz, I[sidor]. Alt-Palästinensischer Bauernglaube ... *Hannover*, 1925. [Review of.] (*Hebrew Union College Monthly.* Cincinnati, 1927–28. v. 13, no. 2, p. 15–17.)
27. A significant controversy between the Sadducees and the Pharisees. (*H. U. C. A.* v. 4, 1927, p. 173–205.)
27a. ——— n. t.-p. [*Cincinnati*, 1927.] p. 173–205. 8.

28. Talmudic-rabbinic view on birth control. [A responsum.] (*C. C. A. R. Yearbook.* v. 37, [1927], p. 369–384.)
28a. ———— n. p., 1927. 1 p. L., 16 p. 8.

1928

29. Hats on or hats off? [port.] (*American Hebrew.* New York, 1928. v. 123, p. 307, 310, 329, 332.)
    "In the present version all technicalities and the numerous references to authorities have been omitted. These, however, will be given in full in the text which will be printed in the Year Book of the Central Conference of American Rabbis next fall."
29a. Should one cover the head when participating in divine worship? [A responsum.] (*C. C. A. R. Yearbook.* v. 38, [1928], p. 589–603.)
29b. ———— n. t.-p. n. p., [1928]. 15 p. 8.
30. מכתב־יד מאת י. מ. טולידאנו :to הערה נוספת. (*H. U. C. A.* v. 5, 1928, p. 412–413.)

1929

31. Abbreviations and their solutions. (*In:* Studies in Jewish bibliography ... in memory of A. S. Freidus. *New York*, 1929. p. 141–149. 8.)
    Paged also: 1–9.
31a. ———— n. t.-p. [*New York*, 1929.] 9 p. 8.
    Paged also: 141–149.
32. The Pharisees and their teachings. (*H. U. C. A.* v. 6, 1929, p. 69–139.)
    Paged also: 1–71.
    "The study here presented consists of three lectures delivered by the writer before the Divinity School of the University of Chicago and the Garret Biblical Institute of Evanston, Illinois in April 1928."
32a. ———— *Cincinnati*, 1929. 1 p. L., 71 p. 8.
    Paged also: 1 p. L., 69–139.
32b. ———— *New York: Bloch Pub. Co.*, 1930. 2 p. L., 71 p. 8.

With dedication: To the memory of my wife Fanny Oberweger Lauterbach.

1931

33. Substitutes for the tetragrammaton. (*American Academy for Jewish Research. Proceedings.* [New York], 1931. [v. 2], p. 39–67.)
33a. ——— *New York*, 1931. 1 p. L., 29 p. 8.
34. The Talmud and the Gospels. [port.] (*The Kallah. Year Book.* Fort Worth, Texas, 5691. v. 4, p. 11–18.)
"This does not represent the entire paper but merely abstracts from it."

1932

35. The naming of children in Jewish folklore, ritual and practice. (*C. C. A. R. Yearbook.* v. 42, [1932], p. 316–360.)
35a. ——— n. p., 1932. 1 p. L., 45 p. 8.
36. Report of Committee on Responsa. (*C. C. A. R. Yearbook.* v. 42, [1932], p. 81–86.)
Contains various responsa.

1933

37. Mekilta de-Rabbi Ishmael. A critical edition on the basis of the manuscripts and early editions with an English translation, introduction and notes. v. 1–3. Philadelphia; Jewish Publication Society of America, 1933–1935. 16. (Schiff library of Jewish classics.)
38. The two Mekiltas. (*American Academy for Jewish Research. Proceedings.* [New York], 1933. v. 4, p. 113–129.)
38a. ——— n. t.-p. [*New York*], 1933. p. 113–129. 8.
39. מדרש ויסעו או ספר מלחמות בני יעקב. י"ל בפעם הראשונה בשלמותו עפ"י כתבי יד שונים עם מבוא והערות. (*In*: Abhandlungen zur Erinnerung an Hirsch Perez Chajes. *Wien*, 1933. [Heb. sec.], p. 205–222. 8.)
Paged also: 1–18.

39a. n. t.-p. [*Wien*, 1933.] 18 p. 8.
　　　Paged also: 205–222.

1934

40. Misunderstood chronological statements in the Talmudic literature. (*American Academy for Jewish Research. Proceedings.* [New York], 1934. v. 5, p. 77–84.)
　　　Paged also: 1–8.

1935

41. The ritual for the Kapparot-ceremony. (*In*: Jewish studies in memory of G. A. Kohut... *New York*, 1935. p. 413–422. 8.
　　　Paged also: 1–10.
41a. ——— n. t.-p. [*New York*, 1935.] 10 p. 8.
　　　Paged also: 413–422.

1936

42. Tashlik; a study in Jewish ceremonies. (*H. U. C. A.* v. 11, 1936, p. 207–340.)
　　　Paged also: 1–134.
42a. ——— *Cincinnati*, [1936]. 2 p. L., 134 p. 8.
　　　Paged also: 2 p. L., 207–340.
　　　With dedication: To my friend Prof. Dr. Samuel Krauss in honor of his seventieth birthday.
43. Unpublished parts of the Yalḳuṭ ha-Makiri on Hosea and Micah. (*In*: Occident and Orient; being studies... in honour of ... M. Gaster's 80th birthday... *London*, [1936]. p. 365–373. 8.)
43a. ——— n. t.-p. [*London*, 1936.] 9 p. 8.

1937

44. ‏... ספר קלונר... מונש לפרופסור יוסף‏ (*In*: ‏מביאורי המכילתא‏ ‏קלונר ליובל הששים‏ [*Tel Aviv*, 1937.] p. 181–188. sq. 8.)

1939

45. The belief in the power of the word. (*H. U. C. A.* v. 14, 1939, p. 287–302.)
     Paged also: 1–16.
45a. ———— n. t.-p. [*Cincinnati*, 1939.] 16 p. 8.

1940

46. Rashi the Talmud commentator. (*C. C. A. R. Yearbook.* v. 50, [1940], p. 360–373.)
46a. ———— n. p., 1940. 1 p. L., 15 p. 8.
47. The origin and development of two Sabbath ceremonies. (*H. U. C. A.* v. 15, 1940, p. 367–424.)
     Paged also: 1–58.
47a. ———— n. t.-p. [*Cincinnati*, 1940.] 58 p. 8.
     Paged also: 367–424.

1941

48. Summarization of C. C. A. R. responsa, contained in year books 1880–1940. [*Cincinnati*]: *Union of American Hebrew Congregations*, 1941. 19 f. sq. 4.
     Mimeographed.
     Contains responsa by Lauterbach.

1942

49. זמן שחיטת הפסח. (*American Academy for Jewish Research. Proceedings.* New York, 1942. v. 12, [Heb. sec.], p. 1–5.)
     A summary of the article in English, by the editor, p. 49–50.
49a. ———— n. t.-p. [*New York*, 1942.] 5, 2 p. 8.

ARTICLES IN ENCYCLOPEDIAS

THE JEWISH ENCYCLOPEDIA
NEW YORK, 1901–5. 12 v. 4.

Volume 7. 1904.

1. Jonathan ben Uzziel. p. 238.
2. Jose the Galilean. p. 240–241.
3. Joseph b. Joshua b. Levi. p. 266.
4. Joshua b. Ḳarḥa. p. 293.
5. Josiah: Tanna of the second century. p. 296.
6. Judah b. Ezekiel. p. 342–343.
7. Judah b. Ḥiyya. p. 343.
8. Judah ben Ilai. p. 343-344.
9. Judah ibn Ḳuraish. p. 345.
10. Judah ben Laḳish. p. 345–346.
11. Judah ben Simeon ben Pazzi. p. 358.
12. Kahana b. Taḥlifa. p. 412.
13. Ketubot. p. 478–480.
14. Ḳiddushin. p. 485-486.
15. Ḳinnim. p. 507–508.
16. Ḳodashim. p. 527–528.

Volume 8. 1904.

17. Megillah. p. 425–427.
18. Megillat Setarim. p. 427.
19. Megillat Ta'anit. p. 427–428.
20. Me'ilah. p. 431-432.
21. Mekilta. p. 444–446.
22. Mekilta de-Rabbi Shim'on. p. 446–447.
23. Mekilta le-Sefer Debarim. p. 447.
24. Melammed. p. 448.
25. Middot. p. 545–546.
26. Middot, Shelosh-'Esreh. p. 546–547.
27. Midrash Halakah. p. 569–572.
28. Miggo. p. 583.

29. Miḳwa'ot. p. 587–588.
30. Miriam. p. 608–609.
31. Mishnah. p. 609–619.
32. Mnemonics. p. 631–632.
33. Mo'ed. p. 640.
34. Mo'ed Ḳaṭan. p. 640.

Volume 9. 1905.

35. Mordecai ha-Kohen of Safed. p. 14.
36. Mordecai b. Shabbethai. p. 15.
37. Morenu. p. 15–16.
38. [Moses] — In rabbinical literature. p. 46–54.
39. Moses b. Benjamin ha-Sofer of Rome. p. 63.
40. Moses Botarel. p. 63.
41. Moses Botarel Farissol. p. 63.
42. Moses ben Joseph ha-Kohen. p. 71.
43. Moses b. Joseph of Rome. p. 71.
44. Moses ha-Levi Alḳabiẓ. p. 73.
45. Maimonides as Halakist. p. 82–86.
46. Moses Nathan ben Judah. p. 92.
47. Moses b. Shemaiah. p. 93.
48. Moses ben Simḥah of Lutsk. p. 93.
49. Moses ben Yom-Ṭob. p. 94–95. (Together with Joseph Jacobs.)
50. Motal, Abraham ben Jacob of Salonica. p. 98.
51. Motal, Benjamin b. Abraham of Constantinople. p. 98.
52. Naḥman bar Isaac. p. 143.
53. Naḥman bar Jacob. p. 143–144.
54. Nahum Eliezer ben Jacob. p. 147–148.
55. Nahum of Gimzo. p. 148.
56. Nahum ben Simai. p. 148.
57. Naresh. p. 170.
58. Nazir. p. 197–198.
59. Nazir, Isaac. p. 198.
60. Nedarim. p. 205–206.
61. Nega'im. p. 206–207.
62. Nehemiah of Beth-Horon. p. 211–212.

63. Nehemiah ben Kohen Ẓedeḳ. p. 212.
64. Nesek. p. 227.
65. Neziḳin. p. 297.
66. Niddah. p. 301.
67. Niederländer, Abraham ben Ephraim. p. 302.
68. Nissim b. Reuben Gerondi. p. 317–318.
69. Nittai of Arbela. p. 318.
70. Nomism. p. 326–329.
71. [Obadiah] — In rabbinical literature. p. 369.
72. [Og.] — In rabbinical literature. p. 388.
73. Onias (Ḥoni) ha-Me'Aggel. p. 404–405.
74. Oral Law. p. 423–426.
75. Ordination. p. 428–430.
76. Orḥot Ẓaddiḳim. p. 433.
77. 'Orlah. p. 435.
78. Ornstein, Jacob Meshullam. p. 437.
79. Orpah. p. 438.
80. Palṭoi b. Abayi. p. 508.
81. Papa. p. 510.
82. Pappos b. Judah. p. 512.
83. Parable. p. 512–514.
84. Parah. p. 520.
85. Passover sacrifice. p. 556–557.
86. Pasuḳ. p. 558.
87. Pe'ah. p. 568–569.
88. Pedat b. Eleazar. p. 577.
89. Peraḥyah b. Nissim. p. 595–596.
90. Pereda. p. 596.
91. Pesaḥ Sheni. p. 649.
92. Pesaḥim. p. 649–650.
93. Peshaṭ. p. 652–653.

Volume 10. 1905.

94. [Philo Judaeus] — His relation to the Halakah. p. 15–18.
95. Phinehas b. Ḥama. p. 20.
96. Pilpul. p. 39–43.

97. Proverbs, Midrash to. p. 231–232.
98. Psalms, Midrash to. p. 248–250.
99. Raba b. 'Ulla. p. 288.
100. Raba (b. Joseph b. Ḥama.) p. 288–289.
101. Raba b. Ada. p. 289.
102. Rabai of Rob. p. 289.
103. Rabbah b. Abuha. p. 289–290.
104. Rabbah Gaon. p. 290.
105. Rabbah b. Ḥana. p. 290.
106. Rabbah bar bar Ḥana. p. 290–291.
107. Rabbah b. Ḥanan. p. 291.
108. Rabbah b. Ḥiyya of Ctesiphon. p. 291.
109. Rabbah b. Huna. p. 291.
110. Rabbah b. Liwai. p. 291.
111. Rabbah b. Mari. p. 291–292.
112. Rabbah b. Matna. p. 292.
113. Rabbah b. Naḥman b. Jacob. p. 292.
114. Rabbah b. Naḥmani. p. 292–293.
115. Rabbah of Parziḳi. p. 293.
116. Rabbah b. Samuel. p. 293.
117. Rabbah b. Shela. p. 293.
118. Rabbah Tusfa'ah. p. 293.
119. Rabbah b. Ufran. p. 293.
120. Rabban. p. 293–294.
121. Rabbiner Seminar für das orthodoxe Judenthum. p. 297–298.
122. Rabin b. Adda. p. 300.
123. Rabina I. p. 300.
124. Rabina II. p. 300.
125. Rabina III of Umza. p. 300.
126. Raca. p. 304.
127. Rafram I. p. 307.
128. Rafram II. p. 307.
129. Rahab. p. 308–309.
130. Rami b. Ezekiel. p. 314.
131. Rami b. Ḥama. p. 314.
132. Rami b. Tamre. p. 314.
133. Abraham Rapoport. p. 320.

134. Ḥayyim b. bär Rapoport. p. 321.
135. Isaac b. Judah ha-Kohen Rapoport. p. 322.
136. [Rehoboam] — In rabbinical literature. p. 363.
137. Reḥumai (I), Rab. p. 363.
138. Reḥumai II. p. 363.
139. Reḥumai III. p. 363.
140. Reischer, Jacob b. Joseph. p. 369.
141. Reuben. p. 386–387.
142. Riblah. p. 402.
143. Rishonim. p. 431.
144. Romaner, Benjamin Zeeb Wolf ben Samuel. p. 443-444.
145. Rosello (Ruscelli), Mordecai Raphael ben Jacob. p. 472.
146. Rules of Eliezer b. Jose ha-Galili, the thirty-two. p. 510–511.
147. Rules of Hillel, the seven. p. 511.
148. Rules of Ishmael, the thirteen. p. 511–512.
149. Rumsch, Isaac Moses. p. 517.
150. [Sacrifice] — Talmudic. p. 625.
151. Sama b. Rabba. p. 665.
152. Sama b. Raḳta. p. 665.

Volume 11. 1905.

153. [Samson] — In rabbinical literature. p. 1–2.
154. [Samuel] — In rabbinical literature. p. 7.
155. Samuel, Midrash to. p. 13.
156. Samuel b. Ḥiyya. p. 17.
157. Samuel ha-Ḳaṭon. p. 21–22.
158. Samuel ben Naṭronai. p. 26.
159. Samuel ben Uri Shraga Phoebus. p. 28–29.
160. Samuel Yarḥina'ah. p. 29–31.
161. Sanhedrin. p. 41–44.
162. Sanhedrin. ("Court"). p. 44–46.
163. [Sarah] — In rabbinical literature. p. 55–56.
164. Sarsino. (Sarcino), Jacob b. Joseph. p. 64.
165. [Saul] — In rabbinical literature. p. 76.
166. Saul, Abba. p. 78.

167. Saul Abba b. Baṭnit. p. 78.
168. Semaḥot. p. 180–182.
169. Semikah. p. 182–183.
170. Senior, Phoebus ben Jacob Abigdor. p. 194–195.
171. Shabbat. p. 213–215.
172. Shamḥazai. p. 228–229.
173. Shammai. p. 230.
174. Shebi'it. p. 236–237.
175. Shebu'ot. p. 238.
176. She'elot u-Teshubot. p. 240–250.
177. Sheḳalim. p. 256–257.
178. Shela. p. 261.
179. Shelah. p. 261.
180. Sherira b. Ḥanina. p. 284–285.
181. Sheshet. p. 285–286.
182. Shila of Kefar Tamarta. p. 288.
183. [Shimei] — In rabbinical literature. p. 290.
184. Shir ha-Shirim Rabbah. p. 291–292.
185. Sihon. p. 335.
186. Simeon. p. 347.
187. Simeon I. p. 347.
188. Simeon II (Ben Gamaliel I). p. 347.
189. Simeon (Ben Gamaliel II). p. 347–348.
190. Simeon b. Abba. p. 348.
191. Simeon b. Absalom. p. 348.
192. Simeon b. 'Aḳashyah. p. 349.
193. Simeon b. Boethus. p. 349.
194. Simeon b. Eleazar. p. 349.
195. Simeon b. Ḥalafta. p. 349–350.
196. Simeon he-Ḥasid. p. 350.
197. Simeon b. Isaac b. Abun. p. 350–351.
198. Simeon b. Jakim. p. 351.
199. Simeon b. Jehozadak. p. 351.
200. Simeon b. Jose b. Leḳonya. p. 351.
201. Simeon b. Judah. p. 352.
202. Simeon b. Judah Ha-Nasi I. p. 352.
203. Simeon of Ḳiṭron. p. 354.
204. Simeon b. Laḳish. p. 354–355.

205. Simeon b. Menasya. p. 355–356.
206. Simeon of Miẓpah. p. 356.
207. Simeon ben Nanos. p. 356.
208. Simeon b. Nethaneel. p. 356.
209. Simeon ha-Paḳoli. p. 356.
210. Simeon b. Pazzi. p. 356–357.
211. Simeon ben ha-Segan. p. 357.
212. Simeon ben Sheṭaḥ. p. 357–358.
213. Simeon Shezuri. p. 358.
214. Simeon of Shiḳmona. p. 358–359.
215. Simeon b. Tarfon. p. 359.
216. Simeon of Teman. p. 359.
217. Simeon b. Yannai. p. 359.
218. Simeon b. Zabdai. p. 363.
219. Simḥah b. Isaac b. Kalonymus ha-Kohen. p. 363.
220. Simḥah b. Samuel of Speyer. p. 364.
221. Simḥah b. Samuel of Vitry. p. 364.
222. Simuna. p. 376.
223. Sinaitic Commandments. p. 383.
224. Solomon Shalem b. Ḥayyim Jeḥiel Cohen. p. 457.
225. Soṭah. p. 471–472.
226. Sukkah. p. 582–583.
227. Ta'anit. p. 653.

Volume 12. 1905.

228. Talmud Hermeneutics. p. 30–33.
229. Tamar. p. 40–41.
230. Tamid. p. 41.
231. Tanḥum b. Ḥiyya. p. 43.
232. Tanḥuma b. Abba. p. 44.
233. Tanḥuma, Midrash. p. 45–46.
234. Tanḥuma b. Skolastikai. p. 46.
235. Tanḥuma b. Yudan. p. 46.
236. Tannaim and Amoraim. p. 49.
237. Ṭebul Yom. p. 72.
238. Temurah. p. 102.

239. Temurah, Midrash. p. 102.
240. Terumot. p. 111–112.
241. Theology. p. 128–137.
242. Ṭohorot. p. 174–175.
243. Tosefta. p. 207–209.
244. Traditions. p. 218.
245. Vows. p. 451–452.
246. Wayiḳra Rabbah. p. 478–479.
247. [Weights and measures] — In rabbinical literature. p. 485–490.
248. Weil, Nethaneel. p. 493.
249. Yadayim. p. 580.
250. Yalḳuṭ. p. 585–586.
251. Yoma. p. 618–620.
252. Yudan. p. 623–624.
253. Yudan ben Ishmael. p. 624.
254. Yudan ben Manasseh. p. 624.
255. Yudan ben Simeon. p. 624.
256. Zebaḥim. p. 643–644.
257. Zeʻera. p. 651-652.
258. Zeraʻim. p. 661.
259. Zerika. p. 662.
260. Zugot. p. 698.

אוצר ישראל, אנציקלופידיא ... New York, 1906–13. 10 vols. 4.

Volume 4. 1910.

1. ויכלו, מדרש. p. 200.
2. ויסעו, מדרש. p. 207.
3. ותודיענו. p. 214.

Volume 5. 1911.

4. כהנא, רב. p. 260–261.
5. כלל ופרט. p. 281–282.
6. לבנה, ברכת. p. 316–317.

Volume 6. 1911.

 7. מדות, ארבעים ותשע. p. 100.
 8. מרימר. p. 295–296.
 9. משה הדרשן. p. 302–303.
 10. מתיא בן חרש. p. 319.

Volume 7. 1912.

 11. נתן הבבלי. p. 126.
 12. סבוראי. p. 133–134.
 13. ספרי. p. 273–275.

Volume 8. 1912.

 14. פלטוי, רב. p. 263.

Volume 9. 1913.

 15. רזיאל. p. 297.

Volume 10. 1913.

 16. שימושא רבא. p. 95–96.
 17. תמורה, מדרש. p. 271.

אשכול, אנציקלופדיה ישראלית ... [Berlin, 1929.] 2 vols. 4.

Volume 1. 1929.

 1. אהלות. col. 728–730.

The Sadducees and Pharisees

The Sadducees and Pharisees

(1913)

I

MUCH has been written about the Sadducees and Pharisees, their respective tendencies, teachings and interpretations of the Law.[1] But no satisfactory presentation of the real motive of their disagreement in regard to the interpretation and application of the Law and of the fundamental principles underlying the peculiar views and opinions of each party, has been given. From Josephus[2] and the Talmud[3] we learn that one of the main differences between them consisted in the peculiar attitude of each towards those laws, not contained in the Pentateuch but merely based upon tradition. The Pharisees considered such laws as of absolute authority and equal to the written laws, while the Sadducees denied them such authoritative and compulsory character. But neither Josephus nor the Talmud has anything to say about the cause and origin of this great difference or of the respective arguments of each party in support of its position. And what we otherwise know about the character and tendencies of the two parties not only does not explain, but apparently makes it even more difficult to understand how each party could have consistently assumed the attitude towards tradition thus ascribed to it.

Judging from their teachings and their interpretations of the

---

[1] About the literature see the bibliography given by Dr. Kohler at the end of his article on the Pharisees in the *Jewish Encyclopedia* IX, 666. Cf. also his article on the Sadducees, *ibid.*, X.

[2] *Ant.* XIII, 10. 6, § 297 and XVIII 1. 4, § 16.

[3] Sanh. 33b (see Rashi there) and Hor. 4a it is taken for granted, though not expressly stated, that the Sadducees denied the authority of the traditional law. This is further evident from the many traditional laws mentioned in the Talmud as having been disputed by the Sadducees, see Suk. 43b and 48b, and 'Er. 68b compared with Hor. 3b–4a.

Law which are preserved to us, we find that the Sadducees held tenaciously to older views and insisted on a simple and literal interpretation of the Law. This we must believe was traditional with them, for we find that the older Halakah, adhering strictly to older traditional ways and principles, follows the same method of simple and literal interpretation and agrees in many points with the teachings and views of the Sadducees (See Geiger, *Urschrift*, p. 134, and *Sadducäer u. Pharisäer*, [Breslau, 1863], p. 15). And it is now considered an historic fact, that the Sadducees were the older party, consisting of the priests, the descendants of the בני צדוק and their aristocratic followers. They were conservative and narrow in their views and strongly opposed to changes and innovations. The Pharisees, on the other hand, were the younger party, broader and more liberal in their views, of progressive tendencies and not averse to innovations. Accordingly we would expect, that the Sadducees, whose priestly ancestors and predecessors had always been the official teachers of the people, the תופשי התורה, the custodians of the Law and presumably also of such tradition as there was, and who themselves were very conservative, the natural advocates of traditional ways and views, would seek to uphold the authority of tradition and the binding character of its laws. On the other hand, we would expect the Pharisees, being the younger, more progressive and liberal party which applied new methods of interpretation and developed new theories, to deny the authority of tradition and reject its laws.

But, instead, we are led to believe that in their attitude towards the authority of the traditional laws the two parties had changed roles. For the conservative Sadducees are said to have opposed the authority of tradition and the binding character of its teachings, while the Pharisees, who in many points departed from traditional ways and favored new views, are represented as the advocates of tradition and of the authority of its laws. Yet there is no reason at all, to doubt the correctness of Josephus' statement in regard to this great difference between the two parties, confirmed as it is by the Talmud. Geiger's explanation, that the negative attitude towards tradition was held not by the older Sadducees but only by the Boethusians who were really of a later date and had no tradition (*Urschrift*, p. 134) is incorrect. For, from the Talmud and from Josephus it is evident that this negative attitude towards tradition was held by all the Sadducees and not merely by the Boethusians. Nor can we accept the other explanation of Geiger (*ibid.*), *viz.*, that the Pharisees instituted some new laws or made additions to older laws, representing them as based upon tradition, and that it was only such traditional laws which the Sadducees refused to accept and demanded for them proof from the Torah.[4] For it is altogether wrong to accuse the Pharisees of representing their own decisions as traditional laws. The Pharisees would never have deliberately invented a tradition to support their own teachings.[5] Nor could they have done so, if they would.

[4] This argument is not only weak but even self-contradictory. It is the best illustration of Geiger's peculiar method of argumentation which has rather weakened the strength of his theory instead of supporting it. In the first place the characteristic attitude, assumed by the Sadducees towards the traditional law, could not have been provoked by and directed against only a few laws which the Pharisees in the course of time may have instituted. This supposition is contradicted by Geiger's own statement that the Sadducees demanded *biblical proof for these Pharisaic laws*. For this implies, that a proof from tradition, even if the Pharisees could have brought such, would not have satisfied the Sadducees. Consequently, the latter must have denied the authority of tradition in general and not merely the few laws which the Pharisees claimed to have derived from tradition. Besides, we find that the reverse was the case. In all their disputes with the Sadducees the Pharisees try to give scriptural proofs for their decisions and they never say, "we have this or that decision as a tradition." On the other hand the Sadducees are unable to furnish for their decisions the scriptural proofs which the Pharisees demanded of them לא היו יודעים להביא ראיה מן התורה (see Scholion to Meg. Ta'an. IV, Neubauer, *Med. Jew. Chr.*, p. 8 and X, p. 16, also pp. 4 and 10 according to the reading of P.).

[5] In the later development of Pharisaism it happened that certain laws and customs, originally taught or instituted by Pharisaic leaders, were erroneously designated as earlier traditions or even as Mosaic laws. But then it was done in good faith. The later Rabbis finding an old law and not knowing its origin any more, really believed it to be an old traditional law, received from the fathers or even from Moses הלכה למשה מסיני. In this manner they credited Moses, Joshua, David, Solomon and Ezra with many laws and institutions which were really of later date and of popular origin. But the Pharisaic teachers would never have deliberately ascribed a law or custom to tradition, if they had known that it was not traditional.

How could they, especially in their earlier disputes, even think of claiming to be in possession of traditions unknown to or denied by their opponents, when the latter were the heirs of the priests who had always been the custodians of the Law and of tradition? Must they not have feared that the Sadducees might ask, how *they* came to have tradition? Yet such a question, as far as we know, was never raised by the Sadducees. Nor do we ever hear in all the disputes between the two parties and in the various arguments of the Sadducees against the Pharisees reported to us, that the former accused the latter of having invented or falsely represented any tradition. This *argumentum e silentio* alone may not suffice to prove that the Sadducees never accused the Pharisees of inventing traditions. For it could be argued that our Pharisaic sources naturally would not record such an accusation.[6] But we have other positive proofs that the disputes between the parties were not about the contents of tradition, but merely about its authority. Josephus expressly states that the Sadducees denied merely the binding character of traditional laws, declaring, that only the written laws were obligatory. So it was never a question whether certain laws were derived from tradition, but whether those laws admittedly derived from tradition were obligatory. The same is also evident from Tosefta Suk. 3.1, where it is stated that the Sadducees[7] or Boethusians did not consent to the observance of the ceremony of beating the willow at the cost of violating the Sabbath. From this we learn, that they did not object to the ceremony as such, because it was merely a traditional custom or law, as Grätz (*Geschichte* III,[5] 696) and Weiss (*Dor* I, 112) assume, nor did they deny that it was a traditional custom. On week-days they would

[6] Though we find that they do report even some ridiculing remarks which the Sadducees made about the Pharisees, as for instance מסורת היא ביד פרושים שהן מצערין עצמם בעו״הז וב״העוה״ב אין להם כלום (Ab. R. N., Version A., Ch. V, Schechter, 26) and בואו וראו פרושים מטבילין גלגל חמה (p. Ḥag. 79d).

[7] The passage reads: לפי שאין הביתוסים מודין שחיבוט ערבה דוחה שבת. But it is evident that the Boethusians were merely expressing the opinion of the older Sadducees on this question. For if the older Sadducees had objected to the ceremony as such and not only to its setting aside the Sabbath, what reason could the younger Boethusians have for accepting the ceremony but merely limiting its performance to week days?

have countenanced the ceremony, but they objected to its observance on the Sabbath, since this meant a violation of the Sabbath laws. In their opinion the observance of a traditional law, not being absolutely obligatory, could not set aside the Sabbath laws. Thus we see that the two parties differed as to the compulsory character of the laws, not written in the Torah but merely derived from tradition.

The question, therefore, remains what principles did the two parties follow in their respective attitudes towards traditional law, and how do these attitudes harmonize with their respective characters and tendencies otherwise known to us? I shall endeavor to answer this question satisfactorily by showing that the attitude towards tradition, ascribed by Josephus and the Talmud to each party was to a great extent the result of its peculiar views about the Written Law and thoroughly consistent with its origin, character and tendencies, as we know them.

II.

Limited space forbids a detailed presentation of the historic conditions leading up to the division into the two parties. I must limit myself to a brief account of the position of the priests and the place of the Law in the theocratic community prior to this division, in order that we may fully understand the character and tendencies of each party. The reorganized community in Judea accepted from Ezra, the priest and scribe, the Book of the Law of Moses as its constitution. They pledged themselves by oath to observe and keep it (Neh. 10.30). The Law was recognized as the only authority in the new community, and the priests, the successors of Ezra, were the official teachers and interpreters of that Law. Though some priests may have fallen short of this ideal, the majority remained true teachers and representatives of the Law. From them alone one could seek instruction in the Torah (Hag. 2.11, Mal. 2.7). Since the Law, as written in the Book, was the only authority, binding upon the people, these priestly teachers could do no more than teach the written Torah with whatever simple interpretations they had to give to it, i. e., the Midrash Torah (see my *Midrash and Mishnah*). They were called Soferim, just as Ezra was called Sofer, because, like Ezra, they occupied themselves with the Sefer ha-Torah, the Book of the Law, taught the Book and from the Book alone. It is doubtful if there were any laymen, i. e., non-priests among the Soferim, but even if so, they had little influence and no official authority. For the priests were the actual leaders and rulers of the community, since they alone were recognized by the Law (Deut. 17) as its official teachers and competent interpreters. Besides teaching and interpreting the written laws, the priests, as the actual leaders of the community, did also introduce some new customs and practices to meet certain needs of their time, being authorized to do so by the right given to them in Deut. 7. Such were the conditions in the Jewish community throughout the entire Persian period.

With the Greek rule conditions changed. During the third century B. C. E. the authority and influence of the priests diminished, while on the other hand, a class of teachers of the Law, who were not priests, gradually arose (see my *Midrash and Mishnah*). At the beginning of the second century these non-priestly teachers already exerted a great influence in the community and began persistently to claim for themselves, as teachers of the Law, the same authority which, till then, the priests exclusively had enjoyed. At first, these teachers of Israelitic and non-priestly descent, חכמי ישראל, probably worked in harmony with the priestly teachers and did not dispute the latter's superior authority. For they could not deny the privileges and prerogatives which the Law gave to the priests and which the latter actually possessed. But the strong desire of the priests for material influence and power and for the maintenance of their own special privileges, could not long harmonize with the purely religious tendencies and the desire to make the Law the common possession of the people that animated the non-priestly teachers. This fundamental difference between the political and worldly aspirations of the priestly aristocrats and the purely religious and spiritual tendencies of the pious lay teachers led to the conflict between the two classes. From the lay teachers developed the party of the Pharisees, while the priestly aristocracy, originally the representatives and leaders of the entire people, became a mere party, *viz.*, the Sadducees.

This difference in tendency which divided them into two parties with different attitudes towards the Law, was already felt before the Maccabean War. It found its primary expression in the first decade of the second century B. C. E. After Judea came under the rule of Antiochus the Great, a senate or Gerousia[8] composed of priests and lay teachers was organized to rearrange and regulate the life of the people according to the laws of their fathers. Both priests and lay teachers, the future Sadducees and Pharisees still stood upon the common ground of Soferic Judaism. Both recognized the Law with all the interpretations given by the Soferim, as absolutely binding upon the people. They also appreciated the teachings of tradition not contained in the written Law. There was absolutely no dispute about these traditions. The priests, especially, had the highest regard for them, since they really were priestly traditions. For up to that time there had been no lay teachers or חכמי ישראל, in an official position who could claim to be the bearers of tradition.[9] But in

[8] Josephus (*Ant.* XII, 3. 3) reproduces an epistle in which Antiochus the Great, gives the Jewish people permission to live according to their own laws, and frees their priests and the members of their Gerousia from all taxes. This epistle may be spurious. But Josephus must have known from other sources that the conditions in Judea, after it came under Syrian rule, were such as described in this epistle so that he could well believe the latter to have been actually written by Antiochus the Great. We can, therefore, learn from this report that under Antiochus the Great the Jews tried to arrange their affairs and live according to their own laws and that their Gerousia or Sanhedrin had many laymen, i. e., non-priests as members. These non-priestly members of the Gerousia must have been acquainted with the laws of the fathers, that is, they were חכמי ישראל (see my *Midrash and Mishnah*).

[9] The Soferim, the official teachers of the people, were, as said above, priests. It was only after the death of Simon the Just, I, the last of the Soferim, about 270 B. C. E. when the authority of the priests was undermined and their official activity as teachers interrupted, that a class of laymen acquainted with the Law, חכמי ישראל, could have grown up (see *Midrash and Mishnah*). Accordingly, these lay-teachers, had never before been in any official position, as recognized teachers. They could, therefore, not claim to have direct traditions from the fathers independent of the priests. They could only go back to the traditions and teachings of the Priest-Soferim.

the hundred years during which Judea was under the political rule and cultural influence of the Greeks, conditions in the community changed so radically that the Law as interpreted by the Soferim together with the traditional laws, such as there might have been, were insufficient to meet the needs of the times and could not provide for all cases, nor regulate all actual occurrences. Many questions of practical life arising from the changed conditions, could not be answered from the Law nor from tradition. How, then, regulate the actual life of the people and harmonize it with the Law? This problem, which had a political, as well as a religious aspect, brought to a climax the difference of opinion between the two elements in the Gerousia, that ultimately developed into two distinct parties, the actual rulers and leaders, the priestly aristocrats, and the would-be leaders, the popular and democratic lay teachers; the Sadducees and the Pharisees.[10]

The aristocratic priests and the ruling classes connected with them, who had always enjoyed a certain measure of authority, now clung fast to the established practices and by extreme conservatism sought to retain their old privileges. They would not see in the changed conditions cause for change in authority or in the modes of applying the Law. Considering themselves as interpreters of the Law, like their fathers, they could see no reason for departing from the rules and methods, or losing the privileges, of their fathers. Like their fathers, they held that

[10] Of course, this does not mean that the names צדוקים and פרושים for distinct parties came into use before the Maccabean War. It only means that the difference between the חכמי כהנים and חכמי ישראל (the two elements that formed the nucleus of the two later parties), was already noted in that first assembly of the reorganized Sanhedrin or Gerousia. It did not, however, come to a complete division at that time, because each group still believed itself able to convince or win over the other. Then came the Maccabean uprising, which the חסידים and the חכמי ישראל supported, expecting as a result of the war the inauguration of a theocratic community according to their ideas and ideals. Only when the Hasmoneans followed the policy of the aristocratic priests and became also Sadduceans, i. e., like the other priests the בני צדוק, only then did the חכמי ישראל separate from them and form a distinct party with the name of פרושים. This probably happened under John Hyrcanus (see below, p. 45, note 21).

there was only one law of absolute authority and this was the Law of Moses, as contained in the Pentateuch, which the people in the time of Ezra had sworn to keep and obey. As we have seen above, the Soferim also taught only the written Torah with its interpretation, Midrash, because it was the sole authority. Accordingly, the priestly group and their followers, who formed the Sadducean party, did not depart in the least from the traditional view, nor differ at all from the former priestly teachers, their ancestors, the Soferim, in their attitude towards the Law. They accepted and followed strictly, the simple, sound interpretations of the Soferim, based upon the plain sense of the words of the Law. They rightly assumed, that as a code of laws the Torah is clear, distinct and unambiguous in expression, that every commandment or law is stated in plain and simple words, easily understood by men for whom the laws and commandments are intended. Or, to use a technical phrase, the Sadducees held דברה תורה כלשון בני אדם, "the Torah speaks in human language,"[11]

[11] The principle דברה תורה כלשון בני אדם which R. Ismael, the last representative of the older Halakah opposed to R. Akiba's tendency to interpret every apparently superfluous word in the Torah (Sifre Num. 112) was, of course, very old. As held by the Sadducees it meant more than merely the rule לשונות כפולות הן as opposed to the tendency to derive laws from certain expressions in the Torah לשונות ריבויין הן as one would judge from p. Shab. 17a. It meant rather that the Torah is to be treated like a human code and its words can mean only what they expressly state in their plain sense. This principle is so thoroughly in consonance with the Sadducean teachings that it needs no proof to show that it was originally a Sadducean principle. Yet one proof may be cited that even among the later rabbis of the Talmud it was still remembered that the Sadducees advanced or followed the principle דברה תורה כלשון בני אדם. In Sanh. 90b a Baraita is quoted which mentions the argument advanced by R. Eleazar b. Jose to prove to the Sadducees [the text has מינים but the correct reading, as given in Rabbinowitz' *Diḳduḳe Soferim*, is צדוקים, as indeed the Sadducees denied the resurrection of the dead] that the belief in resurrection is indicated in the Torah. R. Papa then asks Abaye why R. Eleazar did not prove it to them from the double expression הכרת תכרת, which must refer to a twofold death for the wicked and thus implies another life after resurrection for those not so punished. But Abaye answers him that the Sadducees would have refuted the argument from the expression הכרת תכרת, by declaring that "the Torah speaks the language of man" and such expressions like הכרת תכרת have no special meaning דברה תורה כלשון בני אדם אמרי ליה הוו אינהו. This is not merely a hypothetical answer which, in the opinion of Abaye, the

a principle, which was retained long thereafter even among the Pharisees by the representatives of the older Halakah, which, as has been stated, has many points in common with the teachings and views of the Sadducees. Accordingly, we find them strict in observance of the Law, in its literal meaning, in accordance with traditional[12] methods and principles. They would not devise ingenious methods to explain away a written law or give it a new meaning not warranted by the plain sense of the words. They also held in reverence the unwritten laws and traditional customs and usages, of which, as priests, they were in possession. They observed them in most cases in the same manner as their fathers had done.[13]

Sadducees could have given, but a reminiscence of the principles held by the Sadducees and which they would have applied as an answer.

[12] That their interpretations were the old, traditional ones is evident from the fact that they are in accordance with the literal meaning. In some cases we still find that the older Halakah, adhering strictly to older traditions, followed them, as in the case of עין תחת עין which R. Eliezer takes in its plain literal meaning ממש (B. Ḳ. 84a), exactly as the Sadducees. Of course the Pharisaic sources either suppressed many older Halakoth which followed the Sadducean teachings or did not mention that the Sadducees agreed with them, so that we have not many instances to prove to what extent the Sadducean principles agreed with the older Halakah.

[13] Of course, we can no more ascertain to what extent the earlier Sadducees followed and observed traditional laws, as the Pharisaic sources did not care to report this. But from the very fact, that we hear of only a few laws as being disputed by the Sadducees, we may infer that all the other traditional laws and practices were followed by them. We have, moreover, some positive proofs that confirm this. Thus we never hear that they disputed the law or custom of reading the שמע. The Am ha-Areẓ, described in the Talmud (Ber. 47b) as not reading the Shema, was, in this respect, not a follower of the Sadducees, as Chwolson in his *Beiträge zur Entwicklungsgeschichte des Judentums* (Leipzig, 1910), p. 6 assumes. From the Mishnah Tamid 5.1 we learn that the שמע was read daily by the priests in the Temple, and we know that the Temple service of the priests, was, with the exception of the last 40 or 50 years of the Temple existence, arranged according to Sadducean principles. Accordingly the Sadducees must have observed the practice of reading the שמע, although it is not a biblical law. For according to Samuel (Ber. 21a) it is merely a rabbinic institution קריאת שמע דרבנן היא. It was probably instituted by the Soferim (cf. Pineles, *Darkah shel Torah*, pp. 19–20). And in the case of חיבוט ערבה we have seen above that they objected only to its being performed on a Sabbath day but practiced it on week days. From Matt. 14.11–12

However, they argued in a simple, logical manner — and upon this argument their peculiar view of these laws is based. Since these traditional laws, although some were as old as the written Law, were not incorporated in the Torah, they evidently were not meant to be like the Written Law, always binding upon the people. And they were certainly not accepted by the people as such, for they were not included in the Torah which the people had by oath pledged themselves to obey. For in taking this oath to obey the Law, the people had in mind only the Law as contained in the book read to them by Ezra. And from the very fact, that so many laws and customs although not contained in the Book of the Law and consequently not absolutely obligatory had nevertheless been observed and practiced, with the sanction of the former teachers and priests, side by side with the written laws, the Sadducees drew the logical conclusion, that the Law as contained in the Book was not intended to be all-comprehensive capable of regulating the life of the people in all aspects. At least it was never so understood by the teachers nor regarded by the people. Accordingly, they held that the Torah was meant by its giver and considered by the people who accepted it, to be merely the Book containing the main and absolute laws, to be always observed and never transgressed nor abrogated. But in addition to these absolute laws the representatives and rulers of the people, *viz.*, the priests were free and empowered to adopt such rules and laws, and institute such practices as were required by new conditions to settle new cases and questions bearing upon the public and private life of the people. The passage in Deut. 17, commanding the people to obey the decisions of the priests and follow their instructions, expressly bestows this right upon the priests. For in its literal meaning this passage gives the priests the twofold authority, to teach and interpret

---

where Jesus is said to have warned his disciples against the doctrines of the Sadducees and Pharisees, we also learn that there were some unwritten laws and teachings common to both of them. For Jesus could not have meant the written laws accepted by both the Sadducees and Pharisees. And the phrase דבר שהצדוקים מודין בו (Hor. 5a,b) although it primarily means the written laws, also refers to certain traditional laws which were accepted by the Sadducees and therefore considered as undisputable, like the laws of the written Torah.

the Torah, and also to institute statutes and ordinances, independent of the Written Law.[14] And the historic facts proved that the former priests and teachers availed themselves of this right. For the action of the former teachers and priests in instituting new laws and practices which thus became traditional laws, could be justified only according to the principal rule laid down in Deut. 7, and explained by the supposition that they never considered the Law to be all-comprehensive and all-sufficient.

Standing upon this ground, the Sadducees found a satisfactory solution for the problem that confronted them, *viz.*, how

[14] The passage על פי המשפט אשר יאמרו לך really means: according to the decision or rule which they will tell you *as their own opinion* not in the name of the Law. For if it meant only the decisions which they will give as derived from, and in the name of, the Law, it would be repeating what is said in the passage על פי התורה אשר יורוך. The following passage (Deut. 17.12) threatening punishment to the man who refuses to obey the priest לבלתי שמוע אל הכהן, also speaks of the authority of the priest as such. For if it meant only the man who refuses to listen to the instruction from the Torah, given by the priest, it would say לבלתי שמוע אל דברי התורה. That the passage Deut. 17.11 really meant to give to the authorities the power to decide questions independently of the Torah, is evident from the fact that the Pharisees, after supplanting the authority of the priests by that of the teachers, also interpreted the passage to mean, "even if they tell you about something apparently wrong, that it is right, or vice versa, you must obey them" אפילו מראים בעיניך על שמאל שהוא ימין ועל ימין שהוא שמאל שמע להם (Sifre Deut. 154). The contradiction between this interpretation and the following one, mentioned in p. Hor. 45d: יכול אם יאמרו לך על ימין שהוא שמאל ועל שמאל שהוא ימין תשמע לו ת"ל ללכת ימין ושמאל עד שיאמרו לך על ימין שהוא ימין ועל שמאל שהוא שמאל can be explained by assuming that the Baraitha quoted in the Jerushalmi is older and originated in Temple times. It expresses a protest against the authority claimed by the Sadducees as priests, and emphasizes, that the authorities have a right to demand obedience only if they decide rightly according to the Law על ימין ימין not as the Sadducees do who interpret the Law wrongly and say על שמאל שהוא ימין. The saying in Sifre on the other hand, is much later and originated at the time when the Pharisaic teachers had already supplanted the priests and were the only recognized authorities. It was then declared that their authority was not to be doubted, that their decisions must be obeyed even if they appear to be wrong. See Shir Hashirim r. to 1.2 "Thy love is better than wine"; — "According to the law which they shall teach thee (Deut. 17.11)." It is not written here "According to what the *Torah* shall teach thee" but "according to what *they* shall teach thee." "And according to the judgment which they shall tell thee (*ibid.*)." It is not written here "according to the judgment which *it* (*the Torah*) shall tell thee," but "which *they* shall tell thee."

to regulate the life of the people under the changed conditions of their time. For, as a practical consequence of their standpoint, they claimed for themselves the right and authority which their forefathers enjoyed, *viz.*, to enact new laws and regulations necessary for the new questions resulting from the changed conditions of their time. And they did not hesitate to do so. They laid down their own decisions and rules in a book called ספר גזירתא[15] "Book of Decrees" or "Decisions" to guide them in deciding questions to which no answer could be found in the Mosaic code. They did not deem it right or necessary to invent new rules of hermeneutics, or develop methods of interpretation to enable them to force their laws and decisions into the meaning of the words of the Torah, so as to pass off their own rules and decisions as part of, or derived from, a Mosaic law, thus making them of equal authority with, and of the same binding character as the written Law. For, in their opinion, no other laws could ever acquire the authority of the Laws of the Torah, not even such, as are derived by means of interpretation, מדרש חכמים. For, the Torah itself acquired its absolute authority only from the oath by which the people had pledged themselves to obey it.[16]

[15] Meg. Ta'an. IV (Neubauer, p. 8) reads: בארבעה עשר בתמוז עדא ספר גזירתא. On the 14th day of Tamuz, the Book of Decisions was abrogated. This ספר גזירתא is explained by the glossator to mean the Sadducean code of laws מפני שהיה כתוב ומונח לצדוקים ספר גזירות which was put out of use with the victory of the Pharisees. There is no reason to doubt this report of the glossator, which he no doubt derived from an old reliable source. This code contained all the decrees and laws applied by the Sadducees in deciding civil and criminal cases and not only אלו שנסקלין ואלו שנשרפין. It is probable, that the דיני גזירות mentioned in Ket. 13.1 were such Sadducean Judges, who in their decisions applied this Sadducean code, the ספר גזירות. For this reason they were called in a later Baraitha (Ket. 105a) and also in the Mishnah of the Palestinian Talmud, דיני גזילות. For the Pharisees considered their judgments as incorrect and called them "decrees of robbery."

[16] The idea that the binding character of the Torah is derived from the oath and the promise of the people and from the curse imposed upon those who would transgress it, finds its expression in many passages of the Torah itself where the covenant is mentioned, especially in Deut. 29.9–30.20. It is further evident from the fact that the people in the days of Ezra and Nehemiah actually entered into a covenant and pledged themselves by oath to keep the Law (Neh. 10), that such an oath was considered necessary to secure allegiance

The binding power of the oath, however, could not extend beyond the plain meaning of the words of the Law, as the people

to the Law. According to ancient belief the best way to enforce obedience to the Law, especially to bind future generations to keep it, was to impose a curse upon its transgressors. For an oath was regarded as eternally binding, its violation bringing the curse as a necessary consequence. Thus the oath imposed by Joseph upon his brothers to take his remains along with them was considered as binding upon their descendants (Gen. 50.25; Ex. 13.19). And the curse imposed by Joshua upon any one who would rebuild Jericho (Josh. 6.26) is said to have had its effect after many generations (I Kings 16.34). For this reason the covenant could be made even with those not present on that day and was considered as binding upon the children forever (Deut. 29.13, 14 and 28). Again in Dan. 9.11 the idea is expressed, that as a necessary result of their transgression of the Law the stipulated curse had to come and was poured out upon the people of Israel.

In as much as the people in the time of Ezra and Nehemiah accepted the Law only with reluctance, the oath and the curse were necessary to compel them to accept the Law and to secure obedience to it by future generations. It was, however, natural that, as a result of this process of forcing the Law upon the people by means of the oath and the curse, the tendency developed among the people as well as among the priests, on the one hand, to be very strict and rigorous in keeping the Law, in order to prevent the possible evil effect of violating the oath, i. e., the stipulated curse, and on the other hand, not to keep more than was absolutely necessary to accomplish this end, i. e., to comply with the oath. This attitude towards the Law, based on a superstitious belief in the necessarily evil effect of the curse, was originally common to almost all the people. It was an old belief which the Sadducees still retained. That this was an old belief, firmly rooted in the minds of the people, is evident from the fact that even the Pharisees who opposed the older attitude towards the Law, and tried to base the Law's authority upon its being the Divine Command and not on the promise or the oath with which the people had pledged themselves to keep it, even they could not entirely free themselves from this old superstitious belief. Many sayings in Talmudic literature give expression to this old superstitious belief and show that even in the minds of the later talmudic teachers the binding authority of the Law was associated with the binding force of the oath with which it had been accepted. Thus, for instance, to express the obligation that rests upon the Jew to keep the Law the Rabbis very often use the phrase מושבע ועומד מהר סיני "he is bound by the oath taken at Sinai" (M. Shebu. 3.6 and Shebu. 21b, 22b, 23b, 25a,b and Ned. 8a). Another saying tells us that Moses expressly told the people that he imposed upon them the oath to keep the Law not according to whatever mental reservation they might have in their mind but according to what he, Moses, and God had in mind לא על דעתכם אני משביע אתכם אלא על דעתי ועל דעת המקום (ibid., 25a, cf. also Shebu. 29a). This means that they are

who took the oath understood it. The Sadducees distinguished strictly between the absolutely binding written laws and their own additional laws and decisions.[17] The latter they considered merely as temporary decrees and ordinances, גזירות, issued for the time being by the ruling authorities as necessary for the welfare of the community, to meet certain needs. They were authoritative only as long as they were considered necessary or feasible by the leaders and rulers of the community. For the same reason they did not consider the decisions and practices instituted by their predecessors, the priests and teachers of former generations, which constituted the *traditional Laws* of absolute authority like the Written Law. Hence their peculiar attitude towards the traditional Law and their objection to its authority. They did not deny the existence of these old traditional Laws, for they themselves were the possessors and transmitters of the same. Nor did they reject them as spurious or as without any authority, for, they recognized the right of former priests and teachers to enact such laws. They only refused to consider these traditional Laws as of authority absolute and equal with the written laws contained in the Torah. For the latter, they maintained, the people had accepted in covenant and had pledged themselves by oath to keep them for all times, and there was, in their opinion, no way of freeing themselves from the obligation of the oath. But the traditional Laws the people had never accepted in covenant and had never formally bound themselves to keep,

---

bound to keep the two Torahs, written and oral, according to the meaning intended by Moses, which, of course the Rabbis claim to give in their interpretations. Again in Tanḥuma, *Niẓabim* (Buber 25a) we are told that God had entered with Israel three times into a covenant, and the third time he had fixed a curse upon those who might repudiate it. It should further be noticed, that the idea that the Jew is bound by oath to keep the Law is also found in Karaitic literature (see for instance Bashyazi, *Aderet Eliyahu*, 222d and 225a) which is additional evidence that it was an old and common Jewish belief.

[17] They considered it a violation of the prohibition mentioned in Deut. 13.1 to make other laws of equal authority with the Torah. But in making their additional laws merely for temporary use, and not of equally binding force with the Written Law, they thought that they were not adding anything to the Law as such.

hence they were under no obligation to observe them. The people had observed these traditional Laws, merely in obedience to the ruling authorities and following the instructions and directions of the priests and leaders, who in their time had seen fit to institute these laws. It, therefore, rested with the priestly leaders of the time to decide whether these traditional customs and laws instituted by their predecessors, should be observed or abolished. In this way, only, did they deny the compulsory character of the traditional Laws, as Josephus correctly reports.

Viewed in this light, we find in their attitude towards tradition not the slightest inconsistency. It was quite in keeping with their conservative character and reactionary tendencies. For their apparent denial of the authority of tradition was merely a different interpretation of that authority and of the character of its laws. Psychologically this was the result of their tendency to maintain the old traditional ways, by upholding the exclusive traditional authority of the priests. And logically it was the result of their peculiar attitude towards the Written Law in considering its binding character not as something inherent but as something bestowed upon it from without. For the Sadducees respected the Written Law not because they admired it or considered it the Divine Law, containing the highest truths to which they had to give their inner intellectual consent, but because of the binding force of the oath by which their forefathers had accepted it. The violation of this oath necessarily entailed all the evil consequences of the curse. This peculiar attitude towards the Law had a twofold effect. On the one hand it divorced the Law from life, and on the other hand it made them blind slaves to the letter of the Law without regard for its spirit. It divorced the Law from life, in that it made the two absolutely independent of each other. For if the Law had to be kept only because of the oath, it was altogether sufficient that the oath only be kept. But, since they had never taken any oath to refrain from obeying other laws, life itself could in the main be regulated by other laws of independent origin, instituted and abrogated by the ruling authorities without affecting in the least, the obligation of the oath. On the other hand it made them blind slaves, to the letter of the Law in that it necessarily excluded all possibility of development and progress in the Law. For, since the Law had to be kept only because the people had promised under oath to keep it, then it had to be kept in its plain literal sense as the people who took the oath understood it. It need not meet with the approval of our reason or conscience and, therefore, need neither be interpreted nor explained so as to meet changed conditions and satisfy new views resulting from these changed conditions. The necessary result of such an uncompromising, unprogressive attitude was that the ritual laws gained in prominence and the religious life became centered in such ritual laws as could be maintained and observed strictly and literally. In practical every-day life, outside of the Temple, the Sadducees in the course of time necessarily came more and more to ignore and transgress the religious laws, simply because under the circumstances it was impossible to observe them literally. The religious Law then, thus divorced from life instead of actually controlling it, degenerated into a matter of the sanctuary. It became mere formalism and ritualism, to be observed only in the Temple, where alone it could always be kept strictly in the old traditional way. But it lost entirely all influence upon life.

III.

The חכמי ישראל, i. e., the lay teachers of Israelitic descent, not belonging to the priestly aristocracy had altogether different views about the authority of the Law and Tradition. And the Pharisees, who, as a party, grew out of, and followed, the non-priestly teachers, based their attitude towards the Law and Tradition upon the views held and developed by these teachers.

These חכמי ישראל who had never been permitted to share in the authority of the priests, now on their part refused to recognize this authority of the priests, and began to dispute, not the right of the priests to their privileges as such, but the character and extent of these privileges. Like the priests they also recognized the Law as the only authority. But they claimed that the Law was the heritage of the entire house of Jacob, the common possession of all the people, and that the priests had no monopoly in it. Except that certain functions were assigned to them, which they had to perform and for which they received as compensation certain privileges, the priests, so the lay teachers claimed, were in no way better or more privileged and had no more rights than the rest of the people. Since there was no authority other than the Law, all who knew the Law, i. e., its teachers, whether priests or Israelites, could speak in its name and represent its authority. But, both alike, priests and Israelites could only speak in the name and the authority of the Law and had no authority of their own. Consequently these lay teachers denied the authority claimed by the priests to enact laws necessary for the regulation of the life of the people. In their opinion the passage in Deut. 17, on which the priests based their claim, did not give the priests any special authority besides the Law. It did not bestow upon them the right to institute laws or introduce customs, independent of the Law, not even for temporary use. It gave them only the right to interpret the Law and decide questions according to it. Even this right was not given to them because they were priests as a hereditary class privilege or special family distinction. It was given to them only because and for as long as they were the teachers of the Law, and it was equally given to Israelites who were teachers of the Law, i. e., to the חכמי ישראל. Again, these teachers argued, since, there was no authority other than the Law there could not have been and there never were any other additional laws enacted by priests as ruling authorities. Every rule or decree for the regulation of the life of people to have any authority necessarily must be based on or derived from the Law. For the sovereign authority of the Torah suffered neither repudiation of nor additions to its laws. It expressly forbids in Deut. 13.1, the slightest addition to its commandments, i.e., it prohibits the enactment of any additional laws. The Torah alone is sufficient to regulate the life of the people in all aspects. As a logical consequence of this view these lay-teachers had to expand the connotation of the term Torah beyond the literal meaning of the written word, and make it the basis for new decisions and rules necessary for their times. To achieve this latter end these lay teachers applied new methods of interpretation and developed rules of hermeneutics by which they could read new meanings into the Law and get out of it new decisions and rules.

By that psychological process which makes things dear to us grow in value and importance, it was easier for these lay-teachers to do this, *viz.*, to find the Law all-comprehensive, containing all they needed. For these lay teachers were now new claimants of authority in the name of the Law. And this Law which they thus claimed to represent, and which was to bestow upon them equal rights with the priests and to give them privileges which they had never before enjoyed, naturally meant much more to them, than to the priests, who were not so much dependent upon the Law for their already time-honored privileges and well-established social position. To the lay teachers the Law was a newly acquired כלי חמדה, a precious vessel which contained for them the greatest blessing and they valued it accordingly and revered it more than the priests. For the latter had for so long a time been familiar with the Law and accustomed to administer it that naturally they could not regard it with the same awe and reverence as the new aspirants. The lay teachers looked upon the Torah not as a mere constitution or code to which the people had pledged their allegiance by oath. In their opinion the Torah was much more than a constitution and not to be compared with any other code. It was the תורת יי תמימה the Law of God, most perfect, representing the Divine authority and containing the highest wisdom and loftiest truths. And being such, this perfect, Divine Law had to be sufficient for all times to guide and control the entire life of the people. For as a Divine and perfect Law it must not be understood in its simple sense and in its literal meaing only, like any other man-made law. Its words have deeper meanings, and if properly interpreted, can furnish decisions for all possible cases and give answers to all possible questions. This perfect, Divine Law certainly does not need the priests to complete it by enacting additional laws. For from the principles laid down and from certain indications and peculiar expressions, contained in it, one can derive much better and wiser laws, necessary for the changed conditions, than the ruling priests and chiefs could by their vain reasoning and foolish arguments devise and enact. This principle is expressed in the oft-repeated Pharisaic argument לא תהא תורה שלימה שלנו כשיחה בטלה שלכם.[18]

Of course, a psychological motive, if not the motive, for thus exalting the Law might have been their desire to dispute the rights and privileges of the priestly aristocrats of their own times. By declaring the Law the absolute and all-sufficient authority that neither needs nor suffers any other authority, they invalidated most effectively the claim of the priests that laws additional to the Torah are necessary and permissible and that they, the priests, had the right and the authority to enact them. But once these lay teachers denied to their opponents, the priests of their own times, any authority independent of or additional to the Law, they had consistently to go one step farther, and deny the same also to the priests and leaders of former generations. For there was no principle by which to distinguish between priests and priests. If Deut. 17.8–13, as these lay teachers interpreted it, gives the priests only the authority as teachers to interpret the Law, then the former priests and teachers could by right not have done more than merely interpret the Law and decide questions according to it. They could not have exercised any greater authority nor enacted independent laws, for this the Law did not grant.

But then this question presented itself. By what authority then, if not that of the priests and teachers of former generations, were all the traditional laws and customs enacted which were not written in the Law and yet obeyed and observed by the

---

[18] Scholion to Meg. Ta'an. (Neubauer, pp. 4, 11, 14) and in the parallel passage B. B. 116a. This was an old Pharisaic principle, of which Joḥanan b. Zakkai made use in his disputes with the Sadducees. Later teachers however, knowing that Joḥanan b. Zakkai used this argument against the Sadducees, but not recollecting correctly when so used reported him to have applied it even on occasions when it was not appropriate, and when the Sadducees could rightly reply בכך אתה פוטרני. It is also possible that this principle had originally a positive meaning, *viz.*, our Torah shall not be considered like your idle talk, that is to say it must not be interpreted like a human code, we must apply to it other standards. In this sense the principle was a protest against the Sadducean rule that the Torah speaks in human language and is to be treated like any other law-code (see above, p. 29, note 9).

people? To say, that they were merely customs, observed by the people, or temporary laws instituted by the priests, without any real authority, would mean to admit that the life of the people in the past was controlled not exclusively by the authority of the Law but also by regulations of the people or ruling authorities. This, however, would have defeated the arguments of these lay-teachers and refuted their claim that the Law alone must control the entire life of the people. How could they deny that the life of the people may be controlled by additional laws enacted by the priests, and at the same time admit that this was the practice in former ages? Besides, some of these traditional laws were too highly respected by them and considered by the people as religious laws, to be declared as having been enacted without any real authority. The only possible answer to this question that would be in keeping with this tendency of the lay teachers, to deny the authority of the priests, and yet save the character of these traditional laws, was, therefore, to declare that these traditional laws and customs were not *independent additional laws* enacted by former teachers and priests on their own authority, for they had none, but merely interpretations and applications of the Law, as understood by them, and given in the name and by the authority of the *Law* itself. Consequently these traditional laws are as absolutely binding as the written laws, since they are actually part of the Torah, indicated in it, or implied in its fuller meaning, as the teachers of former generations properly understood it.

This declaration that the traditional laws were not independent laws enacted by former teachers, but part of the Torah, led to the final step, of raising tradition to the importance of the Torah. This position taken by the lay teachers and the Pharisees that followed them had the effect of giving to the Oral Law authority equal to the Written Law. For certain traditional laws and customs could in no way be connected with the written Torah and represented as part, or derived from an interpretation, of a Written Law. Such traditional laws, it would seem, could not but be considered as additional laws to the Torah. How, then, in the face of such existing traditional laws could the Pharisaic teachers maintain their principal contention that they had a

תורה שלימה, a perfect Torah that has no need of any additional laws and to which additional laws were never made? Simply, by giving a broader definition to the term, Torah, and declaring that even those traditional laws which had no basis whatever in the written Book of the Law of Moses, were nevertheless part of the Torah of Moses, but given orally by him and handed down through the generations, by word of mouth and not in written form. For there was a twofold Torah given by God to Moses, written and oral. To this twofold Torah the prohibition in Deut. 13.1, refers, when it forbids to add to or subtract from the laws which Moses commanded. This prohibition was never violated, for nothing was ever added to the laws of Moses. All the laws observed by the Jewish people, were laws of Moses, either expressly stated or indicated in, or derived from the words of the Written Law, or handed down by oral tradition, but none of them originated after the time of Moses, for no additions were ever allowed to the laws of Moses. Not only could not the former priests and leaders but even the prophets never attempted to add any new ordinance to the laws of Moses.[19] Extreme as such conclusions may appear to us, they were none the less arrived at by the old teachers almost unconsciously by what appears to

---

[19] The passage in Lev. 27.34 had been interpreted by the Pharisaic teachers to mean that no prophet could add anything to the Law, after it had been given on Sinai שאין נביא רשאי לחדש עוד דבר (Sifra, Beḥuḳotai 13, end). This interpretation is often quoted as if it were part of the actual text of Leviticus והכתיב אלה המצות שאין נביא רשאי לחדש דבר מעתה (Shab. 104a and parallels) which proves that it is very old. From Tem. 16a we see that this interpretation was understood to apply even to Joshua and Samuel, who when some of the Laws of Moses had been forgotten, could not as prophets have tried to restore them. This shows that the purpose of this saying was to express that the Torah of Moses was absolutely complete and perfect and never needed or suffered any additions. It was directed against the Sadducees, not as Weiss (Dor. II, 7) assumes, against Christianity. The Rabbis would not have used this saying against Christianity, for this would have implied that they admitted that Jesus or Paul had some claim to prophecy and only denied them the right even as prophets to change the Law. Weiss' question, why emphasize this saying when no prophet attempted to change the Law, is sufficiently answered by our explanation that it was to emphasize the idea of a תורה שלימה. And at the time, when this saying was first expressed there was danger of some authorities making new laws, even though they were not prophets.

be a very simple method of reasoning. If the people were to obey only the Law given by God to Moses, then it presumably follows that whatever laws the people did obey must have been given to Moses. And when once it was declared that the traditional laws also were the laws of Moses, even though not contained in the Book, it was easy to include in this category also those traditional laws which apparently were of later origin or even of recent date, thus maintaining consistently that there was not a law observed by the Jewish people which had not been given by Moses. Accordingly, when confronted with laws and practices, known to have been decreed at a certain time and by certain teachers or prophets, the Pharisaic teacher would declare שכחום וחזרו ויסדום[20] that such laws were really Mosaic, but had been forgotten and only afterwards recalled and reintroduced by that teacher or prophet, to whom they were then erroneously ascribed.

These were the ideas and principles of the Pharisees, the party that grew out of and followed the חכמי ישראל.[21] Of course,

---

[20] Although the saying שכחום וחזרו ויסדום is found used only by Amoraim, it is a very old saying which the Amoraim merely quoted and repeated. It is as old as the saying שאין נביא רשאי לחדש דבר מעתה to which it forms a corollary. It is used as an answer to objections raised against the latter principle (Shab. 104a) and to account for innovations said to have been made by the prophets. Thus the contradiction between the statement that the ceremony of ערבה was a Mosaic law הלל״מ and the other statement which described the same ceremony as an institution of the prophets יסוד נביאים is removed by applying the principle שכחום וחזרו ויסדום (Suk. 44a). Another similar way of accounting for some new laws mentioned by the prophets and not found in the Torah, was to assume that such laws were traditional laws received from Moses which the prophets merely happened to mention or express in their writing גמרא גמיר לה ואתא יחזקאל אסמכה אקרא, Ta'an. 17b.

[21] The original name of the party was חכמי ישראל or simply חכמים in contradistinction to the name חכמי כהנים or צדוקים. In M. Mak. 1.6 and in Baraita (Mak. 5b) as well as in the Scholion to Meg. Ta'an. (Neubauer, pp. 1 and 9) the name חכמים is used for the party opposed to the Sadducees. That under חכמים were meant lay teachers of Israelitic, non-priestly descent, follows from the account in Scholion to Meg. Ta'an. (Neubauer, p. 17) that, at first the Sadducees composed the Sanhedrin and with the exception of Simon b. Shetah there was not one Israelite among them ולא היה אחד מישראל יושב עמהם. And when Simon is reported to have succeeded in substituting Pharisaic members for the Sadducees, the report reads (ibid.) נסתלקה סנהדרין של צדוקים וישבה סנהדרין של ישראל where ישראל stands for חכמי ישראל in opposition

all these views and theories did not originate at one and the same time. They developed gradually and it must have taken some time till the system was completed. But we can see clearly how, and by what process, these theories developed, and we find them absolutely consistent with, nay even resulting from, the main tendency of these lay teachers, and of the Pharisaic party that followed them, *viz.*, to dispute the particular privileges of the aristocratic priests and deny them any special authority in religious matters. To dispute successfully the right of the priests to enact new laws necessary for the changed conditions, they had on the one hand to maintain that the priests never had such a right or authority, and on the other hand to insist on the completeness of the Torah and its sufficiency to provide for all cases and conditions. Consequently they had to deny that any of the traditional laws originated from, or were enacted by the priests or teachers of former generations later than the Written Law. They had to insist that they were all enacted by the same auhtor and lawgiver as the Written Law. Thus we see that the Pharisees or the teachers whom they followed, the חכמי ישראל,

---

to צדוקים who were כהנים. This is even more evident from the report about the conflict between John Hyrcanus and the Pharisees (Ḳid. 66a) whence we can learn, when and perhaps also why the name פרושים was first given to these lay teachers. In this report the Pharisees are called חכמי ישראל. Only in the mouth of their accuser Eleazar b. Poʻirah they are called פרושים, when he accuses them of being at heart opposed to the king פרושים עליך לבם של. If the name פרושים was really used by Eleazar, then, we learn from this report that the name was given to them by their enemy, describing them as "separatists." In applying this name to the teachers, Eleazar meant to criticize their attitude and tell the king that they formed a separate group not as loyal to the king as the rest of the people and not sharing in the peoples' joy in his success. But it is also possible that Eleazar used another perhaps disparaging name, for which the word פרושים was later substituted. In this case the phrase ויבדלו חכמי ישראל בזעם "and the Israelitic teachers were dismissed" or perhaps "expelled from the Sanhedrin" will give us the origin of the name פרושים. The wise teachers who were thus dismissed from the king's council and expelled from the Sanhedrin were called נבדלים the excluded ones or expelled ones, or פרושים. This name originally given to them by their enemies they later accepted and it remained the name of their party. Only, they may have interpreted it to mean, not that they had been expelled but that they themselves left the Sanhedrin and separated themselves from the wicked Sadducees with whom they would not sit together.

did not invent any traditions which the Sadducees did not know, or could dispute; they merely invested the traditional Law, common to both of them, with a binding character and greater authority by raising it to the rank of a twin sister to the Written Law.

This recognition of the absolute authority of tradition, and of the superiority of the Torah to any other code or lawbook, not only did not hinder, but even helped and furthered the progressive tendencies of the Pharisees. With all their submission to the Law as the sole and absolute authority, the Pharisaic teachers did not become the slaves of the Law, but rather the masters of it. Their very respect for the Law had the necessary result that they could make of it whatever they pleased, for the Law was now in their hands, capable of development along all possible lines. The declaration that the Law is unlike any other code and does not "speak in human language" implied, that it could be interpreted to mean and contain anything which the teachers would read into it. Again the close and intimate connection between Law and life, on which the Pharisees insisted, also implied the possibility of the growth and development of the Law and its adaptability to the needs of the life of each successive generation. The demand that the entire life of the people be controlled by the Law, necessarily brought about the effect that the Law became in turn controlled by life and its conditions. For the authority of the Law with the Pharisaic teachers, was based not on the binding force of the oath with which the people had pledged themselves to obey it, but on its being the Divine Law, containing all that is true, to which they had to give their inner consent and approval. The result of this view of the Law was that its teachings and commandments had to be interpreted in conformity with the standard of the teachers of each generation, and made to harmonize with their advanced ideas. This was not done by a conscious effort to harmonize. It was accomplished by an almost unconscious psychological process. The teachers, in their admiration for the Law, could not imagine that it could contain anything wrong or express something of which they could not fully approve. Accordingly, when in the course of time and with the development of their ideas of life, they had outgrown a certain law, and could no more accept it in its original meaning they unconsciously gave that law a new and more acceptable meaning.[22]

Thus the element of evolution and progress was injected into the Law. With the ever growing conscience and broadening views of the teachers, the meaning of the Law and the conception of its underlying ideas broadened and developed. For the Law could never mean anything else than what the teachers understood it to mean. This identification of the Law with the ever growing and changing ideas of the teachers, in the course of time even extended the authority of the Law to the very decrees and enactments of the teachers. And after the final victory over the Sadducees, when the Pharisaic teachers alone were the recognized religious authorities, they claimed for themselves the right, which the Sadducees of old had claimed for the priests only, *viz.*, to enact new laws necessary for their time. This right they derived from the very same passage in Deut. 17, formerly used by the Sadducees, which they now applied to themselves instead of to the priests. Thus they derived from the words לא תסור the right to enact new laws binding upon the people. Only they claimed that whatever laws they enacted were in accordance with the actual spirit and the fundamental principles of the Law. It was due to this progressive tendency of the Pharisees, that their interpretation of Judaism continued to develop and remained an ever living force in Jewry. On the other hand Sadducaism, because of its rigid conservatism in following the letter of the Law, gradually lost all influence upon the life of the main body of the Jewish people.

[22] The best illustration of the effect of the broadening conscience of the teachers upon the interpretation of the Law is the change in the interpretation of the law of retaliation (Ex. 21.24–25). Originally this law was understood in its literal meaning ממש as interpreted by the Sadducees and by the older Halakah represented by R. Eliezer (B. Ḳ. 84a). But when the conscience of the teachers developed and their ideas of punishment became more humane, they could not imagine that the Divine Law could decree or sanction such cruelty. They, therefore, could not believe that it was ever meant literally, and in good faith they interpreted it to mean merely ממון monetary compensation. Other illustrations of how the rabbis actually invalidated laws which no more appealed to them, are their interpretations of the Laws of Deut. 21.18–21 and 13.13–18. Cf. also Pineles, *Darkah shel Torah*, pp. 8–9.

A Significant Controversy Between the Sadducees and the Pharisees

A Significant Controversy Between the Sadducees and the Pharisees

(1927)

ONE of the important disputes between the Sadducees and Pharisees was about the manner in which the High Priest should bring in the incense into the Holy of Holies to be offered there on the Day of Atonement. The Sadducees claimed that the offering must be prepared outside of the Holy of Holies. Their practice demanded of the High Priest to put the incense upon the censer outside of the curtain, which separated the Holy of Holies from the rest of the Temple, and, while the smoke of the incense was coming up, to carry the censer with the smoking incense on it into the Holy of Holies and offer it there. The Pharisees, on the other hand, insisted that the incense should not be put on the censer outside of the Holy of Holies, but that the High Priest should enter the Holy of Holies carrying the censer with the fiery coals in his right hand and the spoon full of incense in his left hand. Only after he had entered inside the curtain should he put the incense upon the fiery coals on the censer and thus offer it there.[1]

The biblical law prescribing this offering of the incense in the Holy of Holies on the Day of Atonement is found in Lev. 16.12–13 and reads as follows: ולקח מלא המחתה גחלי אש מעל המזבח מלפני יי ומלא חפניו קטרת סמים דקה והביא מבית לפרכת. ונתן את הקטרת על האש לפני יי וכסה ענן הקטרת את הכפרת אשר על העדות ולא ימות. "And he shall take a censer full of coals of fire from the altar before the Lord, and his hands full of sweet incense beaten small, and bring it within the veil. And he shall put the incense upon

---

[1] See *HaLebanon*, 4th Year, # 9, (Paris, 1867), p. 132 — "Various Notes" — see note 3. An interesting "Pshetil" but at least he assumes a theological difference.

the fire before the Lord, that the cloud of the incense may cover the Ark-cover that is upon the testimony, that he die not." It cannot be denied that the plain meaning of these Scriptural passages favors the Pharisees.[1a] The interpretation put upon these two verses by the Pharisees is syntactically correct. The two consecutive verses prescribe consecutive actions. The priest should first enter within the veil and then, while inside, put the incense upon the fire. It is, therefore, evident that the difference of opinion between the two parties in this specific case was not merely the result of their well-known different methods of interpreting the Law. For as a rule the Sadducees insisted upon a strictly literal interpretation of the Law, while the Pharisees favored a free and more liberal interpretation. In this case, however, they have apparently reversed their positions.

It is also impossible to consider this difference between the two parties merely as the result of their respective attitudes towards the unwritten Law or traditional practice. We cannot assume, as some modern scholars[2] following Maimonides[3] do,

---

[1a] Cf. A. Geiger in *Ozar Neḥmad*, IV, 106; M. M. Kalisch, *A Historical and Critical Commentary on the Old Testament* (London, 1872), to this passage in Leviticus; D. Hoffmann, *Das Buch Leviticus* (Berlin, 1905), pp. 446–447. There seems to be one difficulty in this interpretation of the Pharisees in that it seemingly takes the expression לפני ד' in this verse as designating the Holy of Holies, when in many other passages of the Scriptures the same expression designates also the place outside of the Holy of Holies. This difficulty, however, is only apparent. It is true, that the Babylonian Gemara understood the Pharisees to have based their argument on the interpretation of the phrase לפני ה' in verse 13 as designating the Holy of Holies. But, as will be shown in the course of this essay, the Pharisees did not base their argument upon the interpretation of the phrase לפני ה' and they did not at all stress the interpretation of this phrase as designating the Holy of Holies.

[2] Rudolf Leszynsky, *Die Sadducäer*, (Berlin, 1912), p. 61, without referring to Maimonides says: "Beide Parteien berufen sich auf Schriftverse, aber da der Sinn des Pentateuch-Abschnittes mehr für die Sadducäer spricht, so müssen wir auch hier annehmen, dass die Pharisäer von einer mündlichen Ueberlieferung ausgegangen waren." Against his opinion, that the passage of the Pentateuch favors the Sadducees, see the authorities quoted in the preceding note.

[3] The passage in *Yad, Abodat Yom ha-Kippurim*, I, 7, reads as follows: והיו (הצדוקין) אומרין שקטרת של יום הכפורים מניחין אותה על האש בהיכל חוץ לפרוכת וכשיעלה עשנה מכניס אותה לפנים לקדש הקדשים הטעם זה שכתוב בתורה כי בענן אראה על

that the Pharisees followed an oral tradition when they insisted upon their interpretation of the Law in this case.

In the first place, it is rather difficult to believe that the Pharisees could have been in possession of an old traditional law in regard to the performance of a ritual of which the Saducean priests, who alone had been performing it for generations, were ignorant. Furthermore, such a theory would leave unexplained why the Sadducees in this case refused to follow the alleged traditional practice of the Pharisees, especially when, as we have seen, the literal meaning of the written law also favors this practice. We would then have to find some valid reason or some strong cause that prompted the Saducean priests to depart from the old traditional practice based upon a correct literal interpretation of the Written Law. But above all, the theory which assumes that the Pharisees in this case followed an oral tradition, is without any foundation. There is not the least support for it in the talmudic literature. In the case of other practices, not expressly commanded in the Written Law, but advocated by the Pharisees, we do find that the Pharisaic teachers declare such practices to be based upon an institution of the prophets (יסוד נביאים) or a traditional law handed down from Moses on Sinai (הלכה למשה מסיני).[4] But, to my knowledge, no statement can be found in talmudic literature declaring the manner of offering the incense on the Day of Atonement, as

---

הכפורת אמרו כי הוא ענן הקטרת ומפי השמועה למדו חכמים שאין נותן הקטרת אלא בקדש הקדשים לפני הארון שנאמר ונתן הקטרת על האש לפני ה'. Maimonides does not give any source for his statement that the Pharisaic position was based upon a tradition מפי השמועה. It is also very strange that Maimonides seems to have understood that only the Sadducees interpreted the word בענן as referring to the smoke of the incense, when as a matter of fact the Pharisees never disputed this. Maimonides followed the Babylonian Gemara and understood the Pharisees to have based their argument upon the interpretation of the words לפני ה', in verse 13. Considering this Scriptural proof as not very sound he concluded that the Pharisees must have followed a tradition. Cf. also H. Oppenheim in *Bet Talmud*, (Wien, 1885), IV, 269–271. Oppenheim failed to see the real significance of this controversy, and his explanation of the difference of opinion on this question between the Sadducees and Pharisees is far fetched and pilpulistic.

[4] p. Sheb. 1.7 (33b); b. Suk. 44a.

advocated by the Pharisees, to have been based on an older oral tradition. In the disputes between the Sadducees and Pharisees regarding this ceremony, as reported in the Talmud, the Pharisees do not advance the argument of tradition and no reference at all is made to the older traditional practice as to how and in what manner it was performed. Had the older practice been like the one advocated by their party or had there been an oral tradition favoring their opinion, the Pharisaic teachers certainly would have mentioned it. In such cases an *argumentum e silentio* has considerable weight.

It is, therefore, safe to assume, as will indeed be shown in this essay, that in this case the Sadducees followed the traditional time-honored practice, while the Pharisees were not the advocates of an old oral tradition on this subject but the innovators of a radical reform. No doubt they had a very good reason for seeking to introduce this reform in the Temple service and to change the form of one of the most solemn rites of the Day of Atonement. From the talmudic reports about this controversy it is evident that each party attached great importance to its own special idea about the performance of this ceremony. From this we may conclude that a very important doctrine or a basic theological conception was involved in this controversy. There must have been a fundamental principle underlying this difference of opinion between the two parties. But we cannot obtain any direct and definite information from the ancient sources as to what this fundamental principle was, or what the real reasons were that prompted the two parties to insist so strongly upon their respective interpretation of this ritual law. The talmudic reports apparently content themselves with merely presenting the two opposite opinions held respectively by the two parties and giving the scriptural passages which each party cited in support of its peculiar view. These reports do not tell us, at least not on the surface, whether and how each party met the arguments of the other. We can well understand that the talmudic reports, coming from the Pharisaic circles, would refrain from reporting how the Sadducees answered the arguments of the Pharisees. But strangely enough these talmudic reports mention one apparently very strong argument advanced by the

Sadducees in favor of their position, but do not tell us, at least not expressly, what the Pharisees' answer to this argument was. And even in their presentation of the Pharisees' arguments, which was based upon a correct interpretation of scriptural passages, they do not emphasize the strong points in this argument and apparently fail to make the best of the scriptural interpretation which favors the Pharisaic opinion on this matter. On the whole one gets the impression from the talmudic reports that the Pharisees offered poor arguments though they had a very good cause. Yet, there can be no doubt that the Rabbis of the Talmud were convinced that the Pharisees' position on this question was correct. Why, then, did they not bring out clearly all the good reasons justifying the Pharisaic position? Was there any special cause for this reluctance on the part of the Rabbis to state in full all the arguments of the Pharisees? Were the real motives which prompted the Pharisees to insist upon their interpretation of such a nature as to make the Rabbis hesitate to speak about them openly and expressly? It seems to me that this was the case. A careful scrutiny of the talmudic reports, however, combined with a consideration of what is otherwise known about the character of the two parties, their respective religious outlooks and theological positions, will reveal the fundamental principle underlying this controversy and also explain why the Rabbis of the Talmud refrained from making a clear statement about the real issue involved in the controversy.

Let us, therefore, first examine carefully all the talmudic reports about this controversy, notice the difficulties found in them and see to what extent the information thus obtained can help us, directly or indirectly, to a correct understanding of the respective positions of the two parties.

In a Baraita in Sifra (*Aḥare Mot* III, Weiss, 81b, quoted also in p. Yoma 1.5, [39a,b]) we read the following account of the dispute between the two parties in regard to the offering of the incense on the Day of Atonement. והביא אל מבית לפרוכת ונתן את הקטורת על האש לפני ה' שלא יתקן מבחוץ ויכניס מבפנים שהרי הצדוקים אומרים יתקן מבחוץ ויכניס מבפנים. אם לפני בשר ודם עושים כן קל וחומר לפני המקום. ואומר כי בענן אראה על הכפורת. אמרו להם חכמים והלא כבר נאמר ונתן את הקטורת על האש לפני ה'. אינו נותן אלא בפנים. אם כן למה

נאמר כי בענן אראה על הכפורת מלמד שהיה נותן בה מעלה עשן. ומנין שהוא נותן בה מעלה עשן תלמוד לומר וכסה ענן הקטורת את הכפורת אשר על העדות ולא ימות הא אם לא נתן בה (לא היה) מעלה עשן או שחיסר אחת מכל סממניה חייב מיתה. On the surface this Baraita presents some difficulties. It apparently fails to make out a good case for the Pharisees, though it indicates that they had good reasons for their opinion. By citing the second half of verse 12 והביא אל מבית לפרכת together with the first half of verse 13 ונתן את הקטרת על האש לפני ה', as the scriptural basis for the Pharisaic interpretation, the Baraita clearly indicates, though it does not expressly state it, that the Pharisees derived their positive scriptural proof from the syntactic order of the two verses and not merely from the words לפני ה' "before the Lord" in verse 13.[5] This proof, as we have seen, is very sound. Yet, in arguing with their opponents, the Pharisees, in so far as the Baraita reports it, did not make use of this proof. The Sadducees, as we learn from this Baraita, advanced two arguments in favor of their practice. One was the argument of propriety based upon considerations of respect and reverence for the Deity. It would be disrespectful to God, they claimed, to prepare the incense in His very presence, in the Holy of Holies. If when presenting incense to a human being we do not fix it in his presence but prepare it outside before we bring it in to him, how much the more should we do so when offering incense to God. To this seemingly good argument the Pharisees do not, according to the Baraita, give a direct and clear answer. Their answer, as we shall see, may imply a refutation of the Sadducean position, but it is not a clear and direct answer to the Sadducean argument. The Pharisees reply by saying והלא כבר נאמר ונתן את הקטורת על האש לפני ה' "and is it not said 'and he shall put the incense upon the fire before the Lord?'" They do not give the full scriptural proof for their position as cited in the opening of the Baraita. They do not say והלא כבר נאמר והביא אל מבית לפרוכת

[5] It was thus correctly understood by R. Samson of Sens (1150–1230) who in his commentary to the Sifra, (Warsaw, 1863), makes the following comment upon our passage: שלא יתן מבחוץ ויכניס שהרי כתב והביא ולאחר כן ונתן את הקטורת. R. Aaron Ibn Ḥayyim in his commentary קרבן אהרן (Venice, 1609), however, followed the Babylonian Gemara and understood the argument as being based upon the interpretation of the words לפני ה' as designating the Holy of Holies.

ואחר כך ונתן את הקטורת על האש לפני ה' which would have been a good argument for their opinion. They merely say: והלא כבר נאמר ונתן את הקטורת על האש לפני ה' which on the surface is a very poor answer to the Sadducean position. For the words ונתן את הקטורת על האש לפני ה', which alone they quote here, do not in themselves prove that the incense must be prepared in the Holy of Holies. For the Pharisees certainly could not have denied that the expression לפני ה', "before the Lord," could designate also the place outside of the curtain which separated the Holy of Holies from the rest of the Temple.[6] In fact, they do not say that this scriptural passage proves that the incense must be prepared inside of the curtain, for it is to be noticed, they do not say מלמד שאינו נותן אלא מבפנים. The words אינו נותן אלא מבפנים which follow their answer to the Sadducean argument form an independent sentence in which the Pharisees merely reiterate their position. They are not the logical consequence of the preceding answer to the Sadducees. The answer to the Sadducean argument of propriety consisted merely in the words והלא כבר נאמר ונתן את הקטורת על האש לפני ה'. We shall find that this answer implies a refutation of the Sadducean position but it certainly is not a clear and direct answer to the Sadducean argument.

The second argument of the Sadducees was, according to the Baraita, based upon the scriptural passage כי בענן אראה על הכפורת (Lev. 16.2), which they evidently interpreted to mean, "only through the cloud of the smoke of the incense may I be seen upon the Ark-cover." This is not a strong argument at all. In the first place, the word בענן may simply mean "in a cloud," as the ancient versions understood it,[7] and not refer to the smoke of the incense. Secondly, even if the word בענן meant "through the smoke of the incense," the scriptural passage, taken by itself, would merely say that God may be seen only through a screen of smoke without, however, specifying where that screen of smoke must be produced and started. But strangely enough, weak as this argument is, the Pharisees' answer to this argument seems still weaker. The Pharisees admit that the word בענן in this passage designates the smoke of the incense, but they claim

[6] As e. g., Lev. 1.5; 4.4 and 7 and many others.
[7] See Geiger, *Oẓar Neḥmad*, IV, 107.

that this Scriptural passage merely teaches that in preparing the incense the priest should mix in it a smoke-producing ingredient. Now why did the Pharisees not interpret the Scriptural passage to have no reference at all to the smoke of the incense but merely to mean "with a cloud of glory I shall appear upon the ark-cover," as it was understood by the ancient versions? By admitting that the word בענן here means the smoke of the incense and insisting that the incense must contain מעלה עשן, a smoke-producing ingredient, they rather play into the hands of their opponents. The Sadducees certainly insisted that the incense must produce a cloud of smoke. But they also insisted that the smoke must be produced outside of the curtain, and on this point the Pharisees prove nothing to the contrary. For their interpretation, that the scriptural passage means that the incense must contain a smoke-producing ingredient, does not positively prove that the smoke must be produced inside and not outside of the curtain. Furthermore, after this interpretation of the scriptural passage, according to which the words כי בענן אראה על הכפורת teach that the incense contained a smoke-producing ingredient, the Baraita immediately goes on to ask ומנין שהוא נותן בה מעלה עשן "but how do we know that he must mix with the incense a smoke-producing ingredient?" and in answer it cites another scriptural passage to prove it. But if the requirement of מעלה עשן is prescribed in the words וכסה ענן כי בענן הקטורת את הכפורת אשר על העדות ולא ימות then the words אראה על הכפורת cannot be interpreted to prescribe the same thing, as the Pharisees claimed. This difficulty, as we shall see, was indeed felt by the Babylonian Gemara. Again in closing the argument the Baraita adds something which does not belong to the subject under discussion. Instead of merely stating that if he does not put in a smoke-producing ingredient he deserves death, הא אם לא נתן בה מעלה עשן חייב מיתה, the Baraita says, if he does not put into it the smoke-producing ingredient, or if he omits any one of its ingredients he deserves death: הא אם לא נתן בה מעלה עשן או שחיסר אחת מכל סממניה חייב מיתה. This gratuitous information about the death penalty for omitting any one of the ingredients is entirely out of place here, especially since it is not obvious how it could be derived fom the words וכסה ענן הקטורת את הכפורת וכו'.

CONTROVERSY BETWEEN SADDUCEES AND PHARISEES

The same Baraita is also quoted in the Babylonian Talmud (Yoma 53a) with some significant changes. Here we read as follows: ת"ר ונתן את הקטרת על האש לפני ה' שלא יתקן מבחוץ ויכניס להוציא מלבן של צדוקים שאומרים יתקן מבחוץ ויכניס מאי דרוש כי בענן אראה על הכפורת מלמד שיתקן מבחוץ ויכניס אמרו להם חכמים והלא כבר נאמר ונתן את הקטרת על האש לפני ה' אם כן מה תלמוד לומר כי בענן אראה על הכפורת מלמד שנותן בה מעלה עשן ומניין שנותן בה מעלה עשן שנאמר וכסה ענן הקטרת את הכפורת הא לא נתן בה מעלה עשן או שחסר אחת מכל סמניה חייב מיתה. It appears from this version of the Baraita that the Babylonians did not know that the Pharisees derived their positive scriptural proof from the syntactic order of the two verses 12-13 in Lev. 16. They evidently understood the Pharisaic argument to be derived merely from the words לפני ה' in verse 13, interpreting these words to designate the Holy of Holies, and, therefore, in the opening of the Baraita only verse 13 is cited as the scriptural basis for the Pharisaic opinion. For this reason also the exchange of opinions between the two parties as regards the propriety of preparing the incense in the Holy of Holies is omitted. For on the surface the Pharisees' argument, והלא כבר נאמר ונתן את הקטורת על האש לפני ה' merely repeats the main scriptural proof for the Pharisaic position, as put by the Babylonians in the opening of the Baraita, and does not give any direct answer to the argument of propriety advanced by the Sadducees. Not finding in the Pharisees' reply an answer to the Sadducean argument of propriety, the Babylonians omitted the whole dispute as to the propriety from their version of the Baraita. According to their understanding of the dispute, they would strengthen the position of the Pharisees by suppressing a seemingly strong argument of the Sadducees. They also realized the weakness of the Pharisees' answer to the other argument of the Sadducees from the words כי בענן אראה על הכפורת. For, in commenting upon the Baraita, the Gemara points to the difficulty which we have notice above, namely, that after declaring that the words כי בענן אראה על הכפורת teach the requirement of מעלה עשן in the incense, the Baraita asks for and cites another scriptural proof for the indispensable requirement of מעלה עשן.[8] The Gemara

---

[8] The Yerushalmi also felt this difficulty though it does not express it. For at the close of the Baraita there the additional statement is found: ולא אזהרה זה הרי אראה בענן כי עונש זה הרי ימות which explains why the two verses

pointedly asks קרא לקרא?, "Why pile one Scriptural proof upon another?" It goes on to cite many attempts to explain why two verses were necessary for this teaching. One of this explanations is that from the passage כי בענן אראה על הכפורת we would know only that the incense offered on the Day of Atonement requires מעלה עשן, hence we need the passage וכסה ענן הקטרת וכו', to teach us that the incense of every day in the year also requires מעלה עשן. All these explanations, however, are merely attempts to smooth over an apparent difficulty which they had noticed in the Pharisees' answer to the argument from כי בענן אראה על הכפורת. The real difficulty in this answer of the Pharisees, *viz.*, that even if we accept the interpretation that the passage implies the necessity of מעלה עשן in the incense, it does not prove that the incense must be prepared inside of the curtain; this difficulty is not touched upon nor even hinted at by any of the Rabbis of the Talmud.

We thus see that the Baraita reporting this controversy contains some difficulties and from its presentation of the arguments of the two parties we cannot get a satisfactory explanation of their respective positions.

Let us now seek to ascertain what superstitions or primitive beliefs were connected with the Holy of Holies and especially with the offering brought there on the Day of Atonement, beliefs which no doubt lingered on in the popular mind a long time after the teachers and the enlightened people had outgrown them, and allusions to which may still be found in the talmudic legends. A knowledge of these primitive notions or popular beliefs, connected with the Holy of Holies, may help us to understand the struggle of ideas and the theological issue involved in this controversy between the two parties.

It cannot be denied that the primitive notion was that the Tabernacle, and later on the Temple in Jerusalem, were the residences of God on earth and that the Holy of Holies within the Temple was especially the place where He dwelt, the Ark-cover with the two Cherubim being, so to speak, His throne.

---

were necessary. At the same time this statement seeks to emphasize that the ולא ימות means, so that he shall not incur the penalty of death, and not, that he may not die as a direct consequence of seeing the Deity. See note 23.

The Rabbis often sought to suppress or modify these primitive beliefs, or at least to remove from them the crude anthropomorphic elements, but they were not always successful. These primitive beliefs were retained by the people and echoes of them are found in the Talmud and in the Midrashim.

Thus we are told in the Midrash (Ex. r. 3.4) that the Divine residence on earth resembles in most of its features the Divine residence in heaven. We are also told that, while God had chosen the entire land of Palestine as the place where His presence was manifested, He had especially favored the Temple in Jerusalem and within this Temple He had particularly selected the Holy of Holies as His residence (*ibid.*, 37.4). In this earthly residence He had His throne which was believed to be corresponding to and as it were a projection of the throne in heaven (Mekilta, *Shirata* I, Friedmann, 43b; p. Ber. 4.5, [8c]). This throne in the Holy of Holies consisted of the Ark-cover with the two Cherubim on which was the seat of God (Num. r. 4.13, cf. also Suk. 4b–5a and R. H. 31a; Ex. r. 34.1 and Tanḥuma, *Ki Tisa* 10, *Vayakhel* 6). Because the Ark was the throne of God, the priests, even when moving the Tabernacle, had to take special precautions never to look at the Ark. There was a special spread of blue color (כליל תכלת) with which the Ark and the Cherubim were covered. For as the heavenly throne according to Ezek. 1.26 was of blue color, "as the appearance of a sapphire stone," so also the throne in the Holy of Holies, i. e., the Ark and the Cherubim had to appear in blue color, hence the blue spread to cover it (Num. r., *loc. cit.*, cf. also Men. 43b and Sifre, Num. 115).[9] In the second Temple, in

---

[9] The tendency on the part of the early Halakah to combat these primitive notions and to suppress these anthropomorphic conceptions was, to my mind, the cause of a radical reform in the law of *Ẓiẓit*, prescribed in Num. 15.37–40. The importance of the *Ẓiẓit* consisted in the blue thread, the פתיל תכלת, which was added to them. This blue thread was to serve as reminder to do all the commandments, "that ye may look upon it (the blue thread) and remember all the commandments of the Lord and do them." The blue thread could serve this purpose because it resembled the throne of glory which is also blue in color (Sifre, Num. 115; Men. 43b); the saying in p. Ber. I, 53a: "It is taught in the name of R. Meir: It is not written here 'and ye shall see it (*Otah*)' (i. e., the *Ẓiẓith*) but 'Ye shall see (*Oto*) Him': Thus teaching that

which the Ark was missing, the throne of glory continued to be on the same spot where the Ark once stood. The throne now was on the stone אבן שתיה which took the place of the Ark (cf. Mishnah Yoma 5.2). Commenting upon the verse in Job 39.28, the Midrash (Pesiḳta Rabbati, *Aḥare Mot*, Friedmann, 190) says: סלע ישכון בבנין הראשון שהיה שם ארון ואפילו בבנין השני שלא היה שם ארון אלא אבן שם היה כבודי על שן הסלע ומצודה, cf. also Tanḥuma, *Aḥare Mot*, 3).[10]

---

whoever fulfills the commandment of *Ẓiẓit* it is as if he receives the presence of the Shekinah. Teaching that the blue is like the sea, the sea like grass, the grass like heaven, heaven like the Throne of Glory, etc." The saying suggests an even more anthropomorphic conception, as if God is wrapped in (or appears) blue. The Rabbis, however, at a very early time began to object to the use of the blue thread in connection with the *Ẓiẓit*. Thus R. Eleazer b. Ẓadoḳ (second half of first century) tells us that in Jerusalem it was a strange thing, causing surprise, if one would put the blue thread upon his *Ẓiẓit* (Men. 40a). From Shab. 153a it is also evident that the Rabbis preferred white *Ẓiẓit*. The use of the blue thread was discarded not because the art of producing the special dye necessary for making the תכלת was forgotten (against A. Epstein, *Bet Talmud*, (Wien, 1886), V, 229 ff.) but because the Rabbis wished to suppress or avoid the anthropomorphic idea as if there actually were in heaven a throne of glory blue in color (see my remarks in the *B'nai B'rith Manual*, Cincinnati, 1926, p. 27). Of course, this reform, like so many others, was not effected all at once. The use of the תכלת lingered on and even in Amoraic times they still had the genuine תכלת and, no doubt, some people still used it in their *Ẓiẓit*. In the sixth century however, after the close of the Talmud, the use of תכלת was entirely discarded. See Epstein, *loc. cit.*, p. 305.

[10] Even after the destruction of the Temple the Shekinah, according to some popular beliefs, continued to be present in the place of the Holy of Holies. See the discussion in p. Ber. 4, (8c). According to other legends, however, the Shekinah, after ten wanderings from the Ark-cover to the Cherub, from the Cherub to the threshold, etc., left the Holy of Holies and the entire precinct of the Temple and returned to her pristine abode in heaven (R. H. 31a). R. Petaḥiah of Ratisbon (second half of the 12th century) in his *Sibbub*, ed. Grünhut, (Jerusalem, 1904), p. 35, tells of a legend, current among the Jews in Jerusalem, that the Shekinah left the Temple through the Eastern gate, called the Gates of Mercy (שערי רחמים). Dr. Julian Morgenstern in an essay on "The Gates of Righteousness," which he kindly showed me in manuscript, treats this and other legends about the Eastern gate very exhaustively. He also cites many other references, from Jewish and non-Jewish sources, to the popular beliefs about the visible presence of the Deity in the Temple at Jerusalem. [ed. note: See *HUCA* VI, 1929.]

As a corollary to the belief that God's residence was in the Temple and His throne in the Holy of Holies, there was the other primitive notion that God held court in His residence on earth just as He held court in heaven. For this reason, on the Day of Atonement, when final judgment was passed upon the people by the Divine court, the High Priest, bringing a special offering would enter the Holy of Holies into the very presence of the Deity, in order to obtain forgiveness for the people. At this occasion, when entering into the very presence of the Deity, the High Priest had to be clad in white garments (Yoma 31b, 32b and 35a), in order to appear like one of the ministering angels. For כשירות של מעלן כך שירות של מטן, just as the service in the heavenly abode was performed by attendants dressed in white linen garments so also the service in the earthly abode, in the Holy of Holies, had to be performed by an attendant dressed in white linen garments (p. Yoma 7.3, 44b; Lev. r. 21.11, cf. also Ex. r. 38.3 and 8).[11]

---

[11] The white garments were also aimed to deceive Satan who, when seeing the High Priest dressed in white, would mistake him for an angel and not seek to harm him. The custom, still prevailing in the Synagogue, that the pious worshippers, and especially the reader and the leader in the service, wear a white robe ("Sargenes" or "Kittel") on the Day of Atonement also aims to make the worshippers appear like angels. Like many other ceremonies observed on the Day of Atonement, as fasting, standing up, and not wearing shoes, it has also the effect of causing Satan to believe that the worshippers are like angels and without sin (Pirḳe deR. Eliezer, 46). The custom of burying the dead in a white shroud also had its origin in these primitive beliefs. It aims to make the dead appear like angels and thus gain for them admittance to heaven among the angels. This purpose of the white shroud has been misunderstood, or possibly purposely ignored, by the Babylonian Gemara (M. Ḳ. 27b). It is evident from the Palestinian Talmud (Kil. 9.4, 32b, cf. also b. Shab. 114a) that those Rabbis who were sure of their having lived a righteous life, and, therefore, confident that they would enter heaven and be admitted to the banquet hall, did not hesitate to request to be buried in white garments so as to be properly attired for the banquet (cf. also b. Shab. 153a: R. Eliezer's answer to his disciples and R. Joḥanan b. Zakkai's parable, and 2 Esdras, 2.38–40; further Revelation 3.4–5; 4.4, and 19.14). Other Rabbis, like R. Yannai, whose modesty caused them not to be so sure about their being admitted immediately after death to the banquet hall in heaven, requested to be buried neither in white nor in black but rather in gray garments. They could then, so they expressly say, enter the banquet hall, if found worthy,

When court was held in the Holy of Holies, the Divine residence on earth, it was not God alone, sitting on His throne, upon the Ark-cover or upon the אבן שתיה, that was present there, but also both the pleading and accusing angels assembled around Him. They surrounded Him in the same manner as when court was held in heaven. The Deity, or some manifestation of the Divine presence, as well as a vision of the angels and of Satan, the accuser, could, therefore under favorable conditions, and to especially favored persons, appear in the Holy of Holies on the Day of Atonement. This belief is clearly indicated in the Talmud and in the Midrashim. Thus in Sifra, *Shemini*, I, (Weiss, 43c) we read the following statement which clearly points to the fear that Satan might bring before God accusations against the High Priest when the latter entered the Sanctuary to obtain forgiveness: מלמד שאמר לו משה לאהרן, אהרן אחי אף על פי שנתרצה המקום לכפר על עונותיך צריך אתה ליתן לתוך פיו של שטן שלח דורון לפניך עד שלא תיכנס למקדש שמא ישנאך (ישטינך [read]¹²) בביאתך למקדש. The expression שמא ישטינך בביאתך למקדש alludes to the belief that Satan might be in the Sanctuary, where the Divine court was held, so that Aaron, when entering, might find the accuser facing him. In Pesiḳta Rabbati, *loc. cit.*, (Friedmann, 191), it is expressly stated that Satan was in the Holy of Holies on the Day of Atonement, seeking to accuse Aaron, or the High Priest, but ran away as soon as he saw the merits that entered with Aaron. The passage reads, as follows: ואף אהרן כשהיה נכנס לבית קדשי הקדשים אילולי זכיות הרבה שהיו נכנסות עמו ומסייעות אותו לא היה יכול לעמוד

---

without looking like a mourner dressed in black among the wedding guests. Likewise, in case they should be found unworthy and therefore have to go to the other place where there is mourning and all are dressed in black, they should not be conspicuous by appearing like a bridegroom among mourners. It is, therefore, evident that R. Gamaliel was honored and not (as suggested in M. Ḳ., *loc. cit.*, by the phrase ונהג קלות ראש בעצמו) slighted when he was buried in white garments. The people believed that he had lived a righteous life and that he would, therefore, surely enter heaven and be admitted to the banquet, and they, accordingly, dressed him in the proper attire, i. e., in white garments for his journey to heaven. In the course of time all the people wished to suggest that their departed relatives were worthy of entering heaven and they, therefore, buried their dead in white garments.

¹² So it is quoted by רמב"ן in his commentary to Lev. 9.7.

CONTROVERSY BETWEEN SADDUCEES AND PHARISEES 65

שעה אחת [מפני] מלאכי השרת [שהיו] שם.[13] ועוד שהיה נכנס ביום הכיפורים
והיה השטן בא לקטרג וכיון שהשטן היה רואה אותו היה בורח מלפניו. The
talmudic legends about the High Priest Simon the Just, who
on the Day of Atonement of the last year of his life knew and
told the people that he was going to die during the coming
year, also clearly indicate this popular belief.[14] Thus in Yoma
39b also Men. 109b) the following Baraita is found: תנו רבנן
אותה שנה שמת בה שמעון הצדיק אמר להם בשנה זו הוא מת אמרו לו מנין
אתה יודע אמר להם בכל יום הכפורים היה מזדמן לי זקן אחד לבוש לבנים
ועטוף לבנים נכנס עמי ויוצא עמי והיום נזדמן לי זקן אחד לבוש שחורים ועטוף
שחורים נכנס עמי ולא יצא עמי. אחר הרגל חלה שבעה ימים ומת. We are not

[13] According to this reading suggested by R. Ephraim Z. Margulies in his
commentary to the Pesiḳta, (Warsaw, 1893), on the basis of the reading in the
parallel passage in Ex. r. 38, and accepted by Friedmann in his edition of
the Pesiḳta, the angels would resent the intrusion of a mortal into their
midst, (cf. Shab. 88b). The actual reading in the Pesiḳta, however, is: לעמוד
שעה אחת מלאכי השרת שם. This reading makes no sense. Possibly, this reading
is due to a mistake by a copyist who misunderstood an abbreviation. Originally
the text had: לעמוד שעה אחת מהש' שם. The abbreviation, 'מהש, which stood for
מהשטן, was misunderstood by a copyist to be an abbreviation of מלאכי השרת.

[14] Not Satan alone but a whole band of his subordinates were present in
the Holy of Holies. This is clearly stated in Lev. r. 21.3: אם תחנה עלי מחנה של
קדש סמאל לא יירא לבי שהבטחתני בזאת יבא אהרן אל הקדש. This belief that Satan and
his band had, as it were, an official residence in the Holy of Holies is also presumed in the legend told in Yoma 69b and evidently based on Zech. 5.8.
The returned exiles, this legend tells us, fasted three successive days, praying
that the יצרא דעבודה זרה, the evil one who incites people to idolatry, be delivered unto them. Their prayer was granted and the יצר הרע of idolatry (יצר
הרע is identical with Satan, see B. B. 16a) was delivered unto them. They
saw coming out from the Holy of Holies a fiery young lion נפק אתא כי גוריא
דנורא מבית קדשי הקדשים (I would correct the text to read כי גדיא דנורא) like a
fiery goat for Satan has sometimes the appearance of a goat. Cf. Targum
Jonathan to Lev. 9.3: צפיר בר עיזי מטול דסטנא מימתיל ביה). The prophet told
them that this fiery creature was the יצרא דעבודה זרה and they caught him and
burned him. From that time on they never suffered from idolatrous proclivi-
ties. They also prayed for the delivery of another one of Satan's band but this
was not fully granted them. Now, if the one of Satan's band that was delivered unto them came out of the Holy of Holies, he must have had his residence
there. Dr. Morgenstern, in the essay referred to above, suggests that the
vision in Zech. 3 reflects such a scene in the Holy of Holies on the Day of
Atonement when the High Priest stood before God and Satan sought to accuse
him.

told how, from the fact that an old man dressed in black went in with him and remained there after he went out, Simon concluded that he was going to die during that year. The commentators do not comment on this Baraita. Rashi in Menaḥot, *loc. cit.*, makes only one brief remark. To the words נכנס עמי Rashi remarks, לפני ולפנים, that it means the old man went in with him to the Holy of Holies. The meaning of the whole report, to my mind, is this. The good angels were pictured as dressed in white. The accusing angels, Satan and his band, on the other hand, were dressed in black. When an old person dressed in white went in with him, Simon knew that it was one of the pleading angels who came in to help him and to plead for him. The good angel left with him only after he had succeeded in obtaining for him pardon and a decree of life. When, on the other hand, in the last year of his life he noticed that a man dressed in black went in with him, he realized that he was without a pleading angel and that he was followed by the accuser. And when the accuser remained inside, continuing his accusations, without a pleading angel to refute them, Simon knew that his fate was sealed and that he was going to die. The same Baraita with a significant variation is also found in Tosefta Soṭah 13.8 and in the Palestinian Talmud (Yoma 5.3, 42c) where it is followed by a very interesting discussion. Here it reads as follows: ובשנה אחרונה אמר להם בשנה הזאת אני מת אמרו לו מאיכן אתה יודע אמר להן כל שנה ושנה שהייתי נכנס לבית קודש הקדשים היה זקן אחד לבוש לבנים ועטוף לבנים נכנס עמי ויוצא עמי ובשנה הזו נכנס עמי ולא יצא עמי. בעון קומי ר' אבהו הכתיב וכל אדם לא יהיה באהל מועד בבאו לכפר בקודש עד צאתו אפילו אותן שכתוב בהן ודמות פניהם פני אדם לא יהיו באוהל מועד אמר לון מה אמר לי דהוה בר נש אנא אמר הקב"ה הוה. Here the reference to the accusing angel dressed in black is left out. According to this version of the Baraita, the failure of his good angel to come out with him indicated to Simon his approaching death. For, had the angel achieved his purpose, which was to obtain for him pardon and a decree of life, he would have come out with him as he was accustomed to do in all the preceding years. But the Palestinians also took it for granted that the person dressed in white, who entered with Simon, was an angel. For, in their question to R. Abbahu, some people express their surprise at the angels entering with the High Priest into the Holy of Holies. They quote an old Midrash,[15] which interpreted the passage "and there shall be no man in the tent of meeting when he goeth in to make atonement in the Holy place" (Lev. 16.17), to mean that even those about whom it is written "as for the likeness of their faces, they had the face of a man" (Ezek. 1.10), that is to say even angels, were not allowed to be there. R. Abbahu, however, gives them the following remarkable answer: "What (or who) tells me, that it was a man (or an angel whose likeness is that of a man)? I say it was the Holy One, blessed be He."[16]

[15] I am unable to trace this Midrash to its source. I believe that it originated with R. Akiba and that the questioners, who merely refer to it but do not quote it in full, did not understand its real meaning.

In Sifra, *Vayikra*, II, Weiss 4a, b, after the sayings of R. Akiba and others to the effect that the voice of God that was heard in the Tabernacle came out from between the two Cherubim upon the Ark-cover, there follows another Midrash by R. Akiba and Ben Azzai to the words כי לא יראני האדם וחי (Ex. 33.21), interpreting them to mean that even angels could not see God. This Midrash simply meant to remove the anthropomorphic conception, as if God could at all be visible (cf. Geiger, *Oẓar Neḥmad*, III, 10). R. Akiba thus seeks to make the revelation in the Tabernacle resemble the revelation on Sinai about which it is said: "Ye heard the voice of words, but ye saw no form; only a voice" (Deut. 4.12). He declares that in the Tabernacle, likewise, there was actually heard the voice of God but no visible manifestation of the Deity was to be seen. The same tendency was also followed in the Midrash on the words וכל אדם לא יהיה באהל referred to here. It likewise sought to combat the popular belief that in the Holy of Holies there was visible the presence of God surrounded by angels. The later people, however, misunderstood the meaning of this Midrash as well as the meaning of the other Midrash of Akiba. They understood the latter to mean, not that God was absolutely invisible, but that the angels were not allowed to look at Him; and the Midrash on the passage וכל אדם לא יהיה באהל they understood to mean that the angels were not allowed to enter into the Holy of Holies because God was visible there and they were not allowed to look at Him. See the following note.

[16] As far as I could ascertain, all the commentators as well as Tosafot to Men. 109b, *s. v.*, נזדמן, R. Moses Taku in כתב תמים (*Oẓar Neḥmad*, III, 60), and even R. Jacob ibn Ḥabib (in הכותב to En Jacob) and R. Samuel Jaffe Ashkenazi (in his יפה מראה *ad loc.*) take this answer of R. Abbahu literally to mean that it was God Himself who in the appearance of an old man entered with Simon into the Holy of Holies. Yet one can hardly believe that a teacher like R. Abbahu could have seriously given expression to such a crude, anthropomorphic, almost blasphemous, idea about God. It is true, that R. Abbahu elsewhere (B. B. 25a) speaks of the Shekinah as being in the West, probably

R. Abbahu's answer unmistakably refers to the belief that God was in the Holy of Holies and that a representation of Him could even be seen by the High Priest. The question addressed to R. Abbahu as well as the Babylonian version of the Baraita further indicate the belief that the angels or even Satan would also be present there.

This belief is also alluded to in the following talmudic reports which have direct reference to the controversy between the two parties.

---

meaning in the western part of the Temple, i. e., in the Holy of Holies. Further in Sanhedrin (95b) he reports a legend as to how God appeared to King Sennacherib in the appearance of an old man. But there is a great difference between telling a legend, or speaking of the Shekinah as being in the West, and making a statement to students or in a discussion with people who ask a serious question. Possibly, this answer of Abbahu is not to be taken literally. Had he really wished to say that it was God Himself who entered with Simon into the Holy of Holies, he could have briefly stated הקב״ה הוה. The form of his answer admits the following interpretation. He says to them: "According to your reasoning, which takes the Midrash to mean that the angels, who according to the literal meaning of a passage in Ezekiel have the appearance of man, were also included in the prohibition that no man be in the Holy of Holies, I *could* answer you (אני אומר) that it was God Himself who, in a passage in Daniel (7.9), is pictured as "the ancient of days sitting upon the throne in raiment white as snow, etc." But, of course, you cannot take these passages in Ezekiel and Daniel literally, nor must you take this legend about Simon, which may likewise merely report a vision which Simon had (cf. Isserless in *Torat ha-'Olah*, quoted by R. Enoch Zundel in his commentary ענף יוסף to En Jakob *ad loc.*), literally. What suggests this interpretation of Abbahu's saying, is the fact that in Pesiḳta deR. Kahana, Buber, 178a and in Lev. r. 21.12, after this answer of Abbahu is quoted, there follows another quite different saying of Abbahu. It reads thus: וכהן גדול לאו אדם הוא. "And was not the High Priest a man?" By this R. Abbahu evidently meant to say that if we should understand this Midrash to mean that because God was in the Holy of Holies no man, not even angels, who are like man, were allowed to enter there, then the High Priest could never have been allowed to enter there. Of course, this saying of Abbahu was also misunderstood by the author of the Pesiḳta and by the redactor of Lev. r. who followed him (see Lauterbach, *Jewish Encyclopedia*, XII, 478–479). They took it simply as a question, how could the High Priest be admitted to enter the Holy of Holies? They answered it by explaining that the High Priest was like an angel, not realizing that, according to the Midrashic interpretation of the words וכל אדם לא יהיה באהל, as Abbahu's questioners understood it, even angels were not allowed to enter there.

CONTROVERSY BETWEEN SADUCEES AND PHARISEES 69

ת"ר מעשה בצדוקי In Yoma 19b we read the following report:
אחד שהתקין מבחוץ והכניס ביציאתו היה שמח שמחה גדולה פגע בו אביו אמר
לו בני אף על פי שצדוקין אנו מתיראין אנו מן הפרושים אמר לו כל ימי הייתי
מצטער על המקרא הזה כי בענן אראה על הכפורת אמרתי מתי יבוא לידי
ואקיימנו עכשיו שבא לידי לא אקיימנו.

There is no reason whatever to doubt the historicity of this report, which is also found in p. Yoma 1.5 (39a). It shows that the Sadducees attached great importance to their interpretation of Lev. 16.12, and that they would seek to perform the ceremony according to their own practice, even after the Pharisees had control over the Temple service and were in a position to dictate to the High Priest the instructions for performing his functions. But, following this authentic report, there are given in both the Palestinian and Babylonian Talmudim legendary reports about the punishment which this Sadducean High Priest suffered for his daring to follow the Sadducean practice. The Palestinian Talmud has two different accounts of what happened to this Sadducean High Priest. One account merely reports that he died a few days after the Day of Atonement, but does not specify what manner of death it was, hence it may have been a natural death. But the other report says that when coming out from the Holy of Holies, after having offered the incense, his nose was discharging worms and right in the center of his forehead there was a mark like that of a calf's hoof. We are not told whether and how soon he died as a result of these injuries. But it was understood that both these disfiguring marks on the face of the High Priest were the results of the injuries which he received from the angel in the Holy of Holies. The angel, the soles of whose feet (according to Ezek. 1.7) are like the sole of a calf's foot, kicked the High Priest and hit him squarely in the middle of his forehead right above his nose. The result was that his nose discharged worms[17] and his forehead still showed the impression of the angel's foot. That it was so understood even by the Pales-

---

[17] That the smiting of an angel would have the effect of producing worms, that would eat up the body and cause death, is also assumed in the story about the death of Herod Agrippa as told in Acts 12.23: "And immediately an angel of the Lord smote him because he gave not God the glory, and he was eaten by worms and gave up the ghost."

tinians is evident from the discussion that follows in the same paragraph of the Yerushalmi, the report about the affliction of the High Priest. R. Abbahu, who, as we have seen above, in the discussion of the legend about Simon the Just admits only the presence of God, but denies the presence of angels in the Holy of Holies, was asked to explain this legendary report about the Sadducean High Priest. The questioners ask him how it was possible that the Sadducean High Priest received injuries from an angel in the Holy of Holies when, according to the law in Lev. 16.7 as interpreted by an old Midrash, the angels were not allowed to be in the Holy of Holies at the time when the High Priest entered there. In this case R. Abbahu does not say, as in the case of the legend about Simon the Just, that it may be that God Himself inflicted these injuries upon the Sadducean High Priest. R. Abbahu implicitly admits that these injuries came from an angel, the sign of the calf's foot being indisputable evidence for that. But, says R. Abbahu, the angel was not in the Holy of Holies for he was not allowed to be there. He was standing at the entrace to the Holy of Holies and it was rather when the High Priest sought to enter the Holy of Holies in his Sadducean manner בשעה שהוא נכנס כדרכו, i. e.,[18] carrying the smoking incense in front of him, that the angel hit him.

[18] This seems to me to be the correct meaning of the phrase בשעה שהוא נכנס כדרכו. The interpretations given by the commentators do not make good sense. The author of קרבן העדה gives the following interpretation: בשעה שהוא נכנס כדרכו ומקיים מצות העבודה כתיקונו הוא דאסור לכל אדם להיות שם אבל זה שלא עשה כתיקונו מותרים להיות שם (cf. Tosafot Yeshanim to Yoma, ad loc., who give the same interpretation). This practically assumes that the angels are in the Holy of Holies and only when the High Priest performs the ceremony correctly (כתיקונו) does he succeed in driving them away. Even less satisfactory is the interpretation given by the commentator פני משה which reads as follows: בשעה שהוא נכנס כדרכו לא היה זה בשעה שבא לכפר אלא בשעה שנכנס כדרכו להוציא את הכף והמחתה. This interpretation stresses the words בבואו לכפר בקדש taking them to mean that only at the moment when the High Priest entered to obtain forgiveness were the angels not allowed to be there but before and after that time they could be, and actually were, in the Holy of Holies. This explains only why the angel did not smite the High Priest at the moment when he performed the ceremony. But why did he not smite him outside, immediately when he came out after having wrongly performed the ceremony? Why did the angel have to go into the Holy of Holies and there lie in wait for the High Priest till he came in again to take out the pan and the spoon?

CONTROVERSY BETWEEN SADDUCEES AND PHARISEES 71

The Babylonian Talmud also has two accounts of what happened to the Sadducean High Priest, but they are different from the reports given by the Palestinians. Here we read as follows: אמרו לא היו ימים מועטים עד שמת והוטל באשפה והיו תולעין יוצאין מחוטמו ויש אומרים ביציאתו ניגף דתני רבי חייא כמין קול נשמע בעזרה שבא מלאך וחבטו על פניו ונכנסו אחיו הכהנים ומצאו ככף רגל עגל בין כתפיו שנאמר ורגליהם רגל ישרה וכף רגליהם ככף רגל עגל. One is tempted to believe that the Babylonians knew the Palestinian reports as well as the difficulty raised by the questioners of R. Abbahu and the latter's answer, but they did not find this answer satisfactory. For, if the angel was not in the Holy of Holies but hit the High Priest on his forehead before he entered the Holy of Holies, it is difficult to believe that the High Priest could nevertheless have proceeded into the Holy of Holies and have performed the ceremony there. The angel surely must have dealt the High Priest a blow from which he could not recover. The Babylonians therefore offer another report which presents no difficulty. The High Priest performed the ceremony in his own way since nothing happened to him when he entered. But, after having performed the ceremony and retired from the Holy of Holies, he was smitten by the angel as he came out of the Holy of Holies (ביציאתו ניגף). The angel, who hit him, was not in the Holy of Holies. He came from outside. Indeed, some sort of a noise was heard in the Temple court, which was the noise of the angel rushing in to punish the offender. The High Priest, when he came out from the Holy of Holies, walked backward, so as not to turn his back upon the Holy of Holies (see Yoma 52b and 53a). When he reached the threshold and his back had just emerged from behind the curtain, the angel, who was outside of the curtain, kicked him on his back between the shoulders, and threw him down with his face to the ground. The High Priest fell forward, hitting the floor of the Holy of Holies with his face. He did not recover from this blow; he lay there till his fellow priests came and pulled him out. They then found between his shoulders a mark which looked like a calf's foot. This was proof that an angel, the sole of whose foot is according to Ezek. 1.7, like the sole of a calf's foot, had kicked him. But if he was hit on his back and not on his forehead right over his nose, then the discharge of worms from his nose, of which an old legend spoke, could not have been the result of the injury received from the angel's blow. The Babylonian report, therefore, does not say that immediately when brought out from the Holy of Holies, they saw worms coming out from his nose The Babylonians combine the legend about the worms coming out from his nose with the other report, that he died a few days after the Day of Atonement. The worms came out from his nose because his body was thrown *upon a dunghill*, not having been given a decent burial.

I have discussed these talmudic legends at length, in order to show how all of them clearly point to, if they do not expressly state, the primitive belief about the visible presence of the Deity in the Holy of Holies, entertained by the people even during the time of the second Temple. Of course, the enlightened teachers sought to suppress or at least modify these primitive notions, but they did not succeed in entirely removing them from the popular mind; hence we find allusions to these superstitions even in the later aggadic expressions of the Talmud. It was the attitude towards these primitive beliefs, which brought about the strong controversy in regard to the offering of the incense. The real issue in this controversy was a very important doctrine, a fundamental principle in regard to the God conception. The difference of opinion between the two parties in regard to the preparation of the incense was based upon different theological viewpoints. We can understand the position of each party in this controversy, if we consider its general religious outlook and theological doctrines.

We must remember that the Sadducees were the conservative priestly group, holding on to the older doctrines and beliefs, and cherishing the highest regard for the sacrificial cult of the Temple. They retained many of the primitive notions both about God and the purpose of the service offered to Him in the Temple. They were strongly opposed to any reform in the sacrificial functions of the Temple in which they were so vitally interested and the performance of which had always been their special privilege. The Pharisees, on the other hand, were the progressive literal group of lay teachers, the spiritual successors of the prophets, with a purer God conception and less regard for the sacrificial cult. While not entirely opposed to the sacrificial cult as such, they sought to reform it. They tried as much as it was in their power to democratize and spiritualize the service in the Temple and to remove from it, as far as possible, the elements of crude superstition and primitive outworn conceptions.[19]

In the controversy about the preparation of the incense each party is true to its character. Their respective positions were in perfect agreement with their respective theological views and religious tendencies. The talmudic reports about this controversy present no difficulty. They are not as full and as plain as we would have liked them to be, but by their presentation of the arguments of the two parties, especially if we read between the lines, as well as by their omissions, they clearly indicate what the real reasons were that prompted the two parties to take their respective stands in this controversy.

The Sadducees, as conservative priests, retained and cherished the popular beliefs and primitive notions associated with the Temple and especially with the most sacred place in it, the Holy of Holies. In their service in the Temple, and especially when performing the most solemn rites on the most holy day in the most holy place, they would, therefore, follow strictly the old traditional practice and would not dare to make any change in its ritual.

According to the primitive notions held by them, the entrance of the High Priest into the Holy of Holies on the Day of Atonement was not only a great privilege, offering the rare opportunity of catching a glimpse of the Deity, but was also

[19] See above, *The Sadducees and Pharisees*. The whole attitude of the Sadducees toward the authority of the Law was based upon a primitive conception and superstition about the binding power of the oath. The Pharisees, however, considered the Law authoritative because of the Divine truth it contained.

Dr. Jacob Mann calls my attention to Acts 23.8, where it is said: "For the Sadducees say that there is no resurrection, neither angel nor spirit; but the Pharisees confess both." But this is hardly a correct presentation of the Saducean position. The Sadducees may have denied resurrection, but they certainly did not deny the existence of angels and of Satan, attested to by many passages in the Bible.

fraught with great dangers.[20] There was, in the first place, the danger that he might, even if only involuntarily, look the Deity straight into the face, and, as a result, immediately die; for no man can see the Deity and remain alive. There was also the danger of Satan following him into the Holy of Holies and accuse him there before God. This also might prove disastrous for him. He might be found guilty and punished with immediate death, or, as in the case of Simon the Just, be sentenced to die during the year. All possible precautions had therefore to be taken to protect the High Priest against these dangers, to help him in the successful performance of his function and to secure his coming out unharmed from the trial which he had to face. The old practice of preparing the incense outside of the Holy of Holies and producing a pillar of smoke before bringing it in to offer to the Deity, was a very effective measure of precaution. It afforded the High Priest protection from both dangers that faced him. The smoke coming up from the incense which he carried in his hand protected him from the danger of Satan's accusations. For, Satan, frightened and driven away by the smoke, could not follow him into the Holy of Holies into the very presence of God.[21] The

---

[20] Cf. Mishnah Yoma 5.2 לא היה מאריך בתפלתו כדי שלא להבעית את ישראל and 7.4 ויום טוב היה עושה לאוהביו בשעה שיצא בשלום מן הקדש.

[21] Smoke as such was considered an effective means of driving away Satan and the evil spirits. See Lauterbach, "The Ceremony of Breaking a Glass at Weddings," in *Hebrew Union College Annual*, II, 356–357. The smoke of incense was especially powerful in driving away Satan. This belief has survived to this day in a popular proverb, current among Eastern Jews, who when wishing to describe the horror a person has for something, they say: "He is afraid of it as Satan is afraid of Weihrauch (i. e., smoke of incense)." This belief is very old. According to a legend in the Talmud (Shab. 89a) it was Satan himself (or the Angel of Death who is identical with Satan; cf. the saying in B. B. 16a הוא שטן הוא יצר הרע הוא מלאך המות) who in a generous moment gave away his secret to Moses, telling him that the smoke of incense has the power of stopping his pernicious activities. Thus Moses knew how to put a halt to the activities of the Angel of Death when the plague broke out among the people. He sent Aaron with the pan of smoking incense into the midst of the assembly. "And Aaron stood between the dead and the living and the plague was stayed" (see Num. 17.11–13). Cf. also Tanḥuma, תצוה, 15, and Zohar, *Vayera*, 100b–101a, and *Pinḥas*, 244.

Incidentally we notice here that all the three methods of dealing with the

smoke coming up from the incense also protected him from the danger of seeing the Deity clearly face to face. It formed a sort of screen through which he was allowed to look at the Deity, for "through the smoke of the incense God may be seen upon the Ark-cover." This old practice of preparing the incense outside was, therefore, of the utmost importance for the High Priest. It protected him from the accuser, it prevented him from incurring the penalty of death by involuntarily looking the Deity in the face, and at the same time it afforded him the rare privilege of catching a glimpse of God, of seeing Him, if only dimly, through the screen of smoke. The position of the Sadducees in our controversy was therefore perfectly logical. It was consistent with their theological views and with the primitive notions which they held. Their arguments in favor of the old practice, in so far as they are reported by the Baraita in Sifra and in the Palestinian Talmud, clearly point to these primitive theological views and are quite sound. Their first argument, the argument of propriety unmistakably points to their belief that God is present in the Holy of Holies. They say, since God is present behind the curtain in the Holy of Holies, it would be disrespectful to prepare the incense there in His very presence. Their second argument, the one from the words כי בענן אראה על הכפורת, expresses even more strongly their belief in God's presence in the Holy of Holies. God can be seen upon the Ark-cover, but he may be seen only through a screen of smoke; hence that screen of smoke must be prepared outside, so that at the very moment of entering the Holy of Holies, the High Priest if he should involuntarily look in the direction of the Ark-cover would see God

---

evil spirits, usually employed by the people (see the essay on "The Ceremony of Breaking a Glass at Weddings," *loc. cit.*) were also employed by the High Priest in order to ward off the danger that threatened him from Satan. The white garments were used to deceive Satan, making him believe that the High Priest was one of the angels (see note 11). But there was still the fear lest Satan see through the deception, hence the second method, the one of bribing him, was also used. A gift was sent to Satan in the goat of Azazel (see Pirḳe d.R. Eliezer, 46). But the wicked one was not to be trusted. He might seek to harm the High Priest, even after having received the bribe, hence the third method of fighting him and driving him away by the smoke of the incense was resorted to.

only through the screen of smoke.[21a] The Baraita does not tell us that the Sadducees also pointed out the danger from Satan which could be warded off by their practice. But this need not surprise us. The author of the Baraita may have hesitated to even mention this superstition. More likely, however, he omitted mentioning it because he was not interested in reporting all the arguments of the Sadducees. For this reason also he does not report how the Sadducees met the Pharisees' argument from the syntactic order of the two verses 12–13 which, pointing to consecutive actions, would apparently demand that he put the incense upon the fire after he had entered the Holy of Holies. From the very fact that, as we have seen, the Pharisees did not stress very much this argument of theirs, we may conclude that they themselves did not consider it an irrefutable proof in favor of their position. The Sadducees must have interpreted these two verses in such a manner as to favor their position. The Pharisees must have felt that the Sadducean interpretation of these two verses was as sound as their own; hence they did not

[21a] See Rashbam's comment on this verse (ed. Rosin, Breslau, 1881, p. 159) as follows: "For I appear in the cloud upon the Ark-cover;" its plain meaning is: For behold from the midst of the pillar of cloud I appear always upon the Ark-cover as it is written (Ex. 25.22), "And I shall speak with thee from above the Ark-cover between the two cherubim." Now if the priest would see, he would die. Therefore when he enters on the Day of Atonement, God commands him to burn incense within first in order to darken the house with the smoke of the incense, and then to bring the blood of the bullock of the sin offering and the blood of the goat.

See also A. Sh. Hershberg in *HaOlam*, Oct. 6, 1930, 805–6 as follows: with regard to the incense on the Day of Atonement and the dispute between the Sadducees and the Pharisees, Rashbam says that "I shall appear in the cloud" is to be understood literally and he cites a custom of the Egyptians that the god should not see the priest. According to this, the controversy between the Sadducees and the Pharisees can be explained. But I have not seen anyone who has gone into this thoroughly; for the older teachers said that he should prepare it (the incense) outside (cf. Sifra, *Aḥare Mot*, III, [Weiss, 81b])for the Sadducees were accustomed to follow the Egyptian custom and the literal meaning of the text. But the opinion of the Pharisees was that he should prepare it inside thus to depart from the custom of the pagans. According to that (i. e., the Pharisees') opinion, the incense had a nobler and more spiritual significance.

He almost got the correct idea but not quite.

stress the argument based upon their own interpretation of these two verses. Of course, we need not expect the Pharisaic sources to tell us what the Sadducean interpretation was, especially when it was considered as quite sound. We are left to guess what this interpretation was, and it is not so difficult to guess. The Sadducees, I believe, admitted that the syntactic order of the two verses 12–13 prescribed consecutive actions. The action prescribed in verse 13 was to take place after the action of bringing in the incense and the fire into the Holy of Holies, prescribed in verse 12. But they interpreted the two actions in their own way. The action prescribed in verse 12 was, according to their interpretation, not to carry the incense in one hand and the fire in the other and thus enter the Holy of Holies, as the Pharisees said. It was to bring in the smoking incense, i. e., the incense and the fire together into the Holy of Holies. And the action, prescribed in verse 13 to be performed after the High Priest had entered the Holy of Holies, was not to put the incense upon the fire, as the Pharisees claimed. This had already been done, for he had brought in the smoking incense. The action prescribed in verse 13 was to place before God the incense, which was already upon the fire, that is, to put the pan of fiery coals with the smoking incense on it in front of the Deity.[22]

The Pharisees with their purer God conception were opposed to superstitious notions and primitive beliefs fostered by the conservative priests. They were consistent in their belief in the Divine Omnipresence. God is everywhere, the whole world is full of His glory and no one place is more favored with His presence than any other. Accordingly, they denied that God or any visible representation of Him, or any visible manifestation of His Glory could actually be seen in the Holy of Holies hovering over the Ark-cover, or, in the Second Temple when the Ark was no more, on the Stone (אבן שתיה). They sought to teach the people this purer God conception and were opposed to any teaching or practice which might present to the people a false conception of God or confirm them in their old superstition. They

---

[22] See D. Hoffmann, *Das Buch Leviticus*, p. 446. The interpretation suggested by N. Brüll, *Bet Talmud*, (Wien, 1881), I, 243, is forced and grammatically impossible.

objected to the manner in which the High Priest had been accustomed to perform the ceremony of offering the incense on the Day of Atonement, for no other reason than that this old practice tended to perpetuate crude primitive superstitions and to give the people a false conception of God. They, accordingly, sought to modify this ceremony, at least to remove from it those features which emphasized the crude superstitions. They advocated a radical reform in the performance of this ceremony which would make it much more compatible with their advanced ideas about God. They had no old tradition to back them in their war against superstition, unless it were that the teachings of the prophets of old helped them in forming their ideas about God and determined their attitude towards the sacrificial cult in general. But ancient custom and traditional practice were against them in this specific case. Neither did they have any express statement in the written Law to support them in this fight. They did not have a strong case; they had only a good cause, the cause of advanced religious thought and correct ideas about God. On the positive side of their arguments, they are weak. They have not one strong positive proof in favor of their position. Even their one positive scriptural proof from the syntactic order of the two verses 12–13 in Lev. 16, was, as we have seen, also not unassailable. On the positive side they have only their strong religious convictions to support them. They are, however, negatively strong, as they can show that the arguments of their opponents are not absolutely convincing. In their dispute they, accordingly, limit themselves merely to the task of refuting their opponents' arguments.

To the first argument of their opponents, the argument of propriety, they reply by citing the Scriptural passage from Lev. 16.13, והלא כבר נאמר ונתן את הקטורת על האש לפני ה'. By this they do not insist that the words לפני ה', "before the Lord," designate the Holy of Holies. This, as we have seen, their opponents also admit, except that they claim that the incense, after it had been put upon the fire, should be placed before the Lord in the Holy of Holies. The Pharisees merely say: "But is it not said 'and he should put the incense upon the fire in the presence of the Lord.'" By this they clearly mean: even if, as you say, he puts the incense upon the fire outside of the curtain, he does it also in the presence of the Lord. For right in the preceding verse ולקח מלא המחתה גחלי אש מעל המזבח מלפני ה', the place of the altar outside of the curtain is also designated as מלפני ה', in the presence of the Lord. Hence, no matter where he prepares the incense, he would be doing it in the presence of God and this according to your reasoning would be disrespectful. It is for this reason, that, as we have already noticed, they do not close their argument with the phrase מלמד שאינו נותן אלא מבפנים, for they did not cite this passage as a positive proof for their position. They merely cited it as a negative proof to show how absurd their opponents' argument was in comparing God, who is everywhere, to a human being who can only be in one place and does not notice what is done in another place.

The second argument of their opponents which seeks to prove from the words כי בענן אראה על הכפורת that God is present upon the Ark-cover and may be seen through the smoke, they refute by rejecting their opponents' interpretation of this scriptural passage. They did not want to interpret this passage to mean "with a cloud of Glory will I appear on the Ark-cover," as the ancient versions understood it.[23] For this would admit that

[23] Cf. Geiger, in *Oẓar Neḥmad, loc. cit.* Geiger is not correct in his statement that the ancient versions follow in this case the younger Halakah. The versions here represent but the first attempt of the early Halakah to combat the superstitious beliefs. In this first attempt the Halakah contented itself with merely removing the crude anthropomorphic conception, while still admitting that some ethereal manifestation of the Deity could be visible on the Ark. But the Pharisaic Halakah soon went further and denied even the presence of a cloud of glory or of any other visible manifestation upon the Ark-cover. The opinions of R. Judah and the Ḥakamim (Men. 27b, cf. also Sifra, *Aḥare Mot* I, [Weiss, 80b], which according to Geiger reflect the younger Halakah, do not admit that any visible manifestation of the Deity was present upon the Ark, as Geiger erroneously assumes (see *Jüdische Zeitschrift*, [Breslau, 1863], II, 29–31). On the contrary, they further emphasize the Pharisaic denial of such a Presence by indicating that the Holy of Holies was not the only place, which the priests were forbidden to enter, but that other parts of the Temple were also so forbidden, though the penalty for entering the other parts was not so severe as the penalty for entering the Holy of Holies. But just as the forty stripes which one receives for violating the prohibition of entering the Hekal are a penalty inflicted upon him and not a direct consequence of his entering, so also the death mentioned in the Torah for entering the Holy of

some visible representation of the Deity is present in the Holy of Holies and the High Priest might well seek to shield himself so as not to look at it directly. They insisted that neither in a corporeal form, nor in an ethereal apparition, nor in a fiery manifestation can the Deity be seen in the Holy of Holies. They, therefore, admit that the word בענן in this passage refers to the smoke of the incense. The scriptural passage does imply that a smoke-producing ingredient must be mixed in with the incense, but it does not say anything about God's being seen through the smoke. The Pharisees probably read אֶרְאֶה, instead of אֵרָאֶה, and they interpreted the passage to mean "through the smoke I look down upon the Ark-cover and see whether the ceremony of offering the incense there, which I commanded, has been correctly performed."[24] They sought to reduce the ceremony of offering the incense in the Holy of Holies to a mere ritual חקה, like so many other ritual laws prescribed in the Torah, which we must observe because prescribed by God, though we do not know the reason why God commanded them, but must not seek to explain on the basis of superstitions, or as suggesting to us false beliefs.[25]

Holies is likewise a penalty inflicted upon the High Priest and not a direct consequence of his having seen the Deity, for the Deity is in no manner visible there. They thus make it clear that the prohibition to enter the Holy of Holies was not because of the presence of the Deity there. It was just one of many laws regulating the entrance of the priests into the various parts of the Temple, the reasons for which we do not know. See note 25.

[24] Or, "I will see the smoke which is covering the Ark." I admit that this is merely a guess but I believe it is a good guess. The Pharisees must have given some such interpretation to this verse, namely that God will see the ceremony performed, the smoke covering the Ark, and because of this He will forgive them their sins. Cf. the interpretation given to the words וראיתי את הדם in Mekilta *Pisḥa* VII, Friedmann, 8a. This idea is also reflected in the Midrashic interpretation to the words וכסה ענן הקטרת as meaning that the smoke of the incense will have the effect of covering, so to speak, the sins, hiding them and forgiving them. See Tanḥuma, תצוה 15 and Kohelet r. 4.6 and the remarks of רד"ל there.

[25] Cf. the refusal of R. Yoḥanan b. Zakkai to look for any reason for the ritual of purification by the water of sprinkling (Num. 19) other than that it was so decreed by God, אמר הקדוש ברוך הוא. גזירתו של מלך מלכי המלכים הוא חוקה חקקתי גזירה גזרתי אין אדם רשאי לעבור על גזירתי (Pesiḳta de.R. Kahana, *Parah*, 40b). To observe a ceremony without asking for any reason but merely

The Pharisaic teachers themselves, however, must have detected a certain weakness in this refutation of the Sadducean argument based upon the words כי בענן אראה על הכפורת. The weak point was the admission on the part of the Pharisees that the word בענן means "through the smoke of the incense" and that the passage teaches the requirement of mixing in מעלה עשן with the incense. This requirement of a smoke-producing ingredient in the incense rather helps the Sadducees, for it suggests that it was necessary to produce a screen of smoke. Some of the teachers wondered why the Pharisees make this admission as to the meaning of the word בענן in this passage, when they could just as well have interpreted the passage to mean, through the clouds do I look down from heaven, and omit any reference to the smoke of the incense and the suggestion of the necessity of a screen of smoke to hide something visible in the Holy of Holies.[26] This difficulty

---

because one believes it to be prescribed by God, has some religious significance and is of disciplinary value. To seek to explain the ceremony by accepting the superstitious beliefs which may have motivated its origin is religiously harmful.

[26] In some of the sayings of the Rabbis we can discern a tendency to deny the absolute necessity of מעלה עשן in the קטורת. In the first place מעלה עשן is not counted among the eleven ingredients necessary for the קטרת (Ker. 6a,b) and we are told in the Midrash (Cant. r. 1.14) that it was not good for the קטרת to contain more than these eleven specified ingredients, מיכן בדקו חכמים ומצאו שאין יפה לקטורת אלא אחד עשר סממנים הללו בלבד. It is true that the Baraita in Ker. 6a, after enumerating the eleven ingredients, adds that three other things (not ingredients, see Rashi there, s. v. שס״ה מנים) were also used in the preparation of the קטרת, viz., בורית כרשינה, יין קפריסין and מעלה עשן but it reduces the latter to a minimum, saying that the least quantity of it (כל שהוא) was sufficient. Furthermore, the Baraita goes on to explain for what purpose the other two, i. e., בורית כרשינה and יין קפריסין (or in the absence of the latter חמר חורייו, or מלח סדומית, or כפת הירדן, see comment of R. Moses Cohen quoted in Tosafot there, s. v. מלח סדומית) were used in the process of the קטרת, but does not tell us for what the מעלה עשן was used. Evidently the author of the Baraita hesitated to state that the מעלה עשן was used to produce a screen of smoke. And by stating that only a neglible quantity of it was used, the Baraita suggests that the requirement of מעלה עשן was really not essential. By this the Baraita meant to remove the last vestige of the idea that a screen of smoke was necessary to prevent the High Priest from seeing the Deity. Perhaps the statement of R. Simon b. Gamaliel in the Baraita (p. Yoma 4.5), או שנתן לתוכה מעלה עשן חייב מיתה, really expresses this opposition on the part of some teachers to the use of מעלה עשן in the קטרת. For no matter how one may try

is expressed in the Baraita by the question ומנין שהוא נותן בה מעלה עשן, whence do we know that it was necessary to mix in מעלה עשן, or in other words, why admit that there was any smoke at all? In answer to this question, hinting at the difficulty in the Pharisaic answer, the Baraita cites the passage וכסה ענן הקטורת את הכפורת אשר על העדות ולא ימות, which clearly prescribes, as a specific feature of the ceremony, the covering of the Ark-cover with the smoke of the incense. But lest it be argued that this very passage "that the cloud of the incense cover the Ark-cover that is upon the testimony, that he die not" suggests that some divine manifestation was present upon the Ark-cover and that the High Priest might die as a result of seeing it unless covered by the smoke of the incense, the Baraita wisely and purposely states הא אם לא נתן בה מעלה עשן או שחיסר אחת מכל סממניה חייב מיתה. By this the Baraita indicates that the words ולא ימות do not mean "lest he die" as a result of seeing the manifestation of the Deity. These words mean "so that he may not incur the penalty of death." For the omission of any ingredient of the incense, not only of the מעלה עשן, was an offense punishable by death. And to further prove that the מעלה עשן was just one of the prescribed ingredients of the incense, but was not intended for the purpose of screening the High Priest or covering any manifestation of the Deity, they declared that even the incense which was offered every day, not in the Holy of Holies, but on the altar in the Hekal, where even according to the popular beliefs there was no visible manifestation of the Deity, must also contain the smoke-producing ingredients. They thus declared the מעלה עשן to be merely one of the essential ingredients of the incense and removed the possibility of interpreting its requirement in the incense offered in the Holy of Holies to be for any special purpose.

---

to explain its presence in the קטרת, it still suggests the belief or gives the impression that a screen of smoke was necessary to hide the visible Deity from the eyes of the High Priest. We have no valid reason for correcting the text, as is suggested by the commentator קרבן העדה when he says: ה"נ או שלא נתן לתוכה מעלה עשן חייב מיתה. He has no Ms. variant nor any older source to warrant this correction. He is merely prompted by the desire to harmonize the saying of R. Simon b. Gamaliel with the other sayings in the Talmud which assume the requirement of מעלה עשן in the קטרת.

The above study reveals the great significance of this controversy between the two ancient parties. It also explains why the reports about this controversy do not explicitly state the reasons which prompted each party to take its particular stand on this question. We can well understand why the Pharisaic teachers hesitated to discuss openly and plainly the issue involved in this controversy. They did not wish to mention expressly and publicly the false beliefs which they were fighting even when they could present their refutations of them. They feared that the mentioning of these beliefs, even together with their refutations, would result in advertising them. For, to use a talmudic phrase, איכא דשמע בהא ולא שמע בהא, some people might willingly listen to the presentation of these false beliefs and then refuse or neglect to listen also to the refutations. This was all the more to be feared, since the Pharisaic rejection of these popular beliefs involved also a rejection or a forced interpretation of many biblical passages which speak in anthropomorphic terms of the presence of God in the Temple or in the Holy of Holies upon the Ark-cover. They therefore sought rather to suppress these superstitious notions, believing that in such cases the dictum of the sage כבוד אלהים הסתר דבר, "It is for the glory of God to conceal a thing" (Prov. 25.2), is well applicable. That their apprehensions were not unfounded has been proved by the subsequent development. Not all the Rabbis in later generations could rise to the lofty heights of the early Pharisaic teachers. The superstitious beliefs and primitive notions, which the early teachers sought to fight and suppress, survived among the Jewish people; and echoes of them are found in rabbinic literature. And while the later Rabbis of the Talmud, when speaking about God in the terms of these ancient primitive beliefs, use these terms only figuratively and in an allegorical sense, yet there were some people in talmudic and in post-talmudic times who took them quite literally. The priestly supersititions have not yet died out entirely even among the Jews.

The Pharisees and their Teachings

The Pharisees and their Teachings[1]
(1929)

I

THE PHARISEES

THE struggle of ideas and conflicting tendencies which took place among the Jewish people during the third and second pre-Christian centuries and which finally resulted in the formation of two distinct and separate parties, the Sadducees and the Pharisees, was of momentous significance not only for the history and the development of Judaism, but also for the history of religion in general. For, this struggle, as well as the subsequent prolonged fight between the two parties, was actually and primarily a fight between two different conceptions of religion, between two opposite views of its aim and purpose. The one, whose keynote was fear, sought to bring God down to man, i. e., nearer to the level of man. Its God was an anthropomorphic God and the worship offered to Him was like the homage and tribute paid to a human king or ruler — all but for the purpose of obtaining His favor or warding off His wrath by pacifying and humoring Him. The other, whose keynote was love, sought to raise man to Divine heights and to bring him nearer to God. Its God was a spiritual God and the worship offered to Him

---

[1] The study here presented consists of three lectures delivered by the writer before the Divinity School of the University of Chicago and the Garret Biblical Institute of Evanston, Illinois in April, 1928. I have been urged to publish them. But since I am, at present engaged in another piece of literary work, the preparation of the English translation of my new edition of the Mekilta, I cannot take the time to go into a detailed discussion of all the questions connected with the subject of these lectures. I, therefore, publish them as they were given and merely add a few supplementary notes which embody my answers to the questions that were asked of me in the discussion that followed the lectures.

consisted of praising and glorifying His name by helping man to lead a life of *imitatio dei*[2] and thus to approach Divine perfection.

The victory of the latter conception over the former, which, to anticipate what I hope to prove, was the victory of the Pharisees, determined the course of development of Judaism and thus directly and indirectly exercised great influence upon its daughter religion, Christianity.

For, while the struggle was primarily between the primitive and the spiritual conceptions of religion, it also developed, as time went on, other secondary aspects and later on became "the trial of strength between the purely religious and the political theory of Jewish national life."[3] National life and nationalistic culture naturally go well with primitive conceptions of religion, but do not accord so well with a higher conception of pure religion which of necessity must become universalistic. The victory for higher and purer conceptions of religion, won by the Pharisees, thus necessarily had to result in a broad liberal universalism. And while the Pharisees themselves and the Jewish people that followed them could never entirely give up their national and messianic hopes or their group-consciousness, Christianity, which arose among Pharisaic Jews, set out to carry this tendency towards a complete religious universalism to its logical conclusion.[4] There can be no doubt that Christianity, in the

---

[2] On the Pharisaic ideal of *imitatio dei* see Sifre, Deut. 49, Friedmann 85a; b. Soṭah 14a and especially the saying of Abba Saul (Mekilta, *Shirata* III, Friedmann 37a): "O be thou like Him," לו דמה גא according to the correct reading of the manuscript adopted in my new edition of the text of the Mekilta. Cf. also A. Marmorstein: "Die Nachahmung Gottes in der Agada," in *Jüdische Studien Josef Wohlgemuth zu seinem sechzigsten Geburtstag* (Berlin, 1928), p. 6 ff.

[3] R. Travers Herford, *The Pharisees* (London, 1924), p. 45. Cf. also S. Dubnow, *Weltgeschichte des jüdischen Volkes* (Berlin, 1925), Bd. I, p. xvii, Bd. II, pp. 143 ff. and 571 ff.; and against him I. Elbogen, "Einige Neuere Theorien Über den Ursprung der Pharisäer u. Sadducäer," in *Jewish Studies in Memory of Israel Abrahams* (New York, 1927), pp. 145 ff. Originally and primarily, however, the struggle between the two parties or groups was a struggle of different religious ideas.

[4] The idea of a religious universalism and the tendency of offering its teachings to all mankind were, however, inherent in pre-Christian Pharisaic

main, sprang from Pharisaic Judaism. Jesus and his disciples did not belong to the priestly aristocratic party of the Sadducees. They were of the plain humble people who followed the Pharisees. Paul was "a Pharisee, a son of a Pharisee" (Acts 23.6) and the disciple of a Pharisee (Acts 22.3). And while Jesus may have expressed some teachings different from those of the Pharisees, or on some questions may have argued against the Pharisaic interpretation of the Law, in most of his teachings he is in full accord with the Pharisees and his sayings echo the teachings of the Pharisees.[5]

Yet, important and significant as these two parties were for both Judaism and Christianity, they have not been correctly understood until a comparatively recent date. Both Christian and Jewish scholars were wanting in an adequate knowledge of the origin, development, and relative position of these ancient

---

Judaism from which Christianity took them over. But in the actual carrying out of this idea and in the realization of this tendency Christianity did not go further than, nor even as far as, Pharisaic Judaism. The religious universalism of the Pharisees did not suffer from their refusal to give up the identity of the Jewish group. For they welcomed all other nations to attach themselves to the Jewish nation. They did not discriminate against any race or nation that wished to join the Jewish people and become identified with it. It is true, they insisted upon the performance of certain rites on the part of those who wished to join them, but so do the Christians. Pharisaic Judaism demands circumcision as a condition for admission to the Jewish fold; Christianity demands baptism as the condition for admission to the Church. Pharisaic Judaism demands the acceptance of certain Jewish principles of conduct and rules of ethical life; the Church demands the acceptance of certain dogmatic beliefs. Pharisaic Judaism, however, grants salvation to all who live an ethical and moral life, even if they have not formally entered the Jewish fold; Christianity denies salvation to those outside of its fold. The Church declared that there is no salvation outside of the Church: "nulla salus extra ecclesiam." The Synagogue, however, never said: "nulla salus extra synagogam."

[5] Cf. D. Chwolson, *Das letzte Passamahl Christi* (Leipzig, 1908), pp. 85–121, and Joseph Klausner, *Jeshu haNozri* (Jerusalem, 1922), pp. 227, 243–44 and 396 ff. R. Leszynsky, *Die Sadducäer* (Berlin, 1912) considers Jesus a Sadducee, but his arguments are not convincing. Even Herford who would consider Jesus an *Am ha-Arez* and not a Pharisee, admits that "much of his teaching is substantially what the Pharisees also taught" (*op. cit.*, p. 115). Cf. William R. Arnold, "The Relation of Primitive Christianity to Jewish Thought and Teaching," in *Harvard Theological Review*, (July, 1930), p. 166.

Jewish parties. They did not appreciate the tendencies of the two parties nor did they fully comprehend their ideas. There prevailed, in general, a complete misunderstanding of their relative positions; the older party was considered to be the younger, and the one actually the younger was held to be the older.

The blame for this historical error and gross misunderstanding falls upon some talmudic reports about, as well as some N. T. references to, these two sects or parties. I do not accuse the Rabbis of the Talmud or the Gospel writers of knowingly misrepresenting historic facts for the sake of party interests, though both might have had very good reasons for doing so. I rather think that they both were human and subject to erring. They both could, and in this case, did make mistakes. It is most likely that both the Gospel writers and the authors of some of the talmudic reports no longer knew the actual conditions and the historic forces that caused the division of the two parties, and hence they could easily misunderstand their relative positions and their respective tendencies. We can well understand how they came to make the mistakes which they made. Their misunderstanding of the historical situation was probably due to the fact that in their time the Pharisees had already gained the victory over their opponents. The Judaism of the second half of the first Christian century was already predominantly Pharisaic. And in the first half of the second Christian century the Pharisaic teachers and leaders of Judaism were practically alone in the field.

We must also remember that both the authors of the talmudic works and the authors of the N. T. pursued with their writings only religious and theological, perhaps in some measure also polemical, aims, but certainly no archaeological purposes. At any rate, they were not much concerned with historical critical investigations. They were not intereted in a study of the changes and the developments which had taken place in Judaism and within Jewry during the time of the second Temple. They probably did not know, or would not acknowledge, that there had taken place great developments, or that changes had been made. They both innocently believed that the Judaism of their time, with its conception of the Torah and with its methods of interpreting the Law, was the same as that of the time of Ezra, if not of the time of Moses. And they naively believed that the authoritative teachers and representative leaders of their time were of the same class or type, and represented the same tendencies, as those of former generations. Hence the Rabbis of the Talmud, who were followers of the Pharisees in their teachings and in their methods of interpreting the Law, believed that these interpretations and these teachings, which they considered correct, had also been held by the great teachers of the past; accordingly, they presented them as the traditions of the fathers. Their party, or the teachers, who cherished these ideas and applied these methods of interpretation, were regarded by them as the party of the faithful, loyal to the traditions of old, who ever since the time of Ezra, if not of Moses, have always been the authoritative teachers, upholders of the Torah, and true leaders of the people. On the other hand, the opponents of that party, the Sadducees, who rejected these teachings and disapproved of these methods of interpreting the Law, were regarded by the talmudic authors as an heretical sect that came into being at a comparatively late date, a party of wicked people or groups organized by Zadok and Boethus, two faithless disciples of a great Pharisaic teacher, Antigonos of Soko. These two disciples, so the talmudic legend runs, misunderstood a saying of their master and drew from it the wrong conclusion, denying the doctrine of Divine retribution. They left their master, went out and organized the two groups, or sects, of Sadducees and Boethusians respectively, who forsook the true teachings and the traditional interpretations of the teachers of old.[6] Thus the historic position of the two parties, the Sadducees and the Pharisees, was reversed in the minds of the talmudic reporters.

The writers of the Gospels, who were no more adept in historical criticism than their talmudic contemporaries, likewise made the mistake of identifying, as it were, or putting in one

[6] Ab. R. N., version A. ch. V, version B. ch. X, Schechter, 26. This report cannot be considered historically true, against E. Baneth, *Ursprung der Sadokäer u. Boethosäer*, (Dessau, 1882) who regards it as such. It contains, however, a kernel of truth in that it dates back the beginning of the conflict between the two parties to the time of the disciples of Antigonos. See *Midrash and Mishnah*, below p. 208, note 49.

class, the Jewish religious leaders of their times with the Jewish authorities of the time of Jesus. Now, it is true that the Pharisees who were contemporaries of Jesus never recognized him as the Messiah, but otherwise they showed him no unfriendliness. They could not object to his teachings which for the most part at least were in accord with their own; and they certainly did not persecute him.[7] In the times of the Gospel writers the Jewish teachers and leaders who by that time were all of the Pharisees, of course, continued to refuse to believe in the Messiahship of Jesus, and the Gospel writers, therefore, had to polemize against them. But the Gospel writers, knowing no other Jewish leaders and teachers than those of the Pharisee group of their own times imagined that the conditions of their own times also prevailed in the time of Jesus. They naively assumed that the authorities against whom Jesus preached and whom he strongly condemned,

[7] The Pharisees could not have any reason for persecuting Jesus — if they noticed him at all — the reports of the N. T. to the contrary notwithstanding. Even if his teachings had been different from, or opposed to, their own teachings, the Pharisees would not have sought to harm him. For, according to Pharisaic principles, even the rebellious teacher, the זקן ממרא is punished only if he incites the people to act against the Law, עד שיורה לעשות, but not if he merely holds or preaches heterodox doctrines (M. Sanh. 11.2). And Jesus never incited the people to act against the Law and never preached the neglect of the fulfilment of the commandments. Besides Jesus could at most have been considered a *Talmid* not yet ordained and according to the Mishnah, *loc. cit.*, *Talmid shehorah la'asot patur*. Even if it be true that the Pharisees asked Jesus why his disciples were doing "that which it is not lawful to do upon the Sabbath" (Matt. 12.2 ff. and Mark 2.23 ff.) they did not accuse him of causing his disciples to do so. And the principle with which Jesus is said to have defended his disciples, *viz.*, that: "The Sabbath was made for man, and not man for the Sabbath" (Mark 2.27) was good Pharisaic doctrine. See Mekilta, *Shabbata* I, Friedmann 103b–104a.

Neither could the Pharisees have considered Jesus a blasphemer. If the High Priest declared Jesus a blasphemer he was either ignorant of or in opposition to the Pharisaic interpretation of the Law. For, according to the latter, one can be guilty of blasphemy only if in his alleged blasphemous utterance he mentioned the Tetragrammaton (M. Sanh. 7.5). Jesus, however, used the designation "Power" גבורה and not the Tetragrammaton, aside from the fact that his alleged utterance as such did not consitute a blasphemy. In short, Jesus did not do or say anything which according to the Pharisaic interpretation of the Law was punishable by death. Cf. D. Chwolson, *op. cit.*, pp. 86–92 and especially p. 121.

and the leaders who persecuted him, were of the same class or type as the Jewish leaders of their own times.[8] Hence, they ascribed to the Pharisees of the times of Jesus actions which the latter could never have performed, and tendencies or characteristics which in reality were those of their opponents.[9] In this way, the Gospel writers also confused the respective religious positions of the two parties, and in many instances at least, gave an inadequate presentation and an incorrect picture of the real aims and aspirations of the Pharisees.

[8] The following instance is an illustration of how the gospel writers, projecting into the past conditions or ideas of their own later times, would substitute "Pharisees" for other people or authorities who had been reported as opposing Jesus. The accusation against Jesus that "he casteth out devils through Beelzebub the chief of the devils" was made, according to Luke (11.15), by some of the people who witnessed the performance of driving out the devil. According to Mark (3.22) this accusation was made by the scribes, who were not necessarily Pharisees, since there also were scribes among the Sadducees (cf. E. Schürer, *Geschichte des Jüdischen Volkes*, II, [Leipzig, 1907], pp. 380–381). And Mark himself mentions "the Scribes and Pharisees" as two separate groups (Mark 2.16, cf. also Luke 5.30 and Acts 23.9). But Matthew, who is the most bitter in his accusation of the Pharisees, because of his having to argue against the Jewish teachers of his time who were the followers of the Pharisees, reports that: "the Pharisees said, he casteth out devils through the prince of the devils" (Matt. 9.34). Cf. also Shirley Jackson Case, *Jesus, A New Biography* (Chicago, 1927), pp. 90, 104–105 and 108. Cf. Donald W. Riddle, *Jesus and the Pharisees*, (Chicago, 1928), p. 5, who likewise refers to the disagreement of the Gospel as to the opponents of Jesus. He maintains there, p. 6, that the Christian sources contain confused traditions of Jesus and the Pharisees.

[9] Thus, the accusation that the Pharisees by their interpretation of the laws regarding vows make the commandment to honor father and mother "of none effect" (Matt. 15.3–6) is absolutely false. Such an attitude towards vows, as implied by Matthew, could have been taken only by the Sadducees, who, as far as we know, did not accept the principle that a teacher has the authority to declare a vow void, since this principle has no basis whatever in the written Torah (cf. Ḥag. 10a). The Pharisees, however, taught that vows could be declared void by an ordained teacher when the person who made the vow had a good reason for regretting his having made the vow. The Pharisaic teachers would even suggest to the person who made the vow how he could be released from his vow when it conflicted with the duty of honoring father and mother (M. Ned. 9.4). See Lauterbach, "Vows," in *Jewish Encyclopedia*, XII, pp. 451–52, and cf. Strack-Billerbeck, *Kommentar zum Neuen Testament*, I, (München, 1922), to the passage in Matthew, especially p. 715.

And even the historian Josephus does not give a full presentation or an adequate picture of these two parties. He fails to furnish us with the historical data about their early beginnings and later developments. In his desire to present to his Greek readers the Jewish sects as philosophical schools, Josephus is merely concerned with some aspects of their respective theological positions and with some of their differences in respect of ideas and beliefs, but he does not give any positive historical information about the origin and the respective development of the two sects.[10] No wonder, then, that for centuries, up to recent times, these two ancient parties and their respective tendencies and relative positions, were not correctly understood even by scholars. The source material was deficient in direct and positive historical data.

And yet, in each of these ancient sources there are to be found some details of the conflict between the two parties or some references to one or another of its aspects, which hint at the real differences in their respective viewpoints. Each one of the three sources, Josephus, the Talmud, and the New Testament, gives, implicitly or explicitly, some correct information about these two parties. There is enough factual material as well as significant indications preserved in the Talmud and Josephus — some even in the New Testament — which, if rightly understood and correctly interpreted, throw light on the respective theological positions of the two parties and reveal especially the true character and teachings of the Pharisees. But the mistake made by these ancient reporters in regard to the chronological order and the relative historical position of the two parties made even their correct data and their other valuable information less clear and more difficult to understand. For the one mistake, of necessity, brought others with it. Once the parties were put in a false historical order, or given the wrong historical setting, their views, beliefs, and tendencies were also, to some extent at least, viewed in a false light.

---

[10] Josephus also assumes that the Pharisees were the older sect. For, in describing the sects he refers to the Pharisees as "the first sect" (*Wars* II, 8.2; *Ant.* XVIII, 1.3). And like the Talmud (Ber. 29a) he reports that John Hyrcanus had originally been a disciple of the Pharisees and then turned against them and joined the Sadducees (*Ant.* XIII, 10.5).

If we wish to understand correctly the character and the tendencies of the two parties, we must first correct that error and put each historically in its correct place. We shall then have no difficulty in correctly understanding the ancient reports about them. The information thus gathered from these reports, critically examined and correctly interpreted, will give an adequate picture and a correct presentation of the characteristic tendencies of the two parties. It will thus lead especially to an appreciation of the character, position, tendencies, and teachings of the Pharisees.

Let us begin, then, with the question as to the relative historical postition of these two parties and their respective attitudes towards tradition. The Pharisees were not the older conservative party who preserved the older methods of interpretation and followed the traditional applications of the Law (Torah), although, paradoxical as this may sound, they did advocate the authority of Tradition as such. The Sadducees, on the other hand, were not the heretical group who broke away from the older teachings and denied the true traditions of the fathers. The reverse was the case.[11] The Sadducees were the older, conservative party who adhered strictly to the traditional, simple methods of interpreting the Torah, and who preserved the Torah and the character of its authority. They practiced the ancient laws exactly as prescribed in the Torah. They retained and held to the traditional belief that there is no other authority equal to the authority of the Torah. They would not recognize any other authority as equal to that of the Torah, not even the authority of Tradition; and hence they denied the binding character of the so-called traditional laws. The Pharisees, on the other hand, were the younger, progressive party composed originally of democratic laymen who outgrew some of the older notions, cherished modern and liberal ideas and therefore became separated from the older group and formed a distinct party. They were the liberal separatists, the dissenters who rejected some of the ancient traditional conceptions of religion and who

---

[11] On the question, how the conservative Sadducees came to reject, and the progressive Pharisees came to recognize, the authority of the traditional law, see *The Sadducees and Pharisees*, above pp. 23–48.

broke away from the primitive traditional attitude towards the Torah. They invoked the very authority of Tradition to support them in their fight against some harmful traditions.

These were, generally speaking, the relative historical positions of the two parties and their respective viewpoints. But both parties had their antecedents. Their platforms were not newly made. The opposing parties did not suddenly spring into existence, fully developed and in such shape as we see them when already in actual combat. Even the Pharisees, the younger party, were merely as a party, younger than their opponents; they were comparative newcomers but not entirely newly-born. Though as a party they were younger and of recent date, yet the tendency followed by them was not entirely novel or new. In their spirit and for their ideas they went back, though not in a direct line, to older prototypes; and their opponents, the Sadducees, surely had behind them a long line of predecessors. To understand and appreciate correctly the Pharisees and their teachings, one must go back not only to Ezra and his work[12] but even beyond Ezra and his time to the works of the prophets, just as to understand the Judaism which the Pharisees developed and so strongly modified and spiritualized one must go back to its very source and its basis in pre-exilic times. For the roots of the Pharisaic ideas, the very origin of their principles, the basis of their religious philosophy or theology, are to be found in the teachings of the prophets of old. The Pharisees were the spiritual heirs or the actual, though not the direct, successors of the prophets. They came to their inheritance a long time after the departure of the prophets. But once they entered it they asserted their right to the heritage, persisted in keeping and developing it, and they carried on the fight of their spiritual forbears to a successful victory.

For the fight of the Pharisees against the Sadducean priestly aristocracy with its primitive ideas of religion as a cultus and particularistic conceptions of God, Israel, and the Torah was, practically, but a revival of the old opposition of the prophets to the priesthood. It was a renewal, in a more persistent manner, of

[12] See Herford, *op. cit.*, pp. 18 ff.

the conflict between the prophets and the priestly organization of pre-exilic times. The attitudes and the tactics of the prophets and the Pharisees in their respective struggles show many parallels and striking similarities. Like the prophets, the Pharisees in principle had little use for the sacrificial cult, but tolerated it, when not accompanied by false conceptions of God and not resulting in unethical conduct towards man. They fought it when it tended to lead to wrong conceptions of religion. And just as the prophets in the course of time came to combine the priestly doctrine with the prophetical ideas, made their peace with the sacrificial cult but sought to regulate and improve it, so also did the Pharisees in the course of time, as they prevailed against their opponents, make their peace with the entire priestly ritual and the sacrificial service of the Temple, but they sought to regulate and improve it, spiritualize it and democratize it.[13] In fact, the very secret of their great success lay just in this, that they used against their opponents the very materials accumulated by the latter. They employed for their own higher spiritual purposes their opponent's equipment and institutions. They took over the control of the Temple service and combined with it a higher form of worship. They introduced into the Temple the service of the Synagogue. They retained the ritual of the Temple, but made it expressive of spiritual truths. They prescribed rites but made them symbolize right thinking and just conduct. They developed a ceremonial but it was suggestive of ethical ideals and of advanced religious beliefs. They recognized and admitted the principle adhered to by their opponents, that the Torah is the supreme and only authority and that its laws must be fulfilled by the Jew, but they defined the term Torah differently and extended it to mean more than the *written laws* contained in the five books of Moses. They followed the precepts of the Torah but they first humanized them by interpreting them according to the spirit and not according to the letter.

For the Pharisees were not only heirs of the prophets but

---

[13] And when the Pharisaic teachers after the destruction of the Temple hoped for its restoration, they had their prototype in the priest-prophet Ezekiel.

also disciples of the priests — and very apt disciples at that. A brief review of the history of Judaism, prior to the actual division into the two parties, will show that the two groups, that were later on to become separate and opposing parties, for a long time occupied common ground. The budding younger group started out as alert and eager disciples of the older, priestly group. For a long time, and for a considerable distance, they travelled together along the road of the history and the development of post-exilic Judaism, with but occasional manifestations of minor disagreements. When differences first arose they were not so pronounced and could be settled peacefully; the master, secure in his position and conscious of his authority, yielded a little, and the pupil respectful or reverential, submitted to the authority of his elders. But gradually the disagreements became more frequent and more pronounced, and they were more strongly felt by both groups. The differences increased and became intensified, making it impossible for master and pupil to keep on travelling together. They reached a point where their ways parted and they finally separated from one another completely. The master was indignant and embittered against the ungrateful, disloyal, and pretentious pupil. The pupil, resolute in his zeal, was determined not to let any consideration interfere with his pursuit of righteousness and search for truth — not even respect for his elders. He acted on the principle, later on enunciated and followed by the Pharisaic party, that "where a higher cause is at stake even the honor and the respect due to a teacher are to be disregarded."[14] This brief historical review will show us the immediate causes of the final breach between the two groups, the conditions that prepared and the forces that led up to the formation of the two parties; in other words, Pharisaism in the making.

I said before that the struggle between Pharisees and Sadducees was, in a way, but a renewal of the conflict between prophets and priests of pre-exilic times.[14a] Now, that old conflict had never

[14] כל מקום שיש חלול השם אין חולקים כבוד לרב, Sanh. 82 and Shebu. 30b.

[14a] Cf. Aage Bentzen (Kopenhagen), "Priesterschaft u. Laien in der Juedischen Gemeinde des fuenften Jahrhundert" in *Archiv fuer Orientforschung*, VI, #6, (Berlin, 1931), 280–286. He has a few interesting remarks on the struggle between the priests and what he calls the laity in pre-exilic times.

been fought to a finish. No party had won a decisive victory. A compromise was effected in the Deuteronomic reformation which, for a time at least, seemed to have secured peace without victory. But soon Judea was conquered by Nebuchadnezzar, Jerusalem and the Temple were destroyed, and the people were exiled to Babylon. This national catastrophe, seemingly, decided in favor of the prophetic ideas and dealt a death blow to the priestly conceptions of religion among the Jewish people.

Brooding over the sad fate which had befallen their country and their nation, living in a foreign land, away from the holy city, deprived of a Temple with its sacrificial cult, and without the priestly oracle, the people of Judea could not help learning to appreciate the truth of the prophetic teachings, *viz.*, that God is everywhere and not only in Palestine or Jerusalem, that He is the Lord of all the universe, ruling and guiding the destinies of all peoples, and not only that of Israel; that He can be served by other means than offering sacrifices to Him, nay, that even more than sacrifices He desires a true knowledge of Him and His Law. And, no doubt, the prophetic ideas about the One God and the universality of His Law, the one humanity and Israel's special place in it, took root in the minds of many Judeans and began to be formulated already during their exile in Babylon.

But when the returned exiles rebuilt the Temple and restored the sacrificial cult, the priests were also restored to their former position as religious leaders. The priestly conceptions, then, regained their influence and overshadowed the prophetic ideas. The Jewish people in Judea during the Persian period constituted an autonomous religious community with the High Priest as its chief and highest religious authority, though politically under the control of the Persian rulers. This reorganized community received from Ezra, the priest and scribe, the Law of Moses.[14b]

[14b] Cf. H. H. Schaeder, *Esra der Schreiber*, (Tübingen, 1930). He would assume that Ezra would save the prophetic teachings by putting it in the form of Law. Cf. also Vogelstein in his review of Schaeder's work in *MGWJ*, 1931, p. 385. It could be harmonized with my theory as follows: — While Ezra was a priest he favored the idea of the prophets and expressed it in the law. Other reactionary priests disagreed with him. So in the course of time after Ezra the priestly tendency predominated. Some priests, especially the Soferim

They entered into a covenant and pledged themselves by a solemn oath to walk in the ways of the Law of God which was given by Moses, to obey it and to observe and to do all its commandments, its judgments and statutes (Neh. 10.1 [English translation 9.38] — 29 ff.). In this manner, then, by the binding power of the covenant and solemn oath, the Torah, or the Book of the Law of Moses, became the constitution of the reorganized community in Judea, the Law whose precepts were to be binding upon every Jew. This Law was to be the only authority recognized by the people; but the priests, especially the priest-scribes, the successors of Ezra, were the keepers of the Book of the Law, the official teachers and interpreters of the Torah.[15]

This was as it should be and as it always had been. It was in perfect harmony with traditional usage and in keeping with the old custom that had prevailed in Israel and Judah from time immemorial. The people were accustomed to believe that the priests were the rightful teachers of the Law. They used to say: "For instruction (Torah) shall not perish from the priests" (Jer. 18.18; cf. also Ezek. 22.26 and 44.15–24, Hosea 4.6, Micah 3.11). The two functions of officiating at the altar of God and of teaching the Law of God went together. The priest who ministered to God and brought to Him the sacrifices and offerings of the people, also ministered to the people and brought to them a message from God, and taught them His Law. And the Torah itself, the very Law which the reorganized community had accepted as their authority, points to these two functions of the priests, the sons of the tribe of Levi. In Deut. 33.10 it says: "They shall teach Jacob Thine ordinances and Israel Thy law; they shall put incense before Thee and whole burnt sacrifices upon Thy altar." And in Deut. 17 these priests are designated as the authoritative teachers and competent interpreters of the Law, who alone have the right and the authority to render

---

followed the ideas of Ezra till another חסיד שבכהונה like Ezra — Jose b. Joezer arose. From the reactionary group of the priests the Samaritans got their Torah, hence not in the writing into which Ezra cast it.

[15] See *The Sadducees and Pharisees*, above pp. 27–30 and p. 35, note 16; *Midrash and Mishnah*, below p. 197, note 39, and pp. 208–210; and see below, note 18.

judgments according to the Law and to decide all questions of law, ritual or religious practice. The post-exilic community that accepted from Ezra the Torah as its chief authority, consequently, recognized the authority of the priests, designated by that Torah, as its competent teachers and interpreters. The people were satisfied that "the priest's lips should keep knowledge, and they should seek the law at his mouth" (Mal. 2.7). Under the leadership of the High Priest the priest-scribes no doubt formed some sort of an organization, an official body vested with authority to arrange all religious matters and to settle all questions of the life of the community in accordance with the Law as they interpreted it. Throughout the entire Persian period, then, these priests, while teaching the Torah, naturally taught it according to their primitive understanding of it. They interpreted its laws simply and literally. And while striving to preserve the religion of the fathers and to spread the knowledge of it among the people, it was their own priestly conceptions of that religion which they preserved and sought to perpetuate among the people. No prophet arose to criticize them, to challenge their interpretations of the Law, or to dispute their authority as religious leaders of the community.

But the seed sown by the prophets, which, as we have seen, found a favorable soil in the minds of the people during the exile, was not lost. The prophetic ideas about Israel, God and His Law were not entirely forgotten. They were cherished and preserved at least by some of the choice spirits among the people. And when conditions became favorable, those ideas became more articulate and found their expression in a movement participated in by many of the pious lay people.

These favorable conditions came after the overthrow of the Persian Empire by Alexander which brought Judea under Greek rule and which indirectly helped to weaken and undermine the authority of the priestly organization in Judea.[16] The third century was the period of germination for those ideas of the prophets which had been clearly recognized in the exile but pushed into the background in Palestine during the Persian period.

[16] See *Midrash and Mishnah*, below pp. 193 ff.

The Greek governments under which the Jewish people now lived, while not interfering much with the internal affairs or the religious life of the community, would, of course, not especially favor that priestly organization nor give it much support. The disturbed conditions, brought about by the wars between Alexander's successors and the repeated changes in sovereign rulers, were likewise not favorable to the continuation of the organization of priests as the undisputed official authorities and leaders of the community. As a matter of fact, in the third century B. C. E. there were already among the people many laymen, i. e., Israelites, or rather men of Judah, of non-priestly families, who possessed a knowledge of the Law and of the prophets and of the teachings of their religion. The people were no longer entirely dependent on the organization of the priests for their religious instruction. The lips of the priests were not the sole keepers of religious knowledge, and the people could occasionally seek and obtain instruction in the Torah from the mouths of non-priestly Israelites.[17]

With the spread of the knowledge of the Torah among the people there spread also some ideas arousing doubts as to the privileges and undisputed authority of the priests. From that very

[17] See *ibid.*, pp. 46 ff. Such a lay-teacher was Jesus Siraḥ. Siraḥ was not a priest. Against V. Aptowitzer, *Parteipolitik der Hasmonäer*, etc., (Vienna, 1927), p. 275, cf. Klausner, *Kiryath Sefer* V, 355. He was not one of the older Soferim, for he lived at about 200 B. C. E., after the close of the period of the Soferim. The early Soferim were priests. But during the third century, especially towards the close of it, there were already teachers of both groups, priests and lay people. Siraḥ belonged to the latter. While he cannot be considered a Pharisee, as there was not yet a distinct party of Pharisees in his time, he certainly was not a Sadducee; that is, he did not share the ideas of that aristocratic priestly group that later on came to be known as the Sadducean party. The fact that Siraḥ does not mention the belief in the resurrection of the dead is no argument to the contrary. At most this would merely be an *argumentum e silentio* which has no weight in this case. He may not have had occasion to mention this belief; or this belief may not as yet have become definitely formulated by the lay-group of his time. At any rate, there is no indication in the Talmudic literature that Siraḥ was regarded as a Sadducee. On the contrary, the Rabbis have rather given Jesus Siraḥ positive recognition and have declared that his book was offering some good teachings. This shows that they did not regard him as a Sadducee. Cf. G. F. Moore, *Judaism*, I (Cambridge, 1927), pp. 37 ff., 24 and 44.

Torah, considered as the highest authority by both priest and people, the people learned that they were all meant to be "a kingdom of priests and a holy nation" (Exod. 19.6), and that "the Torah which Moses commanded was intended to be the inheritance of the entire congregation of Jacob" (Deut. 33.4), and not the exclusive possession of one privileged class, the priests. And while the story of the terrible faith of Ḳoraḥ and his associates would deter people from any attempt at rebellion against the priestly leaders, and no one would dare as yet openly and positively to question the authority of the priests, yet people could not help remembering also the words of those ancient rebels recorded in the book of Numbers: "Ye take too much upon you, seeing all the congregation are holy, every one of them, and the Lord is among them; wherefore, then, lift ye up yourselves above the assembly of the Lord?" (Num. 16.3). In their minds, at least, the lay teachers of the third century B. C. E. must have addressed these words to the priestly leaders of their own time.

They may have been encouraged in these vague doubts and questionings of the authority of the priests by their new environment, and by the acquaintance with Greek institutions which not only the Jews in the Diaspora but also the Jews in Palestine had made during the third century. There were in Palestine during the third century many Greek colonies, settled in special cities or communities, which were administered along the lines of Greek democracies. In these democratic communities all free citizens were equal and every member of the community participated in its rule and had a share in the administration of the communal affairs. These ideas of liberty and democratic principles the Jews found to be in accord with the laws of the Torah and the teachings of the prophets. And yet they noticed that their own system of communal government was in one important feature fundamentally different from that obtaining in the Greek democracies. Among the Greeks the priests were the servants of the people and not its rulers, while in their own community the Jews found that their rulers and chief authorities were the priests. The people felt — and it was not a pleasant feeling — that in this respect their system of communal government did not compare favorably with that of the Greeks. The explanation that their community was really ruled by the Torah which they, the people themselves, had accepted as their chief authority, and that the priests were merely the interpreters of the Torah who guide and direct the people in the name and according to the laws of that Torah, could not for long satisfy them. For the lay teachers would naturally ask, why should the priests alone be the authoritative interpreters and official administrators of the Torah? If the Torah is the constitution and the sole guide and law of the community, then knowledge of it alone, and not any inherited family privilege, should qualify one for participation in the government of the community by interpreting and administering the laws of the Torah. Recognizing the Torah as their chief authority and believing it to be the Law of God, perfect and right in all its precepts, true and righteous in all its ordinances (Ps. 19.9–10), these pious lay students of the Law soon came to believe that the Torah indeed never meant to give the priests any special privilege with regard to interpreting and administering its laws. And when the Torah mentions the priests as the authoritative teachers of the law whose interpretations must be accepted and whose decisions must be obeyed (Deut. 17), it merely describes a condition but does not prescribe a rule. They were given the right to interpret and administer the law, not as a hereditary class privilege or family distinction. This right was given to the priests because it just happened in ancient times that they alone had cultivated the Torah and known it; and they, therefore, were in a position to teach and interpret it. This privilege given to that group of teachers because of their knowledge of the law and not because of their being priests, is, therefore, equally to be enjoyed by any one of non-priestly birth who has an adequate knowledge of the Torah. This must have been the line along which the lay teachers reasoned. It was probably the first instance of departure from the literal, simple meaning of the words of the Torah, and the first attempt at interpreting the Torah not strictly according to its letter, but according to the spirit and the purpose aimed at by the Law. Possibly these pious lay teachers were surprised themselves when realizing that they were interpreting the Law in that novel and unheard-of manner. But they persuaded themselves into believing that their interpretation was correct. They probably found a support, if not the suggestion, for their interpretation in another passage of the Torah where it is said of the priests: "They shall teach Jacob Thine ordinances and Israel Thy law" (Deut. 33.10). They found that this declaration, designating the priests as the authoritative teachers, is preceded and, as it were, motivated by the words in verse 9: "For they have observed Thy word and kept Thy covenant." In other words, it was only because the priests had kept the Torah, observed it and studied it, that they were qualified and authorized to teach and interpret it. And, therefore, anyone, not of the priests, who has studied the Torah, acquired a knowledge of it and is thus in a position to teach it, must likewise have the authority to interpret and administer the law. For, "the Torah commanded to us by Moses is the heritage of the congregation of Jacob" and not of the family of Aaron or the tribe of Levi. So the learned pious men of Israel, of non-priestly descent, began to demand their share in the heritage. They claimed the right to have the same authority of interpreting and administering the law, as was enjoyed by the priests. Of course, we have no express records of this phase of the struggle.[18] We cannot tell how boldly and how forcefully this claim was made, nor do we know with certainty the arguments put forth in support of this claim. But this much is certain; the group of Israelitish, non-priestly students of the Torah, the pupils of the elder priestly group, made this demand succesfully. The master, willingly or forced by circumstances, had to yield. And the pupil became the colleague. For in the beginning of the second century we find that the new Sanhedrin, or the Gerousia, the authoritative

[18] See *The Sadducees and the Pharisees*, above p. 34, note, and pp. 39–41. An echo of this ancient struggle between the lay people and the priests is perhaps to be found in the following passage of the Midrash אלה הדברים זוטא, quoted in Yalḳuṭ Shimeoni to Deut. 27.9 (938), which reads: וידבר משה והכהנים והלוים. מה דברים היו שם ללמדך שבאו ישראל ואמרו למשה נטלת את התורה ונתת לכהנים שנאמר ויכתוב משה את התורה הזאת ויתנה אל הכהנים אמר להם משה רצונכם שיכרתו לכם ברית שכל מי שמבקש ללמוד תורה לא יהא נמנע אמרו לו הן עמדו ונשבעו שאין אדם נמנע מלקרות בתורה שנאמר אל כל ישראל לאמור אמר להם משה היום הזה נהיית לעם. This passage expresses a protest against assigning the interpretation and administration of the Torah to the priests.

body in charge of all the affairs of the community, the body interpreting and administering the law, was composed of both priests and Israelites. To use the phraseology of the Zadokite Document, it was an assembly of "men of understanding from Aaron" and of "wise teachers from Israel."[19]

With this admission of lay teachers to the new Sanhedrin, which practically meant a recognition of their authority as interpreters and administrators of the Law and their equality with the priests, the fight between them and the older priestly group was by no means settled. It really just began. It now developed into a conscious, determined fight, fought within that new Sanhedrin which had as its task to arrange and regulate the life of the people according to the Torah which the people in the times of Ezra had pledged themselves to obey and follow. The task of that assembly was a very difficult one. The Torah seemed inadequate for the new life. All the laws contained in the Torah interpreted literally and in in the simple manner, as they were, would seem insufficient to meet the demands now made upon it or to answer the needs of the new situation which had arisen in the life of the community. The conditions of life now prevailing in Judea were very different from conditions in the times of Ezra when the people accepted the Torah and pledged themselves by oath to follow all its precepts. These changed conditions created new situations in life. Questions arose for which no answer could be found in the Books of the Law. There came up unprecedented cases of law, ritual or practice, which could not be decided on the basis of any law or precept in the Torah as traditionally interpreted. The problem before this new Sanhedrin, composed of priests and lay teachers, was, how to find in the old law new rules, answers to new questions, decisions for entirely new cases; in other words, how to harmonize law with life, the old law of the fathers with the new life of the day. Each

---

[19] See *Midrash and Mishnah*, below pp. 47–49. In *Seder Eliahu Rabba* XV, Friedmann, p. 72: — Not to the priests alone is holiness given; but to priests, Levites and Israelites, for it is said (Lev. 19.1, 2): "Speak to the congregation of the children of Israel and say to them: 'Holy shall ye be.'" This statement is perhaps also an old citation echoing the Pharisaic claim to equality with priests.

one of the component groups of that new Sanhedrin looked at the problem before them from a different point of view. Each one of them had a different approach to its solution.

The attempts at solving the problem, the various proposals to meet the difficult situation, brought out in sharp contrast the differences in tendency and outlook, between the older priestly group and the younger group of non-priestly teachers and members, the newcomers to authority. The latter whose very claim to equal authority with the priests was, as we have seen, based upon, or at least supported by, an interpretation of one passage in the Torah according to its spirit, would not hesitate to follow the same method in the case of other passages of the Torah containing laws and precepts. They would be ready to depart from the letter of the Torah and interpret it according to the spirit and its underlying ideas, so as to find in it answers to new questions, or discover in it principles which would guide them in deciding new cases or solving new problems. Again, in seeking to define what constitutes the law of the fathers, these lay teachers would naturally not be as strict and as literal as the older priestly group. The very fact that they claimed for themselves, though they were not of priestly descent, equal authority with the priests, would prevent them from deprecating such customs and practices as had for some time been observed by the people, even though these customs and practices had never been officially sanctioned or recognized by the priestly authorities. After all, to their way of thinking, the priests were not the exclusive authorities, to determine what is religious practice or custom of the fathers. Might not, so these lay-teachers were inclined to argue, the people who introduced or indorsed these practices have had good reasons or reliable authority for these practices, even though the priests had not known them, or refused to recognize them? Might not the Torah, which is not to be understood only literally, be so interpreted as to suggest indorsement of such practices, or so defined as to include all good customs of the fathers, preserved by the people but not expressly written in the words of the Torah, and not recognized by the priests? It was along such lines of reasoning that the lay-group proposed to solve the problem before them.

The older priestly group, on the other hand, could never follow in this direction. They could not entertain such radical notions as to the method of interpreting the Torah, and would not admit the possibility of some popular practices having a religious authority behind them, when they and their forebears, the priestly teachers of old, had never known them. They would, of course, not admit that there ever were any authorities other than that of the priests. They and their priestly forbears alone had always been the sole religious authorities and official teachers of the Law. With their primitive conceptions about the authority of the Torah, and refusing to admit that they, the long established teachers of that Torah, did not understand it correctly, they would hold on to their old methods of interpreting the Law, taking its words according to their literal meaning. And, accordingly, they would naturally propose to solve the problem before them in a manner compatible with their conservative ideas and tending to secure for them their old prerogatives and to perpetuate them in their old privileged position as the authoritative leaders.

These differences in the attempts at meeting the difficult situation were, of course, the expressions of different conceptions of the Torah and of different religious outlooks; but the two groups, as yet, did not recognize their differences as fundamental and irreconcilable. They still hoped to be able to compose their differences and work together. For a time, the two groups in that new Sanhedrin struggled to agree. For about twenty years, according to the Zadokite Document,[20] these two groups worked together, making honest efforts to compose their differences and endeavoring to find the right way for regulating the life of the people in accordance with the laws of the fathers. But the aggressive campaign for Hellenization inaugurated by the Syrian rulers, and abetted by some traitorous priests which soon resulted in religious persecution, interrupted the functioning of that new Sanhedrin. In the face of the great danger that threatened the Torah and the religious life of the community, the two groups who, although differing in tendency and point of view, were both

---

[20] See *Midrash and Mishnah*, below, pp. 207–208.

true to the Torah, as they understood it, and loyal to the religion of the fathers, forgot their differences and their disagreements. The pious men of Israel joined the faithful priests in the fight against the common foe, the enemy of their religion.[21]

But after the Maccabean victory when peace was established and religious freedom secured, when under a government of their own, headed by a King-High Priest, the Jews were to live according to the religion of their fathers, the entire life of the people was again to be regulated and controlled by the laws of the Torah, as interpreted by the rightful authorities. Then the question of who constitutes the rightful authority to interpret the law was again raised, and the differences between the two groups as regards the interpretation of the Torah and the conception of the religion of the fathers again became keenly felt. Both parties now recognized that their differences were fundamental and irreconcilable. The group of lay teachers realized that their conception of the Torah, and their interpretation of its contents and hence their whole religious outlook were radically different from those of the older priestly group. And they concluded that they could no longer continue to work together with that group. The priestly group, on the other hand, now again under the rule of a sovereign of their own, and backed by the power of a political government, were less willing to yield their authority and give up any of their ancient privileges.

So finally, during the reign of John Hyrcanus, the non-priestly teachers, the *Ḥakme Israel* (חכמי ישראל), were excluded from membership in the assembly or the Sanhedrin and branded as Dissenters or Separatists. The name, פרושים, Separatists, was given them by the priestly party and was meant as a taunt, the expelled ones, or, those who are different.[22] They accepted this

---

[21] See I Macc. 2.42 ff. and cf. *Midrash and Mishnah*, below p. 207, note 47.

[22] See *The Sadducees and Pharisees*, above pp. 45–46, and cf. Pseudo-Tertullian, *Against All Heresies*, ch. I. Later on, with the development of their special methods of interpreting the Law, the name "Perushim," slightly chnaged and pronounced "Paroshim" may have been taken as indicating "interpreters" or "expounders" of the Law. A very fanciful interpretation of the origin of the name "Perushim" is given by Solomon Rubin in his *Yalḳuṭ Shlomoh*, (Krakau, 1896), pp. 66–67. According to him, it originally was פרסים

taunt and took up the name of *Perushim*, Pharisees, but interpreted it as a title of honor, the Separatists who separated and held aloof from those who do not follow the right way, who do not interpret the Torah correctly, and who have the wrong conceptions about God and Israel. Thus was formed the party of the Pharisees, who were conscious of their separateness and different from the priestly group that now came to be called the Sadducean party.

How the Pharisees developed their teachings which had their roots in the ideas of the prophets; how, independent of, and in opposition to, the traditional priestly authorities, they created a tradition of their own and developed a traditional Law, interpreting and supplementing the Written Law, and how they developed and formulated their liberal doctrines of Judaism based upon the right conceptions of God, Israel and the Torah, we shall discuss in the next two chapters.

II

THE PHARISEES' ATTITUDE TOWARD LAW AND TRADITION

For a correct understanding and an adequate appreciation of the teachings of the Pharisees, it is necessary to ascertain the fundamental principles underlying their teachings and the ideas which guided them in interpreting the Law and in regulating religious practice. A detailed presentation of their teachings is not within the scope of these lectures nor would it serve our purpose. A mere enumeration of all the differences between them and their opponents on questions of law and ritual, even if accompanied by the arguments said to have been advanced by each party, would not give us an adequate knowledge of their respective ideas and teachings. We would still have to search for the real reasons for these differences and for the motives that caused the Pharisees to oppose this or that ritual practice of their

---

denoting the people who came back from Persia (that is, the Babylonian Exile), but later on it was changed to פרושים, meaning "Separatists" or "Interpreters" of the Law.

opponents, or to interpret this or that law differently. For even when reasons for their differences are stated in the traditional reports, they may not have been the real reasons. And where the arguments they are said to have advanced in their disputes with their opponents are reported, one cannot with certainty learn from them the real reasons for their position in the dispute. For, in the first place, these arguments, even if actually advanced by the Pharisees themselves, may, like most arguments in polemics, have aimed more at confounding the opponents than at explaining their own position and setting forth their own real reasons. Secondly, they may represent later explanations or *ex post facto* justifications of their positions.

On the other hand, if we ascertain the fundamental differences, the ideas and beliefs, that distinguished the Pharisees from their opponents, we can appreciate their whole religious outlook. We shall then, without need of going into details, be able to obtain a correct understanding of all their teachings, and to know the real reasons for all the differences on questions of law, practice and ritual. For the latter are merely the logical, and in some instances psychological, results of the former. It was their religious ideas, their theological principles, that prompted the Pharisees in their opposition to the older priestly party, and determined the interpretation of the Law and the stand they took on certain questions of ritual.

We shall, therefore, consider primarily how the Pharisees understood the three central concepts of Judaism; *viz.*, God, Israel, and the Torah, which are fundamental doctrines in Judaism, or, as one might call them, the Jewish Trinity. For, the understanding and interpretation of these three concepts decides the character of Judaism and determines all its aspects, its laws and rituals, its beliefs and practices. These three ideas are in Judaism intimately connected with one another, and in Jewish thought they are inseparable. To use the words of an older Jewish mystic, "While these three are separate and distinct concepts, they are almost like one, in that they are bound together and cannot be separated from one another."[23] In other

[23] ג' דרגין אינון מתקשרין דא בדא קב"ה אורייתא וישראל וכו' . . . , Zohar, *Aḥare Mot*, (Lublin, 1872), pp. 129 and 145-146. A later Jewish mystic, R. Israel Besht,

words, these three ideas hang together and are inextricably interwoven. A primitive conception of one of them effects also a wrong view of the two others and results in a narrow backward religious outlook. An advanced view of the one of them must by logical necessity lead to a correspondingly advanced understanding of the two others and results in a broad liberal conception of religion, as indeed was the Pharisees' conception. The very fact, however, that these three ideas are so intimately connected, depending upon and conditioning one another, makes it very difficult to discuss one of them apart from the others. One can hardly give a separate presentation of one of them without occasionally repeating, and without getting into a discussion of the other or touching upon some aspect of the third. And yet we cannot discuss all three of them together. A lucid presentation of the Pharisaic understanding of these three concepts demands that we consider them separately and treat each one of them independently of the others, even at the risk of being involved in unavoidable repetitions.

Now, the Pharisees themselves started with some new ideas about the Torah, and, recognizing the Torah as their chief authority, found in the Torah, as they understood and interpreted it, all their other teachings — even their understanding of the other two central concepts, God and Israel. It is, therefore, but logical for us to begin with a discussion of their conception of the Torah. Such a discussion must of necessity include also a consideration of their attitude towards the Tradition of the fathers, which for the Pharisees, at least in their later development, constituted a part or one aspect of the Torah.

The Torah is the cornerstone of Judaism, the basis of all its teachings. But, for the Pharisees, the Torah contained much more than their opponents could or would find in it. As they understood it, the Torah comprised all and expressed all. We have, therefore, to inquire, what, according to the Pharisees, is the Torah? What is its origin? Upon what does its binding authority rest? For whom is it intended? What is its aim and

---

goes farther by saying: קוב"ה ואורייתא וישראל כולא חד (*Keter Shem Tob II*, [Slavita], 2a).

purpose? How is it to be understood and interpreted? We can answer these questions best by first learning the views of the opponents of the Pharisees on these questions. We must, therefore, first make clear to ourselves what was the conception of the Torah held by priests and people before the advent of the Pharisees, the conception which the Sadducees continued to hold even after the Pharisees broke away from them. And then, knowing the points of departure from which the Pharisees started, we shall understand better how radically they differed from the older party in their views on these questions. By contrasting these views with those of the older party, we shall be able to appreciate the great advance their conception of the Torah represents.

Now, the Torah was the common ground upon which both Sadducees and Pharisees stood. The position held by priest and laity alike, before that group of lay teachers, the Pharisees to be, started on their progressive march towards advanced Pharisaism, was, that the authority of the Torah was supreme and binding upon the people, and that every one of its laws had to be carried out strictly and scrupulously. In what light the older priestly group considered the Torah, and what was to them the nature of its authority, what ideas they had about the binding character of its laws, we learn from the account of the procedure at that solemn assembly in which the Torah was accepted by the people. When the people accepted the Torah, read to them by Ezra, they entered a covenant and pledged themselves by a solemn oath to observe and keep its laws. We read in Neh. (10.1, 29–30) as follows: "And yet for all this we make a sure covenant and subscribe it; and our princes, our Levites, and our priests, set their seal unto it ... And the rest of the people, the priests, the Levites ... they cleaved to their brethren, their nobles and entered into a curse, and into an oath, to walk in God's law, which was given by Moses the servant of God, and to observe and do all the commandments of the Lord, our Lord, and His ordinances and His statutes." It is evident from this account that in order to insure allegiance to the Torah and obedience to its laws it was deemed necessary for the people to enter a covenant and pledge allegiance by oath. According to ancient primitive belief, the only sure method of enforcing obedience to the Law, especially on the part of future generations, was to make the people take an oath to keep the Law and thereby to impose a curse upon its transgressors. An oath was regarded as eternally binding and remaining in force for all times, its violation automatically bringing the stipulated curse as a necessary consequence. The Torah then, according to this primitive view, acquired its binding character solely from the oath by which the people had pledged themselves to keep it. This idea, that the authority of the Torah is based upon the oath and the promise of the people and that it derives its binding character from the curse imposed upon or pronounced against those who would transgress it, finds expression in the Torah itself, especially in Deut. 29.9–30.20. It was only by means of the oath and the curse that the covenant could be made even with those not present at the time, and could be considered as binding upon the children of all future generations (Deut. 29.13–14, 28). For, whenever the children would violate the oath and transgress the law, the necessary result would be that the stipulated curse would come and be poured out upon them (cf. Dan. 9.11 ff.). Accordingly, the ideas of the older priestly group in regard to the character, authority, and purpose of the Torah — ideas which the Sadducees retained and continued to entertain even after the Pharisees argued against them — were the following: The Torah is a written document containing laws imposed by God upon Israel, and upon Israel alone, which Israel willingly or reluctantly accepted in order to secure the favor or to ward off the wrath of God, and to keep which the people by solemn oath pledged themselves and their children of all future generations. Transgression of any of these laws contained in the Torah on the part of any Israelite must bring down the curse upon his head. Hence, whether they like it or not, whether they approve of these laws or not, whether they find them kind and just or cruel and harsh, the Israelites whose forefathers had accepted the Torah and pledged themselves and their children to keep it, must carry out it laws, else the curse stipulated in the oath taken by the fathers would come down upon them. But the Torah is not, and need not be, co-extensive with life. It need not be the sole guide of the Israelite for all situations in life, nor must it provide answers to all new questions which may possibly arise in life. For such situations as are not expressly provided for in the Torah, the Israelite may be guided by other rules, and he may and should find answers to new questions in authorities other than the Torah. What is necessary and of the utmost importance is merely that not one single law of the Torah be violated, that not one act prescribed or one obligation imposed by the Torah be neglected. These acts prescribed by the Torah and all the obligations imposed by its laws must be observed rigorously and carried out strictly according to the letter; i. e., according to the literal meaning of the words of the Torah, as the people who accepted it and who entered the covenant understood it. Under the terms of that covenant and according to the oath, then taken, the Israelite merely had to fulfill the laws of the Torah without adding anything to them or subtracting aught from them. He had to do what the document — i. e., the letter of the law — called for, no matter how harsh and cruel and unjust it may have seemed to him. But more than the document called for, more than the letter of the law explicitly required, he was not bound to do; i. e., he was not obliged to do under the terms of the covenant. For no oath had ever been taken by the fathers to keep more than the letter of the Law and, therefore, no curse would or could befall him who fails to do more. Hence, the Sadducees; who retained these ideas, insisted upon a strictly literal interpretation of the written Torah but denied absolute authority and binding character to any law which was not expressly stated in the written Torah no matter by what reliable tradition it may have been vouched for. Because, since such laws were not contained in the written document which the forefathers had pledged themselves by oath to carry out and fulfill, they could not share in that authority and in the binding character which the laws written in the Torah derived just from that oath. The Sadducees did not deny the existence of these old traditional laws, for how could they? — they themselves as the conservative priests were the possessors and transmittors of the old traditions of the fathers. Nor did they reject such traditional laws as spurious, or as without any authority at all, for they did recognize the right and the authority of former priests and teachers to enact rules and regulations necessary for such questions in life as find no explicit answer in the written Torah. They even claimed for themselves, as priestly leaders, the right and the authority to issue decrees and enact laws supplementary to, or altogether independent of, those in the written Torah. But they refused to regard such traditional laws as of absolute authority, and as equal to the laws contained in the written Torah. For the latter, they maintained, the forefathers had accepted by covenant and had pledged themselves and their descendants to keep for all time. And, according to their way of thinking, there was no way of freeing themselves from the obligation of that oath. But the traditional laws the people never accepted in a formal covenant and never pledged themselves by oath to keep. These traditional laws and practices were observed by the people merely in submission to the ruling authorities, and following the instructions of the priest and leaders who in their time, and no doubt for good reasons, had seen fit to institute such laws or to introduce such customs. It, therefore, rested with the priestly leaders of the time to decide whether these traditional laws and customs, instituted by their predecessors, should be continued to be observed or not. In this way only did the Sadducees deny the compulsory character of the traditional laws. And this is probably what Josephus meant when he says that the Sadducees rejected the unwritten laws, saying: "We are to esteem those observances to be obligatory which are in the written word, but are not to observe what are derived from the tradition of our forefathers" (*Ant.* XIII, 10.6); i. e., we are not absolutely obliged to observe them as we are obliged to observe the written laws.[24]

The Pharisees, or those lay teachers who were the forerunners of the Pharisees, entertained entirely different ideas as to the character, authority and purpose of the Torah, but they did not tell us how they developed these ideas and how they came to form their new conception of the Torah. They did not even formulate for us their theories on the subject. We do not find in their disputes with their opponents any direct argument against

[24] See *The Sadducees and Pharisees*, above, pp. 30–32.

the latter's primitive notions. Nor does the talmudic literature which has preserved their teachings contain any express statement as to why or on what ground the Pharisees rejected their opponents' views on this subject and what their own different conception of it was. Of course, we are not in a position to state with certainty the reasons for their reticence or for the silence of the sources on these questions, so interesting to us. Perhaps, neither the Pharisees themselves nor their followers, the talmudic reporters, were interested in the genesis of these ideas; hence, they did not care to report about it. It is also possible that they were so convinced of the correctness of their ideas and considered them so self-evident that they were unaware of any newness in them. They could well believe that these ideas had always been held by all right thinking people in the past, and that no change or development had taken place in their conceptions. Therefore, there was nothing new in regard to this to report about. Their opponents' notions were to them so utterly false and inadequate that they looked upon them as mere aberrations and misunderstandings, hardly worth while reporting about and certainly not deserving formal refutation. But in their teachings they sought to avoid the possibility of a recurrence of such misunderstandings. They interpreted the Law in such a manner as to counteract the mistakes and oppose the erroneous conception of the Torah held by their opponents. It is from the manner in which they interpreted some of the Laws of the Torah, from the emphasis they lay on certain aspects of the Torah, from their general negative attitude towards primitive beliefs and superstitions, from occasional hints they let drop in their disputes, and especially from the lofty praises and the glorification of the Torah found in Psalm 19 and 119, which, if not conceived and written by the forerunners of the Pharisees, were certainly accepted and heartily endorsed by them[25] — it is from these that we can get an adequate picture of their ideas about the Torah and can reconstruct their doctrines as to its character, authority and purpose. Judging from all these indications, we find, in the first place, that, being averse to primitive beliefs and superstitions, the Pharisees would

---

[25] Cf. Herford, *op. cit.*, p. 65.

be disinclined to share in that superstitious belief in the magic power of the oath and in the automatic functioning of the curse stipulated in the oath. Especially did they refuse to make the authority of the Torah rest upon such a superstition, and to make the binding character of its laws for all generations depend merely on the threatening effects of the curse stipulated in the oath with which the people accepted and promised to keep the laws. They believed that the authoritative character of the Torah was not something bestowed upon it from without, awarded it by an assembly or secured by an oath or covenant. In their belief this authoritative character was something inherent in the Torah itself. The Divine origin of the Torah was to them sufficient reason for man to obey it. It is authoritative because it is Divine and not because of any obligation assumed by the fathers or of any promise made by them to observe it.

For the Torah is not a group of laws and commandments imposed by a ruler upon his subjects for purposes of his own, which they in submission to him must obey and carry out, just as they discharge other obligations they owe him. For God derives no benefit from man's obeying the Law nor is He affected by man's violating the Law.[26] The Torah is not for the benefit of God; it is for the benefit of man. It is the Law of truth which God in His lovingkindness revealed to man to serve him as a guide for life, to lead him in the right path and help him live a good life, a godlike life, and thus come nearer to God. And this guide which God vouchsafed to man is a most reliable guide, for it is a perfect Law, its precepts are right, its ordinances are true and righteous altogether (Ps. 19). It is complete and comprehensive and man needs no other laws or authorities for the regulation of his life or for new situations in life. The Divine Law is sufficient for all times for all people and for all possible conditions in life. For, the Torah was not intended for Israel alone, or for Palestine alone, or for a certain period of time and for certain conditions only. It was intended as an eternal law for all mankind. Israel, "the first born son of God" (Ex. 4.22), as it were, i. e., the first one to recognize

---

[26] See Gen. r. 44.1 and Tanḥ., *Shemini*, 12, Buber, 30; and cf. *The Ethics of the Halakah*, below p. 269, note 13.

His fatherhood, received the Torah first, not in order to keep it for himself as an exclusive possession, but to teach it to his younger brothers, to all nations. It was intended for all times and for all conditions; it must, therefore, contain answers to all questions of life. It is sufficient to control and regulate our entire life in all possible situations, if only we understand it aright and interpret it correctly. For, as a Divine and a most perfect Law, it is not to be understood only according to the literal meaning of its words. It must not be treated like a human document. "Our perfect Torah," says a Pharisaic leader, "is not to be considered like your idle talk,"[27] that is to say, it must not be interpreted like a man-made code of laws. We must apply to it other and higher standards of interpretation. For, its words have deeper meanings and subtler connotations.

The Pharisees also believed that one must use his God-given reason in interpreting the Torah. Josephus tells us, that the Pharisees "follow the contract of reason; and what that prescribes to them as good for them, they do; and they think they ought earnestly to strive to observe reason's dictates for practice" (*Ant.* XVIII, 1.3). In other words, they believed it was their duty to listen to reason. The soul within us, so the Pharisees believed, is "the portion of God from above" (Job 31.2), a spark of His light. "It is a spirit in man, and the breath of the Almighty that giveth them understanding" (*ibid.* 32.8). Our reason, the gift of God, "the spirit which is the lamp of the Lord" (Prov. 20.27) and our conscience, the voice of God within us, also tell us what is right and what is wrong. They are but other channels through which truth is revealed to us by God. And truth is one even when revealed through different channels; hence, the laws of the Torah must meet with the approval of our reason and our conscience. In other words, we must so interpret the laws of the Torah that they should harmonize with the truth obtained by our God-given reason. Furthermore, God is still continuously revealing Himself to us. And while He will never change His Law, and indeed He has no reason for doing so, since it contains the

---

[27] B. B. 116a and see *The Sadducees and Pharisees*, above, p. 42, and cf. also Moore, *Judaism*, I, pp. 248–49.

absolute truth, yet He guides us in our deliberations, reveals to us the secrets of His Law, thus helping us to get at its correct meaning. For God is present among those who study the Torah (Abot 3.7).[28] Hence, the Pharisees interpreted the Law according to its spirit and ignored its letter when reason and human conscience were against it. Thus, to give the classic example, the law "an eye for an eye" etc. (Ex. 21.24–25), which, if taken literally, as the Sadducees took it, outrages the human conscience, is cruel and against reason, the Pharisees interpreted as meaning to prescribe *compensation* and not *retaliation*. They did so, because their conscience had developed and broadened and their ideas of punishment became more humane. It was, therefore, to them inconceivable that the Divine Law, that perfect Law of truth and righteousness, could ever have decreed or sanctioned such cruel measures of punishment. They could not believe that these laws were ever meant to be taken literally. In good faith and firmly convinced of the correctness of their understanding of the Law, they accordingly interpreted it to prescribe merely monetary compensation. Such a method, of course, makes of the Torah an ever growing, ever unfolding revelation, capable of developing and assimilating new truths and always being in harmony with reason.

Just as the Torah cannot contradict reason, that other form of inspiration that continually comes to us from the source of truth, and just as it cannot conflict with the dictates of our conscience which is the voice of God within us, so also must the Torah not conflict with Divine truth coming through other channels. It must be in agreement with the voice of God heard through the prophets or recorded in the sacred writings of the inspired sages and seers, with the דברי קבלה, the words of Tradition, as the non-pentateuchal works of the Bible are called, being originally considered as mere tradition.[29] Since the Torah is

---

[28] The idea that God helps one to arrive at the truth and to understand the Torah is common among the Rabbis and finds frequent expression in the Jewish liturgy.

[29] The fact, that the non-pentateuchal works of the Bible were considered as mere traditions (דברי קבלה) was probably responsible for the mistake made by some of the church fathers (Origenes and Hieronymus; see E. Schürer,

not just a group of laws imposed upon Israel, but Divine truth revealed to man, it cannot conflict with other expressions of Divine truth as recorded in the other sacred writings. For, God is not a man that He should in one utterance belie what He said in another. Neither the son of man that He should repent and change His mind, so as to utter other truths and contradict Himself. This idea makes the Torah extend beyond the five books of Moses. It comprises all the sacred writings of accredited inspired seers and prophets, i. e., the whole Bible. Of course, it took some time till the distinction between the Pentateuch and the other Biblical works or between *Dibre Torah* and *Dibre Kabbalah* entirely disappeared. Echoes of this distinction, based upon the primitive notion that the Torah derives its authority from the oath and the covenant, which the other sacred writings cannot claim, are still to be found in the Talmud.[30] But the

---

op. cit., II, pp. 480–481; cf. also Pseudo-Tertullian, *Against All Heresies*, ch. I), in assuming that the Sadducees, like the Samaritans, recognized only the Pentateuch as sacred Scripture. Cf. K. Budde, *Der Kanon des Alten Testaments* (Giessen, 1900), pp. 42–43, and Moore, *op. cit.*, 68.

[30] In the Talmud are found conflicting statements as to whether דברי קבלה are to be regarded as like דברי תורה or not; see Bacher, *Die Exegetische Terminologie der Jüdischen Traditionsliteratur* I (Leipzig, 1899), 166. Significantly enough, the later Amoraim, especially R. Ashi, consider the דברי קבלה to be like דברי תורה (R. H. 19a, cf. also Suk. 32b). It seems to me that this recognition of the authority of the non-pentateuchal books of the Bible was the result of a gradual realization on the part of the teachers, that a strict distinction between the various books of the Bible was incompatible with the belief that the entire Bible was of Divine origin. Cf., however, R. Hirsch Chajes in *Sefer Torat Nebiim* (Zolkiew, 1836), מאמר תורת נביאים או דברי קבלה. The result was that not only the teachings derived from the non-pentateuchal books of the Bible were considered like דברי תורה but even such traditional teachings as had no basis whatever in any passage of the Bible were also designated as דברי תורה. (Cf. R. Hirsch Chajes, *op. cit.*, מאמר תורה שבעל פה, especially, pp. 25–26). This was but the logical consequence of the belief that the traditional law, the תורה שבעל פה also goes back to Moses and was of Divine origin. See below, note 39. Cf. *Ha-Lebanon*, ed. by Jehiel Brill, 3rd year, #16, Paris, Ellul 5626), pp. 250–252, note 13 to the article "General Introduction to the books of the Oral Law" by Elijah ibn Amozegh, as to the reason why the words of the prophets are called *Dibre Kabbalah*. Cf. also note 14. He shows that the Talmud sometimes refers to the prophets as *Rabbanan* as b. Yoma 69b where *Rabbanan* is used as referring to Daniel and Jeremiah.

Pharisees, already at a very early time conceived the idea of including in the Torah the teachings of the prophets and of the other sacred writings. They had to do so as a matter of logical consistency, for, to their way of thinking, there was no reason to make any distinction between one revelation and the other. The Torah, to them, had its authority not because of the oath taken by the people but because of its being revealed truth, the word of God, and the teachings of the prophets also were the words of God. Of course, the Torah of Moses represents the earliest and most comprehensive revelation, aiming at regulating human conduct. The prophet, therefore, cannot make new laws in opposition to the Torah.[31] He does, however, explain and supplement the laws of the Torah,[32] and the Torah must be so interpreted as to accord with the prophetic teachings. The Pharisees would, therefore, often use both the help of reason, dictating higher ideas and broader principles, and the words of the prophets revealing spiritual concepts and Divine truth, for supports and guides in interpreting the Law, thus making it expressive of more advanced religious ideas and spiritual truths. One or two instances will illustrate this point. We have seen that, according to the Pharisees, the Torah was revealed to man for his guidance and his benefit, and does not represent a group of laws just imposed upon him. Accordingly, the Sabbath, as one of the institutions of the Torah, was given to man so that he may enjoy his rest and delight in it, but man was not given to the Sabbath to be a slave to it and suffer inconveniences. To use the older expression of

---

Cf. also Maimonides, *Sefer Hamitzvoth* on the first page of his "Fourteen Points": "What the Sages and *the Prophets* ordained after Moses is also *mi-dRabbanan*." Cf. Ramban's note (*ibid.*). Cf. also Jacob Ibn Safir, *Ha-Lebanon*, 4th year, #5, (Paris, 1867), 84–85, that the meaning of "We do not learn *Dibre Torah* from *Dibre Kabbalah*," refers only to *Gezera Shava*.

[31] Cf. Sanh. 90a, Hor. 4b.

[32] Cf. Bacher, *op. cit.*, I, 154–155. Hence later teachers could say: דבר זה מתורת משה לא למדנו מדברי יחזקאל הנביא למדנו (Yoma 71b. Cf. also R. H. 7a). In spite of the fact that an older principle had declared that no prophet was allowed to inaugurate new laws אלה המצות שאין הנביא רשאי לחדש דבר מעתה (Meg. 2b). See the explanations of this apparent contradiction offered in Yoma 71b and 80a and cf. R. Hirsch Chajes, מאמר אלה המצות, ch. I, *op. cit.*

the Pharisaic teachers: "The Sabbath is given to you and you are not given to the Sabbath" (Mekilta, *Sabbata* I, Friedmann 103b). This idea of the purpose of the Sabbath the Pharisees found expressed in the words of the prophet: "And call the Sabbath a delight ... then shalt thou delight thyself in the Lord" (Isa. 58.13–14). They accordingly could not understand the law in Ex. 35.3 to mean: "Ye shall burn no fire throughout your habitations upon the Sabbath day," as it was understood by other Jewish sects,[32a] like the Samaritans and even the Karaites up to the fourteenth century. For, so the Pharisees reasoned, how could the Sabbath be called a delight if one is to be deprived on it of the comforts of light and heat? They refused to consider the Sabbath a Tabu day to be spent in gloom and cold and darkness. They, therefore, interpreted the law in Exodus 35.3 to mean, "Ye shall kindle no fire throughout your habitations upon the Sabbath day," i. e., you shall not do the arduous work of building a fire or producing light on the Sabbath day. You may, however, nay you should, have in your homes fire and light, so very necessary for your comfort and pleasure, on the Sabbath day; only let the work of preparing it be done before the Sabbath.[33] They even considered it a religious duty and insisted that for the proper observance of the Sabbath it is indispensable to have lights in the home on Friday night, so as to make the home cheerful and the Sabbath a delight. This Pharisaic institution is still observed in Jewish homes. When performing the ceremony of lighting the candles on Friday night, a benediction is recited thanking God for having sanctified us by His commandments and commanded us to kindle the Sabbath light. For, according to Pharisaic teachings, God did command us to have lights in the homes on the Sabbath even though no such commandment is explicitly mentioned in the Torah. He implied it in His commandment, "Observe the Sabbath day" (Deut. 5.12), for this is a

[32a] As to the Sadducees, see Geiger, *Nachgelassene Schriften*, III, 287 ff., who is of the opinion that the Sadducees prohibited the use of fire on the Sabbath. This seems to me to be correct, and in keeping with the general trend of Sadducean doctrine.

[33] Cf. the saying of the Mekilta ביום השבת אי אתה מבעיר אבל אתה מבעיר מערב שבת לשבת. According to the reading of the Yalḳuṭ to Ex. 35.3.

proper form of observing the Sabbath.[34] He commanded it to us through His prophet when he said, "Call the Sabbath a delight," which means to have the home cheerful and bright and not cold, dark and gloomy. Guided by the same principle that the Sabbath is given for man's pleasure, they interpreted another Sabbath law in such a manner as to remove from the Sabbath the character of a Tabu day and teach us an advanced idea of the religious observance of the day. The law: "Abide ye every man in his place, let no one go out of his place on the seventh day" (Ex. 16.29) was interpreted by some sects to mean, that one should not budge from his place and not be allowed to leave the house. This again gives the Sabbath the character of a Tabu day or an unlucky day.[35] The Pharisees, denying that the Sabbath was of such a character, interpreted this law to mean, that one should not leave the town or the village where he dwells, — taking the word "his place" in a broader sense to mean town or village, — and go on a distant journey,[36] and also that one should not go out of the house carrying burdens on the Sabbath day. They learned from Jer. 17.12 ff. that the proper observance of the Sabbath was to refrain from bearing any burdens or carrying forth burdens out of the house. But without carrying any burdens, the Pharisees taught, one may leave the house and take a pleasurable walk even outside of the city or the village, provided it is not too long a distance. For this would be a tiresome effort and no longer a pleasure, hence not in keeping with the spirit of the day.

It was probably the same consideration, viz., to remove from the Sabbath the character of a Tabu day, and to dissociate it entirely from any connection with Saturn, that determined them in their interpretation of the term "Sabbath" in Lev. 23.11 and 15.[37] In seeking to emphasize the idea that the Sabbath was

[34] Cf. b. Shab. 23a as to the justification for the recital of the benediction over the lighting of the Chanukah lights. The same reasons, of course, hold good in the case of the benediction over the Sabbath lights.

[35] See Hutton Webster, *Rest Days*, (New York, 1916), p. 257 and note.

[36] Mekilta, *Vayassa* 5, Friedmann, 51a, 'Er. 51a.

[37] See Men. 64b–66a. It is true that the oldest express reference to an identification of the Jewish Sabbath with Saturn's day dates only from the first pre-Christian century. (Cf. Hutton Webster, *op. cit.*, p. 243 ff.). But

merely a day given for rest and pleasure and that it has nothing to do with Saturn or with other astrological superstitions, they argued that "Sabbath" designates also any other prescribed day of rest even if it be not the seventh day of the week. Every Holiday in which one is to rest from labor is called a Sabbath. They, therefore, interpreted "the morrow after the Sabbath" (Lev. 23.11 and 15) to mean simply, the morrow after the day of rest, that is, after the first day of the Passover festival, or the 16th of the month of Nisan. According to this interpretation, Pentecost which comes 49 days or seven weeks after that, "morrow after the Sabbath," could fall on any day of the week. Their opponents, the Sadducees, as is well known, took the phrase, "the morrow after the Sabbath" literally to mean the morrow after the seventh day of the week, with the result that they would have Pentecost always fall on a Sunday as the church also has it.

As in their views about the character, authority, and purpose of the Torah, so also in their attitude towards the authority of tradition and the binding character of the traditional laws, the two parties differed radically. Josephus in the passage already

---

no doubt the idea is much older and the Pharisees sought to combat it. According to Yalḳuṭ Reubeni to *Jethro* (Warsaw, 1901), p. 108, many of the ceremonies and regulations prescribed for the Sabbath were directed against the practices of those people who believed the Sabbath to be Saturn's day on which they could, by means of certain observances, derive power from Saturn. That the Pharisees were correct in denying that the observance of the Sabbath had any connection with the worship of Saturn, is now admitted by most modern scholars (see Hutton Webster, *loc. cit.*, and cf. A. Büchler, "Graeco-Roman Criticisms of Some Jewish Observances and Beliefs," in *The Jewish Review*, I, [London, 1910], 140–143). But, in spite of this protest of the Pharisees against the identification of the Sabbath with Saturn's day, the idea of such a connection between the two lingered on even in Jewish circles and echoes of it are found in medieval Jewish works. Cf. Abraham Ibn Ezra as quoted by the super-commentary on Ibn Ezra, by Ibn Motot, to Ex. 23.20 in מרגליות טובה (Amsterdam, 1722), p. 73b and also the super-commentary אהל יוסף (*ibid., loc. cit.*). Cf. also S. Rubin, op. cit., pp. 90–91. See A. Epstein, *Mikadmoniyot Hayehudim*, p. 10 and his answer to Chayim Jechiel Bornstein in *Ha-Ḥoker* I, 185–187, with regard to the assertion that before the giving of the Torah the Israelites celebrated a festival dedicated to Saturn, the angel in control of time.

quoted above tells us that "the Pharisees have delivered to the people a great many observances by succession from their fathers, which are not written in the Laws of Moses, and for that reason it is that the Sadducees reject them and say that we are to esteem those observances to be obligatory which are in the written word but are not to observe what are derived from the tradition of our forefathers. And concerning these things, it is that great disputes and differences have arisen among them" (*Ant.* XIII, 10.6). For the Sadducees did not "regard the observation of anything besides what the Law enjoins them" (*ibid.*, XVIII, 1.4). These reports of Josephus are confirmed by statements in the Talmud.[38] This fundamental difference between the two parties presents the anomalous phenomenon, that the older conservative priestly party is opposed to the authority of tradition and denies the binding character of the traditional law, while the younger progressive liberal party of democratic lay teachers advocates the authority of tradition, and considers the traditional laws as binding upon the people and as of authority equal with those of the written Torah. This apparent anomaly in the respective positions of the two parties with regard to the authority of Tradition, is partly responsible for the historical error made by so many people of considering the Pharisees the older party, and regarding the Sadducees as the younger group, the heretical sect. But in the light of our discussion the different attitudes taken by the two parties towards the traditional laws are found to be consistent with their respective views abouth the nature of the authority of the written Torah.

We have already seen that the Sadducees' rejection of the authority of the traditional law was but the logical consequence, the direct outcome, of their narrow views on the written Law. The authority of the latter, according to them, rests entirely upon the oath by which the people pledged themselves to it. And since no oath was ever taken to keep the traditional laws, they cannot have the same authority and binding character as the laws of the written Torah. Likewise, the Pharisees' attitude towards tradition was also but the psychological result and the

[38] Cf. Hor. 4a,b; Sanh. 90b.

logical consequence of their loftier ideas about the written Torah. Their conception of the Torah as revealed Divine law supplemented and explained by the prophetic teachings and in complete accord with truth obtained from other sources or through other channels, naturally disposed them to consider the Traditions of the fathers an additional source of Divine truth. For, as we have seen, the Torah to them was not a burdensome obligation which one has to fulfill for fear of the penalty of the curse, and from which one would seek to free himself by a formal discharge of what the letter absolutely required. It was to them a source of joy and assurance, restoring the soul, enlightening the eyes and rejoicing the heart. It was a Divine guide to lead them through life, to help them and advise them. They loved the Torah, enjoyed its commandments, and rejoiced in the fulfillments of its law. With the Psalmist they would say: "Yea, Thy testimonies are my delight. They are my counsellors" (Ps. 119.24). They would naturally be disposed to welcome more such guides, more direction, and more counsel. They appreciated the great favor God had shown His people in giving them the Torah, and they believed that God gave them much more than was written in the Torah. Perhaps quite unconsciously they felt the need of emphasizing the authority of tradition, if only to dispute the exclusive authority of their opponents. For the written Torah actually favors the priestly authorities, no matter how liberally you interpret it. But if the traditions of the fathers had preserved laws given by God to Moses and handed down to the teachers by words of mouth, the authority of these lay teachers would be established as equal with that of the priests. The Pharisees would, therefore, not limit God's revelation and teachings to the written Torah alone. As one of their followers expressed it: "God desired to ennoble and benefit Israel, therefore He multiplied for them Torah and commandments" (M. Mak. 3.16 end), that is, He gave them more than just the written Torah. And that "more," they believed, was contained in the Traditions of the fathers. Now, they had already, as we have seen, included in the term Torah the words of the prophets and the sacred writings, which were actually called *Dibre Kabbalah*, "Words of Tradition." Why, then, could not the oral traditions of the fathers likewise be regarded as authoritative teachings, explaining and supplementing the laws of the Torah? What reason could there be for making distinctions between "Words of Tradition" embodied in the books of the prophets or other sacred writings, and "Words of Tradition" preserved among the people in unwritten form?

Not only could the Pharisees see no reason to discriminate against such traditions but they even had very good reasons, logical as well as psychological, to favor them and consider them part of the Divine Torah handed down by word of mouth. The Pharisees, as already hinted, were most likely unaware of their radical departure from the older views. They believed their ideas of the Torah to be correct and that their fathers before them had the same ideas of the Torah. To the Pharisees, the Torah was the sole authority for regulating the life of the people. To their way of thinking, their forefathers must have had the same ideas and also considered the Torah alone as their authority. How then, so the Pharisees must have asked themselves, are all these laws, customs and practices, observed by the people, even though not written in the Torah, to be regarded? To reject these popular customs and practices as being without authority was impossible. Some of these traditional laws and practices were considered by the people as religious laws and observances, too highly respected to be declared as having been introduced without any real authority. To say, as their opponents the Sadducees did, that these laws and customs were merely temporary regulations, enacted by the leaders of the time, without any connection with the Torah, and, therefore, without its binding authority, would have meant to admit that the life of the people was not controlled exclusively by the authority of the Torah. It would have meant to abandon their fundamental principle that the Torah is, and always was, the only authority for regulating the entire life of the people. It would also have reflected on the completeness and the all-sufficiency of the Torah. If the Torah was meant to be a reliable guide and faithful help in all situations in life, if its laws were perfect and answering all needs, how was it that it could not and did not supply all the needs of the people, so that the latter had to enact other temporary laws for the regulation of their life? Would not that prove or support the contention of their opponents, that the Torah merely represents a group of laws imposed upon the people which must be strictly carried out to satisfy the demand of the Deity but need not be coextensive with life? Would it not prove the Sadducean claim that for life with all its needs and all new situations the people should be guided by other authorities? And, of course, these other authorities should be the priests, since the written Torah threatens with punishment of death those who would refuse to listen to the authority of the priests. "And the man that doeth presumptuously, in not hearkening unto the priest that standeth to minister there before the Lord thy God, or unto the judge, even that man shall die" (Deut. 17.12).

The only satisfactory answer the Pharisees could give to this vexing question was that all these laws and customs handed down by the fathers and regarded by the people as religious laws and observances, indeed had the same authority as the laws of the Torah and that they derived their authority from the Torah even though not found expressly stated therein. Thus, the Pharisees were led to believe, and they believed it in good faith, that these laws were not regulations enacted by former priests and leaders on their own authority, separate from and independent of the Torah. For, in their opinion these former priests and leaders had no such authority of their own, they had authority only as interpreters of the Torah. And the fathers would not have preserved these laws and customs and would not have regarded them as religious, had they been enacted by an authority other than or independent of the Torah. For, the fathers also had always considered the Torah alone as their only guide and sole authority for their religious life. These laws and customs which the fathers have preserved in their traditions and handed down to their children alongside of the laws of the Torah, were also laws of the Torah, that is, they were interpretations, amplifications, or special applications of certain laws of the Torah. As such, they are implied in, and share the authority of, the laws of the Torah. Even in cases where no such connection with the written Torah could be established, these traditions of the fathers, the Pharisees persuaded themselves to believe, represented additional and supplementary laws of the Torah. They were teachings given by God to Moses on Sinai, together with the written Torah, a sort of companion to it, and handed down from generation to generation in unwritten form as הלכה למשה מסיני, Traditions handed down from Moses on Sinai.

Thus the belief in an Oral Law, a *Torah shebe'al peh*, was developed among the Pharisees. It was a naive, but an honest, belief on their part. They could not escape it; they were led to it by what to them seemed logical reasoning. Their very belief in the absolute authority and in the all-sufficiency of the Torah forced them to believe also in the authority of tradition, but tradition as identical with or as an integral part of the Torah. The Torah which God gave to Moses was really two-fold, a written one תורה שבכתב and an oral one תורה שבעל פה. In short, not all the laws and teachings revealed by God to Moses were committed by him to writing.[39]

Of course, the Pharisees did not blindly accept as authoritative all the traditions current among the people, just as they did not include in their canon of Sacred Scripture all the alleged works of inspired seers current in their times. They no doubt were guided by certain criteria in distinguishing the genuine from the spurious. And in the final analysis it was reason that determined the selection. And their broadening conscience which made them

[39] Thus the theory of a dual Torah, one written תורה שבכתב and one oral תורה שבעל פה, was formulated. The first express reference to the two תורות is ascribed to Hillel (Shab. 31a). A more explicit statement about these two Torahs, that they both were given from heaven, is found in Midrash Tannaim to Deut. (Berlin, 1909), p. 215, in the name of R. Joḥanan b. Zakkai (the parallel in Sifre, Deut. 351 has Rabban Gamaliel). To the argument of the opponent, that the singular form ותורתך (Deut. 33.10) points to only one Torah, R. Joḥanan b. Zakkai answers: לישראל [ך] ותורת שנאמר שתים כן אעפ"י. Even if so, two Torahs are indicated since it says: "And Thy Torah to Israel," which means, besides the one Torah referred to in the preceding sentence: "They shall teach Jacob Thine ordinances" יורו משפטיך ליעקב, they will also teach "Israel Thy other Torah." This seems to me the correct interpretation of the Midrash. A different explanation is given by Hoffmann (*ibid.*, note 100) following the copyist who put a dot over the Resh, suggesting that the word is to be read *Torot*, in the plural form. Cf. J. B. Levinsohn in *Sefer Yehoshafat*, (Warsaw, 1883), p. 83.

interpret the law according to the spirit would also lead them to rationalize some traditional teachings and customs.

This recognition of the authority of tradition as part of the Torah, not only did not hinder but even furthered and helped the progressive tendencies of the Pharisees, for it helped to liberate them from the fetters of the letter of the law. With all their submission to the authority of the Law, the Pharisees did not become the slaves of the Law; they were its masters. And with all their respect for tradition they did not become reactionary but progressive and forward looking. The Torah could be so interpreted as to contain what the teachers read into it, but nothing of which they could not approve. And the Traditions of the fathers, insofar as they contained Divine truths, had to agree with the ever growing and ever unfolding conscience of the people.

Their position was reached by the Pharisees not by a conscious effort at rationalization and harmonization, but by an almost unconscious psychological effort. In their admiration for the Divine Law and Traditions they could not imagine that the Torah could contain anything which they could not fully approve of, or that genuine Tradition could teach any belief to which they could not whole-heartedly subscribe. Hence, any law of the Torah which their broadened conscience could not accept literally had to be so interpreted as to be given a new and more acceptable meaning. And any belief found among the current traditions which they, because of their advanced way of thinking, could not accept was regarded as superstition and as representing a spurious tradition. For the Divine Torah, the written as well as the unwritten, is truth. It cannot teach anything that outrages the human conscience or does violence to human reasoning. Its teachings must meet with the full approval of the human conscience and reason.

We can thus sum up our discussion and answer all the questions about the attitude of the Pharisees to the Torah which we propounded in the beginning of this lecture: The Torah is the Divine revelation to man, contained in the five books of Moses, as supplemented and explained by the teachings of the prophets and by other, unwritten, tradition of the fathers. Its authority is based upon the fact that it is Divine truth. It comes from God. the father of all, and is intended for all mankind. Its purpose is to ennoble man by guiding him in the right way of life. It is to be interpreted in the light of reason, another Divine gift to man, and in agreement with the ever growing and ever broadening human conscience.

How with this conception of the Torah the Pharisees developed their ideas of God, the giver of that Torah, and of Israel, the first recipient of that Torah, we shall discuss in the next chapter.

III

THE PHARISAIC IDEAS OF GOD AND ISRAEL

The Torah, as the Pharisees considered it, was not merely a group of laws imposed upon Israel, but Divine revelation vouchsafed to man for his own good, to guide him aright and help him live a perfect life. For a full and complete life man needs more than rules of conduct and laws prescribing or forbidding certain actions. He needs also directions for right thinking and instruction in true belief. Regarded by the Pharisees as a reliable and complete guide, the Torah had to supply also these needs, which are indispensable for a complete and full life. It must, therefore, teach true ideas about God, His relation to the universe in general and to mankind in particular, and about the nature of the relation of man to man as determined by his relation to God. The Pharisees, accordingly, considered the Torah as the highest authority both for theories and practices, for rules of right conduct as well as for true doctrines.

This, however, did not prevent them from broadening their ideas. Nor did it hinder them in developing new doctrines not expressly stated in the Torah. For, as we have seen, the Torah, to them, was Divine truth, and as such could not conflict with other truths, also coming from God and preserved in other sources, or arrived at by human reason, also a gift of God. This conception of the Torah and the liberal methods of interpretation resulting from it enabled the Pharisees to develop their own advanced ideas of God and Israel, not only without coming into conflict with the teachings of the Torah, but even with the help of the Torah, i. e., by finding support for their new ideas in the very words of the Torah, which was recognized by them as the highest authority.

Since they did not follow the letter of the Law when it conflicted with reason or conscience, they found no great difficulty in harmonizing the teachings of the Torah with their advanced ideas, or, as they naively believed, in finding their ideas hinted at, suggested or implied in the words of the Torah. Such passages in the Torah as reflect primitive ideas about God and a narrow, particularistic conception of Israel they would not take strictly and literally. They would interpret them in such a manner as to be compatible with their own advanced ideas, and as not to be resented by their own reason and conscience. On the other hand, they would emphasize those expressions in the Torah that teach a high spiritual conception of God[40] and a liberal attitude towards humanity. They would lay great stress upon such passages as could be interpreted to give utterance to broader and more universalistic ideas and thus to make all mankind benefit by the Torah.

Whether and how they effected a complete harmonization of all those different ideas and apparent contradictions found in the Torah we have no means of ascertaining. And all for the simple reason that the Pharisees did not leave us any work or special treatise, setting forth all their beliefs and theological doctrines, giving their philosophical reasons and justifications, and citing the Scriptural proofs for them. We have no work on systematic theology by any of the Pharisaic teachers. Most likely the early Pharisaic teachers were not systematic theologians. They certainly were not philosophers, even though Josephus, to please his gentile readers, sought to represent them as a philosophical sect (*Ant.* XVIII, 1.2), "Of kin to the sect of the Stoics" (*Vita* 2.). The Pharisees were not given to philosophic speculation. They did not use philosophical methods in their discussions nor would they cite philosophical arguments in support of their

---

[40] Cf. the interpretation of the passage: "Ye shall not make with Me," etc. (Ex. 20.20) to mean, not to make any likeness or representation of God. (Mekilta, *Baḥodesh* X, Friedmann, 72b).

teachings. They had no reason and felt no need for doing so. They believed that in the Torah, supplemented by the teachings of the prophets and other traditions of the fathers, they possessed the Divine truth as revealed to their forefathers. To the study of this Torah they gave themselves completely and they meditated upon it day and night.[41] They sought to interpret it to the best of their understanding. It was because of their exclusive occupation with the Torah that they were esteemed most skillful in the exact application of their laws (Josephus, *Wars* II, 8.2) and "supposed to excel others in the accurate knowledge of the laws" (*Vita* 37), able "to interpret the laws more accurately" (*Wars* I, 5.2). And the statement of Josephus that the Pharisees "valued themselves highly upon the exact skill they had in the laws of their fathers" (*Ant.* XVII, 2.4) also shows that they themselves valued their interpretations of the Torah and their ability to derive from it their teachings[42] more than philosophical speculations. They were primarily teachers of religion, but religion as comprising the ethical and spiritual truths, the laws and the traditions of the fathers. And they were practical teachers not given much to speculation and theorizing,[43] and perhaps not very systematic. At any rate, the records of their differences and their disputes with their opponents, and the reports which have preserved their discussions and teachings, do not give us a complete or systematic presentation of their theological doctrines. Hence, the great difficulty of getting a clear and orderly view of their body of beliefs and unity of ideas. We certainly cannot content ourselves merely with what is expressly and formally reported about their theological beliefs, such as the report about their belief in the freedom of the will and in the immortality of the soul. For, indeed, this is very little, and very incomplete at

---

[41] Cf. Men. 99b which, however, must be understood as a protest against Greek philosophy only (חכמת יונית) but not against the study of the exact sciences, like astronomy and mathematics, with which one should occupy oneself. Cf. Shab. 75a.

[42] Cf. the saying: הפוך בה והפוך בה דכולא בה, Ab. 5.22, which in Ab. R. N. version A, ch. XII, Schechter, 28a is ascribed to Hillel.

[43] Cf. such sayings as ולא המדרש הוא העיקר אלא המעשה, Ab. 1.17, and והכל לפי רוב המעשה, *ibid.*, 3.15.

that. And, after all, these two beliefs are but aspects of their conception of God and His relation to man, but they are not the whole of it. It is their interpretation of certain passages in the Torah, their institution of a unique and spiritual form of Divine worship in the Synagogue, the manner in which they sought to regulate the Temple ritual and to modify some of its objectionable features, their mode of living, their relation to one another and to the people at large, their activity in spreading the true teachings of the Torah among the people, and their zeal in offering the Torah to all mankind — it is these that tell us about their conception of God. For, in all these activities and attitudes they were guided and prompted by their ideas of God and His relation to man.

That their God conception was based upon the teachings of the prophets goes without saying, since as a party they were opponents of the priests and followers of the prophets whose ideas they accepted and made their own. Thus, while no systematic work of Pharisaic theology has come down to us, the sources contain many expressions of their beliefs and furnish scattered bits of direct and indirect information about them. Upon these we must base our presentation of the Pharisees' conception of God and Israel. And, even though we may not be able to get a complete picture of their theology from all this scattered information, we shall at least be able to form a fairly adequate notion of their conception of God and of His relation to man.

From the prophets the Pharisees learned to think of God as a spiritual being, omnipotent and just, all-wise and all-knowing, all-merciful and like a father loving all His creatures. He is not to be pictured in any image and cannot be likened to any other being. He is not limited to any place but is omnipresent. He is in the heavens above and on the earth beneath. The whole earth is full of His glory, and there is no place in the whole universe where He cannot be found.[44] He rules the whole world with Justice and Kindness.[45] There is no other God besides Him, and no power can frustrate His plans. He is not subject to any

---

[44] ללמדך שאין מקום פנוי מן השכינה, Pesiḳta de R. K., I, Buber, 2b.
[45] ובטוב העולם נדון, Ab. 3.15. And והדין דין אמת (ibid., 3.16).

weakness. All depend on Him, but He does not depend on anything outside Himself. He is not in need of anything and asks of man nothing for Himself. He asks of man only to walk in His ways, to do justly, and to love kindness. All the laws which He gave us are to direct and guide us in these right ways. And even when He chastises us, He does it with the love of a father for our own good: "And thou shalt consider in thy heart, that as a man chasteneth his son, so the Lord thy God chasteneth thee" (Deut. 8.5). "Whatever God the merciful doeth is for the best" (Ber. 60b).

The Torah, as the Pharisees understood it, also taught this God-conception. None of the expressions in the Torah which seem to reflect a more primitive conception of God or speak of Him in anthropomorphic terms are, according to the Pharisees, to be taken literally. For the Torah is truth and it cannot be self-contradictory in its statements, nor can it conflict with the teachings of the prophets. How then is it possible to take literally such an expression as: "And they saw the God of Israel" (Ex. 24.10) when the Torah itself reports God as having said to Moses: "For man shall not see Me and live" (Ex. 33.20) and in another passage it says: "Ye heard the voice of words but ye saw no form" (Deut. 4.12)? And when it is said: "For in six days the Lord made heaven and earth, the sea, and all that is in them, and rested on the seventh day" ((Ex. 20.11) it cannot, so the Pharisaic teachers argue, be taken literally to mean that God had labored six days and needed a rest on the seventh day. For the prophet has taught us that God never wearies: "Hast thou not known? Has thou not heard that the everlasting God, the Lord, the creator of the ends of the earth, fainteth not, neither is weary?" (Isa. 40.28). And the Psalmist declared that merely "by the word of the Lord were the heavens made" (Ps. 33.6) and He did not have to labor. (Mekilta, *Baḥodesh* VII, Friedmann 69b). How is it possible, ask the Pharisaic teachers, to take literally the passage: "And the Lord went before them by day in a pillar of cloud" (Ex. 13.21) when God Himself has told us through the prophet (Jer. 23.24): "Do not I fill heaven and earth?" (Mek. *Besh.* II, Friedmann 25a)? All such expressions must, therefore, be taken not literally but figuratively. The Torah had to use human language and human turns of speech to give concrete expressions to abstract ideas, else human beings could not understand (Mekilta, *Baḥodesh* IV, Friedmann 65a).

That the Pharisees conceived God as the One whom no human being could fully comprehend is especially evident from the manner in which they would refer to Him. Whether and to what extent they were responsible for the prohibition against the pronounciation of the Tetragrammaton is hard to decide.[46] But this we do know, that, except in prayer and in the reading of the Scriptures, they avoided using even any of the other Biblical names of God. They apparently felt that no name could designate His essence or describe the totality of His being. While they interpreted even these Biblical names as merely describing His attributes, as for example, when they interpreted "Elohim" to mean the "*midat ha-din*," the attribute of Justice, they nevertheless feared that the constant use of these names might lead to their being misunderstood and taken for actual proper names of God. They, therefore, referred to Him merely by using some of His attributes. They employed such designations of Him as describe His activity or His relation to the world and to man. Thus, when they had in mind His relation to the world, they would speak of Him as "the Possessor," or "the Creator of the World," "the Master of all works," "the Ruler of the Universe," "He by whose word the world came into being." To indicate His omnipotence, they would speak of Him as גבורה, "Might," the Almighty. To emphasize His omnipresence, they would speak of Him as המקום, "The Place." For, He is the place of the world but not limited to it. The world finds a place and exists only in Him. But the world does not contain Him, for He is in the world and yet beyond it, He is immanent and transcendent. To emphasize that God is eternal, they would call Him חי עולמים, "The One who lives for ever" or חי וקים, "The Everlasting One." To express His relation to man, they would call him, the Father, the Father in Heaven, the Father of all that come into the world, the Lord of Mercy, or shorter, *raḥmana*, the Merciful

---

[46] See A. Marmorstein, *The Old Rabbinic Doctrine of God*, (London, 1927), p. 17 ff.

One. To refer to His revealing Himself to man, or manifesting His presence in the world, they would speak of him as the Shekinah, שכינה, "Divine Presence," and ruaḥ haḳodesh, רוח הקדש, "Spirit of Holiness." The latter two, however, were never taken by the Pharisees or the Rabbis in a hypostatic sense. They never represented separate entities.[47] They were merely used like so many other designations descriptive of some aspects or attributes of God whom no man can fully comprehend.

Intimately connected with the conception of God are, of course, ideas of Divine Worship, that is, how one can properly serve Him. The activities of the Pharisees in this field, their efforts at regulating and modifying the service in the Temple, as well as their fostering in the Synagogue a unique institution of religious worship, outside of, and separate from, the Temple, were but the logical results of their advanced and spiritual God-conception. Once they believed with the prophets and found it also stated in the Torah (Num. 14.21) that the whole earth is full of the glory of God, they necessarily had to believe also that "from the rising of the sun unto the going down thereof, the Lord's name is to be praised" (Ps. 113.2), and that there is no place where God could not be found and reached in prayer. Hence, they concluded that God can and should be worshipped even away from the Temple and outside of Jerusalem. Again, they had learned from the prophets that the multitude of sacrifices is to no purpose unto God and that He delights not in the blood of bullocks or of lambs or of he-goats (Isa. 1.11); and that burnt-offerings are not acceptable to Him (Jer. 6.20). They, accordingly, reasoned: If the Lord has not "as great delight in burnt-offerings and sacrifices, as in hearkening to the voice of the Lord," and if, "to obey is better than sacrifice, and to hearken than the fat of rams" (I Sam. 15.22), then a worship consisting not of bloody sacrifices but of prayer and study of God's Law must be not only as good as the Temple service, but even better and more acceptable to God. Hence, the Pharisees fostered the

---

[47] Cf. Marmorstein, *op. cit.*, pp. 99 and 103. The saying in Pesiḳta Rabbati, Friedmann 12a, merely means to express the idea that God caused the spirit of prophecy to come upon Jacob.

Synagogue. The Synagogue may be considered a Pharisaic institution. Not that the Pharisees first instituted or founded it, for, it must have been in existence long before the advent of the Pharisees. But they developed it and perfected it, raised it to high prominence and gave it an important and central place in the religious life of the people, so that it could rival, if not even surpass, the Temple. Here again the Pharisees merely developed an ancient prophetic idea and based on it a great religious institution. The Synagogue is much older than the party of the Pharisees, its origin probably goes back to the period of the Babylonian exile. We have seen how the people in the exile learned to appreciate the prophets' teaching that God is everywhere. Away from Jerusalem and deprived of a Temple, those who remained loyal to the God of their fathers were forced to content themselves with some kind of form of worship other than sacrifices. Ezekiel tells us that the elders of the people would come to him to inquire of God (Ezek. 14.1 ff. and 20.1 ff.). It is in these visits to the prophet, to inquire about God, that we have the germ of the synagogue. When the people could no longer go to the priest to send through him their offerings to God, they came to the prophet to inquire for a message from God, and the prophet gave it to them. And then they may have come to the prophet again or met together elsewhere to consider the message received from the prophet, to meditate upon the word of God, and to pray to Him. Such meetings with their simple form of worship continued among the people even in Palestine after the Temple was restored and the sacrificial cult reinstituted. No doubt, the forerunners of the Pharisees were among those who cherished this prophetic idea of a religious service without sacrifices and who would assemble in some places outside of the Temple for the study of the Law and the prophets and for prayer and devotion.[48] But after the final breach between the two groups and the formation of the two parties, the Pharisees, in opposition to the priests who naturally favored the sacrificial cult and would have all religious service centered in the Temple, emphasized the

[48] Daniel already performed a religious service consisting of prayer three times a day (Dan. 6.11–12). A religious service consisting of prayer is also presupposed or alluded to in Siraḥ 39.5–6. Cf. also Moore I, 41, note 2.

value of these extra-Temple devotional meetings and assemblies for prayer and study. They found that even according to the Torah, as they understood it, a service without sacrifice and outside of the Temple at Jerusalem was at least as acceptable to God as the sacrifices in the Temple, if not even more so. They interpreted the commandment: "To love the Lord your God and to serve Him with all your heart and with all your soul" (Deut. 11.13) to mean, to serve Him with prayer and by studying His law. Certainly, so they argued, this cannot refer to the sacrificial cult, for into its service one cannot put his heart and soul. It can only mean service with prayer into which one can put his whole soul, and the service of studying the Torah which one can do with his whole heart. As David said (Ps. 141.2): 'Let my prayer be set forth as incense before Thee, the lifting up of my hands as the evening sacrifice" (Sifre, Deut. 41, Friedmann 80a). Thus they developed the Synagogue service which consists of prayer and reading from the Scriptures. This was in line with their democratic tendencies and with their regard for the needs of the people at large which, Josephus tells is, characterized the Pharisees (*Wars* II, 8.2). For this institution of the Synagogue service enabled the people to enjoy everywhere the benefits of their religion, to receive instruction in the Divine Torah, which restoreth the soul, and to pour out their hearts in prayer before their Father in heaven without having to go to the Temple at Jerusalem and without depending upon a priest of a hereditary class. Their very conception of the Torah, that it was intended as a guide for all men, for all times and for all places, forced the Pharisees to believe that the worship in the Synagogue was equal, if not superior, to the service of the Temple. For, certainly the Torah would not be a complete guide if it failed to provide directions for Divine worship, the means of communion with God, for all those who lived away from Jerusalem and far from the Temple. And the Torah certainly could not have meant that those people away from Jerusalem, who could not come to the Temple and yet wished to worship God, should worship Him by offering sacrifices to Him wherever they may be. For, it expressly forbids the offering of sacrifices to God outside of the one chosen place, understood to be Jerusalem: "Take heed to thyself that thou offer not burnt offerings in every place that thou seest" (Deut. 12.13). But the Torah does not specify any particular place where prayer may be offered. On the contrary, it assures us that wherever a human being, a soul yearning for God, will call upon Him in prayer, He will hear him and bless him, For. so the Pharisees understood the passage (Ex. 20.21): "In every place where I cause my name to be mentioned I will come unto thee and bless thee" (Mekilta, *Baḥodesh* XI, Friedmann 73b and parallels).

The Pharisees did not, however, draw the logical conclusion from these ideas about God, so as to oppose the sacrificial cult in the Temple altogether. They tolerated the Temple service but tried to regulate and spiritualize it. What caused them to compromise with the sacrificial cult we cannot tell with certainty. There may have been many causes for their doing so. No doubt, however, the strongest factor which determined their attitude towards the sacrificial cult was the consideration that it is expressly provided for in the Torah. For the Torah does explicitly prescribe sacrifices and regulates the bringing of offerings. These laws about sacrifices, found in the Torah, are too numerous and too explicit to be explained away. And the Pharisees probably did not feel any urgent need for trying to explain away these laws or for objecting to their literal meaning. For these laws and the whole idea of sacrifices were not, in those days at least, regarded as contrary to reason; and they certainly did not outrage the conscience. Furthermore, the Pharisees had a good precedent for their tolerant position, in the attitude of their prototypes, the prophets, who in their time likewise tolerated the sacrificial cult as long as it did not lead to abuse and disregard of the ethical laws and the higher religious duties. Above all, the Pharisees could well believe that, since the Torah was given by God for the benefit of man, these laws about sacrifice also tended somehow to benefit man, else God would not have given them. Some of the followers of the Pharisees expressly state this opinion in regard to the dietary laws. They say: "What difference does it make to God whether one ritually slaughters an animal and eats it or sticks it and eats it, whether one eats clean or unclean food? All these laws were given only in order to discipline and ennoble man." (Tanḥuma, *Shemini*, Buber 15b–30; cf. Gen. r. 44.1).* The early Pharisees may have had the same ideas about the laws for sacrifices. They may have believed that these laws were given to man for some good purpose even though it is not apparent. They may help to train and discipline man, and to cultivate in him the habit of giving up things in obedience to a higher law. But the Pharisees insisted that the sacrifices are of no benefit to God. Like the Prophets, they would fight the sacrificial cult only when its practice would cause a misunderstanding of the religious teachings and would lead to false beliefs, or when it would be made the excuse for the neglect of higher moral duties. One of the Pharisaic teachers, seeking to denounce the idea that sacrifices are gifts to God, indeed makes the bold and sweeping statement, which reminds one of Jeremiah (7.21–22), that God never asked for sacrifices and does not want them. Citing the Psalmist in his support, this teacher says: "Lest you think that He wants your sacrifices because He is in need of food, Scripture says: 'If I were hungry I would not tell thee; for the world is Mine and the fullness thereof . . . Do I eat the flesh of bulls or drink the blood of goats' (Ps. 50.12–13). I have not told you to offer sacrifices. Hence you cannot say: 'I will do His will so that He in turn may do my will.' It is not *My* desire that you sacrifice, it is your own desire to bring sacrifices. For thus it is said: 'When ye offer a sacrifice of peace offerings unto the Lord, ye offer it because of your own desire' (Lev. 19.5), i. e., because you like it and not because God likes it" (Men. 110a). The other teachers contented themselves merely with insisting that the only value in the offering of sacrifices is the thought of God in the mind of those who offer them, their intention to bring a sacrifice in the name of God. Hence, they say, it makes no difference whether one offers much or little, if only his thoughts are directed to God (Men. *loc. cit.*; Sifra, *Vayikra* IX, Weiss 9b).

This consideration was probably one of the reasons why the Pharisees favored and supported the popular ceremony of offering the water libation during the Feast of Tabernacles, to which the Sadducees or the one group of them, the Boethusians,[49] strongly

* [Ed. note: See in this connection the essay "The Ethics of the Halakah."]
[49] In the Talmudic literature the designations Boethusians and Sadducees

objected. The latter objected to this ceremony chiefly because it is not expressly mentioned in the Torah, but probably also because they considered water an inadequate offering to God. The Pharisees believed this ceremony to be based on an old tradition (Suk. 34a and parallels) which to them was as binding as the written law. As regards the appropriateness of the offering, in their opinion, it really could make no difference whether wine or water be offered, since the main and only value of any of the sacrifices is the thought of God in the mind of the sacrificer; and in this case the people thought of God in connection with the performance of this ceremony. Here was a good opportunity of teaching the people that it is not the question of what you offer but in what spirit and with what intentions you offer.

The Pharisees not only sought to remove from the mind of the people the primitive notion that the sacrifices constituted gifts to God but also to combat the superstitious belief that there was any magic power inherent in the sacrifices or in some of the ceremonies connected with them.

In order to emphasize the idea that there is no magic power nor any intrinsic value in the ceremony of purification by the water of sprinkling prepared with the ashes from the red heifer, as prescribed in Numbers 19, one of the outstanding Pharisaic teachers said to his disciples: "By your life, the dead body does not defile nor can the water of sprinkling purify; the whole ceremony is but a decree of the King of Kings" (Pes. deR. Kahana, *Parah*, 40b).[50] In other words, ceremonies prescribed in

---

are used interchangeably to designate the same party or sect. But it seems nevertheless that the Boethusians were a special group of the Sadducees, deriving their name from their leader Boethus. See L. Ginzberg, "Boethusians," in *Jewish Encyclopedia*, III, 285, and Schürer, *op. cit.*, II, 478–79. A fanciful theory about the Boethusians is advanced by R. Azariah de Rossi in his *Me'or 'Enayim* בינה אמרי, III, (Warsaw, 1899), 78–79. According to his theory the Boethusians were identical with the Essenes, and the name ביתוסים is merely a contracted form of the two words בית איסיאי, meaning the house of the Essenes.

[50] The same teacher, R. Joḥanan b. Zakkai, also abolished the ordeal by drinking the bitter waters prescribed in the Law (Num. 5.12–31) for the woman suspected of adultery ((b. Soṭah 47a). His reason for abolishing this ceremony was, according to the Mishnah, that he considered it unjust to have

the Torah were to be observed, according to the Pharisees, merely because they were believed to be prescribed by God. But when the ceremony tended to perpetuate a false belief or to lend support to a superstition, the Pharisees would fight it and abolish it or modify it.

The best illustration of their activity in this direction is their fight against the manner in which the priests would perform the ceremony of offering the incense in the Holy of Holies on the Day of Atonement. To sum up briefly what I have discussed elsewhere at greater length, the fight about the manner in which this ceremony should be performed was a fight between two God-conceptions. The Sadducees, holding to primitive notions about God, believed that God was really present in the Holy of Holies of the Temple, and that His presence could actually be seen there hovering between the two cherubim upon the Ark-cover, or, at a later time when the Ark was no longer there, on the spot where the Ark once stood. The entrance of the High Priest into the Holy of Holies on the Day of Atonement was, therefore, fraught with danger. For, if on entering he should, even if only involuntarily, look in the direction of the Ark-cover and see the Deity he would immediately die. As a precaution against this danger, the old practice of the priests was to put the incense upon the fiery coals on the censer, outside of the curtain which separated the Holy of Holies from the rest of the Temple, and, while the smoke of the incense arose, he would carry the censer with the smoking incense into the Holy of Holies and offer it there. The smoke coming up from the incense protected the High Priest against the danger of seeing the Deity clearly face to face.

---

a double standard of morality, so that the women should be punished for an offence which the men may commit without fear of punishment. It seems to me, however, that this alleged reason based upon the prophetic condemnation of a double standard of morality (Hosea 4.14) was not the real reason, or at least not the sole reason for doing away with this ceremony. For, according to the Rabbis, the ceremony would anyhow be without effect in case the husband was not absolutely blameless and pure from sin מנוקה מעון (b. Soṭah 47b). R. Joḥanan b. Zakkai probably wanted to do away with the superstitions and belief in magic, underlying the ceremony of bitter waters. The utterance of the prophet Hosea merely served as an excuse for the daring act of abolishing a pentateuchal law.

It formed a sort of a screen through which he was allowed to see the Deity. For, "through the smoke of the incense God may be seen upon the Ark-cover," so the Sadducees understood Lev. 16.2.[51]

The Pharisees, on the other hand, insisted that there was no visible manifestation of the Deity in the Holy of Holies. And, in order to teach the people that God has no form in which He could be seen by any human being, and that no semblance or representation of Him could be found or seen in the Holy of Holies, they enforced a modification of this ceremony. The High Priest was not allowed to prepare the smoking incense outside of the curtain. He could not put the incense upon the fiery coals, thus producing a screen of smoke before he entered the Holy of Holies. He had to carry the censer with fiery coals in his right hand and the spoon full of incense in his left, and thus enter the Holy of Holies. And only after he had entered inside the curtain was he to put the incense upon the fiery coals on the censer and offer it there. The Pharisees thus reduced this offering of the incense in the Holy of Holies to a mere ritual like so many other ritual laws or ceremonies which are to be observed because they are prescribed in the Torah though the reason for them is not known. But they prevented this ceremony from being performed

[51] See *A Significant Controversy Between the Sadducees and the Pharisees*, above, especially pp. 73 ff. Arnobius also alludes to the fact that the Sadducees gave form to the Deity. For he says: "And let no one bring up against us Jewish fables and those of the sect of the Sadducees, as though we, too, attribute to the Deity forms, for this is supposed to be taught in their writings" (*Against the Heathen*, III, 12, in the edition of Ante-Nicene Fathers [New York, 1899], vol. 6, p. 467). It is amusing to see how the editors and translators in their desire to find fault with the Pharisees, made the following remark: "It is evident that Arnobius here confuses the sceptical Sadducees with their opponents the Pharisees and the Talmudists" (*ibid.*, note 3). But it is evident that the editors were confused while Arnobius was accurate and knew what he was saying. He had a correct report as to the primitive God conception held by the Sadducees which permitted them to attribute corporeality to God and to make Him dwell in visible form in the Holy of Holies. Kirkisani also says, that the Sadducees believed in the corporeality of God and that they would take the anthropomorphic expressions of the Bible literally. Cf. A. Harkavy לקורות הכתות בישראל in S. P. Rabbinowitz's Hebrew translation of Graetz's *History*, III (Warsaw, 1893), 495.

in such a manner as would suggest the false belief that God is actually present in the Holy of Holies, or that He could at all become visible to the High Priest or to anyone else.

Perhaps the most effective means by which the Pharisees impressed upon the minds of the people the lesson that sacrifices were not the most acceptable form of worship was the institution of a Synagogue in the very precinct of the Temple, and the regulation that the priests hold there every day a religious service of the kind held in a Synagogue. By this institution a sort of combination of the two forms of worship was effected by which the sacrificial cult was spiritualized as it were, and the idea that the value of the sacrifice consisted only in the thought of God which it elicited from the sacrificer was given emphatic support. It certainly put the Synagogue worship on a par with the sacrificial cult. This very fact makes likely the assumption that this institution was forced upon the priests by the Pharisees. But if it was not altogether an innovation introduced by the Pharisees after they got into power and obtained control of the Temple, either in the days of Queen Salome Alexandra or later on, it certainly was fostered and prompted by them. Surely, the Sadducees would not insist upon a daily Synagogue service to be held by the priests in the Temple. It is true that from Josephus' statement, that the Pharisees "are able greatly to persuade the body of the people, and whatsoever they do about Divine worship, prayers and sacrifices, they perform them according to their directions" (*Ant.* XVIII, 1.3) it does not necessarily follow that the Sadducees denied prayer altogether. It may simply mean that the people followed the Pharisees and not the Sadducees in the manner of offering prayer or in the selection and arrangement of certain prayers. The talmudic reports do not say anything about the Sadducean position on prayer. But from the emphasis which the Pharisaic teachers lay upon the importance of prayer and from their eagerness to interpret passages in the Torah as prescribing it,[52] it would seem that

[52] Cf. L. Baeck, *Die Pharisäer*, (Berlin, 1927), pp. 44 f. Whether these interpretations were taken strictly so as to make prayer obligatory according to biblical law מדאורייתא or not is a moot question. There are passages in the Talmud which expressly declare that prayer service is not obligatory by

the Saducees did not believe it obligatory or important. The Sadducees would naturally not favor a religious service, consisting of prayer and study alone, as this would tend to lessen the importance of the sacrifices and thereby weaken their own position as priests. Besides, this kind of service is nowhere expressly mentioned in the Torah, and they had, therefore, no reason to consider it obligatory upon them (cf. Leszynsky, *Die Sadduzäer*, pp. 20–21). Not that they denied that prayer may prevail with God. This they could not do since there are instances in the Torah of prayer having prevailed with God. But, to their way of thinking, offering sacrifices and bringing gifts to Him were more effective methods of securing His favor. For, it was this kind of service, and not prayer, that He stipulated in the covenant and imposed upon Israel in the Torah. Furthermore, this very conception of the Torah made prayer rather superfluous for them. The Torah, to them, was not meant to be coextensive with life. It was a group of laws imposed upon Israel, with rewards promised for obeying it and punishment threatened for disobeying it. Accordingly, all that was necessary to ward off the wrath of God and to secure His continuous favor was merely to fulfill the imposed laws and especially to offer Him the prescribed sacrifices. As for human conduct and activities in general, the Sadducees seemed to have believed that God does not bother with man's affairs, nor does He care what the individual does. As Josephus puts it: "And for the Sadducees they take away fate and say there is no such thing, and that the events of human affairs are not at its disposal, but they suppose that all our actions are in our own power, so that we are ourselves the causes of what is good and receive what is evil from our own folly" (*Ant*. XIII, 5.9). In other words, they did not believe in Divine Providence.[53] Of course, we have to discount Josephus' statement a little. We must not assume, that they denied that God could interfere in

---

biblical law, but is merely a rabbinical institution (e. g., Ber. 21a, ותפלה דרבנן and Suk. 38a). Cf. however, Maimonides in *Sefer haMizvot*, commandment 5 (Warsaw, 1903), p. 6, and Nachmanides, *ad loc.*, and Ḥananiah Casis in קנאת סופרים *ad loc.*

[53] Cf. also Hippolytus, "The Refutation of All Heresies" (*Ante-Nicene Fathers*, vol. V, [N. Y., 1899]), Book IX, chs. xxiii and xxiv.

human affairs. What they seemed to have thought is that God does not care to bother with human affairs. The individual is left to his own resources. To the people as a group, He gives His protection if they fulfill His commands, just as He punishes them for violating the laws stipulated in His covenant. But in matters that are not prescribed nor prohibited by the Law, their conduct is left to themselves, to control their own affairs. And whatever happens to them is but of their own doing, the result of their wise or foolish actions. Surely, there is not much occasion nor reason for prayer when one believes that God does not take notice of all our affairs nor cares for all our needs.

The Pharisees who advocated a religious service consisting of prayer and who believed in the efficacy of prayer, did, indeed, believe that God takes cognizance of all our doings, and orders all human affairs, and that everything that happens in the world is ordained by Him. The Pharisees, Josephus tells us, "ascribe all to Providence and to God and yet allow that to act what is right or contrary is principally in the power of man; although fate does cooperate in every action" (*Wars* II, 8.2). This is confirmed by talmudic reports. With the belief in Divine Providence and Divine Prescience the Pharisees combined the belief in the freedom of will, that is, that man has it in his power to choose between good and evil and determine whether he wants to live virtuously or wickedly. They did not "ascribe the practice of sinners to fortune and fate," as is erroneously stated in the *Apostolic Constitutions* (Book VI, ch. 6). Josephus in the passage just quoted expressly says, that they believed it to be in the power of man to act rightly or wrongly. And in *Antiquities* (XVIII, 1.3) he likewise says: "And when they (the Pharisees) determine that all things are done by fate, they do not take away the freedom from men of acting as they think fit" (cf. also *Ant.* XIII, 5.9). This also is confirmed by talmudic reports of the followers of the Pharisees, who declare: "Everything is in the hands of God but the fear of God" (Ber. 33b), and although "everything is foreseen, yet freedom of choice is given" (Ab. III, 15). But they could not deny God the power of influencing man and determining his choice. This would be incompatible with the belief in His omnipotence. Besides, they knew many instances in the Torah where God did influence men's actions both for good and for evil. For God said to Abimelech: "Yea, I know that in the simplicity of thy heart thou hast done this, and I also withheld thee from sinning against me (Gen. 20.6). And He also said: "And I will harden Pharaoh's heart" (Ex. 7.3). And it is said: "But the Lord hardened Pharaoh's heart and he did not let the children of Israel go" (Ex. 10.20). They knew these and numerous other passages from sacred Scriptures where the possibility of God's influencing man's choice of conduct is presupposed (cf. Suk. 52b and parallels). They, accordingly came to the conclusion that indeed God can, but does not desire to, determine man's choice of conduct. He wants man to choose for himself. However, He is ready to help man carry out his plan to do good, while on the other hand He refrains from hindering him when he chooses to do evil, thus passively at least, cooperating with him. This is what Josephus means, when he says: "Although fate does cooperate in every action" (*Wars, loc. cit.*), that is, even in man's freely chosen actions, whether they are good or evil. As the Talmud more mildly puts it, "If a man chooses to do good the heavenly powers help him. If he chooses to do evil, they leave the way open to him" (Shab. 104a). "In whatever way man desires to go the heavenly powers lead him" (Mak. 10b; cf. Mekilta, *Vayassa* I, Friedmann 46a, band parallels). It is probably this idea which is expressed by Josephus when he attributes to the Pharisees the notion: "that it hath pleased God to make a temperament (?) whereby what he (He?) wills is done but so that the will of man can act virtuously or viciously"[54] (*Ant.* XVIII, 1.3). Josephus is not quite clear in his phraseology. His statement probably means that it is God's will that man do good; He implanted in man not only the impulse

---

[54] Cf. Thackeray's new translation of this passage as given in the *Harvard Theological Review* XXV, No. 1, January 1932, p. 93. Cf. Strack-Billerbeck, *Kommentar zum Neuen Testament*, vol. IV, (München, 1928), p. 344, and Moore, *op. cit.*, p. 457. The passage in Josephus is rather obscure. It may also mean to say that the Pharisees believed there is a prejudgment, determined by God, to let things be done in accordance with its decree, yet allowing man to follow good or evil. In other words, God has prejudged how man, according to his own choice, will act.

to do evil but also the inclination to do good, i. e., a temperament whereby man is led to do God's will but on his own initiative. This idea finds frequent expression in the talmudic literature.[55] Whether this is a satisfactory solution of the problem is not the question. We must remember the Pharisees were not philosophers and probably did not stop to realize all the implications and philosophical difficulties of their naive solution. They were practical teachers of religion and for the purpose of teaching religion and right conduct it was a very practical, if naive, solution. God is omnipotent, nothing is impossible for Him, not even making man choose good or evil. God is also all-knowing and He certainly knows beforehand what choice man is going to make. But man must have freedom of will, if he is to be a moral being which God wants him to be. So God gave him the freedom of will, the power to choose between good and evil. He created him with two impulses, a good one and a bad one, advised him to do good and gave him the Torah as a guide to help him; but if with all this, man chooses evil God does not hinder him. In this manner the Pharisees solved, at least to their own satisfaction, the problem of how man has the power to do evil which is displeasing to God, and how man can be free to make a choice although his choice is foreknown by God. God gives man credit for choosing good, though He helps him in doing it, and holds him responsible for choosing evil, though He could have prevented it.

The belief in man's responsibility for his conduct demands as a corollary the belief in Divine retribution. We have no record of any speculations on the part of the early Pharisees as to the vexing problem of why the righteous suffer and the wicked prosper. From the various discussions of this problem by later Pharisaic teachers, however, we may conclude that this problem occupied the minds of the early Pharisees also. At any rate, they solved the problem by postulating a belief in another life, a life after death.

According to Josephus, the Pharisees believed, "that souls have an immortal vigor in them, and that under the earth there

---

[55] Cf. Sifre, Deut. 53; b. Ḳid. 30b; Suk. 52a,b.

will be reward and punishment according as they have lived virtuously or viciously in this life" (*Ant.* XVIII, 1.3; cf. also *Wars* II, 8.2). According to the Talmud and the New Testament, they believed in the resurrection of the dead. But whether the soul is immortal and continues to live in the beyond, or whether the dead are resurrected and come back to live here on earth, man's career is not ended with death and his existence is not limited to this present life. After this life here on earth there is another life in the future in which the belief in God's retributive justice will be vindicated.

This belief in another world thus makes possible the belief in Divine justice and Divine retribution in the face of all the apparent injustices that may be noticed in this world in the respective positions of the righteous and the wicked, and in spite of the many experiences which show that men do not get their deserts here on earth. Here again the Pharisees found a practical solution to a vexing problem which threatened to tempt man from virtue and cause him to abandon the pursuit of righteousness.

With the question as to the origin of this belief in a hereafter, whether it came from the Greeks or the Persians we are not concerned here. Perhaps we ought not to look to any foreign source for its origin. It may just as likely have been a home-grown product, having gradually developed out of primitive notions about the condition of the dead which had been prevalent in ancient Israel, and as a logical consequence of the belief in the Divine justice. Certainly the Pharisees did not consider it a foreign belief. To them it was a genuine Jewish belief found in many passages of the Scriptures and indicated, or at least suggested, in the Torah itself.

It was probably due to their belief in another world that the Pharisees did not seek to get much out of this world and would not pursue its pleasures and material goods. For, as Josephus tells us, "they lived meanly, and despised delicacies in diet and they followed the contract of reason" (*Ant.* XVIII, 1.3). And according to a talmudic report, their opponents would make fun of them, saying: "The Pharisees hold on to their traditional belief; accordingly, they deprive themselves of the pleasures of this world. But they will get nothing in that future world of theirs" (Ab. R. N., Version A, ch. V, Schechter, 26).[56]

But if they did not seek the material pleasures of this world, they did not slacken their efforts to make it a better world to live in, a world in which the reign of God and His Law should prevail and men live together in peace and mutual goodwill. Their belief in another world did not make them otherworldly. For even more than with the salvation of the individual in the future life of another world were they concerned with the salvation of their people and of humanity, and with the future of this world when all mankind will join Israel in accepting the Torah and believing in the One God. To the attainment of this end the Pharisees devoted most of their thoughts and activities.

For the Pharisees believed in one humanity as they believed in one God. This was but the logical result and the necessary outcome of their whole struggle. They began by fighting the aristocratic priests and disputing the hereditary privileges of the latter as based merely on the accident of birth. They naturally had to end with the belief that Israel, likewise, cannot claim any hereditary privileges on account of mere birth. The distinction Israel has is due not to his birth but to his following the Torah, and any one who accepts the Torah is fully like him.

They found this idea repeatedly stated in the Torah and the prophets. According to the Pharisees, all men are born equal. No man can claim to be of nobler birth than the other, nor can any race claim superiority over another. For all are descendent from one father and one mother, from Adam and Eve. This is the first and most important lesson of the Torah, taught in its opening chapter. Mankind, say the Pharisees, were made to descend from one father, so that no one should be able to say to another, "My father was greater than yours" (M. Sanh. 4.5). Human creatures should, therefore, live in peace together, for

---

[56] The following saying may be regarded as the Pharisees' answer to this taunt of the Sadducees: אמר להם משה לישראל אתם רואים את הרשעים שהם מצליחים בשנים ושלשה ימים הם מצליחים בעולם הזה וסופו לדחות באחרונה שנאמר כי לא תהיה אחרית לרע... ואתם רואים את הצדיקים כשהם מצטערים בעולם הזה בשנים ושלשה ימים מצטערים וסופן לשמוח באחרונה שנאמר להטיבך באחריתך, Sifre, Deut. 53, Friedmann, 86a.

they all have one father even in the flesh, as they have one father in God. God is not only the God of Israel, He is "the God of all flesh" (Jer. 32.27) or, as Moses called Him: "The God of the spirits of all flesh" (Num. 16.22). Now, the Pharisees must have reasoned, if God is not the tribal God of Israel but the God of all peoples, then the conception of Israel as the people of God must also not be limited to the tribes of Israel. Israel potentially embraces all mankind. It can and should be enlarged so as to include all other people. Not that Israel should give up his uniqueness, lose his identity among the other peoples, and become like them. This is impossible. The very thought of it has been denounced by the prophet: "That which cometh into your mind shall not be at all, in that ye say: 'We will be as the nations, as the families of the countries to serve wood and stone' " (Ezek. 20.32). And another prophet declared that Israel shall never cease from being a nation before God (Jer. 31.36–37). And still another one declares in the name of God: "For I, the Lord, change not, and ye, O sons of Jacob, are not consumed" (Mal. 3.6). Israel will remain forever a distinct people. It is a separate family and must retain its separateness among the families of the earth. But he cannot claim any special privileges. The other people are free to join him and become like him. "The stranger shall join himself with them and they shall cleave to the house of Jacob" (Isa. 14.1). "Neither let the alien that hath joined himself to the Lord speak, saying: 'The Lord will surely separate me from His people' " (*ibid.*, 56.3). For God wants all the people to be like Israel. "The Holy One of Israel shall be called the God of all the earth" (Isa. 54.5), the prophet declares. This can only mean, that all the peoples of the earth shall become like Israel in believing in the Holy One and accepting His Law. And it is Israel's duty and function to help the other people to do so. Israel's position among the other nations is that of an older brother. In a religious sense he is the older brother, since he was the first to recognize God as the father. For this reason God called him, "My son, My first-born" (Ex. 4.23). But all the other nations are also children of God, younger sons, as it were. And it is the duty of the older brother to teach and help the younger ones.

According to the Pharisees, it was for that very purpose and with this understanding that God gave the Torah to Israel in the wilderness. The Torah was not given in Palestine, said the Pharisees, for then Israel could have claimed it as their own and withheld it from the other nations. And the other nations could have had an excuse for not accepting it. The Torah was given in the wilderness, in no man's land, so that every one who desires it can accept it (Mekilta, Baḥodesh I, Friedmann 62a and 67a). Before giving them the Torah, God stipulated with Israel that they must be a kingdom of priests (Ex. 19.6), that is, that they should render to the other nations those services which the priests rendered them. The Torah was meant for all men. This is the Torah for men, and not only for Priests, Levites, and Israelites, say the Pharisees. For the Torah does not say: Which Priests, Levites, and Israelites shall do and live by them. It says: "Which a man shall do and live by them" (Lev. 18.5), clearly indicating that the gentile who keeps the Torah is not only like the Jew but even as good as the High Priest (Sifra, Aḥare XIII, Weiss 86b). Not all Israel understood the Torah at once. For quite a time, only the priests knew it and taught it to them. The Israelites must do the same for the non-Israelites. Israel must be the priest-teacher of the other nations, but is not to claim any privilege, for, according to the Pharisees, even the priest of the family of Aaron should have no privileges. As soon as the lay people of Israel learned to know the Torah, the Pharisees claimed, they became like the priests, the sons of Aaron; and likewise as soon as the gentiles learn to know and observe the Torah they become like their priest-teachers, the Israelites. And there were among the leaders of the Pharisees descendants of gentiles, who were great and recognized teachers of the Torah. The Pharisees insisted that a man's religious position is not determined by his birth but by his mode of life. To emphasize this idea and in opposition to the Sadducean priests they called themselves "Disciples of Moses" (תלמידיו של משה, Yoma 4a) as contrasted with the "descendants of Aaron." They preferred to "sit on Moses' seat" (Matt. 23.2) and teach the Torah as Moses taught it, rather than to stand at the altar and offer sacrifices. Not that they disparaged all the functions of the priests. For, just as they appreciated the function of teaching the Law, once performed by the priests but now assumed by them, so also did they appreciate the activity of establishing peace among men, for which Aaron, the brother of Moses, the ideal priest, was famous. But they claimed that even for these functions of the priests, as for the function of teaching, one need not be a descendant of Aaron, for the talent of performing them is not an inherited one. One can acquire it and exercise it and thus be a *disciple* of Aaron, no matter from whom one may be descended. The following report of an encounter between a Sadducean High-Priest and the two Pharisaic leaders, Shemaiah and Abtalion, who were of gentile descent, brings out this position of the Pharisees most clearly: The High Priest in greeting said to them: "Peace be unto the sons of the gentiles," thus alluding to their non-Jewish descent. To this they replied: "Peace be unto the sons of the gentiles who do the work of Aaron, but not unto a son of Aaron who does not do the work of Aaron" (Yoma 71b). Their disciple, Hillel, could well say: "Be of the disciples of Aaron, loving peace and pursuing peace, loving all thy fellow-creatures and drawing them near to the Torah" (Ab. 1.12). These were not merely preachings; the works of the Pharisees were in line with their teachings, for, in truth, the Pharisees practiced what they preached. Josephus tells us, that "the Pharisees are friendly to one another and are for the exercise of concord and regard for the public" (*Wars* II, 8.2). But he does not tell all. The Pharisees, according to the program of Hillel, not only exercised concord among their own people but also sought to establish it among all men. They combined the activities of Moses and Aaron. They thought that the best way of establishing goodwill among men was to bring them to an acceptance of the Torah, whose ways are ways of pleasantness and whose paths are peace. For, according to Pharisaic ideas, the whole Torah aims to establish goodwill among men, כל התורה כולה מפני דרכי שלום (Giṭ. 59b). Or, as Hillel expressed it to the gentile who wished to become converted to Judaism: "What is unpleasant to you do not unto your fellowman, this is the whole of the Torah. All the rest of its contents is but commentary" to this golden rule (Shab. 31a). We show best our true love for our fellowman if we do not withhold from him what would be of greatest use to him in his life. And the Pharisees, prompted by such a love for humanity as was taught by Hillel, did seek to bring mankind to the Torah, or rather to bring the Torah to mankind, to offer to their fellowmen that most precious gift, which they considered of the greatest value in life.

With Micah and Isaiah they believed that at some future time all nations will come up to the mountain of the Lord, to the God of Jacob, to learn His ways, to walk in His paths, and accept the Torah from Zion. But they were not content to wait idly till the end of days when a Messiah will come and realize this ideal. Significantly enough, they did not indulge in speculations about the coming of a Messiah, and the early Pharisees very rarely refer to it.[57] Their plan was that the Torah should go forth out of Zion before the coming of the Messiah and that the word of God from Jerusalem shall spread to all mankind in their own time and by their own efforts. Instead of waiting for the nations to come to Zion seeking the Torah, they went out from Zion taking the Torah with them and bringing it to the nations. They engaged in a very active propaganda for Judaism. They did "compass sea and land to make one proselyte" (Matt. 23.15). And when he became so they made him feel fully as one of their own and showered upon him lavish attention. Such a treatment of the proselyte was repeatedly enjoined upon them by the Torah, as they understood it. The laws of the Torah forbidding certain nations to "enter into the assembly of the Lord" (Deut. 23.4–9) were understood to mean only that intermarriage with them was prohibited. But even this restriction the Pharisees declared could not be applied against any nation on

[57] Cf. J. Klausner, הרעיון המשיחי בישראל, second edition, (Jerusalem, 1927), pp. 250 ff. The one express reference to the coming of the Messiah made by R. Joḥanan b. Zakkai is rather indifferent. It reads as follows: אם היתה נטיעה בתוך ידך ויאמרו לך: הרי לך המשיח בוא ונטע את הנטיעה ואחר כך צא והקבילו, Ab. R. N., version B., ch. XXXI, Schechter, 34a. This simply means: Do not let the coming of the Messiah cause you to neglect your work. Whether the same teacher's saying on his death bed: "Prepare a chair for Hezekiah the king of Judah who has come" הכינו כסא לחזקיהו מלך יהודה שבא (Ber. 28b) expresses the belief in the approaching advent of the Messiah (cf. J. Klausner, op. cit., p. 252, and note 6) is to my mind very doubtful.

earth. They declared that the nations of their time, even though they bore the same names as the nations against whom the Mosaic prohibition was decreed, no longer were identical with them. Wars subsequent to the time of Moses had brought about an intermingling of the various nations (M. Yad. 4.4). And Pharisaic Judaism does not discriminate against any nation, race, or color. Whosoever accepts the Torah and embraces Judaism is in every respect a Jew.

That the Pharisees were successful in their campaign is fully attested by the spread of Judaism throughout the heathen world in the century before, and the first century after, the common era.[58] The success of the apostles and the early Christian missionaries among the gentiles was due in a large measure to the extensive propaganda against heathenism that had been carried on by the Pharisees. In the course of time, however, because of internal and external unfavorable conditions, the Pharisees gave up their active proselytizing propaganda. But they did not change their ideas about the unity of mankind. They welcomed proselytes but did not go out to seek them. They declared that the gentiles even though they do not accept all of Judaism, if they believe in God and live a righteous life, will have a share in the future life (Tosefta Sanhedrin 13.2). Even though they insisted upon the separateness of Israel, they meant him to be but one of the families of the earth, living with all of them in peace and harmony.

These were the fundamental beliefs and guiding principles of the Pharisees. Knowing these, we understand their position. For all their activities, their opposition to the priests, their work among their people, and their proselytizing propaganda were but expressions of these beliefs and means for the realization of their ideal, which was to bring their people and all mankind nearer to God by teaching them to observe the Law of God. If they were

---

[58] Cf. Josephus, *Contra Apionem*, II, 11; Paul in his Epistle to the Romans 2.19–20; Schürer, *op. cit.*, III, 162 ff. and 553 ff. Schürer, however, is wrong when he assumes that these liberal activities for proselytizing were carried on only by the Jews of the Diaspora. Cf. also Moore, *op. cit.*, I, 22–23 and 108. See also A. Sh. Hershberg, "Tenuat Ha-Hitgayyerut Hagdolah" in *Hateḳufah* XIII, (1922), 129–148.

not always consistent, let us remember that practical teachers have to make concessions and cannot always be consistent. If, as it seems to us, they did not draw all the logical conclusions from their advanced ideas and theological premises, let us remember that they were human, subject to error, and that they may not have realized the inconsistencies in some of their positions, as we do. They were far ahead of their time, but perhaps not as far as the twentieth century philosophers and liberal theologians. If they insisted upon the observance of the minutiae of the ritual law, it was not at the expense of the ethical laws, nor to the neglect of the higher spiritual values of the religious teachings of the Torah and the prophets. They demanded the observance of even these minutiae of ritual because they believed them to be part of the Divine Law. The performance of even the least and most trivial act in the belief that God commanded it reminds one of God and brings one nearer to Him.

Of course, some people may have joined their ranks from ulterior motives. Naturally, there were advantages to be derived from belonging to the party beloved by the people. There may have been some people who outwardly imitated them without sharing their high ideals and without understanding their spiritual motives. The Pharisaic leaders themselves were well aware of the presence of some insincere people among their followers. They call them "the sore spots" or "the plagues of the Pharisaic party" (Soṭah 3.4 and 22b). And while they deplored the fact, they had no means of getting rid of them. For, although, as Josephus tells us, "they were believed to have the foreknowledge of things to come by Divine inspiration" (*Ant.* XVII, 2), they could not see into the hearts of all their followers and discover the insincere motives of some of them. In every society or group engaged in some ideal work there will be found some members who have joined without subscribing to its ideals. So, even if it be admitted that Jesus encountered some of that type and denounced them as hypocrites, it would be the height of absurdity to assume that Jesus denounced the whole party, and to regard all the Pharisees as hypocrites. Certainly not all churchgoers are hypocrites although hypocrites have frequently been found among churchgoers. A religious teacher like Jesus could not have failed to appreciate the faithful work of those spiritual teachers of religion with whom he had so much in common.[59] And, even though he may have disagreed with them on some questions or differed with them in some method, he certainly would not misjudge their devotion to God and their quest for righteousness.

With all the occasional setbacks which Pharisaism experienced in the course of time, it persisted in its course as a liberal religious movement. It has contributed much to religious development and to religious liberalism. For, directly and indirectly, within Judaism and outside of it, it has helped much to bring about a finer appreciation of religious ideas, a higher spiritual conception of God, a better understanding of men as the children of God, and of their relation to one another. It has taught man to recognize God as his father and his fellowman as his brother.

In particular, it has enabled Judaism to develop as a spiritual religion without a sacrificial cult, without an hereditary priesthood, and not limited to any one place, but expressing eternal spiritual truths and spreading the ideas of One God and one humanity throughout the world. Verily, "by their fruits ye shall know them."

---

[59] Cf. Shirley Jackson Case, *op. cit.*, p. 305 ff.

Midrash and Mishnah

Midrash and Mishnah

A Study In The Early History Of The Halakah

(1915)

I

THE teachings of the Halakah, as preserved to us in the tannaitic literature, have been given by teacher to disciple and transmitted from generation to generation in two different forms, namely, Midrash and Mishnah. The one, Midrash, shortened from "Midrash Torah"[1] represents the Halakah as an interpretation and exposition of the Torah. It teaches the Halakah together with its scriptural proof, that is, in connection with the passage from the Pentateuch, on which it is based or from which it can be derived, thus forming a halakic commentary to the written law contained in the Pentateuch. This form is especially used in our halakic Midrashim, Sifra, Sifre, and Mekilta, but it is also found in some parts of the collections of our Mishnah and Tosefta, as well as in many so-called Midrash-Baraitot scattered in both the Palestinian and the Babylonian Talmud. The other form, the Mishnah, represents the Halakah as an independent work, giving its dicta as such, without any

---

[1] The term מדרש from דרש 'to search, inquire, investigate,' means 'research, inquiry,' and מדרש תורה accordingly means an inquiry into the meaning of the Torah, an exposition of all laws and decisions which can be discovered in the words of the Torah. In this sense the term 'Midrash Torah' is used in the Talmud (b. Ḳid. 49b) where it designates the halakic interpretation or exposition of the Torah. As we now have many Midrashim to the Torah of a haggadic character, the term Midrash Torah would be too indefinite to designate an halakic exposition of the Torah. A haggadic exposition of the Torah would also be a Midrash Torah. The more specific term Midrash Halakah is therefore now used to designate a halakic interpretation of the Torah. See the writer's article 'Midrash Halakah' in the *Jewish Encyclopaedia*, VIII, 569–72.

scriptural proof, and teaching them independently of and not connected with the words of the written law. For this reason the Mishnah is also designated as "Halakah" or in the plural "Halakot," that is, merely rules or decisions. This form is especially used in our collections of the Mishnah and the Tosefta, but it is also found in many Baraitot scattered in the Talmud and in some parts of our halakic Midrashim.[2] (See D. Hoffmann, *Zur Einleitung in die halachischen Midraschim*, [Berlin, 1887,] p. 3.)

Of these two forms of teaching the Halakah, the Midrash is the older and the Mishnah the later. The Midrash was the original form, and was used in the earliest times, in the very beginnings of the Halakah. This is quite self-evident, as the Midrash was in reality the origin of the Halakah. The dicta of the Halakah had their source in the Midrash Torah, i. e., an inquiry into the full meaning of the Written Law from which alone the earliest Halakah derived its authority.

The returned Babylonian exiles, constituting the new Jewish community, reorganized by Ezra and Nehemiah, accepted the written Torah, so to speak, as their constitution. They entered into a covenant by oath, to keep and follow the laws of Moses as contained in the book read to them by Ezra (Neh. 8 and 10.30). The Book of the Law, therefore, as read and interpreted by Ezra, was for them the only authority they were bound to follow. Whatever was not given in the book, they were not bound to accept. All the religious practices and the time-honored customs and even the traditional laws, if there were such, had to receive the sanction of the written Law in order to be absolutely binding upon the people. This means, that the practices, customs, etc., had to be recognized as implied in the Written Law or contained in its fuller meaning. The teachers, therefore, interpreted the Written Law so as to include in it or derive from it all those customs and practices. Thus, the teachings of the Halakah (for all such rules, customs, practices, and traditional laws con-

---

[2] As the difference is only in form, it is not surprising to find that very many of the Halakot are cast in both forms. Very often the same Halakot which are found in the halakic Midrashim together with their scriptural proofs are also found in the Mishnah and Tosefta without scriptural proofs as independent Halakot.

MIDRASH AND MISHNAH 165

stituted the Halakah) had to be represented as an interpretation or an exposition of the Written Law. This, as we have seen above, means, to be given in Midrash-form.

It is expressly stated of Ezra that he explained and interpreted the Torah to the people, and that he set his heart to search (לדרוש) the meaning of the Law, to interpret it, and to teach in Israel statutes and judgements (Ezra 7.10). We learn from this, that Ezra taught only the Book of the Law with such interpretations as he could give to it. His successors, the Soferim, who were the earliest teachers of the Halakah, did the same. They gave all their teachings merely as interpretations to the Book of the Law. Indeed, the very name Soferim was given to them because it characterized their manner of teaching. This name סופרים is derived from ספר "the Book." It means "Bookmen," and it designated a class of people who occupied themselves with the Book of the Law, who interpreted it and who based all their teachings upon this book exclusively (Frankel, *Hodegetica in Mischnam*, p. 3, and Weiss, *Dor*, I, 47).

For a long period this Midrash-form was the only form used in teaching the Halakah. This is confirmed by reliable traditions reported to us in Rabbinic literature. One such report is contained in the following passage in the Pal. Talmud (M. Ḳ. 3.7, 83b):

איזהו תלמיד חכם? חזקיה אמר כל ששנה הלכות ועוד תורה אמר ליה ר' יוסי הדא דאת אמר בראשונה אבל עכשיו אפילו הלכות.

"Who is to be considered a scholar? Hezekiah says, One who has studied the Halakot as an addition to and in connection with the Torah.[3] Said to him R. Jose, What you say was [correct]

[3] The term ועוד means 'addition,' as, for instance, in the phrase: ויהודה ועוד לקרא 'Is it necessary to mention the custom in Judea as an addition to the law indicated in the Scriptures?' (b. Ḳid. 6a). It is also found in the plural form, ועדות 'additions' (b. 'Er. 83a). The expression ועוד תורה here means, therefore, as an addition to the Torah, i. e., to teach the Halakot not independently but as additions to the passages in the Torah from which they are derived. In almost the same sense it is also interpreted by the commentator Pene Mosheh, *ad loc*.

It should also be noticed that in b. Ḳid. 49a Hezekiah says that to be called a student (שונה) it is enough if one has studied merely detached Halakot.

in former times, but in our day, even [if one has studied merely detached] Halakot, [he is to be regarded as a scholar]." Here it is plainly stated that in earlier times (בראשונה) the only form of teaching Halakot was as an addition to and in connection with the written Law, that is to say, in the Midrash-form. In those days, therefore, one could not acquire a knowledge of the Halakah, i. e., become a scholar, except by learning the Midrash, for the very good reason that the halakic teachings were not imparted in any other form.

Sherira Gaon who no doubt drew upon reliable sources likewise reports in his Epistle (Neubauer, *M. J.*, ch. I, p. 15) that "in the earlier period of the second Temple, in the days of the earlier teachers, all the teachings of the Halakot were given in the manner in which they are found in our Sifra and Sifre," that is, in the Midrash-form.[4] Modern scholars[5] have, accordingly, recognized it as an established historic fact that the Midrash was originally the exclusive form in which all teachings of the Halakah were given.

Not only were those Halakot which were derived from some scriptural passage by means of interpretation taught in Midrash-form, that is to say in connection with the passages which served as proof, but also such Halakot and teachings as were of purely traditional origin — rules, practices, and customs that had no

---

This, however, does not contradict his saying in our passage in the p. Talmud. For תלמיד חכם is a scholar of a higher degree of learning. From b. Meg. 26b it is evident that the student called שונה is not as advanced as the scholar called תלמיד חכם. To be considered a scholar, such as is designated by the name תלמיד חכם, Hezekiah tells us, one must study the Halakot in the Midrash-form. For even after the Mishnah-form had become popular, the Midrash was considered the proper form to be used by advanced scholars. See Guttmann, *Zur Einleitung in die Halakah* (Budapest, 1909), p. 20.

[4] The passage in the letter of Sherira Gaon reads thus: וספרא וספרי דרש דקראי נינהו והיכן רמיזי הילכתא בקראי ומעיקרא במקדש שני ביומיה דרבנן קמאי לפום הדין אורחא הוו תני להון. They taught 'them,' i. e., the Halakot, only in the form used in our Sifra and Sifre, i. e., Midrash.

[5] N. Krochmal in *More Nebuke ha-Zeman*, porta XIII, (Lemberg, 1851), pp. 166–7; Z. Frankel in *Hodegetica in Mischnam*; Weiss, *Dor Dor we-Dorshaw* and *Mabo la-Mechilta*; Oppenheim, 'Toledot ha-Mishnah' in *Bet Talmud*, II; D. Hoffmann, *Die erste Mischna*, (Berlin, 1882); and others.

scriptural basis at all were likewise taught in this manner. The latter were taught in conjunction with some scriptural passage with which they could in some manner be connected, or together with certain written laws to which they were related, either as corollary or modification. (See D. Hoffmann, *Die erste Mischna*, [Berlin, 1882], pp. 5-7.) This procedure was necessary, because the only recognized authority was the written Book of the Law which the teachers used as their text-book in teaching. However, in teaching out of this text-book, they gave not only the meanings of words and the explanations of each written law, but also additional rules as well as modifications to some laws. All of this may be included in an exposition (מדרש) of the Torah and could properly be taught in connection with the text. Thus the Midrash-form could continue to be in exclusive use for teaching the Halakah, even after the latter, in the course of time, came to include traditional laws and customs, as well as new institutions and decrees issued and proclaimed by the teachers themselves in their capacity as religious authorities.[6]

The Mishnah-form, on the other hand, is of a much later date. It was introduced a long time after the Midrash-form[7]

---

[6] Weiss, *Mabo la-Mechilta*, p. iv, remarks about the Soferim: שבכלל תרגומם ופירושם למקרא כללו גם דברים אשר מקורם הגזירה והתיקון. Although the instance mentioned by him as proof for his statement is not a teaching of the Soferim (see below, note 55), yet the statement as such is correct. The Soferim or those who only taught in the Midrash-form could include in their teachings altogether new laws and decrees, issued by themselves as religious authorities, by connecting them with the scriptural laws. Only we may assume that it rarely happened that they taught a traditional law or a decree of their own merely in connection with some scriptural law. In most cases, the Soferim, who had charge of the text of the Books of the Law, could manage to indicate in the text itself, by means of certain signs and slight alterations, any traditional custom or decree of their own. Thus, these same decrees could be taught as interpretations of the written law. See N. Krochmal, *op. cit.*, p. 167. Cf. also below, notes 36 and 37.

[7] Georg Aicher (*Das Alte Testament in der Mischnah*, [Fr.-i.-Br., 1906], pp. 165 ff.) stands alone in the assumption that the Mishnah is older than the Midrash. This cannot be maintained. His statement (p. 64) that "the appearance of scriptural proof in connection with the Halakah was due to the radical changes effected by the catastrophe of the year 70," hardly needs any refutation. The many Halakot in the Midrash-form given by teachers in the time of the Temple as well as the disputes between the Sadducees and

and was used side by side with it. At no time did the Mishnah-form become the exclusive method for teaching the Halakah, because the Midrash never ceased to be in use.[8] At just what date this Mishnah-form was introduced, that is to say, just when the teachers of the Halakah began, for the first time, to teach Halakot independently of the Written Law, has, to my knowledge, not yet been ascertained. Sherira Gaon who, as we have seen, informs us that at some period in earlier times the Midrash-form was the only one in use, does not state exactly how long that period lasted, and does not mention when the Mishnah-form was introduced. Neither is there any other gaonic report to tell us when this happened.[9] Hoffmann (op. cit., pp. 12–13) states that, according to the views held by the Geonim, the Mishnah-form was first introduced in the days of Hillel and Shammai, but he fails to bring proof for this statement. To my knowledge, there is no foundation in gaonic literature for the views ascribed by Hoffmann to the Geonim. Hoffmann bases his theory on the spurious responsum found in *Shaare Teshubah*, § 20, and ascribed to Hai Gaon,[10] in which the following passage is found:

Pharisees, hinging upon different interpretations of scriptural passages as bases for their respective Halakah, ought to have shown Aicher to what extent Midrash was used before the year 70.

[8] We must emphasize this fact against the theory advanced by Weiss and Oppenheim and also by Jacob Bassfreund in his *Zur Redaction der Mischnah* (Trier, 1908), pp. 19–24, that there was a time when the Midrash-form was altogether abandoned, and the teachings of the Halakah given exclusively in Mishnah-form. We shall see that this theory is untenable (below, notes 15, 22, and 53).

[9] The account given in the letter of Sherira stops very abruptly. See the discussion at the end of this essay.

[10] This responsum had been added by some later hand to the responsa of Hai Gaon, but does not belong to the Gaon. Cf. Harkavy, *Studien und Mitteilungen*, IV, xiv. The fact that this report is repeated in *Seder Tannaim we-Amoraim* (Breslau, 1871), p. 29 and in *Sefer Hakanah*, p. 81b, and in S. Chinon's *Sefer Keritut*, Book *Yemot Olam* (Amsterdam, 1709), p. 20a does not in the least alter its legendary character and cannot make it more reliable, for the authors of all these works drew from one and the same source. This source cannot be of a more reliable character than the Midrash Abkir, from which the Yalḳut (Gen., sec. 42) quotes the statement that Methuselah studied 900 orders of Mishnah, משותלח צדיק גמור היה והיה שונה ט' מאות סדרי משנה.

דע מימות משה רבינו עד הלל הזקן היו שש מאות סדרי משנה כמו שנתנם
ה"ב"ה למשה בסיני ומן הלל ואילך נתמעט ונתמסכן העולם וחלשה כבודה של
תורה ולא תקנו מהלל ושמאי אלא ששה סדרים בלבד.

"Know, that from the days of Moses our Teacher until Hillel the Elder, there were six hundred orders of Mishnah just as God gave them to Moses on Sinai. However, from the time of Hillel on the world became impoverished, and the glory of the Law was diminished, so that, beginning with Hillel and Shammai, they arranged only six orders." It is evident that this responsum cannot be taken to represent a reliable gaonic tradition, as it is apparently based on the haggadic passage in Ḥag. 14a, and is accordingly of merely legendary character. Aside from this, the passage does not say what Hoffmann has read into it. It does not even deal with the origin of the Mishnah-form. If anything, we can see from this responsum that its author, quite to the contrary, assumed that the Mishnah-form was very old, and that it was given to Moses on Sinai.[11] He deals merely with the origin of six orders of Mishnah which he assumed to have been extant in the days of Hillel and Shammai. These six orders were in his opinion but a poor small remnant of the six hundred orders which Moses received from God on Sinai and which were extant till the days of Hillel when the world became impoverished and the glory of the Torah diminished. Hoffmann arrives at his interpretation of this responsum by arbitrarily giving two different meanings to one and the same term used by the author twice in one sentence. He states (p. 13) that when the Gaon speaks of the "six hundred orders of Mishnah," he is using the term "Mish-

[11] The belief that the Mishnah was given to Moses on Sinai is repeatedly expressed in the Haggadah. See b. Ber. 5a and p. Ḥag. 1.8 (76d). In the Pirḳe deR. Eliezer, 46, it is said that during the forty days which Moses spent on the mountain, receiving the Law, he studied the Scriptures (מקרא) in the daytime and Mishnah at night. In Pesiḳta Rabbati 5, Friedmann, p. 14b it is said that Moses wished to have the Mishnah written, but God told him that in order to distinguish Israel from other nations it was better that the Mishnah should be given to Israel orally, so that the other nations should not be able to claim it for themselves. See also Tanḥuma, *Ki-Tissa* Buber, pp. 58b and 59a, and p. Ḥag., *loc. cit.* The author of our responsum had as his authority such haggadic sayings when he spoke of the Mishnah which God gave to Moses on Sinai.

nah" in a broad sense to designate traditional law in the Midrash-form and not in the Mishnah-form, but when the Gaon speaks of the reduced "six orders" extant in the days of Hillel and Shammai, he uses the term "Mishnah" in a narrow sense to designate only independent Halakot in the Mishnah-form. This distinction is extremely arbitrary. Furthermore, when Hoffmann concludes his argument with the remark (*ibid.*, p. 13) that "No doubt the six orders of Mishnah introduced in the days of Hillel and Shammai were, like our present Mishnah, composed in the form of independent Halakah, and by this *new form* were distinguished from the earlier form of teaching," he no longer gives the views of the author of the responsum, but his own. And these views are absolutely wrong.[12]

Thus we see that there is no mention in gaonic literature,[13] of the time when this innovation in the form of teaching the Halakah took place. Neither is there any report in talmudic[14] or gaonic sources about the cause of this innovation. We are not told why it was necessary or desirable to introduce a new form of teaching Halakah alongside of the older Midrash-form.

---

[12] There is no doubt that at the time of Hillel and Shammai there were no Mishnah-collections like our Mishnah. The responsum in *Shaare Teshubah*, § 187, which tells us that when a certain Gaon died they found that he had the six orders of the Mishnah of the days of Hillel and Shammai, which had been hidden away, is spurious and legendary. See S. D. Luzzatto, *Beth ha-Ozar*, pp. 55b–56a. Although there were in the times of Hillel and Shammai collections of Halakot composed in Mishnah-form, this form was not new to them and could not be the characteristic which distinguished them from the form of teaching used before. For, as we shall see, there had been even before Hillel and Shammai collections of independent Halakot in the Mishnah-form. And if Hillel himself composed a Mishnah-collection, he did not arrange it in order, and did not divide it into tractates as Pineles (*Darkah shel Torah*, pp. 8–9) and Bassfreund (*Zur Redaction der Mischnah*, p. 25) assume. The arguments brought forward by the latter to prove that Hillel's Mishnah-collection was arranged and divided into tractates are not convincing.

[13] On Saadya's opinion see further below.

[14] There is, however, as we shall see in the course of this essay, a report in the Talmud stating until when the Midrash-form was in exclusive use. This talmudic report has been overlooked or else not correctly understood, for not one of the scholars dealing with the problem of fixing the date of the beginning of the Mishnah-form has referred to it.

Modern scholars have attempted to answer these questions; both to fix the date and to give the reasons for this innovation in the method of teaching. However, the various theories advanced by these scholars are all unsatisfactory. They are the result of mere guess-work — without solid proof or valid foundation. It will be shown that some are based upon inaccurate reasoning, and all of them are in contradiction to certain established historic facts.

We have already seen that the theory which Hoffmann ascribes to the Geonim has no foundation in gaonic literature and that it is altogether Hoffmann's theory. But, no matter whose it is, the theory itself cannot be maintained.[15] In the first place, there were Mishnah-collections before the time of Hillel and Shammai, as Rosenthal has proved (*Ueber den Zusammenhang der Mischna*, Erster Teil, 2te Aufl., [Strassburg, 1909]). In the second place, the introduction of a new form necessarily precedes any collection of Halakot composed in this new form. It must be quite plain that there were individual, detached Halakot taught in the Mishnah-form (and not in the Midrash-form) before any collection of such detached Halakot could be made. Accordingly, if we assume with Rosenthal (*op. cit.*, p. 111) that a collection of such independent Halakot in the Mishnah-form was already arranged in the time of Simeon ben Shetaḥ, we have to go still farther back in fixing the time when the teachers first began to separate the Halakah from its scriptural proof and teach it independently, as Mishnah. This would bring us to about one hundred years before the time of Hillel and Shammai. Not only is this theory of Hoffmann wrong in respect to the date given for the introduction of the Mishnah-form, but it is also unsatisfactory in regard to the cause of this innovation.

---

[15] Cf. also Bassfreund (*op. cit.*, pp. 18 ff.) who likewise seeks to refute Hoffmann's theory. Some of Bassfreund's arguments, however, are not sound. He is altogether wrong in assuming that for a long time before Hillel the Mishnah was the exclusive form used in the teaching of the Halakah, and that Hillel was the first to reintroduce the Midrash-form. He confuses the development of the Midrash methods which were furthered by Hillel with the use of the Midrash-form which had no need of being introduced by Hillel since it was never abandoned (see above, note 8, and below, note 22).

According to this theory, the Mishnah-form was introduced in order to assist the memory in mastering the contents of the traditional Law.[16] However, it is difficult to see how the teachers could have considered the new form of greater aid to the memory than the old form. This new form is on the contrary quite apt to make it more difficult for the memory. It seems to us that it is less of a task for the memory to retain Halakot taught in the Midrash-form. The Written Law, being the text-book, each passage in it, as it is being read, helps, by mental association, to recall all the halakic teachings based upon it. On the other hand, it is much harder to remember detached Halakot given in an independent form, especially when they are not arranged systematically or topically but merely grouped together. This, we must keep in mind, was actually the mode of arrangement used in the earlier Mishnah collections.[17]

Hoffmann himself must have felt that this theory was not satisfactory, for later in his book he advances another and altogether different theory (op. cit., p. 48). According to this second theory, the innovation was not made for the purpose of aiding the memory, and was not made in the days of Hillel and Shammai. Here Hoffmann assumes that the Mishnah-form was first introduced in the days of the later disciples of Hillel and Shammai. The purpose of the innovation, he explains, was to maintain the unity of the Halakah by minimizing the differences of opinion and eliminating the disputes about the halakic teachings which arose among these very disciples of Hillel and Shammai. These disputes, Hoffmann tells us, were in many cases only formal, namely, concerning the underlying Midrash or the

[16] The same reason is also given by Frankel and Weiss. They all seem to have been influenced by the haggadic sayings found in the Talmud, sayings which exaggerate the number of Halakot known to former generations.

[17] Hoffmann makes the mistake of assuming (op. cit., pp. 13, 15, and 48) that simultaneously with the separation of the Halakot from their scriptural basis came the grouping of such detached Halakot into orders and treatises, as we have them. But this is absolutely wrong. The earlier Mishnah went through many different forms of grouping before it was finally arranged according to subjects and divided into treatises and orders. See the writer's article in the *Jewish Encyclopaedia*, VII, 611. The opinions expressed by the writer there on p. 610 (following Hoffmann) are hereby retracted.

scriptural proof for the halakic teaching. The traditional Halakah, as such, was agreed upon by all the teachers. That is to say, there was no dispute about the transmitted rules and decisions which all the teachers received alike. The teachers, however, often did disagree as to the scriptural passages and their interpretations whereon these received halakic decisions were based. One teacher would derive a certain Halakah by interpreting a given passage in a certain manner. Another teacher would deduce the same Halakah from another passage, or even from the same passage but by means of another interpretation. Thus, as long as the Halakah was taught only in Midrash-form there existed many differences of opinion between the teachers, not in regard to the halakic decisions or rules in themselves but in regard to their midrashic proof and support. The teachers of those days who were very anxious to maintain harmony among themselves and unanimity in their teachings therefore decided to separate the Halakah from the Midrash and to teach it independently of the scriptural proof or support. In other words, they introduced the Mishnah-form — the Halakah as an independent branch of learning. By this innovation all the differences of opinion and disputes about the midrashic proof necessarily disappeared. Thus uniformity was restored in teaching the Halakah, and harmony was established among the teachers.

This second theory of Hoffmann is even less tenable than the first. In the first place, it fixes the date for the introduction of the Mishnah even later than the first theory. Consequently, in this respect it is refuted by the same arguments that were brought against the first theory. We have seen above that there were Halakot in Mishnah-form, even collections of such Halakot, at a much earlier date. Furthermore, the explanation of the cause for the innovation put forth in this theory presents a palpable error in reasoning. It presupposes that the decisions of the Halakah, as such, were older than their midrashic connection with the Scriptures, and that at some earlier time they had been transmitted independently of scriptural proofs. For this reason the teachers could well be unanimous in accepting the Halakah and yet find cause for dispute as to methods of proving certain halakic decisions from the scripture by means of the Midrash.

But this means nothing else than that there were some Mishnahs, that is, independent Halakot before the disputes about the scriptural proofs caused their separation from the Midrash. This line of reasoning contradicts itself. It sets out to find the cause for the first introduction of the Mishnah-form, but assumes that before this introduction some Halakot had already been transmitted in Mishnah-form. In other words, this so-called first introduction was really not a first introduction.

If they had taught only in Midrash-form, the alleged evil results which the Mishnah-form, according to Hoffmann, was to remedy could never have arisen. It would have been impossible for the teachers to agree upon a halakic decision, and at the same time to disagree about its scriptural proof. Since every teacher received each Halakah in the same Midrash-form, that is, as an interpretaton of, or connected with, a certain scriptural passage, every one who remembered the decision must have remembered the form in which he received it, that is, the scriptural passage with which it was connected. It is very improbable that a teacher remembering the decision, but having forgotten the scriptural basis, would have supplied another scriptural proof therefor, and then disputed with his colleagues who remembered the right passage on which this Halakah was based. If he did forget the passage for which the Halakah was an interpretation, the mere mention of that passage by his colleagues must have brought it back to his memory. It is evident that there could be no universal acceptance of a Halakah together with disputes regarding its proofs, unless such a Halakah had been taught apart from its proof. This, however, was not done, as long as the Midrash-form was in exclusive use, that is, as long as the Halakah was merely taught as a commentary on the text of the Law.[18]

[18] This would hold true even if we should believe in the genuineness of the so-called הלכות למשה מסיני, that is, that there had been given oral laws to Moses on Sinai and transmitted independently of the written law. For, as Hoffmann himself states (*op. cit.*, p. 7), even all the traditional teachings were taught together with the scriptural laws and connected with them in the Midrash-form. All through the period of the Soferim, and according to Hoffmann till the time of the disciples of Hillel and Shammai, such traditional laws would somehow be connected with the Scriptures. The mental

Quite as unsatisfactory is the theory advanced by Z. Frankel (*Hodegetica in Mischnam*, pp. 6, 7, and 10). According to this theory, the innovation of teaching detached Halakah in the Mishnah-form was made by the last group of Soferim.[19] This was done to overcome three difficulties which Frankel tells us existed in those days. In the first place, the halakic decisions based upon the individual passages had increased to such an extent that the task of studying and teaching them in the Midrash-form became very difficult. In the second place, the absence of inner logical connection between the individual dicta of the Halakah made its study a work of mere mechanical memorizing — a very tiresome and repulsive procedure for the intelligent student. In the third place, the Pentateuch gives the laws pertaining to one subject in many different places. As the Midrash follows the Pentateuchal order, there could be no systematic presentation of

---

attitude of the teachers was not in the direction of separating such traditional laws from the scriptural passages with which they had for centuries been connected. This would have remained their attitude even if they had realized that such a connection was merely artificial (see below, note 27). No differences of opinion were therefore possible as to how such traditional laws were to be connected with the Scripture.

It should be noted that Hoffmann seems to have subsequently abandoned both his theories. In his introduction to his translation of the Mishnah, Seder Nezikin (p. x, note 3), he states that according to the Palestinian Talmud the so-called Number-Mishnahs were already compiled and redacted by the men of the Great Synagogue. He refers to the passage in Shek. 5 (48c), which, like Weiss and Oppenheim, he misinterprets. See below, note 26.

[19] N. Krochmal (*op. cit.*, pp. 174–5) also assumes that even the last of the Soferim began to teach independent Halakot (so also Pineles, *Darkah shel Torah*, pp. 8–9). Like Frankel, Krochmal also gives as the reason the increased number of the Halakot and new decisions which could no longer be connected with the Scripture in the form of the Midrash. There is, however, a great difference of opinion between Krochmal and Frankel as to dates. Krochmal extends the period of the Soferim until about 200 B. C. E., assuming that the Simon mentioned in Abot as 'one of the last survivors of the Great Synagogue' is Simon II, the son of Onias II. Krochmal therefore designates him as the last of the Soferim and the first of the Mishnah teachers, the Tannaim (*op. cit.*, p. 166). According to Frankel, the last member of the Great Synagogue was Simon the Just I, about 300 B. C. E. This Simon, then, was the last of the Soferim in whose days the Mishnah was introduced (*Hodegetica*, pp. 68 and 30–31).

all the laws on any one subject. The laws on one subject, for instance, Sabbath, being derived from widely separated passages in the Pentateuch, had to be taught piecemeal, each decision in connection with its scriptural basis. For all these reasons, Frankel tells us, the last group of the Soferim decided to separate the Halakot from their scriptural bases and to teach them in the new Mishnah-form systematically arranged according to subjects.

Like Hoffmann, Frankel assumes that the plan of arranging the Halakot according to subject-matter was coincident with the very introduction of the Mishnah-form, so that the very earliest Mishnah collections must have been arranged topically. This, as we have seen, is incorrect. The topical arrangement of the Mishnah is of later date. It was preceded by other forms of grouping peculiar to the earlier Mishnah collections. Frankel himself credits R. Akiba with the systematic arrangement of Halakah according to topics (*op. cit.*, p. 115). He also qualifies by the following remarks his former statement concerning the Soferim and their arrangement of the Halakah according to subjects: "We have stated in the preceding chapter that the teaching [of the Halakah] according to subjects began at the end of the period of the Soferim. Nevertheless, a long time undoubtedly passed before all [the Halakot] that belonged to one subject were brought together under one heading. Very often while dealing with one subject they would [not keep strictly to it but] drift to another and pass from one halakic theme to another.... R. Akiba, however, began to arrange the old Halakot to put each in its proper place and [under the topic] to which it belonged."[20] If, however, the order in the Mishnah before R. Akiba was not strictly according to subjects, as Frankel here admits, and if some Halakot bearing on one subject would often be treated among Halakot dealing with another subject, what advantage was there then in separating the Halakot from the Midrash and teaching them in the Mishnah-form? The shortcomings of the Midrash-form, according to Frankel, consisted

[20] והנה כבר כתבנו בפרק הקודם כי לימוד ע״פ העניינים התחיל סוף ימי הסופרים, אבל בלתי ספק עברו ימים רבים טרם נאספו כל השייכים אל עניין אחד תחת דגל אחד, והרבה פעמים בעסקם בעניין זה נמשכו מעניין לעניין ומהלכה להלכה... ור״ע החל לסדר ההלכות הישנות על מכונן וגבולם.

in the fact that the Halakot of one subject could not be taught connectedly but were interrupted by Halakot belonging to another subject. However, according to Frankel's own statement, the same defect was inherent in the Mishnah-form up to the time of Akiba.

Taking up another statement of Frankel, it seems difficult to realize why the study of the written laws together with all the Halakot derived from them, as is done in the Midrash-form, should be such dry mechanical work of the memory, and so repulsive to the intelligent student. One would be inclined to think that the study of the Halakot in the abstract Mishnah-form, especially when not arranged systematically, would indeed be a far more mechanical work and far more tiresome for the student. Again, according to Frankel, it was the alleged lack of inner logical connection between the single Halakot which made the Midrash-form inadequate for teaching purposes. However, this absence of inner logical connection is merely alleged by Frankel, but not proved. If we should even grant that in the Midrash-form the Halakot were not always logically connected and coherently presented, the earlier Mishnah certainly did not remedy this evil. The earlier Mishnah collections were characterized by the most arbitrary modes of arrangement. Halakot bearing upon different themes and altogether unrelated in subject-matter were often grouped together under artificial formulas. Examples of these earlier modes of arrangement have been preserved even in the present form of our Mishnah as, for instance, in the so-called Number-Mishnahs or the En-ben-Mishnahs. The Midrash-form certainly established a better connection between the individual Halakot than did these earlier arrangements of the Mishnah. The mere fact that many Halakot belong to one and the same chapter or are grouped around one and the same passage of the Scriptures, establishes a better connection between them than the accident that they can all be presented under one formula.

Aside from all these arguments, the fundamental position of Frankel can hardly be maintained. In the time of the last group of the Soferim, the halakic material could not have grown to such an extent as to make it impossible to use the Midrash-form and necessitate the innovation of a new form of teaching. The mere volume of the halakic material could by no means have brought about this change of form. This is evident from the fact that our halakic Midrashim, Sifra, Sifre, and Mekilta, present in Midrash-form a mass of halakic material far greater in volume than was extant in the days of the Soferim. Thus we see that all the reasons which Frankel gives for the introduction of the Mishnah-form are insufficient and could not have been the cause of the innovation.

In conclusion, Frankel's admission that the teachers continued to use the Midrash-form even after the introduction of the Mishnah-form[21] is the strongest refutation of his own theory. If the Midrash-form had so many disadvantages, if it was both tiresome for the student and inadequate for presenting the Halakot systematically, why was it not altogether abandoned? How did the new form obviate the evils of the old form if the latter continued in use?

The theory propounded by Weiss in his *Mabo la-Mekilta*, pp. iv and v, and in his *Dor*, I, 66, is somewhat of an improvement upon the ideas of Frankel. Like Frankel, he believes that the Mishnah-form was introduced by the later Soferim, and that the reason for this change was the large increase of halakic material. He avoids two of the mistakes that Frankel made. In the first place, he does not confuse the innovation of teaching detached Halakot in the form of Mishnah with the arrangement of the latter according to subjects. Nor does he assume that the Midrash-form continued in use, after the Mishnah-form was introduced. According to Weiss, the Midrash-form was abandoned because it prove inadequate. It was hard for the student to remember the great mass of Halakot that existed at that time, when taught in the Midrash-form. The teachers, therefore, felt the need of inventing another form which would help the memory retain the increased number of halakic teachings. This help for the memory they found in separating the Halakot from their scriptural bases and in expressing them in short, concise phraseology, and in arranging them according to a number-formula.

[21] *Op. cit.*, p. 7, he says: ודע כי אף שבירדו להם דרך לעצמם בענין הלכה לא עזבו דרך הראשונים לגמרי אבל חיברו גם הם מאמרים למקרא.

The saying of Simon the Just, "The world rests upon *three* things, etc." (Ab. 1.2), and the three Halakot mentioned in 'Eduy. 8.4, which according to Weiss are soferic Halakot, merely reported by Jose ben Joezer, are cited by Weiss in support of his theory that the Soferim taught detached Halakot expressed in concise terms and arranged according to number formulas. Weiss (*Mabo la-Mekilta*, p. v, note 7) admits, however, that the innovation was unsuccessful. The teachers, he tells us, soon found that the Mishnah-form, although superior to the Midrash, in being more easily memorized, had many other disadvantages. As a result, they had to return to the older form of the Midrash after they had abandoned it for a time.[22]

This admission of Weiss that the advantages expected from the new form were not realized, is in itself a strong argument against his theory. Further, we have seen above that the necessity for aiding the memory could not have been the reason for introducing the Mishnah-form. The words of the scriptural text with which the Halakot were connected in the Midrash-form offered sufficient help to the memory. We have also seen above that in the days of the Soferim the halakic material was not so large as to necessitate new forms and arrangements. The Soferim never gave their teachings in any other form but in the Midrash, namely, as interpretations and additions to the written laws. They never arranged them in any other way except in the order

[22] In this assumption, that the Midrash-form had for a long time been abandoned and supplanted by the Mishnah, and that later on objections to the Mishnah-form caused a return to the Midrash, Weiss is followed by Oppenheim ("Ha-Zuggot we-ha-Eshkolot" in *Hashaḥar*, VII, 114 and 116), and by Bassfreund (see above, note 15). It is strange that while these scholars cannot account satisfactorily for one change that really took place, namely, from the exclusive use of the Midrash to the admission of the Mishnah-form, they assume another change which never took place, namely, a return from a supposed temporary exclusive use of the Mishnah to the old Midrash. We have already seen that the Mishnah-form was never in exclusive use, for the Midrash continued to be used side by side with it. Consequently there could have been no return from Mishnah to Midrash. But we shall see that the very reason which Weiss, Oppenheim, and Bassfreund give for the return to the Midrash, namely, the opposition of the Sadducees, was rather the cause for the further departure from the Midrash-form and the extension of the use of the Mishnah-form (see below, notes 72 and 73).

of the scriptural passages to which they belonged. The two passages, cited by Weiss, do not refute this statement. The saying of Simon the Just in Abot is not a halakic teaching but a maxim of the same character as the other wisdom literature of that time. We can draw no conclusions from it as to the form of halakic teachings of that day. As for the three Halakot mentioned in 'Eduyot, these will later be shown to have been the decisions of Jose ben Joezer himself. Consequently they do not prove anything concerning the form of halakic teaching used by the Soferim.

Oppenheim[23] offers a theory that is in reality but a combination of the views examined above. However, he makes a very correct observation concerning the date of the innovation. According to Oppenheim, the Mishnah-form was first introduced during or immediately after the Maccabean uprising. As a result of the persecutions incident to the Maccabean revolution, the study of the law was neglected and the knowledge of it decreased. The teachers, therefore, decided to separate the Halakot from their scriptural bases and to teach them independently, in order to save them from oblivion ("Toledot ha-Mishnah," in *Bet Talmud*, II, 145). They chose this form either because they thought that in this form it would be easier for the student to remember the Halakot, or because they, the teachers themselves, no longer remembered the scriptural bases for many Halakot.

The first of these two reasons is identical with the one given by Frankel and by Weiss, which has been found insufficient. The second one is similar to the one given in Hoffmann's second theory, and, as we have seen, is not plausible. For, if they had not previously studied Mishnah but received the Halakot only together with their scriptural bases, it is hardly possible that the teachers could forget the latter and yet remember the former. The remembered Halakot would have recalled to them the scriptural passages in connection with which they were received.

It seems that Oppenheim himself felt that neither his own nor Frankel's nor Weiss's theory was sufficient to solve the problem. He therefore offered another solution of the problem, and this is

[23] "Toledot ha-Mishnah" in *Bet Talmud*, II, 145, and also in his "Ha-Zuggot we-ha-Eshkolot" in *HaShaḥar*, VII, 114–15.

practically a denial of the fact that there is a problem. After stating that the Soferim taught in the Midrash-form and those who followed them introduced the new form of abstract Halakot, that is Mishnah, he contradicts himself by adding the following remark:[24] "But in my opinion there is no doubt that the Soferim who taught [the Halakah] as a commentary on the Scriptures [i. e., Midrash] also taught independent Halakot." He then proceeds to prove that the Soferim had independent or abstract Halakot in the form of Mishnah.[25] According to this statement there is no problem at all. We need not account for any change in the form of teaching Halakah or explain the reasons for the innovation of the Mishnah, for there was no change and no innovation. The two forms, Midrash and Mishnah, were evidently used together from the earliest times, the Midrash possibly to a larger extent than the Mishnah. This would indeed be the best solution of the problem and would remove all difficulties. The only obstacle in the way of its adoption is that it is contradicted by all historic reports. It is against the tradition that in earlier times all the teachings of the Halakah were given in the Midrash-form only. This tradition, we have seen, is indicated in the discussion of Jose and Hezekiah mentioned in the Palestinian Talmud (Moed Ḳaṭan) and is expressly mentioned by Sherira Gaon.

[24] ולדעתי אין כל ספק כי הסופרים אשר אחזו בפירוש המקראות גם מן ההלכות לא הניחו ידם, "Ha-Zuggot we ha-Eshkolot," loc. cit., p. 114.

[25] This is also the stand taken by Halevi who goes even further and maintains (Doroth ha-Rishonim, I, xiv, 204 ff.) that in the main our Mishnah had already been composed and arranged by the Soferim, but he does not prove his statements. At the most, his arguments could only prove that there had been many Halakot and decisions in the days of the Soferim, and that the earliest Tannaim in our Mishnah in their discussions seek to define and explain these older Halakot and decisions. But it does not follow that these Halakot and decisions were already in the days of the Soferim composed in the Mishnah-form. These Halakot and decisions were originally given in the Midrash-form, as definitions or interpretations of written laws. The later teachers, that is, the earlier Tannaim, discussed and commented upon these decisions and Halakot of their predecessors which they had before them in Midrash-form. Later on, when these decisions and Halakot became separated from the Midrash, they were arranged in the Mishnah-collections as independent Halakot, together with all the comments and explanations given to them by the Tannaim, and in this form they are also found contained in our Mishnah

It is also out of harmony with the generally accepted opinion that the Soferim, as the name implies, imparted all their teachings only in connection with the written book of the Law. It is, further, against an absolutely reliable report in the Babylonian Talmud which, as we shall see, tells us not only that the older form of teaching the Halakah was the Midrash, but also gives us the period of time during which it was in exclusive use.

Thus we see that all these theories examined above have not succeeded in finding a real solution for our problem. None of the theories have given the exact time or the real cause for the introduction of the Mishnah-form.

Probably the strangest feature of the problem is the silence of the talmudic literature about this important innovation. This silence is all the more remarkable when we come to realize that this was not merely a change in form, but an innovation that had great influence upon the development of the Halakah and had great bearing upon the validity of its authority.

The theory proposed in this essay offers what appears to us to be a satisfactory solution for this many-sided problem. In the first place it determines the exact time when the innovation of teaching independent Halakot was introduced. In the second place it describes the conditions that compelled the teachers to make so radical a change. And finally it explains why no explicit report is preserved in talmudic sources regarding this great development in the teachings of the Halakah. This theory I shall now propound.

II

We have seen above that the name "Soferim" designates a class of people who occupied themselves with "the Book" and taught from that "Book" alone. This name has been applied to the earliest teachers of the Halakah, because they imparted all their teachings in connection with the Book of the Law, either as an exposition of it or as a commentary on it, that is to say in the form of the Midrash. This, we have seen, is asserted by tradition and agreed upon by almost all the modern scholars. There is absolutely no reason for assuming that any of the teachers belonging to the group of the Soferim, whether the earlier or later, departed from this peculiar method of teaching. For the name Soferim was given to the teachers because of this method of teaching and continued in use only as long as they adhered exclusively to this method. As soon as the teachers ceased to occupy themselves exclusively with the Book of the Law and its exposition and began to teach abstract Halakot also, the name applied to them was no longer Soferim but "Shonē Halakot" or Tannaim (see especially J. Brüll, *Mebo ha-Mishnah*, [Frankfurt a. M., 1876], II, 2). The haggadic saying of Rabbi Abahu[26] (in p. Shek. 5.1, [48c]) which Weiss and Oppenheim cite as a proof of their contention that the Soferim taught abstract Halakot in the Mishnah-form, does not refer to the Soferim at all. It does not say anything about their methods or form of teaching. It refers to the Kenites, who in I Chron. 2.55 are identified with the families of Soferim, the inhabitants of Yabez, the Tir'atim, the Shim'atim, and Sukatim. In all these names the Haggadah seeks to find attributes for the Kenites, indicating some of their peculiar characteristics. R. Abahu here gives an haggadic interpretation of the name Soferim applied to the Kenites in the same fanciful manner as the other names, Tir'atim, Shim'atim, and Sukatim are interpreted in Sifre, Numbers 78 (Friedmann 20a).

Oppenheim advances still another argument to prove that the Soferim taught abstract Halakot. Since many of the traditional laws designated as הלכה למשה מסיני must have been transmitted by the Soferim, it follows (so Oppenheim) that the Soferim taught independent traditional laws in Mishnah-form. This is not at all convincing. Granted that there were such unwritten laws handed down from Moses to the Soferim, and that

---

[26] The passage in p. Shekalim reads as follows: אמר ר' אבהו כתיב ומשפחות סופרים יושבי יעבץ מה תלמוד לומר סופרים אלא שעשו את התורה ספורות ספורות, ה' לא יתרומו חמשה דברים חייבים בחלה, וגו'.

Weiss (*Dor*, I, 66) refers to this saying in the words: והטיבו אשר דברו בזה חכמי התלמוד (ירוש' שקלים) שהסופרים עשו את התורה ספורות, and Oppenheim (*HaShaḥar*, VII, 114) states: ובירושלמי אמר ר' אבהו שהיו קורין אותן סופרים לפי שעשו את התורה ספורות ספורות כגון ה' לא יתרומו וגו'. Both of them erroneously take this haggadic saying as a characterization of the methods of the Soferim and as a reason for their name.

these formed part of their religious teachings, it does not necessarily follow that these traditional teachings were given in the Mishnah-form. They could as well have been given as additional laws in the Midrash-form, together with the scriptural passages with which they had some sort of relation, though not based on or derived from them.[27] It is therefore absolutely certain that the change in the form from Midrash to Mishnah was not made during the period of the Soferim.

The period of the Soferim came to an end with Simon the Just I about 300–270 B. C. E. In Ab. 1.2 he is designated as being "of the last survivors of the men of the great Synagogue," which means that he was the last of the Soferim. During the time of this Simon the Just I, who still belonged to the Soferim, there could have been no Mishnah. We have, therefore, to look for the origin of the Mishnah-form in the times after Simon I, that is, after 270 B. C. E. We have thus gained at least this much. We have fixed the *terminus a quo*, the beginning of the period during which the innovation of the Mishnah-form could have been made. We have now to find the *terminus ad quem*, namely, the last possible date for the introduction. In seeking to determine this latter date, the only proper way would be to find the oldest authentic Halakah mentioned in talmudic literature without its scriptural proof, that is, in the Mishnah-form. In determining the date when such a Halakah was given, we shall *eo ipso* have determined the date when the change in the form had already been made and the Mishnah-form was already in use. This seems to be the simplest and only logical method of procedure. Strange as it may seem, this method has not been followed by any of the scholars who have attempted to solve our problem.

[27] If, for instance, the regulations about the color of the thongs and the form of the knot of the phylacteries were traditional laws given to Moses on Sinai, הל"מס, as is claimed by some of the Rabbis of the Talmud (Men. 35a,b), these could have been nevertheless taught together with the passage in Deut. 6.8. The teachers could have stated that the commandment "and thou shalt bind them" is explained by tradition to mean, first, to tie them only with black thongs, רצועות שחורות; and second, that the phylacteries must be square, מרובעות; also that the knot must be of a certain shape; and lastly, that the letter, Shin, ש, must be impressed on the outside, etc., etc.

The first teacher in whose name we have independent Halakot is Jose b. Joezer,[28] who died about 165 B. C. E.[29] The sayings of Simon the Just and Antigonos (Ab. 1.2, and 3) are merely wisdom maxims and not halakic teachings. Connected with the name of Jose, however, we have three halakic decisions mentioned without any scriptural proof, i. e., in Mishnah-form (Mishnah 'Eduy. 8.4). The authenticity of these Halakot is not to be doubted. They are certainly decisions given by Jose ben Joezer.[30] In the form in which they are preserved they have

[28] Frankel's statement, כי הלל ושמאי הם הראשונים אשר שמם באו הלכות במשנה ובברייתא, that "Hillel and Shammai were the first teachers in whose name Halakot are mentioned in the Mishnah and Baraita" (*Hodegetica*, p. 38) is, to say the least, surprising. We find Halakot from all the four preceding Zuggot. Thus a Halakah is mentioned in the name of Shemaiah and Abtalion concerning the quantity of "drawn water" (מים שאובים) that is sufficient to disqualify the Miḳwah ('Eduy. 1.3), not to mention the Halakot in regard to the slaughtering of the Passover sacrifice on Sabbath which Hillel is said to have received from them and taught in their name (p. Pes. 33a and b. Pes. 66a). Simon b. Sheṭaḥ mentions a law in the name of the חכמים in regard to the punishment of false witnesses (Mak. 5b). From Joshua b. Peraḥia we have a Halakah in regard to wheat brought from Alexandria (Tosefta Maksh. 3.4), and in the name of Jose b. Joezer we have the three Halakot (Mishnah 'Eduy. 8.4).

[29] The date of Jose's death can only be approximated. He died when Alcimus was still in power (see Genesis r. 65.22). Probably he was among the sixty men whom the Syrian general Bacchides killed at the instigation of Alcimus (I Mac. 7.16). Alcimus died 160 B. C. E. (see Büchler in the *Jewish Encyclopaedia*, I, 332–3).

[30] Jose b. Joezer's authorship of these Halakot was first questioned by Dr. Jacob Levy in *Oẓar Neḥmad*, III, 29. In the course of his discussion, however, Levy arrives at the conclusion that these Halakot were really given by Jose b. Joezer of Ẓeredah. Following Levy's first suggestion, Graetz (*Monatsschrift*, 1869, pp. 30–31) and after him Büchler (*Die Priester und der Cultus*, p. 63) assume that these three Halakot belong to some later teacher whose name was likewise Jose b. Joezer, although such a teacher is otherwise not known. There is, however, no necessity for seeking any other author than the well-known Jose b. Joezer of Ẓeredah who is expressly mentioned in our sources. The fancied difficulties of ascribing the decisions to Jose b. Joezer of Ẓeredah disappear on close examination. The main difficulty is said to be the difference in time between the date of Jose and the date of the Eduyot-collection. How could Jose b. Joezer of Ẓeredah, who died before 160 B. C. E., have testified before the teachers in Jabneh about 100 C. E. on that memorable day when Gamaliel II was deposed from the presidency, and when according to a talmudic report (Ber. 27b) the Eduyot collection was arranged? Were

already been taught by his colleagues or disciples. Thus we find that in the last days of Jose b. Joezer or soon after his death some Halakot were already taught without any scriptural proof, that is, in the Mishnah-form. Accordingly we have found the *terminus ad quem* for the innovation of the Mishnah-form.

We now pass to a consideration of the particular point of time in this period when the new form was introduced. We have good reasons for believing that these decisions of Jose are not only the first mentioned, but in all likelihood the first ever taught in Mishnah-form. Indeed, a reliable report in the Talmud, as well as certain indications in gaonic traditions, points to the last days of Jose as the time when the change in the form of teaching was made. This talmudic report is given in Tem. 15b by Samuel, but it is undoubtedly an older tradition which Samuel merely reported. It reads as follows: כל אשכולות שעמדו להן לישראל מימות משה עד שמת[31] (ימות?) יוסי בן יועזר היו למדין תורה כמשה רבינו מכאן ואילך לא היו למדין תורה כמשה רבינו "All the teachers who arose in Israel from the days of Moses until the death, (or the last

---

this a real difficulty, it could easily be removed by assuming with Levy (*op. cit.*, p. 36) that the word משום "in the name of" was left out in our Mishnah, and that the text ought to read העיד משום רבי יוסי בן יועזר איש צרידה, "a teacher testified in the name of Jose b. Joezer of Ẓeredah." However, no real difficulty exists. The theory that all of the Halakot contained in our Eduyot collection are testimonies that were deposed before the teachers at the assembly at Jabneh, cannot be maintained. Our Eduyot collection contains other Halakot than those testified to before the assembly at Jabneh. It contains also Halakot that were not even discussed at that assembly. To the latter class belong the three Halakot of Jose b. Joezer (see H. Klueger, *Ueber Genesis und Composition der Halakoth-Sammlung Eduyoth* [Breslau, 1895]). It is not necessary to assume, as Klueger (*loc. cit.*, p. 84) does, that these decisions had been found in written form in the archives. These Halakot were simply known to the teachers just as the other sayings and teachings of the Zuggot were known to them. They had been transmitted orally and studied by heart, and at the time when the Eduyot collection was composed or redacted, these three Halakot were incorporated in it. Cf. also Hoffmann in his commentary on Mishnah Eduyot, *ad loc.*

The other difficulties in these three Halakot will be considered later in the course of this essay, when we come to the discussion of the Halakot themselves.

[31] The correction suggested by Graetz (*Monatsschrift*, 1869, p. 23) to read עד ימות יוסי "till the days of Jose," instead of עד שמת יוסי "till Jose died," is very plausible.

days,) of Jose b. Joezer studied the Torah as Moses did, but afterwards they did not study the Torah as Moses did." The discussion that follows in the Talmud endeavors to explain the meaning of this report. We learn that the report was not understood to mean that the teachers until the time of Jose's death were in possession of as many laws as Moses had. Nor was it understood to say that they were all of one opinion and had no doubtful or disputed Halakot. The report, so the discussion ends, can only be understood to say that they taught in the same manner in which Moses taught, מיגמר הוו גמירי להו כמשה.

We are not told what this method was and what it means to study or teach in the manner of Moses, but it is evident that this method can only be the Midrash-form. To give all the Halakot as interpretation of the written word means to study or teach like Moses did. Assuming, as the Rabbis did, that all the interpretations given in the Midrash are correct explanations and definitions of the Written Law, all the teachings given in the Midrash-form were really contained in the words of Moses. And Moses must have taught them in the same manner in which they are taught in the Midrash. For Moses must have read to the people the written laws and interpreted the full meaning of each and explained each passage or each word of the Torah. That the phrase "to study in the manner of Moses" is used to indicate the Midrash-form, can also be seen from another passage in the Babylonian Talmud. In Yeb. 72b we read that Eleazar b. Pedat refuted an opinion of R. Joḥanan by quoting a scriptural passage and giving an interpretation to it. R. Joḥanan, thinking that R. Eleazar, in his argument, was making use of an original interpretation, characterizes his method in these words: ראיתי לבן פדת שיושב ודורש כמשה מפי הגבורה, "I see that the son of Pedat studies in the manner of Moses." Simon b. Laḳish, however, informs R. Joḥanan that this argument was not original with R. Eleazar, but was taken from a Midrash-Baraita in Torat Kohanim, as it is indeed found in our Sifra (*Tazria'* I, Weiss 58b). We see, thus, that to study or teach in the Midrash-form, as is done in our Sifra, is characterized as being "in the manner of Moses" (יושב ודורש כמשה). The report in Tem. 15b, accordingly, tells us that until the death or the last days of Jose all the teachers taught in the Midrash-form, which is called "in the manner of Moses."³²

This seems also to have been the tradition among the Geonim, though for reasons of their own they did not care to express themselves distinctly about this question. We have seen above that Sherira, in describing the period during which the Midrash-form was in exclusive use, employs the term מעיקרא במקדש שני, but does not define how long this "earlier period of the second Temple" lasted. However, we shall arrive at a more exact interpretation of this vague term by comparing its usage in a respon-

---

³² This report in the Talmud might perhaps be confirmed by the report about the religious persecution in the time of Antiochus Epiphanes. Among the many prohibitions against Jewish religious practices devised by the Syrian ruler for the purpose of estranging the Jews from their religion, which are mentioned by the authors of the Books of Maccabees (I Macc. 1 and II Macc. 6), we do not hear of any special prohibition against teaching the Law, as was the case in the Hadrianic persecutions (b. 'Ab. Zarah 17b–18a, cf. Graetz, *Geschichte*, IV⁴, pp. 154 ff.). On the contrary, we learn from the saying of Jose b. Joezer, who lived at that time, that no such prohibition was enacted. For Jose said, "Let thy house be a meeting-place for the wise: sit amidst the dust of their feet, and drink their words with thirst" (Ab. 1.4). Evidently the wise teachers could meet unmolested in private places, and could impart their religious teachings. Yet there is no doubt that the aim and the tendency of the Syrian government were to suppress the religious teachings and to make the Jews forget their Law. We hear that the Books of the Law were rent in pieces and burned with fire, and that the king's command was that those people with whom the Book of the Law would be found should be put to death (I Macc. 1.56–7; Josephus, *Antiquities*, XII, 3, § 256). Evidently the persecutors believed that to burn the books of the Law and to punish any one who possessed them was sufficient to prevent the study of the Law. This was a very correct surmise. Since all teachings were given in the Midrash-form, that is, as an exposition and explanation of the Book of the Law, it followed that to take away the Books of the Law meant to effectually prevent any religious instruction. It was to meet this peculiar situation that Jose uttered his wise saying. Inasmuch as many of the Books of the Law were burnt, and as it was extremely dangerous to use those that had been secretly saved, Jose advised the people to make every home a place where the wise teachers might meet, and where one might listen to their words of instruction even without books.

These peculiar conditions may in some degree have helped to accustom the teachers to impart religious instruction altogether apart from the Book of the Law, namely in Mishnah-form.

sum of R. Ẓemaḥ Gaon. In this responsum[33] the following statement occurs: כל משנה שהיו ישראל דורשין במקדש סתם היה ולא היה בו שם חכם, "All the traditional law (משנה is here used in its broader sense) which they used to teach in the Midrash-form, שהיו דורשין, in the time of the Temple, was anonymous, and no individual teacher is named or connected therewith." The time which Ẓemaḥ Gaon has in mind and which he designates as במקדש cannot include the whole period of the second Temple. Many names of individual teachers living in the time of the second Temple are preserved to us together with their teachings, and these names were no doubt already mentioned in the collections of Halakot that existed in Temple times. R. Ẓemaḥ Gaon can only refer to the time before Jose b. Joezer, when, indeed, no individual names were mentioned in connection with the halakic teachings, the latter being given as interpretations of the Scripture (שהיו דורשין), that is, in the Midrash-form. It is most probable that Sherira by the term מעיקרא במקדש refers to the same period which Ẓemaḥ Gaon designates as במקדש, that is, to the time before Jose b. Joezer. We can therefore reasonably conclude that the new form of teaching the Halakah, i. e., Mishnah-form, was first made use of in the closing days of Jose b. Joezer.[34]

We have, now, to ascertain the reason for the introduction

---

[33] This responsum is quoted by Epstein in his *Eldad ha-Dani*, pp. 7–8, and more fully in Jellinek's *Beth Hamidrash*, II, 112–13. We shall discuss it in detail later on in the course of this essay. Ẓemah's statement that Eldad's Talmud followed the custom of old when they taught the Halakah without mentioning the names of individual teachers, finds corroboration in the manner in which the halakic teachings as quoted by Eldad were introduced. According to Eldad all the halakic teachings were introduced with the phrase אמר יהושוע מפי משה מפי הגבורה. This phrase, like the phrases יושב ודורש כמשה מפי הגבורה and למדין תורה כמשה רבינו, would well describe the older Midrash-form, in which all teachings were given in the name of Moses, i. e., as interpretations of the very words of Moses.

[34] It is perhaps for this very reason that the teachers until the time of Jose were called אשכולות. This is correctly interpreted by Samuel in the Talmud (Tem. 15b and Soṭah 47b) to mean איש שהכל בו, *viz.*, that each man spoke only the opinion of the whole group and that the group spoke for each man, in the sense that the teachers acted as a body, not as individuals. The report that the Eshkolot ceased with the death of Jose b. Joezer, משמת יוסי בן יועזר בטלו האשכולות, means therefore that this concerted action of the teachers ceased with Jose,

of a new form of teaching the Halakah alongside of the older form. Having fixed the time, we must now inquire into the conditions of that time, to see if we cannot find in them the reason for the innovation. An examination of the conditions that obtained during the period under consideration reveals the fact that many great changes had taken place in the life of the Judean community. We notice the presence of various new tendencies. The people's outlook upon life and their regard for the Law had considerably changed. Even among the teachers and leaders we find new and divergent attitudes towards the Law of the fathers on the one hand and towards the new ideas and tendencies on the other hand. All these changes were brought about by the one radical change in the political condition of the people, resulting from the passing of Judea from Persian to Greek rule. This great political change caused the interruption of the activity of the Soferim as an authoritative body of teachers. This interruption of the activity of the Soferim which was coincident with the death of Simon, the last member of that body, in the course of time led to a departure from the methods of the Soferim and necessitated the introduction of a new method of teaching the Halakot, namely, the Mishnah-form. In order to prove this, we must first review the conditions that prevailed in the time of the Soferim and examine the methods of the Midrash used by them.

As said above, the Soferim taught the people only the Book of the Law, ספר התורה, with such interpretations and explanations as they could give to it. Their exegetical rules and Midrash-methods, simple as they were, were nevertheless sufficient for their purpose, which was to give all the halakic teachings in connection with the written Law. There was no reason whatever to make any change in the form of teaching, and there was absolutely no need to teach anything else besides the Book of the Law and its Midrash. The stream of Jewish life, during the period of the Soferim, moved on smoothly and quietly, without any great changes. Under the Persian rule the Jewish people were merely a religious community, at the head of which stood the

---

and after him they began to mention Halakot in the name of individual teachers.

High-Priest,[35] who was the highest religious authority. The conditions which prevailed in this community during the last days of the Persian rule were almost the same as in the earlier days, when the community was first organized by the exiles who returned from Babylon. The Book of the Law accepted from Ezra by these early founders and organizers with the few simple interpretations given to it by the Soferim, was therefore sufficient for almost all the needs of the community throughout the entire Persian period. Of course, some slight changes in the conditions of life must have developed in the course of time. These changes in the inner life of the community probably brought new religious customs. The same changes probably required certain modifications in the interpretation of some of the written laws or even the introduction of new laws and new practices. All these necessary modifications and even the few new laws the Soferim could easily read into the written Law by means of interpretation, or even embody the same in the Book by means of some slight indications in the text itself. Thus they found in the Book of the Law all the teachings they required.

The Soferim were able to do this because they were also the actual scribes whose business it was to prepare copies of the Book of the Law. If they desired to teach a certain law, custom, or practice, because they considered it as part of the religious teachings, although it could not be found in, or interpreted into, the Book of the Law, they would cause it to be indicated by some slight change in the text.[36] For instance, by adding or omitting

* [35] This was the case, at any rate, in the second half of the Persian period. See Wellhausen, *Israelitische und Jüdische Geschichte*, 3rd ed., pp. 198 ff., and Schürer, *Geschichte*, II[4], pp. 267 ff.

[36] As we have received the Torah from the Soferim and only in the textual form in which they cast it (not considering some slight changes and additions that may have been made in the period after the Soferim, see below, note 43), it is impossible now to ascertain the full extent of the changes and corrections made by the Soferim in the original text of the Law. However, there is no doubt that the Soferim did change and correct the text of the Torah which they originally had. A tradition to this effect was current among the Rabbis of the Talmud. The Rabbis often refer to such changes as "corrections of the Soferim," תיקון סופרים (Genesis r. 59.7 and Exodus r. 13.1) or תקנת סופרים (Leviticus r. 40.5). They enumerated many passages in the Scriptures which

a letter, or by the peculiar spelling of a word they could bring

---

in their present form represent the corrected readings introduced by the Soferim (Sifre, Numbers, § 84, Friedmann, p. 22b, and Mekilta, *Beshallaḥ*, *Shirah*, VI, Weiss, pp. 46b–47a). In Tanḥuma, *Beshallaḥ* 15 (on Ex. 15.7) it is expressly stated that all these corrections were made by the Soferim, the Men of the Great Synagogue, תיקון סופרים אנשי כנסת הגדולה; also, אלאשכינו פסוקים אלו אנשי כנסת הגדולה ולכך נקראו סופרים. Even if it should be granted that these statements in the Tanḥuma are of later origin (see R. Azariah de Rossi, *Meor Enayim, Imre Binah*, ch. XIX), it cannot be disputed that the interpretation of the term תיקון סופרים as referring to the corrections made by the Soferim, who were identified with the Men of the Great Synagogue, is correct. This is confirmed by the fact that the same corrections, which in the Midrashim are designated as תיקוני סופרים, are designated in the Massorah, *Oklah We-Oklah* (No. 168, ed. Frensdorf, p. 113), as "corrections made by Ezra" (י"ח מלין תיקון עזרא), who was the first of the Soferim. If this tradition about the תיקוני סופרים conflicts with the later conception of the Rabbis, namely, that the entire Torah is from God, and that the one who maintains that there are some verses in the Torah which were not spoken by God, is a despiser of the word of God (Sanh. 99a), this does not argue against the correctness of this tradition, as R. Azariah de Rossi (*loc. cit.*) assumes. On the contrary, this conflict speaks in favor of our tradition. For it proves that the tradition about the תיקוני סופרים was too well-known a fact to be suppressed by later dogmatic views. All that the later teachers could do was not to deny the fact that changes were made in the text but merely to avoid too frequent mention of it. When forced to mention the fact they pointed to a few harmless changes and omitted (as in Sifre and Mekilta) the direct reference to the Soferim as the authors of these corrections (cf. Weiss, *Middot Soferim*, to Mekilta, p. 46b). It was probably on account of such considerations that the reference to the Soferim, the Men of the Great Synagogue, was omitted from the passage in Tanḥuma, in those old copies which R. Azariah de Rossi (*loc. cit.*) reports to have seen. The statement in the Tanḥuma expressly ascribing the corrections to the Soferim, the Men of the Great Synagogue, is accordingly not of later origin, as R. Azariah assumes. The omission of this reference from certain copies was due to a later hand.

Although the corrected passages pointed out by the Rabbis do not deal with the Law, we may safely assume (notwithstanding Weiss, *loc. cit.*) that the Soferim corrected even the legal portions of the Pentateuch. A correction of the Ketib לא into the Ḳere לו (Lev. 11.21) certainly affected the Law. This change, like most of the Ḳere and Ketib, originated with the Soferim, according to the talmudic tradition (Ned. 37b). The later teachers, for obvious reasons, would not mention the corrections made by the Soferim in the legal parts of the Pentateuch, as it would have cast unfavorable reflections on the authority of the Law and the validity of the Halakah.

about the desired result.[37] They did not hesitate to do so, because they did not in any way change the law as they understood it. The changes and corrections which they allowed themselves to make in the text were of such a nature that they did not affect the meaning of the passage, but merely gave to it an additional meaning, thus suggesting the law or custom which they desired to teach. In this manner they succeeded in grafting upon the written Law all these newly developed laws and customs which they considered genuinely Jewish. Even if the Soferim had desired to introduce a new religious practice or to teach a new law which could not be represented as an interpretation of the Law nor indicated in the text, they would not have been compelled to change their usual form of teaching. They could still have taught that law or custom together with the passage of the written Law with which it had some distant connection, offering it as an additional law or a modification of the practice commanded in the written Torah. Thus, throughout the entire period of their activity the Soferim who, no doubt, formed some kind of an authoritative organization with the High-Priest as its head, remained true to their name, and continued to teach only the Book of the Law with its interpretation — Midrash — and nothing else.

That the activity of the Soferim as an authoritative body of teachers ceased with the death of their last member, Simon the Just I (about 270 B. C. E.) has already been shown. It was the change from the Persian to the Greek rule that caused the interruption of the activity and ended the period of the Soferim. The change in the government brought about many other changes in the conditions of life and in the political status of the people. These, in turn, influenced the religious life and the communal institutions, and had their effect also upon the activity and authority of the teachers. All these changes in the inner life of the community did not come to pass immediately after the people came under Greek rule, for a poeple cannot be

---

[37] For illustrations of this method of the earliest Midrash to indicate Halakot in the text itself, see the writer's article "Midrash Halakah" in the *Jewish Encyclopedia*, VIII, 579 ff.

quickly transformed by mere external influences. It was through a long process, lasting about half a century, that these changes were gradually effected. During the lifetime of Simon the Just, the new influences had not yet overthrown the authority and the leadership of the Soferim as an organized body of teachers. Simon who enjoyed the high respect of the people could maintain the old order even under the changed conditions by the very influence of his great personality. Being the High-Priest and the respected leader of the people, he still preserved the authority of the teachers, and under his leadership they continued some of their usual activities. But with the death of Simon all the influences of the new order of things made themselves felt. The activity of the teachers as an authoritative body ceased. Even the authority of the High-Priest was undermined. He was no more the highest authority of a religious community and its chief representative. Other people assumed authority over the community. Laymen arose who had as much influence among the people and with the government as the High-Priest, and they became leaders.

The people who had now been in contact with Greek culture for half a century, acquired new ideas and became familiar with new views of life, other than those which they had been taught by their teachers in the name of the law of their fathers. The rich and influential classes accepted Greek ideas and followed Greek customs. The leaders of the people were no longer guided by the laws of the fathers, nor was the life of the people any longer controlled solely by the laws and customs of the fathers as contained in the Torah. The teachers were no longer consulted upon all matters of life, as they had been in former days, when, with the High-Priest at the head of the community, they formed an authoritative body. Consequently, the interpretation and the development of the laws of the fathers did not keep pace with the rapid changes and developments in the actual conditions of life. The changed conditions of the time brought forth new questions for which no decisions were provided in the laws of the fathers, and no answers could be found even in the interpretations and traditions of the Soferim, because such questions had never before arisen. These questions were decided by the ruling authorities who were not teachers of the Law, and in some cases probably by the people themselves. These decisions, presumably, were not always in accordance with the principles followed by the teachers of the Law. The decisions in new cases, given by ruling authorities, and answers to new questions, fixed by popular usage, became in the course of a few decades the established practices of the people. This development ensued because the people could not distinguish between decisions derived from the Law by interpretation, and decisions given by some ruling authority, but not based upon any law or tradition of the fathers. Neither could the majority of the people distinguish between generally accepted customs that had been recently introduced, and such as had been handed down by the fathers. To the people at large who were not concerned about historical and archaeological questions, both were alike religious customs sanctioned by popular usage.

Thus many new customs and practices for which there were no precedents in the traditions of the fathers and not the slightest indication in the Book of the Law, were observed by the people and considered by them as a part of their religious laws and practices. No attempt was made to secure the sanction of the authority of the Law for these new practices in order to harmonize the laws of the fathers with the life of the times. The few teachers (disciples of the Soferim) were the only ones who could perhaps have brought about this harmonization. By means of interpretation they might have found in the Book of the Law some support for the new practices, and they might have grafted the new and perhaps foreign customs upon the old, traditional laws of the fathers. But these teachers had no official authority; they were altogether disregarded by the leaders and ignored by a large part of the people.

The fact that there was no official activity of the teachers, in the years following the death of Simon the Just, is borne out even by the alleged traditional report given in Abot 1. The Mishnah, despite its anxiety to represent a continuous chain of tradition and to maintain that the acitivity of the teachers had never been interrupted, yet finds itself unable to fill the gap between Simon the Just I and Antigonos.[38] It does not mention the name of even one teacher between the years 270 and 190 B. C. E., that is, between the latest possible date of Simon's death and the time of Antigonos. Evidently tradition did not know of any teacher during that period. This would have been impossible if there had been any official activity of the teachers in those years.

Even in those days, there were without doubt some teachers who preserevd the traditional teachings of the Law. There were

[38] It is impossible to bridge over the gap in the succession of teachers as given in the Mishnah. It is evident that Antigonos could not have been the successor of Simon the Just I, and the immediate predecessor of the two Joses. Halevi's arguments (*Dorot Harishonim*, I, xii, pp. 198 ff.) are not convincing. The Mishnah speaks of the two Joses as contemporaries. As such they are also referred to Shab. 15a. We cannot for the purpose of upholding the other tradition, namely, that there was an uninterrupted chain of teachers, deny this explicit report and make of Jose b. Joḥanan a colleague of Antigonos and a man older by a full generation than Jose b. Joezer. If Antigonos had been the pupil and successor of Simon the Just I, as Halevi (*loc. cit.*) assumes, he could not have been succeeded directly by the two Joses. We would then have a gap between 250 B. C. E., the date when Antigonos the pupil of Simon the Just I must have died, and 180 B. C. E., the time when the two Joses must have begun their activity. In spite of all the pilpulistic arguments of Halevi against Frankel, it is evident that the latter is right in assuming that Antigonos did not directly succeed Simon the Just I (*Hodegetica*, p. 31). If we still desire to consider the report in the Mishnah as correct, we must interpret it to mean that Antigonos succeeded Simon the Just II (see Weiss, *Dor*, I, p. 95) and not the last member of the Great Synagogue who was Simon the first (against Krochmal, *More Nebuke Ha-Zeman*, pp. 52 and 174). Indeed, the wording in the Mishnah seems to indicate this. For if the Mishnah meant to say that Antigonos succeeded that Simon the Just who is mentioned in the preceding paragraph of the Mishnah and designated as the last member of the Great Synagogue, it would have said קיבל ממנו, as it uses in the following passages the phrase קיבלו מהם. The specific mention of the name in the statement קיבל שמעון הצדיק evidently shows that it was another Simon who is here referred to as the one who preceded Antigonos. This can only be Simon the Just II. At any rate, it is certain that after Simon I there came a time when there was no official activity of the teachers. Even the later tendency to reconstruct the chain of tradition, such as we have in the report in the Mishnah Abot, could not succeed in finding the name of a single teacher who flourished in the period between Simon I and Simon II (see Part IV).

some people who remained faithful to the laws and the traditions of the fathers, and among them some who studied the Law in the manner in which it had been taught by the Soferim. However, these teachers had no official authority. It was merely in a private capacity that they delivered their teachings to those who wished to follow them. However, absence of official authority not only did not prevent but even helped the activities of the teachers to become of great consequence for future developments. It brought about two great results which later became the most important factors in developing the Halakah and in shaping the Jewish life. In the first place, it brought about the popularization of the study of the Law and paved the way for the rise of teachers not of the priestly families. In the second place, it preserved the text of the Book of the Law in a fixed form, which resulted in giving this text a sacred, unchangeable character.

In the days of the Soferim, when the High-Priest was the head of the community, and when the teachers under his leadership formed an official body vested with authority to arrange all religious matters in accordance with the Law as they understood it, the knowledge of the Law was limited to the priests who were the only official teachers.[39] On the one hand, the priests who were in possession of the Law and tradition of the fathers considered the teaching and interpreting of the religious law as their priestly prerogative. They would therefore not impart to the lay people a thorough knowledge of the Law so that they too could become teachers.[40] This would have resulted in curtailing their

[39] The Soferim, up to the time of the death of Simon the Just I, were mostly, if not exclusively, priests. See *Sadducees and Pharisees*, above p. 28. Cf. also Schürer, *Geschichte*, II⁴, pp. 278-9, 373-4, and 455, and R. Smend, *Die Weisheit des Jesus Sirach* (Berlin, 1906), 346. Smend, however, goes too far in assuming that even as late as the beginning of the second century B. C. E. all the teachers of the Law were priests. This is not correct. In the middle of the third century B. C. E., after the death of Simon the Just I, there were already many lay-teachers. In the beginning of the second century B. C. E. they already possessed great influence and were members of the Gerousia. The description of the Soferim as sitting in the senate and knowing the Law, which is given in Sirach 38, refers to both lay- and priest-teachers.

[40] The saying "Raise many disciples," which is ascribed by the Mishnah (Ab. 1) to the Men of the Great Synagogue, does not argue against this statement. It can be interpreted to mean either to raise many disciples among

own special privileges, a sacrifice which priests are not always willing to make. On the other hand, the people had no impetus to study the Law because they could rely on the authority of their official teachers in all matters religious. They were satisfied that "the lips of the priest should keep knowledge and that they should seek the Law at his mouth," and get from him decisions concerning all the questions of life. But when the authority of the High-Priest as the ruler of the community was gone, and the priestly teachers also lost their official authority, the study of the Law was no longer the activity of an exclusive class of official teachers. A knowledge of the Law and the traditions of the fathers no longer gave its possessor the prerogative of sharing in the administration of the community. At the head of the community now stood political leaders who arranged communal affairs according to standards of their own.

The study of the Law now became a matter of private piety, and as such it was not limited to the priests. On the one hand, the priests no longer had any interest in keeping the knowledge of the Law jealously to themselves, as it did not bring them any special privileges. For such influence as the priests still had was theirs, not because they knew or taught the Law, but because they were the priests, in charge of the Temple, and members of the influential aristocratic families.[41] They therefore had no hesitancy in imparting a knowledge of the Law to the lay people. It must be kept in mind that there were at all times some true and faithful priests to whom their religion was dearer than personal advantages and family aggrandizement. These priests were now very eager to spread religious knowledge among the people. On the other hand, the lay people were now more eager than formerly

---

the priests who should carry on the activity of teaching, or to educate many pupils in a knowledge of the religious law, but not to make them authoritative teachers. However, it is very probable that the later teachers ascribed to the early Soferim a motto which they thought the Soferim should have promulgated. As the fact of their being priest-Soferim was forgotten, the later teachers ascribed to them their own democratic tendencies. These tendencies were against the monopolization of the knowledge by the priests, and in favor of spreading the knowledge of the Law among the people at large.

[41] See below, note 50.

to acquire such knowledge. Since there was no official body of teachers to decide authoritatively all religious matters, the pious man who cared for the Law had to be his own religious authority. He therefore sought to acquire a correct knowledge of the laws and the traditions of the fathers. This resulted in the gradual spread of a knowledge of the Law among the pious laymen, and in the rise of lay teachers who had as much knowledge of the Law as the priestly teachers themselves. These new teachers soon claimed for themselves the religious authority which was formerly the prerogative of the priests.

For about half a century, during the ascendancy of the power of the political leaders, these teachers, laymen, and priests had no recognized authority. They were not consulted as to the regulation of the communal affairs, and not called upon to answer questions resulting from the changed conditions of life. They therefore contented themselves with merely preserving the Law and the traditions that were left to them from the past, without trying to develop them further or add to them new teachings of their own. Accordingly, they continued to teach the text of the Book of the Law with the interpretations given to it by the Soferim and the Halakot, which the latter indicated in or connected with the text of the Law. They did not forget any of the interpretations or teachings of the Soferim.[42] Thus they preserved the text of the Law in the exact form in which it was handed down to them by the Soferim, with all of its peculiarities, as well as all the changes and indications made in it by the Soferim. They neither changed the text nor inserted indications of new laws therein. And after the text was for many years in a certain form, that became the fixed and permanent form. In the course of a few decades that permanent form with all its peculiarities came to be considered as sacred, so that no one afterwards dared to introduce textual changes, as the Soferim of old used

---

[42] I must emphasize this point in opposition to Oppenheim who assumes that in the time of persecution they forgot the teachings of the Soferim and for this reason began to teach independent Halakot. The troublesome times might have hindered original activity and the development of the teachings, but could not have prevented the preservation of the older teachings. If they did study at all, they studied what was left to them from the Soferim.

to do,[43] for the purpose of indicating new laws or new meanings to old laws. Thus we see that after the death of Simon the Just I, the conditions in the community and as a result thereof the activities of the teachers differed greatly from those that obtained in the times of the Soferim. There prevailed a state of religious anarchy, wherein the practical life of the people was not controlled by the law of the fathers as interpreted by the religious authorities, nor were the activities of the teachers carried on in an official way by an authoritative body. This chaotic state of affairs lasted for a period of about eighty years, until another great change took place which brought the religious anarchy to an end. This happened about the year 190 B. C. E., when an authoritative Council of priests and laymen was again established. This new Council or Sanhedrin assumed religious authority to teach and interpret the Law and proceeded to regulate the life of the community according to the religion of the fathers.

According to a report in Josephus (*Ant.* XII, 3. 8), Antiochus III manifested a very friendly attitude towards the people of Judea after that province had come under his rule. Following his victory over the Egyptian king at the battle of Panea (198 B. C. E.), he is said to have addressed to his general Ptolemaeus an epistle in favor of the Jews. In this letter, reproduced by Josephus, the following paragraph occurs (142: "And let all of that nation live according to the laws of their own country and let the senate (γερουσία) and the priests and the scribes of the Temple and the sacred singers be discharged from poll money and the crown tax and other taxes also." We learn from this that the Jews under Antiochus III were to live according to their own laws, and that there was, besides the priests, another authoritative body, a senate or a Gerousia, of which

---

[43] We are not considering here the slight changes which according to Geiger (*Urschrift*, pp. 170 f.) were made as late as the time of R. Akiba and according to Pineles (*Darkah shel Torah*, p. 96) even as late as the time of Judah ha-Nasi I. As a whole the text was fixed. Possibly, the Pharisaic teachers, as the party grew in influence and as they became the sole authorities of the religious law, ventured again to make slight changes and to indicate their teachings in the text.

laymen were also members. Otherwise the mention of the *senate and the priests* separately would have no sense.[44]

It is true that some details in the epistle prove the authorship of Antiochus to be spurious. It was evidently not written by Antiochus. It originated at a much later date and was only incorrectly ascribed to Antiochus by some Hellenistic writer whom Josephus followed (see Büchler, *Die Tobiaden und Oniaden*, pp. 158 *et seq.*). However, if the conditions in the Jewish community under Antiochus III had been known to be very different from those described in this epistle, neither Josephus nor his authority would have accepted the authorship of Antiochus. Evidently Josephus on his part had no reason to doubt the genuineness of this epistle, and in his opinion it could well have originated from Antiochus. This can only be explained by assuming that Josephus knew from other sources that, after Judaea had come under Syrian rule, there was a revival of the religious life in the community and a renewal of the official activity of the teachers. From the same source he must have known that the people tried again to live according to their laws and that there was at the head of the community an authoritative body, a Senate or a Gerousia, of which lay teachers also were members. As these events took place under the rule of Antiochus, Josephus linked them in his mind with the political conditions under the same king and believed they were the direct results of Antiochus's friendly attitude towards the Jews. In this supposition Josephus was perhaps right. It is quite probable that the change in the

---

[44] Büchler (*op. cit.*, p. 171) notices this strange feature in the epistle, namely, that the Gerousia is mentioned separately from the priests. He explains it by assuming that the epistle was originally written by a man who lived outside of Palestine and who did not know that in Palestine the senate was composed of priests. While this may explain why the author of the original epistle could have made the mistake, it does not explain how Josephus who was a Palestinian or the Palestinian authority that he followed could have accepted this epistle as genuine. One or the other certainly would have noticed that it did not represent actual conditions. This difficulty is removed by assuming that Josephus knew that at the time of Antiochus the Great the senate in Judea was formed not exclusively of the priests but also of laymen. He, therefore, did not find it strange that the epistle should mention the senate and the priests, i. e., the senate as a body not identical with the priests.

government brought about the change in the internal affairs of the community. As it weakened the influence of the former political leaders, it made it possible for that new organization composed of priests and lay members to assume the leadership of the community. And when Josephus found an epistle, ascribed to Antiochus, which permitted the Jews to live according to their own laws and actually spoke of a senate besides the priests, he could well believe it to have been written by Antiochus.

In a source older than Josephus we indeed find a report of the renewed religious activity by an authoritative assembly composed of priests and lay teachers in the first two decades of the second century B. C. E. I refer to the "Fragments of a Zadokite Work," published by Schechter (*Documents of Jewish Sectaries*, I, [Cambridge, 1910]). There it is stated (Text A, p. 1) that 390 years after God had delivered them (the Jewish people) into the hands of Nebuchadnezzar, the King of Babylon (about 196 B. C. E., i. e., 390 years after 586 B. C. E.), God made to grow a plant (i. e., an assembly) of Priests and Israelites. They (the members of that assembly) meditated over their sin and they knew that they had been guilty [of neglecting the religious laws]. They sought to find the right way [to lead the people back to the Law of God].[45] Again on page 6 the same fact is stated

---

[45] The passage in the text A, p. 1, lines 5 ff., reads as follows: ובקץ חרון שנים שלש מאות ותשעים לתיתו אותם ביד נבוכדנאצר מלך בבל פְּקָדָם ויצמח מישראל ומאהרן שורש מטע לירוש את ארצו ולדשן בטוב אדמתו ויבינו בעונם וידעו כי אנשים אשמים הם ויהיו כעורים וכימגששים דרך שנים עשרים ובן אֵל אל מעשיהם כי בלב שלם דרשוהו ויקם להם (ונוסר) מורה דרך להדריכם בדרך לב. "And at the end of the wrath, three hundred and ninety years after He had delivered them into the hand of Nebuchadnezzar, king of Babylon, He remembered them and made bud from Israel and Aaron a root of a plant to inherit His land and to rejoice in the good of His earth. And they meditated over their sin and they knew that they were guilty men and they were like the blind groping in the way twenty years. And God considered their deeds, for they sought Him with a perfect heart, and He raised for them a teacher of righteousness to make them walk in the way of His heart" (Translation, as given by Schechter). It is evident that the author in describing the origin of the Zadokite sect reviews the conditions that prevailed in Judea prior to the formation of this sect. The period of "wrath" or, as the parallel passage (p. 5) has it, "the desolation of the land," is the time of the wars between Syria and Egypt before Antiochus the Great finally acquired Palestine. It was after this period had come to an end, about three hundred and

even more clearly. There it is said that "God took men of understanding from Aaron (i. e., from among the priests) and from Israel wise teachers (i. e., non-priestly Israelitic teachers) and caused them to come together as an assembly (וַיִּשְׁמְעָם). They dug the well . . ., that is the Torah."[46] This means that the assembled priests and lay teachers together searched the Law of the fathers to find in it a way of prescribing for the religious needs of their time.

The same tradition pertaining to the renewed activity of the teachers and the existence of a Sanhedrin composed of priests and lay teachers in the time of Antiochus, is also found underlying a report in the Mishnah. According to this report, the head of the Sanhedrin at that time was Antigonos of Soko, a lay teacher, and succeeding him were Jose ben Joezer of Zeredah and Jose ben Joḥanan of Jerusalem (Ab. 1.3–4). Of the latter two, Jose ben Joezer, a pious priest, is said to have been the

ninety years after God had given the people into the hand of Nebuchadnezzar (about 196 B. C. E., 390 after 586) that God raised up a plant from *Israel* and *Aaron*. "Plant" here is a designation for an assembly or Sanhedrin (cf. Genesis r., 54.6, ויטע אשל אשל זה סנהדרין, and Ḥul. 92a, והיא כפורחת עלתה נצה אלו סנהדרין).

We learn from this report that in that assembly or the reorganized Sanhedrin, where the nucleus was formed for the two parties, Sadducees and Pharisees, there also arose a third party or sect, composed both of priests and Israelites who differed from the two other groups, the Priest-Sadducees and the Israelite-Pharisees. This third group acknowledged the rights of the lay people to be like the priests, but would otherwise not follow the tendencies of these lay teachers who formed the nucleus of the Pharisaic party. This third group formed a special sect under a teacher of righteousness and emigrated to Damascus.

We further learn from this report that for about twenty years there was harmony between the various elements in this new assembly and that they tried to find a way of arranging the life of the community in accordance with the Law of God, as handed down to them from their fathers.

[46] The passage on p. 6, line 2–3, reads as follows: ויקח מאהרן נבונים ומישראל חכמים וַיִּשְׁמְעָם. The phrase ומישראל חכמים reminds one of the term חכמי ישראל "Lay teachers of Israelitic descent," which later on was the designation of the Pharisees, because these lay teachers in the reorganized Sanhedrin formed the nucleus of the Pharisaic party. See *Sadducees and Pharisees*, above pp. 39 ff. The phrase וַיִּשְׁמְעָם means "he assembled them," like וישמע שאול את העם, I Sam. 15.4.

president and Jose ben Joḥanan, a lay teacher, the vice-president of the Sanhedrin (Ḥag. 2.2). Of course, these reports in the Mishnah, in the form in which we have them, are of a comparatively late date and cannot be considered as historical.[47] They form part of that artificial reconstruction of history, undertaken by the later teachers who aimed to establish the fiction of a continuous chain of tradition and the alleged uninterrupted leadership of the Pharisaic teachers throughout all the past history. Unhistorical as these reports may be, they certainly contain some kernel of truth. This truth consisted in the fact, known to them, that there was some authoritative assembly composed of priests and lay teachers, of which these men, Antigonos and the two Joses, were prominent members. This

[47] It is very unlikely that Jose b. Joezer was president (נשיא) of the Sanhedrin although he belonged to an influential aristocratic family and was a priest (חסיד שבכהונה, Ḥag. 3.2). He and his colleague Jose b. Joḥanan probably were the leaders of that group of pious lay-teachers in the Sanhedrin, the Ḥasidim, who were the forerunners of the Pharisees. This may be concluded from the report in I Macc. 7.12–16, where we read as follows: "Then did assemble unto Alcimus and Bacchides a company of Scribes to require justice. Now the Asideans (Ḥasidim) were the first among the children of Israel (i. e., non-priests) that sought peace of them." These Ḥasidim who are here identified with the Scribes, are also designated as mighty men of Israel (i. e., non-priests), even all such as were voluntarily devoted unto the Law (ibid., 2.42). We learn from these references that, prior to the Maccabean uprising, there were already scribes who were not priests, that is, lay teachers of Israelitic descent, who were mighty and influential in the community, otherwise they could not have assumed the authority to go to Alcimus to negotiate for peace. They evidently were of the same group of lay teachers in that reorganized Sanhedrin, who were the forerunners of the Pharisees. They were distinct from the other members of the Sanhedrin in that they were merely concerned with the religious liberty and were therefore willing to recognize Alcimus if they could obtain from him peace and religious freedom. Jose b. Joezer was among this group, and probably was their leader (see above, note 29). In the mind of the later Pharisaic teachers it was this group of the Ḥasidim in the Sanhedrin which was looked upon and considered as the Sanhedrin. Its leaders were considered as the real leaders of the whole Sanhedrin. Thus originated the tradition about the Zuggot as the heads of the Sanhedrin. For later tradition considers only those teachers who were of the Pharisees as legitimate members of the Sanhedrin, and the Sadducees who constituted the majority of the members and were the actual leaders of the Sanhedrin are regarded as intruders and usurpers.

historical report, the later teachers elaborated to fit into their scheme. They ignored all the other members, probably even the real leaders of that Sanhedrin, and represented those teachers as the real leaders who were pious followers of the traditional Law and who were so to speak the fathers of the Pharisaic party. However, whether Antigonos and Jose were really the heads of the Sanhedrin as tradition represents them, or merely prominent members, or perhaps merely the leaders of the more pious group in that Sanhedrin, the Ḥasidim, this much is sure: there was at that time an assembly or a Sanhedrin, composed of priests and lay teachers with official authority to arrange the religious affairs of the people. The members of this Sanhedrin took up the interrupted activity of the former teachers, the Soferim, and, like them, sought to teach and interpret the Law and to regulate the life of the people in accordance with the laws and traditions of the fathers. But in their attempt to harmonize the laws of the fathers with the life of their own times, they encountered some great difficulties.

It is true, the teachers who were now members of the authoritative council or Sanhedrin, were in the possession of the Book of the Law, in the exact form in which it was transmitted to them by the Soferim. They also knew all the interpretation of the Soferim, as well as all the traditional teachings and additional laws which the latter connected with or based on the written laws of the Pentateuch. But all the laws contained or indicated in the text of the Book together with all the traditional teachings given by the Soferim in connection with the Book of the Law were not sufficient to meet the requirements of the new situation. These laws did not provide answers for all the questions that arose, and could not furnish solutions for the new problems in the life of the people. For all these new problems and questions were the result of new conditions of life now prevailing in Judea, conditions utterly different from those in the times of the Soferim. The problem then became, how to find in the old laws new rules and decisions for the questions and unprecedented cases that now arose.

This difficulty was aggravated by the fact that during the seventy or eighty years of religious anarchy, many new practices had been gradually adopted by the people. In the course of time, these came to be considered as Jewish religious practices, and no distinction was made between them and older religious practices contained in the teachings of the Soferim and based on the traditions of the fathers. Again, the outlook of the people had broadened and their religious concepts had become somewhat modified during those years. Many an old law assumed a new and different meaning or was given a new application, not by the decree of an authoritative body of teachers, but by the general opinion of the people who had outgrown the older conception of that law. Many questions were decided during those years by the people themselves or by such rulers and leaders as they had. Such decisions, though not given by any religious authority and not derived from the written law, became, nevertheless, recognized rules and principles, respected by the people as much as their other laws written or indicated in the Book. It was such new decisions and popular modifications of some laws, as well as the generally observed new customs and practices, that constituted a large part of the traditional laws and practices. These traditional laws naturally had no indication in the Written Law and no basis in the teachings of the Soferim, because they developed after the period of the Soferim.

The reorganized Sanhedrin (after 190) had to reckon with these new laws and customs, now considered as *traditional* because observed and practised by the people for a generation or more. They had to recognize them as part of the religious life of the people. But in order to be able to accept and teach them officially as part of the religious Law, the members of the Sanhedrin had to find some authority for these new laws and customs. They had either to find for them some basis in the traditions and teachings of the Soferim, or to find proof for them by some new interpretation of the Written Law. This, however, was not an easy task to perform. The present teachers, although members of an official body, like the Soferim of old, could not, like these Soferim, indicate new laws in the text by means of slight changes or additional signs, because the pliability of the text was gone. The text was now in a fixed form which was considered sacred, and no changes could be made in it. The simple methods of interpretation used by the Soferim were also inadequate for the needs of the present teachers. These simple methods could not furnish enough interpretations on which to base the new decisions needed for the times. Throughout the period of the Soferim the development of the interpretations of the Law kept pace with the development of the conditions of life. But for the teachers of the reorgnized Sanhedrin, these simple methods were insufficient because their development had been arrested for about eighty years. We have seen above that the development in the conditions of life after the Soferim, took place without a corresponding development in the teachings and interpretations of the Law. Laboring under such disadvantages the new Sanhedrin found it very difficult to solve the problem of harmonizing the Law of the fathers with the life of the people.

Having no reports concerning that time, we cannot trace the activity of the new Sanhedrin from its beginnings. We know only that it was organized after Judea had come under Syrian rule, that is, after 196 B. C. E. Some years must have passed before the above-mentioned difficulties were fully realized and plans proposed for their solution. It was probably not until the time of Antiochus Epiphanes that such definite plans were considered.[48] Different solutions were offered by the various members

---

[48] From the report in the Zadokite Fragment we learn that for twenty years there was harmony among the various elements of that reorganized Sanhedrin and all sought God with a perfect heart and endeavored to order their lives in accordance with His Law (see above, note 44). This means that before the year 175 B. C. E., that is, twenty years after 196 B. C. E., the date of the organization of that new Sanhedrin, the differences of opinion did not lead to an outspoken opposition between the different groups within that Sanhedrin. It was only after the year 175 B. C. E., that is, under the reign of Antiochus Epiphanes, that these differences of opinion became so marked as to characterize the different groups in that Sanhedrin as distinct from one another. This is also stated in the Assumptio Mosis 6.2 where we read as follows: "And when the time of chastisement draws nigh and vengeance arises through the kings who share in their guilt and punish them, they themselves also shall be divided as to the truth." This refers to the time before the Maccabean revolt, and the king through whom they will be punished can only refer to Antiochus Epiphanes. We are accordingly told that in the time of Antiochus Epiphanes, after the year 175 B. C. E., there was a division among the Jews themselves in regard to the truth, that is, as regards their religious laws. The

of the Sanhedrin. This difference of opinion in regard to the solution of this problem caused a breach in that Sanhedrin which ultimately resulted in a division into parties, namely, Pharisees and Sadducees. This breach in the unanimity of opinion was effected during the time of Jose ben Joezer and Jose ben Joḥanan, the successors of Antigonos, and this is possibly the historic fact upon which is based the tradition that ascribes the origin of the two parties, Pharisees and Sadducees to this particular time.[49]

The priestly group in that assembly, whose exclusive privilege it had formerly been to give instruction in religious matters, and who even now participated prominently in the administration of the communal and religious affairs,[50] had a simple solution for the

---

two groups mentioned there are those who later on formed the two parties, Sadducees and Pharisees. Cf. also the Book of Enoch 90.6, where these two groups, the nucleus of the two parties, are referred to as appearing first at that time. This also agrees with the report in II Maccabees, that in the days of Onias III, before Antiochus Epiphanes, the laws were kept very strictly owing to the goodliness of Onias (3.1) who was a zealot for the Law (4.2).

[49] The legendary story in Ab. R. N. (version A, ch. V, version B, ch. X, Schechter, p. 26) contains a kernel of truth in that it dates back the origin of the conflict between the two parties to the time of the pupils of Antigonos. All that the story really tells us is that among the disciples or successors of Antigonos there were already great differences of opinion which divided them into two groups. Only one must keep in mind that the first disagreement was not yet a real division. The complete separation of the two groups and their formation into two distinct parties took place later on in the time of John Hyrcanus (see *Sadducees and Pharisees*, above p. 30, note 10). This seems also to be indicated in the story of Ab. R. N., where the statement הלכו ופירשו להן "they separated" refers to the pupils of the successors of Antigonos. This would refer to the time of Joshua b. Peraḥiah, the successor of Jose b. Joezer, who was the pupil of Antigonos. This explanation will answer the objections raised by Halevi (*Dorot Harishonim*, Ic, VIII, 169 ff.) against putting the date of the origin of the Sadducean party at the time of the pupils of Antigonos.

[50] Even during the period, when the priests did not carry on any official activity as authoritative teachers, they were still not without influence and authority. Their families still possessed political power, and some of them were influential leaders. In the Temple they had an undisputed authority (see Schürer, *Geschichte*, II[4], pp. 279-80). As priests and leaders they had thus become accustomed to exercise authority independently of the Law. Their influence in the last few decades was not due to their being teachers of the Law but to the fact that they formed an influential aristocracy and had control over the Temple and its service.

problem in conformity with the maintenance of their authority. In their opinion, the main thing was to observe the laws of the fathers as contained in the Book of the Law, because the people had pledged themselves, by oath, in the time of Ezra, to do so. If changed conditions required additional laws and new regulations, the priests and rulers were competent to decree them according to authority given to them in Deut. 17.8–13. They maintained that the priestly rulers of former generations had always exercised this authority. For this reason they did not deem it necessary that all the new laws and regulations needed for the changed conditions of life should be found indicated in the Book of the Law or based on the teachings of former generations. Thus the priestly members of that assembly, the future Sadducees, did not feel the need of developing the old laws, or of forcing interpretations into the Written Law. They declared the Written Law with all the traditional interpretations of the Soferim absolutely binding. However, as rulers of the people, they claimed the right to decide by virtue of their own authority those new questions for which the laws of the fathers did not provide.

This apparently simple solution offered by the priestly group in the Sanhedrin did not find favor with the lay members of that body. These lay members who had never had a share in ruling the people, now, because of their knowledge of the Law, claimed equal authority with the priests. They refused to recognize the authority of the priests as a class, and, inasmuch as many of the priests had proven unfaithful guardians of the Law, they would not entrust to them the regulation of the religious life of the people. In the opinion of these democratic lay teachers, an opinion also shared by some pious priests, the right to decide religious questions given in Deut. 17.9 ff. to the priests was not given to them as a family privilege merely because they were priests, but because they were teachers of the Law, and only as long as they were teachers of the Law. The same right was equally granted to the teachers of the Law who were not priests. Both priests and lay teachers had no other authority except that of speaking in the name of the Law. They had merely the right of interpreting the Law and of deciding questions according to their understanding of the Law. They had absolutely no authority to issue new laws or decide religious questions according to principles other than those laid down in the Law, for the Law alone was to be the authority of the Jewish people. The entire life of the people in all its possible situations should be guided and controlled by no other authority than the Law as interpreted by the teachers, whether priest or layman.[51]

Acknowledging the Law of the fathers to be the sole authority, these lay teachers now had to find all the decisions and rules necessary for the practical life of their time contained or implied in the Law. They also had to devise methods for connecting with the Law all those new decisions and customs which were now universally observed by the people, thus making them appear as part of the laws of the fathers.

There were two methods by which they could accomplish this result. The one was to expand the *Midrash* of the Soferim, that is to develop the method of interpretation used by the Soferim and to invent new exegetical rules, by means of which they could derive new decisions from the Written Law, and find sanction therein for various accepted practices. The other method was to enlarge the definition of the term "Law of the Fathers," so as to mean more than merely the written Book of the Law with all its possible interpretations. In other words, it meant a declaration of the belief that not all the laws of the fathers were handed down in the written words of the Book, but that some religious laws of the fathers were transmitted orally, independently of any connection with the Book. Either method, to an extent, meant a departure from the old, traditional point of view, a course which the teachers naturally hesitated to take. In spite of considerable reluctance, the teachers gradually were led to make use of both of these methods. At first they attempted to expand the Midrash, the form which they were accustomed to use. They developed new methods of interpretation by which they could derive from the Law new decisions for current cases and even justify some of the existing practices and find scriptural

---

[51] For further details about the attitude of each group towards the Law see *Sadducees and Pharisees*, above.

support for some decisions which had originally been given without reference to the Written Law. However, the enlarged use of new and more developed Midrash methods was not sufficient to secure proofs for all necessary decisions and find scriptural authority for all existing laws and accepted practices.

There were many practices, generally accepted by the people as part of their religious life, for which even the developed Midrash with its new rules could find no support or proof in the written Law. This was especially the case with such decisions and practices as originated in the time after the Soferim. In the opinion of the teachers, the origin of these laws and customs was Jewish. They reasoned thus: It is hardly possible that foreign customs and non-Jewish laws should have met with such universal acceptance. The total absence of objection on the part of the people to such customs vouched for their Jewish origin, in the opinion of the teachers. Accordingly, the teachers themselves came to believe that such generally recognized laws and practices must have been old traditional laws and practices accepted by the fathers and transmitted to following generations in addition to the Written Law. Such a belief would naturally free the teachers from the necessity of finding scriptural proof for all the new practices. They could teach them as traditional Halakot not dependent upon the Written Law, that is to say — in the Mishnah-form.

However, the theory of an authoritative traditional law (which might be taught independently of the Scriptures) was altogether too new to be unhesitatingly accepted. Although it may be safely assumed that the fathers of the Pharisaic party did not originally formulate the theory of an Oral Law in the same terms and with the same boldness with which it was proclaimed by the later Pharisaic teachers, still even in its original form the theory was too startling and novel to be unconditionally accepted. Even those teachers who later became the advocates of the so-called Oral Law could not at first become easily reconciled to the idea that some laws had been handed down by tradition, side by side with the Written Law and equal in authority to the latter. Accordingly, these teachers applied the term "Traditional Law" only to such practices and rules, whose religious authority was unquestioned and whose universal acceptance went back to the time before the memory of living men.[52] The absence of objection to any such law or custom pointed in itself to an old Jewish tradition as its source, so that the teachers were justified in believing it to be a genuinely traditional law. But even in the case of such generally accepted rules and practices, it was only as a last resort that the teachers would present them independently as traditional laws. They preferred to resort to the developed methods of interpretation, which, although also new and also a departure from the older Midrash, were yet not so startling as the idea of declaring a new source of authority for religious laws in addition to the written Torah. Wherever there was the remotest possibility of doing so, they would seek by means of new hermeneutical rules to find in the words of the Torah support for these traditional laws. They could thus continue to teach them in connection with the Written Law, that is in the Midrash-form, as of old. Only in a very few cases, when it was absolutely impossible to establish by means of the Midrash any connection between the traditional practice and the Written Law, would they teach the same as independent traditional Halakah, that is to say, in the Mishnah-form.[53] This, no doubt, was the very first use made of the Mishnah-form.

However, in this first introduction of the new form with its very limited use lay the possibility of a much wider and more general application. Once it was conceded that, when absolutely necessary, a form of teaching other than the Midrash could be used, it became merely a question of what to consider a case of necessity. This varied with the individual teacher. To some teachers, the Mishnah-form appealed even where the Midrash-

[52] It might perhaps be said that the theory grew and forced itself upon the teachers without any intention on their part to formulate it. They could not ignore certain practices, considered by the people to be religious. They had to teach them. Since they could not trace their origin, they assumed that they were traditions of the fathers. It was but one step, almost an unconscious one, from this to the declaration, that the fathers received their traditional laws together with the Written Law.

[53] Accordingly the Midrash always remained the main form of teaching and the Mishnah only gradually came to be used alongside of it (see above, notes 8 and 22).

MIDRASH AND MISHNAH

form was possible, but not acceptable, as, for instance, when the interpretation of Scriptures offered in support of the decision was not approved. For even the developed Midrash methods and the new rules of interpretation were not all of them accepted by all the teachers. Some teachers would go further than the others. It often happened that rules and interpretations offered by one teacher would be rejected by another. We may presume that it often happened that one teacher would try by means of a new interpretation to support a decision from Scripture, while other teachers, although rejecting that particular interpretation, would accept the decision, either because of the authority of that teacher or because it was accepted by the majority. These other teachers of course could not teach such a decision in the Midrash-form, because they rejected the particular Midrash furnished for the decision. They were compelled to teach such a decision as an abstract Halakah, that is, in the Mishnah-form. Fortunately, we have positive proof that such instances did occur. This actually happened in the case of the oldest Halakot preserved to us in the Mishnah-form, namely, the Halakot of Jose ben Joezer. As will presently be shown, these decisions were taught by the teachers as independent Halakot in the name of Jose, because the interpretations given by Jose in their support were not approved by the other teachers. To prove that this was the case, we have to examine these Halakot in order to ascertain their exact meaning, also Jose's share in them, and the attitude of the other teachers towards them.

These Halakot are found in the Mishnah, 'Eduy. 8.4, and they read as follows:

העיד יוסי בן יועזר איש צרידה על איל קמצא שהוא דכן ועל משקה בי
מטבחיא (דאינון) דכיין ודיקרב במיתא מסתאב. וקרו ליה יוסי שריא.

Jose ben Joezer of Zeredah stated regarding the Ayyal Kamẓa [a certain species of locust] that it is to be considered as clean (i. e., permitted to be eaten), and regarding the liquids of the slaughtering place, that they are to be considered as clean, and that [only] that which has come into direct contact with a dead body becomes unclean. And they [the other teachers] called him "Jose the Permitter." There are a few difficulties in these Halakot which we must point out before we can get at their full meaning and demonstrate their bearing upon our theory.

The first strange feature in these Halakot is their language. They are given in Aramaic and not in Hebrew, in which all other Halakot of the Mishnah are given.[54] Weiss tries to account for the Aramaic language of these Halakot by assuming that they were remnants of the teachings and decisions of the Soferim (*Dor*, I, 66), who according to his assumption delivered all their teachings in the Aramaic language[55] (Introduction to Mekilta, p. iv). Jose, according to Weiss, merely attested to these decisions, but did not originate them. This explanation, however, rests upon false premises. In the first place, if the Aramaic of these Halakot was due to their being decisions of the Soferim, we ought to find many more Halakot in the Mishnah in the

[54] There is no other halakic decision in the Mishnah expressed in the Aramaic language. The Aramaic saying of Hillel (Ab. 1.13) was either uttered by Hillel while he was still in Babylon, or because it was addressed to the people as a popular saying it was given in Aramaic which was then already the language of the people. The latter reason would also account for the other two sayings in Ab. 5.22–3 given in the Aramaic language.

[55] It is surprising to find that Weiss not only contradicts himself, but also reasons in a circle. He himself mentions many proofs for assuming that Hebrew was used by the majority of the people and by the Soferim. He has absolutely no reason for assuming that the Soferim taught in Aramaic. However, just because these three decisions of Jose are expressed in Aramaic, and because in his opinion Jose received these decisions in their form and in their language from the Soferim, he concludes that the Soferim must have taught in Aramaic. And as a proof for his opinion that these decisions are from the Soferim he can only cite the fact that they are expressed in Aramaic, which, in his opinion, was the language of the Soferim. Weiss here follows Krochmal who assumes (in *More Nebuke Hazeman*, X, 52–3) that the language of the people in the time of Ezra was Aramaic. Both Krochmal and Weiss seem to have been misled by the haggadic interpretation of the passage in Neh. 8.8, given in b. Ned. 37b, מפורש זה תרגום, which they understood to refer to an Aramaic translation. Following this Haggadah, they assume that as early as the time of Ezra the Torah had been translated into the Aramaic (see Krochmal, *loc. cit.*, and Weiss, *Dor*, I, 54; cf. also Friedmann, *Onkelos and Akylas*, [Wien, 1896], p. 58). Hence they argue, if an Aramaic translation was necessary, then the language of the people must have been Aramaic. But this is a mistake. There was no translation of the Torah in the time of Ezra, as the people spoke Hebrew, the language in which the Torah was written.

Aramaic language. For there are certainly more teachings of the Soferim preserved in our Mishnah. Weiss himself points out (*Dor*, I, 65) many Mishnahs which, in his opinion, are very old and originated in the time of the Soferim. Why is it then that this one Soferic saying transmitted by Jose has been retained in the original language, the Aramaic, while all the other teachings of the Soferim, which no doubt are preserved in our Mishnah, have been translated into the later Hebrew?[56] Furthermore, the whole premise that the Soferim gave their teachings in Aramaic, declared by Weiss (Introduction to the Mekilta, *ibid.*) to be beyond doubt, is absolutely false. All indications point to the fact that the Soferim gave their teachings in Hebrew, the language which the people spoke. The exiles who returned from Babylon did not bring with them the Aramaic language. They spoke Hebrew, as is evident from Neh. 13.24, where Nehemiah complains that some of the children were unable to speak the Jewish language, that is Hebrew. It certainly cannot be assumed that the Soferim, as teachers of the people, would set the bad example of using any language other than their own.[57] The Aramaic language came into use among the people in Palestine at a much later date[58] (see Schürer, *Geschichte*, II[4], pp. 23–6.)

[56] According to Weiss, then, we would have to account for another radical change in the method of teaching, namely, the change in the language, the medium of instruction, from the Aramaic to the later Hebrew, and one would have to fix the time and find the reason for the change.

[57] Weiss himself says (*Dor*, I, 54) that Nehemiah and the earlier Soferim endeavored to keep up the Hebrew, and only some of the people did not understand Hebrew perfectly. But if so, why did the Soferim give all their teachings in Aramaic?

[58] Schürer points out that the Aramaic of Palestine could not have been brought along by the returning exiles, as the Aramaic spoken in Palestine was the Western Aramaic and not the Eastern Aramaic spoken in Babylon. Friedmann (*op. cit.*, p. 57) assumes that the language of the returning exiles was the Babylonian Aramaic, but that in the course of time this language was changed and influenced by the Aramaic of Palestine. This assumption is without proof. The proofs cited by Friedmann for the use of the Aramaic language do not prove anything with regard to the time of the Soferim. The Aramaic became the language of the Jews in Palestine in the first half of the second century B. C. E. The proofs adduced by Friedmann (*loc. cit.*, p. 58) refer to a much later date than the second century B. C. E. Saadya Gaon, in the preface to his *Sefer Ha-Iggaron* (Harkavy, *Zikron la-Rishonim*, V, 54),

Even after the Aramaic language had become the language of the people, Hebrew remained the language of the school and the teachers, the לשון חכמים. For this reason we have all the Halakot in the tannaitic literature, such as Mishnah and halakic Midrashim, given in Hebrew.

Aside from all these considerations as to the language of the Soferim, it is altogether wrong to connect these three Halakot with the Soferim. They are not Halakot of the Soferim, which Jose merely transmitted and attested to, they are decisions which originated with Jose himself and for which he offered reasons and scriptural proofs. And this brings us to the discussion of the second difficulty in our Mishnah, namely, the introductory term העיד. This term העיד means literally to testify, to state as a witness what one knows or has seen or heard. Some scholars have understood the term העיד in this Mishnah in this very sense, and have declared it to mean that Jose merely testified that these decisions were older traditional laws and practices. As we have seen above, Weiss assumed that they were decisions of the Soferim for the genuineness of which Jose vouched. But it is absolutely incorrect to take the term העיד here in the sense that Jose merely "testified" to older traditional laws and decisions. As far as we know, the method of procedure followed by the teachers of the Halakah in receiving a teacher's testimony in regard to some rule or practice was to consider the testimony alone. They either decided according to it, or if for some reason they would not do so, they stated that reason. Without reflecting upon the testifying teacher, they would seek to invalidate the testimony or to deny its bearing upon the case under discussion (cf. 'Eduy. 2.2; 8.3; Sanh. 7.2; and Tosefta Sanh. 9.11). Nowhere do we find that the hold the testifying teacher responsible for the decision which he reports.[59] Here, in the case of Jose, however, we see

---

states that about three years before the rule of Alexander in Palestine the Jews began to neglect Hebrew and adapted the language of the other nations in the land (i. e., Aramaic). While his date is based upon a wrong chronology (see Part IV), he certainly is correct in his statement as to the fact that the returning exiles spoke Hebrew and that it was only after many years that they began to speak Aramaic.

[59] The case of Akabiah b. Mahalalel (Mishnah 'Eduy. 5.6) whom the other

that they called Jose שריא "the Permitter," thus making Jose responsible for the decisions. If Jose had been merely testifying

---

teachers held responsible for the decisions which he stated before them, cannot be cited as an instance against this statement. It is doubtful, to say the least, whether the four decisions of Akabiah, although likewise introduced with the term העיד, were old traditional Halakot to which he merely testified.

The controversy between Akabiah and the other teachers is shrouded in mystery. The later teachers, for reasons best known to themselves, did not care to report about it in detail. They acknowledged only with reluctance that there were disputes among the older teachers about the traditional laws, that such an eminent teacher as Akabiah protested against what was accepted by others as traditional laws, and that harsh means were used to silence such protests. The knowledge of these facts would reflect unfavorably upon the validity of the traditional law. For this reason one of the later teachers also denied the fact that Akabiah was put under ban (*ibid.*). From the meager reports preserved in our sources it is difficult to obtain a clear account of the nature of the dispute and of what actually took place between Akabiah and the other teachers. It is, however, very probable that Akabiah was the author of these four decisions, and that the term העיד in this case is likewise to be taken in the sense of "stated," "declared," and not "testified." This is apparent from the very demand to retract which the other teachers made. They could not have asked him to take back his testimony, but they could ask him to change his opinion. From this expression used in this demand to retract, חזור בך מארבעה דברים שהיית אומר, it is also evident that Akabiah was his own authority in these four decisions, that he was the one who said these things, and not that he merely testified that others said them. Again, in his advice to his son to follow the majority, Akabiah uses the words מוטב להניח דברי היחיד ולאחוז בדברי המרובים, "It is better to abandon the opinion of an individual and to hold to the opinion of the many" (*ibid.*, 7). From these words it is also evident that the decisions of Akabiah were the opinion of an individual teacher (i. e., himself), and not the opinion of the majority of the teachers from whom Akabiah received them. We must therefore assume that the words אני שמעתי מפי המרובים ... אני עמדתי בשמועתי (*ibid.*, 7), which are put into Akabiah's mouth, are a later addition. They form an attempt on the part of a later teacher to minimize the sharpness of the conflict between Akabiah and his contemporaries. Its purpose was to make it appear as if there had always been perfect harmony among the teachers, and that only in this case each had a different tradition which he had to follow. This, however, is a very poor attempt, for it does not explain how there could have been different traditions. It only shifts the date of the conflict of opinions from the time of Akabiah and his colleagues to the time of their teachers and predecessors.

It is also possible that the same later author who thus attempted to exonerate Akabiah added the word העיד, to introduce Akabiah's decision, thus representing them as being based upon an older tradition which Akabiah had.

to the decisions of former teachers, then those former teachers, the Soferim or whoever they may have been, were the ones who "permitted," and not Jose. Why, then, call Jose שריא "the Permitter?"

This is even more strange since we do not hear that the other teachers gave any argument against his decisions and, as we shall see, they even accepted them להלכה "as a norm of practice."[60] It is therefore evident that these Halakot, though introduced with the phrase העיד יוסי, were not older traditional laws transmitted by Jose as a mere witness, but Jose's own teachings. He was the one who "permitted," and he deserved the name שריא. This is further confirmed by the discussions of the Amoraim in the Talmud who try to explain these decisions. Rab and Samuel in attempting to give a reason for one decision of Jose's, use the word קסבר "he (Jose) held," or "was of the opinion." And when the reason for another decision is asked, the phrase במאי קמיפלגי "in what do they (Jose and his opponent or opponents) differ" is used ('Ab. Zarah 37a,b). Again, when R. Papa ventured to say in regard to one of the decisions that it was an old traditional law, הילכתא גמירי לה, he was promptly refuted (Pes. 17b). Thus we see that in the talmudic discussions about these decisions they are taken as Jose's own teachings and not as older traditional laws.

This correct interpretation removes all the difficulties from our Mishnah. The term העיד is to be taken here in the sense of "declared," or "stated." The Aramaic in which these decisions are expressed is to be accounted for, not by their alleged origin in the early days of the Soferim, but rather by the comparatively late date at which they originated. It is probably also due to the peculiar circumstances which gave them their present form. These decisions, as we have them, are not preserved to us in Jose's own words, nor in the form in which he gave them. Jose gave these decisions in Hebrew and in Midrash-form. He taught

---

[60] Levy erroneously states (*Oẓar Neḥmad*, III, 29–30) that Jose's decisions were ignored by the other teachers. From the talmudic discussion Pes. 16a (cf. also Maimonides, *Yad, Tum'at 'Oklin*, 10.16) and 'Ab. Zarah 37a,b it is evident that the decisions of Jose were accepted by the other teachers and made the norm for practice, להלכה.

them in connection with the several Scriptural passages on which he based the decisions. The teachers, however, who transmitted these decisions, for reasons of their own (to be stated below), detached these decisions from their scriptural bases and expressed them in the Aramaic language. That Jose had scriptural proofs for his decisions, is evidenced by the fact that the Amoraim in the Talmud endeavor to find these proofs or reasons. Evidently the Amoraim were convinced that some scriptural proofs did underlie these decisions, although not mentioned by the teachers who transmitted them. By following the Amoraim, whose analysis of these Halakot probably echoes older tradition, we will be able to find the midrashic proofs given by Jose in support of his decisions.

In the case of one decision the midrashic arguments of Jose and his opponents have fortunately been preserved, namely, in the case of the third decision which is ודיקרב במיתא מסתאב "one who touches a corpse becomes unclean." We must first arrive at the correct meaning of the decision. This decision does not mean simply that one who touches a corpse becomes unclean, for this is expressly stated in the Bible in regard to a human corpse (Num. 19.11) as well as in regard to the carcass of an animal (Lev. 11.27 and 29) or a reptile (*ibid.*, 31). Furthermore, Jose is called "the Permitter," evidently because in all three decisions he permits things that were formerly considered forbidden. He, therefore, could not mean to teach us, in this last decision, concerning what becomes unclean and therefore forbidden. We arrive at the correct meaning of this decision by emphasizing the word במיתא[61] and interpreting it to mean "[only] he who

---

[61] Frankel (*Hodegetica*, p. 32) explains the decision of Jose to mean that Jose decided that one who has come into direct contact with a corpse becomes unclean but one degree less than the corpose itself, i. e., he becomes an אב הטומאה and not an אבי אבות הטומאה. Frankel bases his explanation on the expression מסתאב "becomes unclean," since it is not said מסאב, which could mean also "he makes unclean." But this explanation is wrong. In the first place, if the נוגע במת becomes only an אב הטומאה he could still make others unclean, and thus be a מסאב and not merely a מסתאב. Secondly, as Weiss (*Dor*, I, 100, note) pointed out, the reading מסתאב is not genuine, some editions having indeed מסאב. Moreover, מסאב does not mean "makes unclean," but simply "is unclean." Jose's decision probably was that one can become unclean only

touches a dead body (of a human being or an animal or a reptile) becomes unclean," but one who touches a thing or person that has itself become unclean by contact with a corpse (i. e., דיקרב בדיקרב)[62] does not become unclean. This interpretation of Jose's third decision is given in the Talmud ('Ab. Zarah 37b) and is correct despite the objections raised by Raba. As stated correctly in the Talmud (*ibid.*), the other teachers before and during the time of Jose were of the opinion that דיקרב בדיקרב, one who touches a person who has become unclean by contact with a corpse, also become unclean, מדאורייתא, according to the Law. They must have derived their opinion either from a literal interpretation of the passage in Num. 19.22 כל אשר יגע בו הטמא יטמא, as stated in the Talmud (*ibid.*) or, what is more likely, from the passage in Lev. 5.2, או נפש אשר תגע בכל דבר טמא, which literally means one who touches any object that is unclean. This apparently includes one who touches an object which has become unclean through contact with a corpse. This seems to me to have

---

by direct contact with a corpse, the emphasis being on במיתא. If, however, one touches a thing or another person that had become unclean by contact with a corpse, he does not become unclean, because he did not come in direct contact with the corpse.

[62] The later talmudic teachers seek to harmonize Jose's decision with the later teachings of the Halakah. They therefore modify the meaning of the term דיקרב בדיקרב, and explain it so as to agree with the later teachings of the accepted Halakah. But the original meaning of the term דיקרב בדיקרב, which is apparently identical with the phrase נגע אדם במגע טמאות in Sifra, was altogether different from the meaning given to it in the talmudic discussion. To harmonize Jose's decision with the later teachings of the Halakah, one could interpret it to mean that only certain kinds of דיקרב בדיקרב are clean. That is to say, Jose declared that not everything that has been in contact with a corpse can make a person that touches it unclean. Jose, then, meant to exclude earth, stone, and wood. His decision accordingly was directed against an older Halakah which declared that one who touches wood, stone, or earth that has become defiled by contact with a corpse, becomes unclean. Such an old Halakah seems to be expressed in the "Fragments of a Zadokite Work" (Schechter, *Documents of Jewish Sectaries*, I, 12, lines 15–17). Cf., however, Ginzberg's ingenious explanation of this passage in the *Monatsschrift*, 1912, pp. 560–61). It seems, however, more probable that Jose declared every kind of דיקרב בדיקרב clean, even a person who touches another person who had become defiled by contact with a corpse. Jose, then, is against the later teachings of the Halakah that a טמא מת becomes an אב הטומאה and can make others unclean. See below, note 64.

been the scriptural basis for their theory. But Jose interpreted this scriptural passage differently, so that he could give his decision, permitting a דיקרב בדיקרב, and declaring such a one as clean.

Indeed, we find these two opposing views preserved in Sifra, *Ḥobah*, XII, ed. Weiss 22d. There we read as follows: או נפש אשר תגע בכל דבר טמא, הזקנים הראשונים היו אומרים יכול אפילו אם נגע אדם במגע טמאות יהא חייב ת"ל בנבלת חיה בנבלת בהמה מה אלו מיוחדין שהם אבות הטומאה יצא דבר שאין אב הטומאה "Or if a person touches any unclean thing (Lev. 5.2). The former teachers said: "One might argue [from the expression 'any unclean thing'] that even if a person has touched anything that had come into contact with unclean things, he should also be [considered unclean and consequently] subject to the law mentioned in this passage. The scriptural text teaches us, therefore, [by specifically mentioning] 'whether it be a carcass of an unclean beast, or a carcass of unclean cattle, or the carcass of unclean creeping things' that only these specific objects which are original causes of uncleanness [can by their contact make a man unclean], but it excludes anything else which is not an original cause of uncleanness." The term יכול "one might argue," points to an actual opinion held by some people, which the Midrash seeks to refute. As the view of the זקנים הראשונים here expressed is identical with the view of Jose,[63] *viz.*: that only דיקרב במיתא becomes unclean, the possible opinion introduced by יכול refers to the view actually held by the teachers before Jose, or by those who disputed with him. We can, therefore, ascertain the new method used by Jose from the interpretation given in Sifra in the name of the זקנים הראשונים. This interpretation says that the meaning of the general term בכל דבר טמא is defined and limited by the following special terms בנבלת בהמה חיה או שרץ, so as to include only the latter or such as are exactly like them. Accordingly we have in this instance for the first time the application of the rule of כלל ופרט אין בכלל אלא מה שבפרט. And if we include the passage מה אלו מיוחדין in the original

---

[63] The identity of Jose's decision with the one quoted in Sifra in the name of the זקנים הראשונים is also assumed by Professor I. Levy as quoted by S. Horowitz in *Sifre Zuṭa* (Breslau, 1910), p. 7, note 5.

Midrash, which however is doubtful,[64] Jose or the זקנים הראשונים must have considered the following passage או אשר יגע בכל טומאת אדם as another כלל and formulated the rule כלל ופרט וכלל אי אתה דן אלא כעין הפרט, and accordingly included other אבות הטומאה which are like מיתא.

From a comparison of the explanation given to Jose's first decision in 'Ab. Zarah 37a with Ḥul. 66a we learn that the decision declaring איל קמצא as clean was reached by Jose also by means of applying the rule כלל ופרט וכלל to include כעין הפרט (see Rashi 'Ab. Zarah, ad loc., and Tosefot Yom ṭob to 'Eduy. 7.8). In regard to the decision about the משקה בי מטבחיא, it is hard to find out by what means Jose derived this from the Scriptures, as we are not quite sure as to the exact meaning of this decision. Even the later talmudic teachers held different opinions regarding its meaning. According to Rab, Jose's decision declared these liquids altogether clean and not subject to defilement, דכן ממש, while according to Samuel the decision was merely that these liquids cannot communicate to others their defilement, but in

[64] It seems to me that the passage מה אלו מיוחדין שהן אבות הטומאה is not of the original Midrash of the זקנים הראשונים, but a later addition. For, if it had been a part of the Midrash of the older teachers, then R. Akiba's Midrash which follows it would not have added anything and would have been entirely superfluous. The original Midrash of the older teachers closed with the words ת״ל ... בנבלת שרץ. The older teachers interpreted this scriptural passage as a כלל ופרט, to mean only what is expressly mentioned in the special term אין בכלל אלא מה שבפרט. They excluded even אבות הטומאה. To this R. Akiba added another Midrash according to which only what is not an אב הטומאה is excluded. If, however, we include the passage מה אלו מיוחדין שהן אבות הטומאה in the original Midrash of the older teachers, we must assume that the term אבות הטומאה is used by them in a narrow sense to designate "the original sources of uncleanness," and not in the technical sense in which it is used usually to designate a certain degree of uncleanness (see Horowitz, op. cit., p. 8).

That the זקנים הראשונים excluded even so-called אבות הטומאה is conceded even by Rabed in his commentary on Sifra, ad loc. (This shows that he felt the difficulty of finding a difference between their Midrash and the Midrash of R. Akiba.) Rabed, however, assumes that the older teachers decided this only with regard to punishment for entering the sanctuary in such a state of uncleanness, ואין חייבין עליהם על ביאת מקדש. Levy, as quoted by Horowitz, follows Rabed herein. But it is very unlikely that the older teachers made such a distinction. If a person was considered unclean he would have been punished for entering the sanctuary in his state of uncleanness. If he was not to be punished for entering the sanctuary, that meant he was not at all unclean.

themselves may become defiled, דכן מלטמא טומאת אחרים (see Pes. 17a). Rab's explanation seems, however, to be more plausible and warranted by the plain sense of the word דכן which means, simply, דכן ממש. In this case we may safely assume that Jose arrived at this decision also by means of the method of using the כלל ופרט rule. For in Lev. 11.24, where the defilement of liquids is spoken of, it is said: וכל משקה אשר ישתה בכלי יטמא. Jose saw in the words אשר ישתה "which is drinkable" or "which is drunk out of a vessel," a limiting special term, פרט, which qualifies and limits the general term, וכל משקה, and excludes from the latter the משקה בי מטבחיא which "is not drinkable" or "is not drunk out of a vessel." In the same way Eliezer (in Sifra, *Shemini*, IX, Weiss 55a) applies this principle to exclude משקה סרוח.[65]

Thus we find that Jose derived all his decisions from the Scripture by means of interpretations, and that these interpretations were according to new methods. These new methods, however, were rejected by his contemporaries, because they were novel. The teachers of the next generation and possibly even some of his colleagues, respecting the authority of Jose, accepted his decisions but hesitated to recognize the validity of the new rule of כלל ופרט which Jose used. Since they did not accept this method they could not teach these decisions together with the scriptural proofs given to them by Jose. They therefore merely mentioned them as decisions given by Jose. They would not even teach them in Hebrew, the language in which they taught all their Halakot connected with the Scripture in Midrash-form. They formulated them in the Aramaic language, then already

[65] It is possible that in the saying of R. Eliezer, the representative of the older Halakah, we have the same decision which was given by Jose. Jose, however, directed his decision to a certain kind of undrinkable liquid, the משקה בי מטבחיא, while the older Halakah as represented by R. Eliezer formulated the same decision in a general way, so as to apply it to all undrinkable liquids, משקה סרוח. Accordingly, the statement of Rab (Pes. 17a) that Jose held that there was no biblical law which would subject liquids to uncleanness, קסבר אין טומאה למשקין מן התורה, is not correct. Jose excluded only undrinkable liquids from these laws. It is very unlikely that as early as the time of Jose there was a rabbinical law declaring liquids subject to uncleanness, גזירה למשקין מדרבנן. It should be noticed that there is much confusion about the laws of טומאת משקין, which made it difficult to ascertain the real meaning of Jose's decision, the more so as the later teachers sought to harmonize it with the later halakic rulings about liquids.

popular, just as they would mention decisions given by secular authorities, or just as they would refer to popular customs in the language of the people, rather than in the language of the school.[66] For this reason they introduced these Halakot with the formula העיד יוסי,[67] Jose 'declared,' or 'stated,' i. e., Jose is the authority for these decisions; and they properly called him יוסי שריא 'Jose the Permitter.'

On the same principle and in the same manner, the teachers dealt with another decision given by Jose ben Joezer and his colleague Jose ben Joḥanan of Jerusalem, *viz.*, that glassware is subject to the laws of Levitical uncleanness. An old tradition reports that the two Joses decreed that the laws of uncleanness apply to glassware, גזרו טומאה על כלי זכוכית (Shab. 15a). There is no reason to doubt the genuineness of this report in the Babylonian Talmud, nor are there any reasons for ascribing this decree to other authors as Graetz has done.[68] The reason for this decision

---

[66] In the Midrash form, when the Halakah forms a sort of a commentary on the Hebrew text, the use of the Hebrew language especially recommended itself. In many cases the comment consisted merely in emphasizing the important words in the text, or in calling attention to a peculiar construction or to a special form. All these peculiarities of the Midrash would have made it very difficult to use another language than Hebrew. In this manner Hebrew remained the לשון חכמים, the language of the school. It continued to be used for teaching Halakah even when the latter was separated from the Hebrew text of the Scriptures and taught independently in Mishnah-form.

[67] See above, note 30. There is no doubt that the introductory formula העיד was added by a later teacher. It may be that in the case of Jose, as in the case of Akabiah (see above, note 58) the later teacher who added this formula meant to suggest by it that Jose had a tradition on which he based his decisions, so that he was not the author or innovator of the same.

[68] Graetz, *Geschichte*, III⁴, 707, is inclined to ascribe this decree about glassware to Simon b. Sheṭaḥ and not to Jose b. Joezer. He bases his theory solely on the passage in p. Ket. 8.11, (32c), where it is said of Simon b. Sheṭaḥ, והוא התקין טומאה לכלי זכוכית. The correctness of this statement is questioned by the Talmud on the ground that it conflicts with another reliable report, which ascribes this decree to the two Joses. The explanation is then offered that both reports are correct. The decree was first issued by the two Joses, but was subsequently forgotten or neglected, and then revived and reintroduced by Simon b. Sheṭaḥ. This talmudic explanation may be correct. The hesitancy on the part of the other teachers, Jose's colleagues, to accept the interpretation on which he based his decree may have necessitated another formal decree or a confirmatory act in the days of Simon b. Sheṭaḥ. Graetz, however, evidently

was (as is correctly given by Joḥanan, in the name of Simon ben Laḳish) that glass is made of sand and is therefore the same as

does not think so. He discards this explanation of the Talmud as a poor attempt to harmonize these two conflicting reports. However, granted that this explanation is merely a harmonization, we can reject the explanation but not the objection raised by the Talmud. There is no reason whatever for ignoring all the other reports which ascribe the decree to the two Joses and accepting this one which ascribes it to Simon b. Shetaḥ. This is all the more incorrect as it is apparent that this one report is based on a mistake. Simon b. Shetaḥ decreed against metal-ware, כלי מתכות (Shab. 14b, cf. Graetz, *loc. cit.*, pp. 706, 708). In a report about this decree of Simon some one probably made the mistake of substituting כלי זכוכית for כלי מתכות. R. Jonah's saying cited there in the Talmud (p. Ket., *loc. cit.*) is accordingly another answer to the question raised there about the two conflicting reports. It is introduced for the purpose of correcting the mistake in the one report, and telling us that Simon decreed only against metal-ware כלי מתכות and not against כלי זכוכית. The decree against the latter, then, really came from the two Joses as reported repeatedly in p. Shab. 1.3d, p. Pes. 27d, and b. Shab. 15a.

Graetz is wrong in assuming that the Babylonian Talmud does not contain correct information about this subject, and that the utterance of an Amora Zeera is mistaken in the Babylonian Talmud for a Baraita. The contrary is true. This report is an older Baraita. In the Palestinian Talmud, however, this Baraita is mentioned by the Amora Zeera, as there are many such instances of Baraitot being quoted by Amoraim and appearing as if they were the sayings of the Amoraim (see Frankel, *Mebo ha-Jerushalmi*, pp. 26–7).

From the discussion in the Babylonian Talmud about this report it is evident that they were well informed about this case. Objections are raised against part of this tradition, viz., the report about the decree of טומאה על ארץ העמים. They show that there is another report which ascribes it to the רבנן דשמונים שנה. The two reports are, however, harmonized. But they could not find any contradictory report about the decree against כלי זכוכית.

The reading ועל כלי זכוכית in the report of the activity of the רבנן דשמונים שנה is missing in the older codices. See Zeraḥiah Halevi in *Ha-Maor* to Shabbat, *ad loc*. From the fact that no answer or solution is given in regard to כלי זכוכית it is also evident that the report about the act of the רבנן דשמונים שנה only mentioned the decree of טומאה על ארץ העמים.

Graetz's argument, that this institution presupposes the common use of glassware among the people, a practice which could not have been the case in the time of the two Joses, is rather weak. Although the great majority of the people may not have lived in luxury in the time of the two Joses, yet there were at least some rich people who could and did indulge in the luxury of using glassware. It was just at the first introduction of these vessels to Judea by some rich people that the question about their status in regard to the laws of cleanness came up. The teachers then declared that they were subject to the laws of uncleanness.

any other earthen vessel, כלי חרס (*ibid.*, 15b). The Talmud, discussing this explanation of Simon ben Laḳish, raises the following question: 'If glassware has been declared like כלי חרס because being made of sand it belongs to the class of earthen vessels, why then is it not considered by the Halakah as כלי חרס in all respects?

In the discussion that follows, the Talmud (*ibid.*) finds difficulties in answering this question. We are not concerned with the answer given in the Talmud, because it is merely an unsuccessful attempt to harmonize the decision of Jose with later practice. The significant thing for us is that this question was raised. It indicates that the Amoraim experienced difficulty in understanding the decision, although they were aware of the basis upon which Jose founded his decision. To this question raised in the Talmud we may add the following question which will disclose another weak point in the explanation of the decision. If this decision of the two Joses was reached by interpreting the biblical term כלי חרס so as to include glassware (because it is made of sand) then their decision was in reality a biblical law, as no distinction can be made between vessels of clay and vessels of sand, both being earthen vessels. Why then was this decision ascribed to the two Joses and characterized as an arbitrary decree, a mere גזירה? The following explanation will give the answer to both questions mentioned above and will remove the difficulties experienced by the talmudic teachers in understanding this decision. Jose and his colleague interpreted the biblical term כלי חרס to mean a vessel made of any kind of earth, and, consequently, he included in it כלי זכוכית which he indeed considered in all respects like כלי חרס. The younger teachers, however, would not accept the broad definition given by Jose to the term כלי חרס so as to include כלי זכוכית also. For this reason they refused to follow Jose in considering glassware like כלי חרס in all respects. Out of respect for the two Joses, some of their contemporaries or successors accepted the decision, but designated it merely as a rabbinical decree, a גזירה. They would therefore apply to כלי זכוכית only certain of the laws of uncleanness that pertained to earthen vessels, כלי חרס. These other teachers would therefore not teach this decision in the Midrash-form together with the passage

MIDRASH AND MISHNAH   227

וכל כלי חרס, as Jose no doubt did. They would teach it as an independent Halakah, as a rabbinical law that has no scriptural basis but rested merely upon the authority of the two teachers.

The motive for accepting a teacher's decision without accepting his proof, may be found either in the respect entertained by the younger teachers for the author of the decision, or in their belief, that the author of the decision was in possession of a tradition unknown to them.[69] In either case they had no hesitancy in rejecting the proofs which they considered unconvincing or too novel. Whatever their motives, it is certain that the younger contemporaries of Jose or his successors accepted his decisions and taught them in his name although without his proofs for them. The latter they rejected, because they did not approve of his new methods of interpretation.

This attitude, despite its inconsistency, was quite common among the teachers of the Halakah.[70] The most striking instance of this practice is to be found in the story of Hillel and the Bene Batyra (p. Pes. 33a). In this account we are told that all the arguments and scriptural proofs advanced by Hillel in favor of the decision that the Passover sacrifice should set aside the Sabbath were rejected by the Bene Batyra, although Hillel had learned all or most of these proofs and interpretations from his teachers Shemaiah and Abtalion. But when, at last, he told them that he had received the decision itself from Shemaiah and Abtalion, they forthwith accepted the same. אף על פי שהיה יושב ודורש להן כל היום לא קיבלו ממנו עד שאמר יבא עלי כך שמעתי משמעיה ואבטליון. We need not discuss the historicity of this report, a point which is, to say the least, very doubtful. Whatever we may think of the account, we may be sure that its author pictured accurately the attitude which teachers usually assumed towards the deci-

---

[69] Cf. the idea expressed in the saying: כך היתה הלכה בידם ושכחוה ועמדו השניים והסכימו על דעת הראשונים, often used to explain the acts of the teachers who instituted new laws (p. Sheb. 33b and p. Ket. 32c). It is possible that such an idea was conceived in very early times, and possibly it was such a view that guided the successors of Jose in their acceptance of his decisions.

[70] Cf. the phrase תשובה אם הלכה נקבל ואם לדין יש תשובה (Mishnah Yeb. 8.3 and Mishnah Ker. 3.9) which clearly shows that they were ready to accept a Halakah although rejecting the proof offered for that Halakah.

sions given in the name of older teachers. It is evident from this account that its author certainly believed that teachers or authorities like the Bene Batyra (whoever they may have been) were in the habit of accepting decisions given in the name of a departed teacher, even in cases where they would refuse to accept the proofs for the decisions also given in the name of that teacher.[71] Whether this actually took place in the case of Hillel and the Bene Batyra is of minor importance. Accordingly, we learn from this report that in the time of Hillel there were certain teachers who raised objections to the new methods which Hillel had acquired from the great exegetes דרשנים גדולים, Shemaiah and Abtalion. However, the same teachers would not hesitate to accept a practical decision which Hillel reported in the name of these two authorities. That which happened in the time of Hillel also happened in the time of Jose ben Joezer. When he used new methods of interpretation for the first time, his colleagues hesitated to follow him, although they did accept some of the decisions which he derived from the Scripture by means of these new methods.

We can easily understand the reason for such an attitude, inconsistent as it may appear. To accept the proof for a decision implied approval of the method by which that proof was obtained. This would open the door to further application of these new methods, so that there was no way of telling what decisions might be thus arrived at. Against this danger the teachers attempted to guard themselves, but they never went so far as to decide, in any practical case, against the authority of an older

[71] Cf. Bassfreund (*op. cit.*, p. 19, note 3). All the difficulties which he finds in this story are removed by our explanation. Most likely Hillel had learned from Shemaiah and Abtalion not only the decision but also all the interpretations which he offered as arguments in favor of the same. He also gave these interpretations in the name of his teachers. The Bene Batyra, however, refused to accept these interpretations, because they objected to the new methods developed by Shemaiah and Abtalion. It was their opposition to these new methods of interpretation which kept them from attending the schools of Shemaiah and Abtalion, and not their negligence, as one might judge from Hillel's reputed remark: עצלות שהיתה בכם שלא שמשתם שני גדולי הדור. Their respect for these great teachers, however, led them to accept their decision, even though they would not accept their proofs.

teacher. For this reason they would often accept the decision but reject the proofs.

In the above, we have digressed for the purpose of making clear that difference of opinion concerning methods of interpretation prompted the teachers to sometimes divorce a Halakah from the scriptural proof. We have also seen that the three oldest Halakot preserved in Mishnah-form, namely, the three decisions of Jose, owed their present form to this very reason. They were expressed in Mishnah-form by Jose's disciples who felt constrained to reject the proofs advanced by Jose because of the novelty of his methods of interpretation.

Accordingly, it may be stated with certainty that the Mishnah-form was first used to teach those customs and practices which originated during the time when there was no official activity of the teachers. Having no scriptural basis, they could not be taught in connection with the Scripture, i. e., in the Midrash-form. The Mishnah-form was further used to teach those traditional laws and decisions which some teachers attempted to derive from Scripture by means of new methods of interpretation. While some of their contemporaries or disciples accepted the new methods, and therefore taught these decisions in the Midrash-form, others, and by far the majority, rejecting the new methods, accepted only the decisions. Finding no convincing proofs for such laws in the Bible, they taught them independently of scriptural proof, i. e., in the Mishnah-form. These two motives for teaching Halakot in the Mishnah-form are really one and the same. Whether no midrashic proof could be found for a decision, or whether the midrashic proof suggested was deemed unconvincing, the motive for the Mishnah-form was the same — the absence of a sound Midrash.

To this first motive there soon were added other motives for the use of the Mishnah-form. Certain considerations in the course of time urged the teachers to extend its use even to such Halakot as had, in their opinion, good scriptural proofs and could well be taught in connection with the Scripture in the Midrash-form. These other motives and considerations arose from the disputes between the Sadducees and Pharisees. They became stronger and stronger with the ever-widening breach between the two factions.

As the dispute between the parties progressed, the antagonism between them naturally became sharper. Each party came to assume a distinctive attitude towards the Law, and they consistently worked out their respective lines of attack and defense. The Pharisees came to recognize the binding character of the traditional Law, תורה שבעל פה, and demanded that it be considered of equal authority with the written Law. The Sadducees, on the other hand, became more outspoken in their denial that the traditional Law possessed absolute authority. These differences had their effect upon the forms used in teaching the Halakah.

As we have seen above, the Midrash was used for the purpose of grafting new decisions and practices upon the words of the Written Law, when the latter only was considered the sole authority binding upon the people. To give sanction to any decision or traditional Law, it was necessary to find for it some indication in the authoritative Book of the Law and thus to present it as contained or implied in the Written Law. As soon as Tradition was raised to the rank of the Law and thus recognized as an independent authority parallel to the Written Law, there was no longer that urgent need of connecting each and every Halakah with the words of the written Law in the form of the Midrash. A halakic decision based on a tradition was now considered by the teachers, and represented by them, to be just as authoritative as one derived from the written Torah by means of an interpretation or Midrash. The Halakah as traditional Law could now stand without the support of a scriptural basis, and could therefore be taught independently in the Mishnah-form. Not only was there no more need for teaching all the Halakot together with the Written Law in the Midrash-form, but there were also sufficient reasons for the Pharisaic teachers to teach Halakah as traditional Law without even attempting to connect the same with the Written Law. For, in so doing, they emphasized their belief in the twin-law שתי תורות; that is, the belief that there were two equal sources of religious teaching, one the written Torah and the other the unwritten Oral Law, both of which must be studied alike, and that one is as important as the other. Of course they continued to develop the Midrash method for the purpose of deriving new Halakot from the one source—the Written Law. The Halakot thus derived from the Scriptures were taught together with the latter, in the Midrash-form. In this way, they could well continue to use the Midrash-form even after the Mishnah-form was adopted. They were apprehensive only of using the Midrash-form exclusively, because such an exclusive use might reflect upon their theory of an authoritative Oral Law. The very endeavor to connect all Halakot with the Written Law by means of the Midrash would have meant to acknowledge that there was only one Law, namely, the one contained in the Book. They would thus have conceded to the Sadducees the disputed point that the traditional Law, תורה שבעל פה, was not of equal authority with the Written Law, תורה שבכתב. By the parallel use of both forms, Midrash and Mishnah, they showed that they treated both sources alike. By teaching in Mishnah-form even such Halakot as could be derived from the Written Law and taught in the Midrash-form, they showed that they were not very anxious to find scriptural support for each Halakah. This was a strong expression of their belief in the equal authority of the two Torot, a belief that made it of little consequence whether a Halakah was taught in the Midrash-form, as derived from the Written Law, or in the Mishnah-form, as a traditional Law.

Furthermore, the exclusive use of the Midrash-form threatened to endanger the authority and the teachings of the Pharisees. These apprehensions caused the Pharisaic teachers to make more extensive use of the Mishnah-form and in some cases even to prefer the same to the Midrash-form. For to give all the halakic teachings of the Pharisees in the Midrash-form as based on the Scripture would have exposed these teachings to the attack of the Sadducees. As we have seen above, the hesitancy on the part of some teachers to recognize the validity of the new interpretations offered in support of certain decisions led to their teaching such decisions in Mishnah-form. The new rules and methods gradually found recognition among the Pharisaic teachers, who would admit the validity of interpretations derived by means of these new methods. Thus they were able to furnish a Midrash for almost every Halakah. But among the Sadducees the objection to these new methods was very strong and they absolutely denied their validity. If the Pharisees arrived at a certain decision by means of a new interpretation, the Sadducees could always dispute that decision by refuting the scriptural proof offered for it. It was possible for them to argue that the Pharisaic interpretation was unwarranted and that the scriptural passage did not mean what the Pharisees tried to read into it. The Pharisees feared that such arguments against their teachings raised by the Sadducees might have a detrimental effect upon the young students and draw them away from the Pharisaic teachings. The Pharisees were well aware that some of their interpretations were rather forced, and that their opponents' arguments against these interpretations were sound. Wherever possible, the Pharisees were, therefore, anxious to avoid such disputes, or to prevent their pupils from entering into them. The easiest way to avoid these disputes concerning the validity of the scriptural proofs for the Pharisaic teachings, was to avoid the mention of any such doubtful scriptural proofs at all, that is to say, to use Mishnah rather than Midrash.[72] After the

---

[72] It should be noticed that it was only with the younger students that the teachers pursued this pedagogical method of suppressing scriptural proofs, when these were not quite perfect, and of teaching the Halakot in Mishnah-form without any proof whatsoever. They considered it necessary to take this precaution to prevent the young students from being shaken in their belief in tradition and from doubting the authority of the traditional law. To the advanced students, however, they would unhesitatingly communicate all the scriptural proofs or even artificial supports which they had for their teachings. Hence among the advanced students the use of the Midrash-form was prevalent (see above, note 3).

A few talmudic sayings may be cited here to prove that it was the tendency among the teachers to withhold from the students while young the arguments and reasons for the laws and to keep them from disputes with their opponents. Simon b. Ḥalafta says: בשעה שהתלמידים קטנים כבוש לפניהם דברי תורה הגדילו ונעשו כעתודים גלה להם רזי תורה, "As long as the pupils are young hide from them [some] words of the Torah. When they are more mature and advanced reveal to them the secrets of the Torah" (p. 'Ab. Zarah 2.[41d]). Simon b. Yoḥai says: אין לך רשות לשקע עצמך בדברי תורה אלא לפני בני אדם כשרין, "You are not permitted to enter into a deep discussion of the words of the Torah except in the presence of pious and good people" (ibid.). By "pious and good people," בני אדם כשרין, are evidently meant people who follow the Rabbis and accept the teachings of the traditional law. According to the Gemara (ibid.) the two sayings of Simon b. Ḥalafta and Simon b. Yoḥai go together. There is a subtle

Pharisaic teachers agreed upon deriving a certain Halakah from a given passage, they preferred to teach that Halakah in an

---

connection between them. This connection consists in the fact that both aim at the same purpose, *viz.*, not to give the opponents of the Rabbis and the traditional law any opportunity to attack the traditional law by refuting the arguments or proofs brought for the same by the Rabbis.

We see from these two sayings that even as late as the middle of the second century c. e., when the followers of the Sadducean doctrines were no longer so strong, either in number or in influence, the Rabbis were still anxious to avoid disputes with them, and would therefore not tell the young pupils all their arguments and reasons for the laws, lest the opponents might refute them and upset the beliefs of the young pupils. Cf. the saying of Jose b. Ḥalafta, אל תתנו מקום לצדוקים לרדות, Mishnah Parah 3.3, and see below, note 80.

In the days of the earlier teachers when the influence of the Sadducees and their followers was stronger, this tendency among the teachers of the traditional law, to keep the young students from entering into discussions with the Sadducees, must of course have been stronger. The saying of R. Eliezer: מנעו בניכם מן ההגיון והושיבום בין ברכי תלמידי חכמים (Ber. 17b), probably expresses this tendency to make the young pupils study more the traditional law at the feet of the teachers, and keep them away from studying the scriptural proofs and the arguments for the traditional laws. A very striking illustration of this tendency among the earlier teachers is found in the report of a conversation between Ishmael and R. Joshua b. Ḥananiah. Ishmael asks R. Joshua to tell him the reason for a certain rabbinical law. Joshua, apparently unwilling to state the real reason, gives him an evasive answer. This does not satisfy Ishmael, and he persists in demanding an explanation. Joshua, instead of replying, simply ignores the question, drops the subject, and begins to discuss another subject (Mishnah 'Ab. Zarah 2.5). The Gemara (35a) reports further that Joshua actually commanded Ishmael to stop asking questions about this Law. He plainly told him, חשוק שפתיך זו בזו ואל תבהל להשיב, "Close your lips and be not so anxious to argue." The Gemara then gives the following explanation for this rather harsh rejoinder. It was a rule with the teachers in Palestine not to give a reason for a new law until at least one year after it was decreed. They feared that some people, not approving of the reason, would disregard and treat lightly the law itself: דילמא איכא איניש דלא ס"ל ואתי לזלזולי בה. These words are significant. There was only one class of people who might disapprove the reasons of the Rabbis, and these were the followers of Sadducean doctrines. Ishmael must have been a very young student at that time (see Midrash Shir ha-Shirim r. 1.2), and R. Joshua did not want to give him the reason for this new rabbinical law, for fear that some of the opponents of the traditional law might be able to prove to young Ishmael that the reason for this law was insufficient. (Cf. Joshua's remark against those who question the authority of the traditional law, to be cited below, note 78.)

independent form without citing passage or interpretation. Such a Halakah or decision could then be received in good faith by the students who followed the Pharisees. The pupils would rely on the authority of the teachers believing that they were in possession of valid proofs for their Halakot, although they did not mention them. On the other hand, the Sadducees could never successfully refute the Halakot thus taught. Not knowing on what basis they rested or what proofs the Pharisees offered for them, they were unable to argue concerning them. Their attacks on these Pharisaic teachings would then consist of mere negations without the force of strong argument. As mere negations are not convincing, such attacks on the part of the Sadducees could not greatly harm the Pharisaic followers.

The teachers, all of the Pharisaic party, were influenced by still another consideration. The tendency to teach only in Midrash-form, showing that all the religious teachings were lodged in the written Torah, threatened to take away from the Pharisaic teachers their prestige and to lend support to the claim of the Sadducees that there was no need of the חכמי ישראל, i. e., the teachers of the Pharisaic party. In the report about the conflict between John Hyrcanus and the Pharisees (Ḳid. 66a) we are told that the former, at first, hesitated to persecute the חכמי ישראל of the Pharisaic party because he considered them indispensable as teachers of the Law. He is said to have asked תורה מה תהא עליה "What will become of the Torah" without the Pharisaic teachers? But his Sadducean adviser, who urged the persecution of the Pharisees, told him הרי כרוכה ומונחת בקרן זוית כל הרוצה ללמוד יבא וילמוד, that the Torah would remain, even if the Pharisees would be killed.[73] Also that any one could study it because the Pharisees were not the only teachers of the Law.

[73] It makes very little difference whether this story is historically true in all its details or not. It reflects the idea of the Sadducees that the Pharisaic teachers could be dispensed with, and also the insistence of the Pharisees that they were absolutely necessary for the preservation of the Torah. The story mirrors for us the fears that the Pharisees entertained. As we are concerned merely with the motives that prompted the Pharisaic teachers to make the change in the form of their teaching, this story may be taken as an unconscious but accurate description of the consideration which could have moved them.

If, then, all the teachings and the Halakot were represented as derived from the Torah by means of interpretation, as is done in the Midrash-form, this claim of the Sadducees would appear justified. There would, indeed, be no need of the חכמי ישראל, of the Pharisaic party. Any one else could likewise interpret the Law correctly and derive from it all the Halakot that are implied therein, for a thorough understanding of the text of the Written Law was certainly not limited to the Pharisees. Thus the aim of the Pharisees to assert their authority and to show that they were absolutely necessary for the perpetuation of the religious teachings made it desirable for them to use the Mishnah-form. Even if there had been no objections to their new methods and even if they had been able to find scriptural proofs for all their decisions, they nevertheless thought it advisable not to insist upon connecting their halakic teachings with the Written Law in every case. By separating the two, they made themselves indispensable. If there were Halakot not connected with the Written Law, one must turn for these teachings to the חכמי ישראל, who alone were in possession of them, and who could not therefore be supplanted by others.

That which was at first but hesitatingly proposed, *viz.*, that there was an Oral Law alongside of the Written Law, was now boldly proclaimed. The Pharisaic teachers were represented as the teachers of tradition who received the Oral Law through a chain of teachers in direct succession from Moses. Consequently they were the only reliable authorities for the religious teachings. They insisted that their decisions must be accepted as authoritative, with the understanding that they either derived them from some passage in the Scripture by sound interpretation or based them upon some reliable tradition. The existence of valid proofs was always presupposed. Where no proofs were given, it was implied that they were unnecessary, as the authority of the teachers was beyond doubt. This tendency of the teachers to assert their authority and to maintain the validity of the traditional law did not have its motive in any petty desire for party aggrandizement, but rather in a genuine zeal for the cause, as they understood it. They asserted their authority and the authority of the traditional Law for the purpose of freeing the Torah from the fetters of literal interpretation forced upon it by the Sadducees, and developing the Law according to its spirit.

All these considerations caused the teachers to make more and more use of the Mishnah-form, but were not sufficient to make them abandon the Midrash-form. The Midrash-form still had many advantages. It was the older form to which they had long been accustomed. It also afforded a great help to the memory, as the written word can be relied upon to remind one of all the Halakot based upon or connected with it. Consequently they used both forms. Those Halakot which were based upon a sound and indisputable interpretation of a scriptural passage they taught in the Midrash-form, i. e., in connection with the scriptural proofs, and they arranged them in the order of the scriptural passages. But those Halakot for which the scriptural proofs were in dispute, they taught in the Mishnah-form and grouped them according to some principle of arrangement, such as number-mishnahs or other formulas, for the purpose of assisting the memory. In the course of time, the number of the Halakot taught in the Mishnah-form grew in proportion to the increase and the development of the halakic teachings. A great many of the new Halakot, both new decisions and new applications of older laws, were taught in the Mishnah-form by some teachers, because they could not find satisfactory scriptural support for them. It will be recollected that the decisions of Jose ben Joezer were given in the Mishnah-form for the same reason.

The process of development from the Midrash of the older Halakah to the Midrash of the younger Halakah was marked by constant struggles, in which the older methods tried to maintain themselves as long as possible. In each generation (at least until the time of the pupils of R. Akiba) the teachers were divided as to the acceptance of these new methods. Some teachers clung to the older ways and would not follow the daring applications of some new rules of the younger teachers. With the growth and development of the new methods, which only slowly and gradually won recognition with all the teachers, the number of Halakot connected with the Scriptures by means of these new exegetical rules, also grew. Such Halakot were then taught by different teachers in different forms. Those teachers who approved of all the new methods consequently considered the interpretations reached by these methods as sound, and the Halakot proved thereby as well founded in the Written Law. Accordingly, they would not hesitate to teach these Halakot together with their proofs, that is, in the Midrash-form. But those teachers who hesitated to accept the novel methods and the new interpretations based thereon, but who still accepted the Halakot, did so because they considered them as traditional, or because the same represented the opinion of the majority. Having no sound proofs, in their opinion, for these Halakot, they were compelled to teach them in the Mishnah-form, without any scriptural proof.

We find many such cases in the tannaitic literature. Of these we shall mention only a few; in Sifra, *Zaw* XI (ed. Weiss 34d–35a). R. Akiba tries to prove by one of his peculiar methods of interpretation that a "Todah"-offering requires half a "log" of oil. But R. Eleazar ben Azariah said to him: Even if you should keep on arguing the whole day with your rules about including and excluding qualities of scriptural expressions, I will not listen to you. The decision that a "Todah"-offering requires half a "log" of oil is to be accepted as a traditional law.[74] אפילו אתה אומר כל היום כולו בשמן לרבות בשמן למעט איני שומע לך אלא חצי לוג שמן לתודה הלכה למשה מסיני. The emphatic expression איני שומע לך 'I will not listen to you,' in the statement of Eleazar b. Azariah shows that he strongly objected to Akiba's method of interpreta-

[74] It is very doubtful whether R. Eleazar b. Azariah himself used the term הלכה למשה מסיני to apply to this law (notwithstanding Bacher, "Die Satzung vom Sinai," in *Studies in Jewish Literature published in honor of Dr. K. Kohler* [Berlin, 1913], p. 58). It is more likely that the words למשה מסיני are a late addition and not the words of R. Eleazar. R. Eleazar said merely that this rule was a traditional or rabbinical law, הלכה. A later teacher, who understood the term הלכה to mean "Sinaitic Law," added the words למשה מסיני. There are many such instances where a later teacher enlarges the term הלכה, used by an older teacher, to הלכה למשה מסיני, simply because he, the later teacher, understood the term הלכה in this sense. But this interpretation, given by a later teacher, to the term הלכה which was used by an older teacher, is not necessarily correct. Thus, for instance, the term הלכה used in the statement of the Mishnah והערלה הלכה (Mishnah Orlah 3.9) is interpreted by R. Joḥanan to mean הלכה למשה מסיני (p. Orlah 63b, b. Ḳid. 38b–39a), while Samuel explains it merely to mean simply a law or custom of the land הלכתא מדינה (*ibid.*).

tion, and that he considered such proof, not merely unnecessary, but also unsound. If Eleazar was actually in possession of a tradition for this law, it would have been sufficient to say אינו צריך 'There is no need of scriptural proof.' It is evident that this Halakah could not be based on an indisputable traditional law.[75] R. Akiba, therefore, desired to give it support by proving it from the Scriptures. He, no doubt, taught it in the Midrash-form together with the passage from which he endeavored to prove it. But R. Eleazar b. Azariah, who did not approve the interpretation of R. Akiba, although he accepted the Halakah, naturally taught it as a traditional law, and, of course, in Mishnah-form.

Another example is to be found in the reasoning used to justify the ceremony performed with the willow, ערבה. This, no doubt, was an old traditional custom. Abba Saul, however, declared it to be a biblical law, deriving it from the plural form ערבי נחל used in the passage of Lev. 23.40. This passage, according to Abba Saul, speaks of two willows. One is to be taken together with the Lulab, and the other separately for the special ceremony with the ערבה. Abba Saul, no doubt, taught this Halakah in the Midrash-form as an interpretation of the passage in Lev. 23.40. The other teachers, however, did not accept this interpretation. They considered this ceremony a mere traditional law, הלכה למשה מסיני (p. Sheb. 33b), and, of course, taught it in the Mishnah-form.

The same was also the case with the ceremony of the water-libation, נסוך המים, which R. Akiba, by means of a forced interpretation, tried to represent as a biblical law. The other teachers did not accept his interpretation. They considered it merely a

---

[75] It is absolutely impossible to assume that R. Akiba refused to believe the statement of R. Eleazar b. Azariah that he had a tradition in support of this law. The contrary must, therefore, be true. R. Eleazar rejected the Midrashic proof given by R. Akiba but accepted the law as a mere הלכה, i. e., as a rabbinical or traditional law. It may be, however, that this law was really an older traditional law, though not הלכה למשה מסיני, and that R. Akiba tried to give it a scriptural support while R. Eleazar preferred to teach it as a detached Halakah, i. e., in Midrash-form. Cf. the statement in Niddah 73a in regard to another law which R. Akiba derived from a scriptural passage, while R. Eleazar b. Azariah preferred to teach it as a mere Halakah, לרבי עקיבא קראי לרבי אלעזר בן עזריה הילכתא.

traditional law, הלכה למשה מסיני (*ibid.*), and, of course, taught it in the Mishnah-form. In this manner, the same decisions were sometimes taught by some teachers in the Midrash-form, while other teachers taught them in the Mishnah-form.[76] Thus the two forms continued in use according to the preference of the teachers. The parallel usage of these two forms continued long after Sadduceeism had ceased to be an influential factor in the life of the people, and the Pharisaic teachers had become the only recognized teachers of the Law. The Mishnah-form was retained by the teachers even after the new methods of interpretation had become generally accepted. In spite of the fact that these methods were developed to such an extent that one could interpret any passage to mean almost anything, and thus provide scriptural proofs for all possible decisions, the teachers, having habituated themselves to the Mishnah-form adhered to it. An additional reason for its retention may be found in the fact that the Mishnah-form itself had in the meantime improved. It lent itself to new principles of arrangement and grouping which gave it decided advantage for systematic presentation of the Halakah, and thus made it a desirable form of teaching.[77] The teachers

[76] The very frequency with which the Amoraim declare scriptural interpretations of the Tannaim to be merely artificial supports, אסמכתא בעלמא, for rabbinical or traditional laws (see Bacher, *Die exegetische Terminologie der jüdischen Traditionsliteratur*, II, 13–14), shows that it must have been frequent among the Tannaim to consider some interpretations as mere artificial supports and not real proofs. Otherwise, the Amoraim would not have doubted the validity of a tannaitic Midrash. It was only because they knew that the Tannaim themselves had frequently rejected a Midrash as unacceptable, that the Amoraim dared declare that some tannaitic interpretations were merely artificial supports.

Perhaps we have in the expressions מדרבנן וקרא אסמכתא בעלמא and הילכתא גמירי לה וקרא אסמכתא בעלמא an attempt at harmonization on the part of the Amoraim for the purpose of explaining away the differences of opinion between the older teachers. They mean to tell us that the older teachers always agreed as to which laws were traditional and which were derived from the Scriptures by means of interpretation. However, in the case of certain traditional laws, some of the teachers sought to find an additional artificial support for the same for the mere purpose of connecting them with the Scriptures — not because they doubted their traditional character.

[77] This may seem as if we accepted the view of Frankel and Weiss about the advantages offered by the systematic arrangement of the Mishnah. But

themselves having in the meantime become accustomed to the idea of an Oral Law equal in authority to the Written Law, now considered it unnecessary to seek scriptural proof for each and every law. They would occasionally even separate Halakot, based upon sound scriptural proofs, from their Midrash bases for the purpose of presenting them more systematically in Mishnah-form. R. Akiba, the boldest advocate of new Midrash-methods, was himself the one who helped to retain the Mishnah-form by improving it and introducing therein the principle of topical arrangement.

Thus, out of the one form evolved our Mishnah, a collection of Halakot in independent form arranged topically. Out of the other developed our halakic Midrashim, Mekilta, Sifra, and Sifre, which furnish a running commentary on the Books of the Law.

III

In the above we have ascertained the date and the reason for the introduction of the Mishnah-form, and have traced its gradual adoption by the teachers. Now that we know the motives for its first use, and the causes for its extensive adoption, we may be able to explain the strange silence of the talmudic-rabbinic sources concerning this significant change in the form of teaching and all its important consequences.

For this purpose we need only to review the main points in this whole process and examine them with reference to their possible effect upon the theories of the later Rabbis. We shall then be able to judge whether these later teachers had cause for ignoring these facts and for remaining silent about them.

We have found that the first motive for teaching independent Halakot in the Mishnah-form was the fact that during a period of time when there was no official activity of the teachers, certain

---

it was only after the Mishnah had been long in use and developed its system of grouping that it could be deemed advisable to arrange all the Halakot in Mishnah-form, while Frankel and Weiss assume that these advantages offered by the Mishnah in its later stage only were the cause of the change from Midrash to Mishnah. This, of course, is wrong, as the earlier Mishnah did not offer these advantages.

customs and practices came to be observed by the people. These customs and practices subsequently had to be recognized and taught by the teachers as religious ordinances, although no proof or scriptural basis for them existed. This means that certain religious practices, considered by the later teachers as part of the traditional law, or as handed down from Moses, originated in reality from other, perhaps non-Jewish sources, and had no authority other than the authority of the people who adopted them. This, of course, reflects unfavorably upon the authority of the traditional Law in general. We have, furthermore, seen that the teachers themselves could not agree in regard to the origin of certain laws. While some teachers endeavored to find artificial supports for these laws, using even forced interpretations for the purpose of giving them scriptural endorsement, others preferred to accept them as traditional laws, presumably of ancient Jewish origin. This disagreement among the earlier teachers in regard to the origin and authority of certain laws speaks very strongly against two fundamental theories of the later talmudic teachers, — theories that were considered almost as dogmas. One is the belief in an Oral Law, תורה שבעל פה, handed down from Moses together with the written Torah. The second is the belief in the validity of the laws which the wise teachers derived from the Torah by means of their new interpretations, מדרש חכמים. The disagreement noted above shows unmistakably that in earlier times these two theories were disputed and neither was accepted by all the teachers. For some teachers hesitated to recognize the authoritative character of certain laws merely on the ground that they were traditional. Therefore they felt constrained to seek proofs for these laws in the Torah. On the other hand, there were teachers who objected to the validity of the new interpretations by which certain laws were proved from Scriptures. They pinned their faith to the traditional character of these laws. Thus these earlier differences between the teachers could be used as a strong argument against the authority of their teachings. This fear was actually entertained by the later teachers.

Again, we have seen, that one of the motives for using the Mishnah-form was the desire on the part of the Pharisaic teachers to assert their authority and indispensability. This is apparently at variance with another theory of the Talmud, *viz.*, the belief that from Moses until the Tannaim there was an uninterrupted succession of teachers of the Law, recognized as the chief religious authorities whose direct and undisputed successors were the Pharisees. However, the fact that the early Pharisaic teachers had to assert their authority against the opposition of the Sadducees, shows that these teachers were new claimants to authority. This fact, as we have seen, reveals the true state of affairs, *viz.*, that the priestly teachers, the Sadducees, were originally the authoritative teachers, whom the Pharisees subsequently tried to supplant.

Thus, we see that the real conditions which accompanied the change from Midrash to Mishnah cast many unfavorable reflections upon the theories and views held by the later Pharisaic teachers, the Rabbis of the Talmud. We can, therefore, well understand the silence of the Rabbis about this important change. They did not care to dwell upon facts which, if misunderstood, would reflect on their theories. They hesitated to refer too frequently to circumstances from which some people might, by misinterpretation, draw such conclusions as would shake the foundation of the whole system of the traditional teachings.[78] This was not done with the intention of suppressing

[78] That the Pharisaic teachers had such apprehensions is evident from the following saying of R. Eleazar b. Azariah (or, according to Rashi, R. Joshua b. Hananiah) in Hag. 3b: וכמסמרות נטועים מה נטיעה זו פרה ורבה אף דברי תורה פרין ורבין בעלי אסופות. אלו תלמידי חכמים שיושבין אסופות אסופות ועוסקין בתורה הללו מטמאין והללו מטהרין הללו אוסרין והללו מתירין הללו פוסלין והללו מכשירין. שמא יאמר אדם האיך אני למד תורה מעתה? תלמוד לומר כולם נתנו מרועה אחד. אל אחד נתן פרנס אחד אמרן מפי אדון כל המעשים ברוך הוא (cf. also Num. r. 14.4). We have in this saying both a defense on the part of the Pharisaic teachers for making the Torah grow and increase so as to contain more than its plain words warrant, as well as a refutation of the arguments advanced against them that their very disagreement in many questions speaks against their having reliable traditions. Against this accusation the Pharisaic teachers insist that all their teachings come from the same source, the same leader, פרנס, Moses gave them in the name of God. We see from this that such arguments were raised against the Pharisees by their opponents, for the phrase, שמא יאמר אדם, "lest some might say," is here not meant altogether in a hypothetical sense. It refers to certain people who actually raised the question. Cf. the saying: יצתה בת קול ואמרה אלו ואלו דברי אלהים חיים והלכה כבית הלל, "A heavenly voice was heard declaring that both the

historic facts, as they indeed mentioned these facts. They would speak of them to those pupils who were prepared to see things in their proper light, and were not disposed to misinterpret them. They deemed it unwise to discuss these matters before the pupils at large, fearing that there might be among them some who could be misled by opponents and thus arrive at erroneous conclusions. This is a course of conduct followed by the teachers in regard to still other subjects which they likewise deemed unsafe to communicate to the public at large.[79]

This course was not altogether culpable, seeing that it was animated by no selfish motive, and that it was pursued for the sake of the cause which the Rabbis wished to serve. They were desirous of having their teachings accepted by the people as authoritative. They therefore refrained from dwelling upon the fact that there was once a time when some people did not accept these teachings as authoritative. Instead of reporting in detail the earlier struggles of the Pharisaic teachers for recognition, and their disputes with their opponents, they dwelt more frequently on the continuous chain of tradition by which they received their teachings. They mentioned only those teachers and members of the Sanhedrin who were of the Pharisaic party, whom they considered as having always been the true religious leaders of the people. They quite overlooked the fact that their opponents, the Sadducees, were the ruling authorities in former times. Instead

---

words of the School of Hillel and the words of the School of Shammai [despite their disagreements] are the words of the living God, but the practical decision should be according to the words of the School of Hillel" ('Er. 13b). Cf. also the passage in Giṭ. 6b, where Elijah is reported to have said that God declared both the opposing views of R. Abiathar and R. Jonathan to be the words of the living God. All these utterances were intended to serve as a refutation of the attacks made against the teachings of the Rabbis on account of their disagreements. We see from these covert replies of the Rabbis that the arguments of the Karaites against the Rabbanites (see below, note 85) were not original with the Karaites, but were repetitions of older arguments.

[79] The same was done with the records of the families which the Rabbis did not care to teach or discuss in public, fearing to cause unplesant controversies. They would hand them over to their chosen pupils (b. Ḳid. 71a). The same was the case with certain ineffable names of God which they communicated only to a few chosen pupils, lest the multitude misunderstand the significance of these names (*ibid.*).

of making explicit mention of the origin of the Mishnah-form, which would reveal the late date of so many traditional laws, they assumed the fact that the two Laws, the written and the oral, were both handed down by Moses through the agency of an uninterrupted chain of true teachers, the bearers of tradition. The result was that to most of the later teachers, especially the Amoraim, the origin and development of the Mishnah-form was almost unknown. The time when this change was made, the motives that caused it, and the circumstances that accompanied it, were almost forgotten. They were known only to a very few of the later teachers. These, like their predecessors, the early teachers, did not care to speak about them. The later Tannaim, and even the Amoraim, had the same reasons for avoiding the mention of these conditions that led to the adoption of the Mishnah-form as had the earlier Pharisaic teachers for their silence about these facts. Just as the earlier Pharisaic teachers, so the later teachers, i. e., the Rabbis, had to contend with more or less opposition. They had to combat those who denied their authority and rejected their teachings, i. e., the traditional law.

After the destruction of the Temple and the dissolution of the Jewish state, the Sadducees ceased to be a powerful party and lost their fomer influence among the people. However, it would be a mistake to assume with Büchler (*Der galiläische Am ha-Arez*, [Wien, 1906], p. 5) that in the beginning of the second century C. E. the Sadducees had altogether disappeared. They continued, if not as an influential party, nevertheless as a group of people holding peculiar views about the Torah, denying the binding character of the traditional law and rejecting the authority of the Rabbis who were the advocates of that traditional law. We have evidence of their existence throughout the entire tannaitic period.[80] Many sayings of the later Tannaim

[80] R. Jose b. Ḥalafta declares (Mishnah Niddah 4.2) that the daughters of the Sadducees are to be considered as daughters of Israel, except in cases where we know that they are determined to follow in their observance the ways of their forefathers (i. e., the former Sadducees). The reason for this view of R. Jose is found in his other saying where he states the following: בקיאין אנו בהן יותר מן הכל והם מראות דם לחכמים חוץ מאשה אחת שהיתה בשכונתינו שלא הראתה דם לחכמים ומתה, "We are very well informed about them. They all show

refer to them, though they do not always designate them expressly by the name Sadducees. They even lingered on in the

their blood to the wise teachers (i. e., the Rabbis). There was only one [Sadducean] woman in our neighborhood who would not do so, but she is dead now" (Tosefta 5.3; b. Niddah 33b). Büchler (*JQR*., 1913, 446) erroneously takes this saying of R. Jose to be merely another version of what the high priest's wife told her husband. Such an interpretation of R. Jose's saying is absolutely unwarranted. R. Jose describes conditions prevalent in his own day. He justifies his attitude towards the Sadducean women by the information that, with few exceptions, they follow the Pharisaic regulations in observing the laws of menstruation. This shows that in the time of R. Jose b. Ḥalafta, i. e., about the middle of the second century C. E., there still were Sadducees. Their wives, however, would, in most cases, be guided by the decisions of the Rabbis in regard to the observance of the laws about menstruation. The same R. Jose also says (Mishnah Parah 3.3), אל תתן מקום לצדוקים לרדות, "Do not give the Sadducees an opportunity to rebel (i. e., controvert us in argument)," and this again shows that in his time there were Sadducees who still argued against the teachers.

These Sadducees are also referred to, though not expressly designated by the name Sadducees, in the sayings of other teachers of that time. Thus the passage in Num. 15.31, "He hath despised the word of the Lord," is explained by R. Nathan in a Baraita (Sanh. 99a) to refer to one who disregards the Mishnah, כל מי שאינו משגיח על המשנה, that is to say, one who denies the traditional law. In another Baraita (*ibid.*) it is stated that the expression, "He hath despised the word of the Lord," applies even to such people who would accept the entire Torah as divine but would take exception to a single detail in the traditional interpretation: האומר כל התורה כולה מן השמים חוץ מדקדוק זה מקל וחומר זה מגזירה שוה זה. An anonymous saying in Sifra, *Beḥuḳḳotai* II, Weiss 111b interprets the passage, "But if ye will not hearken unto Me" (Lev. 26.14), to mean, "If ye will not hearken to the interpretation given by the teachers," אם לא תשמעו למדרש חכמים. The saying continues and speaks of people who despise and hate the teachers although they accept the laws given on Sinai. All these utterances were certainly not made without provocation. There must have been people who accepted the Torah and disputed the rabbinical laws.

Another teacher, R. Jose b. Judah, living in the second half of the second century, rules that if a Gentile wishes to accept the Law with the exception of even one detail of the rabbinical regulations, we should not admit him as a proselyte (Tosefta, Dem. 2.5; Bek. 30b). This shows that there must have been Jews who rejected the rabbinical laws. Therefore it could occur to a Gentile that it was possible to become a Jew without accepting all the rabbinical laws.

This is also evident from the following story told in Yerushalmi, Sheb. 9, (39a). A certain man who disregarded the regulations regarding the sabbat-time of the Amoraim.[81] Throughout the entire period of the Amoraim there were certain people who upheld the views and ideas of the old Sadducees. They were opposed to the authority of the Rabbis, and rejected their teachings. They were no longer called Sadducees. They were designated as "Epicureans," אפיקורוס, or referred to without any special name, merely as "people who deny the authority of the Rabbis and reject the traditional law." These anti-rabbinic elements of the talmudic period formed the connecting link between the older Sadducees and the later

---

ical year instructed his wife to be careful in separating the priest's share from the dough (ḥallah). His wife, to whom this conduct seemed inconsistent, asked him why he insisted on the observance of the ḥallah-law when he was disregarding the law about the sabbatical year. His answer was: The law of ḥallah is biblical, the regulations about the sabbatical year are rabbinical, having originated with R. Gamaliel and his colleagues, חלה מדבר תורה שביעית מדרבנן גמליאל וחביריו. This shows beyond any doubt that there were people who observed the Torah strictly but who denied the validity of the rabbinical teachings.

[81] R. Ḥanina and Abba Areka (Rab), Amoraim of the first generation (first half of the third century C. E.), describe the Epicuros as one who despises the teachers, המבוה תלמידי חכמים (b. Sanh. 99b). R. Joḥanan, an Amora of the second generation, and R. Eleazar b. Pedat, an Amora of the third generation (second half of the third century), characterize the Epicuros as one who says (in a tone expressive of contempt), "That teacher," כהן דאמר אהן ספרא, or as one who says, "Those Rabbis," כהן דאמר אילין רבנין (p. Sanh. 10.27d). Büchler makes the mistake of reading כהן instead of כְּהֵן, and therefore makes the saying refer to a "a priest" who uses that contemptuous expression about the Rabbis (Der Galiläische Am ha-Areẓ, p. 187). This is palpably wrong. The same characterization of the Epicuros is given by R. Papa, an Amora of the fifth generation (second half of the fourth century): כגון דאמר הני רבנן (b. Sanh. 100a). R. Joseph, an Amora of the third generation, applies the name Epicuros to a class of people who say, "Of what use have the Rabbis been to us," כגון הני דאמרי מאי אהנו לן רבנן (ibid.). Raba, an Amora of the fourth generation (first half of the fourth century), refers to the family of Benjamin the physician who said, "Of what use have the Rabbis been to us; they have never allowed a raven or forbidden a dove" (ibid.). This is a saying which seems to express that we do not need the Rabbis, the biblical laws being clear enough. These people lived according to the Law, and as stated in the Talmud (ibid.) would occasionally consult Raba concerning some ritual question. Their ridiculing remark about the Rabbis was evidently the expression of their peculiar attitude toward the teachings of the Rabbis and of their opposition to the latter's authority.

Karaites.[82] Knowing that the Sadducean tendencies continued throughout the entire period of the Talmud, and had both open and secret advocates, we can readily understand why the talmudic teachers hesitated to report indiscriminately all the details of the disputes between the Pharisees and Sadducees, and also all the differences of opinion and the disagreement as to methods among the Pharisees themselves. All these, as we have seen, were the causes that led to the adoption of the Mishnah-form. The talmudic teachers were careful not to place weapons in the hands of their opponents.

Thus the strange fact is explained why no explicit report about this matter was preserved in the talmudic literature. Only a few occasional remarks which escaped the teachers hint at the actual historic conditions, and they show us that a knowledge of the real facts did exist among some of the teachers.

The Geonim, likewise, seem to have had a purpose in avoiding the mention of these significant points in the historic development of the Halakah. When occasionally forced to speak about the same, they reveal by their very reticence as much as by their casual remarks that they had knowledge of the facts. We pointed out above the awkward pause in the letter of R. Sherira Gaon. In answer to the question of the people of Kairuan regarding the origin of the Mishnah and the Sifra and Sifre, the Gaon was compelled to speak about the Midrash and the Mishnah. He barely touches upon the subject of the Midrash, saying merely that this was originally the exclusive form. Here he stops abruptly and turns to another subject, *viz.*, the Baraita collections of R. Ḥiyya and R. Oshaya. We might assume that something is missing in the text of the letter.[83] This, however, is improbable. It is almost evident that R. Sherira broke off in the middle of a thought, because he deemed it unwise to say any more about the adoption of the Mishnah-form in addition to the Midrash.

This reluctance on the part of the Geonim to speak about this subject is more noticeable in the responsum of R. Ẓemaḥ Gaon.

[82] Cf. Friedmann in his Introduction to the *Seder Eliahu Rabba*, etc. (Wien, 1902), pp. 97–8, and Harkavy, *Zur Entstehung des Karaismus*, in Graetz's *Geschichte*, V, 472 ff.

[83] See above, note 9.

The people of Kairuan inquired of R. Ẓemaḥ Gaon regarding the attitude to be taken towards Eldad. Eldad reported that in the Talmud of his own people the names of individual teachers were not mentioned. As in our Talmud differences of opinion and names of individual teachers are mentioned, they found this report of Eldad very strange. Ẓemaḥ answered that this was not a reason for doubting the character of Eldad and his teachings, because the method described by Eldad was indeed the earlier mode of teaching. He states that in the time of the Temple, when they taught all the traditional law in the Midrash-form, they did not mention the names of individual teachers.[84] Now, this would seem to be a sufficient answer, and he should have stopped here. But R. Ẓemaḥ Gaon adds the following significant words: והתורה אחת היא בין במשנה בין בתלמוד וממעין אחד הכל שותין ואין נכון לפרש כל דבר, שנאמר כבוד אלהים הסתר דבר, "The Torah is one. It is embodied in the Mishnah and in the Talmud. All draw from one and the same source. It is not advisable to explain everything, for it is said: It is the glory of God to conceal a thing (Prov. 25.2)." Why this mysterious admonition, and what was the secret he sought to hide? The account of the origin of the Mishnah-form, given above, will help us to understand the need for the admonition and the nature of the secret. The Karaites in the time of the Geonim denied that the teachings of the Mishnah and Talmud embodied the true tradition. They characterized these teachings as later rabbinic inventions. In support of their attitude they instanced the numerous disagreements and frequent disputes of the Rabbis of the Talmud. They argued, How could there have been tradition among the teachers when there was no agreement among them as to their teachings and Halakot.[85]

We have seen above that the history of the development of the Mishnah-form reflects unfavorably upon the traditional character of the Pharisaic teachings. This was the reason for the talmudic silence about the origin of the Mishnah-form. The

[84] See above, note 33.
[85] See, for instance, the arguments used by Sahl ben Mazliaḥ (Pinsker, *Likkuṭe Ḳadmoniyyot*, Nispaḥim, pp. 26, 35). The same arguments are raised by many other Karaitic writers.

MIDRASH AND MISHNAH

Geonim were silent on this point for the same reason. Neither Zemaḥ nor Sherira wanted to state exactly how long the Midrash continued in exclusive use, for it would have shown that the Mishnah was of comparatively late origin, and that its adoption was due mainly to the differences of opinion that arose between the Pharisaic teachers and the earlier authorities, the Sadducees. When compelled to refer to the time when Midrash was in exclusive use, both Zemaḥ and Sherira used the vague term במקדש "in the Temple times." This, however, as we have seen, can refer only to the time before the division of the parties.[86] Sherira, who was merely asked about the origin of the Mishnah and the halakic Midrashim could easily avoid mentioning anything he

---

[86] It is possible that the use of the term במקדש in this peculiar sense was suggested to Zemaḥ and Sherira by a passage in Mishnah Ber. 9.5, where the term is likewise used in referring to a custom that was prevalent in the Temple during the time previous to the division of the parties. The passage in the Mishnah reads as follows: כל חותמי ברכות שהיו במקדש היו אומרים מן העולם משקלקלו הצדוקים ואמרו אין עולם אלא אחד התקינו שיהיו אומרים מן העולם ועד העולם. [The text in the editions of the Mishnayot reads משקלקלו המינים, but in the Talmud-editions the reading is משקלקלו הצדוקים, which is the correct reading. Cf. A. Schwartz, *Tosifta Zeraim*, (Wilna, 1890), p. 57, note 189.] Here we have the report of a Pharisaic regulation aimed against the Sadducees who rejected the belief in a future world. Here the term במקדש, while designating the place, i. e., the Temple, also includes an element of time. "In the Temple" evidently refers to the time prior to this Pharisaic regulation, i. e., prior to the division of the parties. The Pharisaic regulation reported in this passage originated in the very early days of the differences between the Sadducees and Pharisees, and not as Buechler (*Priester und Cultus*, p. 176) assumes, in the last decade of the existence of the Temple. This is evident from the fact that in the same paragraph the Mishnah reports another regulation which no doubt originated in the early days of the differences between the priests and lay-teachers. This other regulation prescribed that a man should use the name of God in greeting his neighbor. This was either a reaction against the religious persecution under Antiochus when it was forbidden to mention the name of God (cf. b. R. H. 18b and Meg. Ta'anit VII), or according to Geiger (*Jüdische Zeitschrift*, V, 107; cf. also *Urschrift*, pp. 264 ff.) it was to emphasize the claim of the Pharisees to use the name of God as the priests did. Anyhow, this second regulation originated in the very earliest days of the division of the parties. From this we may conclude that the first regulation also originated at the same time. It is quite evident that the author of this report in our Mishnah mentions these two regulations in the same paragraph to denote their simultaneous origin.

did not desire to state. He limited himself to answering the questions put before him. He stated that the Midrash was the earlier form, used exclusively in the earlier days of the second Temple. He was careful, however, not to define this period. He also told them the history of the Mishnah. He could well refrain from stating why the Mishnah was introduced as an additional form to the Midrash, for he was not expressly asked about this point. His questioners did not ask why a change in the form of teaching was made, and probably did not know that the Mishnah-form was the result of such an important change. Sherira did not find it necessary to enlighten them about this point.

R. Ẓemaḥ found himself in a more difficult position. He was compelled to commit himself to some extent. He was expressly asked why in Eldad's Talmud no names are mentioned, while in our Talmud many names of debating teachers, representing conflicting opinions, are found. This question implied a doubt in the minds of the questioners concerning the authority of our Talmud. R. Ẓemaḥ had to address himself to this doubt. He first admits that originally all teachings were given in the Midrash-form. Since in this form all teachings are presented as interpretations of the written Torah and not as opinions of the teachers, the names of the teachers were therefore not mentioned. He also avoids definite dates, using like Sherira the vague term "in Temple times" to designate the period of the exclusive use of the Midrash. However, he still fears that the people might be led to doubt the traditional character of the Mishnah on account of the disputes and opposing views of individual teachers that are found in it. He therefore admonishes the questioners to entertain no doubts about the Mishnah and the Talmud, but to consider them as coming from the same source as the written Torah and as being one with the Torah. This admonition of R. Ẓemaḥ Gaon is a warning against the Karaites of his day. It is of the same character as the warning uttered by Joshua b. Ḥananiah (Ḥag. 3b) against the Sadducees of his own time.[87]

---

[87] At the end of his responsum (Jellinek, *Beth Hamidrash*, II, 113) Ẓemaḥ repeats his warning not to deviate from the Talmud and the teachings of the Rabbis in the following words: וכבר הודענו לכם שממעיין אחד הכל שותין והתחזקו במה שהחכמים דורשין לכם ובתלמוד שילמדו לכם ואל תטו ימין ושמאל מאחרי כל דבריהם

The result of our inquiry into the cause of the talmudic-rabbinic silence about our subject may be summed up in the following conclusions. The early Pharisaic teachers refrained from pointing to the causes for the adoption of the Mishnah-form, and to its effects upon the development of the Halakah, in order not to strengthen the position of their opponents, the Sadducees. The later talmudic teachers similarly avoided discussion of these subjects out of fear of those of their opponents who followed the old Sadducean doctrines. The Geonim, in like manner, refrained from mentioning these facts in order not to place weapons in the hands of their opponents, the Karaites.

IV

In the course of our discussion, we have proved from a talmudic report as well as from certain utterances of the Geonim, that the first introduction of the Mishnah-form took place in the last days of Jose b. Joezer. There is but one gaonic statement about the beginnings of the Mishnah which seems to be at variance with this conclusion. I refer to the statement of Saadya Gaon in his *Sefer Hagalui* (Schechter, *Saadyana*, p. 5; also quoted by a Karaitic writer, see Harkavy, *Studien und Mitteilungen*, V, 194).

This statement of Saadya places the time for the beginnings of the Mishnah soon after prophecy ceased, in the fortieth year of the second Temple. This is apparently a much earlier date than the time of Jose b. Joezer. A close examination, however, will show that the period to which Saadya assigns the beginnings of the Mishnah is actually the same as the one which we have found given in the Talmud and indicated by the Geonim R. Zemah and R. Sherira, *viz.*, the time of Jose b. Joezer. It is merely due to the faulty chronology, followed by Saadya, that his date appears to be earlier than the one which we fixed on

---

שכן כתוב על פי התורה אשר יורוך ועל המשפט אשר יאמרו לכם תעשו. This repetition of the admonition and the citation of the passage in Deut. 17.11, so often used by the Rabbis in support of the authority of their traditional teachings, further proves that Zemah aimed to allay any disquieting doubts in the minds of the people in regard to the traditional character of the Rabbinical teachings.

the basis of the evidence derived from the Talmud and the statements of R. Ẓemaḥ and R. Sherira.

We must keep in mind that Saadya followed the rabbinic chronology as given in *Seder Olam* and in the Talmud. This chronology, however, at least in so far as it relates to the earlier period of the second Temple, is absolutely incorrect. In order to be able to fix the actual time to which Saadya's date refers, we must first point out the peculiarities of the talmudic-rabbinic chronology which he followed. To account for the errors and the confusion in this chronology, it is sufficient to know its character. It is an artificial chronology, constructed by the later teachers for the apparent purpose of establishing a direct connection between the true teachers of the Law, that is to say, the Pharisees, and the prophets, and thus to prove the authority of the Pharisaic teachers and the traditional character of their teachings. Such a direct connection between the prophets and the Pharisaic teachers of the traditional Law could be established only by utterly ignoring the time during which the priests were the sole religious teachers and leaders, and consequently contracting long stretches of time into short periods. Hence all the inaccuracies in this artificial and faulty chronology.

The Rabbis assume that the Pharisaic teachers received the Law, as well as all their traditional teachings, directly from the prophets. In their chronology, therefore, the prophets are succeeded not by the priestly teachers, the כהנים, but by the חכמים, the wise lay teachers. This is expressed by the Rabbis in the statement: עד כאן נתנבאו הנביאים ברוח הקודש מכאן ואילך הט לבך ושמע דברי חכמים (*Seder Olam Rabba*, XXX; cf. also *Seder Olam Zutta*, VII). By חכמים are evidently meant חכמי ישראל, lay-teachers, or more exactly, Pharisaic teachers, in contradistinction to the priests or Sadducees, the כהנים. This is confirmed by the fact that in passages in the Mishnah and the Tosefta which likewise contain the idea that the wise teachers directly succeeded the prophets, the Zuggot are expressly mentioned. Thus in Mishnah Peah 2.6 and Tosefta Yad. 2.16, we read that the Zuggot, that is to say, the earliest Pharisaic teachers, received traditional laws directly from the prophets, שקיבל מזוגות שקבלו מן הנביאים.

The same idea also underlies the statement in Abot 1, according to which the Zuggot received the Law from the last members of the Great Synagogue. For, according to the Rabbis, this Great Synagogue also included the last prophets among its members. There is only one slight difference between the line of succession as given in M. Abot and that given in M. Peah and Tosefta Yadayyim, namely, that the name of Antigonos is mentioned in the former between the Zuggot and the Great Synagogue. However, in stating the authority from whom the first pair received the Law, the Mishnah (Ab. 1.4) uses the words קיבלו מהם "they received from *them*." This clearly shows that the first pair, the two Joses, did not receive the Law from Antigonos alone. For, if this were the case, the Mishnah would have said: קיבלו ממנו "they received from *him*." The expression קיבלו מהם warrants the supposition that the two Joses received the Law from the last members of the Great Synagogue, or perhaps Antigonos was considered to have been the younger colleague of Simon. According to this supposition there is no discrepancy between all these talmudic reports. They all assume that the last members of the Great Synagogue, among whom were also the last prophets, transmitted the Law and the traditions directly to the Zuggot or חכמים, i. e., the earliest Pharisaic teachers.

This transmission of the Law by the prophets to the wise teachers, or the disappearance of the prophets and the rise of the חכמים, the Pharisaic teachers, took place according to the Rabbis, in the time of Alexander the Great, shortly after the overthrow of the Persian Empire (*Seder Olam Rabba* and *Zutta, loc. cit.*). This rabbinic chronology finds no difficulty in extending the time of the last prophets to the end of the Persian period. For by some peculiar error, which we are unable to account for, the Rabbis reduced the entire period of the existence of the second Temple under Persian rule to thirty-four years. They assume that thirty-four years after the second Temple was built, the Persian rule in Judea ceased and the Greek rule began (*Seder Olam Rabba, loc. cit.*, and Shab. 15a). Accordingly, it was not found strange that Haggai who urged the building of the Temple as well as the other prophets of his time, should have lived to the end of the Persian period and have handed over the Law and the traditions to their successors, the חכמים, or wise lay teachers at that time.

How the Rabbis could identify these חכמים with the Zuggot, so that the latter, living in the second century B. C. E., could be considered the direct recipients of the Law from the last prophets at the end of the fourth century B. C. E., is not difficult to explain. The Rabbis had a tradition that the High-Priest in the time of Alexander the Great was Simon the Just (I) (Yoma 69a). They also had a reliable report of a High-Priest Simon the Just (II) who lived shortly before the time of the Zuggot, either a little before or contemporary with Antigonos. These two Simons they confused with one another. They identified Simon the Just II, who lived about 200 B. C. E., with Simon the Just I, one of the last survivors of the Great Synagogue who lived at the end of the fourth or the beginning of the third century B. C. E. In this manner they established a direct connection between the prophets who were among the last members of the Great Synagogue and the Zuggot or the חכמים, the wise lay teachers, who were the fathers of the Pharisaic party. They were probably unaware of the fact that they passed over an interval of an entire century, or it may be that they consciously ignored it, because, as we have seen, there was no official activity of the teachers during that period.

According to this faulty chronology, then, the Zuggot, or the first pair, Jose b. Joezer and Jose b. Johanan, succeeded the prophets, or the last members of the Great Synagogue, and commenced their activity as teachers of the Law shortly after the overthrow of the Persian Empire by Alexander; that is to say, not much later than the year 34 of the second Temple. And it is actually this time, i. e., the time of the two Joses, that Saadya fixes for the beginnings of the Mishnah. The meaning of the passage in Saadya's *Sefer Hagalui* is now clear, and its date fully agrees with our date for the beginnings of the Mishnah. The passage reads as follows: ויהי כי מלאו למתנה אלף שנים מימי משה איש האלהים לתם יתר הנביאים במלכות מדי ונחתום חזון בשנת הארבעים לבנות הבירה שנית במעט עם בראות הורינו את ההמון כי נפץ בכל הארץ ויגורו על ההגא לבלתי השכח ויאספו כל מלה אשר העתיקו מני קדם למצוה ולחוק

ליהו (לישראל reading the suggests Schechter) ולעדות וימלאום
במדע מלואת תכן ויקראו את שמם משנה.

We may, therefore, assume with certainty that Saadya had a correct tradition that the teaching of Mishnah was first begun in the time of the first pair, the two Joses. But, misguided by the erroneous rabbinic chronology which he followed, he puts the date of this first pair in the year 40 of the second Temple.

The conditions which, according to Saadya, caused the teachers to begin the composition of Mishnah, also point to the time of the two Joses. For, as Saadya assumes, what prompted the teachers to seek to preserve their teachings in Mishnah-form was the fact that the Jewish people were then scattered all over the earth, and the teachers feared that the study of the Law might be forgotten, בראות הורינו את ההמון כי נפץ בכל הארץ ויגורו על ההגא לבלתי השכח. These conditions actually prevailed in the time of the two Joses. From the Sibylline Oracle III, 271, we learn that about the middle of the second century B. C. E. the Jewish people had already scattered all over the earth, and were to be found in every land (cf. Schürer, *Geschichte*, III[4], 4). Indeed, the decree of the two Joses declaring the lands of the gentiles unclean (Shab. 15a) may have been issued for the very purpose of stopping this extensive emigration of the people into foreign lands (see Weiss, *Dor*, I, 99).

Again, from the quotation of Saadya's statement by the Karaitic writer, it would seem that Saadya designated the teachers, who first composed Mishnah, by the name of אבות. If this be so, if Saadya really applied the term אבות to these teachers, he could have had in mind only the earliest Pharisaic teachers, or the Zuggot, who are called in the Talmud (p. Ḥag. 77d) אבות העולם. I am, however, inclined to think that Saadya did not use the term אבות in referring to these teachers. Saadya probably used the term הורינו, as we find it in the Hebrew text (edition Schechter), and which simply means, our forefathers. The Karaitic writer who quotes Saadya's statement translated this Hebrew word הורינו by the Arabic אלאבא.

Our contention that Saadya's date refers to the time of Jose b. Joezer might be objected to on the ground that according to Saadya (Schechter, *loc. cit.*) it took about 500 years from the beginnings of the Mishnah to the final completion of our Mishnah. If, then, Saadya's date coincides with the time of Jose b. Joezer, the actual time between the beginnings of the Mishnah and the completion of our Mishnah is scarcely 400 years. This objection, however, can easily be removed. Here again the mistake is due to the faulty chronology followed by Saadya. Having placed the beginnings of the Mishnah, i. e., the time of the first pair, in the year 40 of the second Temple, and assuming that our Mishnah was completed 150 years after the destruction of the second Temple, Saadya had to extend the period of the Mishnah to 530 years. For, according to the talmudic chronology, the second Temple existed 420 years. Accordingly the period of time which elapsed between the year 40 of the second Temple and the year 150 after its destruction was 530 years. This number was actually given by Saadya, as quoted by the Karaitic writer. The copyist, however, by mistake wrote תק"י = 510, instead of תק"ל = 530 (see Harkavy, *op. cit.*, p. 195, note 6). The number 500 years, לשנים חמש מאות, assigned to the period of the Mishnah in *Sefer Hagalui* (edition Schechter, p. 5), probably represents a round number, as Schechter (*loc. cit.*) correctly remarks.

The Ethics of the Halakah

The Ethics of the Halakah

(1913)

Theory and Practice

THE progress of mankind along the lines of ethical perfection leading toward the goal of a united humanity has been accomplished by two distinct processes: the process of conceiving high ethical ideals and the equally important but nevertheless distinct process of their application to life. Ethical ideals are first conceived and expressed by some great mind — prophet, priest or teacher. Only afterward do the people, striving for moral improvement, make these ethical concepts the basis of law and enactment. Thus they endeavor to make the ideal real. The one process, by a fiction of language, may be called theoretical, the other practical. In the methods whereby each process attempts to accomplish its results there is great difference. The method of the one consists in so expressing the great ethical ideals as to inspire men to achieve them. The other process, seeking to apply these ideals to every-day living, endeavors to create a practical discipline whereby to train men in the observance of the same ideals. This constitutes the difference, in every age, between the utterances of the great moral leaders and the practical, legislative decrees of the lawmakers. Both methods of procedure, complementing each other as they do, are of equal importance for the accomplishment of the ethical perfection of man. If the prophets and seers of mankind give us the ideals that guide our conduct from afar, like lighthouses on the promontories of life, the lawgivers and judges, formulating their practical rules and decisions, place in our hands the humble candles whereby we see how to make the very necessary daily steps of life. And the great journey toward the goal of a united humanity is made up of these humble steps.

In Judaism, which aims to accomplish the ethical and religious perfection of man, we observe the same interplay of these two processes. In one important respect, however, the progress of these two processes in Judaism differs from that in any other historic movement for the moral improvement of mankind. In every other movement radical changes have taken place, from time to time, both in the ethical concepts as well as in their application. It often happened that the practical endeavors succeeded in realizing the ideals to such an extent as to make these ideals become antiquated. The people having outgrown the old ideals, new ideals had to be conceived in order to lead men on to further progress. In Judaism, however, only the practical application of the Divine principles changed from time to time. Certain practices and laws which for one period served as the expression of the ideal become antiquated in another period and had, therefore, to be abandoned. In its outward forms Judaism changed from time to time. At different times and different places, new customs and new practices were adopted to express the same religious ideals. But in its ideals and fundamental principles Judaism has not changed. It has remained the same throughout its history. The ideals as well as the fundamental principles laid down by the God-inspired teachers and prophets of old are of eternal value. They express Divine truths that have neither become antiquated nor have they been surpassed by any teachings of other religious systems. The prophetic ideals are still the loftiest ideals which man has conceived, and the fundamental principles of Judaism, its laws of morality and righteousness, are still the highest principles that have ever been taught.

Prophets and Rabbis

For Judaism to achieve its great aim, it was therefore only necessary that the formulation of its high ideals and noble principles should be followed by endeavors at their practical application in daily life. This actually took place in the course of the history of Judaism. First the prophets, God-inspired men, gave expression to the highest ideals of love and peace, justice and righteousness, and held aloft the vision of a perfect humanity and a true brotherhood of man. Then followed the legislators and teachers of the law who seriously set themselves the task of making the prophetic ideals real, by applying the noble principles taught by the prophets to the actual conditions of life. I do not refer to the biblical legislators who, in the various law codes embodied in the Bible, endeavored to put prophetic ideals to practical use. I refer mainly to those legislators and teachers of the law who were rightly considered the true successors of the prophets, namely, the rabbis and teachers of the Halakah.

Jewish Rabbis and Christian Critics

These ancient Jewish teachers have often been unjustly criticized by Christian scholars. They have been pictured as narrow-minded jurists and pedantic formalists who did not progress along the lines laid down by the prophets. Instead of cherishing and developing the ideals of the prophets they are said to have retrograded and to have marred the beauty of the prophetic religion by the legalistic setting which they gave to it. Their teachings, especially those of the Halakah, are represented to be merely legalistic in character void of the spirit of true religion. They are said to concern themselves merely with the outward conduct without regard to the inner motives. As a result of this criticism it has become quite prevalent among Christian theologians to distinguish between the teachings of the prophets and the teachings of the Rabbis, and to represent rabbinic Judaism as something different and inferior to the religion of the prophets.

These criticisms are based upon misconception and bias. They draw an altogether wrong picture of the ancient Rabbis and give a false characterization of the teachings of the Halakah and of rabbinic Judaism. The accusation of narrow-mindedness does not apply to the ancient teachers of the Halakah as much as to their modern critics, who find it difficult to appreciate anything that is not Christian. The Christian theologians, despite their learning and scholarship, cannot rid themselves of the prejudice which they imbibed from the polemical writings of the New

Testament against the Pharisaic teachers of the Halakah. Without a comprehensive knowledge of rabbinic literature and without a thoroughgoing understanding of the halakic teachings, they proceed to judge the entire Halakah by the few quotations found in the works written by opponents of the Halakah and enemies of the Rabbis. Such a procedure is uncritical, unscientific and unjust. As may be expected, the judgments arrived at by such methods are erroneous and false. It is absolutely wrong to speak of the Judaism of the Rabbis as essentially different from the religion of the prophets. The teachings of the prophets and the teachings of the Rabbis are but slightly different expressions of one and the same religion. Both are teachings of Judaism which have at all times remained the same in essence and principle.

How the Rabbis Conceived Their Duty

The Rabbis who followed the prophets in time were also their successors in spirit. As the age of prophesy came to an end, the age of the Halakah began. The period of the prophets was followed by the period of the wise teachers. To use the words of the Talmud:[1] "the task of prophecy [i. e., to reveal God's truth], was taken from the prophets and assigned to the wise teachers." These wise teachers, the Rabbis, realized the great responsibility that rested upon them, the responsibility of continuing the work of the prophets. They never lost sight of the noble visions of the prophets and never forgot their ethical teachings. They had them constantly in mind and cherished them in their hearts even more than some of their modern critics who are so loud in praising the prophetic teachings with their lips. But the Rabbis believed that the prophets had reached the very highest summit in ethical ideas, and that nothing could be added to their ethical and moral teachings. They, therefore, came to the conclusion that all that was left for them to do as successors of the prophets was to realize these ethical teachings in practice. The Rabbis appreciated the beauty of the prophetic ideals as much as their Christian critics, but they also appreciated the fact which the Christian theologians

[1] B. B. 12a, ניטלה נבואה מן הנביאים וניתנה לחכמים

do not, that ideals lose their value if unaccompanied by actions and remain merely beautiful phrases without any practical influence upon life and conduct. The Rabbis believed that "the main thing is conduct and not theorizing"[2] and that "study is valuable only because it is conducive to good deeds."[3] They, therefore, thought that the noble teachings and beautiful ideas of the prophets were not to be treated as ornaments, but to be turned into articles for common use in the household of humanity. This task the Rabbis set themselves to accomplish in their halakic rules and decisions. And in justice it should be stated that for the advancement of the cause of religion and the promotion of ethical teachings this activity of the Rabbis was not less important than the activity of the prophets. Prophet and Rabbi both directed their efforts to the same goal; they merely used different ways to attain it. The prophets sought to inspire men to good deeds by teaching high ideals and holding aloft noble visions. The Rabbis tried to lead men to a realization of these visions and ideals by training them in the exercise of such good deeds as are expressive of high ideals. The prophets showed the ways of God to man, the Rabbis led man in these ways by teaching him to imitate God in all his doings.[4] Both, however, worked to accomplish the same end, *viz.*, to make man know the Lord and walk in His ways.[5]

[2] ולא המדרש הוא העיקר אלא המעשה, Ab. 1.17.
[3] תלמוד גדול שהתלמוד מביא לידי מעשה, Ḳid. 40b, or as it is expressed in B. Ḳ. 17a, גדול לימוד תורה שהלימוד מביא לידי מעשה. "If one seeks to acquire religious ideas without the intention of putting them into practical use, it would have been better for him if he had not been born. הלמד שלא לעשות נוח לו אלו לא נברא (p. Shab. 1, [3b]) is another saying of the Talmud, insisting that religious ideas must find expression in corresponding good actions.
[4] דברי חכמים מכוונים את האדם הזה לדרכיו של הקב״ה, Pesikta Rabbati, III, Friedmann, 7b.
[5] This is the most characteristic feature of Judaism, prophetic and rabbinic. It is not a system of mere beliefs, nor is it merely a system of religious ceremonies and rites. It is a religion of right conduct and good deeds based upon the belief in the One true God, who is righteous and good, and who wants man to imitate Him by being righteous and doing good. This idea finds its adquate expression in the halakic regulation concerning the reading of the Shema, i. e., the confession of faith recited daily by the Jew. This was so arranged by the Halakah as to impress upon the Jew that he must first take

One thing must be said. As practical teachers the Rabbis had very often to compromise [and make concessions]. At times they had to be satisfied with merely approaching the ideal though not fully reaching it. They believed that a constant training in the exercise of right conduct and continuous practice of right deeds would inculcate in the heart of a man right principles and help him to cultivate noble ideas, thus bringing him nearer to a realization of the ideal. The Rabbis say: "A man should occupy himself with the study of the Torah and the practice of good deeds, even though at first he is not animated by the most ideal motives. In the end he will perform these acts for their own sake."[6] "A wise and practical teacher is sometimes better than a prophetic dreamer," says the Talmud.[7] The practical teacher ready to make concessions when necessary and endeavoring to gain ground slowly but surely, accomplishes more than the idealistic dreamer. The visionary who, with his ideal ever before him, is not satisfied with anything less than the ideal and who uncompromisingly demands either the full realization of the ideal or nothing, will gain nothing. The teachers of the Halakah knew that תפשת מרובה לא תפשת. If you demand too much you gain nothing. They were satisfied to gain a little at a time, thus coming gradually nearer to the full realization of the ideal.

Not Demagogues But Pedagogues

The teachers of the Halakah gravely apprehended the danger involved in continuing the prophetic method. They feared that the people might be led astray by aspiring but mistaken or even false prophets, who, departing from the teachings of the true prophets, would dream strange dreams and see strange visions. Moreover, the teachers felt that merely teaching the ideal with-

---

upon himself the yoke of the Kingdom of God, i. e., acknowledge that there is only one God who alone rules the universe, and then take upon himself the yoke of the commandments, that is, take it upon himself to do what God, the acknowledged ruler of the world, commands him to do (M. Ber. 2.2).

[6] לעולם יעסוק אדם בתורה ובמצות אפילו שלא לשמה שמתוך שלא לשמה בא לשמה (Pes. 50b).

[7] חכם עדיף מנביא (B. B. 12a).

out trying to apply it practically would result in still further removing the ideal from the real. The noble ideas and principles would then become beautiful but empty phrases, with perhaps some shadowy mystic meaning, but without efficacy as guides for practical life. The subsequent history of the development of the religious teachings of the prophets in Judaism and Christianity justifies the apprehensions of the teachers of the Halakah. It argues great wisdom and foresight on their part to have chosen as their activity the practical application of the ideals of the prophets. The talmudic saying, חכם עדיף מנביא, proved itself to be absolutely true. The practical methods of the wise teachers of the Halakah proved to be far more efficacious than the course pursued by some of the aspiring prophets of their day. The application given to the fundamental principle of Judaism by the practical teachings of the Halakah yielded better results than the mere theoretical preaching of that same principle by the writers of the New Testament. Verily, "by their fruits shall ye know them!" (Matt. 7.16).

It is well known that, when Jesus declared the commandment, "thou shalt love thy neighbor as thyself" (Lev. 19.18) to be the second greatest commandment of the Law (Matt. 22.39), he merely repeated what every Jewish teacher before and during his time had taught. There was, however, a great difference between the Jewish conception and application of this noble principle and the Christian understanding of the same. The Jewish teachers in declaring this principle to be the fundamental principle of the religion, the whole Law, taught at the same time that the rest of the Law also had its legitimate place; that the other commandments leading up to this consummation of the Law must also be observed. As Hillel expressed it,[8] "all the rest is merely a commentary," ואידך פירושא היא, but a commentary which one must know, "Go and study it," זיל גמור, in order to learn from it how to apply correctly the one principle, the golden rule. Christianity has accepted the text of Lev. 19.18, without the commentary, the golden rule without the whole system of its practical application. The Law was declared as

[8] Shab. 31a.

abrogated. Paul said, "All the Law is fulfilled in one word." (Gal. 5.14). But the result was that the so-called fulfilment of the Law remained merely a word. The love preached by Christianity did not prove to be that love which "worked no ill to his neighbor" (Rom. 13.10). Quite to the contrary, it wrought great harm. The principle, "love thy neighbor as thyself," was for many centuries upon the lips of Christian nations without any influence upon their character and conduct. They even committed the most horrible crimes and perpetrated the most cruel acts of hatred in the name of that very religion of love. הקול קול יעקב. The voice was the voice of Jacob, repeating the Jewish teachings of brotherly love, but והידים ידי עשו the hands remained the bloody hands of Esau inflicting injury and evil.

The Aim and Purpose of All the Law

The teachers of the Halakah, on the other hand, retained the Law, studied and practiced it, knowing well that it was the necessary and indispensable commentary to the golden rule. Viewing the entire Torah as a commentary to the golden rule, the Rabbis believed that the aim and purpose of all the commandments of the Torah was to establish peace and friendly relations between man and man, כל התורה כולה מפני דרכי שלום.[9] In the light of this belief they, therefore, interpreted the Torah in such a manner as to make all its laws the expressions of ethical ideals, conducive to the promotion of righteousness, peace and love among men. In all their discussions and teachings we find that they aimed at the high ideals of the prophets which they believed to be the purpose of all the commandments. By their explanations and modifications of the biblical laws they sought to give to the latter a moral and religious aspect, and in their own legal enactments they were guided by ethical considerations and based their rules and decisions on sound moral principles.

Before proceeding to prove this thesis by instances from the halakic teachings, it is perhaps proper to show that it was the

[9] Giṭ. 59b.

THE ETHICS OF THE HALAKAH

generally accepted opinion of the Halakah that all the laws of the Torah were merely a means to an end, and that this end was conceived to be the prophetic ideal of a Messianic era, when peace and brotherly love will prevail among all people.

It will also help us to understand the ethics of the Halakah better, if we first make clear to ourselves what views the Halakah held in regard to the origin and character of the laws of the Torah.

TEXT AND COMMENTARY

We have seen above that Hillel declared the whole Torah with all its commandments to be merely a commentary for the purpose of explaining the golden rule and guiding us in its application. This was not the opinion of Hillel alone, it was the opinion held by all the teachers of the Halakah. No mention is made of any objection to this view on the part of any teacher. The idea that the ritual, precepts and ceremonial laws will not be necessary for all time is a logical consequence of this view about the commandments of the Torah. So, indeed, we find that the teachers of the Halakah expressed their opinion that at some future time, in the Messianic age, men will have learned the lesson of brotherly love and will no longer be in need of a commentary to the golden rule. Then the commentary will be dispensed with and all those laws and practices commanded by the Torah for the purpose of training men to follow the ideal, will lose their function, or, to use the words of the Talmud, (Niddah, 61b) מצות בטלות לעתיד לבא. "In the Messianic age the laws will be suspended."[10] The

---

[10] The idea expressed in this saying is also expressed in other sayings of the Rabbis. Thus it is declared by the Rabbis, that in the future age, לעתיד לבא all the sacrifices and all prayers, with the exception of thanksgiving, will be abolished (Midrash Tehillim, LVI, Buber, p. 145a). Likewise in Midrash Mishle IX, Buber, 31a, it is declared that all the festivals, with the exception of Purim and (according to R. Eleazar) the Day of Atonement, will in the future age לעתיד לבא cease to be observed. These sayings show that the rabbis entertained the hope and the belief that the ritual laws will not be necessary and therefore be abolished in the Messianic age. For it is evident that the term לעתיד לבא in these sayings refers to the Messianic era and not to the state of life after death. About the latter state the Rabbis have

teachers, however, believed that inasmuch as the ideal of brotherly love had not been realized and the Messianic era had not arrived, therefore the commentary to the golden rule was still necessary and the laws of the Torah were still to be observed.

THE FALLACIOUS CHRISTIAN CONCEPTION OF THE YOKE OF THE LAW

It should be kept in mind that the teachers of the Halakah believed in תורה מן השמים, in the Divine origin of the entire Torah. According to their belief even the laws and commandments which form the commentary were given by God. God in his goodness desires us to be good, for the purpose of training us to a life of goodness and helping us to attain to holiness. He has prescribed for us all these rules and precepts which we must keep if we wish to realize the ideal. They appreciated the great favor which God has shown them in giving them that "precious article," כלי חמדה, the Torah with all its laws and precepts. (Ab. 3.14). Far from considering these laws and commandments burdensome, they realized their helpfulness. "God was pleased to favor and ennoble Israel," says R. Ḥananya b. Akashya, "therefore he gave them a copious Torah with numerous com-

---

another explicit saying, declaring that in the life after death a man is free from the observance of any law or commandment, כיון שמת אדם נעשה חפשי מן המצות (Shab. 151b), and they do not make any exception regarding thanksgiving or even the Day of Atonement. The claim of Christianity that the Messiah had already come and the law was no more binding, probably had the effect that the Rabbis did not care to express so often the idea that the ritual laws will at some future time be abolished (see my article "Nomism," in *Jewish Encyclopedia*, IX, 328). The same consideration, no doubt, prompted the medieval Jewish teachers to explain away the simple meaning of the talmudic sayings that the laws will be abolished in the future. Thus Tosafot in Niddah, *ad loc.*, *s.v.*, אמר רב יוסף זאת אומרת while admitting that the term לעתיד לבא means the Messianic age, seek to identify this Messianic era with the era after the resurrection of the dead. Likewise R. Solomon b. Aderet, in his Responsa, § 93, interprets the saying, that in the future the festivals will no more be observed, to mean that the many persecutions and great troubles which will fall to the lot of the Jews may compel them to cease to observe the festivals. A very ingenious but nevertheless incorrect interpretation.

mandments."[11] This belief that God gave us all the laws and precepts of the Torah for our own good, finds expression in the very designation רחמנא, "our lover" or the "Merciful One," very often used as the name of God in the halakic discussions.[12] Thus, the Rabbis refer to the author of these laws as the God who because of His mercy and great love for us gave us all these commandments which should help us to lead a noble and pure life. They do not think of Him merely as a stern Lawgiver who issues decrees for purposes of His own and commands His people to obey them for His own pleasure. They realized that God has no profit in these laws and no other purpose than to further the welfare of His creatures. "For, indeed, what difference does it make to God," ask the Rabbis, "how we slaughter an animal, or of what kind of food we partake, except that He desires by such laws and regulations to benefit His creatures, to purify their hearts, and to ennoble their characters."[13]

[11] רצה הקב"ה לזכות את ישראל לפיכך הרבה להם תורה ומצות (Mak. 23b).

[12] By applying this designation to God the rabbis also wished to suggest the thought: Be ye merciful, as your father in heaven is merciful (see Luke 6.36). When they objected to those who would declare this idea to be the sole reason for certain commandments of the Torah (p. Meg. 75c), it was merely a reaction against the antinomian tendencies of the Allegoristic schools. (Cf. my essay on "The Ancient Jewish Allegorists in Talmud and Midrash," in *JQR*, [n. s.] I, 528 ff.)

[13] וכי מה איכפת להקב"ה בין שוחט בהמה ואוכל אותה לנוחר בהמה ואוכל אותה כלום מועילו או מזיקו? או מה איכפת לו בין אוכל טמאות לאוכל טהרות? הא לא ניתנו המצות אלא לצרף בהן את הבריות, Tanḥuma, *Shemini*, Buber, 30. Cf. also Gen. r. 44.1). The idea expressed in this saying greatly helps us to understand the psychological process in the mind of the Rabbis when engaged in minute discussions of ritual or dietary laws. Their firm conviction that God gave us these laws for the purpose of making us nobler and better, forced them to believe that all the details of these laws help to serve this purpose and make us holy. In the minutiae of the ritual of שחיטה they saw a means of teaching us not to be cruel to animals. They believed, that to inflict torture upon animals is forbidden by the law of the Torah צער בעלי חיים דאורייתא (Shab. 128b). In the dietary laws they could not see old Tabu laws, for such a conception would have been out of harmony with their idea of the Divine character of the Torah. They saw in the dietary laws beneficial hygienic laws, or disciplinary rules to train us to control our desires and submit our impulses to a higher will. They also considered them as a means to make Israel distinct as a holy people and keep him separate from all other nations.

Ethical Purport the Primary Concern of the Halakah

In dealing with the laws of the Torah the primary concern of the Rabbis is always to discover the underlying ethical purpose. In some laws of the Torah this ethical purpose is explicitly stated, in others it is implied, and in still others the moral justification is ascertained by the Rabbis only after long and arduous debate. Even the ritual laws of the Torah, where one would least expect to find direct moral injunctions, are studiously and often successfully examined from this point of view.[14] It is irrelevant to discuss whether these ethical purposes inhered in the text or were read into it. For us it is enough that the teachers of the Halakah believed that every law and commandment of the Torah rested on an ethical foundation. Their very success, real or imaginary, in discovering the ethical purport of so many ritual laws, confirmed them in their belief that the commentary, consisting of the ritual and ceremonial law, was necessary for the proper realization of Hillel's moral text, and that every precept of the Torah, be its outward form what it may, served, if not patently, then at least subtly and imperceptibly toward the great and overmastering aim of moral perfection. So strong was their conviction that a moral purpose inhered in every law, that failure to discern the purpose in any particular case did not affect their attitude toward that law. When ingenuity failed to unravel the ethical purpose of an enactment, they nevertheless counseled its observance on the ground that the disciplinary value of implicit obedience is in itself a means to a moral purpose.

The Aim of the Law

But they never lost sight of the fact that the legal enactments and ritual laws of the Torah were merely a means to an end, which is moral perfection. They declared that all the precepts

---

[14] Thus, for instance, in the precept of Lev. 14.36, the Halakah finds indicated the lesson that we must spare and save even the smallest article of the possessions of others, even of wicked people (M. Neg. 12.5). For further illustrations of how the Halakah finds ethical lessons indicated in the ritual laws see below.

and ritual laws of the Torah put together cannot equal in importance one ethical principle of the Torah.[15] They strictly forbade the observance of a ritual precept or ceremonial law, if such an observance involved the disregard of an ethical principle.[16] An act prompted by moral considerations, even though it violates the strict letter of the law, is, in the opinion of the teachers of the Halakah, of greater value than the most careful performance of a prescribed ritual act or ceremonial law, but which is purposeless as far as the ethical motive is concerned.[17] "For," said they, "God desires the heart."[18] They did not set a fictitious value on mere conformity. They did not hesitate to declare that sometimes the abrogation of certain forms of the Law might be the means for preserving the spirit of the Law.[19] When the cause of God, i. e., of true religion requires, then the ritual laws shall be abolished, say the Rabbis.[20] It rests with the teachers of each generation, according to the Talmud, to determine whether the cause of Judaism will be furthered by the abolition of certain ritual or ceremonial laws. They have the authority to abolish even a biblical law.[21]

Such were the views held by the teachers of the Halakah about the origin, character and purpose of the Torah. These views alone should suffice to disprove the current, false opinions about the character of the Halakah, and should vindicate its teachers against the charge of narrow-minded legalism. These general statements made by the teachers of the Halakah reveal to us the true ethical character of the Halakah. They show us that the teachers of the Halakah always held before them the ideal of the fatherhood of God and the brotherhood of man, and that in their discussions and regulations they aimed to help

[15] אפילו כל מצוחיה של תורה אינן שוות לדבר אחד מן התורה (p. Peah 16d).
[16] מצוה הבאה בעבירה (Suk. 30a).
[17] גדולה עבירה לשמה ממצוה שלא לשמה (Naz. 23b).
[18] הקדוש ברוך הוא ליבא בעי (Sanh. 106b).
[19] פעמים שביטולה של תורה זו היא יסודה (Men. 99a,b).
[20] עת לעשות לד' הפרו תורתך (M. Ber., end).
[21] בי"ד מתנין לעקור דבר מן התורה (Yeb. 89b and 90b). About the restrictions to the application of this principle see *Nimuke Joseph* to Yeb., *ad loc.*, and my article "Nomism," in *Jewish Encyclopedia*, IX.

man walk in the ways of God the father and love man the brother. They further demonstrate that the teachers of the Halakah emphasized the true motive power for all moral action, that is, the inner ethical will, and that they insisted not upon outward conformity to the letter of the Law, but on an ethical religious life according to the spirit of the Law.

A detailed examination will prove that the Halakah in all its teachings, whether defining and applying biblical laws or enacting laws of its own, is guided by ethical principles, and by the desire to realize the prophetic ideals. The Halakah comprised the entire life of the Jewish people. An attempt, therefore, to give a detailed discussion of all its teachings would mean to present a complete system of Jewish ethics. This, of course, cannot be given in one paper. I shall, therefore, limit myself to a discussion of those regulations of the Halakah which deal with question of social righteousness, for this part of the Halakah is best fitted to demonstrate the fact that even in its minute discussions and in legal regulations the Halakah endeavored to carry out the prophetic ideas of justice and righteousness. We will, therefore, examine some of the laws and regulations of the Halakah dealing with relations between neighbors, between employer and employee, seller and buyer, benefactor and beneficiary. It will be our endeavor to learn what ethical principles underly the Halakic teachings regulating these various relations between man and man. And if I may be permitted to anticipate the results of my inquiry, I would say that we shall find that the passion for social righteousness characterized the teachings of the Rabbis as it did the utterances of the prophets. The combination of law and religion insisted upon by the Halakah did not result in reducing religion to mere legalism, but resulted in giving to the law the sanction of religion.[22]

[22] The passages in rabbinic literature, expressing the idea that honesty and uprightness are essential for the religious life, are too numerous to be cited here. I shall only quote here one utterance of the teachers of the Halakah which declares emphatically that one cannot believe in God and be dishonest to his fellow-man. Tosefta Shebu. 2.6, it is said אין אדם כיחש בעמיתו עד שכופר בעיקר, a man cannot act treacherously toward his fellow-man unless he denies

Conservation of Life One of the Chief Concerns of the Halakah

We begin our discussion of the ethical principles contained in the teachings of the Halakah by first examining one of the central ideas around which many of the ethical principles are grouped. A very characteristic idea underlying the ethics of the Halakah is the high regard for human life. The idea expressed in the biblical story of Creation that all men are created in the image of God is considered by the Halakah as a fundamental principle of Judaism,[23] second only to the commandment: "Thou shalt love thy neighbor as thyself." This idea teaches that every human being, made in the image of God, has within him a Divine spark — his soul — and is, therefore, capable of helping to realize God's plan in the universe. The Divine spark within him makes every human being an actual or potential ethical factor. His importance lies in the possibility of his rendering service to the cause of humanity and the cause of God. It is a logical consequence of the belief in the God-like nature of man that the highest value attaches to human life. The Halakah accordingly teaches that the life of a human being is to be saved at any cost and his health is to be preserved even at the sacrifice of all laws and precepts. Three grave sins, incest, murder and idolatry, constitute the exceptions to this rule.[24] Excepting the

---

God. In denying the right to his fellow-man he denies the fundamental principle of the religion, viz., that God commands us to be righteous and do justice.

[23] ואהבת לרעך כמוך רבי עקיבא אומר זה כלל גדול בתורה: בן עזאי אומר זה ספר תולדות אדם: זה כלל גדול מזה. Sifra, *Kedoshim*, IV, Weiss, 89b. (Cf. Rabad in his commentary, *ad loc.*, and Yalkuṭ to Genesis, § 40.) Ben Azzai's saying is to be understood in the sense that the belief that man is made in the image of God is not greater in importance but more comprehensive than the commandment, "thou shalt love thy neighbor as thyself." The former gives the reason for the latter. It identifies the commandment, "thou shalt love thy neighbor as thyself," with the commandment, "thou shalt love the Lord thy God." Love thy neighbor as thyself because, like thyself, he is made in the image of God, and by loving man, His creature, you manifest your love for God the Creator. Cf. also the saying in Ab. R. N., Version A, Ch. XVI, Schechter, 32b.

[24] כל עבירות שבתורה אם אומרין לו עבור ולא תהרג יעבור ולא יהרג חוץ מעבודה זרה, גלוי עריות ושפיכות דמים (Sanh. 74a) and בכל מתרפאין חוץ מע"ז ג"ע ושפ"ד (Pes. 25a).

injunctions against these three crimes, no consideration for any religious law should hinder the saving of life.[25] The Halakah teaches that all the laws of the Torah must be ignored when the life or the health of a human being is concerned. For in every human life there is the possibility of service to the cause of humanity, so that the saving of one life may be the saving of the whole world, and the loss of one life may result in the loss of a whole world.[26] We should not hesitate to transgress the law even if it is doubtful whether by such transgression the endangered life will be saved or even when there is doubt as to whether real danger to life exists.[27]

This Concern Based on a Peculiar Weltanschauung

This great importance attached to human life by the Halakah, even going so far as to suspend all the laws in cases where danger threatens, is but the logical result of the two principal views held by the Halakah. The first of these principles is that the purpose of the entire law is the furtherance of the cause of humanity. The second is that every human being is capable of contributing toward the cause of humanity and thus helping in the realization of God's plan. The saving of the individual means, therefore, the preservation of a moral factor in the cause of humanity. The violation of the law for the sake of preserving the life of a human being really becomes the means of helping to realize the purpose of the Law. That this was the reason for ignoring the Law when danger to life was involved, is expressly stated by the Halakah. Thus the halakic principle, "the Sabbath is given to you and not you to the Sabbath,"[28] which means that the Sabbath must be violated when the life or health of a human being is at stake, is supplemented by the further explanation: "Violate one Sabbath for the sake of this individual, so that he

[25] אין לך דבר שעומד בפני פיקוח נפש (Yoma 82a).
[26] המאבד נפש אחת מישראל כאילו איבד עולם מלא והמקיים נפש אחת מישראל כאילו קיים עולם מלא (M. Sanh. 4.5).
[27] אפילו ספק נפשות דוחה שבת (M. Yoma 8.6).
[28] לכם שבת מסורה ואין אתם מסורין לשבת (Mekilta, Ki Tisa, Weiss, 105b).

THE ETHICS OF THE HALAKAH 275

may live to keep many Sabbaths."[29] This means, save life at the cost of violating the Sabbath, for the life thus saved may contribute much to the cause which the observance of the Sabbath is to serve. The principle expressed here in regard to the Sabbath is applied by the Halakah to all the other laws of the Torah. The Halakah subtly emphasizes that they were all given in order that man may live by them and not die because of them.[30] The purpose of the Torah being to guide man in his labor for humanity, it would defeat its own purpose if it deprived itself of laborers by insisting upon a too strict observance of its precepts.

Conservation of Health

Since potential usefulness for the cause of humanity determines the value of life, it follows that the imperative duty of preserving human life applies to all without distinction. The Halakah, therefore, consistently teaches that a person owes the same duty to his life and his health as he owes to the life and health of others.

Conservation of Life

A man has no right to dispose of his life without consideration of his fellow-man. For he does not belong to himself alone. He belongs to humanity at large in whose cause he is to work. He is the עבד לרבים, the servant of the many. He has, therefore, no right to withdraw from his post of duty and deprive humanity of his service. Even if a man sees no purpose in his continuing to live and believes himself to be a burden to society, he has no right to dispose of his life. It may still become possible for him to render some service to humanity. He has no right to deprive society of this possibility, slight as it may be. Suicide, under any circumstances, is, therefore, strongly condemned by the Halakah. It is considered as an act of murder for which God will hold the suicide responsible.[31] The Halakah forbids not only to destroy

[29] חלל עליו שבת אחת כדי שישמור שבתות הרבה (ibid., Weiss, 106a).
[30] וחי בהם ולא שימות בהם (Sifra, Aḥare, XIII, Weiss, p. 86b; Sanh. 74a).
[31] ר'א אומר מיד נפשותיכם אדרוש את דמכם, B. Ḳ. 91b. The decision, declaring

one's life but even to ruin one's health or to inflict injury upon one's body.[32] In discussing the dietary laws the Halakah is guided by the principle that it is much more important to avoid injury to health than to avoid violations of biblical injunctions.[33] Nay, even to hurt oneself by fasting or to deprive oneself of a legitimate pleasure is considered a sin.[34] To care for one's body and keep it in good health is declared by Hillel to be a religious duty,[35] for in doing this we contribute to the public health.

Conservation of Property

Just as one has no right to injure his body or ruin his health because of the evil consequences for the health and welfare of his fellow-man, so he has not the right, according to the Halakah, to waste his property because such an act may result in evil for his fellow-man. Thus the Halakah forbids a man to squander his fortune even for charity, lest he himself become a burden upon society.[36] If a man cuts down young trees, even if they are in his own garden, he should be punished.[37] If a man tears many garments in mourning for the dead, he is to be punished.[38] In either case he has violated the law of בל תשחית, the prohibition against wastefulness. The principle underlying these halakic regulations is the idea, that man is a member of the human family and as such he must have consideration for the interests of this larger family. Although a man has the right to dispose of his property, the exercise of this right should not result in harm to others.

---

suicide, when committed in order to escape disgrace, permissible, which is ascribed to Asheri (Responsa collection, *Besamim Rosh*, 345), is a false decision, and was never given by Asheri. See Jacob Brüll in his notes to his edition of H. Chajes' *Iggeret Bikkoret*, pp. 11b–12a.

[32] אין אדם רשאי לחבל בעצמו (B. Ḳ. 91b).
[33] חמירא סכנתא מאיסורא (Ḥul. 10a).
[34] B. Ḳ., *loc. cit.*, and Ta'an. 11a.
[35] Leviticus r. 34, 3.
[36] המבזבז אל יבזבז יותר מחומש שמא יצטרך לבריות (Ket. 50a).
[37] Sifre, Deut., § 203, Friedman, 111b, Mak. 22a.
[38] B. Ḳ. 91b.

Ramifications of the Same Principle

The Halakah regarded it as a man's duty so to use his own possessions as to increase his usefulness to society and enhance the well-being of his fellow-men. This high regard for the welfare of our fellow-men is the guiding principle of the Halakah in its laws about the relations between man and man. It is not enough that we should not injure the life, health, property, honor and well-being of our neighbors; we should concern ourselves with their preservation and enhancement. According to the Halakah this duty is incumbent upon us even in such cases where we could not be compelled to do so by the letter of the law. This duty extends even to fellow-men who by their own conduct have forfeited their claim upon our consideration.

The Dignity of Man

A few regulations of the Halakah will suffice to show that this was its spirit. "The honor and personal dignity of any human being," declares the Halakah, "are to be so highly regarded as to set aside any prohibitory law of the Torah."[39] Thus, if the observance of a ritual law is apt to subject a man to indignity, that law may be dispensed with. This consideration for personal dignity must, according to the Halakah, be extended even to those who have apparently lost their sense of dignity and degraded themselves by committing a crime. This principle, according to the teachers of the Halakah, is expressed in the Biblical law: "If a man shall steal an ox or a sheep, and kill it or sell it, he shall restore five oxen for an ox and four sheep for a sheep" (Ex. 21.37. English Bible 22.1). They point out that God himself respects the honor of every creature, even of the thief. The fine for stealing a sheep is smaller than for stealing an ox, because in stealing a sheep the thief was probably compelled to carry it on his shoulders. Under these circumstances, the Halakah says, he was certainly put to indignity. It is this humiliation which the law takes into consideration and reduces the fine.[40]

[39] גדול כבוד הבריות שדוחה לא תעשה שבתורה (Shab. 81b).
[40] Mekilta, *Mishpatim*, XII, Weiss, 95b, also B. K. 79b.

Punishment Without Indignity

In meting out punishment we must be careful not to add disgrace.[41] The thief who is sold into servitude must not be insulted by being called a slave.[42] Neither is he to be treated as a slave by being made to do the work of a slave.[43]

Servitude Without Disgrace

The regard for the personal feelings and sensibilities of our fellow-men, taught by the Halakah, is especially shown in its regulations concerning the relations between master and servant. A distinction is here made between servant and slave. The master has no right to humiliate the servant by making him do low or degrading work.[44] He has no right to assign to the servant work which he does not need, merely for the sake of keeping the servant busy. And lest the master pretend that he needs the work, the Halakah reminds him that when the Torah prohibited the master from ruling over the servant with rigor, it adds the words: "But thou shalt fear thy God" (Lev. 25.43), who knows what is in thy heart.[45] The Halakah further enjoins that the servant must be given the same kind of food and the same kind of drink which the master partakes.[46] The principle which underlies these regulations is, that only the product of the servant's labor belongs to the master. This alone the master pays for and has a right to demand. The personal honor and human dignity of the servant are his own sacred rights, which the master dare not infringe upon. The servant is to be treated as a fellow-man in all respects. Even in regard to the Canaanite slave the Halakah rules that the master has only the right to make him work, but not to insult him.[47] R. Joḥanan shared his meat and wine with his slave, declaring that the slave was a human being like himself and applying to him the words of Job 31.15: "Did not He that made me in the womb make him?"[48]

[41] Mak. 22b.
[42] Mekilta, *Mishpatim*, I, Weiss, 81b.
[43] *Ibid.*, Weiss, 82b.
[44] *Ibid., loc. cit.*
[45] Sifra, *Behar*, VII, Weiss, 109.
[46] Ḳid. 20a.
[47] לעבודה נתתים ולא לבושה (Niddah 47a).
[48] p. B. Ḳ., 8, (6c).

The Decision that Broke the Back of the Slavery Law

A most striking illustration of this spirit of the Halakah is found in the following discussion about a slave who has acquired a title to half of his freedom. The school of Hillel at first was inclined to decide that the half-slave should work one day for his master and one day for himself. This arrangement would be just according to the civil law, for to own a slave means to enjoy the product of his labor. In this case, therefore, where there are two owners to the slave, the master and the slave himself, the product of the slave's labor should be equally divided. The school of Shammai, however, pointed out to the school of Hillel the fact that such an arrangement would provide well for the master but ill for the slave. The latter would be wronged by such an arrangement, because it fails to give him a definite status in society. By this arrangement he has neither the advantages of a freeman nor the privileges of a slave. He is not permitted, for instance, to marry a slave, nor has he acquired the right of marrying a free woman. In this way he is deprived of the inalienable right of founding a household. In consideration of these arguments, the school of Hillel agreed with the school of Shammai, that for the betterment of the world and the improvements of the social conditions — מפני תיקון העולם, the master be compelled to give the slave a bill of freedom and receive from the slave a note for the amount which is still due.[49]

The Public Good the Halakic Lodestar of Legislation

The Halakah takes cognizance of the fact that the strict application of the law of partnership would give the master, owning half interest in the slave, the right to continue this partnership and to share the products of the slave's labor indefinitely. However, the Halakah decides that מפני תיקון העולם for the sake of improving the social condition in the world, the master should be compelled

---

[49] מי שחציו עבד וחציו בן חורין עובד את רבו יום אחד ואת עצמו יום אחד דברי בית הלל, אמרו להם בית שמאי תקנתם את רבו ואת עצמו לא תקנתם. לישא שפחה אינו יכול לישא בת חורין אינו יכול... אלא מפני תיקון העולם כופין את רבו ועושה אותו בן חורין וכותב שטר על חצי דמיו. וחזרו בית הלל להורות כדברי בית שמאי, M. ‘Eduy. 1.13.

to consider the slave as a human being with inalienable rights. For the sake of the slave's well-being the master should forego his right of continuous partnership. Compare this high regard for the personal rights of the slave with our modern method of speaking of workingmen as mere "hands." We advertise for "hands," we engage "hands" and discharge "hands." In our industrial world we deal only with "hands," forgetful of the fact that these "hands" belong to human beings with hearts and feelings and with a sense of dignity. Our modern factory legislation could learn from the Halakah to apply the principle of מפני תיקון העולם. Out of regard for the moral improvement of society we owe the laborer more than the stipulated wage. We must regard his personal comfort, his health and his sense of decency.

Employer and Employee

Other regulations of the Halakah dealing with the employer and the employee are prompted by the same ethical spirit as shown above. They seek to protect the laborer and at the same time to show due regard for the rights of the employer. In order to do both and establish friendly relations between employer and employee, the Halakah does not hesitate to modify and even to overrule biblical decrees. In doing so the Halakah expressly declares that we should be guided by ethical considerations even when they make it necessary to decide against the letter of the law. In the following instance, the Halakah finds an exception to the biblical law. According to the biblical law a man who is sued for witholding money or valuables can establish his innocence, in the absence of evidence, by taking an oath. This law, according to the Halakah, is not to be applied in the case of an employer who is sued for withholding the wages of an employee. In this case the Halakah decides against the biblical law and takes the privilege of the oath away from the defendant and gives it to the plaintiff. The employee affirming his claim by oath is awarded the payment of his wages.[50] This decision is

[50] M. Shebu. 7.1.

THE ETHICS OF THE HALAKAH

justified by the Halakah on the supposition that it will please both parties. Even the employer must needs be pleased by such a decision as it will work ultimate advantage in his favor. The Halakah is of the opinion that the strict application of the biblical law, giving the employer the right effectively to deny on oath the claim of the workingman, would ultimately harm the employer. It might earn him a bad reputation and make it difficult for him to secure workingmen.[51]

Extent of Servants' Liability for Damages

Likewise, the Halakah frees the hired laborer from paying the damages for an article spoiled by him accidentally in the process of handling. Only, he must take an oath that the damage was caused by accident or mistake and not by willful negligence. This regulation the Halakah declares to be a rabbinic institution for the purpose of facilitating transactions between the laborer and his employer.[52] The following decision given by Abba Areka in an actual case illustrates the ethical spirit in which the Rabbis administered the law. Rabbah, the son of Huna, engaged certain carriers to transport barrels of wine from one place to another. In handling the barrels, the carriers were evidently careless (see Rashi, *ad loc.*) and broke one barrel, spilling the wine. Rabbah, the employer, took away their mantles in order to secure himself for the payment of the damages, a course of conduct which the law sanctioned. The carriers, however, haled him before Abba Areka, who ordered him to return the mantles. When Rabbah asked, "Is this the law?" Abba Areka answered, quoting Prov. 2.20: "Yes, 'in order that thou mayest walk in the ways of good men.' " The carriers then said: "We are poor laborers; we have spent the whole day on this work and now we are hungry and have nothing to eat." Abba Areka then ordered the employer, Rabbah, to pay them the stipulated wages. To the question of Rabbah, "Is this the law?" Abba Areka answered, quoting the second half of the verse in Proverbs: "Yes, 'and keep the path of the righteous!' " (B. M. 83a). The law gave the employer

---

[51] Shebu. 45a.   [52] שבועה זו תקנת חכמים היא (B. M. 83a).

the right to make the carriers pay for the damage they caused by their carelessness. Abba Areka, however, thought that consideration for the poor laborers should outweigh the letter of the law. He quotes a higher law, "To walk in the way of good men." This higher law should make one forego his legal claims when these affect a poor laborer.[52a] Compare this fine spirit with the modern practice of deducting from the meager wages of the servants and shopworkers for accidental damages caused by them.

NEW RIGHTS OF NEIGHBORS

We turn now to a consideration of some laws of the Halakah which deal with other relations between man and man. The Halakah embraces a whole group of laws defining man's attitude toward his neighbor, which are not directly derived from the laws of Moses and in fact do not properly belong in a legal code. These halakic laws are based upon the ethical principle, that a man must be mindful of his neighbor's welfare. He is not permitted to insist upon his legal rights merely for the purpose of spiting his neighbor. Nor can he argue petty advantage in favor of his conduct. One illustration will suffice to explain this halakic principle.

Two brothers or partners, A and B, divide an estate between them. One of them, A, has another piece of property adjoining the estate in question. The Halakah gives him the option of choosing that part of the estate which joins his other property; the other partner, B, is not permitted to claim the petty advantage which might accrue to him from having his estate protected on both sides by the property of A. The Halakah weighs the advantage of B over against the disadvantage that would arise to A from having his two estates separated, and decided in favor of A. By the letter of the law, B is not bound to consider the convenience of A, and from a legal point of view he could insist upon his right to choose or to have the choice decided by lot. However, such an insistance upon one's legal rights without due regard for the convenience of his neighbor's is condemned by the

[52a] Cf. also b. 'Ar. 30a and b. Ḳid. 20a; a share of the redemption price is also figured out so as to favor the servant.

Halakah and is characterized as the attitude of the wicked people of Sodom. The Halakah assumes the authority to prevent people from acting in such a manner.[53]

Rights of Adjoining Neighbors

The following laws obtain in the case of adjoining neighbors. The Halakah demands that the interests of adjoining neighbors be considered in the disposition of property. The halakic regulations in this regard are called דיני דבר מצרא, "The rights of adjoining neighbors." According to these regulations a property-owner has a prior claim to purchase adjoining property over any other person. If the owner of the adjoining property ignores this right of his adjoining neighbor and sells the property to a third person, the latter may be compelled to turn over the property to the adjacent neighbor, receiving only the purchase price. The Halakah quotes Deut. 6.18: "And thou shalt do that which is right and good in the sight of the Lord" as a justification for granting these rights to the neighbors.[54] The teachers of the Halakah believed that it would be displeasing to God if one should not give his neighbor preference over a stranger.

Some Laws of Partnership

The same tendency of fostering friendly relations is found in other regulations of the Halakah which aim to settle peacefully the differences between partners. Thus, for instance, if one of two partners desires to bring about a dissolution of the partnership, the halakic regulation is as follows: If the property or business to which they are partners can be equally divided, so that each half does not depreciate in value, one can force the other to divide.[55] However, if the property is of such a nature that, when divided in two, each half will have less value than fifty

---

[53] כופין על מדת סדום, *ibid.*, 12a.

[54] *Ibid.*, 108a, b. Cf. also Vidal in his commentary *Maggid Mishneh* to Maimonides' *Yad, Hilkot Shekenim*, end, about the ethical purpose of the laws of בר מצרא.

[55] Mishnah B. B. 1.6.

per cent of the whole, then one partner cannot force the other to divide the property. In this case the dissatisfied partner has the right to fix an equitable price upon his half and force the other either to purchase it or sell him his own half at the same price.[56] In this regulation the Halakah is prompted by the desire to maintain peaceful relations between the partners, realizing that if forced to stay together strife would ensue.

For the same reason the Halakah prohibits one partner from selling his share in the property to a stranger without the consent of the other partners.[57] The new partner may not be agreeable, and should, therefore, not be forced upon the other partners. The teachers of the Halakah made the above enactments for the establishment of good will. They felt themselves justified in doing so, on the principle that the aim and purpose of the entire Torah is to establish peace and good-fellowship among men.[58]

The Ethical Conduct of Business

On the same principle the Halakah prohibits a man from bidding for an article whose purchase is being considered by another.[59] Consideration for one's fellow-man is at the bottom of the halakic prohibition against opening a barber shop or a tailor shop or the like in a neighborhood where one already exists. For the new shop is bound to take away trade from the older one. This restriction, however, does not extend to stores which supply the necessaries of life.[60] In the latter case the opening of new stores may act as a wholesome check upon the monopolization of trade by any one store on any street. The Halakah preferred to encourage legitimate competition in order that the poor consumer might get the necessaries of life as cheaply as possible. Thus the Halakah permits the store-keeper to give little gifts

[56] גוד או אגוד (B. B. 13a). [57] B. M. 108a.
[58] Git. 59b. [59] Kid. 59a.
[60] B. B. 21b. By this distinction between a trade which supplies the necessaries of life and other business, the apparent contradiction between opinion of R. Huna, who followed Simon b. Gamaliel, and the Baraita, permitting the opening of a store which supplies the necessaries of life — or a bath house, which is also considered a necessity — is removed.

to the children who are sent by their parents to make purchases, for the purpose of inducing them to come again.[61] The Rabbis did not consider this a form of rebate, but a form of legitimate competition.

LAWS AGAINST MONOPOLIZATION OF NECESSARIES OF LIFE

The same regard for the needs of the poor consumer was the motive of the halakic regulation prohibiting dealers from putting articles of food into storage for the purpose of raising the price.[62] Similarly, it is prohibited to export articles of food to foreign countries lest this practice would raise the price of these articles at home.[63] Some teachers go even so far as to prohibit the making of profits from dealing in foodstuffs,[64] evidently intending to exclude the middleman. The Halakah also gave the authorities supervision of all dealings in articles of food and power to regulate market prices.[65] The Halakah condemns the practice of adulterating food[66] as well as of selling articles under false labels.[67]

Some of these halakic regulations concerning matters of business may seem quite antiquated in the modern world of business. Possibly this artlessness may spring from the fact that the Rabbis innocently believed that even business furnished a field for the cultivation of the virtues. We are not concerned with

[61] *Ibid., loc. cit.*, Lazarus, *Ethik*, I, 303, incorrectly states that the Halakah forbids this practice of competition. He evidently mistook the opinion of R. Judah for the accepted Halakah. The accepted Halakah, however, follows the opinion of the majority of the teachers who opposed R. Judah and permitted this form of competition. See Maimonides, *Yad, Hilkot Mekirah*, XVIII, 4, and *Shulḥan Aruk, Ḥoshen Mishpat*, 228, § 18.

[62] *Ibid.*, 89b.
[63] *Ibid., loc. cit.*
[64] אסור להשתכר בחיי נפש (B. B. 90a).
[65] *Ibid.*, 89a.
[66] Mekilta, *Mishpatim*, XIII; Weiss, 96a.
[67] Ḥul. 94a. It is forbidden to sell to a non-Jew trefah meat, because the non-Jew buying it in a Jewish butcher shop is misled to believe it to be kosher meat.

the applicability of these laws to modern conditions. We are interested in the fact that the Halakah considered business from an ethical point of view. Quite in keeping with this attitude we find that the teachers of the Halakah were opposed to what is popularly known in our day as "shopping." "If you have no intention of buying, do not ask the price"[68] was the maxim of the Rabbis. They also say, "Do not bargain for any article if you have no money."[69] It is not right to cause the store-keeper unnecessary work and to arouse expectations which we have no intention to gratify. These injunctions of the Rabbis may not prove popular with modern shoppers; in fact, they were probably not popular with ancient shoppers, but their ethical value cannot be denied.

Justice Above Legal Technicalities

Led by the tendency to consider the spirit of the law, the Halakah teaches that a man should not avail himself of a legal privilege whereby he harms his fellow-men. Thus, for instance, the debtor is admonished not to avail himself of the Sabbatical year to avoid paying his debts.[70] The teachers could not very well express this admonition in the form of a law, because according to a law in the Torah (Deut. 15.2) all debts were canceled by the Sabbatical year. Therefore they could only urge upon the debtor to forego his legal right because insistence would work against the spirit of the Torah "whose ways are ways of pleasantness and all whose paths are peace."

In like manner the Halakah strongly condemns certain actions which violate the higher moral law, although they do not constitute a violation of the civil law. The verdict of the Halakah in such cases is: "He is free according to the laws of men, but guilty according to the judgments of God."[71]

[68] לא יאמר לו בכמה חפץ זה והוא אינו רוצה ליקח, Sifra, *Behar*, IV, Weiss, 107d.
[69] לא תעמוד על המקח בשעה שאין לך דמים, M. B. M. 4.10; Tosefta, 3.25.
[70] המחזיר חוב בשביעית רוח חכמים נוחה הימנו, M. Sheb. 10.9.
[71] פטור בדיני אדם וחייב בדיני שמים, Tosefta Shebu. 3; B. Ḳ. 55b.

Halakah Does Not Hesitate to Abolish Biblical Laws

We now turn to a consideration of those cases, wherein the Halakah found it necessary to abolish certain biblical laws which it conceived to be out of harmony with the spirit of the Torah. In such cases they would justify their procedure on the principle mentioned above that: "When the cause of true religion demands, certain laws may be abolished," 'עת לעשות לד הפרו תורתך. As peace and brotherly love is the aim of religion, they would abolish such laws of the Bible, as, in their opinion, tended to lessen peace and brotherly love. A few instances may be cited here.[72]

First is the well-known institution of the Prosbul. This practically nullifies the law (Deut. 15.1–2) which declares that the Sabbatical year cancels all debts. This institution was introduced by Hillel because he observed that the effect of the biblical law was to deter people from loaning to the needy, a practice which violates the higher moral command of the Torah (Deut. 15.9) which enjoins upon us not to refrain from lending to the poor.[73]

Another instance of abolishing a biblical law is found in the halakic enactment, tending to facilitate the collection of debts. The biblical law requires the same severe examination of evidence in civil as in criminal cases. This would obviously complicate the collection of debts and discourage the creditor from lending. As this would ultimately work harm to the borrower, the Halakah therefore, ignores the biblical law, giving as its reason "in order not to close the door against the prospective borrower."[74]

The following is another instance, where the Halakah changes a biblical law, realizing that its application might become the cause of unfair dealings and the source of friction in business

---

[72] I cite here only such cases in which the Halakah avowedly declares that it consciously changes or modifies the biblical law for some ethical reason. There are, however, many other instances in which the Halakah, influenced by its higher ethical conceptions, unconsciously, so to speak, explained away or changed biblical laws.

[73] M. Sheb. 10.3.

[74] כדי שלא תנעול דלת בפני לווין, Sanh. 2b–3a; Ket. 88a.

relations. According to the biblical law a purchase of chattels is consummated by payment of purchase price. The teachers of the Halakah feared, and no doubt their fears were based upon actual experiences, that the application of this law would be productive of evil results under certain conditions. If, for instance, the purchaser failed to remove the purchased article immediately, there is a possibility that the seller, having received the price, would not take such care of the article, as if it were his own. In case of danger by fire, for instance, he might be tempted not to put forth any effort to save it. Even if he made such an effort and failed, the suspicion of carelessness would arise in the mind of the purchaser. Thus the application of the biblical law might result in mutual distrust and ill feeling. To avoid this the Halakah rules, contrary to the biblical law, that purchase is consummated only by actual acquisition.[75] Here again, we are not concerned with the relative merits of the biblical and halakic laws. We are merely interested in the fact that the change made by the Halakah was prompted by the ethical consideration of avoiding strife and dispute. This further proves that the teachers of the Halakah made the laws of the Torah measure up to their ethical standards.

It was only because of their conviction that the aim and purpose of the Torah was to establish peace and love, justice and righteousness, that the Rabbis dared apply to the biblical laws the test of ethical valuation. When they realized that under the changed conditions a given law could no longer serve that high purpose of the Torah, they did not hesitate to modify it.

Some *Obiter Dicta* Which Serve to Show the Mind's Construction

We have endeavored to ascertain the ethical standards of the Halakah by examining some of its direct enactments and certain changes made by it in the biblical laws. We now pass to a consideration of a number of indirect statements made by the teachers of the Halakah which will serve to confirm these deductions. The ideas expressed in debates, the arguments advanced

[75] B. M. 47b.

THE ETHICS OF THE HALAKAH

in the discussions of various laws, the casual remarks made in explaining certain biblical enactments, are very telling indications of the principles which guided the teachers of the Halakah. These impromptu remarks, expressed in discussions, reveal the character and the moral outlook of the disputants. This is especially the case when we find the teachers of the Halakah raising objections to some of the laws or to certain applications of the Law on the ground of ethical consideration. I shall cite a few instances of such discussions which reveal the ethical ideas always in the mind of the Rabbis. I shall select these instances from themes which seem to offer very little scope for the expression of ethical principles.

Sabbath Burdens and the Messianic Era

Thus in discussing the prohibition against carrying a burden on the Sabbath, the rule is laid down that a man may carry on his person that which is generally considered an article of adornment or decoration. One of the teachers expressed his opinion in favor of permitting a man to wear his armor on the Sabbath on the ground that armor is an adornment, תכשיטין הן לו. However, the other teachers objected to this opinion, giving as a reason that weapons do not constitute an adornment but a disgrace to mankind. Because it is said: "And they shall beat their swords into plowshares, and their spears into pruning hooks, nation shall not lift up sword against nation, neither shall they learn war any more."[76] (Isa. 2.4). Our efforts to realize the ideal of peace must begin with learning not to glory in weapons of war. Here we see that the prophetic ideal of peace was in the minds of the teachers of the Halakah even when they discussed purely ritualistic laws.

Court Appearances and the Position of Woman

Likewise in discussing certain points of the law of the Levirate marriage, the teachers of the Halakah were influenced in their decisions by considerations for the feelings of the woman. They

[76] M. Shab. 6.4.

would in certain cases not countenance the application of the law because it would put an indignity upon the woman. They justify this, their attitude, with the statement that such an application of the law would not be in accord with the spirit of the Torah "whose ways are ways of pleasantness and all whose paths are peace."[77]

VOWS AND HUMANITY

Another such instance is found in the discussion of the laws pertaining to vows. It must be said parenthetically that the Rabbis were strongly opposed to the popular practice of making vows, especially as some of these vows were often made in the heat of anger. The Halakah discusses the conditions under which a man may retract his vow. If a man makes a vow under an illusion concerning facts or under a misapprehension concerning consequences, the vow is voidable. Upon ascertaining the correct facts or upon realizing the grave consequences he may apply to the court (Beth Din) to declare the vow null and void. The procedure of the court was to examine the person with the view of ascertaining whether he was correctly informed, when he made his vow, both as to facts and as to possible consequnces. To this end the court permitted itself to point out any grave consequence that might have escaped the notice of the person, but which, if known, would have deterred him.

R. Meier advised that we should ask the person, if at the time of making the vow he was aware of the fact that his vow might involve the violation of a moral law. The court should say to him, "If you had known that in taking such a vow you were violating the law, 'Thou shalt not avenge or bear any grudge' (Lev. 19.18), and the law, 'Thou shalt not hate thy brother in thy heart' (*ibid.* 19.17), and the law, 'Thou shalt love thy neighbor as thyself' (*ibid.* 19.18) and the law commanding you to give assistance to the poor, expressed in the words of Lev. 25.36, 'That he may live with thee.' Did you consider that the person against whom you vowed might become poor

[77] Yeb. 15a and 87b.

and thus you would be prevented from rendering succor unto him?" If he says, "Had I known all this I would not have vowed" — that man is free from his vow.[78] What stronger proof do we need than the examples quoted, that the Rabbis were always animated by the highest ideals. We may disagree with them as to the whole subject of vows, but we must admire the high moral plane whereon they discussed this purely formalistic subject.

Erub Ceremony and Neighborliness

Another instance of this kind is found in the rules of the Halakah concerning the *Erub Hazerot*. By the ceremony of the *Erub,* the families living in one court are fictitiously united into one household by taking a meal in one common room, accessible to all. In this ceremony the teachers of the Halakah saw a way of establishing peace and friendly relations between the inhabitants of the same court or the neighbors on the same street.[79] A story is told of two enemies who became reconciled through this ceremony. And the Rabbis conclude, that in this manner is illustrated the truth of the saying that all the ways of the Torah are ways of pleasantness and all her paths lead to peace.[80]

The same thought suggests itself to the Rabbis, when they discuss the selection of the palm branch as one of the four plants to be used on Sukkoth.[81]

Universalistic Tendencies

The Rabbis tried further to carry out the purpose of the Torah by enacting a whole group of laws for the sake of furthering peace among all men, Jew and gentile alike.[82] Thus, for instance, the Halakah enacts that we should do charity to the poor, of non-Jews also, that we should bury their dead and attend to their

---

[78] M. Ned. 9.4.
[79] מערבין בחצרות מפני דרכי שלום, p. 'Er. 3, (20d).
[80] הדא הוא דכתיב דרכיה דרכי נועם וכל נתיבותיה שלום, *ibid., loc. cit.*
[81] Suk. 32b.
[82] M. Giṭ 5.8, and Tosefta, 5.4–5.

funerals and deliver for them funeral addresses and condole with their mourners just as we would do all these things to Jews, in order that peace and goodwill might prevail among all men.[83]

THE TALMUDIC IDEA THAT CHARITY IS JUSTICE, NOT EXCESS OF LOVE

The last-mentioned regulations bring us to a discussion of the halakic rules concerning charity. This subject I will only touch upon very briefly because it has been exhaustively treated by several authors. In these rules the tendency of the Halakah to make man fulfil the commandments, "Thou shalt love thy neighbor as thyself," and "that he may live with thee," clearly manifests itself. Here again, the teachers of the Halakah realized that it was not sufficient merely to preach high ideals. They realized the necessity of establishing laws, whereby those who were able should be compelled to give charity and whereby the community would be compelled to render assistance to its dependents. Here, as elsewhere, they realized that practical legislation must be content to achieve what is possible under the circumstances. Thus, whatever lofty ideas about spontaneous charity they expressed in their haggadic utterances, and they have many such ideas, in their legal enactments they confined their efforts to what they considered practical. They aimed to secure for the poor the help that he needed and to impress upon the rich the obligation that rested upon him. In other words, they tried to make of charity what its Hebrew term, צדקה, connotes, namely, justice to the rights of the poor. This idea of justice in charity, demands that charity be collected only from those who are able to give and distributed only among those who really need it. The Halakah, accordingly, regulated by law, the collec-

---

[83] Tosefta Giṭ, *loc. cit.* That the meaning of the phrase מפני דרכי שלום is "for the sake of furthering peace and good will among all men" and not "merely to maintain peaceful relations with the heathen," as some Christian theologians would interpret it, has been proved by Lazarus, *Ethik*, I, 182–83, and F. Perles, *Bousset's Religion des Judentums*.

tion and distribution of charity. They determined by law those who must contribute and in what proportion to their income. They also determined those to whom charity should be given and how it should be rightly administered.[84] They permitted one exception to the rules regarding investigation. A hungry person should be fed without investigation.[85] In all these laws laid down in the Mishnah and the Talmud and embodied in all the later halakic codes, there is a spirit of brotherly love and true sympathy for the poor. These laws lay especial stress upon protecting those who are compelled to take charity. Assistance should be rendered in such a manner that the recipient be made to feel that he is receiving justice and not charity. In this manner the idea is emphasized that we are all brothers, children of one Father in Heaven. If we give from our abundance to the poor, we are, according to the Halakah, acting as stewards in our Father's household and we give to the poor brother what our Father entrusted to us for that purpose, for we and our good belong to the Lord.[86]

Concluding Thoughts

I feel that the above examination of the halakic laws and regulations concerning man's relation to his fellow-man will convince the unbiased that the Halakah, in interpreting and applying the biblical laws, as well as in its own legal enactments, was guided by the highest ethical principles. We have seen that as practical legislators, they often had to content themselves with merely approaching the ideal, but they never forgot the two fundamental principles, the fatherhood of God and the brotherhood of man. They constantly kept before them the vision of a united humanity worshiping the one true God.

---

[84] Mishnah and Tosefta Peah, and in sayings scattered throughout the Talmud, see, also, Maimonides, Yad, *Mattenot 'Aniyyim*, and *Shulḥan Aruk Yore Deah*, 246–259.

[85] אין בודקין למזונות, B. B. 9a, according to the opinion of R. Judah, which is supported by a Baraita.

[86] Ab. 3.8.

A Priest People Must be Distinct

Even when occupied with those halakic regulations which tended to keep Israel separate from the other peoples, as, for instance, the dietary laws, the peculiar customs and religious ceremonies, the teachers of the Halakah did not forget these lofty ideals. It was not contempt or hatred for other people that prompted the teachers of the Halakah in upholding and developing these ritual laws and ceremonial customs. Neither did the teachers consider these laws of perennial value. As we have heard above, these laws were considered merely a commentary, which at some time and under certain conditions might even be dispensed with. All these ceremonial laws and customs were conceived by the teachers of the Halakah to be a useful means to a noble end. They served, in the opinion of the teachers, to make Israel a distinct and holy people and to enable him to teach his moral and religious truths to the other peoples of the world. In their haggadic sayings these teachers often expressed their hope for the ultimate conversion of all nations to the worship of one God. They displayed a readiness to receive and welcome proselytes. They even recognized the religious equality of the pious ones among the gentiles, the חסידי אומות העולם, although not formally converted to Judaism. With all that, the teachers of the Halakah were convinced — and we share their conviction — that it was absolutely necessary for the priest and teacher of the nations to preserve his identity, that Israel as a religious people should remain distinct. In their opinion the dietary laws and the peculiar customs were the surest safeguards of the Jewish identity and most conducive for the preservation of the distinctive religious character of the Jewish people. No student of Jewish history can dare say that they were wrong. Nobody can deny that these ancient Jewish teachers accomplished their purpose. By their halakic regulations they preserved the Jewish people and through it the heritage of the prophets, Judaism. Moreover, these ancient teachers of the Halakah have showed how to preserve Israel and his teachings. In their path the Jewish teachers of all subsequent generations have followed.

Continuity of Jewish Thought

We, the present-day teachers of Judaism, also follow in the path of those ancient teachers. We preserve the continuity of Jewish teachings and Jewish religious thought. In spirit and in purpose, in principles of conduct and in essentials of belief, we are at one with those ancient teachers in Israel. We differ from them in the details of practice, but these are minor differences. It is true, that many of the laws and regulations of the talmudic Halakah have been discarded by us. Many of the practices taught by the ancient teachers have been abolished because they have outlived their usefulness. Many of the ritual forms and religious ceremonies which served the ancient teachers as vehicles for religious ideas, being no more in harmony with our modern ideas, have been changed or modified. Indeed, the whole system of civil law which formed a great part of the talmudic Halakah has been relegated to the civil authorities. This, too, paradoxical as it may sound, is in keeping with a talmudic principle which declares דינא דמלכותא דינא that, "the civil law of the country is to be considered as the civil law of the Jew."[87] However, all these differences in custom and practice do not constitute essential differences between us and our predecessors, the Rabbis of old. The existence of these differences does not indicate an interruption in the continuity of the Jewish tradition. On the contrary, their very presence emphasizes this continuity, for change does not always indicate a break with the past.

The Modern Halakah

In instituting these changes, we are merely doing the same thing which our ancient teachers did. The Halakah, as a complex of laws, forms and customs, is not something fixed or permanent. Its very name, Halakah, הלכה, suggests movement and progress. There has always been an older and a newer Halakah. From its very beginning, the Halakah was constantly changing and developing. Ours is the youngest Halakah, representing its latest

[87] Giṭ. 6b.

development, but it is still the living stream of Jewish Halakah. We also have a complex of laws, forms and customs, whereby we regulate our religious life — our Halakah. In a good and sufficient sense we are also separatistic, as were our forefathers. We also keep ourselves distinct and separate from all other peoples in our religious life. We have a ritual of our own and religious ceremonies of our own, which are for the most part the same as those of our forefathers, only modified and adapted to our time and country. We also have certain peculiar forms for expressing our religious ideas. We have our Jewish festivals, our historic Jewish Sabbath. We worship in our own way and in our own houses of prayer. Thus, we are, in a religious sense, separatistic as were the ancient teachers of the Halakah. Like them, we also want to maintain our Jewish identity; we seek to preserve the priest-people Israel. We use the means we think best fitted for our time. The ancient teachers used the means they thought best fitted for their time. The modern Halakah, just as the ancient Halakah, aims to accomplish the same end, to preserve Israel as the priest-teacher of the nations. Nobody would think of accusing us of having forgotten the prophetic ideals of love, justice, righteousness and universal brotherhood in spite of the fact that we are in a sense separatistic.

It is just as illogical to accuse the ancient teachers of the Halakah of having forgotten the prophetic ideals because of the separatistic tendencies found in their halakic teachings. The ancient teachers of the Halakah realized that if Israel was to accomplish his task of spreading the knowledge of God on earth, they must preserve the agent who is to do this work, they must see to it that Israel should not become submerged among the nations of the world. And we, today, whose task it is to continue the work of the prophets and of the ancient teachers of Judaism, likewise realize, that in order to carry out our mission, it is absolutely necessary that we preserve our Jewish religious individuality. We must keep ourselves religiously separate from the other peoples and be an עם קדוש, a holy nation. Thus alone can we accomplish our mission and bring nigh the time when "the earth will be full of the knowledge of God as the waters cover the sea."

Tashlik

Tashlik

A Study In Jewish Ceremonies
(1936)

RELIGIOUS ceremonies are the best conservers of religious ideas and beliefs. They may properly be designated as storehouses in which religious ideas and beliefs are safely put away and preserved. In a storage place new wares are very often added to those already stored there. Sometimes these new articles are placed around or on top of the things which have been placed there before. The old articles may thus become inaccessible, or they may even be hidden from sight, almost buried under the newer articles, but they do not become destroyed nor do they get lost. They may not be seen, their presence may not be noticed and they may be hard to reach, but they remain there, in the place originally assigned to them. In fact, they are all the more safe and secure in their original place because they are hidden away, covered and protected by the newer wares.

It is the same with the ideas and beliefs embodied in a religious ceremony. The ceremony very often experiences changes and modifications in the course of time. It receives new interpretations, becomes a repository for new ideas, and new beliefs become associated with it. But whatever new interpretations the ceremony may receive in the course of time, no matter what additional meanings are given to it, or how many new ideas are put into it, it never entirely loses its original, simple meaning. Very rarely does it dissociate itself completely from the ideas which at one time had been invested in or connected with it. The newer ideas do not crowd out the old ones. The latter are not removed from the domain of the ceremony. They linger on persistently and continue to be attached to the ceremony for all time.

Even after the enlightened and more advanced people have come to regard these old ideas as foolish notions or even harmful superstitions to which they strongly object, the people at large still fondly hold on to them and do not discard them. In the popular appreciation of the significance of the ceremony the old and primitive ideas find a place where they remain undisturbed and continue to retain their old connection with the ceremony.

It is true that they no longer occupy a conspicuous place, they no longer hold a prominent position in the realm of the ceremony. They are very often entirely overlooked by superficial observers or even intentionally ignored by those who like to see and recognize only the newer and more modern ideas. But this very fact is the salvation of the older idea or belief. For just because it is ignored or not sufficiently noticed, such an old belief or superstition is able to survive. Its very inconspicuousness renders it safe from attack. It does not attract attention and, consequently, it is not affected by the fight against the class of ideas to which it belongs. It is not disturbed by the storm of enlightenment which sweeps away the other old superstitions. It remains quietly and safely hidden away in the obscure place reserved for it in the popular mind. There it bides its time till at some subsequent period, under more favorable conditions, it may have an opportunity to come out of its obscurity. Then it again makes its public appearance and again figures prominently in the observance of that religious ceremony with which it has always been connected. At any rate, there is always a chance for it to be brought to light again, recognized and identified by the student who will explore the whole domain of that ceremony.

Ceremonies retain not only the original ideas and beliefs which had once been connected with them, but also the various modifications which these ideas assumed in the course of time. And since the ceremonies in the course of time assume new meanings and become associated with new ideas, all of which they tenaciously hold and preserve, they very often present strange combinations of different ideas and exhibit peculiar products of syncretistic tendencies.

The various ideas connected with one ceremony become, so to speak, attached to one another by the mere force of propinquity. The very fact that they are contained in the same vessel or vested in the same symbolic form causes these various ideas somehow to associate and combine with one another, although originally they were entire strangers or even extreme opposites.

In one single ceremony, therefore, one may find various layers of beliefs or superstitions, which have been accumulating in it in the course of time, as well as separate parallel lines of thought or distinctly different ideas and beliefs, running alongside of one another.

These various strata of superstitious beliefs and parallel currents of ideas, represented in one ceremony, frequently commingle and become so entangled with each other as to confuse the observer and even perplex the student.

However, even in these curious combinations of ideas, so frequently represented by a single religious ceremony, the original component elements remain intact.[a] The complete record both of the various beliefs which are embodied in the ceremony and of the peculiar combination of ideas represented by it can be deciphered by the patient and diligent student who pursues a scientific study of the religious ceremony, applying to it the analytic method.

Such a method would be, first to seek to ascertain the original, simple meaning of the ceremony, disregarding such explanations as were apparently superimposed upon it by a later rationalizing tendency. Then, the different thought-elements, ideas and beliefs, contained in the various interpretations given in the course of time to the ceremony, must be searched out and separated from the combinations into which they entered. The results obtained by such an analysis enable the student to recognize the different systems of beliefs or currents of thought represented in the ceremony, to distinguish them from their

[a] Cf. Robert Briffault, *The Mothers*, I (New York, 1927), 80-81, interesting remarks as to the persistence of ideas and superstitions bearing out my theory.

parallel and cross-currents, and to trace each one of them to its respective origin.

It is this prospect of obtaining from the record of the ceremony correct information about the superstitious beliefs expressed in it, and thus arriving at definite conclusions in regard to the origin and the development of the religious ideas connected with it, that makes the scientific study of religious ceremonies of such vital interest and great importance for the history of religions. The ultimate results obtained by such a scientific study of religious ceremonies would amply reward the labor involved in the tedious, yet fascinating, process of analyzing the meaning of each part of the ceremony and examining in detail its various aspects.

A careful and thorough investigation of one particular religious ceremony with all the ideas contained or implied in it may throw light on many other religious ideas and beliefs, embodied in other ceremonies of the same religion. It may also help us to understand similar ceremonies and practices found in other religious systems. Sometimes the history of the development of one ceremony may even give a complete record of the various stages in the development of the religious system to which it belongs.

Such a record of the various phases of Judaism in the different stages of its development is, to my mind, to be found in the history of the Tashlik ceremony, a study of which I shall attempt to present in this essay.

Insignificant as this ceremony may at first sight appear, it is, nevertheless, of great importance, because of its long and interesting history. It offers us a wealth of information about certain Jewish religious ideas and their development. It also shows how Judaism in the various periods of its history either assimilated, or reacted against foreign ideas and heathen superstitions.

To the superficial observer it might seem that this ceremony was introduced for the first time in the middle ages, and that it had its origin in the obscure source of the contemporary popular beliefs possibly borrowed from a non-Jewish environment. Indeed, with but very few exceptions, the modern scholars who have paid any attention at all to this ceremony, have treated it from this point of view.[1] But, as will be shown in the course of this essay, such a point of view is but the result of a very superficial observation.

It is true that in the peculiar manner and in the special form in which this ceremony is now generally observed by orthodox Jews it made its first appearance during the latter part of the middle ages, about the fourteenth century. But in a scientific study of religious ceremonies one must make a distinction between the observance of the ceremony itself and the peculiar form in which it finds expression at a particular time. In the fourteenth century our ceremony may have assumed the special form which in the main is identical with the one in which it is now still observed. But the ceremony itself, i. e., the custom of going out to a place near water for the purpose of worshipping there, or of performing some kind of propitiatory rite, is much older. It is in fact even older than Judaism itself. It is a ceremony taken over by Judaism from older primitive religions. It has accompanied Judaism through the various stages of its development on its long journey from early antiquity down to modern times. It experienced many changes together with other Jewish religious customs and in keeping with the general development of religious thought and Jewish practice. It assumed different forms at different periods of time and in different countries. Its observance was frequently modified and adapted to suit the ideas prevailing among the representative religious authorities. At certain times it was strongly objected to and efforts were made to suppress it altogether, so that it almost disappeared. It became almost unknown or unrecognizable, but in reality it existed in one form or another all the time. Whether observed by all the Jews or only by some of them, whether practiced by the main body of Jewry or merely by one of its groups or sects, whether officially recognized or merely tolerated, whether approved of or objected to, it always remained a Jewish

---

[1] See the writings of Isaac B. Levinsohn (below, note 165); Jacob Reifman (below, note 166); Wolf Wertheim (below, note 167); R. Kirchheim (below, note 169) and Abraham Berliner (below, note 145). Cf. also *Jewish Encyclopedia*, XII, *s. v.* "Tashlik."

custom, observed at least by some Jews in one country or another. The Tashlik ceremony observed near a body of water, particularly a river, may well be compared in the course of its development to a river. It is a very long and mighty stream. It has its main source in far away lands, in hoary antiquity. For a certain distance, or a certain time, it flows on the surface in different directions, spreading in turn over a larger or smaller area and alternately increasing or diminishing in volume, according to special seasons or periods of time. Then its floods gradually wear a deeper channel, it forms its own bed, becomes a river, and continues to flow regularly in its adopted course. Soon, however, it meets with obstructions which put a stop to its course. It is forced out of its bed, flows over the adjoining lands, turns in different directions, and is almost lost. At least it disappears from the surface and is lost to the eye of the observer. But, although not visible to the eye, it continued to flow on subterraneously, and soon it appears again on the surface at some strange spot. It then regathers its waters and resumes its visible current. It cuts for itself a new, deeper and wider bed in which it continues to flow openly and proudly as a mighty river. In the course of these long travels across many lands and through different territories, not only has its stream been diverted and apparently intercepted so that the connection between its parts has become unrecognizable, but its very contents also have changed considerably and have assumed a different aspect. For all along its long course it has washed away from its banks various substances and has picked up many foreign elements in the wild lands which it has traversed. Many little rivulets have joined it on its way, flowed into it, and become its tributaries. All these foreign influxes and influences have given various colors to its waters and have greatly affected the character of its contents.

The result is that the untrained observer does not recognize in the modern large river the old stream which had its origin in the distant lands of far antiquity. He misses the connection between the different parts and does not recognize that, in the main, the contents of the new river are essentially those which flowed in the old stream, though a little differently colored, and slightly changed in character and in substance.

Let us now follow this stream of old on its long journey, trace its main current and see what tributaries have flowed into it, and how they affected its currents and contents.

The main and characteristic feature of the Tashlik ceremony as it is now observed is the recitation of prayers or hymns near a river or any other large body of water. The idea underlying this practice is, no doubt, the belief that prayers recited at such a place will reach God and be heard by Him more readily than those recited at any other place. This means that a spot near water, more than any other place on earth, is a locality especially suitable for prayer, because God or one of His angels is always near it and can easily be found there. In other words, the presence of God, or of some Divine Being, manifests itself especially in or near water.

This idea is very old and was entertained by the ancient Hebrews in the very earliest days of their history. It may be said to go back to the days when the story of creation was first told in Israel. It can be found in Jewish thought and literature of all periods of history though, of course, in different forms and with various modifications.

The idea expressed in the Genesis story of creation, that "the spirit of God moved upon the face of the waters," lingered on consciously or unconsciously in Jewish thought throughout all the ages. It was somehow felt or believed that God had never entirely abandoned the place in which He first moved about. His spirit continued to hover on or about the water. The water, or the place near it, ever since remained His most favored haunt. Here He receives His chosen ones and here He chooses to reveal Himself to His prophets. Near the water He receives the offerings and praises of man, and here man can best approach Him with supplications and petitions and be favorably answered. Such were the ideas, or at least the popular beliefs, which have always been found among the Jews. Jewish literature abounds in references to sacred wells, to solemn proceedings or important events taking place near a river or a well, to temples built upon wells, to houses of prayer erected preferably near water, to special ceremonies performed near the water, to occasional prayers offered at a place near water, all of which point to the popular belief, that God is to be found especially at a place near water.

The Tashlik ceremony of today is but a survival of these ancient popular Jewish beliefs, which were merely modified and changed in the course of time. This thesis I propose to prove by an investigation of the history and the development of those beliefs. My method will be historical, i. e., to collect and examine all indications of such beliefs found in the Bible, and to investigate the references to them found in the Talmud and its contemporary literature of Jewish origin. We shall then trace their gradual development, the many changes and various modifications which they received in post-talmudic times, till they found expression in the form in which the modern Tashlik ceremony is observed.

Indications in the Bible of the belief that God and His angels are to be found preferably near water are many and varied in character.

In the first place, we find references to special wells, probably sacred wells, distinguished because God was believed to be present or to reveal Himself near them, or because of the fact that angels were seen or appeared there. Thus, the well near which the angel of the Lord met Hagar (Gen. 16.7 ff.) and which was called Beer-lahai-roi, that is, "the well of the Living One who seeth me" or, according to Onkelos, "the well where the angel revealed himself"[2] (*ibid.*, v. 14) was such a sacred well. Most likely the well was considered a sacred spot where people would come to seek God and to pray to Him. It was not by accident that the angel found Hagar there. Hagar came thither to pray to God and complain to Him,[3] and there the angel revealed himself to her and answered her. Now a place whither people go to pray is believed by them to be the place where

---

[2] בירא דמלאך קימא איתחזי עלה. According to Jonathan, *ad loc.*, the well was designated as "The well where the Eternal revealed Himself," בירא דאיתחלי עלה חי וקים.

[3] See Gen. r. 60.13, and cf. commentaries of Ramban and Sforno to Gen. 24.62.

God can especially be found, or the place where His presence dwells.

Likewise, the well at Beer Sheba, where both Abraham and Abimelek swore and made a covenant (Gen. 21.31–32) was no doubt such a sacred well, considered as sacred to, or favored by the presence of, a deity. They swore either by the sacredness of the well or by the deity of the well. At this "Well of the Oath" Abraham planted a tamarisk tree or a grove, and there he called on the name of God (*ibid.*, v. 33).

Likewise, the well En Rogel where Adonijah assembled his friends to offer sacrifices (I Kings 1.9) was no doubt such a well. The sacrifices offered there by Adonijah were evidently intended to help secure for him the succession to the throne, either by securing for him the favor of the deity present there, or by having his assembled friends pledge themselves there, in the presence of the deity, to support him in his ambitious plan.

The same must be said of the well Gihon at which Solomon was anointed king (*ibid.*, v. 33). It must have been considered a sacred well or a place especially favored by God with His presence. It was purposely chosen for such an important act, for it was deemed a place most fit for the performance of the ceremony of crowning the king.

These wells, En Rogel and Gihon, had in the popular belief the same character as the place Gilgal where the people proclaimed Saul king in the presence of God (I Sam. 11.15). In other words, they were sanctuaries,[4] for kings are crowned and anointed in sanctuaries, i. e., in places where God dwells or is near, and where His favor can more easily be obtained. That there was a definite purpose in selecting the place at Gihon for the anointing of Solomon cannot be doubted. In fact, it was so understood even as late as talmudic times. An old Baraita preserved in the Talmud (Hor. 12a and Ker. 5b) not only tells us that there was such a definite purpose but also hints that the purpose was to secure for the newly anointed king a long and successful reign. The Baraita reads as follows: תנו רבנן אין מושחים את המלכים אלא על המעיין כדי שתמשך מלכותם שנאמר ויאמר המלך להם

---

[4] See I. Benzinger, *Hebräische Archäologie* (Tübingen, 1907), p. 317.

קחו עמכם את עבדי אדוניכם וגו' והורדתם אותו אל גיחון וגו' ומשח אותו שם.
"The Rabbis taught that they anoint kings at no other place but at a well, in order that their reign may be continuous and prolonged, for thus it is said, 'And the king said unto them, Take with you the servants of your lord and cause Solomon, my son, to ride upon mine own mule and bring him down to Gihon. And let Zadok, the priest and Nathan, the prophet, anoint him there king over Israel.' " The words: כדי שתמשך מלכותן are a later reinterpretation of the ancient practice, aiming to give a rationalistic explanation of the significance of this ancient practice. Thus the act is represented as having had merely a symbolic character, that is, to suggest that the days of the reign of the anointed one may flow smoothly and continue for a long time. But by this rationalistic interpretation the original meaning of the ancient practice is not altogether hidden or obscured. For even this interpretation as much as tells us that the purpose of the practice was to help secure the favor of the deity for the newly anointed, so that his reign be long-lasting and undisturbed. Such favor, in the popular belief of those days, could best be obtained at the residence of the deity, i. e., near a well. We see from this that even in talmudic times, when the tendency prevailed to explain away old popular superstitions or heathen beliefs, the belief that the Divine favor can more easily be obtained at a place near a well or a river still survived, although a somewhat different meaning was read into it by the teachers, who sought to explain it as having had only symbolic significance. We may be assured that in biblical times this belief was understood, by the people at least, in its more primitive and simple meaning, that God can be found near the water, because the water was regarded as His dwelling place. It is in keeping with this ancient belief that we find that among ancient peoples temples were erected near water or built upon wells, a practice which no doubt existed also among the ancient Hebrews. Traces of such an intimate or close connection between the Temple at Jerusalem and a body of water are found in the Bible and in post-biblical Jewish literature. Thus Ezekiel sees in his vision rivers of water coming forth from the Temple (47.1–12) and Joel (4.18) has a vision of a fountain that shall come forth out of the house

of the Lord. Likewise, a rabbinic legend has it that the foundation of the Temple at Jerusalem reached down to the wells or springs of the great deep (Mak. 11a).

These references clearly show that in ancient times the idea of a close connection between the abode of the deity and a body of water was prevalent. Hence a Temple or sanctuary, taken to be the abode of the deity, had to be near or upon a body of water. This does not necessarily mean that the biblical authors still cherished the primitive belief that God dwells upon or in the water. It merely shows that a relic of this belief can still be traced in the ideas found in the Bible, connecting a sanctuary or place of worship with a place near water. Of course, since superstitions do not die so easily, we may assume that in the minds of the people, the popular primitive belief that God actually dwells upon or near water still lingered on, even after they had been taught that God is in the heavens above and in the earth beneath, and that the whole earth is full of His glory.

This belief that the presence of God was to be found near water was probably the basis of the practice of worshipping near water, references to which we find also in those later books of the Bible, which even according to the most orthodox beliefs were written after the Judeans came in contact with the Babylonians, that is, during or after the Babylonian exile.

Thus Daniel and his companions who were at the side of the great river (Dan. 10.4) probably assembled there for devotion or worship. There Daniel also saw a vision; it was there that the angel of God appeared to him and spoke to him. Perhaps, the people who sat by the rivers of Babylon and wept (Psalm 139) meant to cry to God, because the places near the rivers were considered as fit places of worship. Hitzig's[5] remark that they assembled at synagogues situated near the rivers, is not quite correct. But this much seems plausible, that in the absence of any Temples of their own in the strange land, the people assembled for prayer at places which of old had been considered as the abode of God, i. e. near rivers.[6]

[5] *Die Psalmen*, part II (Heidelberg, 1836), p. 203.

[6] In the Midrashim the question is asked, why did they cry at the rivers of Babylon, מה ראו ישראל לבכות על נהרות בבל, Pesiḳta Rabbati 28 (Friedmann,

Ezekiel also received his revelation at the river Kebar (Ezek. 1.1–3). Ezra proclaimed a fast at the river Ahava that the people might afflict themselves there before God and pray to Him Ezra 8.21). The first religious service held by the returned exiles in solemn assembly on the first of Tishri was conducted in a broad place in front of the water gate[7] (Neh. 8.1 ff.) which is identical with the broad place before the house of God (Ezra 10.9). It may, therefore, be stated that in biblical times the idea was prevalent among the Jews that God's presence was found preferably near water. This is further supported by such expressions as: "the voice of the Lord is upon the waters ... the Lord is upon many waters" (Ps. 29.3) and: "His voice was like a noise of many waters" (Ezek. 43.2; cf. also 1.24).

There is one ceremony mentioned in the Bible which seems to me to express the idea that the deity dwells in or near water, and which in many other respects bears striking resemblances to the ceremony which is the theme of this essay. In fact, it is a ceremony like that of Tashlik, both seeking to obtain forgiveness for sin, or to ward off the punishment for a crime. This ceremony we shall discuss here before we proceed to trace the development of the idea in post-biblical times. I refer to the ceremony of killing a young heifer as a sort of expiation for murder, described in Deut. 21.1–9. The real significance of this ceremony was no longer known to the later Jewish teachers; perhaps even the author or redactor of Deuteronomy no longer knew its real meaning, else he would have hesitated to embody or retain it in his book. The ceremony is a relic of an old, crude, primitive, heathen conception of a suitable means of expiation of the sin of blood-shed. The heifer, after its neck was broken, was thrown into a mighty stream as an offering to the deity or the demon

---

135a); Midrash Tehillim 137.3 (Buber, p. 522). And two different explanations are given. According to the one they cried because the water of the Euphrates was injurious to their health, and many of them died as a result of the bad water. According to the other, they cried at the Euphrates because it was at the Euphrates that Jeremiah left them (Midrash Tehillim, *loc. cit.*). Neither one of these explanations is correct. The real reason was that at the rivers, they believed, they could reach God best.

[7] See below, notes 28, 29 and 30.

dwelling there, in order to pacify the avenging wrath of that deity. The elders would wash their hands in that very stream while putting into it the sacrificed heifer. In this manner they believed that they washed away the guilt that might be on their hands in connection with the murder. Or it may be that they washed their hands from the stains of the blood of the heifer which they sacrificed and that this was a symbolic act suggesting by a sort of sympathetic magic that the blood of the murdered person which may have been on their hands was also washed away. This, I believe, was the significance of the ceremony. The נחל איתן into which the heifer was brought down was not a "rough valley" nor even a "valley with running water" but a "mighty stream" or "a river flowing mightily." It was thus understood by Aquila who translates it by Χείμ αρρος στερεός:[8] Maimonides[9] also takes it in the sense of נחל ששוטף בחזקה "a river that flows with might." Of course, if there were no mighty stream in the neighborhood of the town any brook or rivulet would do, as the Mishnah (Soṭah 9.5) and also Sifre Deut. 207 expressly state: אף על פי שאינו איתן כשר. The insistence upon the elders' washing their hands in the water just where they put the sacrificed heifer also suggests the magic significance of washing away the blood from their hands (cf. Sifre Deut. 209, Midrash Tannaim p. 125, and b. Soṭah 46a,b). The apparent contradiction between the act of offering an expiatory sacrifice to the deity or demon of the water and at the same time praying to God for forgiveness need not surprise us. A similar syncretism is found in the ceremony of the Day of Atonement when the goat which was to be sent as an offering to Azazel[10] into the

[8] See D. Hoffmann, *Midrash Tannaim*, (Berlin, 1908), p. 124, note ת.
[9] *Yad*, *Hilkot Roẓeaḥ* 9.2, and Commentary to the Mishnah, Soṭah 9.5; cf. also *Tosefot Yomṭob* on that Mishnah.
[10] That the עגלה ערופה and the שעיר לעזאזל were both sacrifices offered to Satan for the purpose of bribing and pacifying him was recognized by many medieval authorities. Thus R. Menaḥem Recanati in his טעמי המצות (Basle, 1581), p. 18a, says: לערוף את העגלה כדי שתחול מדת הדין עליה ולא בעולם והוא כדוגמת העזאזל. And in his פירוש על התורה (Venice, 1523), section אחרי מות, he explains that the Israelites were permitted to offer a sacrifice to Satan, one of the subordinate officers of the heavenly administration, since it was done only to please God who had commanded them to give something to His servant.

wilderness was first presented alive before the Lord. The High Priest then, while placing his hands upon this offering to Azazel, made confession and asked forgiveness of God (Lev. 16.10; Yoma 6.2).

After the God of Israel had been recognized by the people as the one great and mighty God, the other gods, the gods of the other nations and of the other lands, were not denied all existence altogether. They were regarded as inferior gods. They were degraded to demons and relegated to some obscure domain, some to the wilderness and some to the depths of the sea. The water beneath the earth and the desert had of old been regarded as favorite places selected by the gods for their residence. Even at the time when each god was assigned a special territory and each land was believed to be ruled by its own sovereign deity, the water and desert, not inhabited by man, had been considered a sort of neutral territory where all gods could reside without encroaching upon each other's territorial rights. In the popular mind, accordingly, these places continued to be the favorite abode of the gods. And the deposed gods, now stripped of their sovereign power and deprived of their territorial possessions in the inhabited lands, were believed to have retired, voluntarily or involuntarily, to these old resorts of the gods. We need not expect consistency in the popular beliefs. Although the degraded gods were deposed from their exalted position and banished from the habitations of men, they were nevertheless still feared by

---

Baḥya b. Asher in his commentary on the Pentateuch to Deut. 21.1 (Warsaw, 1878), pp. 55, says: ענין עגלה ערופה בנחל איתן שהוא מקום חורבן כענין צפורי מצורע הצפור החיה... היתה משתלחת על פני השדה לפורחות השדה... וכן השעיר המדברה... וכן בכאן בעגלה ערופה בנחל איתן... הענין לשר הנחל... והוא השר הממונה עליו שהוא כח תקיף וחזק. Cf. also his comment to Lev. 16.7 (pp. 50–51) on the purpose of the goat to Azazel where he gives the same explanation as is given by Recanati as to how it was that they were allowed to offer a sacrifice to Satan. And in his comment on Deut. 21.8 (p. 56), he declares that in both cases, in the case of the עגלה ערופה and in the case of the שעיר לעזאזל we can ask and expect that God will forgive us, only after the accuser has received his portion. Likewise R. Menaḥem b. Meir in his ספר ציוני (Cremona, 1560), p. 100b, says: והסוד כן שעגלה ערופה דומה לשעיר, and on p. 48d he gives the same explanation as given by Recanati and Baḥya, as to how it could have been permitted to offer a sacrifice to Satan. See below, note 70. Cf. also R. Todros Abulafia in his אוצר הכבוד (Warsaw, 1879), p. 58.

men. The people would be afraid to provoke them. Hence, they would occasionally send them gifts, even though worshipping and praying only to the true God. On the Day of Atonement they sent an offering to the demon dwelling in the wilderness and at the occasion of an unascertained murderer, they offered a sacrifice to the demon dwelling in the waters beneath the earth. The ceremony of throwing gifts, bread and wine to the water as sacrifices to the deity dwelling there is not infrequently found among Semites (*see* W. R. Smith, *Religion of the Semites*, 2nd edition, p. 177).

After this long digression which, as will be seen in the course of this essay, was necessary for a proper understanding of our theme, let us again follow the course which the idea that places near water are favorable to the presence of God, took in post-biblical times.

In the talmudic period we find but a few indications of this ancient belief, but these few are sufficient to prove the existence of this belief even in that period. The reason why we do not hear more about this belief during that period is that the teachers of post-biblical times, advanced in their theology, recognized the religious harm inherent in such a belief and sought to suppress it. But these very attempts at suppression clearly point to the prevalence of the belief. It continued throughout the entire talmudic period, though somewhat modified and changed. It found different expressions and assumed different forms in Palestine and outside of Palestine.

Official Judaism in Palestine was opposed to this belief and sought to suppress it. Hence, we find but a few traces of this belief in authentic talmudic literature. But these few remarks of the rabbis of the Talmud enable us to trace the further development of this idea and the different aspects it assumed in Palestine and outside of Palestine. Two teachers of the second century, R. Judah and R. Nehemiah, discuss this idea and their sayings are reported in a midrashic comment on Ex. 12.1 which reads as follows: " 'And God spoke to Moses and to Aaron in the land of Egypt,' this proves that before the land of Israel was especially consecrated, all countries were fit places for the divine revelation, but after the land of Israel had been especially consecrated, the prophets in all places (outside of Palestine) received their revelations only at a place near water, for thus it is said, 'The word of the Lord came unto Ezekiel ... by the river Kebar' (Ezek. 1.3), and it is also said, 'And I saw in a vision and I was by the river Ulai' (Dan. 8.2), 'As I was by the side of the great river which is Hidekel, etc.' (Dan. 10.4–5). Likewise with Jonah God spoke only near or upon the water. R. Judah says, even formerly (i. e., before Palestine was consecrated) God would speak with the prophets only near water. R. Nehemiah says, formerly He would speak with the prophets at any place."[11] R. Judah b. Ilai who usually gives exact reports about historic and archaeological questions has here also preserved to us the actual belief of the people as it had been entertained in ancient times. In his concise remarks he has really given us an exact report of the development of this ancient belief and of how it was changed in the course of time. We learn from his report that according to the belief of the people, God would in former times reveal Himself only at places near water. But in the course of time Palestine was especially chosen by Him and declared a holy land. It was distinguished from all other lands in that it was declared to be like a temple of God. The entire territory of Palestine was holy and God could reveal Himself in any part of it, on land as well as on the waters. The other countries, however, were not so favored by God, and remained in their former condition. They had not been consecrated and they were not fit places for divine manifestations. Consequently, whenever God had to reveal Himself to prophets in any of the countries outside of Palestine, He did it only at a place near water, which, as of old, still remained a suitable place for the divine presence. This was the actual process of the

[11] ויאמר ה' אל משה ואל אהרן בארץ מצרים מלמד שהיו כל הארצות כשרות לדבור עד
שלא נתקדשה ארץ ישראל אבל משנתקדשה ארץ ישראל לא היה דבור על הנביאים בכל מקום
אלא על המים שנאמר (יחזקאל א', ג') היה היה דבר ה' אל יחזקאל בן בוזי הכהן בארץ כשדים
על נהר כבר: ואומר (דניאל ח', ב') ואני הייתי על אובל אולי (דניאל י', ד') ואני הייתי על [יד]
הנהר הגדול הוא חדקל: וכן יונה לא היה מדבר עמו אלא על המים. ר' יהודא אומר אף בתחלה
לא היה מדבר עם הנביאים אלא על המים שנאמר היה היה. ר' נחמיה אומר בתחלה היה דבר
עם הנביאים בכל מקום, *Mechilta deR. Simon b. Joḥai*, ed. Hoffmann (Frankfurt a. M., 1905), p. 5.

development of this ancient popular belief. Two popular beliefs clashed with one another — the older belief that the water was the abode of the deity, and the new belief that Palestine was the land which God has chosen for His habitation and where His presence revealed itself. The outcome of this clash between the conflicting ideas was a compromise. It was believed that Palestine was, as it were, His only land estate and His specially favored residence. But outside of it, He favors with His presence only the places near water, the usual abode of gods.

This process had its effect upon the selection of places for worship. For, as we have seen, the two ideas are inseparable. Where God reveals Himself there He can be found by those who seek Him, and there is the right place to worship Him and pray to Him. This explains the fact that, as we shall show below, the custom of praying at places near water did not prevail in Palestine during the time of the second Temple, but was quite prevalent in the lands of the Diaspora. Palestine was the holy land in which God dwelled and in which He could be found everywhere; hence, any place there was suitable for a place of worship, and the idea of God's nearness to, or residence at, the water was almost suppressed, at least in the circle of the authoritative teachers of Judaism. But outside of Palestine, where the land was considered impure and unholy, the only place fit for worship was a spot near water. It should be noticed, however, that the idea of pure and impure lands, or the distinction between Palestine and other lands on the ground of purity and impurity, represents a higher stage of development in the popular belief as to the abode of the deity.

Originally the real distinction between Palestine and the other countries, according to the popular belief, was that Palestine was the domain of the God of Israel and the other countries were the domains of other gods. God could not reveal Himself in any other country which belonged to another god. Neither could He be worshipped in any other country outside of Palestine. For the people living in any country could worship only the god of the land under whose rule and protection the country stood (cf. I Sam. 26.19 and comment on this verse in b. Ket. 110b). God in the popular belief could have revealed Himself outside of Palestine only in neutral territory, i. e. at a place near water or outside of the inhabited districts, just as the other gods might have come to the rivers and lakes and the deserted places or the wilderness in Palestine. But after the God of Israel had been recognized as the God of the whole world and with the advanced thought that God's presence is everywhere and that He can be found outside of Palestine as well as in Palestine, the distinction between Palestine and other lands could not be maintained in its primitive form, *viz.*, that in Palestine God dwells throughout the entire land and in the other lands he dwells only in the old neutral territory near water. A slight modification was made, therefore, in the idea of the distinction between Palestine and the other land by introducing into it the motive of purity. It was declared that Palestine was pure; hence, in it God would reveal Himself and could be prayed to anywhere. But the other lands were impure, except for the spots near water; hence, man could not receive a revelation from God nor commune with Him in prayer, except in these clean and pure places near water. This modification of the primitive idea is indicated in the passage of the Mekilta deR. Ishmael,[12] where the result of the process mentioned above is briefly stated, in the saying: אף על פי שנדבר עמהם בחוצה לארץ ובזכות אבות לא נדבר עמהם אלא במקום טהרה של מים: "Even though He did speak with the prophets outside of Palestine, and because of the merits of the fathers, He did it only at a pure spot near water." The words במקום טהרה "at a pure spot" are significant. They represent a later stage in the development of the idea that God prefers places near water. It is taken for granted that it was merely the purity and cleanliness of the place which is the necessary condition for God's manifestation there, although God is present everywhere and the whole world is ruled by Him and by no other gods.

In this way, the belief that the revelation of God takes place near water and the old custom of seeking to pray near water which is connected with it were given a seemingly rational interpretation. But this very interpretation made it impossible for

---

[12] *Pisḥa* I, ed. Lauterbach (Philadelphia, 1933), I, p. 6.

the idea to survive in Palestine, especially in the circles of official Judaism. For, if the main condition for the manifestation of God at a given place is merely the purity of the place, then every place in Palestine, the pure and holy land, met this requirement; and consequently, in Palestine every place was fit for worship. Hence, we do not find there synagogues or places of worship erected near water. Of course, we must not assume that the suppression of this old superstition was accomplished in Palestine at one stroke. Even in Palestine the superstition lingered on for a time, for superstitions die very hard. Some of the people retained the old preference for places near water and may have tried to harmonize it with the belief that the entire land of Palestine was holy and pure. The people, in preserving the custom of praying at places near water, may have persuaded themselves to believe that the reason for their preference for such a place was, not that it was purer than any other place in the holy land, but that it was more convenient for the performance of the ritual purifications, for there they could more conveniently take their baths and perform their washing which was considered necessary before prayer and study.[13]

But even with this new interpretation the custom of praying near water could not maintain itself for long in Palestine. For, in the first place, the authoritative teachers of Judaism, the Pharisees, apparently were opposed to the custom of taking ritual baths every morning, and this practice was observed only by a certain sect, the Hemerobaptists, טובלי שחרית (see Tosefta Yad., end); even the requirement of a ritual bath for a בעל קרי was abolished in the course of time. Secondly, the Pharisaic Jews in Palestine would perform their ritual bathing and purifications in artificial water pools, *Mikwaot*.[14] Such *Mikwaot* could be built near a synagogue or within its courtyard in any place, even away from rivers or lakes. Thus the excuse for having synagogue or prayer-houses near the water in order to facilitate the taking of ritual baths by those who needed or required them would not be valid.

[13] Cf. Rosenmüller, quoted by I. Wiesener, *Scholien*, (Prag, 1859), I, 6.
[14] Cf. also W. Brandt, *Die jüdischen Baptismen* (Giessen, 1910), Beiheft XVIII to the *ZAW*.

The result was that in Palestine, especially in the circles of official Orthodox or Pharisaic Judaism, where the idea that God manifests Himself and can be found wherever He is sought but preferably in the pure and holy land of His people Israel was fully understood, the old superstition that God dwells near water and that consequently places near water are most fit for prayer and worship was almost entirely suppressed. To what extent it lingered on in the minds of the common people we cannot ascertain. Neither can we ascertain whether certain sects in Palestine persevered in the practice of having their places of worship near water. The Essenes, to whom the Hemerobaptists belonged, may have had their places of worship near water to facilitate their daily bathings, but we have no definite proof of it and, as stated above, a *Mikwah* would have served their purpose just as well. If the idea of the association of prayer with places near water lingered on in Palestine, it may have been only among such groups or sects as were not strictly following the Pharisaic teachings. Official Pharisaic Judaism in Palestine was opposed to this idea, recognizing its heathenish character and considering it incompatible with their conception of God. According to their teaching, God's presence fills the whole world, and there is no reason to believe that He may be found preferably at places near water.[15] As stated above, we cannot ascertain whether and to what extent the ancient belief that God dwells in or near water continued to be held by the common people in Palestine. But even if we assume that the teachers succeeded in weaning the people from this belief as far as the supreme God in whom they believed was concerned, there is reason to believe that the idea that other deities or spirits have their abode in water or in places near water continued to be prevalent among the people in Palestine.[16] After all, it is very difficult

---

[15] On the God conception of the Pharisees see above, *The Pharisees and their Teachings*, pp. 135 ff.

[16] See T. Canaan, *Studies in Palestinian Customs and Folklore, II, Haunted Springs and Water Demons in Palestine* (Jerusalem, 1922). There is no reason for assuming that the present common beliefs and primitive notions prevalent among the Palestinian peasants are later importations. They are rather native superstitions, survivals of ancient beliefs persisted in by the people

and almost impossible to eradicate from the popular mind ancient, deep-rooted beliefs.

We have seen above that in earlier times it was believed that in the countries outside of Palestine the God of Israel, being so to speak on foreign territory, revealed and manifested Himself only near water. In other words, it was believed that in these countries He actually was dwelling near the water. Now, according to the popular notion, there must have been a reciprocal arrangement between the gods of the different countries. We may, therefore, safely assume that in the popular mind foreign gods were to be accorded the same privileges in Palestine which the Palestinian God enjoyed in foreign lands. Hence, in Palestine foreign gods were also believed to dwell in or near water, the neutral territory, since they could not be thought of as occupying any other place in the holy land which was under the exclusive sovereignty of the God of Israel.

These popular notions persisted even in post-exilic times for, although the people had by that time fully learned the lesson that the God of Israel is the God of the whole world, they still could not altogether deny the existence of foreign gods. The latter, as we have seen, were merely reduced to subordinate powers or degraded to the rank of demons. But they still had some existence in the popular belief; hence a place of residence had to be assigned to them. Accordingly, the natural thing for the popular belief to do was to assign to these demons or degraded gods the old haunts of the gods. In other words, the people believed that these spirits or demons dwelt in the sea or in the rivers where they still had some authority and from where they could still exercise some influence and power. Not only to degraded foreign gods was the water assigned as an abode somewhat in keeping with their former position, but also other subordinate divine beings were believed to dwell in the sea or in some river or lake and have power over its domain. This belief lingered on among the people, and we hear of a "Ruler of the Sea," שר של ים, and that some people were suspected of worship-

---

in spite of all efforts on the part of enlightened teachers to combat and suppress them.

ping him and offering sacrifices to him.[17] Likewise we hear of the practice of offering sacrifices to rivers, which evidently were intended for the deity dwelling in the rivers.[18]

The Mishnah forbids these practices, condemning them as idolatrous. Even when slaughtering an animal not intended as a sacrifice, it was forbidden to let the blood flow into the sea or a river lest it might appear as if it were offered to the deity of the water. These mishnaic regulations prove that the practices of sacrificing to the deity dwelling in the water still lingered on among the people in tannaitic times, else there would have been no need of forbidding them. They also show how strongly the religious authorities were opposed to these superstitious ideas. And, indeed, as already stated, we find no reference to the preference for erecting places of worship near water in Palestine.

It was different, however, in the lands outside of Palestine. Here the influence and the authority of the Pharisaic teachers were not so strong as to successfully combat this ancient superstitious belief. Consequently, the belief persisted that God is to be found preferably at places near water. And we find many references to the custom of praying near water, or of having places of worship erected near water, in countries outside of Palestine. The Jews in the Diaspora may have given different explanations of the custom prevailing among them. They may have accepted from their brethren in Palestine the distinction between Palestine and other countries, that Palestine is a pure country, hence God can be found there in any place; while the other countries are unclean and only their rivers and lakes or places near them are pure spots where God can be found, hence suitable for places of worship. In the course of time, they may have also assumed that the consideration of convenience was underlying their ancient custom. They may have explained their custom of having their places of worship at spots near water on the ground that such spots near water recommend themselves for places of worship because of the convenience which they offer for the ritual washing which might be necessary before

---

[17] דאמרי לשרא דימא קא שחיט, Ḥul. 41b.   [18] *Ibid.*, 40a.

prayer. But whatever explanations or justifications may have been given for this custom there can be no doubt that underlying it, or its real and original reason, was the ancient belief that God dwells in or near water, and that especially in foreign countries under the rule of other deities the God of Palestine could find an abode only in the neutral territory of the waters. The oldest express reference to the custom among the Jews of the Diaspora of praying near water or having their synagogues near water is found in the decree of the people of Halicarnassus (Josephus, *Ant.* XIV.10, 23), granting the Jews permission to celebrate their Sabbaths — and to "have their *proseuchae* (prayer-houses, or prayer-meetings) at the seaside according to the customs of their forefathers."[19] It is evident that "the customs of their forefathers" here mentioned refers to the general custom among the Jews of the Diaspora to have their *proseuchae* near the water, or at the sea-side,[20] and not as L. Löw (*Gesammelte Schriften* IV, 25) assumes, to the peculiar local custom of Halicarnassus where the Jews just happened to have their prayer-house built near the water. This decree is supposed to have been given about the year 120 B. C. E. and "the custom of the forefathers" herein mentioned must have been much older. In other words, in the beginning of the second century B. C. E. this custom was already prevalent.[21]

---

[19] See below, note 171.

[20] See Schürer, *Geschichte* (Leipzig, 1907), II, p. 519; S. Krauss, *Synagogale Altertümer* (Wien, 1922), pp. 281 ff.; and E. L. Sukenik, *Ancient Synagogues in Palestine and Greece* (London, 1934); also in *Tarbiz*, I (Jerusalem, 1929), p. 146, note 2.

[21] Accordingly this custom could not have been the result of the law decreeing a state of uncleanness upon the foreign lands, as assumed by Wiesener (*loc. cit.*), Konstantin Hartte, *Zum Semitischen Wasserkultus* (Halle, 1912), p. 6, and Sukenik, *Ancient Synagogues*. For the law decreeing uncleanness upon the land of the gentiles, טומאה על ארץ העמים, is said to have been decreed by Jose b. Joezer of Zeredah and Jose b. Johanan of Jerusalem (b. Shab. 14b) about 170 B. C. E. and as appears from the discussion in the Talmud (*ibid.*, 16a,b) it was not in full force till another decree was issued about 10 B. C. E. Besides, the uncleanness of the lands of the Gentiles included rivers entirely within the territory of foreign lands. Cf. Tos. 'Oh. 18.5; b. Naz. 55a. Cf. Alon, *Tarbiz*, VIII, 2 (January, 1937), 159, note 71. Alon assumes however that the "uncleanness" dated from pre-Hasmonean times.

This custom of having the synagogues near water is also reflected in the report given in the Letter of Aristeas,[22] about the arrangement and preparation made by the Egyptian king for the translators of the Pentateuch. There we are told that the king assembled the wise men "in a house which had been built upon the sea-shore" (301). This was not accidental. This house near the shore was built for, or assigned to, the Jewish translators in order that they may have the opportunity of performing their devotions in accordance with the Jewish custom of praying near water. This is, perhaps, further indicated in the following passage: "And, as is the custom of all the Jews, they washed their hands in the sea and prayed to God and then devoted themselves to reading and translating" (305). Now there is no "custom of all the Jews" requiring "washing the hands in the sea" before prayer. And had they been accustomed to pray at another place away from the sea, it would have been quite sufficient for them to wash their hands merely with water drawn in a vessel. But the author, an Alexandrian Jew, merely describes the custom prevalent among the Jews in the Diaspora to pray near the water, and hence, he declares that they washed their hands right there in the water, near which they prayed; in this case, it was the sea. For it is to be noticed that it is not said that they washed their hands and entered the house to pray; therefore, we must assume that they prayed outside, right at the sea-shore. It is quite likely that the author here reflects the later interpretation of the custom of praying near the water, *viz.*, that it is observed merely because of the facility such places offer for the ritual washing. It may also be that the place was selected for the translators not only for the purpose of offering them the opportunity of praying near water but also because such a place was regarded as most fit for receiving the divine inspiration necessary for their work. For places near water were not only regarded suitable for worship, but were also considered as very favorable to the study of the Law.[23]

In a papyrus from Egypt of the end of the second century

---

[22] See Charles, *Apocrypha and Pseudepigrapha* (Oxford, 1913), II, 120.
[23] Cf. b. Hor. 12a.

B. C. E., there is also mentioned a Jewish prayer house, προσευχή
'Ιουδαίων, which was situated near the water.[24]

A plain and unmistakable evidence of the custom of the Jews in Egypt to pray at a place near water is given by Philo (in *Flaccum* XIV). There we read as follows: "And when they had spent the whole night in reciting hymns and songs, they poured out through the gates at the earliest dawn, and hastened to the nearest point at the shore, for they had been deprived of their usual places of prayer, and standing in a clear and open space they cried out: 'O most mighty King of all mortal and immortal beings, we have come to offer thanks unto Thee to invoke earth and sea and the air and the heaven and all the parts of the Universe and the whole world in which alone we dwell, etc.' "[25] There are a few interesting points in this report which we must discuss in detail in order that we may understand it correctly and see clearly its connection with the medieval Tashlik ceremony.

In the first place, we have to examine this report and see whether Philo gives any special reason for their having gone out to the shore to pray. At first sight it might appear that in the statement: "For they had been deprived of their usual places of prayer" Philo means to explain why they had to go to the shore, namely, that the reason for doing so was because their synagogues had been taken away from them.[26] This, of course, would speak against the supposition that it was an established ancient custom to pray near water. It would rather prove that this practice was an unusual one, prompted by necessity, since they had no other place where they could assemble for prayer. Such an interpretation of Philo's statement, however, is not correct. For, in the first place, Philo had not definitely stated that the Jews had been deprived of their property, whether private houses or public houses of worship. And while he states that many Jewish homes have been destroyed, he does not say that any synagogue was destroyed. On the contrary,

---

[24] See Schürer, *op. cit.*, pp. 500 and 519, note 63.
[25] I quote according to C. D. Yonge, *Philo Judaeus* (London, 1855), IV.
[26] So it was understood by Wiesener, *loc. cit.*, and A. Jeremias, *Babylonisches im Neuen Testament* (Leipzig, 1905), p. 113.

we are told that the non-Jewish mob had rushed into the synagogues and put there images or statues of the Emperor. So the synagogues were not destroyed, nor taken away from the Jews. Furthermore, it is evident from Philo's statement that the Jews still owned their houses of prayer or assembly places and they still could assemble and worship in them. For we are told that they went to the shore early in the morning "after having spent the whole night in hymns and songs." Evidently then they had assembled in some place during the night where they recited hymns and songs. They just as well could have stayed in the same place to recite the prayers in the morning, had there been no special reason for going to the sea-shore to say the prayers there. It seems, therefore, that Philo does not mean to give an explanation as to why they went to the shore for the purpose of reciting their prayers. This was an old established custom and required no further explanation.

It seems to me that Philo does not mean to imply that their synagogues or houses of worship had been taken away from the Jews. What he means to say is that they had been deprived of certain privileges which they had previously enjoyed. The Jews, enjoying the rights and privileges of citizens, must have had special places near the shore assigned to them by the city magistrates, where they were permitted to assemble at special occasions when, following their ancient custom, they would recite their prayers near the water. The privilege of having such public places near the water assigned to them for their prayer meetings, it seems, had recently been taken away from the Jews together with other rights and privileges of which Flaccus had deprived them. To this withdrawal of the old privilege Philo refers in the words, "They had been deprived of their usual places of prayer." By this statement he merely seeks to give a reason, not for their going out to the shore to pray, but why they hastened to "the nearest point at the shore" and not to their usual places there. These "usual places of prayer" near the shore, or the privilege of using them, having been taken from them, they were compelled to hasten to the nearest point at the shore before their enemies would gather to disturb them in their devotions, and at first clear and open space to which they came, they recited their prayers. It should be noticed that Philo uses the term προσευχή. *Proseuche*, however, does not necessarily mean a prayer-house, but can also mean any place of prayer, even an open place[27] at the shore. In this sense, the word *proseuche* in the decree of Halicarnassus is to be understood. Conditions in Halicarnassus must have been similar to those which prevailed in Alexandria up to the time of Flaccus and we can thus understand the real significance of the decree of the people of Halicarnassus. It really meant that the Jews should have the privilege, which their forefathers had enjoyed, of assembling near the shore for prayer, and that they should not be disturbed in doing so. If this decree had merely meant to give the Jews the right to buy land, near the shore, on which to build synagogues, it would not have conferred such a great privilege as to merit special mention. Why should we assume that there were any restrictions as to the locations where the Jews might own or acquire property? If, however, the reference is to the privilege of using a certain public place near the shore for their undisturbed prayer meeting (*proseuche*), we can well understand why its being granted in a special decree should deserve special mention.

To come back to Philo. We thus learn from his report that in his days the Jews would at special occasions go to the shore to recite their prayers. Of course, they had synagogues and assembly houses near or far from the shore; but they also had the special privilege, granted to them by the city authorities, of using a special square or clear and open space near the shore for assembly and prayer at certain occasions. This privilege had now been taken away from them. Hence, when one of the occasions at which they were accustomed to pray near the shore came, they hastened to the nearest clear and open space at the shore, and there recited their prayers.

We now must seek to ascertain at which occasion or at what time or season of the year it was especially customary to assemble for prayer near the water. In general, it can be assumed that this was done whenever they had to pray or thank for special

[27] Cf. Schürer, *op. cit.*, p. 522, notes 72–73.

favors. But in this particular case there is an express mention in the report of Philo as to the time when this took place. This offers other suggestions as to the occasion for such prayers near the water. Philo mentions that this happened during the autumnal Festival. This immediately suggests that this custom is identical with one of the ceremonies observed during the Sukkoth festival in the Temple at Jerusalem in connection with the festivities of the שמחת בית השואבה. At the latter they would also spend all night in songs and hymns and in the early morning they would go down to the well of Shiloaḥ and draw the water for the water-libation (Suk. 4.9 and 5.4). It may, therefore, be that this ceremony among the Egyptian Jews corresponds to the ceremony observed by the Jews of Jerusalem. But in the diaspora this ceremony had been preserved in its more primitive form, and they would go out to the water to pray there. In Jerusalem, on the other hand, where, as we have seen, all such superstitions that God is found near water had been suppressed, the ceremony was somewhat modified. It was made but one feature of a whole cycle of ceremonies. It was explained that they went out to the well, not in order to pray near the water, but merely for the purpose of drawing water for the libation upon the altar in the Temple. This explanation of the purpose of the ceremony, however, is, to say the least, very doubtful. For one may rightly question whether such a solemn ceremony of marching out to the Shiloaḥ had no other purpose than to secure the water necessary for the libation. They certainly could have had the water brought in on the previous day by a few attendants, not by all the people marching out to draw it from the well, or they could have obtained it not direct from the well but from the large basin, כיור, in the Temple itself, as they actually did when securing the water for the libation on the Sabbath day (Suk. 4.10). Furthermore, it should be noticed that one feature of the ceremony as described in the Mishnah was that when they reached the water-gate after having drawn the water from the well they would blow the horn and shout. This water-gate, שער המים, was not one of the Temple gates which was given this name just because through it the water for the libation on Sukkoth was brought in. R. Eliezer b. Jacob correctly explains the name שער המים as the place where waters bubble and come up;[28] in other words, the gate near the well. The שער המים or "water-gate" mentioned here is accordingly the same place before which the people in the time of Ezra assembled on the seventh month and held their religious services (Neh. 8.1). This stopping at the "water-gate," i. e., at the gate near the water, where the first religious service was held in the time of Ezra, was probably due to the old custom of assembling there for prayer,[29] which persisted from the time of the returned exiles. This feature shows that there still lingered on in the ceremonies observed in Jerusalem at the festivities of the שמחת בית השואבה an echo of the ancient practice to assemble for prayer at a place near water.[30]

But whatever the real significance of the ceremony in Jerusalem may have been, in Alexandria, at any rate, it was the custom, according to Philo, to go out to pray near the water during the autumnal festival. Let us now consider some of the popular beliefs connected with the autumnal festival or with any special day thereof. We may then be able to fix the exact day of the festival on which this ceremony took place, and to show its connection with the later Tashlik ceremony. Now, we find that to a certain degree Sukkoth in the popular mind has the character of a day of Judgment, just like New Year's day.[31]

---

[28] See Tosefta Suk. 3.3.

[29] The saying, למה נקרא שמה בית השואבה ששמש שואבין רוח הקודש (p. Suk. 5.1, 55a) may perhaps echo the old belief that at this place, near the well, God reveals Himself.

[30] L. Venetianer, "Die eleusinischen Mysterien im jerusalemischen Tempel" (in Adolf Brüll's Populärwissenschaftliche Monatsblätter, XVII, pp. 121–125 and 169–181), maintains that the ceremonies connected with the water libation were an imitation of the eleusinian mysteries in which the going out to the sea or well formed a prominent feature. It is, however, very unlikely that a foreign heathen cult could have been introduced into the Temple service at Jerusalem, if there had not been a similar native custom among the Jews. The going out to the water gate or the Shiloah well to pray or to receive inspiration was an old established ceremony in Jerusalem (cf. Paul Volz, Das Neujahrsfest Jahwes [Tübingen, 1912], p. 56, note 57). This old native ceremony may have facilitated the introduction of the foreign ceremony which in some features resembled the native one.

[31] See Midrash Tehilim, 118.2 (Buber, p. 241), and cf. also Volz, op. cit., p. 19.

Like New Year's day it is one of the four times in the year in which the world is judged. On this Festival it is especially decided whether the world should get enough rain (R. H. 1.3). This, of course, may have suggested the idea of going *near* water to pray *for* water. However, we find that Sukkoth was considered not only as the time in which the people were judged in regard to the water or the supply of rain, but it was regarded also as a time of judgment in general, a time when the judgment begun on Rosh Hashanah was brought to a close (cf. Pesikta deR. K., Buber 180a,b).

But especially has this character of a Judgment Day been given to the last day of the Sukkoth festival, i. e., Hoshana Rabbah. This last day of the Sukkoth festival is put on a level with Rosh Hashanah. They are described as the two outstanding days of the year in which the people make a special effort to seek God.[32] This, no doubt, means that on these two days when the people are judged for the whole year, they seek God in order to obtain from Him a favorable verdict. And in the Midrash Tehillim 17 (Buber 128–129) it is expressly stated that the final decision of the heavenly court is reached and given out on Hoshana Rabbah. In New Testament times this day was considered a very important day. For "the last day, the great day of the feast" (John 7.37) designates Hoshana Rabbah, which is the last day of the Sukkoth festival and not Shemini Azeret which is an independent festival[33] by itself merely following closely upon the Sukkoth festival. In post-talmudic literature this idea is commonly accepted and Hoshana Rabbah is declared to be a day of Judgment, יום דינא or יום חתימת הדין, the day of the final judgment or the day on which the court decision is signed, sealed and issued.[34]

[32] See p. R. H. 4.8 (59c). There was a custom among some people to fast on Hoshana Rabbah, though Simon Duran forbids the practice (*Tashbez* III, 160), see H. Zimmels "Nachtalmudische Fasttage," in *Jewish Studies in Memory of G. A. Kohut*, p. 610, notes 90 and 91. Cf. also *Siddur Ozar Hatefiloth*, p. 1163 — *Arugat ha-Bosem*. Another interesting feature of Hoshana Rabbah is the custom of some pious people to have Kapparot. See Agnon, *Yamim Nora'im*, p. 212.

[33] שמיני רגל בפני עצמו, Tosefta Suk. 4.17 and b. Suk. 48a.

[34] תשב"ץ, 554 (Warsaw, 1875), p. 93; *Shibbole ha-Leket*, 371 (Buber, p. 334);

It is also stated that on the night preceding Hoshana Rabbah the judgment is sealed and it is for this reason that the day is considered the end of the year.[35] The ritual and service for this great day are in many features as solemn as those for New Year's and Atonement Day. It is also the custom to spend the whole night preceding Hoshana Rabbah in religious devotions,[36] as a sort of last effort to obtain favorable judgment. While this custom is mentioned at a comparatively late date, there is no doubt that it originated at a very early time. I am, therefore, inclined to assume that the custom described in Philo also took place at the close of the autumnal festival, i. e., on Hoshana Rabbah. The people already in the days of Philo considered this day as the day of final judgment; hence, they were up all night, spending it in religious devotions;[37] then in the early morning they went out to the water to assemble there in prayer and make the final appeal to God. In other words, the final and most strenuous effort at obtaining forgiveness was made by approaching God in His very residence, i. e., near the water. This act thus resembles that of the High Priest in the Temple at Jerusalem on the Day of Atonement, when in order to obtain forgiveness he entered the Holy of Holies where God was believed to reside.[38]

Let us now consider the third important point in Philo's

Tanya Rabbati, 87 (Warsaw, 1879), p. 192. See also המנהיג (Berlin, 1855), p. 69 and Zohar צו (Lublin, 1872), pp. 62–63, but cf. also Zohar ויחי, p. 220, where the eighth day of the Festival שמיני עצרת and not Hoshana Rabbah is declared to be the day on which the decree is sealed and issued.

[35] בליל הושענא רבה חותמין ולכך נקרא בצאת השנה, *Sefer Ḥasidim*, ed. Wistinetzki, 1544 (Frankfurt a/M., 1924), p. 379.

[36] *Shibbole ha-Leḳeṭ*, loc. cit.

[37] Another instance of a practice reported by Philo reappearing among medieval mystics is the custom of being awake all through the night preceding the Shabuot festival (see מנן אברהם to *Sh. 'Ar., Oraḥ Ḥayyim*, 494, i). This custom is reported by Philo ("On a Contemplative Life," in C. D. Yonge, *Philo Judaeus* [London, 1855], IV, 19) as having been the practice of the Therapeutes, and the Zohar, *Emor* (p. 195), describes it as the practice of the ancient Ḥasidim חסידי קדמאי, or Essenes. Cf. I. Heinemann, "Die Sektenfrömmigkeit der Therapeuten" in *MGWJ*, LXXVIII (1934), p. 106.

[38] See *A Significant Controversy between the Sadducees and the Pharisees*, above pp. 61 ff.

statement, the prayer itself. In the prayer, the people say: "We have come to invoke the earth and sea, etc." This might indicate that the purpose of coming to the sea-shore was to invoke the sea, or the "sea-lord." Yet it would be a mistake to assume that the people at that time still worshippped the sea or the deity dwelling in the sea. For, actually, they address God as "the most mighty King of mortal and immortal beings." But they seem to have invoked the sea and asked it to intervene in their behalf with the most mighty King. We have seen above in the case of the ceremony of breaking the neck of the heifer that the people were also syncretistic in their strange practice of praying to God and at the same time offering a sacrifice to the demon or deity of the brook. At the time of Philo the people were more advanced and must have felt the irreconcilable elements in such a syncretism; hence, they modified it a little. They merely asked the sea or its deity to intervene for them with God whom alone they worshipped. In other words, the deity of the sea, formerly worshipped, is now regarded as a subordinate deity that can only be employed as a mediator but cannot be considered as an independent deity besides God. This is a familiar process. After the people came to recognize the God of Israel as the only God they declared the other former gods either mere demons or subordinate heavenly princes who, under the sovereignty of God, are the patrons of those people by whom they were formerly worshipped.

In the same manner the former deity dwelling in the sea is now merely a subordinate, immortal being whose mediatorship can be sought. But lest it appear as though they still consider the sea or the "sea-lord" as a god, they expressly acknowledge God as the most high King even of the immortal beings. Such a declaration was deemed necessary at any occasion when, to judge by appearance, it might seem as if other beings were given divine homage. The idea of asking the sea to pray to God in one's behalf is also found in talmudic-midrashic literature. Thus Moses went to the great sea asking it to pray for him to God ((Tanḥuma, *Vaethannan*, Buber, p. 12). Of course, this is merely an echo of the time when the sea was an independent deity, or the habitat of an independent deity. That this is so is further indicated by the saying of the Midrash, there, that after being unsuccessful with the sea, Moses goes to the heavenly Prince of the Interior, or שר הפנים and solicits his mediatorship. Thus the sea and the angel of the Interior are both immortal beings, or degraded deities. Likewise, in Philo's prayer the sea is apparently regarded as one of the immortal beings, i. e., degraded gods subordinate to the One God. Now, it is also possible that Philo gives his own rationalistic interpretation of the attitude of the people, *viz.*, that they merely came to invoke the sea and solicit its mediatorship. The real attitude of the people, or at least of many of them, may have been the original and primitive attitude of people believing that the deity dwelt in the water; they actually worshipped and prayed to the God whose dwelling they believed to be there. At any rate, we have here a report of an ancient custom among Jews to go to a place near the water and pray there to God, and an echo of the ancient belief that the water is the habitation of the deity.

This custom is also attested to by the report in Acts 16.13, where reference is made to a place outside of the city by a riverside "where prayer was wont to be made" or where there was supposed to be a place of prayer, a *proseuche*. It does not state that there was a building of a synagogue, or a house of prayer. It may have been merely an open place where prayer was customarily offered. It may be that prayer was customarily offered there only at special occasions. It is also significant that, as stated there, the women used to come together to that place. It would thus seem that it was not the regular prayer-house.[39] Only the women who are superstitious and more apt to preserve ancient beliefs would come thither for prayer, even on ordinary Sabbaths. More clearly is this custom of the Jews in the Diaspora described by Tertullian, who gives us also a few details which will help us to trace the development of this early custom into the later Tashlik ceremony.

Tertullian (*ad Nationes*, XIII) mentions the *orationes litorales* or "the prayers at the sea-shore" as a Jewish institution. It is evident that Tertullian does not refer here to the general

[39] Cf. August Neander, *Geschichte der Pflanzung und Leitung der christlichen Kirche durch die Apostel* (Hamburg, 1832), I, 218, note 2.

custom of the Jews to have their synagogues preferably near water, nor say that their prayers were usually held at a place near water, for then he could hardily describe them as an institution and call them by a special name. "The prayers at the sea shore" or *orationes litorales* are evidently special prayers of a distinct character different from the usual prayers. Tertullian refers to an established custom among the Jews to go out to the sea-shore on special occasions and there recite special prayers. These special prayers recited at such occasions he designated by a special name *orationes litorales*. On what day or at what occasion this custom was observed, Tertullian tells us in another work. In his treatise *On Fasting (de Jejunis*, XVI) Tertullian makes the following statement: "A Jewish fast, at all events is universally celebrated; while neglecting the temples, throughout all the shore in every open place, they continue long to send prayer up to heaven."[40] Before proceeding to explain the full significance of this statement for the development of the Tashlik ceremony, we must first refute the interpretation given to this statement by L. Löw (*Gesammelte Schriften*, IV, 25). Löw absolutely refuses to admit the existence of an ancient custom among the Jews to pray near the water. He, therefore, interprets this report of Tertullian as referring to the ceremony of the special religious service held on a fast day proclaimed for the purpose of praying for rain, as mentioned in Ta'an. 2.1. On such fast days, the Mishnah tells us, it was the custom to take out the Ark from the synagogue into the public square of the city and there hold special religious services. The square of some cities in Palestine, so Löw tells us, was situated near the water. Tertullian, so Löw argues, made the mistake of considering this practice as a custom of praying near the water when actually they merely

---

[40] The passage in the original reads: "Judaicum certe (perhaps it should be "certum"?) jejunum ubique celebratur, cum omissis templis per omne litus quocumque in aperto aliquando jam precem ad coelum mittunt" which can be translated: "There is indeed a (or if we read "certum" instead of "certe" a certain) Jewish fast which is universally observed, when, neglecting the temples, they send a prayer to heaven at every open space along the whole shore." Cf. Neander, *op. cit.*, p. 241, and A. Jeremias, *Babylonisches im Neuen Testament* (Leipzig, 1905), p. 113.

prayed in the open square which by local coincidence happened to be facing the water. This may be very ingenious but is hardly plausible. It is very unlikely that Tertullian could have made the blunder of calling such mere open air service by a special name *orationes litorales*. Granting the supposition of Löw, that there was some connection between the prayers near the water reported by Tertullian and the prayers in the public square due to the proximity of the square in some cities to the water, it seems more reasonable to assume that there was a development in a direction opposite to that which Löw assumes, namely, that the custom of praying on such fast days in the open square was but a relic of the custom to pray at a place near water, and not that the latter is merely a mistaken substitution for the former. One can hardly accept Löw's reason for the custom to pray for rain in the open square, *viz.*, that it was due merely to the fact that the synagogues could not accommodate the large crowds assembled at such occasions. There certainly must have been another reason for transferring the Ark and with it the place of prayer from the synagogue to the public square. It is more likely that the original custom was to pray for rain at an open place near water. This was considered a fit place for such a religious service. For, as we have seen above, part of the ceremony on Sukkot when they prayed yearly for rain consisted of going down to the well of Shiloaḥ and assembling at the שער המים. In Palestine, as we have seen, the custom of praying near the water was discouraged and the idea underlying such a custom, *viz.*, that God is to be found near water more than elsewhere, was suppressed. Hence, they emphasized the fact that this service was to be held in the open air, under the sky, from which rain was expected. In cities where the square faced the water such a displacement of ideas in the mind of the people could easily take place, for it was both near the water and in an open space. The people thus got used to consider the essential feature in the ceremony to be the prayer in the open square. Accordingly, even in cities where the square did not face the water front, they also assembled for prayer on the public square. The Mishnah in describing the ceremony merely states that the service was held in the public square, omitting to specify whether the square was near the water, or whether the service was originally held near the water.

To come back to Tertullian. He certainly could not have had in mind a communal fast day declared for the purpose of praying for rain. For he speaks of a fast day that is universally celebrated. This can only mean the Day of Atonement which is both a fast day and a festival. Löw points to the mistake of the church historians in that they understood Tertullian's remark as referring to festivals,[41] when he expressly speaks only of a fast day. But the church historians may have understood Tertullian correctly, since the Day of Atonement is also a festival. Furthermore, the church historians may have known of such a custom among the Jews on the festivals from other sources;[42] hence, they understood Tertullian to have in mind the general custom observed by the Jews on all festivals, although explicitly he speaks only of the one festival which is also the great universally celebrated fast day. Accordingly, we have here an early reference to a custom among the Jews to leave their synagogues on Yom Kippur and go to places along the shore there to send their prayers to heaven. The same custom, as we have seen in Philo, was also observed by the Jews in Alexandria during or at the close of the Sukkot festival, i. e., on Hoshana Rabbah. We thus notice that this ceremony was observed on a day on which, according to the belief of the people, so much depended. On such a day in which they were judged or on which the final decree about their life and welfare was issued, the people would naturally take particular pains to make their prayers heard. The ancient belief in the special efficacy of prayer recited at places near water and the notion that God can best be found in such places, could not be entirely ignored. For in moments of crisis or of especial anxiety people are more likely to fall back upon older beliefs or superstitions which they may have

[41] Löw does not give any reference to the church-historians and I cannot ascertain whom he had in mind. But Neander, *loc. cit.*; Wiesener, *loc. cit.*; Hartte, *loc. cit.*, and Jeremias, *loc. cit.*, all understood Tertullian as referring to a custom observed by the Jews on the Festivals.

[42] As will be shown in the course of this essay, traces of the observance of a Tashlik ceremony on the festivals are found in Jewish sources.

outgrown and which in normal times they discard. What other ideas may have been connected with this custom of going out to the water on Yom Kippur we may learn perhaps from certain allusions in later mystic literature to be discussed in the course of this essay.

Thus we see that this ancient custom was observed especially on the day of the final judgment, the day on which the people believed that their fate was being sealed. This day, however, was not the same for all classes of people. For, according to Jewish belief, the heavenly court passing yearly judgment upon the people which begins on Rosh Hashanah and concludes on Hoshana Rabbah, holds three important sessions at three distinct periods. The perfectly righteous people, the צדיקים גמורים, are given a favorable verdict on the very first day when court opens, i. e., on New Year's day. On the same day also the thoroughly wicked, the רשעים גמורים, are given an unfavorable verdict. The middle class, the בינונים, however, are not immediately judged definitely. They are given a chance of improving their status up to the Day of Atonement (b. R. H. 16b). And finally, there is, as it were, a last day of appeal for all, Hoshana Rabbah, when all decrees are signed, sealed and issued. We can thus understand how the date for this ceremony, constituting the final effort at obtaining forgiveness, shifted from Hoshana Rabbah to Yom Kippur and lastly to Rosh Hashanah. It was first observed on Hoshana Rabbah, which is the last day of judgment for all classes. Then some people observed it on Yom Kippur, when for the average people, the בינונים, judgment is sealed, and finally it was shifted to New Year's day when the judgment is sealed for the righteous. Now it is a common phenomenon that in religious practice the people like to imitate the very pious ones, especially when in doing so they may be benefited thereby or get some prestige. Hence, in our case, every Jew hoped and wished to be considered as belonging to the best class, the perfectly righteous, צדיקים גמורים upon whom a favorable judgment is passed on the very first day of the court, on New Year's day. Accordingly, he would perform this ancient ceremony on the first day of the New Year's festival, and this, in the course of time, became the general practice.

Before we proceed to trace the course of the later development of this ancient practice, it might be advisable first to sum up the results so far reached in our inquiry. We have found that there was an ancient custom among the Jews to pray near the water, and that this custom had its origin in the primitive belief that water is the dwelling place of the deity. Such a primitive belief about the Deity was in the course of time found incompatible with the more advanced teaching of Judaism that God's presence is to be found everywhere, and was accordingly discarded, insofar as the God of Israel was concerned. But it was not incompatible with the current Jewish conceptions of the false or degraded gods or spirits. Hence the belief that these degraded gods or spirits dwelt in the water continued among the people. The official teachers of Judaism, therefore, discouraged the practice of praying near water even to God, lest it might appear as if the worshippers pray to one of the spirits or false deities dwelling in the water. In Palestine where Pharisaic Judaism succeeded in spreading its religious teachings among the people, the custom of praying near water disappeared almost entirely. Hence, no express reference to it is found in the authoritative Jewish literature of Palestine.

Outside of Palestine the practice of praying at places near water, at least on certain special occasions, continued. But even in the Diaspora this practice did not retain its primitive significance. It was reinterpreted and a somewhat different meaning was given to it in order to remove from it its primitive heathenish character. It was explained as serving the purpose of invoking the mediatorship of the "Lord of the Sea" or the spirit of the water, but not as praying to them or worshipping them as gods. With the spread of Pharisaic teachings and their general acceptance by the large masses of the Jews even in the Diaspora, this ancient practice, incompatible with the pure belief in one omnipresent God, was opposed by the religious authorities everywhere; consequently, it disappeared from official Jewish circles, even in the Diaspora. It may have been preserved among certain Jewish sects or mystic groups in Palestine and outside of it, but since these sects gradually drifted away from Judaism and became entirely separated from the main body of the Jewish people, official Judaism and its authoritative literature entirely ignored this superstitious practice and made no express mention of it.

But although the practice was not countenanced by the religious authorities, some ignorant and superstitious Jews may have persisted in observing it privately or occasionally. For, usually the common people do cling to their favorite practices, even though the enlightened official teachers condemn them. At any rate, the ideas and superstitious beliefs underlying this practice did not completely die out. They continued among the people, or at least among certain Jewish groups. In a modified form they were even tolerated by some of the teachers. Indeed, we find that while the talmudic literature ignored this superstitious belief and the practice resulting from it, it does contain quite a few sayings which show not only that the people maintained these beliefs — to be sure in a somewhat modified and less objectionable form — but also that some of the teachers. Indeed, we find that while the talmudic literature ignored this superstitious belief and the practice resulting from it, it does contain quite a few sayings which show not only that the people maintained these beliefs — to be sure in a somewhat modified and less objectionable form — but also that some of the teachers did not even object to these milder forms. Aside from the sayings in the Talmud referred to above, which aim at combatting these superstitions and thus indirectly prove that they were still entertained by some of the people, there are a few positive indications of the existence of these superstitions found in the talmudic-midrashic literature. Thus it is reported in the Talmud (b. Hor. 12a) that Meshershaya, a prominent Babylonian Amora of the fifth generation, advised his sons to study at a place near water. He said to them: "When you study, study at a place near a stream of water, so that your studies may run smoothly and continue, just as the water runs continually" כי גרסיתו גריסו על נהרא דמיא דכי היכי דמשכן מיא משכן שמעתתייכו. Of course, the reason "so that your studies may continue as the water runs continually" was merely the explanation given by R. Meshershaya of this practice. The real reason, no doubt, was that there still lingered on in the minds of the people the idea that near water one can receive inspiration because it is a place where God can be found.

Another reference to the persistence, among the people of talmudic times, of the belief that spirits dwell in the water is the following story related in Midrash Lev. r. 24.3: Abba Jose of Zitor was studying near a well and there appeared to him the spirit that dwelled there and said to him: "You know that for so many years I have been dwelling here (in this well) and you, people of the town, and your wives, you frequently came out here by day and night and were never hurt. And now, know ye that a certain evil spirit wishes to take up his residence here and he is of the kind that harms and hurts human beings." Then Abba Jose said to the spirit: "What shall we do?" And the spirit said to him: "Go warn the townspeople and tell them, that every one of them who has a hammer, a shovel, or a spade should come out here tomorrow morning at the dawn of day and they should watch the surface of the water. At the moment when they will notice a disturbance in the water they should beat with their iron instruments and cry aloud: 'Our spirit will be victorious!' and they should not leave the place until they see a drop of blood upon the water." The story continues to relate that Abba Jose did what the spirit told him; the townspeople came out with their iron weapons, and with their help the friendly spirit did defeat the evil spirit who tried to dispossess him from the well. The story is also found in Midrash Teh. 20 (Buber 88) where we are told that this Abba Jose was a very pious man or a חסיד. What we learn from this story is first that some pious people, mystically inclined, would still observe the practice of studying near the water. Secondly, it confirms our idea suggested above, that the purpose of studying near the water was in order to receive inspiration or to commune with the spirit that dwells there, as, in this case, the pious man actually did converse with the spirit. At any rate, we learn that the people still believed that the water is the dwelling place of spirits, so that when the evil spirit was looking for a place in which to dwell he was about to turn out another, good, spirit from his residence. This legend of the well, where a good spirit dwelt,[43] reminds us of the well where the angel of God appeared to Hagar; both reflect the old belief that God dwells in the water. Of course, in the time of the Midrash, people could no longer believe that God Himself dwelt in the water, but they could still believe that inferior gods or spirits dwelt there. That they would occasionally try to obtain favors from and in turn do some service to these spirits dwelling in the water is but natural; for if, as is told in this story, they feared that the unfriendly spirit might harm them, they certainly must have believed that a friendly spirit would do them some good. Hence they helped him in his fight against the evil spirit. The people would sometimes seek to offer some gifts to the spirit dwelling in the river or lake near their town. If they considered him a friendly spirit, it was an expression of thanks for his favors. If it was an unfriendly spirit, the gifts were intended to pacify him. The practice of throwing something into a lake or river is condemned by the Rabbis as דרכי האמורי, a heathenish custom.[44] But in spite of its being forbidden by the teachers, the people continued it and believed that such practice might bring them good results.[45] This belief of the people is reflected in the following story related in the Midrash Koh. r. 11.1: A certain man used to observe the following practice: every day he would take a loaf of bread and throw it into the great sea. One day he bought a fish and when he opened it he found in it a treasure. The

[43] Cf. the legend about the pool of Bethesda in Jerusalem, that "an angel went down at a certain season into the pool and troubled the water" (John 5.4).

[44] הסמונה ומשליך צרורות לים או לנהר הרי זה מדרכי האמורי, Tosefta Shab. 6.1.

[45] Possibly the story told in Ḥul. 105b reflects such a belief. The crumbs of bread thrown into the water together with the grass were an offering to the good spirit dwelling in the water, and in return for this offering the good spirit prevented the "demon of poverty," שרא דעניותא, from harming the man. If, however, one throws away the crumbs instead of offering them to a protecting good spirit, he brings down upon himself the wrath of the demon of poverty who might harm him and make him poor and wanting in food. Cf. also Zohar, פנחס, p. 491. See below note 111. To both cf. Frazer, *Golden Bough* (1 volume edition), pp. 200–201 about Tabu on leaving food uneaten. By sympathetic magic, it was believed one can harm a person by getting a hold of the leftover of his food.

people then said, "This is the man whose loaf of bread stood him in good stead," and they applied to him the verse, "Cast thy bread upon the waters, for thou shalt find it after many days"[46] (Eccl. 11.1). There can be no doubt of the meaning of this story. The man was offering a daily sacrifice to the "sea-lord" or to another spirit dwelling in the water. When he once found a jewel or a pearl in a fish that he bought, it was understood by the people that this was sent to him by the spirit to whom he gave bread every day, as a reward for his offerings.

The belief in water demons, or in evil spirits that dwell in rivers or lakes who might hurt the people, especially when the latter try to get water from their dwelling place, is also expressed in a Baraita of the Talmud (Pes. 112a) which reads as follows: "A man should not drink water from rivers or lakes during the night, and if he does drink, his blood is upon his head, because of the danger." Commenting upon this Baraita, the Gemera asks: What is the danger? And it gives the answer, that there is the danger of *Shabriri*. R. Samuel b. Meir in his commentary *ad. loc.* explains שברירי to mean blindness; hence, it would simply mean that there is a danger of becoming blind. But the explanation of Rashi that *Shabriri* is the name of a water demon is more correct.[47] For the Gemara there prescribes that in case one is thirsty and must drink he should recite a certain incantation containing also the words שברירי ברירי רירי ירי רי. This no doubt was believed to have the power of rendering the spirit harmless. By gradually dropping letters and thus reducing the name of the demon, his power also becomes reduced.[48] I believe that the other Baraita (Pes. 112a) which warns people against drinking water on Wednesday night and Friday night because of the danger of the evil spirit, also means to prohibit the drinking only of the water from a well or river, but not of the water which

[46] The passage in the original reads as follows: עובדה הוה בחד בר נש דבכל יום הוה נסיב חד עינול ומקלק לימא רבא חד יומא אזל וובין חד גון קרעיה ואשכח ביה סימא. אמרו ליה היידי הוא גברא דקם ליה עינולה וקרון עלוי שלח לחמך על פני המים.

[47] In 'Ab. Zarah 12b Rashi explains שברירי to be the name of the demon who has the power to inflict blindness: שד הממונה על מכת סנורים.

[48] Cf. Lauterbach, "The Naming of Children in Jewish Folklore, Ritual and Practice," in *Yearbook of the Central Conference of American Rabbis*, XLII (1932), 3.

had been drawn from the well at daytime and kept in a vessel in the house.[49] The reason is that on these two nights of the week especially, the evil spirits have power to harm people (cf. Pes. 111b and 112b about the queen of the demons, Agrata, the daughter of Maḥlat); hence, they might harm anyone who comes near their dwelling place or dares to take some water from there. As a charm to protect one from harm, if he absolutely needs the water, there are prescribed certain formulas by which to drive away the demon. One is also advised to make some noise and thus drive away the demon, or, and this is very significant, to first throw something into the well before drawing the water to drink,[50] that is, to pay for it or pacify the demon by offering him something.

With the exception of these few indications of popular beliefs and practices resembling somewhat the later Tashlik ceremony or reflecting the ideas underlying it, we do not find in the talmudic-midrashic literature any express mention of such a ceremony or any direct reference to the custom of praying near water in talmudic times. It would, however, be a mistake to believe that the ancient custom disappeared entirely. In the first place, the silence of the talmudic authorities about such a practice of the people would not necessarily prove that it was not observed in their times. Secondly, it can be inferred from the few talmudic passages cited above that the ancient custom with the ideas underlying it persisted, though in a modified form, even in later amoraic times. It is evident from the few indications in the Talmud that during the amoraic times a change took place both in the manner in which some of the people continued to observe the ancient practice as well as in the attitude of the teachers towards the ideas underlying its modified form. In the fight against the superstitious beliefs underlying the ancient practice the Rabbis of the Talmud won only a partial victory; to be more correct, they apparently directed their attacks only against a certain aspect of the practice or against some of the popular beliefs, especially those incompatible with their pure God conception, not, however, against all of them. They fought

[49] Against Rashi in 'Ab. Zarah, loc. cit., cf. Tosafot there, s. v. לא ישתה.
[50] נישדי בה מידי והדר נישתי, Pes. 112a.

insistently against the belief that God dwells in or near water and that prayer offered to Him at a place near water is more readily answered. In this they were successful. The people at large had learned the lesson that there is only one God to whom alone prayer may be offered and that no other being besides Him, angel, demon or spirit, may be worshipped as a god. They also had got the correct conception of God and believed that the whole universe is full of His glory and that the water is not His favorite abode; hence, prayers offered to Him at a place near water are not more efficacious than prayers offered to Him at any other place. For this reason we do not find any reference to the custom of offering prayers near water or of building synagogues near water in later talmudic times.

But the Rabbis did not successfully fight, or perhaps did not even seriously try to fight, against the popular belief in the existence of angels and demons, good and evil spirits, who as subordinate beings have the power of helping or harming people. They did not combat the popular beliefs that angels dwell in heaven and that other spirits, good or evil, dwell in the water. Probably some of the Rabbis even shared these popular beliefs. Hence we have found that in amoraic times no objection was raised to the practice of throwing bread into the sea, which no doubt was intended as a gift to the spirit dwelling there. We have also found that in amoraic times some of the Rabbis themselves recommend the recitation of certain biblical verses or of other incantations as a means of protection against the harm that might come to one from the spirit dwelling in the water. They even recommend throwing something into the river as a gift to the spirit dwelling therein, in order to pacify him — a practice which in tannaitic times, when there was still the danger that some people might be worshipping the spirit of the lake or the river, was condemned as a heathenish practice (Tosef. Shab. 6.1). In other words, with the danger that these popular practices might affect the correct belief in the One God removed, the Rabbis did not strongly object to these practices or to the ideas underlying them. As ceremonies aimed merely at securing favors from or protection against spirits subordinate to God, these practices were tolerated by the Rabbis. This changed attitude of the Rabbis made it possible for the ancient custom to survive, though in a modified form. Instead of being a religious rite accompanying the service offered to God, it became merely a popular practice, intended to secure favors from demons or to ward off the harm they might cause. In the course of time, due to the gradual rise of mystic tendencies, certain developments in theological concepts took place. Some elements of the primitive beliefs were differently formulated and made more acceptable; some component ideas underlying the ancient practice assumed a more definite form, found bolder expression and became more and more recognized by the people. This process gradually prepares the way for the reappearance of the ancient custom as a religious rite and for its acceptance as a Jewish religious ceremony in the form of the later Tashlik.

Let us, therefore, first analyze these elements of the ancient ideas and see how they were developed and in what form they were believed by the people during the later talmudic and the early gaonic period. This may enable us to find the connecting link between the ancient custom and its modified form in the later Tashlik ceremony.

We have seen that during the talmudic period the Jewish people had outgrown the primitive belief that God dwelt in or near the water, but the idea that the water, of old the residence of God, was the abode of degraded gods or spirits still lingered on. We also find that Satan, the head of the demons, and Lilit, their queen, as well as the fallen angels, were believed to have their abode in the depths of the sea. These ideas must have been prevalent among the people even in the early talmudic times, though authoritative Jewish literature of that period does not mention them. Thus we read in Rev. 20.1–3, "And I saw an angel coming down out of heaven, having the key of the abyss and a great chain in his hand. And he laid hold on the dragon, the old serpent, which is the Devil, and Satan, and bound him for a thousand years, and cast him into the abyss, and shut it and sealed it over him, that he should deceive the nations no more, until the thousand years should be finished; after this he must be loosed for a little time" (cf. also vv. 7 and 10). The same ideas are repeatedly found in a later midrash and in post-talmudic mystic literature. Thus we read in Midrash Abkir[51] that the demons and evil spirits hide in the dark mountains and in the depths of the sea. In the Zohar[52] we are told that Uza and Azael the revolting angels who were cast down from heaven are bound with iron chains and kept down in the abyss. According to another statement in the Zohar,[53] Lilit, the queen of the demons, fled or was thrown into the deep sea, where she still dwells, ready to harm people and to lead them astray. As a protection against her evil devices, there is prescribed an incantation, containing in part the following words: "Go back, go back (i. e., to your place in the sea), the sea is roaring for you, its waves are calling you.[54] Samael or Satan himself was also thrown, together with the Egyptians, into the sea.[55] And in passages of the Zohar[56] Satan is identified with the depths of the sea. While these ideas are found only in later post-talmudic sources, there can be no doubt that they are of much earlier origin and are only openly expressed in the post-talmudic times when mysticism became more and more tolerated, and, to a certain extent, even recognized.

Another important theological development which took place in the later talmudic and early gaonic periods was in regard to the position of the angels and their possible function as mediators between God and man. The idea that the angels, although subordinate beings and not independent deities, have, nevertheless, a definite function and, as it were, some share in the heavenly administration, was not altogether foreign to the Jews even in earlier times. But the enlightened teachers sought to suppress it. It was thought incompatible with the pure monotheistic Jewish belief. Accordingly, it was taught that the angels cannot interfere with God's administration of the world,

---

[51] Ed. by A. Marmorstein in הדביר II (Berlin, 1924), 139. Cf. also L. Ginzberg, הגדות קטועות, in *Hagoren*, IX, 60 and 67.

[52] הקדמת ספר הזהר, p. 9b, and פנחס, p. 465.

[53] בראשית 19b and ויקרא 37.

[54] Zohar ויקרא, *loc. cit.*

[55] ספר החשק (Lemberg, 1815), 6b; cf. also Jubilees 48.15 for Mastema, and see Zohar בראשית, 40 and 48, and תרומה, 326.

[56] תצוה, 371 and אמור, 203.

and that God ignores or rebukes them whenever they argue against His plan or contemplated action (b. Sanh. 38b and 103b). The authoritative teaching of Judaism was that a man need not fear any other being besides God, neither may he ask favors of any other heavenly being besides Him. He can, and should, pray to God directly and he needs no mediator to intercede in his behalf; he need not ask Gabriel or Michael to help him or to plead his cause before God.[57]

In spite of these enlightened teachings of Judaism, however, the other more primitive ideas developed more and more. It was believed, at least by some teachers, that God takes counsel with the angels and that He does not do anything without consulting them.[58] Now, if they are consulted, so popular belief argued, might they not be able to influence God, or somewhat affect and modify the Divine plan? Hence, the belief is occasionally expressed that the angels sometimes plead successfully the cause of Israel or of the righteous man.[59] It was, therefore, believed by the people, as well as by some teachers, that the angels could help one by presenting his cause or bringing his petition before God.[60] For this reason one of the teachers considered it inadvisable to make a supplication to God in the Aramaic language, which the ministering angels do not understand.[61] For, not understanding, or unwilling to recognize, the language of the petition, the angels might fail to present it before God and be unable to recommend its being granted.

---

[57] See p. Ber. 9.1 (13a), and cf. K. Kohler, *Jewish Theology* (New York, 1918), p. 186 f.

[58] אין הקב״ה עושה דבר אלא אם כן נמלך בפמליא של מעלה, Sanh. 38b.

[59] See Soṭah 12b; Sanh. 44b and 96b; B. B. 75b.

[60] This belief is clearly expressed in the following Midrash quoted in *Shibbole ha-Leḳeṭ*, 282 (Buber, Wilna, 1886), p. 266: במדרש שיר השירים על פסוק השבעתי אתכם אומרת כנסת ישראל למלאכים העומדים על שערי תפלה ועל שערי דמעה הוליכו תפלתי ודמעתי לפני הקב״ה ותהיו מליצי יושר לפניו שימחול לי על הזדונות ועל השגגות ונאמר אם יש עליו מלאך מליץ אחד מני אלף וגו׳. Cf. L. Grünhut in his edition of Midrash Shir Hashirim (Jerusalem, 1897), p. 39, note 7.

[61] Shab. 12b. Cf. *Shibbole ha-Leḳeṭ, loc. cit.*; also Rashi to Soṭah 33a, *s. v.* שאני בת קול, and Asheri quoted in *Bet Joseph* to Oraḥ Ḥayyim, 101, who interprets שאין מכירין to mean, they would not recognize. See also Lauterbach, *op. cit.*, p. 44, note 74.

With the further development of mystic tendencies in the post-talmudic times this idea of the angels acting as helpful mediators was objected to by but few enlightened teachers. In gaonic times the idea becomes more and more popular and the angels are frequently invoked for protection or for help in bringing prayers before God.[62]

With this development in the attitude towards the angels or good spirits, there also went a definite development in the attitude towards Satan and the evil spirits in general. For, like the angels, Satan, even though only a subordinate being, also occupies, in the popular belief, a certain position in the heavenly councils, and has a definite function to perform in God's plan of judging and ruling the world. If the good angels who favor Israel and the righteous ones can do some good and help the people by pleading their cause or recommending their petitions to God, Satan, whose function is to accuse people and to seek to harm them, might on his part likewise try to interfere with the heavenly administration and prevent it from granting favors to the people. Methods of dealing with Satan and of preventing him from using his influence to harm the people, therefore, had to be devised. There were two methods of dealing with Satan, in use even in very early times. The one was to use friendly means of persuading Satan to desist from his evil work. This was done by bribing and offering him gifts. An echo of this early belief that Satan could be bribed is found in the Sifra, where it is said that Moses advised Aaron to use this method of placating Satan, *viz.*, to send him a gift before entering the Holy of Holies to obtain forgiveness from God.[63] This idea of offering

---

[62] Some of the Geonim justify the practice of addressing the angels and asking them to present the prayers before God or even to intercede with God in behalf of the petitioner. See A. Harkavy, תשובות הגאונים (Berlin, 1885), pp. 188–189. On the question of תפלה ע"י אמצעי see R. Aryeh Leib Gordon in his Introduction (מבוא) to the סדור אוצר התפלות (Wilna, 1923), pp. 14–20. The reference to the responsum of R. Israel Bruna given there as סימן רע"ה is to be corrected to סימן רע"ד (Stettin, 1860), p. 114b. Cf. also Jacob ibn Habib in עין יעקב to הכותב Shab. 12b and ספר תוספת מעשה רב (Jerusalem, 1896), שאלתות, No. 128, p. 18b for R. Elijah Gaon of Wilna's objection to the recitation ברכוני לשלום addressed to the angels.

[63] מכילתא דמילואים, Weiss, 43c. The passage reads as follows: שאמר לו משה

a sacrifice or sending gifts to Satan was objectionable to the Rabbis. They considered sending gifts to Satan a form of worshipping him, or they may have feared that the people, if allowed to indulge in such practices, might be led to worship or pray to Satan — which their religious conscience could not tolerate. Accordingly, the Rabbis discouraged this method of dealing with Satan, and, with the exception of this one passage in Sifra, echoing the older primitive belief, the idea of bribing Satan is to my knowledge not found in the Talmud.[64] The other method of dealing with Satan was to fight him and seek to frustrate his evil designs or hinder him in the performance of his function as accuser. This method is theologically less objectionable than that of bribing him, for the very belief that one could fight Satan precludes the danger of worshipping him. Even this method, however, was not equally approved by all the Rabbis, Some of the Rabbis, seeking to emphasize the belief in the One God who alone rules the world in justice and mercy and whom alone

לאהרן אהרן אחי אף על פי שנתרצה המקום לכפר על עונותיך צריך אתה ליתן לתוך פיו של
שטן שלח דורון לפניך עד שלא תכנס למקדש שמא ישנאך (ישטינך read) בביאתך למקדש.
Cf. *A Significant Controversy between the Sadducees and the Pharisees*, above pp. 64–65. This passage implies that Moses knew that it would not be displeasing to God if Satan were bribed and silenced. Cf. above, note 10.

[64] An echo of this idea is perhaps to be found in Targum Jonathan to Lev. 9.3 which reads, as follows: ועם בני ישראל תמלל למימר סבו ברם אתון צפיר בר עזי מטול דסטנא מימתיל ביה מטול דלא משתעי עליכון לשון תליתאי על עיסק צפיר בר עזי דנכיסו בני יעקב.... ואמר בר שתיה מטול דידכר לכון זכוותא דיצחק דכפתיה אבוי הי כאימרא. The words מטול דסטנא מימתיל ביה suggest the idea that the purpose was to bribe Satan by offering him something which resembles him and which he likes, and thereby prevent him from talking evil against Israel. Then, as if to weaken the idea that God Himself commanded them to bribe Satan, there is added the other idea that the purpose was rather to counteract Satan's accusations by showing that the children of Israel who killed a שעיר עזים when committing the crime against Joseph, also kill a שעיר עזים as an offering to God. It is, however, also possible that in the words מטול דסטנא מימתיל ביה we have already a suggestion of the idea later developed by Lurya (see below, note 128) that the purpose was to fight and weaken Satan by killing something that resembles him and that might be taken, as it were, as his representative. It is also interesting to note that according to Jonathan the other offering consisting of a lamb was to be offered at the same time for the purpose of reminding God of the עקידת יצחק the merit of which should help Israel against Satan. See below, note 83.

we must fear and worship, taught that the best method of fighting Satan was to invoke the help of God against him. Were it not for the help of God — declares one of the Rabbis in the Talmud (b. Ḳid. 30b) — no man could prevail against Satan or the evil desire, as it is said, "The wicked (i. e., Satan) watcheth the righteous and seeketh to slay him. The Lord will not leave him in his hand, nor suffer him to be condemned when he is judged" (Ps. 37.32–33). R. Judah ha-Nasi would, therefore, in his private prayer, uttered every day, include also the petition that God may deliver him משטן המשחית, from Satan who might seek to destroy him (b. Ber. 16b, cf. also *ibid.*, 46a). R. Joḥanan b. Nappaḥa said, "A man should pray that the heavenly powers should assist him and that he should not have any adversaries in heaven" (b. Sanh. 44b), and R. Simon b. Laḳish said, "Whoever makes a strenuous effort in prayer here below will have no adversaries in heaven," i. e., need not fear the adversaries in heaven (*ibid.*, *loc. cit.*). This position of the enlightened Rabbis, however, is rather inconsistent, for once the existence of Satan as the official accuser, appointed by God to his task, is admitted — and the Rabbis did not deny it — it cannot be expected that God would interfere with Satan's activities and hinder him in the performing of the function which He Himself assigned to him.[65] Of course, one may pray to God not to believe the accusations of Satan and not to listen to his suggestions for punishment, but then the danger remains that Satan may be so eloquent in his charges against the people and so insistent in his demands that they be justly punished, that God will listen to him rather than to the pleadings of the people on trial.

The popular belief, shared in by many of the Rabbis, was, therefore, not content to leave it to God to hinder Satan in his

---

[65] Not all the Rabbis, however, were consistent in this idea. According to scattered sayings in the Midrashim God employs against Satan the same methods used by man for the purpose of frustrating Satan's designs (see Lauterbach, "The Ceremony of Breaking a Glass at Weddings" in *HUCA* II [Cincinnati, 1925], 356 f.). He seeks to bribe him (see Gen. r. 57.3 and cf. Zohar אמור, p. 202); He seeks to deceive him (see Pesiḳta Rabbati, Friedmann, pp. 185–186, and cf. Zohar, *loc. cit.*, p. 201) and, of course, He fights him by rebuking him and stopping him in his work.

work, for God in His justice may find that Satan is correct in his accusations. The popular belief thought it advisable to use all possible means of preventing Satan from appearing before God and bringing his accusations against the people. Especially during the period of judgment, beginning on Rosh Hashanah and closing on Hoshana Rabbah, were the people very anxious to hinder Satan in the exercise of his function as accuser. Many of the ceremonies performed during this season were calculated to have a restraining effect upon Satan. Thus one of the purposes of blowing the Shofar on New Year's day, according to the Talmud, was to confound Satan so that he should not be able to accuse the Jews on this first day of judgment.[66] Likewise on the Day of Atonement, notwithstanding the fact that some of the Rabbis taught that on this one day in the year Satan has no power at all to function in his capacity as the accuser (b. Yoma 20a),[67] the people sought to prevent the possibility of Satan's harming them. Many ceremonies observed on this day were calculated to confuse Satan and cause him to believe that the Jews were as sinless as angels (Pirḳe deR. E. 46). During the Sukkoth festival, in performing the ceremony of waving the ethrog and the palm-branch, some people aimed to hurt Satan or, as it is expressed by the Rabbis, to "send arrows into the eyes of Satan" (b. Suk. 38a and Men. 62a).

In the course of time, however, the people began to question the wisdom of the practice of attempting to fight Satan by cursing him, sending arrows into his eyes, and seeking to confound him. It occurred to the people that after all Satan might not be so bad. If he accuses the people, he is merely performing a task imposed upon him, for he has been appointed by God to the office of accusing the people. Personally, he may not relish

[66] למה תוקעין בר"ה ... כדי לערבב השטן; R. H. 16a,b. See commentaries and cf. B. M. Lewin ערבוב השטן בראש השנה in התור VI (1926), No. 40, pp. 6–8.

[67] For in some circles the opposite idea was prevalent, viz., that just on the Day of Atonement Satan is given full authority to accuse Israel; see Pirḳe deR. Eliezer, 46 and cf. R. David Lurya in his commentary ad loc. From the story of Simon the Just (Yoma 39b) it is also evident that it was believed that Satan had authority to accuse Israel on the Day of Atonement. Cf. A Significant Controversy, etc., above pp. 65 ff.

it. If, however, people curse him and seek to fight him, he may become provoked and more bitter in his accusations, which otherwise he might perform merely in a perfunctory manner. Accordingly, we find in the later talmudic period that the service of pointing with the palm-branch at Satan and cursing him by saying, "Arrows into the eyes of Satan" was declared to be an unwise thing, for it might provoke him (b. Men. 62a).

The legend told in the Talmud (b. Ḳid. 81a,b) suggests even more strongly this change of attitude towards Satan. Pelemo — so this legend runs — was in the habit of cursing Satan every day by saying, "Arrows into the eyes of Satan." One day, it happened to be on the eve of the Day of Atonement, Satan disguised himself and appeared in the form of a poor man standing in front of the door of Pelemo's house, asking for bread. When it was given to him he said, "On a day like this (a sort of holiday) when everybody is inside shall I alone be left outside?" So they asked him in and put food before him. He then said, "On a day like this when everybody sits around the table shall I sit alone?" They then asked him to come to the table. While sitting at the table he brought upon himself boils and running sores and made himself very repulsive. Pelemo then said to him, "Sit decently and do not act so disgustingly." The poor man (Satan) then sank down and feigned death. Voices were heard crying, "Pelemo killed a man." Thereupon Pelemo, very much frightened, ran to hide. Satan followed him and, seeing how worried Pelemo was over the supposed murder, had compassion on him and disclosed his identity to him, thus showing him that in the first place the supposed poor man was no man at all and, secondly, that he was not killed. Satan then reproached Pelemo, saying to him, "Why do you always curse me thus (i. e., by saying, "Arrows into the eyes of Satan")?" Pelemo then asked him, "How else can I protect myself against you?" Satan then answered, "You should say, 'May God restrain Satan.'" (This is as much as to say, release him from his duty of acting as the accuser.)

This legend clearly expresses the idea that Satan is not to be blamed for performing his duty and accusing the people. As long as he is not discharged from his office he has to do its duties. He has to fulfill the task imposed upon him unless stopped by his superior, i. e., told by God that he should cease to function in the capacity of accuser. We further learn from this legend that in the popular belief Satan was capable of having sympathies and acting kindly toward people, as he did in this case when he had compassion on Pelemo and relieved him from his fear and worries. This idea is also expressed in the legend in b. Shab. 89a, where we are told that Satan or the angel of death was rather generous to Moses and taught him how he might counteract his destructive activities.[67a]

These popular beliefs caused the people in later talmudic times to change their tactics against Satan. The older idea of seeking to bribe Satan and thus make him rather friendlily disposed to the people was thus gradually revived. And in post-talmudic times this idea becomes more prevalent, and is boldly expressed. A change in the attitude towards Satan takes place. It is expressly taught that Satan might be won over by gifts and sacrifices; hence, the people might try to pacify him and silence him by bribes. Thus the Midrash Abkir states that Azazel is identical with Azael,[68] one of the fallen angels who refused to repent and who continues in his evil practice and still seeks to lead man into sin. (Accordingly, it is but another name for Satan.) It was for this reason, concludes the Midrash, that in order to pacify or reconcile him, that he may tolerate their sins, Israel offered to him a sacrifice on the Day of Atonement, similar to the one which they offered to God, in order to obtain forgiveness — this is the Azazel mentioned in the Torah[69] (Lev. 16). This idea is even more plainly expressed in Pirḳe deR. Eliezer, ch. 46, where it is stated that the goat which

---

[67a] Cf. also B. B. 16a saying of R. Levi about the purpose Satan aimed at with his accusations against Job, which assumes that Satan was very friendly towards the descendants of Abraham.

[68] An identification of, or a connection between, Azael and Azazel is also suggested in b. Yoma 47b.

[69] The passage from Midrash Abkir, quoted in Yalḳuṭ Shime'oni to Gen. § 44, reads as follows: עזאל לא חזר בתשובה ועדיין הוא עומד בקלקולו להסית בני אדם לדבר עבירה בבגדי צבעונין של נשים ולכך היו ישראל מקריבין קרבנות ביום הכפורים איל אחד לה׳ שיכפר על ישראל ואיל אחד לעזאזל שיסבול עונותיהם של ישראל והוא עזאזל שבתורה.

was sent to Azazel on Yom Kippur was a bribe which Israel offered to Satan in order that he should not attempt to prevent the divine acceptance of Israel's sacrifice. It also goes on to explain the manner in which the bribe becomes effective with Satan — really a justification of him. For practically it shows how he could honestly become derelict in his duty. All the sins of Israel were piled upon the goat, so that Satan while receiving the gift does not look at the gift nor at the pile of sins attached to it; he merely looks at the givers and, scrutinizing them as he may, he actually finds in them no sins, since they had been transferred to the goat. He can honestly, therefore, refrain from accusing them since he finds no fault with them. From Saadia (*Emunot We-de'ot*, ed. Slucki, III, 73) we also learn that in his time there were people who believed that Azazel was the name of a demon to whom the sacrifice was offered. This was indeed one of the arguments of Ḥivi Al-Balkhi (v. S. Poznanski in *Hagoren*, VIII, 112–37; cf. also I. Davidson, *Saadia's Polemic against Ḥivi Al-Balkhi*, [New York, 1915], p. 90). Of course, Saadia is opposed to this idea and he explains Azazel to have been the name of a mountain. The fact remains, however, that many people in the 9th century believed that Azazel had been the name of one of the fallen angels, or of Satan, and that a sacrifice in ancient times had been offered to him on Yom Kippur to bribe him and thus prevent him from making accusations against Israel.[70]

To sum up, then, we may say that the ideas prevalent during

---

[70] See Zohar צוה, p. 369, and אמור, pp. 202–203. Ibn Ezra and Ramban in their respective commentaries to Lev. 16.8 also assume that the goat to Azazel was in a manner an offering to Satan. Ramban explains that Israel was commanded to do this by God Himself in order to silence Satan. This idea of Ramban was further developed by Baḥya b. Asher, and Ẓiyoni (see above, note 10. Cf. also Ibn Shuaib דרשות על התורה [Krakau, 1573], p. 51d). Another ingenious explanation of the purpose of this offering to Satan is given by Recanati in his טעמי המצות (ed. Abraham Kanaryvogel, Przemysl, 1888), p. 16b. According to this explanation this offering carried with it a warning and a threat. It was to serve notice to the accuser that if he should persist in bringing accusations against Israel accusations would also be brought against him, recalling the sins which he, Azael, had once committed. Cf. Lauterbach, "The Ritual for the Kapparot-Ceremony," in *Jewish Studies in Memory of George A. Kohut* (New York, 1935), p. 419.

the gaonic period, at least among certain circles of the Jewish people, if not among all, were as follows: (1) Spirits — including the fallen angels and Satan, too — have their residence in the depths of the sea or in water, which originally had been considered the favorite dwelling place of the gods. (2) The mediatorship of the angels and spirits was sought, and it was thought permissible and advantageous to secure their favor. (3) It was believed that even Satan himself might be made favorably disposed, and his frienship won if he be offered gifts and sacrifices. All these ideas, of course, were old and traces of them are to be found in the earlier literature, but in the gaonic period there seems to have been less objection to them on the part of the official and authoritative teachers. They were entertained even by people of orthodox beliefs, and they found expression even in some of the literary productions of the period. The revival in the gaonic period of these ideas of the power of Satan, and the need of reconciling rather than fighting him, would naturally have the effect of causing people inclined to mystic thought, as they were in gaonic times, to try to reintroduce certain ceremonies similar to the ancient sacrifice to the Azazel. Such ceremonies would have the same purpose, i. e., to win the favor of Satan. In other words, we would expect that certain gifts would be offered to Satan at the time of New Year's day and the Day of Atonement. Again, since Satan's residence was believed to be in the water, we would not be surprised to find that certain gifts intended for Satan were thrown into the water, i. e., brought to him into his home. Again, since sacrifices cannot be made except when the one who offers them is present, and since they must be accompanied by some petition, we would expect the people to go out to the residence of Satan and there personally present him with their offerings. In other words, the people would try to employ the same means of securing a favorable decision on the Day of Atonement, as were, in their belief, effectively used in the Temple and in olden times. They would, accordingly, revive the ancient custom of going out on the great fast, i. e., Yom Kippur, to a place near the water to pray there to God, and to ask the sea, also, to be favorable to them — even to intercede on their behalf, as suggested by Philo. Even more, in order to secure the favor of Satan who dwells in the depths of the sea, and silence all his possible accusations, they might try to offer him some gifts like the goat which had been offered to him in olden times. These gifts we would expect the people to throw into the sea, the dwelling place of Satan (identified with the Serpent and the Dragon), just as the goat in ancient times was sent to the wilderness, likewise a dwelling place of the demons and of Satan.

To repeat, then, if we would find such a custom in the gaonic times we would not be surprised. But we do not find an express record of such a ceremony having been observed in gaonic times, although we do find that some people in that age observed ceremonies almost identical with the one we would expect. We must remember, however, that progress, or retrogression, in religious practices, as elsewhere, does not follow a straight line, but follows rather a zigzag course. This also happened in our case. The objections to the old primitive superstitions, while not so very strong and while raised only by a few enlightened teachers, were yet not entirely overcome. These objections were still strong enough to hinder the introduction of a ceremony in such a form as would be clearly a reverting to old primitive superstitions. It was due to the wholesome influence of rabbinic law and ritual, that that tendency to observe the ceremony in a form which would fully express the popular beliefs was checked. The ceremony had to be changed and modified so as not to encounter strong rabbinic objections. There resulted a compromise between the popular beliefs and the rabbinic teachings. Such compromises are evident in the varied forms of the ceremonies which were actually introduced or at any rate officially recognized in gaonic times. Let us make a short digression to discuss these ceremonies and then we shall come back to continue tracing the development of the Tashlik ceremony.

Two ceremonies appearing in gaonic times seem to have been performed for the purpose of securing a favorable verdict in the season of judgment — between the New Year and the Day of Atonement. These two ceremonies, as we shall see are in reality but two different forms of one ceremony. Of these two forms, the one that became more generally accepted and has survived, even to this day, is the so-called Kapparot ceremony. On the eve of the Day of Atonement or sometimes a day or two earlier, every male in the house takes a rooster, and every female a hen, swings it around the head a few times and recites the prayer, "May this be my substitute, etc.," and slaughters it. This ceremony is mentioned by the Geonim[71] and forms the subject of many of their responsa. I quote here in full the responsum of Sheshna[72] in the collection of *Shaʻare Teshubah* (Leipzig, 1858), No. 299, in which this ceremony is fully discussed and described in detail.[73] It reads as follows: "As to your question,

---

[71] Dr. Rothschild in Rahmer's *Literaturblatt* XII (1883), No. 48, pp. 189–190, assumes that the *Kapparot* ceremony is not older than the times of the Geonim and that it was the result of Christian influence. Neither one of these assumptions is correct. It is true that in the form in which the ceremony is still observed it is first expressly mentioned by the Geonim. But this does not mean that it was first introduced in Gaonic times. As will be shown in the course of this essay the origin of this ceremony goes back to talmudic times. J. H. Schorr in *Heḥaluṣ* VI, 56, cites a parallel to this ceremony from the Persian religion.

[72] Sheshna, also called משרשיא בר תחליפא (cf. S. Krauss, "Beiträge zur Geschichte der Gaonim," in *Livre d'homage a la memoire du Dr. Samuel Poznanski* [Warsaw, 1927], p. 136 and V. Aptowitzer, "Untersuchungen zur Gaonäischen Literatur" in *HUCA* VIII–IX [Cincinnati, 1932], 437, note 41) was Gaon in Sura about 650.

[73] The full text of the original reads as follows: וששאלתם האי שאנו רגילים לשחוט ערב יוה"כ תרנגולים ואין אנו יודעים מנהג זה למה אי משום תמורה מ"ש תרנגול מבהמה וחיה הא ודאי קושיא היא. וי"ל יש בה שני טעמים אחד שתרנגול מצוי בביתו של אדם מבהמה וחיה ועוד יש במקומנו עשירים שעושים תמורה אילים ועיקר מבעלי קרנים דמות אילו של יצחק אבינו לפיכך לא דבר קבוע הוא. ועוד שמענו מחכמים ראשונים שאעפ"י שיש מי שעושה תמורה בבהמה שדמיה יקרים תרנגול מובחר לפי ששמו גבר כדאמרינן מאי קריאת הגבר אמר רב קרא גברא דבי רב שילא אמרי קרא תרנגולא ותניא כותיה דר' שילא היוצא קודם קריאת הגבר דמו בראשו וכיון ששמו גבר תמורת גבר בלבד וטפי מהני ומעלי. וכך צריך אוחז שליח תרנגול ומניח ידו על ראש התרנגול ונוטלו מניחו על ראש מתכפר ואומר זה תחת זה וזה חילוף זה זה מחול על זה ומחזירו עליו פעם אחרת ואומרים יושבי חשך וצלמות כו' ויוציאם מחשך וצלמות כו' אווילים מדרך פשעם כו' כל אוכל תתעב נפשם וגו' ויצעקו אל ה' בצר להם וגו' ישלח דברו וירפאם יודו לה' חסדו וגו' ויחננו ויאמר פדעהו וגו' נפש תחת נפש. ועושה כסדר הזה ז' פעמים ואח"כ מניח ידו על ראש תרנגול ואומר זה יצא למיתה תחת זה ומניח ידו על ראש מתכפר ואומר תכנס אתה פלוני בן פלוני לחיים ולא תמות ועושה כסדר הזה ג' פעמים ומניח מתכפר ידו על ראש תרנגול תבנית סמיכה וסומך עליו ושוחטו לאלתר הבנית תיכף לסמיכה שחיטה. Cf. Responsum No. 15 in שו"ת הגאונים published by Ch. M. Horowitz in his *Halachische Schriften der Geonim* (Frankfurt a/M., 1881), p. 50. See also

'What is the significance of the practice, which we are accustomed to follow, of slaughtering roosters on the eve of the Day of Atonement. For we do not know what the purpose of this ceremony is. If it is to serve the purpose of offering a substitute (for the person who performs the ceremony), then why use especially a rooster and not any other animal?' This surely is a difficult question. One might say that there are two reasons for the choice of a rooster for this ceremony. One of the reasons for choosing the rooster is that the rooster is more frequently found in a household, or more easily obtainable than any other animal. And, indeed, there are still some rich people in our community who use a ram for this ceremony of offering a substitute. The essential thing — according to these people — is that the animal should be of the kind that have horns, like the ram that was offered instead of our father Isaac. Accordingly, there is really no definitely fixed rule. There is still another reason. We have a tradition from former teachers that, although some people perform this ceremony with an animal that is more expensive, it is preferable to perform the ceremony with a rooster, because the latter is called *Geber*, and since its name is *Geber* which also means 'man,' it alone can be a proper substitute for man, and the ceremony performed with it will be better and more effctive.

"And thus should the ceremony be performed. The agent who performs it takes hold of the rooster and places his hand upon its head. Then, removing his hand from the head of the

---

Responsum of Naṭronai Gaon in חמדה גנוזה (Jerusalem, 1863), No. 93, p. 17b; Responsum No. 16 in Horowitz, *loc. cit.*, and Responsum published by Halberstamm in Kobak's גנזי נסתרות III (1872), pp. 4–6. Cf. also Rashi in ספר האורה (Lemberg, 1905), p. 109; ספר פרדס הגדול (Warsaw, 1870), No. 186, p. 69; Vitry, p. 273; Asheri, *Halakot*, Yoma VIII; *Ṭur, O. Ḥ.* 605; Mordecai, Yoma 723; תשב״ץ (Warsaw, 1875), No. 125, p. 21; *Kol Bo* (Lemberg, 1860), 68, p. 33a; Abudirham (Lemberg, 1857), p. 94b; *Or Zaru'a* II, 257; and *Shibbole ha-Leḳet*, 283 (Buber, Wilna, 1886), p. 266. Cf. also Lauterbach, "The Ritual for the Kapparot-Ceremony," *op. cit.*, Judah Modena in his *The History of the Present Jews*, English translation by Simon Ockley (London, 1707), p. 141, says: "But this custom (Capora) is laid aside, both in the Levant and in Italy, as being superstitious, and not built upon any foundation.

rooster, he places it[74] upon the head of the person for whom the ceremony is performed and says, 'This (rooster) shall be instead of this (person); this rooster shall be the substitute for this person; this rooster shall be the ransom for this person (or, this person is to be redeemed[75] by this rooster).' He then swings the rooster around the head of the person for whom it is to be a substitute, while reciting the following words: 'Such as sit in darkness and in the shadow of death, etc. He brought them out of darkness and the shadow of death, etc., crazed because of the way of their transgression, etc. Their soul abhorred all manner of food, etc. They cried unto the Lord in their trouble, etc. He sent His word and healed them, etc. Let them give thanks unto the Lord for His mercy, etc.' (Ps. 107.10–21). Then He is gracious unto him and saith, 'Deliver him from going down to the pit, I have found a ransom'[76] (Job 33.24). 'A life for a life.' He does this seven times. He then places his hand upon the head of the rooster, saying, 'This rooster shall go out to death instead of this person.' Then he places his hand upon the head of the person who is to receive atonement by this ceremony, saying, 'Thou, so and so, the son of so and so, shalt enter into life and thou shalt not die.' This he does three times. Then the person for whom the substitute is offered places his hand upon the head of the rooster, as a sort of סמיכה (the ceremony of laying the hands upon the sacrificial animal). He lays his hand upon it (the rooster) and slaughters it immediately, thus in a manner following the rule prescribed for sacrifices, *viz.*, that the slaughtering of the sacrificial victim must follow immediately the ceremony of the laying on of the hands."[77]

[74] The words ונוטלו מניחו על ראש מתכפר may also mean, he takes the rooster and puts it upon the head of the person for whom the ceremony is performed.

[75] The reading מחולל for מחול is given by Asheri, *loc. cit.*, *Ṭur*, *loc. cit.*, and Abudirham, *loc. cit.*

[76] I give the verses as rendered by the Bible translations. The meaning of these biblical phrases as used in this recitation, however, must have been: "O ye dwellers in darkness ... He will bring them out ... So let him then be gracious unto him and say ..." See below.

[77] Sheshna speaks frankly about the ceremony of סמיכה בבעלים to be performed on the animal used for the Kapparot ceremony, as if it were a regular sacrifice, קרבן. The earlier authorities who quote this responsum or mention

A careful scrutiny of the responsum of Sheshna and a comparison of it with the utterances on this subject by other Geonim, as quoted by the medieval authorities, will reveal to us the real significance of this ceremony and its bearing upon and relation to the Tashlik. In the first place, we learn from this responsum that the ceremony had been observed in the very earliest days of the gaonic period, if not already in the later talmudic period. For in Sheshna's time[78] it was already an old and long established

the ceremony likewise unhesitatingly speak of the סמיכה to be performed on the Kapparot animal (see *Pardes*, Asheri, Mordecai and *Ṭur, loc. cit.*). Later rabbinic authorities objected to the laying of the hands upon the head of the rooster on the ground that such a performance would make it appear as if the animal were offered as a regular sacrifice, קרבן, which is forbidden outside of the Temple at Jerusalem. Still the performance of the סמיכה on the rooster persisted. The people who favored it must have reasoned that, since the rooster was a gift to Satan like the שעיר לעזאזל (see below, note 81), the סמיכה should be performed on it as it used to be performed on the latter. They may have wished to unload their sins upon the head of the rooster, as was done upon the head of the goat to Azazel which transfer, it was believed, could be effected by the laying on of the hands (see Seforno to Lev. 1.2 and cf. *JE* XI, *s. v.* "Semikah," p. 183). Hence they thought that such a סמיכה was not exactly the kind performed on a regular sacrifice (see Emden, סדור בית יעקב [Warsaw, 1910], p. 196). Others argued that since the rooster was not the kind of animal that could be offered on the altar, there is no danger that it might be regarded as a regular sacrifice, even if the סמיכה were performed on it (see R. David Halevi in *Ṭure Zahab* to Sh. '*Ar., Oraḥ Ḥayyim*, 605, 3). Hence R. Shneor Zalman of Ladi in his *Shulḥan 'Aruk*, 425, recommends the performance of the סמיכה on the rooster but urges against using pigeons for the ceremony of Kapparot for in that case, since the pigeons were eligible for sacrifices upon the altar, the סמיכה performed on them would make it appear as if they were offered as regular sacrifices: אבל אם אין לו תרנגולים ולוקח שאר בעלי חיים לכפרה לא יקח תורים ובני יונה שהם ראוים למזבח ואם יסמוך ידו עליהם יהא נראה כמקדיש קדשים לשוחטן בחוץ. Cf. Dr. A. Y. Braver: "Miparashat Masaotai b'faras" in *Sinai*, first year, § 14 (2nd Adar, 5698), 437: — On the eve of Rosh Hashanah they made a Kapparot with small or large animals; on the eve of Yom Kippur with fowl. In Ispahan I heard about additional Kapparot on Hoshana Rabbah — apparently it was performed only by especially pious individuals. Cf. above note 32 as to Agnon's reference about additional Kapparot.

[78] Sheshna was Gaon in Sura about 650 (see above, note 72) and he speaks of this ceremony as an old established custom about which he had "a tradition from earlier teachers," מחכמים ראשונים. The origin of the ceremony then must have gone back to talmudic times. See below, note 98.

practice. We further learn that the ceremony had undergone certain modifications in the course of time, for the teachers before the time of Sheshna had already made or suggested some changes in it, such as the substitution of the rooster for the cattle or horned animal. And we also learn from the question addressed to Sheshna, if we read between the lines, as well as from the express utterances by other Geonim, that in spite of the changes and modifications made in the ceremony in the course of time, which no doubt aimed at meeting some objections to it, the objections did not entirely cease and the ceremony was not universally approved of.

Now for a special analysis of the question addressed to Sheshna and his answer. The questioners asked two questions: What is this ceremony for, or what is its meaning? And if its purpose is to offer an animal as a substitute for the person, why then just a rooster and not any other animal? To the first question, which implies a certain objection to the ceremony or at least a doubt as to its propriety, Sheshna does not give any direct answer. He rather seems to admit that it is difficult to answer. For when he says, "This surely is a difficult question," he can only refer to the first question, and not to the second, which he found no difficulty in answering, and for which he had even more than one answer. Evidently, Sheshna hesitates to make a clear statement or to give a definite answer about the meaning and purpose of the ceremony. He contents himself with merely answering their second question, *viz.*, why use a rooster rather than any other animal for this ceremony? He admits indirectly that the purpose of the ceremony is to offer a substitute for the person. His answers to their second question — for there is more than one answer — are very significant and they actually give us more information about the ceremony than the questioners asked for. It is especially significant that he tries to explain the practice of those who performed the ceremony with a ram. As a reason why the ram may be used for this ceremony of offering a substitute, or why the people choose a ram, he gives the fact that at one time, in the case of Isaac, the ram was actually offered and accepted as a substitute for Isaac; hence, it is to be assumed that it can be used also in this ceremony as a substitute for any other person. Now, about all this he was not asked at all. On the contrary, the questioners took it for granted that an animal could be used as a substitute offering. What puzzled them about this ceremony, if its purpose be to offer a substitute for the person, was why a rooster and not any other animal is chosen to be the substitute. This Sheshna has sufficiently explained by first stating that there is no fixed rule to use a rooster since, indeed, other animals are also used, at least by the wealthy in his community, and that the rooster is used by the people at large merely because it is more easily obtainable. He then reverses his position, declaring that according to a tradition there is a good reason — not merely one of economic convenience — why a rooster should be used. This reason, which makes it even preferable to the more expensive horned animal, is that being called by the name *Geber*, which means "man," the rooster is a more suitable substitute for man.[78a] Now, since some of his remarks would seem to be gratuitous, he did not have to drag into the discussion the consideration of the fitness of the ram for use in this ceremony and why it is also acceptable as a substitute for man. He evidently wished to suggest that there is some connection between this ceremony and the sacrifice of Isaac, or that this ceremony has a secondary meaning, *viz.*, to serve the purpose of recalling the sacrifice of Isaac. The same was done by later rabbinic authorities who, as we shall see, sought to establish some connection between the Tashlik ceremony and an incident which happened when Isaac was led by his father to Mount Moriah to be sacrificed there. But there must have been some reason which prompted Sheshna first to suggest this connection between the intended sacrifice of Isaac and the Kapparot ceremony. Again the statement ועיקר מבעלי קרנים, "the main thing is that the substitute be of those animals that have horns," is very suggestive. The detailed description of the manner in which the ceremony is to be performed and the peculiar incantation, consisting of several biblical verses, recommended to be recited during the performing of the

[78a] For another interesting ceremony in which the rooster is used as a substitute for man see Ḥai Gaon's responsum in the collection *Shaare Ẓedeḳ* (Salonika, 1793), p. 76.

ceremony, also indicate that this ceremony had another significance besides merely serving to offer a substitute for the person. Besides, Sheshna is persistently silent as to the real significance of this offering of a substitute. He does not expressly state whether and how it achieves its task; he does not tell us to whom this substitute for the person is offered. Is it an offering to God or a gift to Satan? The expectation of such a clear statement in answer to these questions is especially justified, when one considers that there were some people who not only objected to this ceremony as magic and witchcraft, but even ridiculed it as a foolish superstition. And even some of those Geonim who tolerated or approved of the ceremony were forced to admit that it was a sort of magic, but they claimed that it was a sort of good and effective magic. Thus the responsum supposed to have been sent by the Palestinians to some people in Babylon, in which this ceremony is defended opens with the following significant words: ששחקתם ואמרתם שאנו נחשים ניחוש, "You have laughed (at us) and said that we are practicing magic" (in that we perform these ceremonies). From this we see that there were some people who ridiculed the ceremony and considered it an act of magic. And those who defend the practice say: בכוונה טובה אנו עושים, "We do it with a good intention."[79] In other words, the ceremony may seem to be an act of magic, but we do not do it in that sense; we give to it another good meaning. Likewise Naṭronai[80] calls it נחש לטובה, "magic for a good purpose." Also in the responsum of Geonim, quoted by *Or Zaru'a*, Hilkot Rosh Hashanah, 257, this and other ceremonies related to it are described as acts of magic but at the same time declared to be good, being based mostly on scriptural and agadic passages: וזהו הניחוש טוב הוא ורובו מיסוד המקרא והגדרות. From all these statements in gaonic literature as well as their persistent silence in regard to certain features of the ceremony, we can draw our conclusion as to the real meaning of the ceremony, the reasons for the many changes made in it and the different interpretations given

---

[79] *Ginze Nistarot, loc. cit.*; Mordecai, Yoma 723. The reading ששחקתם is correct against Halberstamm, *Ginze Nistarot, loc. cit.*, note 2. Cf. Lauterbach, "The Ritual for the Kapparot-Ceremony," *loc. cit.*

[80] In חמדה גנוזה, *loc. cit.*, *Shibbole ha-Leḳeṭ, loc. cit.*, also calls it a נחש לטובה.

to it in the course of its development from the very earliest times of the gaonic period till the times of Sheshna and even later.

The real significance of this ceremony was that it represented a revival of the old idea of bribing Satan or the demons by offering to them a sacrifice, as had been done in the times of the Temple.[81] Some people would indeed use a he-goat for this ceremony in exact imitation of the sacrifice to Azazel of old. The he-goat was especially chosen because it was believed somehow to resemble Satan and because its name in Hebrew, *Sa'ir*, was also used as a name for demons[82] (Isa. 34.14 and Lev. 17.7). But there were some objections to this revival of the ceremony of offering a goat to Azazel. The objection was especially to the use of a he-goat, which unmistakably declared the sole purpose of the ceremony to be a sacrifice to Satan. The people, therefore, began to use rams for this ceremony and thus consciously or unconsciously deceived themselves by interpreting its purpose to be also that of serving as a reminder of the sacrifice of Isaac.[83] That the real purpose, however, still was

[81] The similarity in character and purpose between the Kapparot and the goat to Azazel is expressly declared by *Vitry*, p. 373, who says: ויהא כפרתו כמו כפרת שעיר המשתלח, and by Żemaḥ in נגיד ומצוה, p. 74b (see below, note 140) and by של"ה (quoted below, note 127); cf. Lauterbach, *op. cit., loc. cit.*

[82] See Cheyne-Black, *Encyclopedia Biblia* (New York, 1903), IV, 4301, *s. v.* "Satyrs." According to Ber. 62a the demon found in the water closet resembles a goat, see Rashi *ad loc., s. v.* שעיר.

[83] The attempt to achieve both purposes, preventing Satan from accusing, and recalling the merit of עקידת יצחק, simultaneously is already suggested in Jonathan to Lev. 9.3 quoted above, note 64. But while Jonathan suggests that the two purposes were to be achieved by two different animals, the preventing of Satan's accusation by the goat and the recalling of the עקידת יצחק by the lamb, the people in Gaonic times sought to achieve both purposes by offering one animal. By selecting a ram for the Kapparot they suggested to Satan that just as God accepted a ram as a substitute for Isaac, he, Satan, may likewise accept a ram as a substitute for the man. They also indirectly and subtly reminded him that the merit of the עקידת יצחק, just recalled to God, might be in their favor, counteracting his accusations if he should persist in making them. A similar attempt to achieve the two purposes by one ceremony was according to the Talmud made with the blowing of the Shofar. The purpose of the blowing was to confound Satan, לערבב השטן (R. H. 16b). But it was performed with the horn of a ram to recall the merit of Isaac: תקעו לפני בשופר של איל כדי שאזכור לכם עקדת יצחק בן אברהם (*ibid.*, 16a).

to offer Satan a bribe is evident from the fact that the people were particularly anxious that it should be an expensive animal, בהמה שדמיה יקרים, for the more expensive the bribe the more effective it will be. And Sheshna plainly tells us that it need not be especially a ram — which alone could serve as a reminder of the sacrifice of Isaac. Any other expensive animal would do. The main thing, according to Sheshna or according to those that practiced it, was that the animal used in the ceremony should be a horned animal. In other words, it must be an animal that somehow resembles Satan or the demons who are horned[84] and who prefer horned animals as sacrifices or gifts. A calf also was considered a proper gift to Satan.[85] And, as we have seen, in the ceremony prescribed in Deut. 21, it is presupposed that a heifer is acceptable to the demon. Still, the objections were not silenced. People hesitated to declare boldly that this was a sacrifice to Satan though they were willing to consider it a bribe to him. This may seem inconsistent, but such inconsistency is usually found among people who like to retain superstitious customs but are unwilling to openly profess the underlying crude superstition, and hence, try to make the ceremonies appear less objectionable. Now, in using a horned animal for this ceremony, one would have to declare openly that it is intended for Satan. If it is not expressly so declared, it might appear as if it were a sacrifice offered to God outside of the Temple of Jerusalem, a practice which is strictly forbidden by the Halakah. People who would not be willing to appear as if they were violating the law against offering sacrifices outside of Jerusalem, i. e., שחוטי חוץ, as well as those who were not wealthy enough to afford a horned animal, would, therefore, select for the ceremony an animal against which the objection on the ground of the law against שחוטי חוץ could not be raised, which was less expensive than the horned animal and which at the same time could accom-

---

[84] The Devil was commonly believed to be horned. Cf. I. Scheftelowitz, Alt-palästinensischer Bauernglaube (Hannover, 1925), pp. 11 ff.

[85] Some demons resemble a calf. See Tanḥuma נשא, 23. See also Ta'an. 25b, האי רידיא דמי לעגלא, and cf. Kohut, Aruk Completum, s. v. רד 8. And the prince of darkness resembles an ox: שר של חשך דומה לשור (Pesiḵta Rabbati 95a, according to the correct reading of Friedmann).

plish the main purpose of the ceremony just as effectively as the horned animal. They used a rooster, a species of animal which, according to rabbinic law,[86] was not admitted as an offering upon the altar, and hence could in no way be considered as שחוטי חוץ, and yet was believed to be as acceptable to Satan as the horned animals. For the rooster also has some resemblance to Satan or the demons, the latter's feet being of the shape of the feet of a rooster.[87] As we have seen, Sheshna favors the use of a rooster and declares it to be even more effective, although it is not as expensive as a horned animal, and he gives some reason for it. But here again we may question his explanation.

We may safely assume that the reason given by Sheshna why the rooster is preferable for this ceremony was not the real reason why the people chose the rooster. The teachers hesitated to admit openly that the purpose of this ceremony was to offer a sacrifice to Satan and that for this reason the rooster, being acceptable to Satan, is preferable. They, therefore, sought to explain the preference for a rooster for this ceremony as being due, not to its acceptability to Satan, to whom it is offered, but to the fact that its name, *Geber*, is also the designation of "man." By this reinterpretation of the original reason for the choice of a rooster, however, Sheshna merely avoids stating expressly that the sacrifice was intended for Satan. He does not, however, completely conceal this fact. For, even according to this reinterpretation, it is still apparent that the sacrifice was intended as an offering to Satan, whom one might deceive by offering one

---

[86] Some of the Karaites held that the rooster was the תור mentioned in the Torah (Lev. 1.14 *et al.*) which was permitted as a sacrifice upon the altar (see Pinsker, *Likkuṭe Ḳadmoniyot*, נספחים, p. 84; Hadasi, אשכול הכופר, 98 [Goslow, 1836], pp. 41d–42a, and Harkavy, *Studien u. Mittheilungen* VIII [St. Petersburg, 1903], pp. 154–155). On the other hand Anan is said to have declared the תרנגול as unclean and forbidden to be eaten (see Harkavy, *loc. cit.*). Rabbinic law holds the middle position between these two extremes. It considers the תרנגול as clean, טהור וכשר לאכילה, but insists that it was not eligible as a sacrifice upon the altar: ואינו ראוי לגבי מזבח.

[87] See Ber. 6a: ובצפרא חזי כי כרעי דתרנגולא, where it is assumed that the footstep of the demons are like those of a rooster, and Rashi to Giṭ. 68b *s. v.* בדקו בכרעיה says: שרגליו של שד דומות לשל תרנגולים. See also his comment to Giṭ. 69a, *s. v.* אסא כלבא.

kind of a *Geber*, i. e., a rooster, for another kind of a *Geber*, i. e., the human person whom he has selected as one of his victims. Certainly, one could not think of deceiving God by offering Him a rooster as a substitute for a man.

That the sacrifice was intended for Satan, and that this ceremony was a revival of the old practice of sending a goat to Azazel is also evident from the detailed description of it as given by Sheshna. The person who brings the sacrifice, or the one for whom the sacrifice is to be a substitute, does not himself perform the ceremony. An agent, acting as a sort of priest, performs the ceremony. He is called here השליח, which reminds one of the priest who dispatched the sacrifice to Azazel and who is likewise called השליח.[88] He places his hand upon the head of the rooster, reciting a prayer, just as the High Priest placed his hands upon the goat intended for Azazel and made confessions over it (Yoma 6.2). The person for whom the substitute is offered performs the ceremony of *Semikah* as in the case of other sacrifices. But in this case it most likely had also the additional significance of transferring the sins of the person to the rooster,[89] so that Satan when accepting the offering and looking at the one who gave it to him could not find any fault with the latter.

Furthermore, the prayer prescribed to be recited during the performing of the ceremony, although consisting of biblical verses, was originally an incantation intended to placate Satan or hinder him from doing harm. For Satan is not unfamiliar with the Scriptures and occasionally himself cites passages from them. So one may cite passages when pleading with him. It was an incantation of the kind prescribed in Pes. 112a to be recited against an evil spirit, which latter incantation likewise consists of seven verses from Psalms. The contents of the verses quoted by Sheshna, however, allude to Satan and Azazel (or

---

[88] See p. Yoma 6.3 (43c) though his usual designation is המשלח (Lev. 16.26). At any rate he was conceived of as the agent, שליח, of the community to bring the offering to Satan.

[89] Just as Aaron, acting as the representative of all Israel, by his סמיכה on the goat to Azazel placed upon it all the sins of Israel (Lev. 16.21). Cf. above, note 77.

Azael). Probably the incantation originally was intended to be addressed to Satan and his band, the fallen angels, who dwell in darkness, chained in iron fetters because they rebelled against God.[90] And it contained a petition directed to Satan, in which the words of Job 33.24 were used in the sense of "May he be gracious unto him (i. e., the victim) and say: 'Deliver him from going down to the pit, I have found a ransom.'" Sheshna, of course, did not understand the incantation in this sense. He no doubt already understood it as a prayer addressed to God. But there must have been some people who understood it correctly as an incantation to Satan and used it thus. It was for this reason that later Rabbis added to these biblical verses constituting the incantation the words בני אדם,[91] "sons of man," to indicate that it is not an incantation addressed to Satan and his band, those who dwell in darkness, but a prayer to God on behalf of human beings who dwell in darkness or are afflicted with disease.

As to the day on which the ceremony was to be performed, some changes have been made in the course of time due both to certain theological beliefs and to considerations for certain rabbinical laws. In the attitude of the Rabbis towards superstition there has always been the following peculiar feature: They are, as a rule, opposed to superstitious practices and seek to suppress them. In many cases, however, they abandon their efforts at combating the false popular beliefs and tolerate some superstitious practices because they realize the futility of their protests and their inability to make the people give up their cherished superstitions. In such cases they content themselves with merely suppressing the superstitious beliefs underlying the practice by

[90] See Rev. 20.1–3 quoted above; הקדמת ספר הזהר, p. 9b, and Zohar פנחס, p. 465 (above, note 52); also Zohar בראשית, 48 (above, note 55).

[91] These two words appear first in Abudirham, and according to מחזור אהלי יעקב II (Jerusalem, 1910), p. 7a, they were first added by or in Abudirham: וברד"א (=ברבי דוד אבודרהם) נתיספו שתי מלות בני אדם. From there they were copied by later printers and put into the later editions of Asheri's *Halakot*. It may be that originally the incantation contained the address בני אלהים written in abbreviation ב"א which abbreviation was misunderstood to stand for בני אדם Cf. Lauterbach, "The Ritual for the Kapparot-Ceremony," *op. cit.*

giving the practice another explanation, thus making it religiously harmless or even of some possible value. But whenever such a superstitious practice involves the violation of an ethical or ritual law, the Rabbis, as guardians of the law, are unyielding in their fight against it. They will not allow the observance of a superstitious practice which conflicts with the religious law, though they may tolerate the same practice if modified so as not to involve a violation of the ritual or ethical law. This happened also in the case of our ceremony.

As we have seen, the ceremony was an imitation or a revival of the ancient custom of offering a sacrifice to Satan or Azazel. To be consistent, then, the proper time for the performance of this ceremony would have been the Day of Atonement, just as the sacrifice to Azazel was made on that day. But here the Halakah interfered. Outside of the Temple in Jerusalem it was forbidden to do any work on the Day of Atonement. Hence, they could not perform this ceremony on that day, inasmuch as it involved the work of slaughtering, which was not permitted on this holy day. The ceremony, therefore, was shifted to the day preceding the Day of Atonement. Once this change was made and the ceremony was no longer observed on the very Day of Atonement — as was its prototype, the ceremony of the Azazel sacrifice — some people considered it advisable to perform it still earlier, that is, on any one of the penitential days, the days preceding the final Judgment on Yom Kippur. They did so in order to be more sure that it would reach Satan before the Day of Atonement, so that he would refrain from accusing them on that day. Some people even went further. Wishing and hoping to be counted among the righteous for whom a favorable judgment is passed on Rosh Hashanah, they thought it advisable to propitiate Satan on the day preceding Rosh Hashanah, so that on Rosh Hashanah at the opening of the court, Satan, having been made more friendlily disposed to them, would not accuse them, and they would thus be found to be among the righteous who are on the first day of the court session inscribed in the book of life. And, indeed, we are told by the Geonim that some scholars as well as pious laymen, חכמים ובעלי בתים, performed this ceremony twice, once on the day preceding Rosh Hashanah and a second time on the day preceding Yom Kippur.[92] The repetition of the ceremony on the day preceding the Day of Atonement, was, of course, a measure of precaution. They sought to protect themselves so that, if for some reason or other they were not found to be perfectly righteous and the decision of their case had been postponed till Yom Kippur, Satan, reminded by another gift, would be friendly to them and not hinder the favorable verdict being passed upon them on Yom Kippur.

As to the disposal of the sacrifice after it was slaughtered, i. e., whether and how it was offered to the party for whom it was intended, we have no definite record. It is true that Naṭronai tells us that it was customary to give it to the poor.[93] But this could not have been the original and the only way of disposing of the sacrifice. The people must have tried to deliver the sacrifice or part of it to Satan for whom it was intended. For though Satan sometimes is disguised as a poor man, coming around for food on the day preceding the Day of Atonement, as we are told in the legend about Pelemo, yet to give the sacrifice to the poor could not have been considered a safe method of delivering it to Satan. For not every poor man is Satan in disguise. Hence, there must have been other methods of disposal. Asheri[94] tells us that it was the custom to throw the entrails of the sacrificed

---

[92] ויש חכמים ובעלי בתים שעושים כן בערב ר"ה ובערב יום הכפורים, *Ginze Nistarot*, *loc. cit.*; Mordecai, *loc. cit.*, and *Shibbole ha-Leḳeṭ*, *loc. cit.* See also *Maḥzor Soncino* II (Casal Maggiore, 1485–86), p. 10. Cf. also N. Slouschz, *Travels in North Africa* (Philadelphia, 1927), p. 207. Joḥanan Treves in his commentary קמחא דאבישונא to מחזור מנהג רומא II (Bologna, 1540) is not correct when he says: האומנם שהלועזים נוהגים לשחוט הכפרות האלו בערב ר"ה הוא כנגד הפוסקים והמנהגים הקדמונים מהותיקים. The לועזים had good authority for their practice. According to Naṭronai's responsum (Horowitz, *loc. cit.*) there were people who would perform the ceremony twice, once on the first day of Rosh Hashanah and again a second time on the day preceding the Day of Atonement. He says: וביום טוב הראשון של ראש השנה ובערב יום הכפורים שוחטין תרנגולין... וחכמים ובעלי בתים עושין כן. Cf. also ראב"יה to ראש השנה (ed. Aptowitzer, 1935) II, 246.

[93] In חמדה גנוזה, *loc. cit.*, and Horowitz, *loc. cit.* See also Asheri, *loc. cit.*; *Ṭur*, *loc. cit.*; תשב"ץ, *loc. cit.*, and *Kol Bo*, *loc. cit.* This, however, was a later innovation, seeking to combine with the ceremony the feature of charity, which delivers from death.

[94] *Loc. cit.*; also *Ṭur*, *loc. cit.*, and תשב"ץ, 526.

rooster upon the roof. This custom must have been very old, for he connects it with a practice alluded to in the Talmud (Ḥul. 95b), thus assuming that already in talmudic times it was the custom on the day preceding Yom Kippur to throw the entrails of the slaughtered animals upon the roof or into a free and open place from which the birds could pick them up and carry them away.[95] If this custom of so disposing of the entrails of the rooster or of the other animals used for the Kapparot ceremony was observed also in gaonic times, or, as suggested by Asheri, even in talmudic times, its significance becomes clear to us. It was one of the methods whereby part of the sacrifice offered to Satan was made to reach him. The demons were believed to dwell also upon the roof;[96] hence, part of the sacrifice was sent up to their dwelling place. That only part of the sacrifice was thus delivered to them and not the whole of it, need not surprise us. It was in this respect treated like other sacrifices (though not like its prototype, the goat to Azazel) from which

[95] It was not done in order to give food to the birds, showing thereby that we show mercy to other creatures hence we merit that God should show us mercy, as suggested by תשב"ץ, *loc. cit.* For this purpose could have been achieved by merely throwing them away in the courtyard as food to any of the domestic animals. There was a special purpose in throwing them upon the roof, and this special purpose represented a heathen superstition, דרכי האמורי, to which Ramban strongly objected, as suggested by the author of חמדת הימים, see below, note 137.

[96] These עופות to whom the parts of the sacrifice were thrown were the פורחות or פורחות השדה another designation of the demons. Cf. Ramban, commentary to Lev. 14.4 and 53 and Ibn Shuaib, *op. cit.*, p. 46d, also Baḥya to Deut. 21.1. In *Darke Moshe, O. Ḥ.*, 605, 3; also in *Matṭeh Moshe* by R. Moses Premysla No. 836 (Warsaw, 1876), p. 168, it is suggested that the Kapparot are offered to an angel. This angel, as his name חתך, "Cutter," suggests must have belonged to the army of Satan or the angel of death. Cf. Lauterbach, "The Ritual etc.," *loc. cit.* See also below, note 121. There is a custom observed in East European countries of throwing grain to the birds on the Sabbath on which the section בשלח is read שבת שירה. Some authorities object to this custom on the ground that since it is not our duty to feed the birds we are not to do any work connected with feeding them, on the Sabbath. See מגן אברהם to *Sh. 'Ar., Oraḥ Ḥayyim*, 324, 7. This reason for the objection, however, is disputable, see מחצית השקל, *ad loc.* I suspect that in spite of the various fanciful explanations of this ceremony the Rabbis were afraid that the people intend this food not for the ordinary birds, hence their objection.

only parts were offered upon the altar. But it is significant that the parts thrown upon the roof are those parts which are especially acceptable to demons. The liver and the lobe were regarded as the symbols or the representatives of Samael (Satan) and his female consort. Just as the goat and the rooster were considered acceptable offerings to Satan because they resemble him in some features, so also the parts of the animals which somehow resemble him most or are favored by him were considered suitable offerings to him.[97]

It may be stated, therefore, without hesitation that in its original form the ceremony of Kapparot also contained another feature, *viz.*, the mode of dispatching the sacrifice or part of it to Satan's residence. On this the Geonim are purposely silent. They may have sought to suppress it. The custom of throwing the entrails upon the roof may safely be assumed to be a relic or a modification of the earlier practice of sending the sacrifice to the residence of Satan — to the water.

This assumption will be confirmed by an analysis and discussion of the other ceremony reported by the Geonim. The ceremony in question is reported by Rashi in his commentary to Shab. 81b *s. v.*, האי פרפיסא in the name of the Geonim, and is described as follows: "About two or three weeks before Rosh Hashanah they make baskets from the leaves of the palm tree and fill them with earth and manure. For every young boy or girl in the house they make such a basket into which they sow Egyptian beans, or other kinds of beans or peas. They call it *propitio*. On the day before New Year's each person takes his or her basket, turns it around his or her head seven times, saying: 'This is for this (evidently pointing to the basket and to himself or herself), this is to be in exchange for me, this is to be my substitute,' and then he or she throws the basket into the river."

[97] That these parts of the animal either belong to or are especially favored by Satan is suggested by such sayings as כבד ויותרת סמאל ונחש (Zohar, פנחס, p. 224) and לסמאל ונחש כבד ויותרת יצר הרע ובת זוגו (*ibid.*, רעיא מהימנא, p. 464). It should be remembered that these parts of the animal were also offered upon the altar (Lev. 3.2–4 and 10 *et al.*). They must have been considered as food for the gods, hence not despised by the degraded gods, the demons. Perhaps the saying קרבים לאו בשר ואוכליהן לאו בר אינש (Me'il. 20b) echoes the ancient belief that those who eat these parts are not human beings.

The passage in the original reads as follows: האי פרפיסא עציץ נקוב
שזרעו בו, ובתשובות הגאונים מצאתי שעושין חותלות מכפות תמרים וממלאים
אותם עפר וזבל בהמה וכ"ב או ט"ו יום לפני ר"ה עושין כל אחד ואחד לשם כל
קטן וקטנה שבבית וזורעים לתוכן פול המצרי או קיטנית וקורין לו פורפיסא
וצומח ובערב ר"ה נוטל כל אחד שלו ומחזירן סביבות ראשו שבעה פעמים
ואומר זה תחת זה וזה חליפתי וזה תמורתי ומשליכו לנהר.

There can be no doubt that this custom, mentioned by the Geonim, was originally identical with the other custom of Kapparot mentioned by the Geonim, Sheshna and Naṭronai. It is merely a variation due, perhaps, to local conditions or to individual circumstances. Just as in ancient times there were three kinds of sacrifices brought as sin offerings in order to obtain forgiveness, e. g., an offering of a goat or a sheep for the rich; an offering of pigeons or doves for the poor; and a meal-offering for the very poor (Lev. 5.1–13); so also in this revived form of a sacrifice offered to Satan or the demons there were rams for the rich, roosters for the less wealthy, and this vegetable offering for the poor. But all three were of the kind acceptable to and liked by the demons, to whom they were offered, for beans also were considered an especially fit food for the demons. Consideration for the taste of Satan, as well as the desire to avoid a conflict with the rabbinic law determined the choice of the substance of the last two kinds of offerings. We have seen above that some people objected to the offering of a ram or goat because it might be construed as a violation of the law against שחוטי חוץ. Hence, in selecting the fowl for the offering to Satan, they chose the rooster, both because it is acceptable to the demons and at the same time is not of the kind which was offered upon the altar. The same consideration determined the choice of the substance of the third-class offering. They had to offer something which had not been offered upon the altar in the Temple in Jerusalem. Hence, the poor offered beans to the demons instead of the fine flour which had been the poor man's offering in the times of the Temple. But the one important and distinctive feature in this form of the ceremony is the sending of it to the right address. It was thrown into the river, the residence of Satan for whom it was intended.

Another very interesting point in the report of this variation of the ceremony is that its name, indicating its purpose, has been preserved. They called it פרפיסא which is no doubt a corruption of *propitio*. This name clearly indicates the character and the purpose of the ceremony. It plainly tells us that the purpose of the ceremony was to propitiate and pacify some evil power. It is also evident that this evil power was believed to dwell in the sea or river since the offering intended for it was thrown there. And we have found that Satan and the demons were believed to dwell in the water; hence, this offering no doubt must have been a sacrifice to Satan. Now, since this ceremony is cited by the Geonim in explanation of the word פרפיסא of which Abaye speaks and we have no reason to question the correctness of this gaonic interpretation, it must be concluded that already in Abaye's time (about 280–338) this ceremony, as described by the Geonim, was observed. In other words, this form of the ceremony of Kapparot dates back to talmudic times.[98] This makes the connection, suggested by Asheri, between the custom in later times of throwing the entrails of the Kapparot upon the roof and the custom in talmudic times of throwing away the entrails of the animals slaughtered on the day preceding the Day of Atonement very plausible. In other words, already in talmudic times some people may have performed the ceremony of Kapparot with sheep or goats, the entrails of which they

[98] A ceremony resembling the Kapparot ceremony and believed to be effective in getting rid of sickness is mentioned in the Talmud (Shab. 66b). The passage reads, as follows: לישקול כוזא חדתא וליזיל לנהרא ולימא נהרא נהרא ליה אוזפן כוזא דמיא לאורחא דאיקלע לי ולהדר שב זימני על רישיה ולשדין לאחוריה ולימא ליה נהרא נהרא שקול מיא דיהבת לי דאורחא דאיקלע לי ביומיה אתא וביומיה אזל, "The person who is afflicted with the sickness should take a new pitcher and go to the river and, addressing the river — or the spirit of the river — should say: 'River, river, lend me a pitcher of water (otherwise it is dangerous to take from the water of the river belonging to the spirit) for a guest who happened to come to me.' Then he should take the pitcher of water, swing it around his head seven times, and, with his face turned away from the river, throw it back into the river, saying: 'River, river, take back the water which thou hast given me, for the guest who happened to visit me came and went away on the same day.'" Cf. also b. M. Ḳ. 25b. "When Raba came to the Tigris river, etc." Is there an allusion here to a Tashlik ceremony? It is not stated at what occasion it was that Raba went out to the river Tigris. At any rate, we have an instance of a prayer recited at the water.

would throw away, though eating the rest of the animal. In talmudic times they may have hesitated to so openly reintroduce a ceremony of offering to Satan a sacrifice resembling the ceremony of the Azazel goat. But, even in talmudic times, some people performed the ceremony of Kapparot with goats or fowl just as some performed it with baskets of beans. That we do not have a report about it in the talmudic literature need not surprise us. The Rabbis of the Talmud objected to it; hence, they did not care even to mention it. Even the ceremony performed with a basket of beans they do not report directly; they merely allude to it. They would not have mentioned it at all had it not been for the fact that it was necessary to discuss the law as to whether such a basket may be moved on the Sabbath day or not.

Having established the identity of the offering of the beans with the offering of the goat or the rooster, there is no reason to think that different methods of dispatching the offering to the one for whom it was intended were used for the different forms of the offering. In other words, we have no reason to assume that the method used for dispatching the basket of beans to its destination was not also used for dispatching the offering of the goat or the rooster. We may, therefore, safely assume that at least some of the people who performed the ceremony with a goat or a rooster originally threw part of the sacrifice, if not the whole of it, into the river,[99] thus sending it directly to the residence of Satan for whom it was intended. In the course of time, however, this feature of the ceremony was abolished in cases when the offering consisted of an animal. This was due to the strong opposition of the rabbinic law. In talmudic times when the ceremony was not tolerated by the Rabbis the latter did not attempt to change any feature of the ceremony even though it may have been more harmful or more objectionable than the others, since they objected to the ceremony altogether. But when in gaonic times the ceremony

[99] Cf. Heinrich Zimmern, "Das babylonische Neujahrsfest" in *Der Alte Orient* XXV, 3 (Leipzig, 1926), p. 11, for an interesting parallel in connection with the Babylonian New Year ceremonies.

became more prevalent and was even recognized and approved by many of the teachers, the latter considered it their duty at least to remove from it such features as were more objectionable or could be construed as violations of some rabbinic law. We have seen above that the rabbinic law, as laid down in Mishnah and Talmud (Ḥul. 41a,b), prohibits the slaughtering of any animal — even when not intended as a sacrifice — near a river or lake and letting the blood flow into the water, lest it might appear as if the person doing this was offering a sacrifice to the lake or the river. This prohibition was still in force in gaonic times and the same reason for it which was given in the Talmud is also given in gaonic times, *viz.*, that it might seem as if one were offering a sacrifice to the sea, ונראה כמקריב לים. Later teachers sought to abolish this law on the ground that in their time there was no longer the danger that such an act might be construed as a form of idol worship.[100] But in gaonic times this prohibition was still strong, evidently because there were still some people who used this form of worshipping the sea, river or lake, or the spirit dwelling in them. This rabbinic law caused the Geonim to object to the practice of throwing part of the animal used for the ceremony of Kapparot into the sea. They rightly feared that it might be or at least look like an act of worshipping a being or power dwelling in the sea. In other words, it would be evident that the ceremony is a form of offering a sacrifice to Satan who dwells in the sea. For it must be remembered that in the case of the basket ceremony the incantation זה חליפתי וזה תמורתי was made near the water immediately before throwing in the basket, exactly as in the later Tashlik ceremony the prayers are recited near the water immediately before throwing in some crumbs of bread. When performing the ceremony with a goat or a rooster, the incantation was recited immediately before slaughtering the animal. To recite the incantation near the water before throwing in the slaughtered animal would have amounted actually to slaughtering it and letting its blood flow into the water — exactly what the rabbinic law prohibited. There was, however, no law

---

[100] Thus *Or Zaru'a* I, 385 says: שאין איסור לשחוט לתוך ימים כי זה היה רק לפנים שהיה מנהג עבודה זרה.

prohibiting the throwing into the water of bread or vegetables which were not used as offerings upon the altar. On the contrary, as we have seen from the story in Midrash Koh. r. cited above, such a practice was tolerated and even favorably commented upon. The original feature in the ceremony of offering a sacrifice to Azazel-Satan, *viz.*, the dispatching of it to his residence in the water, could therefore well be preserved — and be tolerated by the Rabbis — in connection with that form of the ceremony in which vegetables were used instead of animals. But when an animal was used in performing the ceremony the Rabbis insisted that it should not be dispatched to the sea or river, since they considered such an act to be in violation of a rabbinic law. The idea that the purpose of the ceremony was to offer a sacrifice to Satan, though never expressly stated and even glossed over by the teachers, was, however, well-known and cherished by the people. The interpretation given by the teachers that the ceremony was a sort of offering of a substitute did not actually combat this idea; it rather helped to foster it in the popular mind. For since the teachers carefully avoided mentioning to whom this substitute was offered, there was no doubt in the popular mind that it was offered to Satan, who might be deceived into accepting the rooster called *Geber* for the man called *Geber*. The people, therefore, preferred performing the ceremony with a rooster, admittedly a proper substitute for man, to performing it with a basket of beans, even though in the latter case they could dispatch the offering to the residence of Satan by throwing it into the water. They were, however, reluctant to give up entirely the idea of sending the sacrifice to the residence of Satan. For then the offering is not actually brought to him. And if the offering does not reach him, it cannot accomplish its purpose. They were very anxious to have the sacrifice reach Satan. They would have liked to send it to the depths of the sea, but to this the rabbinic law strongly objected. The people, therefore, had to content themselves with sending part of the sacrifice to the roof, another dwelling place of Satan and the demons. Against this there was no rabbinic prohibition. Thus, the ceremony of Kapparot performed with a rooster became more and more prevalent while the other forms of the ceremony requiring the use of vegetables which could be cast into the water and thus dispatched to the main residence of Satan apparently fell into disuse.

It would, however, be a mistake to assume that this latter form of the ceremony entirely ceased to be observed among the Jews. It is true that for about two or three centuries we do not hear anything about it. The rabbinic authorities mention only the one form of the ceremony, i. e., the Kapparot performed with a rooster, some objecting to it and others approving of it and recommending it. But to the ceremony of throwing baskets of beans into the water no explicit reference is, to my knowledge, to be found in the rabbinic literature of the 12th, 13th and 14th centuries. However, all that we can rightly conclude from the persistent silence about this ceremony on the part of the rabbinical authorities is that the official authorities in Judaism did not indorse it, and hence did not care even to mention it. But the ceremony continued to be observed by the people, perhaps in a modified form, even though the Rabbis objected to it. For, when it appears again in the beginning of the 15th century and finds recognition among the Rabbis, it appears not as a recent innovation but as an older well established practice.

Furthermore, there are some positive indications pointing to the continuous observance of this ceremony by the people, if not by the Rabbis. The ceremony could not have been entirely neglected or forgotten even during these centuries in which the rabbinical authorities persistently avoided mentioning it. For we find that the ideas underlying it were current among the people and even found expression in the literature of these centuries. We have seen above that the idea that Satan and the fallen angels dwell in the depths of the sea is found in the Zohar, which made its appearance in the thirteenth century. The Zohar plainly identifies Satan-Azazel with the depths of the sea. It mentions the ceremony, which is described in Pirḳe deR. Eliezer, how Satan is bribed by receiving the gifts offered to him by Israel and how with their gifts he also takes away from them their sins. But the Zohar significantly adds that this process or this ceremony is expressed or indicated in the scriptural words, "And thou wilt cast their sins into the depths of the sea" (Micah 7.19), and even plays upon the words ותשליך במצולות ים which gave our ceremony its peculiar name Tashlik. Of course, all these ideas were old, but the very fact that they were again circulated by the Zohar shows that they were not forgotten during the 13th century. And if the ideas underlying the ceremony were not forgotten, the ceremony itself could not have been forgotten or neglected. From the Zohar we can conclude that a ceremony, such as our Tashlik, or like the one performed with the basket of beans in gaonic times, was known and performed, by some people at least, during the 12th and 13th centuries. For, if the sins are removed from Israel by being placed upon the gift sent to Satan, and this act is also described as throwing all the sins into the depths of the sea, then the gift sent to Satan upon which the sins were heaped up, as it were, must have been sent to the depths of the sea. In other words, the gifts intended for Satan were thrown into the water.

The silence of the rabbinical authorities about such a ceremony can, therefore, only mean that they objected to it and would not indorse it. The Rabbis could not entirely forget that these ceremonies were based upon superstitious beliefs not quite compatible with Jewish religious teachings. Of course, not all the Rabbis equally recognized the incongruity of these practices with Jewish doctrines. In Spain, where the Rabbis were more rationalistic and philosophical, where even the Ḳabbalah was more of a speculative-theoretic order, the ceremony could not find popularity. There the teachers could more readily recognize the superstitions underlying these ceremonies and felt more keenly their incompatibility with Jewish religious doctrines. Even in the form of the Kapparot the ceremony was strongly opposed by Spanish authorities.[101] Among the German Jews, however, who were less inclined to philosophical thinking, and who cultivated rather the practical Ḳabbalah, these ceremonies could more readily find acceptance. At least the objections to them, even on the part of the rabbinic authorities, were not so strong. Among German mystics, close followers of gaonic mysticism, these ceremonies of gaonic times could have been

[101] Ramban and Salomon b. Abraham Adret; see *Bet Joseph* to *O. Ḥ.* 605.

preserved, even if some of the rabbinical authorities had objected to them. To the Kapparot ceremony, performed with a rooster, there was, as far as we know, no objection whatever on the part of the German Rabbis. To the other form of the ceremony, however, consisting of throwing food into the water while reciting an incantation or prayer, there may have been some objections.[102] But these were not strong enough to suppress the ceremony altogether. All that they could and did accomplish, was to effect slight changes or modifications in the ceremony.

Indeed, it would seem that during the few centuries of silence, when we do not hear any explicit report about it, the ceremony went through a process of development and received new interpretations so as to meet the objections raised against it by the Rabbis. The observance of the ceremony, though in a modified form, was even extended to other festivals besides those of the annual period of Judgment.[103] The people continued its observance and no doubt gave some excuses for doing so when the Rabbis tried to hinder them. Then again, we find that the ancient belief that a spot near water is the most suitable place for prayer was revived.[104] And some people, justifying the practice of this ceremony, could have interpreted it as merely serving the purpose of going out to a pure place near water in order to pray there.[105]

[102] The false accusation of poisoning the wells raised against the Jews in the 14th century may have caused the Rabbis to be over-careful and to object to the one feature of the ceremony, *viz.*, the throwing of food into the water — a feature to which R. Shalom of Vienna and Maharil still objected, though they gave other reasons for their objections, see below, note 108. Some of the Rabbis may have objected to the ceremony on the ground of חוקת הגוי, since the non-Jews observed a similar ceremony; against Kirchheim who assumes that the Jewish ceremony was borrowed from the non-Jews, see below, note 169.

[103] I advisedly say "the period of Judgment" for in the course of time it was observed on different dates within that period. See below, note 144.

[104] Thus Jacob Asheri in בעל הטורים to Gen. 16.7 says: שטוב הוא להתפלל על המים כדכתיב מקול מחצצים בין משאבים שם יתנו צדקות ד' וכן התפלה נמשלה למים דכתיב שפכי כמים לבך.

[105] A. M. Luncz in his *Jerusalem* XI–XII (Jerusalem, 1916), p. 5 says that during the 12th and 13th centuries it was the custom among the inhabitants of the towns near the Jordan to go out to the Jordan and recite there

The following custom observed by German Jews during the 12th and 13th centuries on the Shabuot festival clearly points to the continuation of our ceremony and its extention to other festivals besides Rosh Hashanah. It was customary in those days for boys to enter the religious school on the Shabuot festival. The children who had passed their fifth birthday and reached the school age of those times were brought to the Synagogue on Shabuot and with elaborate ceremonies initiated into their school work and given their first lesson. After these ceremonies were over and the boys had received their first lesson, they would be led to the banks of the river in order that, since the Torah is compared to water and since it is said, "Let thy springs be dispersed abroad," the boys in this manner might acquire a broad mind,[106] ולאחר הלימוד מביאים הנער על שפת הנהר. על שם שהתורה נמשלה למים ועל שם יפוצו מעינותיך חוצה ושיהא לנער רחב לב. This ceremony was more than a mere symbolic act, suggesting that from now on the child was to go to school to study the Torah which is comparable to water, and that the wells of his wisdom might overflow and be dispersed abroad. For the wish that the boy would acquire a broad understanding could not have been realized by the mere going out to the water. It is evident that this account in the *Sefer Asufot* does not give us a full report of this ceremony of going out to the water. The people did more than merely lead the boys to the banks of the river. They most likely went to the river and threw in some food, probably remains of the honey cakes and the boiled eggs used in the initiation ceremony, as gifts to the spirits in order to make them friendly to the child and prevent them from harming him in his school career. They also must have recited a prayer near the water for the success of the child, addressed to God or Purah, the spirit who protects people from forgetfulness, פורה שר של שכחה. In other words, the same ceremony which they

---

hymns and prayers. As his reference he gives Parḥi in כפתור ופרח. But Parḥi merely says: כפתור ופרח) ואנחנו הורגלנו לומר בראותנו הירדן כך, Jerusalem, 1897, Ch. VII, p. 121). But this does not necessarily mean that it was an established custom to go out to the Jordan and recite prayers there.

[106] *Sefer Asufot* MS. quoted by M. Gaster in *Report of the Judith Montefiore College Ramsgate* (London, 1893), p. 60.

used on Rosh Hashanah for the purpose of obtaining a favorable verdict was performed on Shabuot for the purpose of insuring a successful career for the child.

We also learn from another source that a ceremony similar to our Tashlik was performed by the people in the 14th century, on all holidays and not only on Rosh Hashanah. R. Jacob Moelln (Maharil, 1365–1427) reports[107] that his teacher R. Shalom of Vienna objected strongly to those people who went out on holidays to walk on the banks of rivers or lakes to observe the fish swimming, and who carried with them food to throw to the fishes and watched them gather around the food and swallow it. He says: אמר מהר"ש הני בני אדם ההולכים בי"ט לטייל אצל נהרות ויאורים לראות את הדגים ששטין שם ונושאים עמהן אוכל להשליך אל הדגים לראותם כשנתאספו לבלוע המאכל תרתי רעות הן עושין חדא מוציאין חוץ לעירוב ועוד דגם אם נזדמן להם גוי אצל המים אסור לישראל לקחת ממנו אוכל ולהשליך אל הדגים דמאחר דמחוסרין צידה הוי מוקצה ולא מתקרי לכם. וכללא הוא כל שנאסר במגע משום מוקצה אסור ליתן לו מזון. There can be no doubt that these people went out to the lakes or rivers, not merely for a walk but for a definite purpose. This purpose was to bring offerings of food to the spirits dwelling in the water. For this reason they would watch to see the fish swallow the food, for then they could believe that the offerings reached their destination, since they could assume that the fish would bring them to the spirits dwelling in the depths of the sea. It was because the Rabbis objected to such a ceremony of offering gifts to the spirits that the people pretended merely to take a walk along the banks of the river. They would also privately arrange with some non-Jew to be there on the spot with the food necessary for the ceremony. The people would thus avoid openly carrying the food from their homes to the river. They could then pretend that they merely took a walk and happened to find a Gentile with food near the river; so they took it from him and threw it to the fish to have some fun watching them swallow the food. R. Shalom, however, objects even to this disguised form of the ceremony on the ground that, as he claims, it involves the violation of two rabbinic laws. But his objections were of

[107] *Maharil*, Hilkot Yomṭob (Lemberg, 1860), p. 33a.

no avail. The people simply persisted in performing this ceremony, and soon gave up even the pretense of merely taking a walk and accidentally throwing food to the fishes. They openly performed this ceremony of going out to the river to recite prayers and to throw food as a gift to some being dwelling in the water. After some slight modification in its features whereby the very objectionable characteristics were removed and after some reinterpretation of its significance, the ceremony is accepted even by the rabbinic authorities, though they record it merely as a popular custom and not as a prescribed rite. And the pupil of R. Shalom of Vienna, Jacob Moelln, himself performed the ceremony to which his teacher so strongly objected. And beginning with the 15th century, we find this ceremony mentioned by rabbinic authorities who discuss its features and seek to explain its significance.

Let us now consider the description of this ceremony as it was recognized and adopted by the authorities of the 15th century, and trace its development in the subsequent centuries. We shall find that it experiences many reinterpretations. Some of its features are modified while others are left unchanged, with the result that the ceremony as a whole contains contradictory elements. In the first place, some of the very ancient ideas, e. g., the offering of prayer to God at a pure place near water, are again revived and are predominant in the ceremony. The ceremony thus becomes a religious ritual. It is now one of the forms of a religious service to God. Likewise the idea of pacifying Satan by gifts still persists, though this feature of the ceremony is strongly objected to by the Rabbis, ostensibly on the ground that it would involve a violation of a ritual law. In reality, however, the authorities, objected because, consciously or unconsciously, they felt that any appeal to Satan is a form of worship forbidden to the Jew who must worship God alone. To meet these rabbinical objections the very characteristic feature of the ceremony, i. e., the throwing of food into water, is so reinterpreted that it no longer appears as offering a gift to Satan. Even the very act of going out to the water is given an interpretation calculated to suppress the idea that they were going to the residence of Satan. Yet reference to Satan as having some connection with the ceremony is retained. Many other reinterpretations are attempted in order to make the ceremony less objectionable and more acceptable as a religious rite. All this, however, merely shows that the religious conscience of the Rabbis could not so easily be persuaded to overlook the heathenish ideas and superstitious beliefs underlying this ceremony. After many centuries of general observance the religious genius of R. Elijah Gaon of Wilna still feels that it is incompatible with the Jewish religion, and, as we shall see, the liberal teachers of Judaism finally drop it altogether. But we are running too far ahead.

Let us go back to the first appearance of this ceremony in its modified form. It appears as popular a custom among German Jews, and the first one to mention it and to comment upon it is Jacob Moelln, the pupil of Shalom of Vienna, mentioned above. In the *Sefer Maharil*, Hilkot Rosh Hashanah (Lemberg, 1860), pp. 54–55, the following comment is found: אמר מהר"י סג"ל מה שנוהגין לילך בראש השנה אחר הסעודה אצל ימים ונהרות להשליך במצולות ים כל חטאתינו משום דאיתא במדרש זכר לעקידה שעבר אברהם אבינו בנהר עד צואר ואמר הושיעה ה' כי באו מים עד נפש והוא השטן שנעשה כמו נהר להעכיב אותו מן העקידה. ומהר"י סג"ל נהג גם כן להלוך אצל הנהרות ואמר כשהולכין אל הנהרות ביום טוב אל יוליכו עמהם שום מזון כדי לזרוק אל הדגים שבנהרות להראות להם לשמוח בהן דאית ביה חילול יום טוב גם אם יזדמן לו כותי אצל הנהר אל יקח ממנו לחם להשליך אל הדגים משום דמוקצים הם לישראל משום דמחוסרין צידה ואין מאכילין ביום טוב אלא לדבר הראוי לו. אם כן הנושא מזון עמו תרתי ריעותא עבדי דנושא חוץ לעירוב ומאכיל את המוקצה וכל שכן כשחל ראש השנה בשבת דאין לעשות. It is evident from this statement that the custom had been observed long before the time of Maharil, for he merely comments upon it and tries to suggest some new ideas about its significance. But he seems to be particularly anxious to modify it, or to prohibit certain features of the ceremony to which he objects, apparently[108] on the

---

[108] I say "apparently" for in reality the objections on the ground of an involved violation of the law are not valid. It is not correct to consider carrying food outside of the city to feed the fish a חלול יום טוב. Neither one of the two alleged evils תרתי לריעותא applies in this case. As regards the first one, *viz.*, דנושא חוץ לעירוב, it does not apply to a holiday. The laws prohibiting the carrying out of things לרשות הרבים apply only to the Sabbath but not to holidays

ground that they involve a violation of a ritual law. His description of the ceremony and his emphatic objections to certain features of it clearly show that this ceremony is identical with the custom which we have found to be observed in the gaonic times, though somewhat modified. Thus Maharil takes it for granted that the purpose of the ceremony was to get rid of one's sins. But he does not explain how this was to be accomplished. However, if we remember how according to Pirke deR. Eliezer, Midrash Abkir and Zohar, quoted above, the sins were placed upon the gift or the lamb offered to Satan and thus they were removed from Israel and transferred to him, we may safely conclude that the throwing away of the sins, to which Maharil refers, was also done by throwing into the water some gift which took the sins with it. The gift consisted of food which, Maharil tells us, the people used to take along with then when going to the river and which they threw to the fish. Maharil does not say that Satan was believed to be the recipient of the gifts or the food thrown to the fish. But from the strong objections which he expresses to this feature of throwing food into the river, one may conclude that he knew well for whom this food was intended by the people. The idea that Satan is associated with the river is explicitly stated by Maharil, though he somewhat modifies it. He does not countenance the popular belief that Satan dwells in the depths of the seas and that the fish who swallow the food thrown in by the people, carry it to him. Satan, according to Maharil, is brought in connection with this ceremony merely because at one time in the past Satan had assumed the form of a river. Maharil refers to a Midrash where the following legend is related: "When Abraham was on his way to Mount Moriah to sacrifice his son, Isaac, Satan, anxious to prevent him from doing the will of God, sought to hinder his progress.

---

for אין איסור הוצאה ליום טוב (see Bezah 12a and *Sh. 'Ar., Orah Hayyim*, 495, 1). The second evil likewise does not apply in this case. The objection to giving food to fish that are מוקצה is only because one might seek to catch them. But where there is no danger that one might seek to catch them, especially when throwing food to them from a distance, ברחוק מהם, as in this case when the food is thrown into the river there can be no objection (see the commentary מגן אברהם to *Sh. 'Ar., Orah Hayyim*, 497, 2).

He changed himself to a river and tried to drown Abraham, who however would not be deterred by the water, In answer to Abraham's prayer God rebuked the river-Satan, and it immediately dried up and disappeared. Abraham and Isaac then proceeded on their way to obey the command of God."[109] Like the Geonim who, as we have seen above, sought to interpret the Kapparot ceremony as being a reminder of the intended sacrifice of Isaac, Maharil would have the Tashlik ceremony also serve the purpose of a reminder of the sacrifice of Isaac. Maharil speaks rather vaguely about the relation of this ceremony of going out to the water to the reminiscence of the 'Aḳedah. We are not told for whom this reminder was intended. Was it to remind God how Abraham risked his life in wading through the water when going to do his will — an act which should earn consideration for his descendants — or was it to suggest to us, while praying near water, that on this day we have to face the accusations of Satan who resembles or is identical with a river of water, and that like our father Abraham, who was once in a similar position, we should trust in God and pray to him to deliver us from "the waters that are come in even unto the soul," i. e., save us from Satan? But no matter whom this reminder is for, this much is certain, that Maharil wishes to understand the ceremony as a reminder of the intended sacrifice of Isaac of or some event that happened to Abraham and Isaac at the occasion when the latter was to be sacrificed. Hence, he objects strongly to those features of the ceremony which could in no way be connected with the sacrifice of Isaac, and which reveal the real character of the ceremony as it was understood by the people. That in the popular mind the ceremony had a meaning different from the one which Maharil would have liked to give to it is quite evident. For Maharil expressly tells us that the purpose of the ceremony was to throw away the sins, that is, that the people believed that by this ceremony they could relieve themselves of their sins. Maharil further tells us that the ceremony was observed right after the festal meal (אחר

---

[109] This Midrash is quoted in Yalḳuṭ Shimeo'ni to Gen. § 99. Cf. also Tanḥuma Buber, וירא, p. 114.

הסעודה), which is quite significant. For it no doubt means that when the people had finished eating, they took some food, left over from their meal, and went to the river to throw it into the water. Maharil objects to this very strongly. But from the very arguments that he raises against this feature, we can learn how the original custom of throwing baskets of beans, mentioned by the Geonim, developed into that feature of the Tashlik ceremony which consists of throwing crumbs of bread into the water while reciting the prayer. We see here again the strong influence of rabbinic law upon popular superstitious customs. The power of the rabbinic law was great and could not be trifled with. Any custom or ceremony which would conflict with some rabbinic law had to be modified so as to avoid the violation of the law. We have suggested above that the ceremony of throwing the basket into the sea was performed on the day preceding Rosh Hashanah, and not on Rosh Hashanah itself, because on the holiday itself the performance would have involved a violation of a rabbinic law. These baskets, or pots of beans, not intended for human food, were considered as מוקצה, *mukzeh*, i. e., forbidden for use, and could not be moved or carried about on a holiday. Even when the people pretended that they threw these beans into the river merely as food for the fish, they were not permitted to carry them out to the river on a holiday. For, not being food for human beings and not having been prepared as such, these beans, especially since they were still attached to the earth in which they grew, were still considered as *mukzeh* and could not be carried about on a holiday. But the people were very anxious to perform the ceremony on the New Year's day, the very day when judgment begins, when the good will of Satan is of great value. Hence, in order to avoid the violation of a law, they modified the ceremony somewhat. Not being allowed by the law, the use of beans in this ceremony was abandoned by the people, although they knew that beans were a favorite dish of the demons and a most acceptable gift to Satan. They persuaded themselves into believing that other food might do just as well, and they decided to offer him part of their own festal meal. Such food could by no means be regarded as *mukzeh*, hence no objection could be raised to its being moved or carried about on a holiday on the ground of any rabbinic law. At certain times, however, when even food prepared for human beings could not be carried out of the house, as when New Year's day happened to fall on a Sabbath, they must have made arrangements with non-Jews to have food or bread ready at a place near the river, so that they would not have to carry it out of their house through the streets.[110] That such arrangements were occasionally made with non-Jews is clearly indicated by Maharil. For when, like his teacher R. Shalom, he speaks against taking the bread from a non-Jew who, "accidentally," may happen to be near the water, we may safely conclude that this Gentile was there by pre-arrangement and not "accidentally."

Had the objections to this feature been merely on the ground of the rabbinic law against carrying things out of the house on Sabbath, or moving things that are *mukzeh* on a holiday, these modifications would have satisfied the objectors. In truth, however, the objections had a much deeper and more valid reason. The Rabbis felt that it was a sort of offering to the demon, an act which is like idolatry.[111] Even the explanation that it was meant as food for the fish or "to show them food, to rejoice with them" could not appease the qualms of the religious conscience of the Rabbis. They could not entirely ignore the original meaning of the ceremony — that it meant offering a gift to Satan. This is the real reason for Maharil's objection. That he argues merely on the ground of the requirements of the ritual law, *viz.*, that food for fish in the river or brook was not to be carried on a holiday, need not surprise us. He may have been averse to the explicit mentioning of the real reason for his objections, which would have made the entire ceremony of Tashlik objectionable. It is possible that he may have resented it merely

---

[110] As to throwing it into the water there could have been no objection since it is a כרמלית ומקום פטור. Cf. Jacob Reischer in his Responsa שבות יעקב II (Metz, 1727), *Oraḥ Ḥayyim*, No. 50.

[111] Even to leaving remains of the meal on the table the Rabbis objected because they knew that the people who did it intended it as an offering to the demons. See Sanh. 92a, the saying of R. Eleazar and cf. Rashi *ad loc.* See also *Sh. 'Ar., Yore De'ah* 178, 3 and 179, 17. See above note 45, the reference to Frazer.

because, subconsciously, so to speak, he felt that it was an offering to Satan, but he was not clear and definite about it himself. So he could not expressly say to the people, "You cannot offer a gift to Satan" when they maintained, truthfully or not, that they merely gave food to the fish. But he suspected them, hence his objections. At any rate, we see that he strongly objects to the feature of the throwing of food into the sea even though allegedly it was meant as food for the fish. To the ceremony of going to the water and in some mystic way ridding oneself of one's sins, he does not object. In fact he himself observes it. Evidently this custom was too well entrenched in the popular practice and too well established to be abolished on the ground of the objections by the Rabbis to some of its details. It was the force of popular usage that helped to preserve this ceremony. It is significant that the rabbinical authorities, even when recognizing it, speak of it merely as a custom of the people. They say: "the people are accustomed," ונוהגין or ורגילין, etc. It was a custom that persisted among the masses, but was more or less resented by the authorities. Even when all possible violations of a ritual law connected with it were avoided, rabbinic Judaism was not pleased with this ceremony, as though feeling instinctively that the ideas underlying it were heathen and superstitious. But popular custom, or *minhag*, plays a prominent part in Jewish religious life. The fact that this custom, in one form or another, was so long observed by the people made it a "Jewish practice" (מנהגן של ישראל), or a "custom of the fathers" (מנהג אבותינו), which carries with it the weight of religious authority in Judaism.[112] This consideration forced the rabbinic authorities to recognize it. But this recognition was not granted all at one time. It was slowly and gradually wrung from the Rabbis. Neither was this full recognition accorded to all the features of the ceremony alike. This recognition was given grudgingly and piecemeal. At one time some of the features which were modified in order to meet the objections of the religious consciousness of the Rabbis were permitted, while the other features were still

---

[112] See *Tosafot*, Men. 20b s. v. נפסל and Isserles in *Sh. 'Ar., Yore De'ah*, 242, 14.

rejected. But later the latter likewise were modified or reinterpreted and accepted. We have just seen that Maharil accepted the ceremony, but objected to the feature of throwing food into the river. But this was an untenable position, and the same force of the popular custom which compelled the authorities to accept the ceremony as such, persisted, and gradually succeeded in forcing the authorities to accept even the objectionable features after they too had been slightly modified or reinterpreted. We shall indeed find that after Maharil the ceremony became generally accepted, and practically all its features were tolerated by the authorities. They merely sought either to find in the ceremony and in each of its features new meanings which would make it expressive of such ideas as would meet with their approval, or at least to give the objectionable features a harmless meaning. In other words, they subjected the ceremony to a process of reinterpretation and to slight modifications. This process proceeded along two distinct lines, the rationalistic-rabbinic and the mystic-rabbinic. The rabbinic authorities, who were prompted by the principle מנהג של ישראל תורה היא or מנהג אבותינו תורה היא to accept this custom, tried to rationalize it and to interpret it so as to make it a Jewish rite of some religious significance. They accordingly ignored all the heathen ideas connected with its origin; indeed, some of them may no longer have had full knowledge of these heathen ideas. They also sought to suppress the crude superstitions which in the popular mind were associated with the ceremony. Whenever possible, they gave a symbolic meaning to the objectionable features and interpreted them in such a manner as to make them compatible with their theological views. When this was impossible they utterly ignored the objectionable features and did not mention them at all, not even to protest against the popular practice that still continued to retain these features in the ceremony.

Thus R. Isaac Tyrnau, a younger contemporary of Maharil, in his *Sefer ha-Minhagim* (Warsaw, 1909), p. 23a, merely records the ceremony as a popular custom, without giving it any interpretation and without mentioning its objectionable features. He merely says, "The people are accustomed to go to the river and to say, 'He will again have compassion upon us, etc.,' (Micah

7.19) and they look at the living fish," ונוהגין לילך אל הנהר ולומר ישוב ירחמנו וגו' ורואין דגים חיים. He does not say that the people went to the river in order to cast away their sins, though he, no doubt, knew that this was the purpose of the ceremony according to the popular belief. Evidently he is unable or unwilling to explain how this purpose was achieved, hence he refrains from mentioning it. He likewise fails to mention that the people took along food to throw into the water, though there can be no doubt that the people of his time did it, just as it was done in the days of Maharil, and as it continued to be done by the people in later times. It would seem that the Rabbis abandoned their efforts to combat this feature of the popular practice, realizing the futility of such efforts. Hence, Tyrnau does not even record a protest against it. Possibly he avoids even mentioning it in the hope that if he records the ceremony without it the people might be led to observe the ceremony without this objectionable feature. It would further seem that the Rabbis themselves — or at least some of them — gradually came to deceive themselves into believing that the throwing of the food into the water was not intended as a gift to Satan to whom the fish would carry it, but merely as a means of attracting the fish to the shore, so that the people could see them. Of course, if thus understood, there is no harm in the feature of throwing food into the water. And by emphasizing this meaning of the feature, the Rabbis felt justified in not protesting against it. This might explain why Tyrnau mentions only the feature of "looking at the living fish." As a matter of fact the "looking at the living fish" was merely one part of the feature of throwing food into the water, as will be shown immediately. This is especially evident from the description of the ceremony given by John Pfefferkorn (1469–1521) in his *Der Juden Beicht* (Cologne, 1508), p. 5.[113] According to Pfefferkorn, the people would come near the water, shake their garments, (in which they carried the food) and, throwing the food into the water, they would cry out to the fish, "We throw our sins to you." In a woodcut reproduced in Pfefferkorn's work, there is a representation of the ceremony in

---

[113] The same description of the ceremony is also given by Anthonius Margaritha in his *Der gantz jüdische Glaub* (Augsburg, 1530), p. 17a,b.

which the people are shown holding up the skirts of their garments, which served as a sort of basket for the food, and emptying them into the water. The fish are shown as having come up near the shore and poking their heads through the surface of the water in their eagerness to receive the food.

We have no reason to doubt the accuracy of this representation of the ceremony. The people did throw their food and with it meant to throw their sins to the fish and would call to the fish to take the sins away with them. They thus merely repeated the practice of the people in Temple times who while pulling the hair of the goat to be sent to Azazel, would call to it, "Take (our sins) and go, take (our sins) and go" (Yoma 6, 4). But of course Tyrnau, like the other rabbinic authorities who followed him, did not care to mention these details of the ceremony.

The next rabbinic authority to discuss our ceremony is R. Moses Isserles (1520–1572) who in his annotation to the *Sh. 'Ar., Oraḥ Ḥayyim* 593, as well as in his *Darke Moshe* to *Ṭur, O. Ḥ.* 593, mentions the custom, with the interpretation given to it by Maharil, *viz.*, that it was to serve as a reminder of the sacrifice of Isaac. Isserles, like Tyrnau, also omits mentioning the fact that the people would throw food into the water, though this was the practice of the people in his time, as can be seen on the woodcut referred to above, which is also reproduced in *Der Gantz Jüdisch Glaub* by Antonius Margarita, a contemporary of Isserles. Isserles also says, quoting Tyrnau's *Minhagim*, that one of the features of the ceremony was to look at the living fish, and he seeks to explain the purpose or significance of this feature. He says, "Possibly it is to serve as a good omen, suggesting that no evil eye should hurt us and that we should increase and multiply like fish."[114] He does not explain how the mere looking at the fish can have the effect of warding off the danger of the evil eye. It may be that he meant that this was to be obtained by a prayer to God to make us like fish over whom the evil eye was supposed to have no power. But it is more likely

[114] ואיפשר שהוא לסימן שלא תשלוט בנו עין הרע ונפרה ונרבה כדגים, *Darke Moshe, loc. cit.* Fish were believed not to be subject to the evil eye. See Soṭah 30b: כדגים שלא שלטא בהוא עינא בישא. Cf. also M. Auerbach in Rahmer's *Literaturblatt* X (1881), No. 40–41, p. 61.

that the warding off of the harm of the evil eye was to be achieved by reciting an incantation while throwing the food into the water, the very feature which Isserles refuses to mention. For, according to a popular belief still prevalent among east-European Jews, the effects of the evil eye are removed by throwing crumbs of bread into a glass of water and reciting an incantation. Be this as it may, we see that Isserles suppresses the objectionable features, and mentions only the feature of looking at the fish, which is rather harmless and which he seeks to explain as suggesting a good omen. The casting of bread into the river he does not mention. Evidently Isaac Tyrnau as well as Isserles shared Maharil's objection to this feature; hence, they do not mention it.

But Isserles does not seem to have been completely satisfied with the meaning of the ceremony as interpreted by Maharil and Tyrnau, so he tries to give it another, more rationalistic, interpretation. In his *Torat ha-ʻolah* he says in essence, as follows: When one goes to the river one observes the mighty wonders of the Creator who has made the sand as a boundary to the sea, that its waters should go so far and no further. One then reflects on the great mystery of the depths of the seas, and realizes that the world was created by God *ex nihilo*. Thus one recognizes God, and becomes confirmed in the belief in His existence, and accordingly repents of all his sins and obtains forgiveness for them. In this manner his sins are thrown into the depths of the sea.[115] This ḳabbalistic philosophic interpretation does credit to Isserles as seeking to free Judaism from super-

---

[115] The passage in the original reads, as follows: ומנהג של ישראל תורה היא במה שהולכים על מים ואומרים תשליך במצולות הים כל חטאתינו להיות כי מן מצולות יש ניכר ענין בריאת העולם כי מצולת ים הוא התהום והוא המקום היותר עמוק בים והנה לפי הטבע של היסודות שהמים יכסו הארץ והארץ הוא המרכז והוא מקום הנמוך בכל העולם. והנה הארץ לצורך בני אדם ולדרים עליה אינו בלא כוונת מכוון והוא אשר חדש העולם כרצונו לתכלית ישוב הארץ ולכן אנו הולכים על המים לראות אשר שם חול גבול לים ואמר פה תבוא ולא תוסיף וכשאנו הולכים שם אנו רואים גבורתו של יוצר בראשית ולכן אנו הולכים על המים בראש השנה שהוא יום הדין לשום כל אחד על נפשו ענין בריאת העולם ושהשם יתעלה מלך הארץ ועל זה נאמר תשליך במצולות הים חטאתינו כי באמת המתבונן בענין מצולת ים ומכיר שהעולם מחודש על ידי זה עומד על מציאות השם יתעלה ומתחרט על ידי זה כל עוונתיו וחטאיו נמחלים ועל ידי זה נשלכים החטאים במצולות הים, *Torat ha-ʻolah* III, ch. 56 (Lemberg, 1848), p. 48b.

stitious beliefs, and to read into its customs suggestions of higher truths, but it certainly was not the original meaning of the custom, nor was it so understood by the people who practiced it even in Isserles' time.

The next rabbinic authority to discuss this custom is R. Mordecai Jaffe (1530–1612). In his *Lebush Tekelet* (Prague, 1701), No. 596, he mentions this custom as one which the people are in the habit of observing. He gives to it the usual explanation, that it is to serve as a reminder of the occasion of the intended sacrifice of Isaac, referring to the Midrash, cited by Maharil, about the legend of Satan becoming a river. He says: ורגילין לילך על הנהר זכר לעקידה משום דאיתא במדרש כשהלך אברהם אבינו לעקוד את יצחק בנו הוליכו השטן עד שבא עד צוארו במים ואמר אברהם הושיעה יי כי באו מים עד נפש וניצול. But he is not quite pleased with this interpretation of the purpose of the ceremony, or, in other words, he does not apparently wish to accept the ceremony as thus understood. He therefore, gives it a slight modification. He attributes to the ceremony an additional feature, which gives an altogether new interpretation of the purpose and significance of the ceremony, thus lending it more of a religious value. He continues thus: ורגילין לילך למקום שרואין שם דגים לזכר שאנו משולים כדגים חיים הללו במקום שנאחזים במצודה כך אנו נאחזים במצודת המות והדין ומתוך כך נהרהר יותר בתשובה. "It is customary to go to a place where we can see fish in order to remember that we are like these fish who live in a place where they can be caught with a net. For we also can be caught in the net of death and of judgment.[116] By such contemplations we shall be led to think more about repentance."

We learn from Tyrnau, Isserles, and Jaffe that watching and observing the fish was a specific feature if not the main feature of the ceremony. The ceremony accordingly was performed primarily and preferably near a body of water in which living fish could be seen, as is evident also from the picture in Pfefferkorn's book. This idea, though first expressly mentioned by these authorities, is no doubt much older. Even Maharil

---

[116] The idea of comparing men to the fish of the sea was suggested to Lebush by the saying in the Talmud 'Ab. Zarah 3b–4a.

assumes that the ceremony was to be performed at a place where there were living fish. For he interprets the purpose of throwing food into the water as being to give food to the fish "to look at them and rejoice or amuse oneself with them." Maharil innocently believed that the food thrown into the river was intended for the fish whom we look at and whose joy in obtaining food we share. But Tyrnau, Isserles and Jaffe rather emphasize the feature of seeing and observing the fish, and attach to it great importance. How did this feature of "looking at the fish" come to attain such prominence, and why do these teachers not mention the other component parts of this feature? I believe that this can be explained in the following manner. When in former days the people cast their food into the water as a sacrifice to Satan, who dwells in the depths of the sea, they were very anxious that their gifts should reach him. They would accordingly watch to see whether the gift was received. When the fish would swallow the food and swim away from the shore, the people could believe that the fish rushed away with it to the master of the sea, just as in the case of sacrifices offered to God in Heaven when a fire came down upon the altar and consumed the sacrifice it was believed to have been favorably accepted by God. The fish could have been considered by the people as messengers of the sea-lord, Satan. It, therefore, became customary for the people, when performing the ceremony, to watch the fish come up close to the banks of the river, and, after swallowing the food, swiftly swim away. Thus even in the popular mind the belief became established that in performing this ceremony it was essential to see the fish. Lebush, who like Isserles, ignores the feature of throwing the food into the water, accordingly notices only the fact that the people are very anxious to see the fish. In his desire to find in this old ceremony a suggestion of some religious idea, he takes this feature, *viz.*, the watching and observing of the fish as expressing the sole purpose and significance of the ceremony. From the fish, he believes, we may learn a wholesome lesson. The lesson is that we, like the fish, are liable to be caught in the net, and this thought should cause us to contemplate repentance more seriously, which is so necessary on New Year's day. The same explanation of the ceremony is also given by the contemporary of Lebush, R. Moses of Premysla.[117] According to this interpretation the entire ceremony lost its original significance. It is performed only for the sake of the one feature in it which has some religious significance, namely, the watching and observing of the fish which are so easily caught. This is to suggest to us a lesson appropriate for New Year's day. Thus we see that the rabbinic authorities endeavored, each in his own way, to explain the ceremony as a mere symbolic reminder of our dependence on God in order to cause us to repent of our sins, and to seek His mercy.

Had it been left to the strict and rather rationalistic rabbinic authorities, the original significance of the ceremony with its superstitious meaning and heathen ideas would, as a result of the process of reinterpretation, have been entirely forgotten, at least in rabbinic circles. No one could have recognized the origin of this ceremony after Lebush had given it such a splendid, ethical, religious interpretation. But Jewish thought and Jewish teaching are not determined by the rationalistic Rabbis alone. The mystics also share in shaping them. And in the mystic circles the idea that this ceremony has something to do with Satan, that its purpose was to prevent or somehow counteract his accusations, survived and was even further developed though also somewhat modified. Now, since some of the rabbinic authorities were also students of the Ḳabbalah and mystically inclined, they too could not and would not entirely ignore the ḳabbalistic interpretation of the ceremony. The result was, as we may expect, that the original mystic ideas connected with the ceremony were not entirely forgotten even in rabbinic circles, but rather revived after the strict rabbinical teachings had almost succeeded in utterly hiding them under their symbolic explanations.

Thus, R. Isaiah Horowitz (1555–1630), a prominent rabbinical authority and a great Ḳabbalist, mentions this custom in his *Shene Luḥot ha-Berit* I (Josefow, 1878), p. 139, and discusses its meaning, according to the rabbinic interpretation, as well as according to the interpretation which it received in the Lurya

[117] In his מטה משה, 820 (Warsaw, 1876), p. 166.

school of mysticism, to be discussed below. Here we can only consider the one interpretation of the ceremony given by Horowitz which is but slightly mystic and in which, like Tyrnau, Isserles, and Jaffe, he stresses the feature of looking at the fish. After giving Jaffe's interpretation, Horowitz continues thus: "I have also heard that there is an important and adequate symbolic suggestion in this ceremony. We go to the water in which there are fish because, since the fish have no eyelids and hence their eyes are always open, we thereby arouse and awaken, as it were, the 'Open Eye Above,' which symbolizes great mercy. For, 'behold He that keepeth Israel doth neither slumber nor sleep' (Ps. 121.4), but His eyes are open. Hence it is also said: 'Awaken! Why shouldst thou sleep?' (Ps. 44.24). It is also written, 'Why doth Thine anger smoke against the flock of Thy pasture?' (Ps. 74.1). For smoke is hard on the eyes and induces them to close. But we pray that they be open." (עוד שמעתי רמז גדול ונכון כי הולכים למים שיש בהם דגים יען כי להדגים אין גבינים ועיניהם תמיד פקוחות כדי להתעורר עינא פקיחא דלעילא שרומז על רחמים גדולים והנה לא ינום ולא יישן שומר ישראל רק עיניו פקוחות ועל זה נאמר עורה למה תישן וכתיב למה יעשן אפך בצאן מרעיתך כי קשה העשן לעינים וגורם שיהיו פקוחות סגורות ואנחנו מתפללים שיהיו פקוחות.) It is to be noted that "Observing the fish," according to this interpretation, was not to serve the purpose of making us realize how, like the fish, we are exposed to danger, liable to be caught in the net, and thus cause us to contemplate sincere repentance. It was rather a sort of sympathetic magic. We pray to God, and by concentrating our attention upon the fish at the same time, we suggest to Him that He let not the smoke of His anger close His eyes, but keep His eyes open and look upon us with favor.

Before we proceed to discuss the reinterpretation of the ceremony as given in the mystic circles, especially in the school of Lurya, it might be advisable first to sum up the results of the endeavors of the rabbinic authorities at reinterpreting this ceremony and at suppressing the crude superstitions connected with it, so as to determine what measure of success they achieved in their efforts. If we consider non-rabbinic reports and descriptions of how the ceremony was observed in the 16th and 17th centuries, and the manner in which the ceremony is actually performed to this day, especially by Jews in east European countries, we find that the Rabbis were not successful in removing the superstitious elements from this ceremony. Their interpretations of the significance of certain features of the ceremony had no effect upon the popular conception of the significance of these features. The people continued to perform the ceremony in their own way. They practically ignored all the ingenious interpretations which the Rabbis gave to some features of the ceremony. They performed these features but for a purpose other than that suggested by the rabbinic interpretations. And they also retained those features of the ceremony which the Rabbis sought to suppress. We have seen that both the Rabbis and some of the mystics emphasize the feature of "looking at the fish," as if in it alone lay the whole significance of the ceremony. The mystics, as we shall see, attach great importance to the feature of shaking the garments. Both these features, however, were mere accompaniments of the main feature of the ceremony — the throwing of food into the water or sending gifts to Satan. This main feature is suppressed by both the Rabbis and the mystics. The people, however, correctly considered the two features of shaking the garments and observing the fish as aids to the main feature of the ceremony, *viz.*, the sending of gifts to Satan, which they continued to practice. They shook their garments merely to empty them of the food carried in them, thus sending it as a gift to Satan. They observed the fish to see whether these carriers received the gifts entrusted to them for delivery to Satan. In other words, they performed the ceremony merely for the purpose of pacifying Satan by sending him a gift and with it their sins; the ceremony was, in their belief, a repetition of the ancient ceremony of sending a goat to Azazel. This is confirmed by the non-Jewish reports about the ceremony from the 16th and 17th centuries, as well as by the ideas still prevalent about it among present-day east European Jews. The latter still preserve the custom of shaking their garments and emptying their pockets of crumbs of bread which are thus thrown into the water, believing that they thereby cast off their sins, which Satan is to receive together with the crumbs.

We have seen from the woodcuts in the works of Pfefferkorn and Margarita that the people threw food into the water from the folds of their garments, and watched the fish reach for it. But Pfefferkorn and Margarita also report the following significant form of the ceremony. When they (the Jews) cannot find a place near water, so these two converts report, they go to an open space where the wind blows, turn their backs to the wind, and shake their garments, so that their sins may be carried off by the wind. From this it is evident that the people ignored all the interpretations of the purpose of "observing the fish" given by the Rabbis. To the popular mind, the fish were merely the carriers of both the gifts and their sins to Satan. When they could not send their gifts and their sins by way of water, they would dispatch them through the air, and the wind replaced the fish as a carrier. They thus repeated the practice which, as we have seen above, they followed in connection with the Kapparot ceremony. When they were hindered from throwing the Kapparot into the water, they threw parts of the rooster upon the roof or into an open space from which the wind or the birds might carry them away. This further proves the identity of purpose of both the Tashlik and the Kapparot ceremonies. We have no reason to doubt the accuracy of the description of this special form of the ceremony given by the two converts Pfefferkorn and Margarita. For, as we shall see, some of the Jewish mystics in prescribing the ceremony also emphasize that the place where the ceremony should be performed must be outside of the city and not necessarily at a place where there are fish. Thus, it seems that the fish were not essential to the performance of the ceremony. There were in the popular belief many roads leading to the residence of Satan. Just as the goat to Azazel was sent to the wilderness and, from the precipice there, dispatched to a place where Satan was supposed to reside, so the people believed that their gifts to Satan, laden with their sins, could be sent to him through the air from any free or deserted place outside of the city. For the people considered their ceremony to have the same function as the ancient practice of sending the goat to Azazel. This is expressly stated by John

Buxtorf (1564–1629) who in his *Juden-Schul*,[118] describes this ceremony as follows: "Nach dem Essen, gehen Mann, Weib und Kinder Junges und Altes an ein Wasser oder auf eine Brucken Taschlich zu machen, das ist, ihre Sünde in das wasser zu werfen, wie geschrieben steht: Er wird sich wenden und sich über uns erbarmen, unsere Missethaten wird er hinwegnehmen und alle unsere Sünden in die Tieffe des Meers werffen. Wann sie nun fisch sehen halten sie es für ein gutes Zeichen, springen vor Freuden auf, schütteln ihre Kleider[119] tapffer und werffen ihre Sünde auf die fisch, dass sie darmit hinweg schwimmen, gleichwie der Widder in den Alten Testament mit des Volcks Sünde in die Wüsten geloffen ist, wie man solches in den dritten Buch Moysis lieset. Andere schreiben, es geschehe zur Gedächtnis Abrahams; als derselbe am Neuen-jahrs-Tag mit seinem sohn Isaac gangen, ihn zu opffern seye ihm der Sathan begegnet und hab sich in ein grosses Wasser verkehret, welches erst nur knie tieff bald aber ihnen biss an den hals gangen, dass er vermeinet, sein leben allda zu lassen. Als er aber zu Gott geschriehen, hab ihm Gott einen trockenen weg durch das wasser gemacht, wie man im Medrasch Vajoscha lieset." It is to be noticed that Buxtorf, when mentioning the interpretation of the ceremony as being a reminder of the occasion of the intended sacrifice of Isaac, uses the introductory phase: "Andere schreiben," "Others write," which clearly indicates that he got this interpretation merely from books. From this we may conclude that the other interpretation, *viz*., that it was to serve the same purpose as the ancient ceremony of sending a goat to Azazel, he did not get from books but heard from the people, and that the people in general so understood the significance of the ceremony. This is also confirmed by another non-Jewish writer, L. Addison, who

[118] *Synagoga Judaica oder Juden Schul* (Frankfurt u. Leipzig, 1738), Ch. XIX, p. 447–448. Cf. also Bodenschatz, *Kirchliche Verfassung der heutigen Juden*, part II (Erlangen, 1748), p. 125.

[119] The shaking of the garments originally simply in order to shake out the food carried in the folds of the garments came also to be regarded as a shaking off of the sins, since the latter were to be placed on the food constituting the gift to Satan. Later on it was explained to be a means of shaking off the evil spirits or קליפות created by the sins. See below, notes 133, 134 and 136.

in his work, *The Present State of the Jews (more particularly relating to those of Barbary)*, (London, 1675), p. 192, gives the following account of our ceremony: "The Jews have had a Custom on this day, i. e., on New Year's Day, to run into the Rivers, and there to shake off their sins, that according to Micah 7.19. 'they may be carried into the depths of the sea.' If at this Lustration they have the good Fortune to see a fish, they shake themselves lustily on purpose to load it with their Sins, that it may swim away with them, and be as the Scape-goat of old, which carried the peoples Sins into the Desert. Some among them would have this repairing to the running-Water, to be in memory of Abraham's being led by an Evil Spirit into a River (when he went to Sacrifice his Son) where being in great danger of Drowning, he prai'd unto God, and the River upon the sudden became dry Land."

In his preface the author states that the account which he gives of the Jews and their customs and beliefs was not gathered from books but from personal communication with the Jews: "This being the result of conversation, and not of report." These conversations Addison had with Jews of Barbary during the years (1662–1670) in which he served as chaplain of the garrison at Tangier. We may, therefore, assume that the ceremony which he described was observed by the Jews of Barbary. There is one peculiar feature of this ceremony which is not found among European Jews. It seems that instead of merely throwing food and with it their sins to the fish to be transferred to Satan, the Jews in Barbary would jump into the water[120] and thus come into direct contact with the fish and unload their sins upon them. Addison does not say whether the people threw food to the fish or not. It may be that this feature was not so prominent among the Jews of Barbary. They may have considered the fish themselves as the goat sent to Azazel, and by jumping into the river and coming into close contact with the fish they unloaded their sins upon them, which like the goat, carried the sins to Satan. In doing so they merely repeated what the people in

---

[120] A similar practice was observed by the Jews of Kurdistan. See below, note 143.

ancient times did with the Azazel goat when they sought to touch it, pull its hair, and thus directly unload their sins upon it, saying: take our sins with you and go out to Satan. It may also be that they already knew that shaking the garments was to serve the purpose of shaking off the sins and evils clinging to them, an interpretation given by the Lurya mystics to be discussed immediately. For this reason they could not content themselves with merely throwing food to the fish, or with merely shaking their garments, for some of these sins and evils might stick to the garments and not fall off by mere shaking. They therefore jumped into the water in order to wash away their sins. At any rate it is evident from the reports of Buxtorf and Addison that in the popular belief this ceremony of Tashlik served the same purpose which the ceremony of the goat to Azazel served in Temple times. It should further be noticed that both Buxtorf, *op. cit.*, p. 450–52, and Addison, p. 186, when describing the Kapparot ceremony, also say that in popular belief this ceremony, too, served the same purpose as that of sending the goat to Azazel. By throwing the entrails of the slaughtered rooster upon the roof the people believed that with the entrails they throw away their sins also.[121] This further confirms our theory that both the ceremonies of Tashlik and Kapparot were originally identical and that both are survivals of sending an offering to Azazel. This identification of the two ceremonies, Tashlik and Kapparot, with the ceremony of sending a goat to Azazel is also assumed by the mystics of the Lurya school, though, as we shall see, they give a new interpretation to the significance of these ceremonies.

In the attitude of the mystics of the Lurya-Vital school towards these two ceremonies we notice a reversion to older ideas. This, it seems to me, was the result of the reassertion of the fundamental Jewish doctrine in regard to the God conception. The repeated rabbinic objections to any form of worshipping or paying homage to any power or being besides the One God,

[121] Buxtorf expressly says: "So stecke auch die Sünde auf dem Ingeweyd des Hahnen, sollen derohalben die Raaben kommen und mit des Juden Sünde hinweg in die Wüsten fliehen, wie der Bock im alten Testament mit des Volks Sünden ist in die Wüsten geloffen."

had their effect upon these mystics. The strict belief in the unity of God, which these mystics shared with the rationalistic Rabbis, did not permit them to recognize besides God any being with independent power, to whom one could pray or offer sacrifices. They could think of hosts of subordinate beings participating in the heavenly administration. They could also distinguish the different divine attributes of which they spoke in terms of personification, but they considered them as united in the one God-head. According to their way of thinking, such personifications of the divine attributes did not conflict with the monotheistic Jewish conception of one supreme power. However, they could not and would not recognize an independent evil power, and hence they had no great respect for the position held by Satan, though they by no means denied his existence or his evil desire to harm people. In their dealings with this low and subordinate official, they do not follow the methods of reconciliation. They do not seek to pacify him by bribes or gifts. They revert to the older methods of fighting him by their own good works and frustrating his evil designs by appealing to his Superior to withdraw support from him and to refuse to listen to his malicious accusations. These are the underlying ideas of the new interpretation of both the Tashlik and the Kapparot ceremony given by the Lurya-Vital school. Thus R. Jacob Ḥayyim Ẓemaḥ[122] in his work נגיד ומצוה (Leghorn, 1785), p. 74, containing Lurya's explanations of the ritual and the ceremonies, as collected from the writings of Ḥayyim Vital, mentions the ceremony of Tashlik in the following words: נוהגין באשכנז ביום ראשון דראש השנה ללכת למעין המים להשליך העונות ואומרים שם י"ג תיקוני דיקנא עילאה דא"א שהם מי אל כמוך ומנהג טוב הוא וצ"ל אחר מנחה קודם שקיעת החמה וטוב הוא אם הוא חוץ לעיר על שפת הים או מעין או באר מים חיים. Here it is plainly stated that the purpose of the ceremony is "to throw away the sins," in other words, to make it impossible for Satan to find fault with us and accuse us. How this purpose is achieved is explained in a rather lengthy Ḳabbalistic discussion which may be summed up in the following few sentences. The prayer and the prescribed verses, if recited with

---

[122] Ẓemaḥ fled from Portugal in the year 1619. See *JE*, VII, 656.

the proper intention, with adequate devotion, with a correct understanding of their full meaning and of all their mystic implications, have the effect both of making Satan helpless and of freeing the worshipper from his sins, thus securing for him atonement. Satan, who according to the Zohar is identical with the depths of the sea, is not the sovereign of the sea. He has no independent realm in the sea. This realm of the sea belongs to the heavenly "Powers" (גבורות) or to the divine Strict Justice (דינין). Satan dwells in the very depths of the sea and occupies a very low position. Figuratively speaking, he represents the lowest part of the sea, he is "the dross of the silver," "the dregs of the sea," but the sea itself symbolizes the heavenly powers, the ים קדישא (cf. Zohar, Emor, p. 202). Satan has no power whatsoever except the little support or strength which he draws from the דינין, or Strict Justice above. That is to say, the divine attribute of Strict Justice cannot refuse to listen to the malicious accusations of Satan when he can actually point to the sins of the people and thus substantiate his charges. In other words, justice supports the accuser when he can prove his accusations. Now, by reciting the prayer, and the special verses with the proper intention, we are successful in our appeal to the divine attribute of Justice (מדת הדין or דינין). Strict Justice relaxes, as it were; it becomes softened and sweetened and does not so readily yield to the demands of Satan. It does not accept his accusations and rather withdraws the support from Satan. Justice can honestly do so because due to another effect of the recitation of these verses, Satan becomes actually unable to substantiate his charges, for he cannot point to our sins. The recitation of the prayers accompanied by sincere repentence rids us of our sins, and of their effects, i. e., those evil spirits which cling to us as a result of our sins. For just as every good deed creates an angel, every evil deed creates an evil spirit or an accuser.[123] The evil spirits, thus created by sins, increase the host of Satan or the army of accusers. These accusers cling to the person by whose sins they were created; they are constantly around him, thus giving evidence, as it were, of the sins which

[123] Ab. 4.11.

he committed. At the same time they tend to subject the person to the further influence of Satan, since they are of his army, creatures of evil. The recitation of the prayers has the effect of driving away these evil creatures. They are thrown into the depths of the sea, i. e., they are forced back upon their chief, Satan or Samael, who thereby becomes powerless. For his people, the evil spirits created by man's sins no longer cling to the person who brought them forth, for he has shaken them off and thrown them back to Satan. They can no longer help Satan to substantiate his charges, for they are no longer around the man to testify to his sins. Neither can Satan receive any strength and support from Strict Justice (דינין), for, as a result of the recitation of the prescribed formula, the latter have become mollified and have been prevailed upon by divine Mercy (חסד) to withdraw support from Satan. The latter thus becomes utterly helpless and can do no harm. These are in essence the ideas underlying the Luryanic explanation of the significance of the Tashlik ceremony, so far as one can express these intricate mystic notions, with their hints and allusions, in rational language. The same explanation is also given by R. Isaiah Horowitz (*op. cit., loc. cit.*) who connects it more directly with the passage in Zohar, *Emor* p. 202, and insists most emphatically that sincere repentance must accompany the ceremony.

According to this interpretation of the meaning of the ceremony, some of the features, which according to the previous rabbinic interpretaion were prominent in it, lose their significance and are utterly ignored. Even the time for the performance of the ceremony is changed. We notice that according to Lurya the ceremony shoud be performed, not immediately after the noon meal as Maharil had it, but later in the day, after the *Minḥah* prayer, before sunset. We also notice that no mention is made of the fish, or of any food thrown into the water. This is in keeping with the new interpretation. The change in time had to be made because of the development of the new ideas connected with the ceremony. We have seen that the performance of the ceremony right after the noon meal was due to the fact that its purpose was considered to be the bringing of a sacrifice or offering a gift to Satan. If the purpose was to send food to

Satan, or even, as it was naively explained, to give food to the fish, it was but natural that the people should do so right after the meal when they could conveniently take along with them the remnants of the meal. But if, as understood by Lurya, the purpose was not to offer Satan any gift but to fight him and to hinder him in his malicious work by the recitation of certain formulas and prayers, addressed to the Heavenly Judge, then there was no reason for doing this right after the meal. It was rather thought advisable to look for a more favorable time, an especially propitious moment when such prayers would be heard. The time after the *Minḥah* was believed to be such an auspicious moment. For Elijah, when praying to God for help in his fight against the false gods, was answered only at *Minḥah* time.[124] The same time, it was felt, would also be favorable for a prayer to God to subdue the false Satan and deprive him of any power to harm people. It had, however, to be done before sunset, since its aim and purpose were to secure a favorable verdict. The heavenly courts observe the same rules as the courts on earth. In cases of life and death the courts sit in judgment only during the day and are not allowed to judge at night. The ceremony therefore had to be performed before sunset, i. e., before the close of the court session.

With the shifting of the time for the performance of the ceremony due to the modification of its purpose, the features of shaking the garments and of observing the fish necessarily lost their real significance and had to be abandoned or given a new meaning. These two features, as we have seen, were merely accompaniments of that part of the ceremony which consisted of sending a gift to Satan. The shaking of the garments was done in order to empty into the water the food which the people carried in the skirts of their garments. The watching of the fish was done merely to see whether they received the food which they were to carry to the Sea Lord. But when no gift is to be offered to Satan and no food is to be thrown into the water or to the fish, there is no occasion for shaking the garments or

---

[124] See Ber. 6b: לעולם יזהר אדם בתפלת המנחה שהרי אליהו לא נענה אלא בתפלת המנחה.

observing the fish. Hence Lurya does not say that the ceremony is to be performed near a body of water in which there are fish. He seems to lay more stress upon performing the ceremony outside of the city; whether near the sea where there are fish or near a well or a spring where there are none, is of no relevance. In fact, this ceremony, as understood by Lurya, could be performed away from water. For the effectiveness of the ceremony depends only on the prayer recited with the intention of throwing the sins back to Satan, figuratively designated as the depths of the sea, and hence the ceremony need not necessarily be performed near a body of water. Zemaḥ merely says that it is preferable to recite these prayers near water: ולכן טוב לומר זה על שפת הים או מעין או באר מים חיים. This all but suggests that there was an element of sympathetic magic underlying the preference for reciting these prayers near water.

We shall see how these features of going to the water, shaking the garments and watching the fish, which persisted in the popular practice, were retained even by the mystics of the Lurya school and reinterpreted so as to fit in with their interpretation of the significance of the ceremony. First, however, we must consider how the Lurya-Vital school, with its changed attitude towards Satan, reinterpreted the Kapparot ceremony which like the Tashlik was a relic, or revival, of the ceremony of sending a goat to Azazel.

In explaining the ceremony of Kapparot, Zemaḥ[125] says that like the Tashlik it also serves the purpose of softening or tempering the attitude of strict Justice. The rooster, called גבר, is a sort of representation or symbol of the Powers, (גבורות), in which there is the attribute or quality of Strict Justice (דינין קשין). The rooster is slaughtered early in the morning of the day preceding the Day of Atonement, because at that time of the day Mercy is strong and the rule of Mercy prevails in the world;[126] hence, it is an auspicious moment to subdue the Powers or Strict Justice. By slaughtering the rooster, the symbolic representative of גבורות, and by withdrawing its blood

---

[125] *Op. cit.*, pp. 74b–75.
[126] Cf. also של"ה II, פרק תורה אור, הלכות תשובה (Josefow, 1878), p. 15.

from it we somehow subdue the גבורות and soften or temper them. This ceremony is like that of sending the goat to Azazel. For both the rooster and the goat are symbolic representatives of Strict Justice. For just as the rooster, called גבר, symbolizes the Powers, גבורות, so also the goat represents one of "their party," i. e., of the party of Satan and the demons who draw their support from the גבורות. For the goat is called in Hebrew שעיר which is also a name for the demons, as suggested in Isa. 12.22, where it is said, "And Satyrs shall dance there" (ושעירים ירקדו שם). The goat represents the stronger power, hence it was necessary to send it away to the wilderness, outside, beyond reach of us, as it were. The rooster, on the other hand, represents the weaker power, and for this reason it is not necessary to send it away but it is sufficient if we slaughter it and thus weaken the power represented by it. This in essence is the explanation given by the Lurya school to the ceremony of Kapparot.[127] This explanation not only shows the identity of purpose of the two ceremonies, Tashlik and Kapparot, and their connection with the ceremony of sending a goat to Azazel, but also gives an altogether new reason for the choice of a rooster for the Kapparot ceremony, different from the one given in gaonic literature and accepted by all the rabbinic authorities. The rooster, according to this interpretation, is not a substitute for man, with whom he shares the name גבר, and is not a sacrifice to Satan. Rather the rooster represents Satan or the demons, and in slaughtering it we kill, or at least weaken, the demons and Satan who draw their support from the Powers of Justice. This interpretation also seems to suggest that the purpose of the ceremony of sending the goat to Azazel, the prototype of the Kapparot and Tashlik ceremonies, was, likewise, not to offer a sacrifice to Satan, but

[127] Cf. also של"ה II, *loc. cit.*, who gives the same explanation in the name of the disciples of Lurya, whom he quotes as saying: אנו (הדינין) לכן להמתיק זה שוחטין תרנגול לבן שנקרא גבר... אנו לוקחין אותו תרנגול ושוחטים אותו באשמורת הבוקר כי אז בעת ההיא חוט של חסד גובר בעולם ואנו שוחטים אותו להכניע הגבורות ומוציאים ממנו דמו להכניעו והרי זה כמו שעיר המשתלח... כי הגבר רומז אל הגבורות והשעיר גם הוא מסטרא דילהון כענין שנאמר ושעירים ירקדו שם... ולכן נקרא התרנגול כפרה כמו שעיר המשתלח הנקרא כפרה.

rather to hurt Satan and his people by sending to destruction the goat which is a representation of Satan.[128]

As already stated above, according to the interpretation of the Tashlik ceremony as being a means of hurting Satan rather than bribing him, the features of shaking the garments, and of looking at the fish, apparently lose all significance and are unnecessary, since the ceremony could effectively be performed even away from water. But these features had become very closely connected with the ceremony and, according to the popular practice, formed an integral part, almost the very essence, of it and the mystic interpretation could therefore not ignore them. And we find indeed that the Lurya school did retain or reintroduce all these features but explained their significance in such a manner as to make them agree with their new interpretation of the ceremony.

The author of the חמדת הימים,[129] a younger contemporary of Jacob Ẓemaḥ, and likewise an exponent of Lurya's ideas about ceremonies and ritual, also discusses the two ceremonies of Tashlik and Kapparot, and gives in a somewhat clearer form and with more details the Luryanic interpretation as presented by Jacob Ẓemaḥ. In the second volume of his work,[130] in the part dealing with New Year's Day, he commends the Tashlik ceremony and describes it as follows: ואחר תפלת המנחה יום א' דראש השנה קודם שקיעת החמה יש ללכת אל הים או אל באר המים או מעין אשר מחוץ לעיר לומר הי"ג מדות עליונות של מי כמוך והטעם נודע לבאים בסוד ד'... ולכן הולכים אל המים המורים על חסדים וגם במקום שיש בו דגים שרומזים על עינא פקיחא להמתיק הדין הקשה... ויגביה שני צדי הגלימה מחציה וכשיגיע לותשליך במצולות ים אז ישלשלם וינערם וכן יעשה ג' פעמים. He also prescribes a long prayer, to be recited while performing the ceremony. In this prayer, expressing the ideas quoted by Ẓemaḥ, the following passage is significant since it

[128] See above, note 64.
[129] He is supposed to have been Nathan Ghazzati (1644–1680), the follower of Shabbatai Ẓevi (see *JE*, V, 651); cf., however, David Frankel, in *Alim, Blätter für Bibliographie u. Geschichte des Judentums*, Heft II (September 1934), p. 54, note 1.
[130] Ch. VII (Leghorn, 1764), p. 52c,d.

expresses these ideas more clearly and at the same time explains why, even according to the Lurya interpretation, the ceremony must be performed near the water. It reads thus: ובכן תשליך במצולות ים העליון לס"מ ולילית ונחש וכל המשחיתים אשר נבראו על ידינו ואל יהי להם יניקה משמות הקדושים אדני' אלהים' שכבר נמתקו. We notice here a new interpretation of the main feature of the Tashlik ceremony — i. e., "going to pray near the water" — namely, that the reason for it is that "Water is indicative of Mercy." Since according to the Lurya idea the purpose of the ceremony is to pray to God to restrain Satan, to withdraw support from him and to let Mercy prevail over Justice, it is necessary to perform the ceremony near water, which suggests mercy. Furthermore, by the act of casting our sins and all the evil spirits that were created by them into the water, we also suggest to God, as if by a sort of sympathetic magic, that He likewise subdue Satan, or as it is expressed in the passage of the prayer quoted above: "And thus mayest Thou throw into the depths of the 'Sea Above,' Samael, Lilit, and the Serpent together with the evil and harmful spirits which were created by us (i. e., by our sins) so that they should not draw any support from the Holy Names *Adonai Elohim* (representing the Attributes of Justice) that have already been softened and sweetened." The other feature of the ceremony, i. e., looking at the fish is also retained, but merely for the reason that fish symbolize the Open Eye, and thus the ceremony suggests to Mercy to soften Strict Justice.[131] For the same reason it is also advisable according to this author to eat fish cooked sweet, but not sour or sharp, on New Year's Day. "For the fish have no eyelids and their eyes are always open. Thus the Open Eye Above which is a symbolic expression for Great Mercy will be aroused," etc.[132]

The feature of shaking the garments is also retained and even given great weight. It is prescribed that this performance of shaking the garments be repeated three times. This feature is very important, for by it we throw away our sins and the evil spirits created by them, which cling to our garments. That

[131] וגם במקום שיש בו דנים שרומזים על עינא פקיחא להמתיק הדין הקשה.
[132] *Ibid.*, ch. IV.

this was the purpose of shaking the garments is not expressly stated here by the author.[133] But we can learn it from another statement of his. In discussing the ceremony of blessing the new moon,[134] he says: והמנהג לנער אחר כך שולי בגדיהם להבריח החיצונים. The same idea is also expressed by Zemaḥ, who says:[135] "he should shake the skirts of his garments to drive away the accusations and the *Outsiders*, i. e., the evil spirits," וינעור שולי בגדיו להבריח הקטרוג והחיצונים. The belief that the evil spirits cling to the garments is very old, and is already suggested in the Talmud.[136] Hence if we wish to drive them away we must shake our garments in order to throw them off. By thus shaking our garments and throwing the sins and evil creatures into the water, while reciting the words, ותשליך במצולות ים, we suggest, as if by sympathetic magic, that God in His Mercy may throw Satan and his people into the depths of the Sea Above and let Mercy prevail over Justice.

Thus all the features which were characteristic of the ceremony when it was understood as intended to bribe Satan or to offer him a gift, were retained, even after its purpose was interpreted as being that of fighting Satan.[137]

The interpretation of the Tashlik ceremony, as given by the Lurya school, represents its last important development. In the subsequent period the ceremony shows practically no further development. No important changes were made in the observance of the ceremony itself and no new features were

---

[133] It is, however, indicated in the prayer prescribed by him to be recited while shaking the garments.

[134] *Ibid.*, II, ch. V, p. 28b. Cf. also ספר שם טוב קטן by Benjamin B. Cohen of Krotoshin (Berlin, 1740), p. 19a.

[135] *Op. cit.*, p. 66a.

[136] Ber. 6a: הני מאני דרבנן דבלו מחופיא דידהו; cf. Rashi *ad loc.*

[137] About the Kapparot ceremony חמדת ימים (IV, p. 64) gives the same explanation as Zemaḥ but even more clearly indicates that its purpose is to kill Satan: לכוין בשחיטת הגבר אשר דרכו לגבר נסתרה. It is interesting that he considers the feature of the throwing of the entrails upon the roof a heathenish superstition, to which alone, he claims, Ramban objected, but not to the ceremony of Kapparot as such. He says: ומה שחרה לו להרמב"ן ואמר למנוע אותו משום דרכי האמורי היינו מפני שזורקים הבני מעיים על הגגות ובאים העופות ואוכלים אותם דודאי בדבר זה היטב חרה לו אמנם בענין הכפרה עצמה אין שייך דרכי האמורי. Cf. above note 35.

added to it. The rabbinic authorities who cite or recommend the ceremony do not advance any new theories about its significance. They do not offer any new ideas in explaining its function, nor do they give any new reasons for its observance. They content themselves with merely repeating what had already been said by their predecessors, at most but slightly modifying one or the other feature of the ceremony. According to their personal inclinations or mental attitudes, rationalistic or mystic, the various authorities selected one or the other of the ideas advanced by preceding authorities, and emphasized it as the underlying idea or the correct explanation of the ceremony. And, since so many ideas had been connected with this ceremony, so many different interpretations had been given to it, and such a variety of reasons for its observance had been offered, it was not difficult for anyone, no matter what his intellectual preference may have been, to accept the one or the other explanation, and to find in the ceremony some feature that appealed to him or some idea which made the observance of the ceremony worth while.

There was but one great rabbinical authority of the eighteenth century, R. Elijah Gaon of Wilna (1720–1797), who would not be deceived by all the various rationalistic or mystical interpretations of this ceremony. With his religious genius he perceived that, despite all the explanations given to it and despite all the changes and modifications made in it in the course of time, this ceremony was incompatible with the purely monotheistic belief and the religious teachings of Judaism. He must have recognized the origin and the heathen character of this ceremony even in the disguise of later interpretations; and for this reason, no doubt, he refused to observe it.[138] But he stood alone among his contemporaries. All the other rabbinic authorities of the eighteenth century, accepted the one or the other of the various interpretations of the ceremony and considered it a valuable Jewish religious custom which they observed themselves and

[138] See ספר תוספת מעשה רב (Jerusalem, 1896), No. 202, p. 12, where it is said about the Gaon of Wilna לא היה הולך לנהר לומר תשליך. His disciple, R. Ḥayyim of Wolozyn likewise refrained from performing this ceremony (*ibid.*, *loc. cit.*, note 60).

TASHLIK 411

led others to observe. The result was that, from the eighteenth century on, the ceremony gradually came to be universally accepted. Even in communities that followed the Spanish-Portuguese ritual, the ceremony came to be observed. The rabbinic authorities of the Spanish school evidently recommended, or at least did not disapprove of, the observance of this ceremony.[139] The ceremony spread to the remotest Jewish communities. Thus the native Jews in Dagestan,[140] who in the main followed the Spanish ritual, observed this ceremony of Tashlik on the first day of Rosh Hashanah, in the afternoon. And among the Krimchaki, the oldest Jewish settlers in Crimea, the ceremony was also observed.[141] Likewise the Jews in Kurdistan observed the Tashlik ceremony on the first New Year's Day. They are reported to have performed it in the usual manner but to have added one peculiar and primitive feature. After reciting the Tashlik ritual, instead of shaking their garments, as is done by the European Jews, they jumped into the water and swam around like fish. It was their belief that by so doing they would be effectively cleansed from their sins, for the water would wash

---

[139] The first non-Ashkenazic rabbinical authorities who endorsed or recommended the ceremony were also Cabalists who followed the Lurya school. These are the two Italian Rabbis, R. Moses b. Mordecai Zacuto (died 1697) and R. Joseph Ergas (1685–1730). Both these authorities approved of the ceremony and differed only on the question as to whether it should be observed even in case the first day of Rosh Hashanah falls on a Sabbath. The former opposed, the latter recommended, its being observed on a Sabbath (see Ḥ. J. D. Azulai in his ספר יוסף אומץ [Leghorn, 1803], 18a No. 17). But from the 18th century on, it seems, the ceremony was generally observed in the Italian communities (see Lampronti פחד יצחק s. v. ראש השנה and R. Abraham Chalfon ספר חזון אברהם, הלכות ימים נוראים [Leghorn, 1826], No. 298, p. 46). The ceremony is also observed in the Sefardic communities, in Algiers (see ספר זה השולחן by Elias Gigi [Algiers, 1889], p. 52), and in Egypt (see נוה שלום by Elijah Ḥazan [Alexandria, 1894], p. 24b, and נהר מצרים by Raphael Aaron ibn Simeon [Alexandria, 1908], p. 42b). In all these communities it is observed on the first day of Rosh Hashanah even when it falls on a Sabbath. The last two works refer also to the custom in Jerusalem of observing the ceremony on the first day of Rosh Hashanah even when it falls on a Sabbath.

[140] See Joseph Judah Chorny in ספר מסעות edited by A. Harkavy (St. Petersburg, 1884), p. 6.

[141] See Isaac B. Markon, "Ueber das Maḥzor nach Ritus Kaffa" in Harkavy's *Festschrift* זכרון לאברהם אליהו (St. Petersburg, 1908), p. 454.

away all the sins which they had committed during the year that had passed.[142] But even this feature does not represent a new development of the ceremony. It is in reality but a revival of an older form in which the ceremony had been observed in some other part of the world. We have seen above that the Jews in Morocco likewise observed the ceremony in this manner, though the reason given by them for so doing was that it enabled them to come into closer contact with the fish.[143] And, of course, the idea that by the ceremony they became cleansed from their sins, or that the water washed away the sins, is also not new. It can, therefore, still be maintained that no new idea as to the function of the ceremony was advanced by the rabbinic authorities, nor any new feature added to it after the interpretation given to it by the Lurya school.

But, if no change was made in the ceremony itself, nor any new development in the ideas underlying it, some changes were made in the time fixed or in the date prescribed for its observance.

We have seen that changes in the date fixed for the performance of this ceremony had been effected already in very early times. We have found that while originally the ceremony of praying at a place near water may have been observed at any time, it nevertheless became, already in ancient times, limited to the fall of the year or to the season of judgment,[144] which extends from the first day of Rosh Hashanah to the last day of the feast of Tabernacles, or Hoshana Rabbah. During the season of judgment, more than at any other time, the people naturally felt the need of using some efficacious method for securing a favorable verdict. They, therefore, quite naturally fell back upon a practice which from of old was considered apt to secure such favorable results. It is true that in the course of time the observance of this ceremony was extended to other

[142] See ספר מסעי ישראל by Israel Joseph (Benjamin II) (Lyck, 1859), p. 30.
[143] See above, note 120.
[144] See above, note 103. It may be stated that in one form or another it was observed in ancient times on Hoshana Rabbah (Philo), on the Day of Atonement (Tertullian) and, in the form of פרפיסא, in talmudic times on the day preceding New Year's Day. Then it was shifted to the New Year's Day.

holidays and festivals,[145] which, while they may have been considered days of judgment[146] in regard to one thing or for one particular need, yet were outside of the season of the yearly general judgment. We have already seen above that on the Shabuot festival a sort of Tashlik ceremony was observed by the German Jews in medieval times.[147] We also have a specific reference to the observance of the Tashlik ceremony on the last day, or at the end, of the Passover festival. This reference is found in two different sources, though it is not certain whether both these sources refer to people of the same period of time or of the same country. According to J. E. Budgett Meakin,[148] "the Jews in some parts of Morocco have the curious custom of going out to the sea to say the Kadesh and the Tephilot on the last day of the Passover festival." Possibly it is this custom of some Moroccan Jews that is mentioned in a manuscript from the sixteenth century, containing a super-commentary to Rashi's Pentateuch commentary and also divers matters from various prayer rituals.[149] In this manuscript, which is now in Cambridge, there is found on folio 109a the following reference to a Tashlik ceremony at the end of the Passover festival: במוצאי פסח הולכין אל נהר ואומרים תשליך במצולות ים כל חטאתם ויש בזה סוד, "At the end of the Passover festival — this can mean either the evening following the last day of the festival or the day after — they go out to the river and recite: 'thou wilt cast all their sins into the depths of the sea.' And there is some mystic reason for doing this." We thus see, that the ceremony was observed, at least at some time and in some country, also on the other festivals and not only on New Year's Day. In fact, the statement of R. Shalom

---

[145] See A. Berliner, *Aus dem Leben der deutschen Juden im Mittelalter* (Berlin, 1900), pp. 37–38. Berliner there erroneously assumes that the custom of going to Tashlik on Rosh Hashanah is of later origin and developed out of the older custom of going out to the water on Saturdays and holidays. As a matter of fact the reverse was the case.

[146] See R. H. 1.2, בארבעה פרקים העולם נידון וכו'.

[147] As reported in *Sefer Asufot*, see above, note 106.

[148] See *JQR*, O. S., IV (1892), p. 389.

[149] See Schiller-Szineszy, *Catalogue of the Hebrew Manuscripts in Cambridge* (Cambridge, 1876), p. 78. I am indebted to my friend Prof. I. Davidson for this reference.

of Vienna quoted by Maharil in reference to "those people who on a holiday go out to the river" etc., which we cited above, also justifies the assumption that the ceremony was observed, by some people at least, on any holiday and not only on New Year's Day. For R. Shalom speaks of a holiday in general, ביום טוב, and not of the holiday of New Year in particular.

We have also reason to believe that the observance of this ceremony was not limited to the festivals alone but that it was observed by some Jews, in one place or another, on every Sabbath, and by some Jews, in one country at least, even on every day. The original idea connected with this ceremony, namely, that it is appropriate to pray at a place near water, was never entirely forgotten nor completely dissociated from the ceremony. And, according to this understanding of the ceremony, there was no reason at all why it should not be observed every day. There certainly was reason for its observance at least on days when the community met in solemn assembly and held its communal religious service, as on Sabbaths and holidays. But, even according to the interpretation of the ceremony as serving the purpose of pacifying Satan and silencing his accusation, the ceremony could have been considered as necessary and helpful for every day. For, indeed, one is in danger of Satan and his hosts every day, since according to the opinion of some Rabbis at least, "A man is being judged by the heavenly powers on every day."[150] This being so, Satan is likely to bring up his accusations every day; hence it could have been deemed advisable to seek every day to prevent him from doing so by means of this ceremony. And we do, indeed, find references to what looks very much like an observance of the Tashlik ceremony on every Friday evening, that is, on the entrance of every Sabbath, and, in one country at least, on every day.

Thus Isserlein (Israel b. Petaḥiah Ashkenazi, died 1460) in his Responsa, *Terumat ha-Deshen*, I (Sadilkow, 1835), p. 3a cites a report about a custom which had been observed long before his time in the city of Krems on every Friday evening, which suggests the character of a Tashlik ceremony, though

---

[150] ר' יוסי אומר אדם נידון בכל יום, R. H. 16a.

it is not expressly described as such. The custom in Krems, according to the report cited by Isserlein, was to hold the Friday evening service in the Synagogue in the daytime long before nightfall. This was done in order that the Rabbi and the prominent men of the community should have enough time to go out, after the first Sabbath meal on Friday evening and take their walk along the Danube, and yet be able to return and come home before it was dark. These are his words: גם שמעתי בישיבה מפי אחד מהגדולים ששמע וקיבל כי בימי הקדמונים בקרימש התפללו ערבית וקראו את שמע בערב שבת בעוד היום גדול כל כך שהיה רב העיר שהיה מהגדולים הקדמונים הוא וכל טובי הקהל עמו הלכו לטייל אחר אכילה של סעודת שבת על שפת הנהר דונאי והיו חוזרין לבתיהם קודם הלילה. It seems very unlikely that this walk taken by the Rabbi and the elders of the community was just a walk for pleasure. It would have been strange, to say the least, if the arrangement to have an early service on Friday evening, which even though it could be permitted by talmudic authority nevertheless involved some irregularity, had been made for no other reason than to enable the Rabbi and the elders to have the pleasure of a walk in daytime after their evening meal. There must have been some good reason for taking this walk other than mere pleasure. Furthermore, it could not have been accidental that they walked along the banks of the river. Indeed there would have been no purpose in telling where they walked if that walk had been a walk for pleasure only. Of course, Isserlein is merely interested in the fact that for some reason the arrangement of having the Friday evening service already during the daytime was permitted. He is not interested in questioning this reason nor in telling us whether it was a valid reason or not. All he cares to tell is that it was for the purpose of enabling the elders to have their customary walk on the banks of the Danube. But he does not tell us what the purpose of this customary walk was. He may not have known it himself. For he never witnessed the custom personally and, of course, he never participated in it himself, as he never was Rabbi in Krems.[151] Isserlein merely reports

---

[151] It is strange, indeed, that Berliner (*op. cit.*, p. 38) could have misunderstood Isserlein to say that he, Isserlein himself, took that walk with the

what he had heard from one of the authorities who in turn had received a tradition in regard to a custom that had obtained in Krems in former generations. The custom, he was told, was observed by the Rabbi and the elders or representatives of the community. This custom, it would seem, had to be observed at daytime and yet after the first Sabbath meal. It was considered of sufficient importance to justify the irregularity of the arrangement for the Friday evening service to be held at daytime, a few hours before dark so as to enable the Rabbi and the representatives of the community, to have their Friday evening meal and then to observe this custom of walking along the river and to return home before nightfall. Considering all this, one is justified in concluding that it was not just a pleasure walk in which the Rabbi and the elders wished to indulge and for which they arranged the time for the Friday evening service to suit their pleasure. There must have been some religious practice connected with the walk along the banks of the river. This practice must have been a sort of Tashlik ceremony which, as we have seen, had to be observed in the afternoon before dark and after a meal. The people in Krems who observed this custom must have thought that what is good for the festivals is also good for every Sabbath.

A similar custom, which even more resembles the Tashlik ceremony, was observed by the Jews of Kurdistan every day. According to the report of Benjamin II,[152] it was the custom of the Jews of Akra in Kurdistan to go out to a place near the river on every day before the *Minḥah* service. At that place by the river they would all eat their meal together and then recite their prayers. The report does not say whether they threw part of their meal, or the remnants thereof, into the river. Nor does the report clearly state what prayers they recited there, whether it was the regular *Minḥah* prayer or some special prayers in connection with this ceremony of having their meal

---

representatives of the community. He says: "Auch Isserlein erzählt, dass er als Rabbiner mit den Vertretern der Gemeinde am Freitag abend den Spaziergang an den Ufern der Donau machte."

[152] ספר מסעי ישראל (Lyck, 1859), p. 30.

in common near the river. It may even be that the report means to say that after their meal at the water they retired to the nearby Synagogue and recited there the *Minḥah* service. But the very custom of assembling at *Minḥah* time near the water and having there a sort of community meal in itself suggests a sort of Tashlik ceremony. The purpose of their gathering for a meal near the river must have been to have the opportunity of throwing part of their meal into the river before they recited their prayer, and they no doubt wished to recite their prayers near the water.

However, while it may be true that there were times when, and places where, the ceremony was observed by some people on all holidays and even on Sabbaths or on every day, in the main the observance of the ceremony, at least from the fifteenth century on, was limited in European countries to the first day of New Year, that is, the day of the first session of the heavenly court. But in the second half of the seventeenth century and during the eighteenth, and possibly also in the early part of the nineteenth century, after the ceremony had received its interpretation and latest development in the Lurya school, and partly as a result of this interpretation, changes in the time set for the observance of the ceremony were made. One of these changes was due, in part at least, to the very interpretation given to the ceremony by the Lurya school. The other was due to a reassertion, as it were, of the authority of the Halakah and to the revival of certain halakic scruples against the performance of the ceremony on a Sabbath day. To begin with the former change, which has some connection with the Luryanic interpretation of the ceremony, we have seen that in the Lurya school, emphasis was laid upon the recitation of the thirteen attributes of God, contained in the verses of Ex. 34.6–7, during the performance of the Tashlik ceremony. The recitation of these thirteen attributes, שלש עשרה מדות, has always been considered a most effective means of obtaining forgiveness. Now, on the day preceding the eve of the Day of Atonement, i. e., on the eighth of Tishri, the recital of these thirteen attributes occupies an especially prominent place in the liturgy of the day. The penitential prayers, סליחות, recited on that day early in the morning before the regular morning service, contain, according to the Polish ritual, a prayer the refrain of which consists of the verses in Exodus containing these thirteen attributes.[153] The whole penitential ritual of the day, in fact the day itself,[153a] is generally designated as the day of the recitation of the thirteen attributes, סליחות של שלש עשרה מדות. It must have occurred to some people that, if the recital of the thirteen attributes during the performance of the Tashlik ceremony is important and necessary in order to assure success for the efforts at silencing or overcoming Satan, then it might be advisable to perform the ceremony on the very day when a special prayer, סליחה, containing a recitation of the thirteen attributes is said. On that day, so some people must have thought, one could expect more success in obtaining the assistance of the attributes of Kindness and Mercy against the attributes of Strict Justice, and thus to be more able to overcome Satan. Even the thought of the association of the ceremony with the offering of Isaac would according to some cabalistic notions not be in the way of shifting the date of the ceremony from the first day of New Year to the day preceding the eve of the Day of Atonement. In fact, it would rather favor the latter day. For while according to the Midrashim the offering of Isaac, עקידת יצחק, took place on New Year's Day, according to the Ḳabbalists it took place on the Day of Atonement.[154] Of course, even according to the Ḳabbalists the ceremony commemorating this sacrifice of Isaac could not have been performed on the Day of Atonement itself, as it may have been observed in very ancient times. There were many considerations against performing the ceremony on the Day of Atonement. In the first place, it might involve a violation of the laws governing that holy day. Secondly, since according to the Luryanic interpretation the Tashlik had to be performed

---

[153] This פזמון beginning with the words אלה אזכרה is by Amitai, cf. *Sefer Ḥasidim*, ed. Wistinetzki, 415 (Frankfurt a/M., 1924), p. 123. It is found in the סליחות of the Polish Ritual No. 82 (Krakau, 1887), p. 166.

[153a] Cf. Agnon, *Yamim Nora'im*, p. 202, as follows: "The eighth of Tishri which is the eighth of the Ten days of Penitence is called "The 13 attributes," etc. Cf. also p. 204 *ibid*.

[154] See L. Ginzberg in *HaẒofeh* III, pp. 186 ff.

after the *Minḥah* service, to perform it at such a late time on the Day of Atonement would have been too late. Nor could they recommend it to be observed on the eve of the Day of Atonement, for on that day the time after the *Minḥah* service is taken up with the final preparation for the fast. Furthermore, on the eve of the Day of Atonement it is forbidden to fast and some pious people may have deemed it advisable to fast on the day, in the afternoon of which they would perform the Tashlik ceremony. The day preceding the eve of the Day of Atonement was, therefore, considered very appropriate for the performance of this ceremony. Most people are, after all, not sure of themselves in regard to their record in heaven. They consider themselves as belonging to the בינונים, that is, the class of people who are neither condemned nor acquitted on the first day of New Year but whose sentence is suspended until the Day of Atonement. The people who felt that way realized that a respite was given them during which they had a chance to improve their status, and they utilized the penitential days between New Year and the Day of Atonement for that purpose. They would do penitence and fast[155] during these "Days of Repentance," ימי תשובה. On the last day of these voluntary penitential fast days — for on the eve of the Day of Atonement they were not allowed to fast — they could believe themselves to have sufficiently improved their status so as to merit the aid and the assistance of the attributes of Mercy in subduing Satan. Hence, late in the afternoon of that day, after the *Minḥah* service, was deemed a very propitious time for performing the Tashlik ceremony, the aim of which is to prevent Satan from accusing the people and seeking to harm them. We cannot ascertain exactly when and by whom this change in the date set for the Tashlik ceremony was first made. All that we know, is that already in the nineteenth century, especially among the followers of the Ḥassidic Rabbis of the dynasty of R. Israel Friedmann of Ruzhin (later of Sadigora), the ceremony of Tashlik was performed not on New Year's Day but on the day preceding the eve of the Day of Atonement.[156]

---

[155] See Lev. r. 30.7 and cf. *Shibbole ha-Leḳeṭ*, 306, also ראב"יה II, p. 247.
[156] See Ḥayyim Knoller, דבר יום ביומו (Przemysl, 1909), p. 7b and 13b.

The other change in the date set for the observance of the ceremony has no connection at all with the Luryanic interpretation. It was rather the indirect result of the older understanding of the ceremony as serving the purpose of bribing Satan by gifts. The change represents a revival of the older reactions on the part of the Rabbis to the popular crude notions about the ceremony and to some of its features which the people adhered to obstinately. This change, furthermore, was not a permanent one; it was made only for a Rosh Hashanah that might fall on a Sabbath. In that case some authorities objected to the performance of the ceremony because of the possibility of a violation of the Sabbath laws in connection with it; and, not wishing to abandon the ceremony altogether, they recommended its being performed on the second day of the holiday.

The first one, to my knowledge, to advocate this change was R. Jeḥiel M. Epstein (flourished in the second half of the seventeenth century), the author of the קיצור שני לוחות הברית. For in this work (Lemberg, 1864), p. 79, he says: "When the first day of Rosh Hashanah falls on a Sabbath, the Tashlik ceremony should not be performed until the second day, lest people come to be involved in a profanation of the Sabbath."[157] There can be no doubt that he objected to some popular form of observing the ceremony which involved a violation of the Sabbath laws. For he also argues against the popular belief that by the Tashlik ceremony one throws off all one's sins. He objects to those who say: "I will go to shake off my sins." From this we see that he objected to the popular notions about the ceremony, and, no doubt, he objected also to certain features of the ceremony which expressed these false notions. He does not say how or which feature of the performance of the ceremony might involve a violation of the Sabbath laws. It may be that the mere shaking of the garments, or the throwing out of the crumbs of bread from their folds or pockets, was regarded as work which one should not do on the Sabbath. This assumption would seem to be supported by the statement of R. Joseph

---

[157] ואם חל יום ראשון של ראש השנה בשבת לא יעשה תשליך עד יום שני כדי שלא יבואו חס ושלום לידי חלול שבת.

Josepha. In his work, נוהג כצאן יוסף (Hanau, 1718), p. 73c, the latter says that when Rosh Hashanah falls on a Sabbath, they do the shaking of the garment — a feature in connection with the Tashlik ceremony — on the second day, ואם יום ראשון דראש השנה בשבת מנערין ביום שני. He does not say anything about the other features of the ceremony, as the going out to the water or the recitation of the prayers; he does not indicate whether these are to be performed on the first day and only the one feature, the "shaking" — which could not be done on the Sabbath, is to be performed on the next day, or that the entire ceremony is to be postponed to the second day. It may be that for him the main significance of the ceremony lay in the act of shaking the garments whereby the evil spirits and the sins are shaken off. For in describing the ceremony he says: והולכים אל הנהר ונוערים שולי בגדים להסיר הקליפות (*ibid.*, *loc. cit.*). By saying that the "shaking" is to be done on the second day he may, therefore, actually mean that the whole ceremony be postponed to the second day. At any rate it is evident that there was objection to the shaking of the garments on the Sabbath, and Epstein may have shared this objection. It is, however, more likely that Epstein's objection was to the carrying of food outside of the city, which is forbidden on the Sabbath. Epstein, then, merely re-echoes the objection of Maharil. The people, as it seems, continued to take along with them food to throw into the water, when going to Tashlik, in spite of the fact that Maharil and other authorities had forbidden it. If they did not do it openly they would carry some food hidden in the folds of their garments or some crumbs of bread in their pockets, which they would empty into the river after reciting the Tashlik prayer — as, indeed, it is still done to this day by most of those who observe the ceremony. Epstein, or his authority, may have objected to this feature altogether as did Maharil. But, realizing that the people could not be prevented from doing this in connection with the Tashlik ceremony, he, or his authority, sought, at least, to prevent their doing so on the Sabbath, a time when carrying something outside of the house or the enclosed court constitutes a violation of the law. He did tolerate it on the holiday when it fell on a week day, since there is no law against carrying things out of the house on a holiday.[158] For this reason he advocates that the ceremony be performed on the second day when the first day of the holiday happens to be a Sabbath day.

It would seem that this shifting of the date of the ceremony to the second day of Rosh Hashanah was a compromise. Other people, as it seems, would, for the same reasons, neglect the ceremony altogether in case the first day of Rosh Hashanah fell on a Saturday. This seems to have been the custom in Fürth, where they would omit the Tashlik ceremony in years when Rosh Hashanah fell on a Sabbath. For, in the work מנהגי ק"ק פיורדא by R. Israel and R. Kopel § 26 (Fürth, 1767), p. 5b, after the statement that the custom of going to the river for the Tashlik ceremony is observed on the first day of Rosh Hashanah, it is added ואם חל בשבת אין הולכים אל הנהר, "But if the first day of New Year's falls on a Sabbath they do not go to the river." It does not say that they would go the next day or at any other time before the Day of Atonement. They seemed to have been of the opinion that since in this case the ceremony could not be performed on its proper date, that is, on the opening day of judgment, then it need not be observed at all. Other people, however, like Epstein and his authorities, were loathe to give up the ceremony altogether. And, having in mind the idea that the two days of Rosh Hashanah are regarded as "one long day," they considered it advisable and proper to observe the ceremony at the end of that "long day," that is, on the afternoon of the second day. In this manner they retained the observance of the ceremony on the Rosh Hashanah day without incurring the risk of thereby violating the Sabbath law. This change of the date, however, was not generally accepted. There were rabbinic authorities who had come to regard the ceremony as a good Jewish religious custom and utterly ignored the implications involved in the still persistent popular abuses of it. Since they strictly forbade these objectionable features, they could not and would not recognize them as integral parts of the ceremony. Accordingly they could not see any reason why the ceremony should not be observed on a Sabbath. For, if observed strictly

---

[158] אין איסור הוצאה ליום טוב; see above, note 108.

in the manner prescribed by the authorities, that is, without carrying out food to cast into the river, or without shaking the garments, there could be no objection to it on the part of the Halakah. Among these authorities urging the performance of the ceremony on the first day, even if it happened to be a Sabbath, R. Jacob Reischer (died 1733) is especially noteworthy. In 1725 the first day of Rosh Hashanah fell on a Saturday, and Reischer was asked whether the ceremony of Tashlik should be observed on the first day or be postponed to the second. His answer was that he did not know the least possible objection to observing the ceremony on the first day even if it be a Sabbath day. On the contrary, so he argues, since the authorities have prescribed this ceremony to be performed on the first day of Rosh Hashanah, pious people should be eager and prompt to perform a religious ceremony and should not delay it for another day. Referring to Epstein who taught that the ceremony should be observed on the second day, Reischer says: "Recently there was printed the work of קיצור שני לוחות הברית in which the author states that one should not go to the river for the Tashlik ceremony on a Sabbath day, but without any reason or proof for his statement. He certainly must have overlooked what Maharil says on this question."[159] This last statement of Reischer, however, is neither fair nor correct. Epstein gives a very good reason for objecting to the ceremony's being observed on a Sabbath, namely, that it might lead to a violation of the Sabbath laws. He certainly did not overlook the opinion of Maharil. On the contrary, he based his objection on the very apprehension, which was felt by Maharil, that the people might carry food with them for the performance of the ceremony and thereby violate the Sabbath laws. It was rather Reischer, and not Epstein, who missed the implication in Maharil's discussion of the ceremony, namely, that there might be a possible profanation of the Sabbath in connection with the ceremony as it was commonly observed by the people.

---

[159] ומקרוב נדפס קיצור שני לוחות הברית שכתב שם שאין לילך אל הנהר ביום השבת בלי טעם וראיה ובודאי נתעלם ממנו דברי מהר"יל, Responsa, שבות יעקב No. 42 (Metz, 1729), p. 21b. Against Reischer see Azulai, *op. cit.*, p. 18.

However, be this as it may, the question whether the ceremony should be performed on a Sabbath or not, was not definitely decided. The opinions continued to be divided, and the custom accordingly varied in the various communities. The later rabbinical authorities all recognized the right of local option on the part of the communities in regard to this question. And even those authorities who, like Reischer, were of the opinion that the ceremony should be observed on the first day of Rosh Hashanah even if it be a Sabbath, nevertheless mention also, and without any expression of disapproval, the custom in certain communities of performing the ceremony on the second day of Rosh Hashanah if the first day happens to be a Sabbath day.

Thus R. Jacob Emden (1697–1776), while he declares that the ceremony should be observed on the first day of Rosh Hashanah even if it be a Sabbath day, also mentions that there are some people who in such an emergency perform the ceremony on the second day.[160]

Likewise R. Ephraim Zalman Margolioth (1762–1828) is of the opinion that the ceremony should be performed on the first day of Rosh Hashanah even if it be a Sabbath day. He insists, however, that the people must be careful, when going to the river outside of the city, to refrain from carrying anything with them, and especially not to take bread or other food with them to throw to the fishes.[161] In this way he meant to obviate the danger of a violation of the Sabbath law feared by Maharil and Epstein. He mentions, however, that in some communities it is customary to perform the ceremony on the second day of Rosh Hashanah if the first day happened to be on a Sabbath. He also declares that, if for some reason it was not possible to perform the ceremony on the first day, it may or should be performed on the second day. Thus we see that he is not so strict regarding the particular time set for this ceremony. He goes still further in allowing another change in the time — from the time after the *Minḥah* service to any time in the early after-

---

[160] See סדור בית יעקב (Warsaw, 1910), p. 108.
[161] See מטה אפרים עם אלף למטה § 598, 5–6 (Lemberg, 1858), p. 25a.

noon, before the *Minḥah* service.¹⁶² This may seem to be simply a reversion to the older custom of the time of Maharil when they used to perform the ceremony before the *Minḥah*, in the early afternoon, right after the noon meal, אחר הסעודה. But there is more to it. In this change from the time after the *Minḥah* to any time before it, there may be seen the expression of a reaction against Lurya's understanding of the ceremony. For according to the latter it was absolutely necessary that the ceremony be performed after the *Minḥah* service. A reaction against the Luryanic interpretation of the ceremony on the part of R. Ephraim Zalman Margolioth may also be found in his insistence upon the ceremony's being performed, if at all possible, near a river in which there are fish,¹⁶³ and especially in his explanation of the feature of shaking the garments while performing the ceremony. The shaking of the garment, according to his explanation, is not in order to shake off the evil spirits that cling to one as a result of his sins. It is merely a symbolic gesture to remind us that we should set our heart upon abandoning our evil ways and in the future we may examine our conduct and search our ways, so that we may be pure of all sin.¹⁶⁴

Of course, the main idea, that the purpose of the ceremony was to silence Satan and hinder him from making accusations, persisted among the people as well as among the mystically inclined rabbinical authorities. But this interpretation of the ceremony by R. Ephraim Zalman Margolioth as a mere symbolical act probably helped to make the ceremony less objectionable, if not altogether acceptable, even among the enlightened and more critical people who would have opposed all the mystic ideas connected with it according to the Luryanic interpretation. It is also possible that it was due, partly at least, to this interpretation by R. Ephraim Zalman Margolioth that the heathen superstitions underlying the ceremony were obscured and not recognized by the enlightened non-rabbinic scholars of the nineteenth century. The general acceptance of this ceremony naturally awakened the interest of these scholarly writers and

---

¹⁶² *Ibid.*, 598, 7.   ¹⁶³ *Ibid.*, 598, 4.
¹⁶⁴ *Ibid., loc. cit.*, ומנערים שם שולי הבנדים והוא לרמז בעלמא ליתן לב להשליך החטאים ולחפש ולחקור דרכים מן הוא והלאה שיהיו בנדיו לבנים ונקיים מכל חטא.

called their attention to it. The interpretation of R. Ephraim Zalman Margolioth, giving the ceremony merely symbolic significance, made it easy for these enlightened people to accept the ceremony and even stimulated them to try on their part to give it a rationalistic interpretation which would make it an unobjectionable Jewish ceremony. We accordingly find quite a number of scholarly writers of the nineteenth century who manifest a scientific interest in this ceremony and try to trace its origin, to explain its significance, and to give it a rationalistic meaning.

The writers who discuss this ceremony may be divided into two groups. The one group, misled by the fact that the ceremony is first explicitly mentioned in the fifteenth century by a German authority, Maharil, and is never mentioned nor referred to by any authority of the Spanish school, assumed that the ceremony had its origin in Germany and that it was first introduced among the Jews in Germany at about the beginning of the fifteenth century. Of course, these writers also assume, or at least do not deny, that the German rabbinical authorities who introduced the ceremony may have had the idea for such a ceremony suggested to them by some indication of a similar practice found in the earlier literature; but the ceremony as such according to their views was an innovation of the later German authorities. The other group rightly ignores the fact that the ceremony is first explicitly mentioned in the fifteenth century, and seeks to trace its origin to some ancient practice or to some idea or belief expressed in Bible or Talmud. They fail, however, to trace the ideas underlying it to their very origins. They do not show how the entire development of the ceremony took its course, nor how and in what forms it persisted up to the time when it made its first appearance in its fully developed form in the late middle ages in Germany.

Of the former group the first to be mentioned is Isaac Ber Levinsohn whose theory is that the Tashlik ceremony, like the ceremony of blowing the Shofar, is a symbolic act, indicating that we again accept upon ourselves the rule and the Kingdom of God. He says: "By blowing the Shofar on every New Year the people again renew their pledge of loyalty to the Ruler of the world and accept Him as their King. Therefore, it seems to me, that for the very same purpose later authorities instituted the custom of going on New Year's day to the rivers or wells in order there to renew the pledge of loyalty to God and to accept Him again as their King. For the Rabbis of the Talmud (Hor. 12a) said: 'They anoint kings only near a well, as it is said: "And bring him down to Gihon ... anoint him there ... and blow ye with the horn" ' " (I Kings 1.33–34).[165] Levinsohn is correct in assuming that the purpose of the Tashlik ceremony is the same as the purpose of the ceremony of blowing the Shofar. But he is not correct in believing that that purpose was to renew our declaration that God is our King. The purpose of the blowing of the Shofar, as stated in the Talmud (R. H. 16b), was to confound Satan, כדי לערבב שטן, and to prevent him from accusing the people. And so also the purpose of the Tashlik ceremony was to silence Satan and to prevent him from bringing his accusations against the people. And just as the Shofar ceremony is of very ancient times, so also the Tashlik ceremony has its origin in very ancient times, and is not an innovation of the אחרונים, the later German rabbinic authorities, as assumed by Levinsohn.

Like Levinsohn, Jacob Reifman also assumes that the Tashlik is of late origin. He ascribes the institution of the ceremony to some unknown German authorities. The idea for such a ceremony was suggested to them, he says, by the saying of Abaye in the Talmud (Hor. 12a) who recommends the practice of looking at (or eating?) certain vegetables on New Year's Day which may serve as a good omen, auguring a successful year. These unknown German authorities, therefore, thought that it would be good to go out on New Year's Day to the river and look at it; this likewise would serve as a good omen, since according to a saying of R. Joshua b. Levi in the Talmud (Ber. 56b) a river is a symbol of peace. The idea of throwing the sins into the river, however, originated, according to Reifman, much

---

[165] אבני מילואים, the second part of בית האוצר (Wilna, 1841), p. 300; also ספר יהושפט (Warsaw, 1883), p. 94. This idea is also advanced by Ch. M. Eliaschow in *Hamagid*, XI, No. 39, p. 310.

later, in the mind of the ignorant masses who misunderstood the original significance of the ceremony.[166]

Against Reifman's theory, R. Wolf Wertheim, quoted by Hirsch Bodek, rightly contends, that from the very passage in the Talmud (Ber. 56b) referred to by Reifman one could argue equally well that a river might also be a bad omen, as suggested by the passage: "For distress will come like a river" (Isa. 59.19). Hence the custom of going to the river could not have been for the purpose of securing a good omen. Wertheim, therefore, thinks that the idea for the ceremony was suggested to the later authorities who introduced it, by the saying of the Talmud to the effect that an act performed near the water, whether the anointing of a king or the study of the law, will have lasting effect and continue in its result, as the water flows continually. He says: "And no doubt it was on the basis of this idea expressed in the Talmud, that some of the later great authorities instituted the custom of going out to wells or rivers on New Year's Day in order that the stream of God's mercy may flow upon us continuously as the stream flows from the well continuously."[167] Bodek himself, after quoting Wertheim's discussion, proceeds to give his own opinion about the Tashlik and he has a few interesting and very suggestive ideas. Bodek thinks that the ceremony of going out to the river is a relic of the time when the people would go out to the river to meet the

[166] Zion, edited by Jost and Creizenach, I (1840–1841), p. 184. See against Reifman the remarks by Bodek in Zion II (1841–1842), p. 48. In השחר II, p. 434, Reifman gives another explanation of the Tashlik ceremony. Zweifel in לקוטי צבי, p. 81, quotes Reifman as explaining the purpose of the ceremony to be להשריש בלבנו קדושת מלכותו. But this is not Reifman's own idea. Reifman merely quotes (השחר, loc. cit.) R. Solomon Klueger. The latter in his ספר החיים (Zolkiew, 1825), השמטות, p. 8, explains the significance of the ceremony, as follows: ולפענ"ד נראה ליתן טעם חדש על דרך שאמרו חז"ל אין מושחין מלכים אלא על המעיין כדי שתמשוך מלכותן כמעיין ולפי"ז כשמגיע ר"ה ובכל שנה ושנה מקבלין אנחנו על עצמנו עבודת הש"י... ועל כן הולכין למעיין להתפלל שיהיה נמשך מלכותו של הקב"ה עלינו כמעיין ולא יפסוק... ולכך נראה לילך דוקא לנהר הנמשך ולא לבאר ובור מכונס. Cf. Ezechiel Ratner who in his work מבשרי אחזה, 34 (Wilna, 1874), p. 39, gives the ideas of both R. Epharim Z. Margoliouth and R. Solomon Klueger without mentioning their names.

[167] Zion II, loc. cit. Cf. also M. Auerbach in Rahmer's Literaturblatt, X (1881), No. 40–41, p. 161.

king after he had been crowned there. He also suggests that it is to remind us of the crossing of the Red Sea, so that we may remember that God helped us against our enemies when we were at the sea and brought us out from slavery to freedom. The rise of the custom, according to Bodek, was due to the spread of the Cabalah in the time of Maharil. Maharil was not in favor of the ceremony and would very much have liked to suppress it but was unable to do so. For the rabbinic authorities have always been on the lookout to fight against superstitions and false beliefs. "Had it not been for the watchfulness of the rabbinic authorities," says Bodek, "who knows but what we should have had to this day preserved to us superstitious customs and false heathen rituals of going to the river and praying to and asking petitions of the spirit of the river or the god of the sea."[168] Bodek correctly sensed the struggle between the strict rabbinical authorities and the heathen superstitions in connection with this ceremony.

And finally, among the writers laboring under the delusion that since the ceremony is first specifically mentioned by Maharil, it must have been introduced not long before Maharil's time, is to be mentioned R. Kirchheim,[169] who assumes that the Jews in Germany borrowed this ceremony from the Christians in the Rhein province. For, a ceremony exactly like the Tashlik was observed by the Christians in Cologne in the fourteenth century as noticed by Petrarch on his visit there. The same theory is also advanced by M. Spaniel,[170] who evidently did not know that Kirchheim preceded him with this theory.

In the other group of writers who felt that the ceremony was of more ancient origin there is first to be mentioned K.

---

[168] מי יודע אם לא היה נשאר לנו עד היום הזה מנהגי כזב ועבודת שקר לילך אל הנהר ולבקש תחנה ובקשה משר הנהר או משר של ים (Zion, loc. cit.). One is inclined to suspect Bodek of disguising in this remark his characterization of the ceremony as understood and practiced by the people.

[169] Geiger's *Jüdische Zeitschrift für Wissenschaft und Leben*, IV (1868), p. 238.

[170] Rahmer's *Literaturblatt*, X (1881), No. 38. Cf. also Alexander Zederbaum in *Hameliẓ*, VI (1866), No. 39, p. 589, who finds a resemblance between the Tashlik ceremony and the Christian custom of marching on the 6th of January from the church to the river.

Schulmann, who rightly suggests that the Tashlik ceremony may have some connection with the practice of the Jews in Halicarnassus, mentioned by Josephus to which reference has been made above.[171] Again, according to a rabbinical authority, quoted by Ch. M. Eliashow,[172] the Tashlik ceremony originated in the time of Ezra and Nehemiah. For, as reported in Nehemiah (7.37–8.3), on the first day of the seventh month, that is, on the day of Rosh Hashanah, Ezra assembled the people for the reading of the Torah in front of the water gate. This, then, was a religious service near the water on the day of Rosh Hashanah. This rabbinical authority seeks even to trace the feature of shaking the garments at the Tashlik ceremony to Nehemiah (5.3) where the shaking of the garments is mentioned apparently as an act symbolic of throwing something off.

R. Hirsch Segal of Rovno[173] correctly recognized that the Tashlik and Kapparot ceremonies were originally but one, or, at least, had one and the same origin. He traces them to the practice in gaonic times, as reported in the gaonic responsum, cited by Rashi to Shab. 81b, which we have discussed above. The going to the river, according to Segal, is but a relic of the practice of going to the river to throw in the baskets of fruit. The baskets of fruit have in the course of time been replaced by fowl and the date for disposing of them shifted to the eve of the Day of Atonement, while on Rosh Hashanah there remained but the old habit of going to the river. Segal failed to take notice of the fact that even in later times it was not a mere walking out to the river, but that the people continued to carry with them food and to throw it into the river. He also is mistaken when he considers the gaonic custom as the beginning of the ceremony, when as a matter of fact, the gaonic custom itself represented already a development from a much older custom, as we have shown above.

David Isaac Landesberg[174] agrees with Segal and recognizes the original identity of the two ceremonies, Tashlik and Kap-

[171] In *Hameliz*, VIII (1864), No. 14, p. 106. Cf. above, note 19.
[172] *Hamagid*, XI, No. 39, p. 310.
[173] In his לקוטי צבי edited by E. Zweifel (Zytomir, 1866), p. 80.
[174] In *Hameliz*, 1866, Nos. 33–34. Cf. above, note 102.

parot. He assumes, however, that besides being in the course of time divided into two separate ceremonies, changes were at some time effected in the ceremony, in that it was deemed preferable to go to rivers instead of to wells and that the authorities began to object to the throwing in of the baskets. The reason for these changes, according to Landesberg, was that the observance of the ceremony by throwing the baskets into the wells may have been the cause of the false accusations of poisoning the wells which were raised against the Jews. For, so he argues, the Gentiles might have misunderstood the purpose of this ceremony and imagined that the Jews were throwing poison into the wells. All this is very ingenious but not correct. In the first place, there is no ground whatever for assuming that originally they would throw these baskets into wells instead of into rivers. Secondly, even in later times they would go to wells in places where there was no river, and they still continued to throw food — which the Gentiles could have just as easily mistaken for poison — into the river or well. Furthermore, the accusations against the Jews that they poisoned the wells were not raised before the beginning of the Black Death in 1348. But Petrarch on his visit to Cologne (about 1333–34) already noticed a similar custom among the Gentiles. How, then could the Christians have misunderstood the purpose of the ceremony observed by the Jews when Christians themselves also had a similar ceremony?

An anonymous writer, author of the essay בקרת מנהגים,[175] is opposed to the theory of Segal and Landesberg because he finds it difficult to explain how the ceremony, if originally one, became divided into two. He also finds it implausible that the baskets of vegetables should have been replaced by fowl and that the date for the Kapparot should have been changed from New Year's Day to the eve of the Day of Atonement. He, therefore, assumes that the Tashlik ceremony, or at least the original idea underlying it, was the expression of the belief that, as suggested in many passages of the Bible, "The glory of God hovers over

---

[175] In *Hameliẓ*, XIX (1888), No. 75, pp. 1204–5. בקרת מנהגים מאת י. ה. ו. פ. מבריסק דליטא.

any body of water, seas or rivers; these are, therefore apt to arouse holy sentiments in the hearts of those who come near them." How the whole Tashlik ceremony in its later form developed out of this original idea, and how the notion of throwing away the sins came in the course of time to be connected with it, he admits that he is unable to explain.

We thus find that even among modern scholarly writers the Tashlik ceremony was frequently discussed,[176] various reasons for its observance were offered, and explanations of its meaning suggested.[177] All these discussions and rationalizing interpretations did not in the least harm the ceremony nor reduce its popularity. On the contrary, they even helped to preserve and perpetuate it. For, certainly a ceremony that lends itself to so many different interpretations and can be made to suggest so many different ideas, could not be ignored and was rather considered worth while observing. The rationalizing interpretations had merely the effect of pushing to the background the false ideas underlying it. It helped to explain in a symbolic way some of the objectionable features connected with it, thus making them appear harmless, if not even useful. Even Isaac Erter's famous parody[178] could be taken as directed against the popular misunderstanding of the significance of the ceremony, and not against the ceremony itself, and certainly not against any of the good ideas which were interpreted into it by the more enlightened Rabbis and scholars.

As a result the ceremony is still observed to this day. It is true that among liberal Jews, or in the Reform wing of Jewry, the ceremony has been discarded. But among the conservative

[176] Israel Abrahams discusses the Tashlik ceremony in the *London Jewish Chronicle*, September 1889, pp. 15–16. But he failed to see the real significance of the ceremony and was totally unaware of the development which it went through.

[177] The following is a new suggestion about the significance of the Tashlik ceremony offered by R. Meir Posner in his work on the *Shulḥan 'Aruk*, בית יראה שהוא על שם הפסוק שמואל א. ז' וישאבו מים וישפכו :93 .p ,(1876 ,Josefow) מאיר לפני ה' ומתרגם יונתן ושפיכו לבהון בתיובתא כמיא קדם ה'. ורש"י פירש סימן הכנעה הרי אנו כמים הללו הנשפכין לפניך. Cf. also מחזור אהלי יעקב I (Jerusalem, 1908), p. 149a, where it is suggested that the ceremony is to remind us of Adam's repentance.

[178] In his הצופה לבית ישראל (Wien, 1864), pp. 64–80.

and orthodox Jews, who constitute the vast majority of Jewry, the ceremony is still observed. In the last few years, however, the popularity of the ceremony has suffered a great setback due to the fact that the Jews are mostly city dwellers and concentrate in large cities. The Jews who live in large cities encounter a physical difficulty in observing this ceremony, in that it is hard for them to get to a river or well. In most cases a river or lake cannot be reached from a city residence by walking. To get to the river or lake it is often necessary for the city dweller to take a long ride in some kind of vehicle, and this the Halakah forbids on a holiday. The long struggle between the Halakah and the superstitious practice must, therefore, end with the defeat of the latter. The Halakah, the arch-enemy of superstition, will ultimately be the cause of the complete abolition of the Tashlik ceremony which in spite of all rationalizing interpretations and symbolic meanings given to it, has its roots in ancient heathen superstitions.

The Sabbath in Jewish Ritual
and Folklore

The Sabbath in Jewish Ritual and Folklore

THE Sabbath has always played a very important role in the social and religious life of the Jewish people. It is a unique institution, conceived and developed by the Jewish genius, without any equivalent among the similar institutions of other people. There were in ancient times other peoples who observed every seventh day as a day of rest and of cessation of all work. The Babylonian "Shabbatu," connected with and determined by the phases of the moon, while it may have had some superficial resemblances to the Jewish Sabbath, was in reality of an entirely different character. It is true, in the Bible,[1] the Sabbath is mentioned together with the new moon, and it may originally also have been connected with the phases of the moon. But as understood and developed in post-biblical times the Jewish Sabbath is altogether different from the Babylonian "Shabbatu."[2] Again, there were people who observed rest days as tabu days or unlucky days.[3] But the Jewish Sabbath, although it may perhaps originally have had some aspects or features resembling a tabu day,[4] and even though survivals of such features may still be traced in some of the Sabbath rituals, yet in spirit and in character is anything but a tabu day. Many of its features are such as to show it to be just the opposite of a tabu day, and some of its ceremonies seek to emphasize that it is not at all an unlucky day.

---

[1] Amos 8.5; Hosea 2.13; Isa. 1.13; 66.23; Ezek. 45.17; 46.1, 3; II Kings 4.23; I Chron. 23.31; II Chron. 2.3; 8.13; 31.3.

[2] See Hans Meinhold, *Sabbat und Sonntag* (Leipzig, 1909), pp. 6–7; Hutton Webster, *Rest Days* (New York, 1916), p. 242 f.; also C. H. Toy, *Introduction to the History of Religions* (Boston-New York, 1913), pp. 252–53.

[3] Toy, *op. cit.*, p. 253.

[4] Toy, *op.* cit., pp. 251–252; *idem*, "The Earliest Form of the Sabbath," *Journal of Biblical Literature*, 1899.

Again, the Jewish Sabbath is not and never was regarded by the Jewish people as a day sacred to Saturn, as some Roman writers believed.[5] For there is no indication at all in ancient Jewish literature of any connection between the Jews and Saturn which would justify the assumption that the latter was especially honored by the Jews.[6] The very interpretation of the Pharisees of the term Sabbath to mean not only the seventh day of the week but also any holiday proclaimed by the law as a day of rest from work, seeks to deny any connection between the observance of the Sabbath and the worship of Saturn.[7] And according to Yalḳut Reubeni to *Jethro*[8] many of the ceremonies and regulations prescribed for the Sabbath were directed against the practices of those people who believed the Sabbath to be Saturn's day. According to another, later, mystic writer, the secret of the Sabbath and its real significance is rather to emphasize the belief that God is the sole ruler of the world, and Saturn, though he rules every seventh day, has absolutely no power or influence on the affairs of men.[9] And modern scholars agree that there is no connection between the Jewish Sabbath and Saturn.[10] For the Jewish Sabbath is not of a negative character, that is, it is not merely a day on which one must refrain from doing work, or a day of idleness as the Stoic philo-

[5] See A. Büchler, "Graeco-Roman Criticism of Some Jewish Observances and Beliefs," *Jewish Review* I, (London, 1910), 140–143; also Hutton Webster, *op. cit.*, p. 245.

[6] A. Epstein's suggestion that in very ancient times prior to the revelation on Sinai the Israelites may have observed a festival in honor of Saturn, מקדמוניות היהודים, (Wien, 1867), p. 10, is but a guess lacking any confirmation. And when in later Jewish works an astrological connection between Saturn and the Jews is mentioned, it is emphasized that the Jews observe the Sabbath rather to demonstrate their independence of Saturn, that they need no help whatever from him, but rely on God alone. See ספר מרגליות טובה, (Amsterdam, 1722), p. 71b.

[7] See Lauterbach, *The Pharisees and Their Teachings*, above p. 124 and note 37.

[8] Warsaw, 1901, p. 108.

[9] See עמק המלך by Naftali Hirz b. Jacob Elḥanan, שער עולם הבריאה, ch. 23, (Amsterdam, 1648), p. 177. See also זהב חדש to יתרו, (Warsaw, 1901), p. 73. Also Baḥya שופטים, (Warsaw, 1878), p. 50.

[10] b. Berakot 57b; Büchler, *op. cit.*, p. 143; Watson, *op. cit.*, p. 243.

THE SABBATH 439

sopher Seneca considered it.[11] It is of a most positive character, performing a definite function in the life of the people, saving, strengthening and preserving it. It is a day crowded with pleasurable and spiritual and intellectual activities which refresh the soul and give it a foretaste of the bliss and joy of the future world, שבת מעין עולם הבא.[12] The Sabbath, according to rabbinic views, is a divine institution antedating the selection of Israel and the Revelation on Sinai, which only gradually in the course of time, after having been cherished by the patriarchs, became more and more identified with their descendants and then became the unique though not exclusive possession of the Jewish people. It was first instituted at the very beginning of creation and God Himself observed it.[13] Then the first man, Adam, was given the commandment concerning the Sabbath[14] and he observed it, was comforted by it and was saved from all evil.[15] The Patriarch Abraham observed even the minutiae of the Sabbath regulations.[16] The Patriarch Jacob likewise observed the Sabbath.[17] Joseph observed the Sabbath[18] and spent that day studying what he had learned from his father.[19] The Israelites in Egypt also observed the Sabbath. They were exempted from doing any labor, a privilege which Moses, before he fled from Egypt, had obtained for them from Pharaoh.[20] They also observed the day actively with a sort of religious and educational activity. They had in their possession certain writings or scrolls, containing cheerful messages promising them that God would deliver them from their bondage. From these scrolls they would read on every Sabbath day and comfort themselves.[21] After they

[11] See J. Hugh Michael, "The Jewish Sabbath in the Latin Classical Writers," in the *American Journal of Semitic Languages and Literatures*, XL (1923–24), 121.
[12] b. Ber. 57b; also נובלת העולם הבא שבת (Gen. r. 17.5), the Sabbath is a sort of an incomplete variety of the future world.
[13] Gen. 2.2; Gen. r. 11.2 and 6; Pirḳe deR. Eliezer 20.
[14] Gen. r. 16.8.   [15] Pirḳe deR. Eliezer, *loc. cit.*
[16] b. Yoma 28b.   [17] Gen. r. 11.8 and 79.7.
[18] Gen. r. 92.4 and Num. r. 14.9.
[19] See ליקוטים ממדרש אבכיר, ed. S. Buber, (Wien, 1883), p. 9; also Yalḳut Shime'oni, Gen. 146.
[20] Gen. r. 1.32.   [21] *Ibid.* 5.22.

departed from Egypt and on their wanderings reached Marah[22] the law about the Sabbath, together with the commandment to honor father and mother, was given to them in a special revelation.[23] These two laws were later merely repeated on Sinai and were given together with the other commandments. The intimate relation between these two commandments and the ideal of a life of holiness is suggested in the Scriptual passage: "Ye shall be holy, for I the Lord your God am holy. Ye shall fear every man his mother and his father and ye shall keep my Sabbaths."[24] And the effectiveness of these commandments is enhanced and their interrelation is strengthened by the very manner in which the Sabbath is, and has always been, observed. The main center of the Sabbath observance is in the family circle at the home and many of its ceremonies are calculated to strengthen the bonds of love and affection between the members of the family, to emphasize the parental care and duties, and to increase the filial respect and reverence for the parents. A man, working or engaged in business during the six days of the week has not much time to spend with his family. "But when he rests and is free from business on the Sabbath he has the opportunity to become really acquainted and pleased with his children and reconciled with all the members of his household."[25] The parents have time to instruct and occasion to inspire the children, and reverence for the parents causes the children to pay respectful attention to the parental instruction. Thus they receive all the teachings which have traditionally been transmitted by parents to children from generation to generation. In this manner the Sabbath observance in the home cultivates and preserves in the family circle all the Jewish ideals and religious teachings, leading its members to the love of God and His law.

But not only in the home and among the members of the family does the Sabbath create a spirit of love and reverence. It also encourages a spirit of friendliness and of good fellowship in the whole community and among the entire people. For the Sabbath is observed by the community in public assemblies in

---

[22] Ex. 15.23–25. [23] b. Sanh. 56b. [24] Lev. 19.2–3.
[25] *Seder Eliyahu Rabbah* I, Friedmann (Wien, 1902), p. 4.

the synagogues, prayer houses and houses of study. These assemblies were always devoted to religious worship, studying and expounding of the Law and the Prophets, as is evidenced by numerous references to such Sabbath observances in the talmudic literature[26] as well as in the N. T. literature[27] and in the contemporary works of Philo[28] and Josephus.[29] And when they assemble in the synagogues, they not only pray and study, but also cultivate a spirit of friendship, learning not to hate or insult each other and not to be jealous of one another.[30] In this manner the Sabbath leads to the study of the Law and to the keeping of the Commandments. "The Sabbath," says the Talmud[31] "is equal to all the laws of the Torah taken together." And the Midrash[32] says: "God said to the Israelites, if you only keep the Sabbath I will account it to you as if you had kept all the laws of the Torah." For the very observance of the Sabbath in the proper manner and in the right spirit will make them learn all the laws of the Torah and appreciate the religious truths. The Sabbath thus preserves the Jewish people and their ideals, trains them to cherish their lofty teachings and to admire their glorious traditions. The faithful keeping and correct observance of the Sabbath can indeed save Israel and bring them redemption.[33]

It is because of this great importance of the Sabbath for the life of the Jewish people, and because its observances and

[26] See b. Shab. 115a and 116b; p. Soṭah 1.4 (16d); Gen. r. 17.7; p. Shab. 15.3 (15a); Pesiḳta Rabbati xxiii, Friedmann 121a; *Seder Eliyahu Rabbah* I, Friedmann, 4; also Midrash Mishle xxxi, Buber, p. 108.

[27] Matt. 4.23; 9.35; Mark 1.39; Luke 4.15, 44; Acts 13.5.

[28] *De Septennario* II, 282. Cf. M. Friedländer, *Synagoge und Kirche in ihren Anfängen* (Berlin, 1908), pp. 37–38. The ideas expressed in *Seder Eliyahu Rabbah loc. cit* and in p. Shab. *loc. cit.* might well be considered as reflecting a parallel conception of the Sabbath on the part of Pharisaic Judaism; against Friedländer, *ibid.*, p. 38 note 1. Cf. also J. Mann, "The Observance of the Sabbath and the Festivals" etc. in the *Jewish Review* IV, (London 1913–1914), 433 ff.

[29] See *Ant.* XVI, 2, 4, and *Contra Apionem* II, 7, and cf. Mann, *loc. cit.*

[30] Midrash Shir ha-Shirim 8.15.

[31] p. Ned. 3.14 (38a).

[32] Ex. r. 25.16.

[33] b. Shab. 118b; p. Ta'an. 1.1 (4a) and Ex. r. 25.16.

ceremonies, if correctly understood, all teach the Jewish spirit, suggest religious ideas and help to reinforce the sense of Jewish solidarity among the members of the Jewish household, and impart to them a knowledge of and a love for Judaism — it is because of all these functions of the Sabbath that a correct understanding of the manner in which the Sabbath is and should be observed and a full knowledge of the ceremonies connected with it are so very necessary for adequate and effective instruction in Judaism both in the religious school and in the home.

In this essay I shall endeavor, as far as I am able, to give full information about the Sabbath observance and all its ceremonies to the extent that such information can be gathered from the various sources, and especially from the works of Jewish literature; and wherever possible I shall also attempt to trace the development of each ceremony. For to understand correctly the significance of the ceremonies of the Sabbath and to appreciate their value for the religious life, one must keep in mind the process of development which religious ceremonies in general undergo. In the course of time, the advanced beliefs and more enlightened thoughts of succeeding generations, cause ceremonies to be subjected to a process both of modification and reinterpretation. By this process they receive ever new meanings and fresh significance in keeping with the more advanced ideas of the people of each successive period or generation, meanings which are entirely different both from their original significance and from the meanings given them in earlier or preceding times.[34]

One must remember the intimate relation between Jewish ritual and Jewish folklore. It has often happened in the course of development of Jewish ceremonies that while the ritual has been spiritualized and the ceremonies modified and reinterpreted so as to harmonize with the advanced beliefs of the teachers, the popular mind, retaining some of the earlier notions or primitive beliefs, would cling to some forms of the ceremony or to some features of the ritual which were characteristic of an earlier and lower stage of the religious development. Thus the

[34] See Lauterbach, "The Ceremony of Breaking a Glass at Weddings" in *HUCA*, II (Cincinnati, 1925), 353–354.

THE SABBATH 443

ceremony is made to preserve and continues to suggest ideas and beliefs long abandoned by the progressive teachers.[35] The ceremonies of the Sabbath will furnish us with many illustrations of such arrested developments or interrupted progress. We may find in the popular form of an observance of some of the Sabbath ceremonies certain features which represent either a residuum of older superstitions or a relapse into a more primitive stage of popular belief and folklore. On the whole, however, we shall find that the teachers, representing the advanced mode of thinking and the progressive Jewish genius, in every generation try to eliminate from the ritual such survivals of crude superstition, to reinterpret even the popular notions and to give them a higher ethical meaning and a purely religious significance, thus bringing them up to the cultural and spiritual level of their times and generation. We shall thus find that the Sabbath, as understood by the best minds of the people, its representative teachers, and as observed by the more enlightened groups of the people, is indeed, as the Scripture declares it to be, "a sign between Me and you throughout your generations, that ye may know that I am the Lord who sanctify you."[36] For only a God-inspired people, a people consecrated to God and filled with the spirit of true religion could have developed such an institution as the Jewish Sabbath, constantly reinterpreting and spiritualizing its ceremonies, thus transforming the crude ore of superstitious notions and astrological beliefs into the pure gold of higher ethical teachings and true religious ideas.

We shall treat first the ceremonies observed at the entrance of the Sabbath, then some special ceremonies or characteristic features of the observance of the Sabbath day,[37] then the ceremonies at the closing of the day or the going out of the Sabbath,

[35] See *Tashlik*, above p. 299-302.
[36] Ex. 31.13.
[37] I shall deal only with the positive elements or the active side of the Sabbath observances, i. e., what the Jew is to do and observe on the Sabbath, and not with the negative or passive side, i. e., what is forbidden to do. In exceptional cases when the negative laws in reality have positive character, as when certain prohibitions express a protest against some older superstitious laws, or otherwise have some folkloristic value, I shall point them out. Neither shall I deal with the details of the liturgy except to point out par-

to be followed by a discussion of the final farewell to the Sabbath, or Saturday night observances.[38] In explaining the individual ceremonies we shall proceed chronologically, discussing first their original meaning and significance when and wherever it can be ascertained, then arranging in chronological order the various subsequent meanings attached to or superimposed upon them in the course of time by the process of modification and reinterpretation. Thus, in many cases at least, we shall present a complete picture of their development.

From what has already been said about the character of the Sabbath, it is evident that the Jewish Sabbath is not a Puritan Sabbath; it is not a gloomy or a sad day. It is rather a day of joy and of pleasure, and as will be shown in the course of this essay, all the restrictions imposed upon us during this day, as e. g., to refrain from work and travel,[39] are intended primarily not to impose burdens upon us,[40] but rather to give us full

---

ticular ideas concerning the character of the Sabbath which are expressed in certain parts of the liturgy.

[38] [Dr. Lauterbach's discussion of the Sabbath eve and night observances was published separately in the *HUCA* XV, 1940 under the title, "The Origin and Development of two Sabbath Ceremonies." See editor's note, below p. 470. L. H. S.]

[39] The halakic regulations prohibiting travel were at the time of their inauguration not a restriction but, paradoxical as it may sound, rather a liberation of the movements of a person on the Sabbath. For by restricting the Biblical injunction which prevented a man from going "out of his place" to mean only an interdiction of long distance travel, they aimed at permitting travel at least to a certain distance, thus removing from the Sabbath the character of a tabu day. For some sects interpreted the law: "Abide ye every man in his place, let no one go out of his place on the seventh day" (Ex. 16.29) to mean that one should not budge from his place and not be allowed to leave his house. Remnants of a sect who observed such a literally strict interpretation of this Sabbath law were still found in the second half of the twelfth century. See סבוב ר' פתחיה ed. Grünhut (Jerusalem, 1904), p. 4 where it is reported about them ויושבים במקום אחד כל היום. See *The Pharisees and Their Teachings*, above p. 124, and see below, note 97.

[40] This is not to deny that in the course of time by an accumulated excess of minutiae they may have become burdensome to some people. But the pious Jew joyfully accepted and submitted even to all the details of these accumulated regulations. Cf. Schechter, *Studies in Judaism* (Philadelphia, 1905), First Series, pp. 244–248.

leisure and thus to increase our joys and our pleasure on this sacred day. Our spiritual as well as our material life is to be made richer, more pleasant and more delightful by our leisure on the Sabbath day and by the observance of its ceremonies. It is a religious duty to have pleasure and delight, עונג שבת,[41] on this day. This is especially expressed by the prophet when he says, "If thou turn away thy foot because of the Sabbath from pursuing thy business on My holy day, and call the Sabbath a delight, and the holy of the Lord honourable; and shalt honour it, not doing thy wonted ways, nor pursuing thy business, nor speaking thereof, then shalt thou delight thyself in the Lord."[42] The same idea is repeatedly stated in the Talmud. It was considered not a burdensome obligation but a great privilege to have such an institution as the Sabbath.

God said to Moses: "I have a precious gift stored away in my treasury which I am now going to give to Israel. It is the Sabbath." So runs a legend in the Talmud.[43] Israel gladly received this beautiful gift and knew how to value, appreciate and keep it. They compared it to a beautiful bride whom they called the "Princess Sabbath" or the "Queen Sabbath," and whom they were eager to welcome on her weekly visits.[44] They thought of her the whole week, anticipating the pleasure of her visit. And whatever desirable portion they happened to find or acquire during the week, they would say, "Let us keep it for our beautiful guest, the Sabbath."[45] And on the day preceding her arrival the whole house was cleaned and decorated in her honor. A pleasurable excitement prevailed in the home. Every-

---

[41] The Sabbath pleasure or *luxus sabbatarius*, however, never degenerated into debauchery and violent excesses, as some church fathers would make us believe, even though pious Jews would serve sumptuous meals and give pleasant entertainments on the Sabbath and even though dancing as such was allowed on the Sabbath (see *Sh. 'Ar. Oraḥ Ḥayyim* 339, 3, especially Isserles' remark, and cf. I. Abrahams' *Jewish Life in the Middle Ages* [Philadelphia, 1903], p. 381). For it was always done with moral restraint and in the consciousness of doing it in honor of the Sabbath. See also Hutton Webster, *op. cit.*, pp. 265–266.

[42] Isa. 58.13–14. [43] b. Shab. 10b. [44] *Ibid.* 119a.

[45] Mekilta deR. Ishmael, *Baḥodesh* VII (ed. Lauterbach, II, 253); b. Beẓah 16a; Pesiḳta Rabbati 115b.

one in the household delighted to do part of the work in preparing to welcome her; everybody in the house was eager to help in making her visit a delight.[46] The appearance of the house was entirely different at the arrival of this honored guest.

When Does the Sabbath Begin?

Before we proceed to describe the ceremonies of the entrance of the Sabbath we must ascertain the exact time of her appearance, that is, at what time of the day the arrival of the Princess Sabbath was expected. This will help us to understand better certain features in the arrangements for welcoming her. As the Sabbath is the seventh day of the week and extends over one whole day, a brief discussion[47] of the development of the Jewish system of reckoning the day is necessary to determine the time of the coming in and the going out of the Sabbath.

There can be no doubt that in pre-exilic times the Israelites reckoned the day from morning to morning. The day began with the dawn and closed with the end of the night following it, i. e., with the last moment before the dawn of the next morning.[48] The very description of the extent of the day in the biblical account of creation as given in Gen 1.5 presupposes such a system of reckoning the day, for it says: "And it was evening and it was morning, one day." This passage was misunderstood by the Talmud,[49] though significantly enough when the Tosefta[50] asks מנין שהיום הולך אחר הלילה, it cites in proof Esth. 4.16 where the order לילה ויום occurs, but does not cite the passage in Genesis, or was reinterpreted to suit the later practice of a different system. But it was correctly interpreted by R. Samuel b. Meir (1100–1160) when he remarked:[51] "It

---

[46] b. Shab. 119a.

[47] In another still unpublished paper I deal with this subject at greater length. Cf. J. Morgenstern, "The Sources of the Creation Story," in *The American Journal of Semitic Languages and Literatures*, xxxvi (1919–1920), 176, note 1 to p. 179. [The unpublished paper referred to is *The Calendar of Jewish Festivals and Seasons* and is in possession of the editor.]

[48] See Ed. Koenig in *Z. D. M. G.*, LX, 606–612.

[49] b. Ber. 26a; p. R. H. 2 end. (58b). [50] Ta'an. 2.5.

[51] See his פירוש התורה, edited by D. Rosin (Breslau, 1881), p. 5.

THE SABBATH   447

does not say that it was night time and it was day time which made one day; but it says 'it was evening,' which means that the period of the day time came to an end and the light disappeared. And when it says 'it was morning,' it means that the period of the night time came to an end and the morning dawned. Then one whole day was completed."

There are many more indications in the Pentateuch pointing directly or indirectly to the mode of reckoning the day from morning to morning. To mention but a few such indications; when prescribing that a Thanksgiving offering must be consumed on the very same day on which the sacrifice is slaughtered, the Law states "on the same day it shall be eaten, ye shall leave none of it till the morning"[52] which directly indicates that the day comes to an end on the next morning.[53] And when in special cases, as e. g., in regard to the Day of Atonement, where the Law wishes to make the fasting on it stricter than on any other fast day so as to include also the preceding night, the Law specifically states that it should begin with part of the preceding day and therefore expressly says: "And ye shall afflict your souls in the ninth day of the month at even, from even to even shall ye keep your Sabbath."[54] This indirectly but

[52] Lev. 22.30; see also Lev. 7.15.

[53] For further proofs see Morgenstern, *loc. cit.*, to which I will add one point from the Passover legislation in Ex. 12 which is not pointed out there. The law in Ex. 12 prescribes that the Paschal lamb be slaughtered on the fourteenth day of the month and eaten at the following night and that nothing be left till the next morning (verses 6–10). And we are told that on the very same day, i. e., the fourteenth of the month God brought out the children of Israel from the land of Egypt (*ibid.*, verse 51). And in verse 42 of the same chapter we read as follows: "It is a night of watching unto the Lord for bringing them out of Egypt." Now then, if they came out at night, that is, in the night following the fourteenth day, and it is said on the very same day, that is on the fourteenth day, they were brought out, it clearly indicates that the night following the fourteenth day is still part of that day.

[54] The Rabbis of the Talmud who nowhere allude to and probably no longer knew of the earlier mode of reckoning the day felt the difficulty in the phrase: "Ye shall afflict your souls on the ninth day," and when commenting on it they say: "But are we to fast on the ninth day?" (Yoma 81b, R. H. 9a,b). A very sound objection indeed. For if the day had in Bible times been reckoned from evening to evening, as it was in talmudic times, then the phrase: "In the ninth day of the month at evening" contains a

unmistakably points to a mode of reckoning the day from morning to morning.[55] In post-exilic times, however, probably not later than the beginning of the Greek period,[56] a change in

---

contradiction in terms, for the evening is already part of the tenth day. Besides the special injunction "from even unto even shall ye keep your Sabbath" would be entirely superfluous, for any other day also extends from evening to evening. The talmudic explanation that the meaning of the passage: "Ye shall afflict your souls on the ninth day" is to say that one who eats on the ninth day performs a Jewish religious duty, and it is accounted to him as if he had fasted both on the ninth and tenth days (*ibid.*, *loc. cit.*) is, of course, a homiletical subterfuge. The fact is that the Rabbis of the Talmud no longer knew or would not acknowledge that in ancient times there was another mode of reckoning the day according to which the evening preceding the tenth day still belongs to the ninth day. In the case of the Day of Atonement the Law especially prescribes that the fast be observed in a new manner, covering part of the ninth and part of the tenth days.

[55] See also H. J. Bornstein in *HaTekufah* VI, 254 and 303 ff., and especially 313.

[56] See Morgenstern, *op. cit.*, p. 179, note. Also "Three Calendars of Ancient Israel," in *Hebrew Union College Annual* X (Cincinnati, 1935), 146, note 236. The fact that the Samaritans also reckon the day from evening to evening would not be any argument against the fixing of this period for the innovation. For, in the first place we do not know the exact date when the Samaritans finally and absolutely separated from the Jews. Furthermore they may have accepted Jewish practices even after the separation, or they may, independently of the Jews, have interpreted the passage in Lev. 23.32: "From even to even shall you keep your Sabbath" to apply to every Sabbath and Holiday and not only to the Day of Atonement. In my paper referred to above (note 47) I expressed the idea, which was accepted by Morgenstern ("The Sources of the Creation Story," *op. cit.*, p. 179, note) that the statement in the Talmud (b. Ber. 33a) that the men of the Great Synagogue instituted the ritual of Ḳiddush and Habdalah, also points to the time of the beginning of the Greek period for the innovation of the system of reckoning the day from evening to evening, since the ceremonies of Ḳiddush and Habdalah are now observed on Friday evening and Saturday night respectively. I would, however, now qualify this idea somewhat to the extent that we must understand the talmudic statement to refer to the last generation of the men of the Great Synagogue, who lived after the beginning of the Greek period. It is, however, possible that the reference is to the earlier Men of the Great Synagogue. Yet this would not necessitate the fixing of the date for the innovation of the system in reckoning the day before the Greek period. For the talmudic statement only says that they instituted a ritual for consecrating the Sabbath at its entrance and for marking its distinction from the week days at its going out, but does not say when the

the system of reckoning the day was made, and the day was reckoned as extending from the preceding to the following evening. As might be expected, such a radical innovation was not immediately generally accepted. It took some time before it entirely supplanted the older system. In certain spheres of the population the older system continued to be in use, either exclusively or side by side with the newer system. Thus in the Temple service the older system continued all through the time of the existence of the second Temple, and there the day was reckoned from morning to morning, or as the Talmud[57] puts it בקדשים הליל הולך אחר היום "In sacrificial matters the night follows rather than precedes the day."[58] In some circles[59] or among some

---

coming in and going out of the Sabbath at the time when these rituals were first introduced, took place. According to the Talmud (*ibid.*, *loc. cit.*) some changes as to when or where the ritual of the Habdalah should be recited were made even during the period of the Men of the Great Synagogue. It is therefore not impossible that another change in the time for reciting these rituals also took place during the period of the Men of the Great Synagogue. When the older generation of that period first instituted these rituals they may have been recited at Sabbath morning and at Sunday morning respectively. Then, when the reckoning of the day was changed, the times for reciting these rituals were correspondingly shifted to Friday and Saturday night respectively. (See below note 58.) The passage in Neh. 13.19–21 does not necessarily prove that already at the time of Nehemiah, the night preceding the Sabbath was part of the Sabbath as assumed by Bornstein (*op. cit.*, p. 305). See Morgenstern, "Three Calendars of Ancient Israel," *op. cit.*, p. 22, note 36.

[57] Ḥul. 83a.

[58] This simply means that in the sanctuary the conservative priests persistently held on to the older practice though in all other spheres of life it had been abolished or changed. The fact that in the Temple service the night followed the day is another support for the theory that the innovation was introduced in the period of the Men of the Great Synagogue (see note 56). For had it been introduced earlier in that period in the time of Ezra and Nehemiah, before the Temple was rebuilt and the sacrificial cult restored, it would have been introduced into the Temple service also. The Temple may have been slow in admitting changes in practices that were continuously observed, but when the service was instituted anew and everything reorganized, there would have been no reason to go back to a practice which had been observed in pre-exilic times, but discontinued for a time and changed.

[59] According to the Talmud (p. Ned. 8.1 [40d]) even among the common

Jewish sects[60] the older system continued and the Sabbath was observed from Saturday morning to Sunday morning. For those groups, as for the people of the time prior to the introduction of the new system, the night following the Sabbath and not the night preceding it formed part of the Sabbath, and the morning of Saturday — not Friday evening — marked the entrance of the Sabbath. But the majority of the people, following the teachings of the Halakah,[61] reckoned the day from evening to

---

people the older system continued and in the popular language בלשון בני אדם, the day included the following and not the preceding night. See commentary פני משה *ad loc.* and cf. also Bornstein, *op. cit.*, p. 311. Likewise the author of the Gospel according to Matthew has preserved the older system, for we read there 28.1: "In the end of the Sabbath, as it began to dawn towards the first day of the week." So according to him the Sabbath extended towards the dawn of Sunday morning.

[60] Benjamin of Tudela (second half of the twelfth century) reports about a certain Jewish sect on the island of Cyprus whose members observed the Sabbath from Saturday morning to Sunday morning, or as he puts it, who desecrated the night preceding but keep holy the night following the Sabbath day. See מסעות ר' בנימין מטודילה, ed. L. Grünhut, I (Frankfurt a. M., 1904), p. 23. According to S. A. Poznanski in his *Introduction to Eliezer of Beaugency's commentary to Ezekiel and the twelve minor prophets* (Warsaw, 1913), p. 43, Ibn Ezra's attack in his אגרת השבת (*Kerem Ḥemed* V [Prague, 1839], 115 ff.) was directed not against R. Samuel b. Meir and his interpretation of Gen. 1.5, but against those heretical sects who drew practical conclusions from this interpretation and observed the Sabbath from morning to morning. Cf. also Bornstein, *op. cit.*, p. 304.

[61] But even among those who followed the Halakah allusion to the continuance of the older system and traces of an extension of the Sabbath rest to the night following Saturday are to be found. Thus in commenting on the different expressions זכור and שמור used respectively in connection with the commandment about the Sabbath in the two versions of the Decalogue (Ex. 20.8 and Deut. 5.12) the Mekilta says: " 'Remember' and 'Observe.' Remember it before it comes and observe it after it has gone." (Mekilta deR. Ishmael, *Baḥodesh* VII [ed. Lauterbach, II, 252]). How to remember the Sabbath before it comes is well illustrated there (*ibid.*, p. 253), but no illustration is given as to how the Sabbath is to be observed after it is gone. Instead of such an illustration there is added the remark about the conclusions which the teachers drew from the interpretation of the word "Observe" as meaning "observe it after it has gone." This remark reads: מכאן אמרו מוסיפין מחול על הקודש. Hence the teachers said: "We should always increase what is holy by adding to it some of the non-holy." But no illustration of the observance of the Sabbath after it has gone is given in the

THE SABBATH   451

evening and the entrance of the Sabbath for them came after the sunset of Friday or on Friday evening.

All the arrangements for welcoming the Sabbath and the ceremonies connected with it were set for Friday evening. And

---

Mekilta. Such an illustration, however, is furnished elsewhere in the statement that the Jewish women refrained from work on Saturday night even after the Sabbath had gone (p. Pes. 4.1 [30c,d]). This custom of the women is disapproved by the teachers and declared to be not a proper custom אינו מנהג. But in spite of the disapproval of the teachers the custom has persisted among pious Jewish women to this day. It is evident that this custom of the Jewish women, which is supported by the saying of the Mekilta, is a relic of the ancient practice of keeping the Sabbath till the dawn of Sunday. The teachers, insisting that the Sabbath extends only from evening to evening, objected to this custom but they were unable to suppress it. They had to tolerate it, hence they tried at least to limit it to only a part of Saturday night עד יפני סדרא (*ibid.*, *loc. cit.*). And even this approved refraining from work during part of the time of Saturday night they explained to have its reason not in the assumption that Saturday night or part of it was still part of the Sabbath, but merely in the rule that it was a good custom "to add part of the non-holy to the holy." And to be consistent they said that such an addition should not be one-sided, i. e., not only part of the day following the Sabbath but also part of the day preceding it, should be added to the Sabbath. The women, while persisting in their practice and refusing to confine it to the limits fixed by the Rabbis for Saturday night, were nevertheless not unwilling to accept the reason for their practice as given by the Rabbis, and hence agreed that an addition to the Sabbath should also be made on the day preceding it. But they seem to have assumed that such an addition should consist not of a mere fraction of the day but of the whole day of Friday, just as the addition at the going out of the Sabbath consisted — in their practice — of the whole night following the Sabbath. Thus they would refrain from doing any work during the entire day of Friday. This practice was likewise disapproved by the teachers and declared not to be a valid custom אינו מנהג (p. Pes., *loc. cit.* [30d]). Here also the teachers insisted that only part of the day of Friday should be added to the Sabbath. And a Baraita in b. Pes. 50b declares that whosoever does work on Friday afternoon after the Minḥah time and on Saturday night — significantly enough no time limit is specified as to what part of Saturday night — will not be successful. But it should be noticed that while the Rabbis were sucessful in persuading the women to do work on Friday, adding only a part of that day to the Sabbath, they did not succeed in making them abandon their practice of refraining from work on Saturday night, evidently because the latter custom was a survival of the ancient practice of observing the Sabbath till the dawn of Sunday.

late in the afternoon of Friday, the day which now came to be designated as ערב שבת,[62] the eve of the Sabbath, or in Aramaic as מיעלי שבתא the day ushering in the Sabbath, the Jewish home has a festive aspect and all members of the family are attired in their best in honor of this holy visitor.[63] Besides the general festive appearance which the Jewish home is given on Friday evening, there are special arrangements for the ceremonies which are to mark the reception of the "Princess Sabbath." Some of these arrangements seek to emphasize the idea that the Jewish home is like the Temple of the Lord. Hence, in imitation of the arrangement in the Tabernacle where the Candelabrum was placed on the south side and the table with the show bread was on the north side,[64] so also in the Jewish home on Friday evening it is so arranged that the table, covered with a white cloth, is put on the north side, and opposite it on the south side are the lamps or candlesticks.[65] And where the lamps or candlesticks are placed on the table, they are put on the south end of the table and the Sabbath loaves on the north end. This is also expressed by Isaac Lurya in his song for welcoming the Sabbath on Friday evening, one verse of which reads אסדר לדרומא מנורתא דסתימא ושולחן עם נהמא בצפונא ארשין. This arrangement of שולחן בצפון may have originally been intended as a protest against the Parsee religion which forbids the placing of food towards the north

[62] With the change in the reckoning of the day and the fixing of the Sabbath as extending from evening to evening, the meanings of the two terms respectively designating the periods of time preceding and following the Sabbath, ערב שבת and מוצאי שבת were also changed. Originally מוצאי שבת designated Sunday morning or the entire day of Sunday. See *Seder Olam Rabbah*, xxx, ed. Ratner (Wilna, 1897), p. 74 and also b. 'Ar. 11b where, declaring the day on which the Temple was destroyed to have been a Sunday, the phrase אותו היום מוצאי שבת היה is used. ערב שבת designated the evening preceding the Sabbath or Friday night after sunset. After the change מוצאי שבת came to designate Saturday night, and ערב שבת came to designate the entire day of Friday, so that when it is desired to specify the time of the afternoon one says ערב שבת מן המנחה למעלה or ערב שבת אחר חצות היום. Cf. Bornstein, *op. cit.*, p. 280 note.

[63] See above pp. 445–446.
[64] See Ex. 26.35.
[65] See b. B. B. 25b.

side, because it would look as if the food were offered as a sacrifice to the demons who were believed to have their place in the North.[66] And although, as appears from Jewish sources,[67] the belief that the North was the place of the demons is also found among the Jewish people, it may be that the desire to emphasize the idea that the Jewish home was to be regarded as a Temple was so strong as to make them ignore the fear that the placing of the bread on the north end of the table might be misunderstood as a sacrifice to the demons.[68]

In many Jewish homes[69] flowers are placed on the table either for the purpose of decorating the table or for the purpose of enjoying their fragrance.[70] This is either a survival or a resurrection of an old custom.[71]

---

[66] See I. Scheftelowitz, *Die Altpersische Religion und das Judentum* (Giessen, 1920), p. 59.

[67] See Pirḳe deR. Eliezer III; Pesiḳta Rabbati, Friedmann, p. 188; Midrash Konen in Jellinek's *Beth ha-Midrash* II, 30, and מדרש אבכיר, ed. A. Marmorstein, in דביר (Berlin, 1923), 121.

[68] The Rabbis objected to practices which might give the impression that sacrifices were offered to the demons. The saying in b. Sanh. 92a כל המשייר פתיחים על שולחנו כאלו עובד עבודה זרה is a protest against the practice of leaving food on the table. Cf. Lauterbach, "The Ceremony of Breaking a Glass at Weddings," in *HUCA* II, 358, note 2. But they seem to have made a distinction between leaving crumbs or part of the food left from the meal, which might well appear as though the demons were given a portion of the meal, and the placing of whole loaves even on the side where the demons dwell. The fact that these loaves were yet whole was, in the minds of the Rabbis, sufficient indication that they were meant to be used at the meal and were not an offering to the demons.

[69] In the Middle Ages it was customary among the German Jews to decorate the home and the table for Sabbath with flowers. See Berliner, *Aus dem Leben der deutschen Juden im Mittelalter* (Berlin, 1900), pp. 34 and 37. It is still customary in some Jewish homes.

[70] See b. Shab. 119b description of the table on Friday evenings or on the Sabbath in a rich man's home. Among the things mentioned as being on the table are spices וכל מיני בשמים, though these three words are missing in the quotations of this passage in שאלתות I (Wilna, 1861), p. 6, in *Or Zaru'a* II, 10 and *Shibbole ha-Leḳeṭ*, p. 43 (See דקדוקי סופרים).

[71] This old custom has been fully discussed in an article "The Origin and Development of Two Sabbath Ceremonies" in *HUCA* XV, 1940.

The Sabbath Lights

The outstanding ceremony of Friday evening is the kindling of the Sabbath lights or the lighting of the lamps, performed in the Jewish home at the very moment of the entrance of the Sabbath. This is the oldest and one of the most striking ceremonies observed in connection with the welcoming of the Sabbath. It is unique and, as we shall see, interesting from many points of view. It no doubt had a long struggle before it came to be universally accepted. Then it went through a process of development, was subjected to modifications and reinterpretations, until it acquired a fixed form and a definite ritual and was recognized as a characteristic part of the Jewish Sabbath observance.

The custom of kindling lights in a Jewish home on Friday evening is very old. The Mishnah[72] already presupposes it as an old and undisputed practice and merely discusses some details, such as what materials should or may be used for the lamps. Among the Greek and Roman people of the first Christian century it was known as one of the ceremonies characteristic of the Jewish observance of the Sabbath. Persius Flaccus, a Roman satirist, writing between 34 and 62 C. E. mentions it.[73] The Stoic philosopher Seneca (first century) refers to it in a letter in which he wrote: "The lamps on the Sabbath (lighted by the Jews) should be prohibited, for the gods do not want light and men do not like the smoke."[74] Josephus[75] says: "For there is not any city of the Grecians, nor any of the barbarians, nor any nation whatsoever, whither our custom of resting on the seventh

---

[72] Shab. II.

[73] Satire V, 180. Cf. A. Büchler, "Graeco-Roman Criticism of Some Jewish Observances and Beliefs," in the *Jewish Review* I (London, 1910), 133.

[74] Büchler *op. cit.*, *loc. cit.* See also J. Hugh Michael, "The Jewish Sabbath in the Latin Classical Writers," in the *American Journal of Semitic Languages and Literatures* XL, No. 2 (Jan. 1924), 117. It should be noticed that Seneca objects to the ceremony as being disagreeable to God and men. Evidently he knew that a significance was ascribed to it as being not only useful to men, but also desiring or pleasing to God or the angels.

[75] *Contra Apionem* II, 40.

THE SABBATH 455

day hath not come, and by which our fasts and lighting up lamps and many of our prohibitions as to our food are not observed." By "lighting up lamps" he most likely means the custom of lighting the Sabbath lamps on Friday evening,[76] although he might possibly have reference to the Ḥanukkah lights.

While we know that this was an old custom we do not know exactly how old it is. We cannot ascertain with accuracy the time when it was first introduced. We can only guess and find an approximate date and we shall attempt to do so. There is no indication of such a custom in the Bible. Neither does the Talmud indicate when or by whom it was first introduced. The statement made in Midrash Leḳaḥ Ṭob to *Vayakhel*[77] that it was a traditional law handed down from the days of Moses to kindle lights on Friday evening שקבלה היתה לישראל מימי משה רבינו להדליק הנר is rather an exaggeration and cannot be taken seriously.[78] Neither can we consider the saying in Gen. r. that Sarah and after her Rebecca had lights burning in their tents every Friday night[79] a reference to the origin of our custom. And there is no reason to assume with Landesberg that this custom was borrowed from the Parsees.[80] In fact, as we shall soon see, there are many reasons against such a theory. In the first place it is very unlikely that a ceremony borrowed from the Parsees could have assumed such importance. Secondly, the ceremony could not have been observed at a time when the

---

[76] See Schürer, *Geschichte des Jüdischen Volkes* III (Leipzig, 1909), 166, note 49. Probably Tertullian (second half of the third century) "Ad Nationes" I, 13 (*Ante-Nicene Fathers*, III [New York, 1899], p. 123) in his statement: "And Jewish also are the ceremonies of the lamps" refers to the lights on Friday evening and not to the Ḥanukkah lights.

[77] Ed. Buber (Wilna, 1884), p. 106a.

[78] Leopold Landesberg in his essay הדלקת נר שבת in חקרי לב part IV (Szatmar, 1908), 82–89, is also inclined to assume that the custom originated in the time of Moses, though he also has another theory about the origin of the custom (see below, note 80). But his essay contains much pilpul and has no scientific value whatever.

[79] The passage 60.15 reads as follows: כל ימי שהיתה שרה קיימת היה נר דלוק מלילי שבת ועד לילי שבת וכיון שמתה פסק אותו הנר וכיון שבאת רבקה חזר . . .

[80] *loc. cit.*

day was reckoned from morning to morning and the Sabbath began with the dawn of Saturday. And as we have seen above, the change in the mode of reckoning the day to make it extend from evening to evening, with the result that the entrance of the Sabbath took place on Friday evening, was not made before the Greek period.[81] Our ceremony, accordingly, could not have been introduced or observed before the Greek period. This is further supported by the fact that the Samaritans did not know, and would have strongly objected to such a ceremony. For they would not have any light or fire in the house on the Sabbath even if kindled before the Sabbath.[82] Likewise the Falashas never had and probably objected to such a ceremony.[83]

[81] See above note 56. We can perhaps go further and fix more nearly the date for the introduction of this ceremony. It may have been introduced after the introduction of the Ḥanukkah Festival, and the latter may have been a contributary cause of our ceremony. We have seen above (note 28) that the Samaritans also accepted the reckoning of the day from evening to evening. And we never hear of the Sadducees objecting to this innovation, although the priests in the Temple continued the old system of reckoning the day from morning to morning. Having accepted the practice of reckoning the Sabbath from evening to evening, the Samaritans and the Sadducees applied the law of Ex. 35.3 to Friday night also, since it was now part of the Sabbath. But after the introduction of the Ḥanukkah Festival with the feature of kindling lights for eights days including Friday, there arose a difficulty in regard to the lighting of the Ḥanukkah lights on Friday evening. It was solved by ordering that on Friday the Ḥanukkah lights be kindled before sunset, i. e., before the entrance of the Sabbath. This opened a wedge into the prohibition against having light on Saturday. The Pharisees then extended this device for the kindling of lights before the Sabbath to all other Fridays, since in one case on the Sabbath of the Ḥanukkah week, the law in Exodus had to be interpreted in a sense of allowing light prepared before the entrance of the Sabbath to continue to burn. This interpretation enabled them to make the Sabbath a delight by having lights on Friday night, and they insisted on this practice.

[82] See R. Kirchheim, *Karme Shomron* (Frankfort a. M., 1851), p. 27; and J. A. Montgomery, *The Samaritans* (Philadelphia, 1907), p. 33.

[83] See A. Epstein, מאמר על הפלשים ומנהגיהם in his *Eldad ha-Dani* (Pressburg, 1891), p. 173, who says (כהשומרונים והקראים) בלתי מבעירים אש ונרות. A. Z. Aeskoli in תרביץ VII, p. 39 says: אין מבעירים אש ואין מדליקים נר לשבת אפילו מערב שבת but see his note 49. Against him, see J. Faitlowitch (*ibid.*, p. 374), who says אין אצלם איסור להדליק נר ביום הששי קודם שקיעת החמה ולהשאיר את המאור בביאתה בליל שבת. At any rate they do not have such a ceremony. They merely would

THE SABBATH 457

But we may go further and assert that it was instituted by the Pharisees in opposition to the Sadducees and other sects and that its original significance was to protest against the superstitious belief that the Sabbath was a tabu day. We certainly cannot assume that the purpose of this ceremony was merely to make the home cheerful and bright, so that peace and joy might reign in it on the Sabbath, as would seem from the statements in the Talmud.[84] This would not agree with the other statement הדלקת נר בשבת חובה[85] and it could hardly explain the emphasis laid on this ceremony and the great importance attached to it. The promise that because of the observance of the ceremony of the Sabbath lights God will show the people the lights of Zion in the future[86] and the belief expressed in the Talmud[87] that the family observing regularly the ceremony of the Sabbath lights will be blessed with scholarly sons, learned in the Law, as well as the statement that the neglect of this ceremony is one of the sins for which women die in childbirth[88] clearly indicate that great importance was attached to this ceremony, and that it was not merely a device to provide comfort for the people. There must have been some special purpose which the Rabbis aimed at by emphasizing the importance of this ceremony and declaring it to be a duty חובה to perform it.

We may reasonably assume that the early teachers of the Halakah wished to remove from the minds of the people the idea that the Sabbath was a sort of a tabu day or unlucky day on which no light or fire was allowed in the house, a superstition which is found among primitive people today and which was also found among the peoples of antiquity.[89] To impress upon the people the idea that they need not fear evil spirits on

---

not object to a light being kindled before the Sabbath which would continue to burn during the evening of the Sabbath. About the Sadducees and Karaites see below.

[84] b. Shab. 23b and 25b.
[85] *Ibid.* 25b.
[86] Yalkut, *Beha'aloteka* 719.
[87] b. Shab. 23b.
[88] M. Shab. II, 6.
[89] See Hutton Webster, *Rest Days* (New York, 1916), pp. 9, 12, 15 and especially 258.

the Sabbath day the Rabbis insisted that the lights be kindled even though the gods of Seneca[90] or the evil spirits might not want it. There was even more reason for emphasizing that this ceremony was a duty, since it apparently was in violation of a biblical law if understood literally. Certain Jewish sects interpreted the law in Ex. 35.3: "Ye shall burn no fire throughout your habitations on the Sabbath day" not merely as a prohibition against making a light or building a fire on the Sabbath day, but also of having any light or fire in the house, even if made or prepared before the entrance of the Sabbath. We know that the Samaritans so understood this law.[91] And though we have no express statement to this effect, it seems that the Sadducees likewise understood it so.[92] The Pharisees, however, who insisted that we must interpret the Law in the light of reason and follow the spirit and not the letter, could not accept such an interpretation of the law in Ex. 35.3. They learned from the prophet that the Sabbath was to be a delight: "And call the Sabbath a delight.... then shalt thou delight thyself in the Lord."[93] They also taught that "the Sabbath is given to you but you are not surrendered to the Sabbath."[94] Hence they reasoned, if the Sabbath is given to us and is to be a delight, the law could not mean that we should spend that day in darkness. They accordingly interpreted the law in Exodus to mean: "You shall kindle no fire .... upon the Sabbath day," but you

---

[90] See above, note 40.

[91] See above, note 46.

[92] See Geiger, *Nachgelassene Schriften* I, 280 f., who assumes, and I believe correctly, though he does not give any proof for it, that the Sadducees like the Karaites would not allow a light to burn on the Sabbath even if it had been kindled before the Sabbath. Perhaps the saying in Tanḥuma, *Gen.* I, which reads as follows: וקראת לשבת עונג זו הדלקת הנר בשבת. ואם תומר לישב בחשך אין זו עונג שאין יורדי גיהנם נדונין אלא בחשך is taken from an older source and represents a polemic argument against the Sadducees and not against the Karaites as assumed by Zunz, *Gottesdienstliche Vorträge* (Frankfurt a. M., 1892), p. 247, note d.

[93] Isa. 58.13–14.

[94] לכם שבת מסורה ואין אתם מסורין לשבת Mekilta deR. Ishmael, *Shabbata* I (ed. Lauterbach, III, 198). Jesus merely quoted this rabbinic dictum, when he said, "The Sabbath was made for man and not man for the Sabbath." (Mark 2.27).

can and should have fire and light prepared before the entrance of the Sabbath, so that the Sabbath be spent in a bright and cheerful home.[95] They therefore laid special emphasis upon the ceremony of having lights on Friday night.[96] It was as a protest against the Samaritans and the Sadducees.[97] For this reason they exaggerated the importance of this ceremony and declared it a duty, חובה, essential to the proper observance of the Sabbath. It was in this polemical spirit that the exaggerated statement in Midrash Leḳaḥ Ṭob referred to above was made, ascribing the origin of the ceremony to a mosaic tradition.

Having made the lights a feature of the Sabbath observance it was but natural that a similar ceremony was also introduced for the eves of every holiday נר יום טוב. But although the Talmud declared it an obligation to have lights on the Sabbath הדלקת נר בשבת חובה and it was an essential feature in the Sabbath observance, there was, to our knowledge, in talmudic times no benediction prescribed for the performance of this ceremony. Nowhere in the Talmud[98] is it said that one who kindles the

---

[95] Probably the talmudic explanation of the purpose of the lights משום שלום בית alludes to or means to suggest this idea, namely that the Sabbath should be made a day of joy and not considered an unlucky day.

[96] Cf. Lauterbach, *The Pharisees and Their Teachings*, above p. 123.

[97] See Geiger, *Nachgelassene Schriften* III, 287–289. Jacob Reifmann in his treatise on נר שבת in מאמר משלוח מנות (Prague, 1860), also correctly explains that the special emphasis laid on the ceremony of having lights on Friday evening more than on any other ceremony or form of עונג שבת Sabbath delight, was due to a desire to protest against the Samaritans and later against the Karaites. As to the arguments of R. Ch. J. Pollack against Freimann in עברי אנכי (1877), No. 37 see Chaim Erdstein in his שדה פרחים (Wien, 1892), pp. 80–84 and 87–89.

[98] In מרדכי to Shab. II, #273 (71a) it is said that according to the Yerushalmi one is required to pronounce a blessing when lighting the Sabbath lamps, as well as when lighting the holiday lights. He says: ובירושלמי דפרק הרואה גרסינן המדליק נר של שבת צריך לברך להדליק נר של שבת וכן ביום טוב של יום טוב. Likewise in הגהות מיימוניות to הלכות שבת ch. V, it says: וכן איתא בירושלמי פרק המביא כדי יין המדליק נר ביום טוב צריך לברך אשר קבמ"ו להדליק נר של יו"ט. ובפרק הרואה ירושלמי גרסינן להדליק נר לכבוד יו"ט ודכוותיה בשבת אומר לכבוד שבת .... But neither in the place in Ber. פרק הרואה nor in the place in Beẓah פרק המביא כדי יין is such a statement found in our Yerushalmi. See Aptowitzer in *Rabiah* שבת 199, p. 263, note 10, references to other authorities where this alleged Yerushalmi is quoted. Aptowitzer assumes that these authorities quoted

lights of the Sabbath should recite a benediction, as we find it in the case of the Ḥannukah lights.[99] Such a benediction was introduced in gaonic times and was probably intended as a more emphatic protest against the Karaites[100] who objected to this ceremony, considering it a violation of the biblical law in Ex. 35.3.[101] It is mentioned in Halakot Gedolot[102] in the name of R. Naṭronai Gaon, and also in Amram.[103] Ha-Manhig[104] quotes R. Aḥa of Shebḥa as requiring a benediction over the Sabbath lights, although in our editions of the Sheeltot such a statement is not found. The Geonim must have had some difficulty in finding sanction for prescribing such a benediction, a difficulty experienced also by the Rabbis of the Talmud in regard to the benediction over the Ḥanukah lights.[105] In the latter case the difficulty was removed by declaring that on the basis of the law in Deut. 17.11 commanding the people to do as the teachers of each generation tell them,[106] they are justified

from a "ספר ירושלמי" the author of which may have *added* the gaonic insitution of the benediction to a Yerushalmi text. See also *Vitry*, p. 80, note 2.

[99] b. Shab. 23a.

[100] The early Karaites interpreted the passage in Ex. 35.3 to mean "not to let burn any fire or light in the house." See Hadasi, *Eshkol*, p. 54d and Aaron of Nicomedia in his *Keter Torah, ad loc.* Cf. also Ibn Ezra in his commentary to this passage in Exodus. Anan (second half of the eighth century) and the early Karaites objected strongly to having lights on Friday night. The later Karaites, however, permitted one to have lights. See Elijah Bashyazi אדרת אליהו ch. 17–19, and especially ch. 20, where he mentions his grandfather Menaḥem Bashyazi (1450) and others who permitted the practice of having lights on Friday night. Cf. also Danon, "Karaites in European Turkey," *J.Q.R.* (Jan., 1925), p. 305 ff. About the early Karaites protesting against having the lights in the synagogue on Friday nights see Pinsker, *Likkute Kadmonioth*, p. 39. Cf. also Jonas Gurland, *Ginze Israel* (Petersburg, 1866), p. 22 ff. See also סבוב ר' פתחיה (1175–1190) ed. Grünhut (Jerusalem, 1904), I, 4 about the מינים, no doubt Karaites, who eat their meal on Friday evening in darkness, ואוכלין בחשך. See also *ibid.*, II (German Translation), 4–5, notes 8 and 9.

[101] See Weiss, *Dor* IV, 97.

[102] Ed. Hildesheimer, p. 86.

[103] P. 24b.

[104] P. 25.

[105] b. Shab. 23a.

[106] *Ibid., loc. cit.*

in reciting the benediction, and declaring that God had commanded them to do whatever the teachers commanded them. In the case of the Sabbath lights the Geonim must have followed a similar reasoning.[107] or they may have considered the ceremony as included in the commandment to keep and observe the Sabbath, hence it is not incorrect to recite the benediction, declaring that God had commanded us to light the Sabbath lights. By requiring a benediction for the performance of this ceremony the Rabbis made their protest against the Karaites more emphatic, which was necessary especially in gaonic times when the challenge of the Karaites was very strong.[108] The fact that originally the holiday lights נר יום טוב did not require a ברכה[109] would also support this idea. For in the case of נר יום טוב no protest was intended and therefore no emphasis needed. But the Sabbath lights needed this emphasis very much, hence they prescribed a benediction for it. Later on in the course of time the Yom Ṭob lights were also assigned an appropriate benediction.

[107] See Lauterbach, *op. cit.*, above p. 124, note 34. As to Yerushalmi, see *Or Zaru'a* II, end of Section 11, Laws of the Eve of the Sabbath. Cf. Higger, *Ozar ha-Baraitot* II #56, pp. 254–255 and p. 319. See also *Vitry*, p. 80, who expressly gives the reason given in the Talmud for ברכת נר חנוכה as the reason for the benediction over the Sabbath lights. He says: הילכך צריך לברך והיכן ציונו רב אויא אמר מלא תסור .... But this is said in the Talmud only in connection with the benediction over the Ḥanukkah lights. In *Sefer ha-Ittim*, ed. Schor (Berlin, 1902), p. 18, it correctly reads: מברך נר של שבת. והיכן ציונו מלא תסור כדאמרינן בענין נר של חנוכה.

[108] Polemics against the Karaites' attitude on the question of the lights on Friday evening continued after the gaonic times. See *Sefer Ḥasidim* (1147) (Lemberg, 1862), pp. 84–85, answer of R. Meshullam to those heretics (Karaites) who would not have lights in their houses on Sabbath because of the law in Ex. 35.3 זאת התשובה השיב רבינו משולם נ"ע למינין שאינן מדליקין נרות בבתיהם בשבת מפני שאומר הפסוק לא תבערו אש בכל מושבותיכם ביום השבת השיב להם כך כתיב ויברך אלהים את יום השביעי אין אנו יודעים במה ברכו אלא ממה שאנו רואים בקללות שקלל איוב את יומו שקיללו בחשיכה שנאמר הלילה ההוא יקחהו אופל וגומר יקו לאור ואין מכלל שהברכה שברך הקב"ה השבת היא אורה שהיא שלום הבית וכל מה שאמר איוב בקללה יש לומר להפך גבי לברכה באיוב כתיב אל תבא רננה בו מכאן שיש לו לרנן בשבת בשירות ותשבחות. See also *Sefer Ḥasidim*, ed. Wistinetzki, 622, p. 166. In Yalḳut Reubeni to the passage in Exodus (Warsaw, 1901) p. 180 it is said ולאפוקי מקיראים דלית להון בוצינא דדליק ביומא. דשבתא עלייהו כתיב ורשעים בחשך ידמו ...

[109] See *Ha-Manhig*, p. 26.

Who Is to Perform This Ceremony?

If the purpose of the Sabbath light is for the comfort and peace of the family, משום שלום ביתו then it is incumbent upon both the man and the woman to perform the ceremony. And indeed, either one of them may do so. Again, if this ceremony had been a real obligation included in the commandment to observe the Sabbath, then according to the rule וכל מצות עשה שהזמן גרמא אנשים חייבין ונשים פטורות, "the observance of all positive commandments dependent on a special time is incumbent only upon men but not upon women,"[110] only men and not the women would be obliged to perform this ceremony. But since it is not an express commandment and actually is merely a rabbinic institution, its performance has been assigned to the woman where there is one in the household. Of course, where there is no woman in the household, the man performs this duty. While it is quite natural that the woman, the housewife, as the mistress of the home should perform this ceremony, the alleged purpose of which is to make the home cheerful and bright, yet the Rabbis tried to give special reasons for the performance of this ceremony by the women. One of these reasons is as follows: God said to the woman: "I gave you a soul which is called light, נר, therefore I command you the duty of kindling the Sabbath light."[111] This is rather a fine compliment to the soulfulness of women.

But not all the Rabbis were so complimentary to women. The Haggadah in the Palestinian Talmud[112] connects this obligation of the women with the offense which is supposed to have been committed by the first woman, Eve. Here we read that Eve extinguished the light of Adam and caused his death by inducing him to eat of the forbidden food. Therefore she must atone for this sin by observing the law of kindling the Sabbath light.[113]

---

[110] M. Ḳid. 1.7. [111] b. Shab. 32a.
[112] p. Shab. 2.6 (5b).
[113] The passage in Yerushalmi reads as follows: אדם הראשון נרו של עולם היה שנ' נר אלהים נשמת אדם. וגרמה לו חוה מיתה. לפיכך מסרו מצות הנר לאשה.... See also Genesis r. 17, end, and Abot deR. Nathan B., IX Schechter p. 25 (י״ג) and Tanḥuma נח, I, p. 28–29.

THE SABBATH

But this assumption that Eve caused Adam's death is, to say the least, open to doubt.[114] It is interesting to notice that in Gen. r.[115] there are cited many opinions why death was decreed upon Adam, למה נקנסה מיתה על אדם, but none of them refer to Eve and the fruit of the tree of knowledge.[116]

As a matter of fact, according to the biblical account,[117] Eve was merely prevented from *prolonging* Adam's life. They were driven out of Paradise before she had a chance to try to taste also of the fruit of the tree of life עץ חיים. But aside from this, this attitude towards women based on Eve's conduct is not fair and the conclusion that she did a great wrong is unjustified, for even if it were true that she caused Adam's physical death, she also caused him to acquire intelligence and thus helped him to a fuller life. If it had not been for Eve, we would all still be monkeys. Eve set a fine example to all her daughters to urge their husbands to seek knowledge. It was due to Eve that Adam made an effort to get knowledge. And ever since there have been many great scholars who owed their achievements to the urging and encouragement of their wives.[118] The lighting of the candles on Friday evening by the woman is symbolic of her efforts to keep the light of religion and truth burning in her home.

A similar thought is expressed in the Zohar to Bereshith.[119] After mentioning the idea expressed in the p. Talmud and Gen. r. cited above, the Zohar continues in quite a different

---

[114] M. Friedmann in an essay on "The Sabbath Light," *JQR*, III [o. s.] (1891), 707 ff., is inclined to interpret this saying of the Palestinian Talmud as meaning merely that woman could extinguish the light of man just as she is capable of maintaining it. But this is rather pilpulistic. In general the essay of Friedmann surprisingly does not contain any new or interesting idea and has no merit at all.

[115] 9.5.

[116] The question of death as the result of the advice of the serpent בעטיו של נחש, needs a fuller consideration into which I cannot enter here. See מפתח התלמוד *s. v.* אדם הראשון p. 637.

[117] Gen. 3.22–23.

[118] One need think only of the story about R. Akiba who became a scholar chiefly by the encouragement of his wife. See b. Ned. 50a. Ab. deR. Nathan A, VI, Schechter p. ט״ו (29) and p. Shab. 6.1 (7d bottom).

[119] Lublin, 1872, p. 48b.

strain as follows: "The secret of the thing is this.... it is a great privilege and an honor shown women in imposing upon her the duty to kindle the lights because in doing so she will have her children grow up to be great lights in the Torah and she prolongs the life of her husband." Eve once gave the light of reason to man and so she should continue to keep the light of religion in her home. Baḥya ben Asher of Saragossa (14th century) in his commentary to the Bible, to section *Jethro* also says that the good woman has always been and still is the cause for the Torah being received by the people. Commenting on the verse: "And Moses went up unto God, and the Lord called unto him out of the mountain, saying: 'Thus shalt thou say to the house of Jacob, and tell the children of Israel' "[120].... he says: Tell it to the *house*, means according to the Rabbis, tell it to the women first and then it will be done. The woman is qualified and worthy to recite special prayers for herself, her husband, and her children at the moment when she lights the candles, says Baḥya, because a prayer which is recited together with the performing of a religious ceremony or the fulfillment of a religious duty will be heard and answered; and because the woman kindles the light, she will have her children grow up in the study of the Torah which is also called "Light."[121]

While these are very pure religious ideas about the significance of the ceremony and the importance and efficacy of the prayers recited by the performer, these ideas did not prevent other less rational ideas from becoming connected with the ceremony and with some of its details in the course of time. It is a strange irony that a ceremony which, as we have seen above, was introduced with the intention of combating superstition should itself in turn engender superstitious belief. But superstitions will not be downed and if suppressed on the one side they will crop out on the other. Thus, the one superstition con-

---

[120] Ex. 19.3.

[121] In his work דעת משה to section תרומה R. Moses Eliakim Beriah (died 1825, see *JE* IX, 65) writes that he had heard that the mother of R. Samuel Kaidenower whenever she performed the ceremony of kindling the Sabbath lights used to pray in Russian that her son should become a scholar and that her prayer was answered, for her son did become a great scholar.

nected with the Sabbath lights is that they will drive away all the evil spirits which according to some authorities have sway on Friday night.[122] This is especially expressed in the prayer, תחנה, recited by the women at the performance of this ceremony in addition to the benediction. It reads as follows: "May my lights burn clear and pure in order to drive away all the evil spirits, demons and destroyers of the hosts of the daughter of Mahalat and all that come from *Lilith*, so that all of them take flight before the lights which I kindle in Thine honor and in honor of the Torah and of the Sabbath, so that these evil spirits be unable to do any harm to any man, woman, or child of Thy people Israel."[123]

Another superstition which seems to have grown up in connection with the Sabbath lights is that angels come down

[122] There are many statements in the Talmud to the effect that on Friday night the evil spirits have special powers and more freedom in plying their evil trade. Thus in b. Pes. 11b it is said: בלילי שבתות ובלילי רביעיות שרו מזיקין. *Ibid.* 112a, ת"ר לא ישתה אדם מים לא בלילי רביעיות ולא בלילי שבתות . . . מפני סכנה מאי סכנה רוח רעה. [With this is connected the saying: השותה מים בין השמשות בערב שבת כאלו גוזל את מיתיו reading of R. Meshullam (see *Beth Joseph* to *O. Ḥ.* 291), not as found in our Midrash Tehillim 11 (ed. Buber, p. 102), where it reads only בין השמשות. Some read בין השמשות בשבת (*Tur, O. Ḥ.* 291). The reason for this is that the spirits rushing out from Hell run into the wells to cool off and need all the water. See *Shibbole ha-Leḳeṭ* 157. Though the authorities reading ביה"ש בשבת would probably imagine that before returning to Hell on Saturday night the spirits try to take in a supply of cooling water . . . . At any rate these spirits may harm human beings, whether on Friday evening or on Saturday evening.] Likewise in Pes. 112b it is said לא יצא יחידי בלילה לא בלילי רביעיות ולא בלילי שבתות מפני שאגרת בת מחלת היא . . . מלאכי חבלה יוצאין . . . לחבל. Also Rashi to b. Shab. 24b *s. v.* משום סכנה where he explains סכנת מזיקין. Cf. Aptowitzer *Rabiah*, Berakot, p. 8, note 12 and Shabbat, p. 240. This belief conflicts with the theory that on the Sabbath the Jews are protected from evil spirits (see תניא רבתי #13, p. 37, and other sources). But the people feared the demons even on Friday evening and believed the lights would protect them from harm.

[123] See סדר תחנות (in the Yiddish-deutsch) נייאי טייטשי תחינות (Amsterdam, 1873), p. 137a. I transcribe here the original: "Meine Lichter sollen hell und lauter brennen zu vertreiben alle die böse רוחות und שדים מזיקים בת מחלת alle die da kommen von לילית, dass sie alle sollen fliehen vor die Lichter, die ich da anzünde Dir und der תורה and dem שבת zu ehren, dass sie nicht sollen können beschädigen kein Mann noch kein Frau noch kein Kind unter Dein Volk Israel."

through or rest upon the flames of the candles.[124] We have seen elsewhere[124a] that the scholars recommended that one stand by or in front of the lights while reciting a greeting to the angels,[125] a

[124] The notion that angels appear in a flame and disappear by means of a flame is found in the Bible, Ex. 3.2: "And the angel of the Lord appeared unto him in a flame of fire" (though there it may refer to God Himself). But then the Shekinah could be seen in a flame. Cf. however Ex. r. 2.9: מתחלה לא ירד אלא מלאך אחד שהיה ממוצע ועומד באמצע האש ואח"כ ירדה שכינה ודברה עמו. And Judg. 13.20: "For it came to pass when the flame went up toward heaven from off the altar that the angel of the Lord ascended in the flame of the altar.

[124a] [EDITOR'S NOTE: The reference is to the material in the article cited in note 71, which was originally part of this paper].

[125] The recitation of שלום עליכם was addressed to these angels who come down with the additional soul. For it was believed by some people — especially by those who did not perform, or objected to the ceremony with the myrtle — that the angels came down, or rested, in the flames of the candles lit for the Sabbath. Hence the practice was to stand in front of the lights, or to look at them while reciting this greeting. See ספר מנהג טוב edited by Meir Zvi Weiss in הצופה תרפ"ט (Budapest), p. 12, # 36, סימן ל'ו where it is said: ומנהג טוב בליל שבת כשבאין מבית הכנסת לילך מיד אצל הנרות הדליקים לכבוד שבת ושנתברך עליהם ולעמוד כנגד שתיהן ולומר מלאכי רחמים ושלום בואכם לשלום עליכם שלום הלכות שבת אהרן מריינישבורג בעצמו. And in Maharil וכולכם שלום וכן מצאתי שהנהיג הר' אמהר"ש שראה מאביו מה"ר יצחק ז"ל כאשר היה (Lemberg, 1860), p. 37 it is said: מקדש בליל שבת היה תולה עיניו ומסתכל בנרות הדולקות על גבי השולחן וכו'. And even Lurya, though believing, as it seems, that the angels came down and rested upon the myrtle branches which were used in the Sabbath eve ceremony nevertheless urges that one also look at the candles: הסתכל באור הנר שברכו עליה לשבת ותכוין .... Shulḥan Aruk Ari, loc. cit. Cf. also discussion of the ceremony of lighting the candles, below, p. 469. At any rate this greeting was not addressed to the two angels who accompany the man on his way home אחד טוב ואחד רע as is commonly understood, for why should they welcome the bad angel, and why call him מלאך השלום? Besides these two angels accompany the person all the time (See Lauterbach, "The Belief In the Power of the Word," *HUCA* XIV, 1939) and there would be no reason to greet them especially on Friday evening. Perhaps, however, the closing words וכולכם שלום contain an allusion to the two angels who regularly and also on Friday evening accompany a person (b. Shab. 119b) and of whom one is a מלאך רע, suggesting that he too may be one of peace. This greeting, addressed to the angels who *come down* on Friday night was an old one, but may have fallen into oblivion with the general suppression of the belief that angels come down. Then it may have been reintroduced by the Ḳabbalists in the beginning of the eighteenth century. In this sense only can we accept the statement in סדור אוצר התפלות (Wilna, 1923), p. 615 that the recitation of the

THE SABBATH

statement which makes sense only on the assumption that the angels were there on the lights or in the flame.[126] It is possible that an allusion to such a belief is also found in the passage in the Zohar *Terumah*[127] which reads as follows: רב המנונא סבא כד הוה סליק מנהרא במעלי שבתא הוה יתיב רגעא חדא וזקיף עינוי והוה חדי והוה אמר דהוה יתיב למחמי חדוה דמלאכי עלאי אלין סלקין ואלין נחתין... The interpretations given to this passage[128] are not satisfactory.

שלום עליכם on Friday evening dates only from the beginning of the eighteenth century: ... ולא נמצא הפיוט הזה בסידורי הקדמונים והונהגה אמירתו על פי המקובלים זה כמאה ושמונים שנה. This can be correct only as referring to the form of the recitation פיוט as found in our prayer books.

We can now understand what the objections to our ceremony were. Some people may have addressed prayers and petitions to those angels whom they believed to have come down. This was objectionable as it involved the belief in intermediaries. We know that R. Elijah Gaon of Wilna objected to part of this recitation, to the verse ברכוני לשלום "Bless me, O ye angels of peace" on the ground that we should pray to God alone and not to angels. (See ספר תוספות מעשה רב [Jerusalem, 1896] in the part שאלתות No. 128, p. 18). The same objections may have been raised by former teachers against reciting prayers to the angels coming down on Friday night. Of course they could not deny the talmudic statement that angels accompany one from the synagogue to the home, and they explained that the greeting was addressed to them and not to other angels believed to have come down especially on Friday night. And of course there is no harm in *greeting* angels as long as one does not petition them.... They also inserted the phrase ממלך מלכי המלכים הקב"ה which seems tautological after מלאכי עליון as if to indicate that we greet them, or even if we petition them we do so only in the sense that we address the messengers of God, i. e., we pray to God through his messengers. Significantly enough, in the older recitation, i. e., of מנהג טוב there is merely a greeting and no petition, no phrase like in the later ברכוני לשלום. The latter form could only have been introduced by later Kabbalists.... The words וצאתכם לשלום refer to their leaving on Saturday night, which also points to the angels who come to stay for the whole Sabbath day, as it would hardly be polite if addressed to the two accompanying angels — to greet people at their arrival and immediately tell them to leave in peace.

[126] See above, note 68, especially the reference to ספר מנהג טוב, the author of which was an Italian of the thirteenth century. It may be that, as in the case of the myrtle, the angels who come down on the flames are the ones who drive away the evil spirits, as expressed in the prayer cited above, note 66.

[127] (Lublin, 1872) p. 136b.

[128] In ספר השבת (Tel Aviv, 1936), p. 171 this passage of the Zohar is quoted and rendered into Hebrew by: ערב שבת עם יציאת הכוכב. This is not correct, for מנהרא cannot be a designation of the evening star, though it

It is therefore possible that מנהרא means the light or flame of the Sabbath lamps — not the star — and the passage means that when the flame of the lights on Friday evening rose, Hamnuna would look at them with joy, seeing, or imagining, the angels going up and coming down in this flame. What is the significance of the number "Two?"

The reason why two candles are lit is not given in the Talmud. In fact the number is not fixed by talmudic or gaonic authorities. Possibly the number is for the smallest family consisting of husband and wife.[129] and the two candles are to represent them symbolically and thus suggest that their lives should be bright.[130] It has also been suggested that the two candles are to remind us of the two different versions of the

---

might mean the dawn or the morning star (see Jastrow, *Dictionary*, s. v., p. 798). So סליק מנהרא could possibly stand for עלה השחר but not for צאת הכוכבים in the evening. Likewise the English translation of this passage as given by Sperling *et al.*, which reads as follows: "When R. Hamnuna the Ancient used to come out from the river on a Friday afternoon, he was wont to rest a little on the bank, and raising his eyes in gladness, he would say that he sat there in order to behold the joyous sight of the heavenly angels ascending and descending," is not correct. For what significance could there be to his coming up from the river (reading מְנַהֲרָא = מן הנהר)? Does it mean after he took his bath in the river? But what difference does it make whether he took his bath in the river or in any other body of water, or מקוה? I am not so sure of the correctness of my interpretation as given here in the text. But at any rate it makes better sense than the other interpretations.

[129] Cf. *Ta'ame ha-Minhagim* I, 36 quoting Elijah Rabba as giving this reason for two candles on the evenings of the holidays, and cf. *Shelah*, Sec. Sabbath, p. 133b who also says that there are other reasons for the two lights besides the one given by *Tur*.

[130] Hence the number may vary with the number of the members of the family. This will also explain the peculiar superstition in connection with these lights — similar to that referring to the one lit on the Day of Atonement — namely, that if the light does not burn smoothly, or if the candle melts away or is extinguished it is considered a bad omen, auguring death to the person whom the light represented. As a charm to prevent the candle from melting away and thus insure its burning smoothly to the end — symbolizing that the person represented by it will live out his full life — superstitious people place a whole loaf, חלה, opposite the melting candle. This is possibly a gift to the demon, who thereby desists from threatening the person, and the melting of the candle is stopped.

commandment about the Sabbath found in the two versions of the Decalogue; the one in Exodus reading "Remember," זכור, the other in Deuteronomy reading "Observe," שמור.[131] It has been suggested that the two lights also symbolize the two souls possessed by the Jew on Sabbath.[132]

The Rabbis repeatedly state the importance of this Mitzvah which is one of the three commandments given to women, the other two being the laws concerning menstruation and Ḥallah. The merits of observing these three laws will be remembered to women in the critical moment of giving birth to a child, and they will have an easy delivery. Those who neglect these duties are in danger of being punished just at the time of childbirth.[133] No doubt this belief on the part of the women helped much to insure the observance of this ceremony. For after all, people do not court danger, especially when the ceremony in itself is easily performed.

I should add that no special color of the candles is required, though it is customary to use plain white ones. Nor does it make any difference of what material they are prepared, provided the material is such as would cause the light to burn smoothly and not need trimming and fixing. An electric Sabbath lamp would be permitted,[134] but it would take away much of the peculiar charm and the quaintness of the ceremony and therefore should not be advised.

The special feature accompanying the performance of this duty, namely that the woman covers her eyes while reciting the benediction is explained as follows. The performance of this ceremony constitutes for the woman the welcome of the Sabbath. For her Sabbath begins with the moment when she performs

[131] The same as in the case of the myrtle bunches. [EDITOR'S NOTE: See "The Origin and Development of Two Sabbath Ceremonies," *HUCA*, XV 1940]. Perhaps the candelabrum having three candles was intended for the three angels who come down with the soul, and in this respect also the candles are an alternate for the myrtle, making the latter superfluous. *Kol Bo* 31 (Lemberg, 1866), 25c; *Tur, O. Ḥ.*, p. 263.

[132] Perishah to *Tur, loc. cit.*

[133] M. Shab. 2.6.

[134] See R. Isaac Schmelkes in his Responsa בית יצחק part of *Yoreh De'ah* No. 120, 4; also *Ta'ame ha-Minhagim* III, 85.

this ceremony. Ordinarily, a benediction, to be recited in connection with the performance of a duty, must precede the act of the performance כל המצוות מברך עליהן עובר לעשייתן.[135] In this case, then, the benediction ought to be recited before lighting the candles. This, however, cannot be done. For when reciting the benediction, the woman accepts the Sabbath, and she could no longer do the work of lighting the candles which is forbidden on the Sabbath. Therefore, she first kindles the lights, then covers her eyes, so that she does not see them. It is then as if she were in darkness. She recites the benediction and removes her hands from before her eyes, and then enjoys the light. The enjoying of the light is then considered the act following the benediction. This, however, may be a later rationalizing interpretation. I believe that the original significance of the woman's covering her eyes with her hands was that she was afraid she might see the angels coming down on the flames of the lights. Then she might have peeped through between the fingers of her outspread hands. She also believed that through the spaces between her fingers, the angels would still see her and bless her.[136]*

---

[135] b. Pes. 7b.

[136] Cf. Midrash Shir ha-Shirim r. 2.21; The comment on מציץ מן החרכים, that God loves us from between the fingers of the pirests when they recite the blessing, מבין אצבעותיהם של כהנים. The Zohar, *Kedoshim*, p. 167 gives as the reason why it is forbidden to look at the hands of the priests when they recite the blessing (b. Ḥag. 16a) that the glory of God is there.

* [Ed. note: The essay referred to in note 38 above dealt with the ceremonies at the beginning and end of the Sabbath. This essay while promising to deal with "some special ceremonies or characteristic features of the observance of the Sabbath day," did not do so. Dr. Lauterbach did not, unfortunately, indicate what else specifically he intended to deal with. L. H. S.]

Jesus in the Talmud

Jesus in the Talmud

A STUDY of the relation between Judaism and Christianity, their reactions towards one another and their mutual appreciation or deprecation is of interest not only to the Jewish and Christian theologian, but also to the student of religion in general. In such a study a comparison of the Talmud with the N. T., or an examination of their respective teachings, their agreements or disagreements on fundamental theological questions, occupies a very prominent place. For in the literature of these early centuries, comprising the formative period of Rabbinic Judaism and the beginnings and unfoldment of Christianity, we can best study the fundamental difference between these two religions and their attitudes towards one another. In later years these two religions became more estranged, with the result that frequently only differences are recognized and emphasized while agreements are but rarely acknowledged and appreciated. Both mother and daughter frequently lost their tempers in later years. And whatever parental love and filial respect there may have existed in the earlier days was almost completely forgotten. The representatives of both religions became embittered and irritated, and they spoke harsh words of and to one another and rather sought to deprecate and minimize the truths contained in the religion of their opponents.

We must first seek to ascertain whether the Talmud and the authentic Midrashim have some information to give us about Jesus and his disciples and the birth of Christianity. We must leave out of our discussion later rabbinic works on this subject as well as works of Jewish legendary literature about the life of Jesus in their various forms and versions, such as *Tam u-Mu'ad, Toledot Yeshu, Ma'aseh d'oto v'et B'no*.[1] We may indeed consider

[1] See S. Krauss, *Das Leben Jesu nach Jüdischen Quellen*, (Berlin, 1902), for the various versions; also L. Ginzberg, מעשה ישו, in *Ginze Schechter*, (New York, 1928), 324 ff.

them occasionally insofar as they may sometimes throw light on older works and help us to a better understanding of the authentic reports or allusions in the Talmud. For while it is possible that all these later works depend upon older sources and in some of their statements go back to older works of Talmudic times, they are not authentic Midrashic works. They do not cite their sources nor mention them by name, so that we cannot judge the character of these supposed sources nor decide upon their reliability. Furthermore, it is most likely to assume that whatever information these later works may have drawn from older authentic works is not reproduced in its original form. It is given in a later legendary form, embedded in layers of popular fancies. We are not so much interested in this study at least, in popular Jewish sentiment toward Jesus. We want to know what the authorities of Judaism, as represented in the literature of the Talmud and the authentic Midrashim, have to say about the beginning and very earliest history of Christianity. We want to find out whether the authentic literature of the Talmud and Midrashim have some information to give us about Jesus and his disciples — and what this information is. And in examining the information on these subjects which we may find in the Talmud, we must be careful to distinguish between such as comes from early sources, or sources contemporary with Jesus, and such as comes from later times. For the Talmud embodies documents and teachings originating in the four pre-Christian as well as in five or six Christian centuries. And some of the contents of the Midrashim represent material of even later centuries. Accordingly, the statements found in the Talmud are not all of equal value, and the reports found in the Talmud and in the Midrashim are not all of equal historical reliability. A report about any event given by an eye-witness is of course of greater historic value and more reliable than a report by a later historian or teacher, who may have drawn his information from older records but may also have obtained it from mere hearsay. In other words, we shall have to consider who the authors of the information found in the Talmud were, and when and where they lived. And yet we cannot set out to ascertain what these early teachers of Judaism actually knew about Jesus and Christianity. We can only seek those reports which were embodied in the literature that has come down to us.

For it is quite possible that these earlier teachers knew more about the origins of Christianity than they cared to report or had occasion to express even to their contemporaries and disciples. If for one reason or another they did not care to speak about these things publicly and explicitly, it would be futile for us to attempt to find out what they knew about them. We cannot make them talk now. We can only guess sometimes and draw conclusions from a veiled allusion or from a side remark about other questions that may have been prompted by what they knew or thought of early Christianity. But all our interpretations of such allusions or indirect remarks cannot claim absolute accuracy and certainty. They are only guesses. Again, it is quite conceivable that not all the information given by these early teachers and embodied in the original works of the Talmudic literature have been preserved to us. Perhaps in their original form the Talmud and Midrashim contained some information about the New Testament characters or some express references to Christianity which in the course of time were eliminated either by Christian censors, by Jews themselves for fear of censors,[2] or even because such information was not considered worth preserving by the later Jewish editors. Some of this early material may have been omitted or lost by sheer negligence or accident without any intentional effort by friend or foe, just as so much other literary material even of an halakic nature, which was certainly regarded as important, as well as haggadic information from ancient times, became lost in the course of the centuries before the age of printing. We must content ourselves with an investigation of the material which is available to us.

---

[2] Even in some Spanish MSS some passages were omitted. See H. L. Strack, *Einleitung* ..., 68 and R. N. Rabbinovicz, מאמר על הדפסת התלמוד, 24. Jewish printers like Soncino exercised censorship. See Strack, *ibid.*, 84 and 88. Cf. also the letter of the Jewish authorities in Poland in 1631 demanding elimination of references to Jesus in printed editions, see Strack, *ibid.*, 87. Censor-free editions are Bomberg I, 1520–1523; II, 1531; Justinian, 1548. (First censored, Basel, 1578–80, Amsterdam 1644–48 partly restored the omitted passages.)

That is to say, we must deal with the literature as we have it now and consider the talmudic-midrashic works in the form in which they have come down and been preserved to us in those early editions or manuscripts which were, comparatively speaking, free from censorship.

In the later editions the censors expunged passages from the Talmud which though not expressly mentioning Jesus or Christians, were considered by the censors as unfavorable to Jesus or Christianity. Some of these omitted or stricken passages are found in the older editions or have been saved and preserved in separate works.[3] But, as already stated, there may have been many more passages stricken out from the Talmud before the first printed editions appeared or even before the time of the oldest existing MSS.

I said that this study is of interest to both Jew and Christian. But I should add that this interest is — or should be — purely scientific and not apologetic or polemic. It should not aim to prove or disprove the New Testament reports about the central figure of Christianity or its earliest advocates and teachers. For, it must be acknowledged, that from a strictly scientific point of view, the question of the historicity of Jesus cannot be answered either way on the basis of the little information about him found in the Talmud or the lack of such information in the contemporary Jewish literature, that is, in those parts of the Talmud which date from the first century of the common era.

The lack of available information about Jesus in contemporary talmudic literature, i. e., in sayings by Tannaim of the first generation, even if it could be assumed with certainty that the talmudic literature never contained any such passages would not necessarily argue against his historicity. Such an *argumentum e silentio* in this case cannot be regarded as valid or cogent. Such silence may have been purely accidental, in that the earliest redactors of the Talmud may not have had an occasion to embody a report about Jesus by a contemporary in their collections; or such a silence may have been due to ignorance about him on the

[3] Like ס״ש חסרונות ספר or ההשמטות קבוצת והוא חסרונות (Krakau, 1893); another edition ס״ש חסרונות למלאות קונטרס (Königsberg, 1860); and השכחה אומר קונטרס, 1861; also אבדה השבת ספר (Lemberg [?] 1858).

part of his contemporaries who may not even have noticed his existence or his activity, the reports in the New Testament as to the great excitement caused by Jesus in his days notwithstanding.[4] After all the Talmud does not furnish a complete history of *all* the important events or great personalities of the first century of the common era. Many such events and personalities may have gone unnoticed by the earlier teachers and actually are not mentioned in the Talmud. Jesus and his activity may have been one of these. But aside from these considerations, accepting the historicity of Jesus, the silence could be explained on other grounds. Thus it might be assumed that the Jewish authorities of his days did not consider Jesus of sufficient importance or worth to discuss him or report about him.

But above all, there is the other possibility, that the Jewish teachers of his time *did* discuss Jesus and did refer to him, favorably or unfavorably, but their references to him and their statements about him were later suppressed and ultimately became lost to us.

On the other hand, the scanty references to him that are still to be found in the Talmud and in the Midrashim do not at all prove his historicity, any more than the records of the New Testament.

The references and allusions to Jesus found in the Talmud and in the Midrashim are of such a nature that they cannot be considered convincing proof that he actually existed. For, as will be shown, not even one *single statement* preserved to us in the talmudic-midrashic literature can be regarded as authentic in the sense that it originated in the time of Jesus or even in the first half century of the Christian era. The Talmud does not record even one *talmudic teacher* who lived at the time of Jesus or in the first half century of the Christian era as mentioning Jesus by name, telling something about him, or expressly referring to him in any way. In other words, the Talmud does not furnish any contemporary evidence for the historicity of Jesus.

The references to Jesus recorded in the Talmud are mostly

[4] This is actually assumed by Klausner as one of the causes of the *silence* of the contemporary Jewish authorities about Jesus. See his ישו הנוצרי, 4th ed., (Jerusalem, 1933), 9. Cf. however M. Guttmann in *MGWJ*, (1931), 252.

from teachers who lived a long time after Jesus. A very few of them come from teachers who lived in the beginning of the second century of the common era, or at the earliest, in the later part of the first century, but not earlier than the first or the original authors of the synoptic gospels.[5] Whatever these teachers have to say about Jesus simply refers to the person *legendary* or historical — who was believed by the people of their time, especially by the Christian sect, to have been the originator of the Christian sect. The rabbis may have contented themselves with, or relied upon, current stories about him. They certainly knew, and came into contact with, the Christians of their days. And in the second century most of the synoptic gospels, giving the life story of Jesus as the originator of the new faith or the founder of the sect and of the new religion were already redacted. The Christians of the second century among whom these were circulated, certainly believed in a Jesus, as the originator of their new faith or the founder of their new religion. The Jewish teachers of that time, in polemics or in casual references, merely referred to that person, the real or alleged founder, who was the central figure of Christianity. They never argued the question whether such a figure had actually existed or not, since Christianity was an actual reality. They probably were not even interested in this question. For their purpose or from their point of view, which concerned itself merely with the truth or falsehood, the correctness or the incorrectness of the Christian teachings, it really was of no great consequence, or at least it made no difference to them, whether the person in whose name these teachings were given had actually lived or not. To deny that he had lived would not have disproved the teachings ascribed to him. They could accept or believe the legends current about him, and believe that such a person had lived, and nevertheless dispute his greatness or reject and argue against his teachings. But they had no interest in inquiring whether and when he

---

[5] The composition of the present Mark dates from about 70 C. E., that of Matthew and Luke between 70 and 110 C. E. All of them used older sources or gospels, which go back to about the year 50 C. E. though not earlier. See James Moffatt, *Introduction to the Literature of the New Testament*, (New York, 1923), 212 ff.

lived. They usually did this only in case of people in whom they were especially interested or in whose teachings they believed, e. g., when they seek to determine who Elijah was,[6] or from what tribe he came,[7] or fix the time and generation of Job.[8] But they probably did not care to inquire whether a person whose teachings they rejected and whose mission or importance they did not believe, actually lived or was merely a myth. Hence, we need not expect to be able to decide the question of Jesus' historicity on the basis of the references made to him by those rabbis of the Talmud who lived after his time. Of course there is a possibility that these references to Jesus by Rabbis of the second century, came from earlier times. Sayings or teachings quoted in the Talmud in the name of a teacher may sometimes be not his own original teaching, but such as he received from older teachers. It is therefore possible — though not plausible — that these later rabbis of the Talmud, when mentioning Jesus or making any statement about him or his disciples, do not give their own original views, but merely quote or repeat what they have heard from their teachers or received by tradition from teachers of former generations — among whom there may have been contemporaries of Jesus. In the latter case, then, we would have the evidence as to Jesus' historical existence coming from his contemporary Jewish teachers, preserved to us and quoted by Rabbis who lived a long time after him. But since in the case of any statement made by a teacher without giving the source, we cannot decide whether that teacher gives his own saying or the view of another teacher, and if this latter is so, when that other teacher lived, it still remains doubtful, to say the least, whether the information contained in that saying, is of an older or of recent date. So the statement that we cannot find in the Talmud *contemporary* evidence of the historical existence of Jesus remains unchallenged.

Yet these references to Jesus made by later rabbis of the Talmud are of great importance and of interest to us. For even if they cannot help us to decide the question of the historicity

[6] B. M. 14b. פנחס זה אליהו.
[7] Gen. r. 71.12 אליהו משבט גד (או) משבט בנימין; אליהו כהן היה.
[8] B. B. 15a,b מעולי גולה or איוב בימי משה היה etc.

of Jesus, we can still learn from what the rabbis of the Talmud, beginning with the second century, thought about Jesus. It is of no small interest to know what the reaction of Judaism to Christianity, in its formative period, was, and what the rabbis thought about Christianity, its teachings and its alleged or real founder. In other words to know, what information the authoritative Jewish literature, the Talmud and the Midrashim, has about the attitude of the Jewish people, as voiced by their representative teachers, toward Christianity in the first three or four centuries of its history.

In seeking to answer this question we shall proceed in the following manner. We shall first seek to find out what information the Talmud and Midrashim have to give us about Jesus himself — whether they have something to say about the person of Jesus; whether they mention him by his name, Jesus, or designate him by any other name, or refer to him under any special designation like פנטירא בן or בן סטדא or under the disguise of a biblical name like בלעם or allude to him by certain terms unmistakably pointing to him like אותו האיש, פלוני or describing his personality when speaking of him as "man" or "son of man."

Then we shall see whether any mention is made in the talmudic-midrashic literature of his family, relatives, mother and brothers, disciples and followers. In the case of the latter we shall seek to discover also whether some of them are mentioned by their real names, by a substitute name, or merely referred to under the general designation of his disciples, followers or Christians, נוצרים. In connection with a discussion of the latter group, we shall also consider whether, and in which cases, the designation מינים refers to Christians or merely designates heretics in general. Then again we shall consider the various heretical writings or books mentioned in the Talmud ספרי מינים, or ספרי קוסמים, to determine whether they refer to or include also writings of the early Christians or collections of their teachings; also what other general reference to the New Testament, as עון גליון or גליונות or אורייתא אחריתא are found in the Talmud, and whether quotations from it, agreeing or disagreeing with the existent versions of the New Testament, can be discovered in the talmudic-midrashic literature.

Beginning with the question whether Jesus is mentioned by his name in the Talmud, we shall first consider the following passage which connects him with an older teacher, a teacher living long before the time in which the Jesus of the Gospels is supposed to have lived.

In the Tractate Sanhedrin[9] of the Babylonian Talmud in a Baraita which reads: ת״ר לעולם תהא שמאל דוחה וימין מקרבת ולא כאלישע שדחפו לגחזי בשתי ידים, there are — although omitted in the present censored editions but found in the Munich manuscript (written 1343) as well as in the older uncensored editions (i. e., those printed before the edition of Basel 1578–81) — following the words בשתי ידים, this additional remark: ולא כיהושע בן פרחיה שדחפו לישו הנוצרי בשתי ידים.[10] This Baraita then declares that Jesus had been a disciple or follower of Joshua b. Peraḥyah by whom he was then repulsed. On the same page in the Talmud about ten lines below, after the words א״ר יוחנן גיחזי ושלשת בניו there is found in the MSS and in the earlier editions a story which seeks to explain the unrelenting attitude of Jeshua b. Peraḥyah towards Jesus referred to in the above Baraita, and to explain how, when and why the latter left Judaism after having been excommunicated and repulsed by his teacher. It reads as follows: ר' יהושע בן פרחיה מאי הוא כדקטלינהו ינאי מלכא לרבנן אזל רבי יהושע בן פרחיה וישו (כת״י מ הנוצרי) לאלכסנדריא של מצרים כי הוה שלמא שלח ליה שמעון בן שטח מיני ירושלים עיר הקודש ליכי אלכסנדריא של מצרים אחותי בעלי שרוי בתוכך ואנכי יושבת שוממה קם אתא ואתרמי ליה ההוא אושפיזא עבדו ליה יקרא טובא אמר כמה יפה אכסניא זו אמר ליה רבי עיניה טרוטות אמר ליה רשע בכך אתה עוסק אפיק ארבע מאה שיפורי ושמתיה אתא לקמיה כמה זמנין אמר ליה קבלן לא הוה קא משגח ביה יומא חד הוה קא קאי קריאת שמע אתא לקמיה סבר מידחא לקבולי אחוי ליה בידיה הוא סבר מידחא דחי ליה אזל זקף לבינתא והשתחוה לה אמר ליה הדר בך אמר ליה (כת"י מ ישו) כך מקובלני ממך כל החוטא ומחטיא את הרבים אין מספיקין בידו לעשות תשובה ואמר מר ישו (כת״י מ הנוצרי) כישף והסית והדיח.[11] Let us consider first a few minor details and the meaning of some words in this story before

---

[9] Sanh. 107b.

[10] The designation הנוצרי after לישו is omitted in some of the older prints; see R. N. Rabbinovicz, *Diḳduḳe Soferim, ad loc.*

[11] Read the text in the Venice edition; also Soṭah 47a, Amsterdam edition, or in חסרונות הש״ס (Krakau, 1893).

we examine its contents as a whole to determine its reliability and accuracy. The name ישׁ by which Jesus is here mentioned is probably merely a shortened form of the name ישׁוע (the abbreviation sign on top is a later addition.)[12] But since such an abbreviated form of the name is not used in any other case of a person named ישׁוע or יהושׁע, but persistently and consistently used when the name refers to Jesus, it may be assumed that this shortening of the name was probably an intentional mutilation by cutting off part of it. The rabbis mention other instances of the names of persons being shortened because of their misconduct,[13] but here in the case of the name Jeshua there may have been an additional special reason for shortening it into Jeshu. Elias Levita[14] thinks that the reason was that the Jews, unwilling to even suggest that Jesus might have been a savior, or redeemer, which the name ישׁוע with an *ayin* at the end signifies, dropped the letter *ayin* from his name.[15]

At any rate, here in the talmudic text, this shorter form of the name was *not* meant to represent the curse ימח שמו וזכרו, "May his name and memory be blotted out," although in the later Jewish works about the life of Jesus this form of the name was understood to be an abbreviation of the three words constituting this curse.[16]

The meaning of the designation הנוצרי which, as we have seen, the MS text adds to the name ישׁ in our passage, we shall discuss further on in connection with the name נוצרים used as a designation for the Christians.[17] Here I will only point out that

[12] Cf. the shorter form עדו in Zech. 1.1 and in Ezra 5.1 and see S. Krauss, *op. cit.*, 250; also אשתמוע, Josh. 21.14, shortened to אשתמה and Keri אשתמו, *ibid.*, 15.50. See Ch. D. Ginsburg ed. of the Hebrew Bible.

[13] See Mekilta, *Amalek* III, (Friedmann 576, Lauterbach II, 165), the case of עפרן for עפרון and יונדב for יהונדב.

[14] Tishbi as quoted by Krauss, *op. cit.*, 250.

[15] שהיהודים אינם מודים שהוא היה המושיע לפיכך אינם רוצים לקראו ישוע והפילו העין וקורין לו ישו. See also H. L. Strack, *Jesus Die Häretiker und die Christen, nach den Ältesten Jüdischen Angaben*, (Leipzig, 1910), 8.

[16] Thus the author of the מעשה דאותו ואת בנו in Krauss, *op. cit.*, 68 says ואז החרימו חרם בישראל שלא יקרא שמו יהושע אלא ישו כלומר ימח שמו וזכרו וכן קראו משם ואילך בזה השם.

[17] b. Ta'an. 27b. See older editions and *Diḳduḳe Soferim*.

JESUS IN THE TALMUD

the derivation of this name from Nazareth, presents many difficulties.[18] First, it is doubtful whether there was at that time a town by that name. If, however, there was, we would have to read the name Nozáret נוצרת or Nozerah נוֹצְרָה in order to derive the gentilic נוצרי after the fashion of תמני from תמנה.[19] In the Greek text of Matthew 2.23 and John 19.19, he is called Ναζωραῖος, i. e., Nazoraios. This would be a transliteration from נוֹצְרָיָה, which cannot mean "a man from Nazareth," but must be derived from נוֹצֵר or ·נוֹטֵר, "observe," "watch." נוצרי then would mean "an observer" equal to שומר, נוטר, in this case an observer of a rule or of the law. נוצרי or נצורא, the Syriac name for Christians, would be a *nomen agentis* equal in form to סָבוֹרָא, אמורא and in the plural נְצוֹרַיָא would designate people characterized as being strict "observers" or "keepers of the law" נוצרי תורה or שומרי תורה. It may have designated a group from a much older period than the time of Jesus, whose name the Christians, wishing to be regarded as of similar character, as the true observers of the law, or the observers of the new or true law, borrowed.[20]

Another detail in this report concerns the meaning of the expression זקף לבינתא, "put up a brick." We do not know of any satisfactory explanation for this phrase as it stands, for it can hardly be assumed that even in a later report Jesus should have been accused of having worshipped an idol consisting of a "brick." R. Jeḥiel of Paris in his disputation which took place in the year 1240 in Paris, suggests that the brick was in the form of a cross.[21] According to these emendations or explanations,

---

[18] Some Christians would derive the name from נצר = צמח = משיח.

[19] See Herford, *Christianity in Talmud and Midrash*, 52, note, 164–170, 344 and 379.

[20] See Mark Lidzbarski, *Mandäische Liturgien*, (Berlin, 1920), XVI ff., and *Ginza, Der Schatz oder das grosse Buch der Mandäer*, (Göttingen and Leipzig), 1925, IX. See below the discussion of passage in Matthew and Talmud Taanit.

[21] ויכוח רבינו יחיאל, ed. Grünbaum, (Thorn, 1873), 5; ed. R. Margulies, Lemberg, (s. d.), 17. He says, והכי משמע שהשתחווה ללבינה איכא למימר דההיא לבינה עשויה כשתי וערב כמעשיהם. In the work תם ומועד (no date or place of publication given) 10, it is suggested that there were two bricks — reading לבינתא — one placed on top or across the other and held by magic: וילך הרשע וזקף לבינה על גבי לבינה בכשפים.

this sentence would contain a reference to the worship of the cross. But how could Jesus worship the cross before he was crucified? Had the cross some significance before the crucifixion? The same allusion to the cross is found in this sentence, if we emend the text with A. S. Kamenetzki to read צליבתא instead of לבינתא.[22] But there is no basis for this emendation in the MSS. At any rate, the phrase as it stands in our text makes no sense.

Another detail in the report is the phrase אפיק ד׳ מאה שיפורי ושמתיה. "He sounded four hundred trumpets and excommunicated him." We find a similar statement in b. M. K. 16a in the report that Barak declared the ban over Meroz (Judg. 5.23) with four hundred blasts of the trumpet, which may also mean that four hundred trumpets were used in declaring or announcing the ban בד׳ מאה שיפורי שמתיה ברק למרוז. Meroz there is taken by some to have been a person and by some a star,[23] but in this case the trumpets may have been for purposes of proclamation or making it known to the whole camp. What, however, would be the significance of the four hundred trumpets here? To proclaim it to the whole world? As to the use of the Shofar in connection with proclaiming a ban, we have the statement מאי שיפורא שנפרעין ממנו[24] which seems to pre-suppose the use of a Shofar when proclaiming a ban. The significance of its use appears to derive not from its *sound*, but from the mere name שופר which, as a pun on the word שנפרעין ממנו was to serve as a sort of reminder either to the people that the heavenly powers *will*, or to the heavenly powers themselves that they *should*, exact punishment of the man put in ban. Since other definite explanations of the use of the Shofar, or express prescription that it should be used in connection with the act of proclaiming a ban are, to my knowledge, not found in tannaitic literature, it is doubtful whether Joshua b. Peraḥyah used it. I cannot even find any reference to it in a Palestinian source. In b. Sanh. 7b it is said that R. Huna when going out to hold court would say, "Bring

---

[22] A. S. Kamenetzki in התקופה XVIII, (Warsaw, 1923), 511, וכבר בארתי במקום אחר שבמקום "לבינתא" צריך להיות "צליבתא" (זקף מורה בארמית "תלה" "צלב") ובכן יש כאן רמז אנדי על עבודת הצלב לנוצרים.

[23] Cf. also b. Shebu. 36a.

[24] b. M. K. 17b.

out for me the implements of my office, the whip, the staff, the Shofar and the sandal;" which Rashi explains to mean שופר לשמעתא ונדוי. So here, if Rashi is correct the Shofar was one of the means used not only for proclaiming but actually in imposing or pronouncing a ban. Although even here it may mean only to announce the ban, that is, to make it known to the public by means of the Shofar. Likewise the saying of Samuel, "The blow (the sound of the Shofar) binds; the blow releases"[25] is understood by R. Ḥananel[26] and Rashi[27] to mean that by the sound of the Shofar the ban is pronounced or imposed and by the sound of the Shofar the ban can also be removed or lifted. This would mean then that the Shofar sound in itself was the very means of imposing the ban and making it effective.[28] There seems to have been the practice in later, amoraic times, and certainly in gaonic times of using the Shofar as a means by which a ban was pronounced.[29] At any rate we do not find any reference in tannaitic sources to the use of the Shofar in connection with the imposition of ḥerem, though in Tannaitic times it may have been used to proclaim the ban. The manner in which Joshua b. Peraḥyah is reported to have excommunicated Jesus reminds one rather of the later amoraic or gaonic practice and speaks against the authenticity of this report. The whole tone of the story is legendary. At any rate it is not a contemporary document. It is a later report and as a whole has no real historic value, though it may have some elements of truth in it, as we shall see.

In the first place, the whole report about Joshua b. Peraḥyah's flight to Egypt is questionable. It is rather doubtful whether

[25] b. M. K. 16a, טוט אסר טוט שרי.
[26] *Ad loc.*   [27] *Ad loc.*
[28] Cf. however, Tosafot Men. 34b, *s. v.* טט בכתפי where one explains the phrase טוט אסר in the saying of Samuel to mean two scholars or judges can pronounce the ban, and two others have the power or authority to remove it. According to this interpretation Samuel had no reference at all to the Shofar.
[29] A full description of the חרם with the use of the Shofar and other horrifying means is given in a responsum of R. Paltoi Gaon in תשובות הגאונים (Lyck, 1864), No. 10, page 8. [May it also have been used to ward off danger from the persons who pronounce the ban?] Cf. also as to the use of the Shofar for mere announcing or proclaiming a prohibition the saying in 'Ab. Zarah 40a, ושרי..... נפק שיפורי דרבא ואסר שיפורי דרב הונה.

Joshua b. Peraḥyah ever went to Egypt. One report which, as we shall see, seems more authentic, names Judah b. Tabbai, and thus casts doubt on our story, which names Joshua.[30] It is very likely that the story in the Babli is but a modification of the other report found in p. Ḥagigah[31] about Judah b. Tabbai who had to run away to Alexandria and later on was recalled to Jerusalem. A later reporter who had heard the story about Judah b. Tabbai confused him with Joshua b. Peraḥyah and mixed with the story other legendary reports about persons who went from Palestine to Alexandria. Out of this confusion of the story about Judah b. Tabbai with other stories, emerged the story as we have it in the Babli, with the suspiciously legendary features of the "brick" and "four hundred shofars" and the specific name of Jesus.

The story about Judah b. Tabbai in p. Ḥagigah[32] reads as follows: מאן דאמר יהודה בן טבאי נשיא עובדא אלכסנדריא מסייע ליה יהודה בן טבאי הוון בני ירושלם בעון ממניתיה נשיא בירושלם ערק ואזל ליה לאלכסנדריאה והיו בני ירושלם כותבין מירושלם הגדולה לאלכסנדריאה הקטנה עד מתי ארוסי יוסב מרתא דביתא דקבלתן מה הוות חסירה (חסידה?) א"ל חדמן תלמידוי רבי עיינה חות שברה א"ל הא תרתי גבך חדא דחשדתני וחדא דיסתכלת בה מה אמרית ואייא ברייא לא אמרית אלא בעובדא וכעס עלוי ואזל. This story has nothing legendary about it and may actually have happened. The expression ואזל at the end may mean simply, "he went away," that is, left the teacher, without any other implication as to the subsequent career of the disciple. It may, however, also mean, he went away and left Judaism, corresponding to the phrase יצא לתרבות רעה. Possibly also it means that he died אזל מן עלמא. Z. Frankel assumes that the whole account of Joshua b. Peraḥyah's going to and coming back from Alexandria is unhistoric. But if we should assume that there is some truth in this legend, and it is based on a traditional report that Joshua b. Peraḥyah had a disciple by the name of Jesus who was expelled by the teacher and who left Judaism, it would not prove anything in regard to the Jesus of the Gospels, who is reported to have been born about 130 years after Joshua b. Peraḥyah. And indeed, some people assume on the basis of this story that there were two

---

[30] See Z. Frankel, *Darkhe ha-Mishnah*, 35–36.
[31] II, 2, (77d).   [32] *Loc. cit.*

men named Jesus.[33] Some Christian scholars likewise assume that there had been a pre-Christian Jesus. Some of those who deny the historicity of the Jesus of the Gospels claim that the Jesus of the Gospels is unhistorical and that the story of the Gospel is but a myth woven around the name of Jesus b. Pandera, a certain person who had been put to death under the reign of Alexander Jannai (106–79 B. C. E.).[34]

One Christian scholar assumes that Jesus indeed lived in the time of Joshua b. Peraḥyah, but that the Gospel writers confused him with a false prophet who lived in the time of Pontius Pilate.[35] He assumes, then, that our story has some historical value. In fact, many of the later Jewish sources do put Jesus in the time of Joshua b. Peraḥyah and Simon b. Shetaḥ.[36]

Likewise, Abraham ibn Daud (1110–1180) in his *Sefer ha-Kabbalah*[37] says: וכותבי זכרונות בישראל אומרים שיהושע בן פרחיה רבו של ישו הנוצרי.[38] He takes notice of the difference between this and the non-Jewish reports and concludes with what he considers a true tradition: קבלת אמת בידינו כי בשנת ארבע לאלכסנדר המלך נולד ומת בן שלשים ושש בשנת שלש למלכות אריסטובולים בן ינאי. This would put Jesus about 70 years before the Gospel date. At any rate, the Jesus of the Gospels, said to have been born under the reign of Herod the Great, could not have lived in the time of Alexander Jannai and could not have been the disciple of Joshua b. Peraḥyah.

The story about Jesus as given in our passage in b. Sanhedrin

---

[33] See R. Jehiel in his ויכוח, ed. R. Margulies (Lemberg), 16–17, who says that this story refers to another Jesus.

[34] For the literature, see Albert Schweitzer, *Von Reimarus bis Wrede, eine Geschichte des Leben Jesu Forschung*, (Tübingen, 1906).

[35] Cf. Maurice Goguel, *Jesus the Nazarene, Myth or History*, (1926).

[36] See S. Kraus, *op. cit.*, 65, 118, 147. In a MS of a Midrash in the British Museum, (Margoliouth, *Catalogue* II, [1915], 21) there is found the following statement, דע שישוע הנצרי היה קודם חרבן הבית כמאה וחמש ושלשים שנה. Cf. Margoliouth's reference to Steinschneider as to another MS containing the same statement.

[37] Neubauer, *Medieval Jewish Chronicles* I, 53.

[38] Why does he not say "The Talmud says" if our passage in the Talmud was regarded as authentic? In other words the story in our Talmud passage was not regarded by him as קבלת אמת, true tradition.

cannot be considered an historical account of the Jesus of the Gospels and certainly cannot be considered as contemporary evidence or as proof for his historicity. It is merely a legend. In this case we can at least guess, if not explain, how this legend originated and on the basis of the following assumptions show the process by which it may have developed and how it became associated with the name of Joshua b. Peraḥyah. It may be considered a historic fact that when in the second half of the second century B. C. E. one of the teachers of Jerusalem, Judah b. Tabbai (or Joshua b. Peraḥyah) went to Alexandria, he was accompanied by some of his disciples. It may also be assumed as historically true, as we have no reason to consider it improbable, that one of the disciples accompanying the teacher, coming under the influence of the Alexandrian heretical doctrines, disgraced himself and left Judaism. Such a sad occurence seems to be supposed in the saying of Abtalyon in Ab. I 12: אבטליון אומר חכמים הזהרו בדבריכם שמא תחובו חובת גלות ותגלו למקום מים הרעים וישתו התלמידים הבאים אחריכם וימותו ונמצא שם שמים מתחלל. Whether it happened to a pupil of Joshua b. Peraḥyah or to one of Judah b. Tabbai is of no significance. At any rate it was not Jesus. It must have happened to a disciple of one of the teachers preceding Shemayah and Abtalyon, for Abtalyon apparently based his saying on this unfortunate event. It seems more likely that it happened to a disciple of Judah b. Tabbai as the story in the Yerushalmi has it. This story does not mention Jesus, in fact, it does not give any name but merely refers to "one of his disciples." In the Babylonian Talmud, however, the story was enlarged and the name Jesus added. One might argue that the original story named Jesus but the Yerushalmi omitted the reference. This, however, would not be likely. We can well understand how the original story about "one of the disciples" was misunderstood in Babylon as referring to Jesus. They may have heard the legend told in the gospels, that Jesus had been to Egypt.[39] They also heard that Jesus was a wizard, who wrought witchcraft, and enticed and led men astray. They also had heard, as we shall see below, that Jesus was originally a disciple but

[39] Matth. 2.13–15.

later became corrupted in his doctrine.[40] And so they jumped to the conclusion that the disciple who became corrupt and who was in Egypt was Jesus. Hence they told the story about Jesus instead of about "one of the disciples." (Of course it is possible that even in the Babli the name Jesus is a later insertion.)

There was also another confusion of persons and names which may have caused the Babylonians to assume that this "disciple" was Jesus. The Babylonians had heard of a Jesus Sirach, the grandson of the older Sirach, who came to Egypt about 132 B. C. E., approximately the time of Joshua b. Peraḥyah, and translated his grandfather's work into Greek. This book of ben-Sirach was regarded as one of the external books, ספרים חיצונים.[41] Thus the Babylonians knew of a Jesus who was the author or translator of one of the ספרים חיצונים, for they confused Sirach the grandfather with Sirach the grandson who went to Egypt, that is, the author with the translator. There were many legends about this Jesus Sirach, the author of the book, which resemble the legends about Jesus of Nazareth. His mother, too, was a virgin, the daughter of Jeremiah, who conceived indirectly from her father Jeremiah, (the numerical value of whose name ירמיהו is the same as סירא=271)[42] by means of a bath-tub.[43] These legends the Babylonians may have vaguely known, just as they vaguely knew or heard of the legends about Jesus who was taken as a child to Egypt. Having in their mind identified the two men named Jesus, they, therefore, assumed that it was Jesus of Nazareth who went to Egypt about the year 132 B. C. E., the time that Jesus Sirach, the younger, went. Likewise, they made him go not as a child with his father Joseph but with his teacher. The name Jeshua may indeed have suggested the teacher's name Jehoshua b. Peraḥyah instead of Judah b. Tabbai, that is a יהושע

---

[40] תלמיד שהקדיח תבשילו ברבים, Ber. 17b, Sanh. 103.

[41] See p. Sanh. 10.1 (28a), ספרים חיצונים כגון ספרי בן סירא ובן לענה and b. Sanh. 100a where Rab Joseph forbids the reading of Ben Sirach.

[42] See *Yuḥasin* 103, s. v. אבוה, in the name of Judah ha-Nasi. See also Rashi to Ḥag. 15a, s. v., כאמבטי.

[43] See Steinschneider's edition of אלפא ביתא דבן סירא (Berlin, 1858), 16b, 17, a work containing parts from different ages, one from about the end of the Gaonic period and another part of later date.

with a ה to contrast him with his pupil. The teacher with ה in his name had the true belief in God which saved him.[44] The disciple did not have a ה in his name and was lacking in the true belief in God hence was not saved from the bad influence, the מים הרעים of Alexandria.[45]

To sum up, then, the story in b. Sanhedrin is a later legend about Jesus and not a contemporary report, not even a reliable tradition, as is evident from R. Abraham ibn Daud. It merely reflects the vague knowledge of the legends about Jesus that were current about Jesus in later times, about the fifth or sixth century of the Christian era. All it knows of him is that he left Judaism, and caused others to do so and leave their true Jewish religion. He is an enticer who led Israel astray. It knows him as a sorcerer, or one practicing witchcraft, which was the common opinion among the Jews even in the time of the Gospel writers.[46] But it is significant that they speak of him as a one time disciple. Even the later rabbis of the Talmud among whom this legend circulated considered Jesus as having once been a disciple, as one שהקדיח תבשילו, i. e., held false doctrines and followed the practices of magic.

The next passage in the Talmud in which Jesus is mentioned by name and in which he is also referred to and described as a misleader, מסית, is — or rather was — to be found in b. Sanh. 43a,b. It is omitted in the later editions but is found in the earlier printed editions and in the manuscripts. It reads as follows: לפניו אין מעיקרא לא והתניא בערב הפסח תלאוהו לישו והכרוז יוצא לפניו ארבעים יום קודם שהוא ליסקל על שכישף והסית והדיח את ישראל כל מי שיודע לו זכות יבא וילמד עליו ולא מצאו לו זכות ותלאוהו בערב פסח: אמר עולא ותסברא בר הפוכי זכות הוא מסית הוא ורחמנא אמר (דברים י"ג) לא תחמול ולא תכסה עליו אלא שאני ישו דקרוב למלכות הוה: Before we consider this Baraita let us first attempt to ascertain on what day Jesus was executed so as to be able to decide whether this Baraita could have had reference to Jesus and whether it agrees or disagrees

---

[44] Cf. Soṭah 34b, the case of Joshua the son of Nun — יהושע = יה יושיעך מעצת מרגלים.

[45] Cf. in addition R. Herford, *Christianity in Talmud and Midrash*, 54 and Heinrich Laible, *Jesus Christus in Talmud*, (Berlin, 1891), 41 ff.

[46] See Matth. 9.34 and 12.24.

with the New Testament reports about his execution. Now, according to the Synoptic Gospels,[47] Jesus was executed on the first day of the Festival.[48] But according to John 17.8 ff. it was on the fourteenth of Nisan, before the priests prepared and ate the Passover lamb, that Jesus was executed, although Jesus had already eaten his Seder meal the evening previous.[49] Yet they all agree that he was executed on Friday, for on the third day thereafter, on Sunday, he is said to have arisen. Was Friday *Yom Ṭob*,[50] so that Jesus could have held Seder on the preceding night, Thurday evening, as assumed by the Synoptists, or was it *Ereb Yom Ṭob*, i. e., the fourteenth of Nisan, as John assumes, and if so, how could Jesus have conducted his Seder before? The answer is given by Daniel Chwolson.[51] Friday was *Ereb Yom Ṭob*, but in certain groups בין הערבים was understood as twilight, i. e., בין השמשות. Those who held that אין פסח דוחה שבת, for even after Hillel there were some who did not accept his decision that פסח דוחה שבת,[52] could not slaughter the lamb on Friday at twilight because בין השמשות ספק יום, hence ספק שבת. John must have had a report that Jesus was supposed to have belonged to one such group, hence he reports him as having offered the Passover sacrifice and celebrated the Seder the night before.[53] According to John, then, the day in which Jesus was executed was the fourteenth of Nisan, Friday, *Ereb Shabbat* and also *Erev Pesaḥ*. The other contradictions in the Gospels do not concern us.

Not let us consider our Baraita and see whether it does have

[47] Matth. 26.17 ff. and parallels, Mark 14.12 and Luke 22.7.
[48] Cf. Matth. 27.15 ff. We need not concern ourselves with the difficulty of Matth. 26.17 "The first day of unleavened bread."=יום ראשון דחג המצות, i. e., the 15th of Nisan. See Chwolson, *Das letzte Pessahmahl Christi*, (Leipzig, 1908), for it is possible that the fourteenth day, on the afternoon of which leaven is already forbidden — though Matzah could not yet be eaten — was regarded by some as the first day of the unleavened bread.
[49] See John 12.2 ff.
[50] The rule לא בד"ו פסח is of a later date.
[51] *Op. cit.*
[52] b. Pes. 66a.
[53] [Ed. note: See J. Lauterbach, "זמן שחיטת הפסח" *Proceedings American Academy for Jewish Research*, (New York, 1942), vol. 12, Heb. section 1–5.]

reference to Jesus. It contains a few minor difficulties but they are sufficient to prove that the Baraita is comparatively young and not entirely authentic. We must remember that this Baraita is merely cited in a discussion seeking to understand the Mishnah which says והכרוז יוצא לפניו. The Gemara challenges the implied interpretation of לפניו as "immediately before but not previous to that time," by quoting this Baraitha, the authenticity of which is at all times open to question as is not infrequent in talmudic discussion.

In the first place, the statement והכרוז יוצא לפניו ארבעים יום, is rather strange. Does it assume, taking לפניו literally, that for forty days they would, on each day, lead out the victim with the herald walking in front of him proclaiming that he was going to be executed.

But such a procedure is unknown in Jewish law. Aside from the fact that the Mishnah[54] speaks only of the herald actually going in front of the victim on his way to the place where he was to be executed, there is no precedent for forty days of such announcements. One might possibly expect such a precedent in the case of a זקן ממרא, a rebellious teacher[55] whose execution was announced sometime before it actually took place.[56] But there it is said that they would announce it through letters — but not by a herald. And even there, no mention is made of a period of forty days. All it says is: וכותבין ושולחין בכל המקומות which was probably an announcement of the execution yet to be performed. It is possible, however, that someone computed as follows: if a "rebellious elder" (whose execution had to take place during the time of a pilgrim festival) was judged and convicted on the first day after Pesaḥ, they would keep him till the next pilgrim festival, i. e., till Shabuoth. Of course, they would not execute him on the holiday itself (for the phrase "they execute him at the festival" means at the time or season of the festival)[57] but on

[54] Sanh. 6.1.   [55] Mishnah Sanh. 11.4.

[56] As to whether Jesus could have been considered a זקן ממרא, see above, *The Pharisees and Their Teachings*, page 92, note 7, to which is to be added that Jesus was merely a תלמיד, not yet a זקן and תלמיד שהורה לעשות פטור (Mishnah Sanh. 11.2).

[57] "Zur Festzeit;" see N. Brüll, *Jahrbücher*, VII, 96.

the day before, which was close to the time of the festival when all the prilgrims were already assembled in Jerusalem. In this case, there would be forty days between the sentence and the execution. This Baraita, then, would regard Jesus as a זקן ממרא, "rebellious elder," who denied the traditions of the teachers, and in such a case an elapse of forty days between the sentence and the execution was possible. The author of this Baraita must then have assumed further that Jesus was sentenced about forty days before Pesach, so that they had to keep him forty days until Pesaḥ. To fill out these forty days with some activity, the reporter put in the unheard of practice of the *herald* proclaiming for forty days, instead of the sending out of the letters. But even if we assume this, it will show that the author of this Baraita was badly confused.[58]

Unless we assume that the author of our Baraita somehow heard or believed that Jesus was sentenced about forty days

[58] It is interesting to note the theory of M. Joel, *Blicke in die Religionsgeschichte usw.*, (Breslau, 1882), II, 58, who assumes a similar confusion in a Baraita. In Tosefta Sanh. 11.7, (Zuckermandel, 432), the rule about משמרין אותו עד הרגל which the Mishnah applies only to זקן ממרא is extended to others, *viz.*, to מסית ומדיח ונביא השקר which would fit the case of Jesus. The Tosefta passage reads: ומשמרין אותן עד הרגל וממיתין אותן ברגל שנ' וכל העם ישמעו ויראו ולא יזידון עוד דברי ר' עקיבא אמר לו ר' יהודה וכי נאמר וכל העם יראו ויראו אלא כל העם ישמעו ויראו ולמה מעניו את דינו של זה אלא ממיתין אותו מיד וכותבין ושולחין בכל המקומות איש פלוני נגמר דינו בבית דינו של פלוני ופלוני עדיו וכך וכך עשה וכן עשו לו. That the execution of these other offenders should be delayed is said to be the opinion only of R. Akiba. Now Joel maintains that this opinion was constructed by him on the basis of a guess. Akiba had heard the report that Jesus was executed on the first day of Pesach, as the Synoptic Gospels expressly say. He considered Jesus a מסית ומדיח ונביא השקר, if not a זקן ממרא and he accordingly concluded that since in this case Jesus a מסית etc. was executed on the holy day — (or if we take ברגל to mean "Zur Festzeit;" i. e., on Erev Pesaḥ, so that the "first day" in Matthew would be on the 14th of Nisan as in Pes. 5a י"ד נקרא ראשון — the day on which the paschal lamb was sacrificed) then the law must be that a מסית or זקן ממרא should be kept until the time of the festival. The Baraita here, however, had already heard the latter report found in John (18.25 ff.) that Jesus was executed on Erev Pesaḥ, hence it says expressly ותלאוהו בערב פסח. The Mishnah which Joel assumes is also later than this passage in the Tosefta left out מסית ומדיח and speaks only of זקן ממרא whom they ממיתין אותו ברגל. See Brüll, *op. cit.*, *loc. cit.*, against Joel's theory. Joel does not explain how the Tosefta came to include in the practice בן סורר ומורה and עדים זוממים for whom there was no such alleged precedent.

before Pesaḥ, we cannot account for the statement הכרוז יוצא לפניו ארבעים יום. Heinrich Laible[59] says that there is nothing in the history of, or in the legends about, Jesus to account for this period of forty days reported by our Baraita. He suggests that perhaps the practice now obtaining in the church of fasting forty days before Easter was already observed in the ancient church by some people, and the Jews believed that the reason why the Christians fast forty days around that time is because Jesus suffered those forty days before the crucifixion by being led out every day to the execution place with the herald before him. Hence the mistake of our Baraita. But the custom of Lenten fast, which begins about six weeks before Easter, is not mentioned by any church father before the Council of Nicea, 325 C. E. Before that time they fasted only a few days. Even after the Council of Nicea they fasted only six weeks, excluding Sundays, which are only thirty-six days. At any rate the forty days of fasting originated in the seventh century, probably in imitation of Jesus' fasting forty days[60] and thus could not influence our text.

Strack, in a note to Laible's work[61] suggests that perhaps the report of Jesus' fasting forty days may have caused some Jews to think that he fasted that period because his execution was delayed for that period. He also suggests that the forty days are an echo of the forty days between the day of resurrection and the "Feast of Ascension" held forty days after Easter.[62]

Another difficulty in our Baraita is furnished by the phrase ותלאוהו, "they hanged him," which follows the statement יוצא ליסקל, "he is going out to be stoned." Indeed, according to this Baraita, Jesus was guilty of the crimes of witchcraft, enticement and misleading for which death by stoning is prescribed.[63] Thus,

---

[59] *Op. cit.* 81.   [60] Matth. 4.2.   [61] *Loc. cit.*

[62] See *Britannica*, (11th Ed.) I, 717 s. v. This festival was celebrated already in the 4th century, though it may have been from even an earlier time.

[63] Mishnah Sanh. 7.4, אלו הן הנסקלין... המסית והמדיח והמכשף. The Gospel reports do not mention his having been tried and found guilty of these offenses. But this would only prove that neither the Gospels nor the Talmud knew the exact circumstances of the trial and execution of Jesus.

the phrase תלאוהו cannot refer to a mode of execution, for he had been killed by stoning. It must therefore mean, they *hung* him up after he had been stoned to death, merely to expose the body. This would represent the opinion of Rabbi Eliezer only who holds that *all* who have been stoned must be hanged.[64] According to the majority of the teachers, however, only he who is stoned for blasphemy is afterwards exposed in this fashion. Now the question is: Was Jesus a blasphemer? According to Matthew 26.64-65 and Mark 14.63-64, Jesus was accused of blasphemy, but this is rather doubtful. Joel[65] claims that Jesus was not a blasphemer, for according to M. Sanh. 7.5, a blasphemer is one who curses the Name, a crime of which Jesus was not guilty.[66] N. Bruell,[67] however, proves that according to Sifre[68] Jesus, while not literally blaspheming, could have been considered a blasphemer because of his claim to have the same power as, or share in, the power of God, or "because he called himself the son of God."[69] I personally cannot see how he could have been regarded as a blasphemer, מגדף.[70] At any rate our Baraita itself says that he was convicted as having been a wizard, enticer and misleader but not as a blasphemer.

Still it may be that our Baraita is correct on this point. Rabbi Eliezer the *traditionalist* has probably preserved the correct tradition in his statement that all those who were stoned were hung. So Jesus was first stoned as an enticer and misleader and then hanged. This tradition has also been preserved in Acts 5.20, "Jesus whom ye slew and hanged on a tree;" and also Acts 10.39 "whom they slew and hanged on a tree."[71] Our

---

[64] Mishnah Sanh. 6.4.   [65] *Op. cit*. II, 48 ff.

[66] The Mishnah there says עד שיפרש השם which may however have been understood to mean merely "pronounce the Divine Name," an offense of which Jesus may have been guilty. See *Mekilta*, ed. Lauterbach, III, 48, note 6.

[67] *Loc. cit*.

[68] To Deut. 22.1, מה מגדף מיוחד שפשט ידו בעיקר אף כל שפשט ידו בעיקר.

[69] John 19.7.

[70] See *The Pharisees and Their Teachings*, above p. 92, n. 7.

[71] Cf. also Harold P. Cooke, "Christ Crucified — and by Whom," *Hibbert Journal* XXX, (Oct. 1930), 61-74, though he relies too much on the later work תולדות יש״ו which also assumes that Jesus was actually first killed by the Jews and then hanged on a tree.

Baraita then would also report a stoning and a subsequent hanging. But it is rather strange that our Baraita does not mention the stoning. It does not say וסקלוהו ותלאוהו. Maybe it merely wants to emphasize the fact that the Halakah is according to R. Eliezer and although Jesus was not tried or sentenced as a blasphemer he was nevertheless hanged. It did not deem it necessary to explicitly state that he was stoned for this is implied in the words יוצא ליסקל.

There is no doubt that the Baraitha here has no explicit reference to the execution as such, but merely to the subsequent exposing of the body. Certainly the expression ותלאוהו does not mean: they crucified him. To express this the Baraita would have said וצלבוהו. When the Mishnah wishes to designate one executed by crucifixion, it uses the expression צלוב[72] so there is no reason to assume that the Baraita here uses the term ותלאוהו to indicate crucifixion as assumed by Laible.[73] It is true that Onkelos to Deut. 21.22 renders the words ותלית אותו על העץ with ותצלוב יתיה על צליבא from which it would seem that תלה can mean also צלב. But the Mishnah or Baraita does not use it in this sense. Laible's reference to the Targum on Esth. 7.9 does not prove anything. In Esther, the word תלה means 'henken,' i. e., execute, kill. In our Baraita here the word תלאוהו after יוצא ליסקל, necessarily refers to the exposing of the corpse for a while after death, according to the law in Deut. 21.22. This hanging or exposing of the body after the person had been killed is expressly distinguished from hanging as a mode of execution, whether by strangulation or crucifixion.[74]

There is another difficulty in our Baraita. It assumes that the Jews executed Jesus by stoning and then exposed him by hanging, all according to Jewish law, and the Romans had nothing to do with the whole procedure. The Gospels on the one hand do not report any stoning and on the other hand

---

[72] See M. Yeb. 16.3.
[73] *Op. cit.*, 81 ff.
[74] See Sifre, *loc. cit.*, where it says: יכול יהו תולים אותו חי כדרך שהמלכות עושים ת"ל והומת ואח"כ ותלית, "perhaps they are to follow the practice of other nations and hang him alive? No!, Scripture explicitly says, "he shall die" and afterwards "Thou shalt hang."

expressly mention that the Roman soldiers crucified him.[75] It is not likely that the Gospel writers would have made any changes in the accepted report about the execution in order to exonerate the Jews. It is more likely that they reported correctly that the Romans executed him by crucifixion. Our Baraita then does not represent an authentic historic account. It seemingly represents a later legend, consisting of confused and contradictory reports. The author had heard the report that Jesus was hung upon a beam, עץ. He did not know that this hanging was crucifixion. He also heard another legend preserved in Toledot Jeshu and reflected in Acts, that Jesus was actually hanged on a tree. He had heard that Jesus was accused of being a wizard, enticer and misleader and he knew that as such he had to be stoned. So our author reconciled the report of Jesus having been hung, i. e., crucified, with the other report that he was a misleader, etc., for which he was to be punished by stoning. He assumed that the hanging was not crucifixion, but was performed in compliance with the law of Deut. 21.22 as interpreted by Rabbi Eliezer. In other words, the account of this Baraita is a legend made up by guesswork and misunderstanding of various legends and popular reports about Jesus. Herford[76] suggests that Jesus was known as a תלוי (i. e., hanged one) in early times, and the Jews may have known of him as *a* or *the* תלוי. Perhaps Onkelos' translation of Deut. 21.22 כי קללת אלהים תלוי by ארי על דחב קדם ד' אצטלב is an allusion to Jesus hinted at as a תלוי or צלוב. Thus Paul in Galatians 3.13: "Christ redeemed us from the curse of the Law, having become a curse for us, for it is written: 'Cursed is everyone that hangeth on a tree.' " applied the phrase קללת אלהים תלוי to Jesus. The Jews then having heard of a Jesus as a תלוי deemed it correct to use in the report in connection with the execution of Jesus on the eve of the Passover the phrase ותלאוהו בערב פסח.

This brings us to the discussion of another statement or expression in this report made by the Gemara — or by Ulla — which also points to a late date of the whole report, showing that it does not represent a knowledge of facts. This statement

[75] Matth. 27.27–35; Mark 15.16–32; Luke 23.36.
[76] *Op. cit.*, 85–86.

is: שאני ישו דקרוב למלכות הוה, "The case of Jesus was different for he — or it (the case) — was near the kingdom or government." The meaning of this phrase is very doubtful to say the least, and many suggestions have been offered to explain it. We have to explain the meaning of each word, and each word can have several different meanings. ישו can refer both to the person, Jesus, as well as to the *case* of his death. קרוב can mean related, near, connected with or of concern to. מלכות can mean the kingdom of God, the kingdom of the house of David, the kingdom or government of Rome, or the kingdom of the Messiah. With these various possibilities of the meaning of each word in the report, the report as a whole naturally likewise can have many different interpretations. Krauss[77] would understand this phrase to mean: קרוב למלכות בית דוד, alluding to a relationship or connection with, or descent from, the house of David claimed for Jesus. This interpretation, however, is not plausible. Of course, from the reports in the Gospels, the Jews could have heard that Jesus claimed to be the "son of David" or a descendant of the Davidic house. And in later Jewish works like מעשה דאותו ואת בנו,[78] Miriam, the mother of Jesus, claimed to have come from the Davidic family: אמרה מרים ממשפחת דוד המלך אני. This is the same legend which is reported in the Book of James, or Protoevangelium[79] where Mary is said to have been of the tribe or the *House of David*. But it is nowhere stated that the Rabbis believed Mary, or that the Jews admitted this claim of Davidic descent for Jesus. And it is likely that even if it had been true the Rabbis would rather have hesitated to admit it. Furthermore, it is not clear how this fact, assuming that it was a fact, that he was related to the house of David would have changed the course of law, so as to delay his execution for forty days. We do not find any reference to a special procedure in the announcement of the execution of one sentenced to death, in the case of princes of the

[77] *Op. cit.*, 215.
[78] Krauss, *op. cit.*, 67.
[79] See *The Apocryphal New Testament*, by M. R. James, (Oxford, 1924), 43, "The child Mary, that she was of the tribe of David;" and "Protevangelium des Jakobus," 10, Hennecke, *Neutestamentliche Apocryphen*, 2te Auflage, (1924), 89.

house of David. Above all, in the time of the Second Temple there was no longer a Davidic kingdom, and hence one could not claim connection with such a kingdom. The people who claimed descent from the Davidic house, like the family of Hillel and others, are usually described as ממשפחת דוד or מבית דוד as even Miriam in *Ma'ase d'oto v'et B'no* said: ממשפחת דוד המלך אני.[80] Nowhere, to my knowledge, can we find that people claiming descent from David are described as קרובים למלכות בית דוד, related to the royal house of David. The expression קרובים למלכות[81] usually means connected or influential with the Roman government. So the מלכות here cannot mean מלכות בית דוד which no longer existed at that time. We may, therefore, take the phrase קרוב למלכות in the sense of קרוב למלכות רומי. This statement then would allude to the reports in the N. T. that Pilate hesitated to execute Jesus.[82] The Rabbis may have heard of those legends and concluded that Jesus stood in the good graces of Roman government. The report then would mean that the Jews were afraid to execute him immediately, but showed the governor, who was friendly to Jesus, that they were giving Jesus a fair chance to find proof for his innocence; they were making an exception in his case and allowing an announcement of forty days to find evidence justifying a new trial.[83]

It is also possible that this statement of the Gemara echoes the report in Luke 23.8–12, that Herod (probably Herod of Chalcis) was friendly to Jesus; hence the later legend describes Jesus as being close to royalty, taking קרוב למלכות as referring to a *ruler* of the House of Herod. Of course, such an interpretation would presuppose that the Babylonian teachers (or Ulla?) knew the reports of the Gospel and even accepted these reports. While the latter may be unlikely and as Herford[84] remarks, it is

---

[80] *Loc. cit.*

[81] See B. K. 83 where it is used for the descendants of Hillel.

[82] John 18.38–19.16. Cf. also Matth. 27.19–24 where Pilate's wife sends word to him: "Have thou nothing to do with that righteous man," and Pilate washes his hands, saying: "I am innocent of this .... man's blood." Also Mark 15.12–15 and Luke 23.13–20.

[83] Cf. Laible, *op. cit.*, 80–81 and Herford, *op. cit.*, 89, both of whom favor this interpretation of the passage.

[84] *Loc. cit.*

not at all warranted to assume a knowledge of the Gospel reports by the Rabbis, yet it is not altogether impossible. In a vague and confused manner some of the Gospel reports may have penetrated into the circles of the Rabbis even in Babylon. Herford's suggestion, that because Jesus spoke so often of the "Kingdom," meaning the kingdom of heaven, some people may have misunderstood him to boast of his connections with the earthly government, and this gave rise to a current belief about his being related to or connected with royalty, is far fetched. Perhaps some people may have made a joking or ironical remark, that he was — according to his preaching — so near to the kingdom of heaven, or the coming of the kingdom.

All these interpretations of the phrase קרוב למלכות are not satisfactory. Hence one may offer still another interpretation which, at least, is not less satisfactory than all the others.

I suggest that since this statement שאני ישו דקרוב למלכות הוה was made by Ulla, an Amora of the third generation living in the first half of the fourth century or by the Gemara in answer to Ulla's argument, it may refer to the Roman government. At that time, i. e., after Constantine's conversion, the government was friendly to and even associated and connected with Christianity. The people of the fourth century, judging from conditions of their own times, assumed that the friendly relations between Christianity and the government must have existed also in the time of the founder of Christianity; hence they called Jesus "close to the government," in the sense of having influence with the Roman government.[85]

Another direct reference by name to Jesus is found in b. Sanh. 103a ונגע לא יקרב באהלך שלא יהא לך בן או תלמיד שמקדיח תבשילו ברבים כגון ישו הנוצרי.[86]

---

[85] Like B. K. 83a של בית ר"ג קרובים למלכות. This is also echoed in the later legend of the *Toledot Jeshu* (Krauss, 131) according to which Mary the mother of Jesus is related to Queen Helen. This legend confuses Helena, wife of Monobaz of Adiabene (about 50 C. E.) with Helena, mother of Constantine the Great — called St. Helena (247–327 C. E.).

[86] Thus in the old printed editions and MSS. See *Dikduke Soferim*, *ad loc.* Parallel to this is b. Ber. 17b, אין פרץ .... שלא יהא לנו בן או תלמיד שמקדיח תבשילו ברבים כגון ישו הנוצרי, in MSS and uncensored texts. Some MSS read כישו הנוצרי in place of כגון ישו הנוצרי.

The phrase שמקדיח תבשילו, 'spoil the soup' or 'burn the food' is figurative. It means spoil the teaching, causing the good food, the doctrines of Judaism to become spoiled, harmful and of bad taste.[87] As to the word ברבים, among the masses, it means that the masses take this *corrupted Judaism* for the genuine Judaism, the real spiritual food. Thus the Aruk *s. v.* קדח has כגון ישו הנוצרי שהיה מעמיד ע״ז בשוקים וברחובות. It seems the author considered the later Christian practice of burning incense before shrines and images as idolatrous, and assumed that Jesus, the founder of the religion, was the author of these practices.[88] The date of these two sayings is about the second half of the third century. The saying in Berakot, if it be by R. Joḥanan (died 275) or his disciple R. Eleazar b. Pedat, is not earlier than the second half of the third century. The saying in Sanhedrin is given by Ḥisda, a Babylonian Amora of the third century (died 309) in the name of R. Jeremiah b. Abba, an Amora of the second generation, a pupil of Rab who for a time lived in Palestine where he probably heard this saying with its reference to Jesus and thus is also not earlier than the third century. Both sayings, then, are of a comparatively late date, at any rate, they are not tannaitic and certainly not contemporary with Jesus. It is, however, interesting to note that Jesus was still considered as a disciple of the wise, though he disgraced them by corrupting the teachings which he received from them. In the later *Toledot Jeshu* he is also described as having once been a disciple; they simply could not imagine anyone who had never studied capable of leadership or even of heresy.

The next passage which in the uncensored editions contains a reference to Jesus by name, is in b. Giṭ. 56b–57a where it is reported that Onkelos the nephew of Titus conjured up the spirit of Jesus, or brought him up from hell, or dragged him up from the grave, and asked him for his advice in regard to the attitude to be assumed toward the Jews. Before we discuss this passage it may be advisable to examine first the passage in 'Ab.

---

[87] Jastrow's "disgraces his education" misses the point.
[88] See Strack, 39; Laible, 50: also Herford, 56–62, who has some interesting remarks.

Zarah 10b–11a and its parallel in Midrash Deut. r. 2.15 in order to identify this Onkelos.

The passage in 'Ab. Zarah speaks of an Onkelos b. Clonimos. Clonimos is probably corrupted from Clemens and the passage has reference to Flavius Clemens, a Roman Consul and nephew of the Emperor Domitian, hence also a nephew of Titus, who was sentenced to death and executed in the year 95 or 96 on the charge of atheism, i. e., of having denied the Roman gods. He was probably a proselyte to Judaism, hence he was confusedly identified with Onkelos or Akylos אונקלוס הגר or עקילס הגר who lived (a little later?) in the time of R. Eliezer and R. Joshua.[89] The similarity of names often led to the confusion and identification of different personalities. In passing, I may remark that probably the Titus who is so condemned in the Talmud as טיטוס הרשע and who is charged with having burned the Temple and committed other crimes, was not Titus the son of Vespasian who later became emperor and who is so highly spoken of by Josephus and other historians. It was a stepson of Vespasian whose name likewise was Titus and who was in command of the soldiers who burned the Temple.[90]

Now to return to our story in Giṭ. 56b–57a. Clemens or Onkelos called Jesus up from Hell, for the term אסקיה, "brought him up," suggests that he was believed to have been somewhere down below, unless we interpret it simply "dragged him up from the grave" which is very unlikely since the expression בנגידא, "by necromancy," points to his spirit coming up.

Jesus is described here — in the substitute reading as פושע ישראל — in the original form as one who scoffed at the Pharisaic teachings or the rabbinical interpretation of the law. This legend then echoes, or presupposes a knowledge of the charges reportedly made by Jesus against the Pharisees.[91] It is to be noticed that he is still regarded as a Jew — even in the substitute reading of "transgressor," with sympathies for his people, advising others

---

[89] See Graetz, *Geschichte*, IV, 4th ed., 109–110 and note 12, 402 ff.

[90] Cf. Mendel Wohlman התלמוד ויוסיפוס פלאויוס in the periodical מזרח ומערב edited by Abraham Almaleh, vol. V, (June, 1930).

[91] Matth. 15.3 ff., against tradition; 16.6–12 against the leaven of the Pharisees *et al.*

to do good and no harm to the Jews. He is markedly distinguished here from Balaam in his attitude towards the Jews. He is still one of them.[92]

Likewise the later legend about Simon Peter[93] — שמעון כיפא, who told the Christians to be friendly to the Jews, טובתם תדרוש, and the legend of an Elijah (אל יה?) חכם אחד שנקרא אליה, who simulated Christianity and proclaimed to the Christians in the name of Jesus, ולא תעשו רע ונזק ליהודים לא בגופם ולא בממונם,[94] echo this report here that Jesus wished the Jews well and did not want his people to suffer. Whether the Jews really believed this of him, or whether it was put forward by them as a precaution against possible persecutions on the part of the Christians, we cannot decide. In ancient times the former may have been the case; in later times the latter motive may have prompted the legend.

In the above passage we have seen that Jesus is mentioned by name or as פושע ישראל alongside of, but distinguished from, Balaam. Let us now consider another passage in the Talmud which is understood by some to refer to Jesus though not mentioning him by his real name but alluding to him by the name of Balaam.[95]

The passage is found in Sanh. 106b (the preceding part and saying of Rab Papa on 106a will be considered later) and reads as follows: א"ל הוא מינא (צדוקי) לר' חנינא מי שמיע לך בלעם בר כמה הוה א"ל מיכתב לא כתיב אלא מדכתיב אנשי דמים ומרמה לא יחצו ימיהם בר תלתין ותלת שנין או בר תלתין וארבע א"ל שפיר קאמרת לדידי חזי לי פנקסיה דבלעם והוה כתיב ביה בר תלתין ותלת שנין בלעם חגירה כד קטיל יתיה פנחס ליסטאה א"ל מר בריה דרבינא לבריה בכולהו לא תפיש למדרש לבר מבלעם הרשע דכמה דמשכחת ביה דרוש ביה. We must first seek to ascertain the identity of the persons in this dialogue. R. Ḥanina b. Ḥama, a Palestinian Amora of the first generation, pupil and successor to Judah Ha-Nasi, flourished in the first

---

[92] See M. Friedmann, *Onkelos and Akylos*; and Marmorstein, *HUCA*, X, (1935), 228, note 22.
[93] Krauss, 86–88.   [94] *Ibid.* 84.
[95] The other passages mentioning the name ישו but referring to his disciples and followers as תלמידי ישו will be discussed later. Here we deal only with references to his person.

half of the third century. But who was the heretic or Sadducee who conversed with him on this question? If we assume that he was a Christian, then it is difficult to maintain that the person about whom he sought information was Jesus. A Christian would not have spoken about Jesus in such a disrespectful manner referring to him as "lame Balaam." Against this one might argue that, possibly, we have not in this report the exact words of the heretic. The latter may have used, in his question as well as in his reference to the Book=פנקס which he later cites, the real name ישו, but the reporter — or a later copyist, perhaps a very later scribe, fearful of the censor — changed the name and substituted בלעם חגירא for ישו הנוצרי. But there is another difficulty in identifying this heretic as a Christian, if we assume that he sought information about Jesus. Why should a Christian ask Ḥanina whether he knows or had heard how old Jesus was? It would, therefore, be more likely to assume that this heretic or Sadducee was a non-Christian heretic, a member of one of the many sects that existed in Palestine in those days. He agreed with Ḥanina's attitude toward Jesus and in denying his claims to Divinity or messiahship and may have sought only to obtain information or compare notes with him about Jesus. On this assumption there is at least no objection to assuming the possibility that Jesus is meant when they talk about "Balaam the lame." But we have, as yet, no positive reason for the assumption that Jesus is here designated as Balaam. We must therefore examine the contents of the dialogue and see whether there is any positive justification for identifying the Balaam mentioned here with Jesus. It has been suggested that the Balaam mentioned here is a designation of Jesus.[96] פנחס ליסטאה[97] would then be a corrupted form of Pontius Pilate. This description might fit Jesus who was probably 33 years old when he was executed, for according to Luke 3.23, Jesus was about thirty years old[98] when he began his teaching and his career did not

[96] See J. Levy, *Wörterbuch*, s. v. בלעם, 236; and Geiger, "Bileam und Jesus" in *Jüdische Zeitschrift*, VI, 34 ff.

[97] J. Perles in *Monatschrift*, (1872), 266–7, suggest here פנחס פליסטאה.

[98] This, by the way, was said in order to make him resemble Moses who, according to the Midrash, Num. r. 14.29, began his teaching at the age of thirty-two.

last more than three years. The *Pinkas* which this heretic here cited could then have been one of the Gospels, containing the life story of Jesus. The name Balaam might have been chosen as a designation for Jesus to indicate as the Talmud elsewhere[99] fancifully explains the meaning of his name, that he is עם בלא, "without the people," or as the Aruk *s. v.* בלע reads בלא עם ישראל עם חלק לו שאין פירוש, "*Belo'-'am* means that he had no portion in Israel,"[100] or it might mean בלע עם, *Bala'-'am*, "one who sought to devour, i. e., destroy and harm, the people" by leading them away from God — alluding to the charge that he sought to lead Israel away from their Father in Heaven.

The description חגירה, "the lame one," cannot so easily be made to fit Jesus, since there is no record elsewhere of his having been lame. There is not any record in the Bible about Balaam having been lame either. It was merely a tradition among the Rabbis that Balaam was lame on one foot.[101] It may therefore be argued since the Rabbis were accustomed to refer to Balaam as "the lame Balaam" when they came to use his name as an epithet for Jesus, in order to characterize him as being like Balaam, they applied to him the full name with the adjective "the lame."

Perhaps the saying of Jesus in Mark 9.45: "If thy foot cause thee to stumble, cut it off: it is good for thee to enter into life halt, rather than having two feet to be cast into Hell" suggested to some people that Jesus was lame on one foot. There may have been some legend current among the Jews that Jesus was lame. It is possible that the legend found in the later *Toledot Jeshu*[102] that Jesus was polluted by Judas Iscariot and thrown down to the ground from the air where he was flying, originally also contained the additional statement that Jesus became lame as a result of the fall.[103]

---

[99] Sanh. 105a.

[100] No portion with all Israel in the world to come?

[101] Sanh. 105a; R. Joḥanan said: Balaam limped on one foot. The proof verse Num. 23.3 is of course questionable. Perhaps the tradition is based on Num. 22.25 "and crushed Balaam's foot against the wall."

[102] Krauss, 43–44.

[103] Thus Simon Magus who was brought down from the air by Peter — in the story which is the prototype of the story of the fight in the air between

It may also be that since according to the legend in *Toledot Jeshu*,[104] Jesus is supposed to have cut open the flesh on his hip or thigh and put into the open wound the pieces or parchment containing the letters of the sacred name and then closed again the wound with the skin of the flesh, some people assumed that he limped as a result of this operation and they called him "the lame." It is also possible that since the Christians considered Jesus "the lamb," i. e., the lamb of the Passover sacrifice, פֶּסַח, the Jews in derision made a pun on this designation and called him פִּסֵּחַ, "the lame one," in Aramaic חגירא.[105] These are all possible, though far fetched, interpretations which might explain how the designation "Balaam the lame" could have been chosen as a descriptive epithet for Jesus.

Likewise Phineas the robber besides being possibly a corrupted form of Pontius Pilate, might be an allusion to the High Priest who in his zeal was instrumental in the apprehending and crucifying of Jesus, thus proving himself a worthy descendant of the great zealot Phineas the son of Eleazar, the son of Aaron — who was zealous for his God.[106] Of course, this Christian source cited by the Sadducee (heretic) characterized Phineas as a murderer instead of a zealot. It will thus have to be assumed that the reporter in quoting the Sadducee (heretic) substituted for the name Yeshu used by him the epithet Balaam the lame, but left the uncomplimentary characterization of Phineas, as "the murderer" unchanged, which would be rather strange. Of course it is also possible that this Sadducee (heretic) belonged to a sect that objected to acts like that of Phineas, hence he called him "Phineas the robber" to indicate that he, his successors, descendants or imitators, were to be thought of as murderers. However, while he regarded Jesus as an innocent victim of these priestly zealots, he rejected him and described him as "Balaam the lame."

Jesus and Judas Iscariot — became lame. See Krauss, 175 and B. Heller in *MGWJ*, (1932), 36.

[104] Krauss, 40.
[105] See Rashi *ad loc.* חגירא תרגום של פסח.
[106] Num. 25.11–13.

Then again "Phineas the robber" may be a variation of the name פאפא בן רצצתא or another characterization of the person by that name, who according to *Toledot Jeshu*[107] betrayed Jesus, thus causing his death.

Admitting that all these possible interpretations are rather forced, it may nevertheless be said that at least it is not impossible to assume that Jesus was the subject of the discussion between R. Ḥanina and the heretic and that he is designated by them, or at least by one of them, as "the lame Balaam." I say advisedly, it is not impossible. But is it plausible? We must ask ourselves the question: what cogent reason is there against taking this report about the discussion between Ḥanina and the heretic in its plain and literal meaning, as referring to the Biblical personage, Balaam, the contemporary of Balaḳ and Moses, whom Phineas the son of Eleazar, the commander of the army in the campaign against the Midianites is said to have killed as stated in Num. 31.8: "Balaam also the son of Beor they — i. e., the soldiers under the command of Phineas — slew with the sword."[108] Balaam's Chronicle which the heretic cites may have been an apocryphal work containing the story of Balaam with some additions to and embellishments of the biblical story.[109] Perhaps it was a gnostic work, and the circles among whom this book was preserved rather favored Balaam and hence called Phineas who killed him, a robber, since Balaam was a lame and helpless man who could not defend himself. Perhaps indeed in that apocryphal book it was reported that Phineas personally slew Balaam with the sword, not "they slew" as in Numbers.

There seems to be no reason at all to assume that the name Balaam was used by the Rabbis as a substitute for the name

---

[107] Krauss, 78–79.

[108] See Rashi here *s. v.* כד קטיל יתיה where it is said פנחס שר צבא ואפילו קטליה אחר כל המלחמה נקראת על שמו.

[109] Perhaps the פרשת בלעם mentioned in b. B. B. 14b "Moses wrote his Book [presumably the Pentateuch] and the פרשת בלעם" refers to such a separate story about Balaam and not to the account in Numbers, which was part of Moses's Book. See Isaiah Horowitz של"ה (Fürth, 1764), 362a where it is indeed assumed that the Talmudic saying refers to such a separate book written by Moses in addition to the Pentateuch and subsequently lost.

Jesus. Such usage could not have been meant to indicate or to suggest that Jesus was in character like Balaam, for, as we shall see below, such was not the case. Since, we find that in many passages he is called by his real name Jeshu, why then should another name have been substituted in this passage? Even if there had been some reason for not using his real name, a better substitute could have been used, either the term פלוני or אותו האיש or even פושע ישראל and not the name of an ancient heathen prophet. The use of the latter name as a substitute would not be advisable as it might mislead people into thinking that it was actually the ancient heathen prophet who was meant and not another person who was supposed to have been like him and therefore called by his name.[110]

This argument becomes even stronger, since, as we have seen in the passage in Giṭṭin,[111] Jesus is distinguished from and contrasted with Balaam, the heathen prophet, in that he is called פושע ישראל, "a Jewish sinner." Against this it might be argued that not all tractates of the Talmud were redacted by the same person or even the same school, hence the terminology need not be alike in all the tractates. While the redactor of Giṭṭin may have distinguished Jesus' character from that of Balaam, the redactor of Sanhedrin may have identified them and hence he called Jesus by the name of Balaam. But the mere fact that some people, like those who redacted the tractate Gitttin, made a distinction between Jesus and Balaam, shows that it was not a general practice to designate Jesus as Balaam. Why then should we assume that the redactor of Sanhedrin used as a substitute for Jesus a name which some people might take literally when he could have used any of the other substitutes about which there were no disputes and which were less likely to be misunderstood? Above all, we would have to assume that both the heretic and R. Ḥanina regarded Jesus as having had the same character as Balaam and hence both would call him by that name. But we do not find anywhere else that the Rabbis of the Talmud ascribed to Jesus the sins and vices of Balaam.

---

[110] See also W. Bacher in *JQR* [o. s.], III, (1891), 356–357 against Geiger.
[111] *Supra*.

Why then assume that R. Ḥanina did characterize him as another Balaam? An examination of the passages of the Talmud describing the character of Balaam provides no justification for interpreting them as referring to Jesus. Thus the passage in Ab. 5.19, characterizing the followers or disciples of Balaam, as possessing "an evil eye, a haughty spirit and a proud mind," does not refer to the Christians, the disciples of Jesus.[112] The Christians were not regarded by the Tannaim as having a haughty spirit, proud mind and an evil eye. Hence the application of the verse Ps. 55.24 "Men of blood and deceit shall not live out half their days," applied also by R. Ḥanina to Balaam, could not refer to the disciples of Jesus who preached meekness and a humble spirit.[113] But the description actually fits the biblical Balaam as understood by the Rabbis.[114] This condemnation by the Rabbis of Balaam and his disciples cannot refer to Jesus and his followers, especially since the same condemnation of Balaam and his disciples was current among the Christians and finds strong expression in the N. T. writings, where it certainly cannot be thought of as an allusion to Jesus and his disciples. Why then should we assume that the same condemnation when found in Talmudic literature refers to Jesus and his disciples?

The following are the references to Balaam and his disciples in the N. T. writings: In the second Epistle of Peter 2.1–3 and 10–15 there is a reference to a false sect which indulged in lust and "forsaking the right way, they went astray, having followed the way of Balaam the son of Beor." In verse 18 we read "For uttering great swelling words of vanity, they entice in the lusts of flesh by lasciviousness," which latter description compares with the Rabbinic characterization of Balaam.[115] Further reference is made in Revelation 2.14–15: "But I have

---

[112] Cf. Herford, *Pirke Aboth*, (New York, 1925), 140–141, where he modifies his former opinion about the undercurrent of a reference to Jesus in the Balaam passages, expressed in his *Christianity in Talmud and Midrash*, 69.

[113] Matth. 5.3–12.

[114] See Midrash Num. r. 20.9.

[115] In the Midrash Num. r. 20.8 עמד בלעם והטעה את הבריות בעריות, and in b. Sanh. 106a שנתן לו עתה על הזנות. Cf. Graetz, *Geschichte* IV, 4th ed., 92.

a few things against thee, because thou hast there some that hold the teachings of Balaam, who taught Balak to put a stumbling block before the sons of Israel, that they might eat food sacrificed to idols and practice immorality. So hast thou also some that hold the teachings of the Nicolaitans in like manner." This description agrees with the description of the disciples of Balaam in Abot[116] and fits those gnostic sects or the Nicolaitans but not the Christians. Hence, even if we did not take the name Balaam in our passage literally, as referring to the ancient heathen prophet — which as we have seen is not the case — and we had to assume that Balaam is a epithet for a person who lived in later times, it would be more likely that the person referred to was the founder or teacher of the Nicolaitans, or of another gnostic sect referred to also in N. T. writings.[117]

Dr. H. P. Chajes in *Markus Studien*[118] declares that in those passages of the Talmud where Balaam's lasciviousness and immorality are emphasized or described, the reference is to the Nicolaitans and not to Jesus or the Christians.[119] Even Geiger, who interprets our passage in Sanhedrin as referring to Jesus admits that Balaam is not a substitute for Jesus in all the passages of the Talmud.[120] In other words, he admits that it was not the general practice of the Rabbis to refer to Jesus under the name of Balaam. What reason then have we to interpret any passage in which Balaam is mentioned as referring to Jesus, if we can just as well interpret it to refer to the Biblical personage himself or to some other person of whom we know at least that he had the characteristics or was of the type of Balaam, like the Nicolaitans?[121]

---

[116] *Loc. cit.*
[117] See M. Friedländer, *Der Antichrist* (Göttingen, 1901), 191–193.
[118] Berlin, 1899, p. 25.
[119] Cf. also Klausner, *Jeshu Hanozri*, p. 23, note 3.
[120] *Jüdische Zeitschrift* VI, (1868), 36–37.
[121] In the passage from the Yalkut to be discussed later on, where Balaam is opposed to Jesus and utters a prophetic warning against him, there may be an illusion to Balaamites or some other false sect who were against Jesus and the Christians. See Friedländer, *Antichrist, loc. cit.* Hyamson's statement

Coming back to our passage in Sanhedrin, we have seen that it could well be interpreted as referring to the biblical Balaam himself, and there is no reason whatever to interpret it as referring to Jesus. It is, however, possible that the redactor of the Talmud or the compiler of this Tractate, in putting this report about the discussion between Ḥanina and the heretic in this particular setting and context, knew that certain people did sometimes consider Jesus, the would-be Jewish prophet, in a class with the heathen prophet Balaam. Hence he put this passage next to the saying of R. Papa (106a) which may contain an allusion to Mary, the mother of Jesus. R. Papa, to illustrate the saying of R. Joḥanan about Balaam, cites a popular proverb about a woman who was the wife or daughter of princes and rulers and yet has so fallen that she would go a whoring after carpenters היינו דאמרי אינשי מסגני ושלטי הואי אייזן לגברי נגרי. This may also be interpreted that she had to marry a carpenter after she had become a whore. We then would have to supply another word like אינסבא after the word אייזן. Or it may mean she committed adultery after being married to a carpenter like זנתה תחת אישה הנגר. This then would allude to Mary who claimed descent from princes, the royal house of David and yet had to be married to a lowly carpenter and then — or because — she committed adultery. But the saying of R. Joḥanan refers to Balaam himself and not Jesus. In commenting upon the passage in Josh. 13.22 בלעם בן בעור הקוסם, "Balaam also the son of Beor, the soothsayer, did the children of Israel slay with the sword," the question is asked קוסם? נביא הוא!, "Soothsayer? But he was a prophet!" And R. Joḥanan's answer בתחלה נביא ולבסוף קוסם, "First he was a prophet then he became merely a soothsayer," no doubt refers to the biblical Balaam, who, so R. Joḥanan thought, started out as a prophet, for the Torah reports that God spoke to him, but later degenerated and became a magician קוסם or a soothsayer.

If one should interpret this saying of R. Joḥanan as an

---

that "there are many references to Jesus in Talmudic literature." But the references are veiled under the name of Balaam, (*JQR*, [n. s.], XXII, Oct. 1931, 216) is rather hazardous and certainly not proven.

allusion to Jesus then it would mean that the Rabbis actually acknowledged that Jesus had originally been a prophet or possessed prophetic powers and then lost them, which is very unlikely. We have seen that the Rabbis considered him as a disciple who spoiled the good doctrine but we never find any reference to his having had, misused and subsequently lost any prophetic powers. Of course, one could argue that the Rabbis were making fun of him when they said בתחלה נביא and meant that originally he started out with prophetic pretensions although he was most certainly not such. But it was too serious a question for the Rabbis to joke about.[122]

The passage in the Mishnah Sanh. 10.2 that mentions Balaam as one of the four commoners who had no share in the world to come, has also been understood by some scholars as referring to Jesus under that name and not to the Biblical personage. The argument, given in favor of this interpretation, is that since those four are mentioned as exceptions to the rule that all Israel, or every Israelite, has a share in the world to come כל ישראל יש להם חלק לעוה"ב they must be a part of Israel. Hence the Balaam mentioned could not refer to the heathen prophet of old.[123] Klausner's counter-argument[124] that Doeg the Edomite, also mentioned as one of the four exceptions, was likewise not a Jew, is not strong enough to disprove this theory. For, in the first place, Doeg was considered by the Rabbis as a Jew, even though he may have been of Edomitic descent. Secondly, as Klausner himself notices, the scholars who consider the name Balaam in this Mishnah passage an epithet for Jesus also consider the other three biblical names, Doeg, Ahitophel and Gehazi as substitutes for the real names of some of the disciples of Jesus, as we shall see below. But there is no cogent reason to assume that Balaam is a substitute for Jesus. Since, according to the Rabbis, the pious men of the gentiles have a share in the world to come,[125] there was reason to state that Balaam though a prophet and as such expected to be counted among the צדיקים

[122] See below discussion of passage in Num. r. 20.7.
[123] Geiger, *Jüdische Zeitschrift* VI, 32–33; Laible, *op. cit.*, 52–53; Herford, *Christianity etc.*, 66.
[124] *Jeshu Hanozri*, 4th ed., 23.   [125] Tosefta Sanh. 13.2.

JESUS IN THE TALMUD 513

באומות or חסידי אומות העולם who have a share in the world to come, is excluded from this privilege.

The passage in Midrash Num. r. 20.7 describing Balaam as one who began as an interpreter of dreams, then turned (חזר does not necessarily mean, returned), to magic or soothsaying and then turned to — became a recipient of — the holy spirit, or to prophecy ויש אומרים בתחלה פותר חלומות חזר להיות קוסם וחזר רוח הקודש is interpreted by Stier[126] as referring to Jesus and describing his career, as first performing miraculous cures (קוסם?) and then claiming the holy spirit. As a reason for his thus interpreting this midrashic passage, Stier assumes that the Rabbis, wishing to criticize Jesus and fearing to do so openly, mentioned him under the disguise of Balaam.[127] But this is a very poor reason. As we have seen, they mention his name ישו when they criticized him as a מכשף and מסית ומדיח and as a disciple who spoiled the good doctrine, why then should they be afraid to mention him by his name when they rather compliment him by saying חזר לרוח הקודש? Stier's interpretation, that this merely means "claiming prophecy" is not correct.

His argument, that Jesus was like Balaam in that both of them used their prophetic powers to hurt Israel is also weak. For this would mean that the Rabbis admitted that Jesus, like Balaam of old, was actually a prophet and not merely a prophetic claimant. Furthermore, Jesus never, in the opinion of the Rabbis, sought to do harm to Israel. We have seen above, that the Rabbis believed him friendly to his people, so that even after his death he is supposed to have given advice to do good and no harm to the Jews. He certainly cannot be held responsible for all the harm that has come to the Jews as a result of the misunderstanding of his teaching on the part of his followers. Besides, the first stage of Balaam's career as described in this passage, that of being an interpreter of dreams פותר חלומות does not fit Jesus. Further קוסם soothsayer or even magician, does not necessarily mean one who performs miraculous cures by magic, as Jesus was accused of doing. So it seems to me that it is very

---

[126] In Rahmer's *Das Jüdische Literaturblatt* X, (1881), Nos. 31 and 32.
[127] *Ibid.*, 122.

questionable, to say the least, whether this midrashic passage can mean all that which Stier would read into it. And we still have to find proof for the statement that Balaam was used as an epithet for Jesus.

There are still other names by which, according to some modern scholars and even some Amoraim, Jesus is supposed to have been mentioned in tannaitic literature. One of these is the name Ben Satada or Ben Sateda בן סטדא.[128] There has been so much speculation about this alleged designation of Jesus, both by the Amoraim in the Talmud and by modern scholars, that for the sake of clarity, it is advisable to divide the material. We shall, therefore, first consider the older material, that is, the references found in the tannaitic statements. We shall examine these statements and seek to ascertain their meaning independently of the amoraic comments on them. For it is doubtful, to say the least, whether the latter's interpretations of the tannaitic statements are correct. At any rate, we have a right to investigate for ourselves the meaning of the tannaitic statements, and we must not be prejudiced by the amoraic comments.[129] Then after we have independently come to some conclusions as to the meaning of the tannaitic statements, we shall proceed to consider the amoraic comments separately. For even if we should find that the Amoraim did not correctly interpret or even misunderstand the tannaitic utterances on this point, the amoraic remarks are in themselves of interest to us, as we can at least learn from them that some of the Amoraim referred to Jesus under the name of בן פנטירא or בן סטדא and how they understood these names as fitting Jesus or adequately describing him.

---

[128] The passages in which this name occurs are: Tosefta, Shab. 11.15 Zuckermandel, 126); Sanh. 10.11 (Zuckermandel, 431); b. Shab. 104b and b. Sanh. 67a; p. Shab. 12.4 (13d); p. Yeb. 16.6 (15d end).

[129] A method of procedure which I pursued with good results in interpreting the statements about the three books found in the Temple "The Three Books found in the Temple at Jerusalem" *JQR*, [n. s.] VIII, (1917–18), 385–423, and about the chronological data concerning the Second Temple "Misunderstood Chronological Statements in the Talmudic Literature," *Proceedings of the American Academy for Jewish Research* V, (New York, 1934).

In Tosefta Shab. 11.15 the question is discussed of whether tattooing, or scratching and making marks on one's body, המסרט על בשרו, is to be considered a form of writing, so that one who does this on a Sabbath has violated the Sabbath law prohibiting writing. R. Eliezer, against the opinion of the majority of the teachers, considers tattooing a form of writing and cites in support of his opinion, the case of a certain person, whom he designates as בן סטדא, who used this method of writing only. Said R. Eliezer to the other teachers: "But did not Ben Satada learn [what?] (or teach) only by this form of writing?" אמר להם ר' אליעזר לחכמים והלא בן סטדא לא למד אלא בכך. To this, his opponents, the other teachers, answer: "Because of one fool shall we lose or destroy all sane people?" אמרו לו מפני שוטה אחד נאבד את כל הפקחין. Here we are not told what this man learned in this manner, nor is it clear how through or because of (this) one fool we may lose or destroy all sane people. Does it mean that although one man, a fool, used tattooing as a form of writing, we cannot consider it as such, for to do so would in effect destroy all sane people by sentencing them to death, should they happen to do tattooing on a Sabbath? This would certainly be an exaggeration to say the least. For not all sane people tattoo, and even those who do, do not all do so on the Sabbath. Besides, we do not say that we lose or destroy people when we forbid them to do any other, more useful, work on Sabbath, even though the performance of such prohibited work involves a death sentence. Why then should we specifically consider the prohibition of tattooing on the Sabbath a cause of losing or destroying people, even though as in other cases one's disregard of this law might lead to a death sentence? This Baraita as it stands in the Tosefta is certainly cryptic. But we may learn more about the subject under discussion from the versions in which this Baraita is reported or quoted in the palestinian and babylonian Talmuds.

In p. Shab. 12.4 (13d) we read תניא אמר להן ר' אליעזר לחכמים והלא בן סטדא לא הביא כשפים ממצרים אלא בכך? אמרו לו מפני שוטה אחד אנו מאבדין כמה פקחין? And in b. Shab. 104b we read: תניא אמר להן ר' אליעזר לחכמים והלא בן סטדא הוציא כשפים ממצרים בסריטה שעל בשרו? אמרו לו שוטה היה ואין מביאין ראיה מן השוטים. The difference between these two versions is only that the Palestinian version still retains an allusion to the loss or destruction of many (not all!) sane people in connection with or as a result of the insane conduct of Ben Satada, while the Babylonian version ignores or does not know of these sad consequences but simply says: "We cannot cite in proof the action of a fool or insane person." Both the palestinian and the babylonian versions, however, agree that it was magic formulae, incantations or charms, that Ben Satada wrote on his body.[130] They also tell us that he brought these magic charms from Egypt, or he came from Egypt with these magic formulae tattooed on his body, thus bringing them to Palestine. The presumption is that the officials in Egypt, or the custodians, who watched over the palace-library, museum, or archives where these charms were kept, would not allow anyone to make copies of them. Ben Satada, therefore, could not copy them on papyrus or parchment, for he feared such copies, if found on him, would be taken from him. Hence he resorted to the unusual method of tattooing or writing them on his body. The Ben Satada, then, here alluded to was a magician who came to Palestine from Egypt, and apparently directly or indirectly caused the destruction of many innocent and sane people; or many naive people came to harm as a result of his coming to Palestine; or at least were threatened with harm; though it is not clear what kind of harm or destruction was done or threatened and how it was connected with Ben Satada's appearance. The question presents itself, why did R. Eliezer not mention this magician by his own name, but only mentions whose son he was? And if this should be an allusion to Jesus, who was believed to have been a magician and to have visited Egypt, why did not R. Eliezer mention him by the name by which he, himself, elsewhere designates Jesus, namely ישוע בן פנטירא.[131] Considering the fact that the

---

[130] The word למד in the Tosefta version then means למד כשפים.

[131] Tosefta Ḥul. 2.24 (Zuckermandel, 530). Of course one could assume that בן סטדא is indeed a mistake for or corruption of בן פנטירא though it would be forced and as we shall see, unnecessary, even though we ourselves assume that סטדא is a slightly corrupt form of another name. R. Hananel in his commentary to Shab. 104b reads בן פטיא and not בן סטדא so it may just be the name of an unknown man. See *Aruk* II, 180, s. v. בר פטר where he says פירוש שם

JESUS IN THE TALMUD   517

reading סטדא is not certain, and many suggestions as to the
original of which it may have been a corrupted form have been
made previously, one feels justified in making a slight emendation
which would suit the context in which this name occurs. I
propose to read סרטא instead of סטדא. Further the term בן does
not here mean son, so that the words Ben Satada, or better
Ben Sarata does not intend to give the parentage of the person
referred to. The term בן means rather "adept" or "expert" as
in בן תורה or בר אוריין and in בן חמסן or בן קמצן.[132] Ben Sarata
then means an *adept at tattooing* or *an expert tattooer*. R. Eliezer,
interested merely in proving his point that סריטא is a form of
writing and as such is prohibited on the Sabbath, cites as evidence
the case of a certain expert tattooer without giving his proper
name or the name of his father or mother. There is no reason
whatever to consider either term סטדא בן or the reading בן סרטא
a designation for Jesus.[133] True Jesus was also considered a מכשף

אדם. See also *Aruk*, *s. v.* בר פחתי or בר פאתי, though the *Aruk* reads here סטדא;
see also Kohut, *ibid.*, *s. v.* סטדא where there is much material but not correctly
understood. B. Königsberger in Rahmer's *Literaturblatt* XX, (1891) No. 36,
140–141 suggests that Satada (or as R. Ḥananel reads פטיא) is corrupted from
פטרא and refers to Peter. בן would mean not son but disciple. He says: Ohne
Zweifel ist nämlich פטיא und סטדא corruptiert aus פטרא, das nichts Anderes
bedeutet als "Petrus".... Das בן ist dabei vielleicht überflüssig (wenn nicht
als "Jünger" zu übersetzen)." See *Magyar Zsido Szemle*, (Juli, 1891), 458,
to which Königsberger refers. He could have made a better suggestion by
referring it to "pater" "son of the father." See below, the discussion of בן
פטורי.

[132] Tosefta, Soṭah 13.8. N. Brüll, *Jahrbücher* VII, 95 also suggests that
originally it read בן סירטא. But he thinks it refers to Jesus who was so designated
to distinguish him from בן סירא. In this he is wrong. The designation never
referred to Jesus and there is no reason to seek to distinguish him from Ben
Sira.

[133] After having written this, I found a remark (by Reifman?) in *Ha-
Lebanon* V, No. 8, (Paris, 1868), 116, as follows: ונראה לי ברור כי תחת בן סטדא
צ"ל בן סרטא וכן הוא אמת הגירסא בתוספתא שבת פ' י"ב. ונקרא כן לפי שסרט על בשרו כישופי
מצרים וקסמיהם (מיסטעריעון?) כאמור (תוספתא שם ושאר מקומות וכאשר האמינו גם הרומים
ועיין גרטץ ח"ד) והתוספת בן לפעל היתה נהוגה הרבה בימי קדם להורות על מי שדרכו בפעולה
ההיא כמו (תוספתא סוטה פ' י"ג) מעשה בכהן אחד בציפורי שנטל חלקו ... והיו קורין אותו
בן חמסן. ועיין פסחים מ"ט וקרו ליה בר מחים תנורי .... בר מרקיד בי כובי (וללא צורך
בנו ליה לבנו שם: קרו ליה רש"י שפירש מה). Königsberger in Rahmer's *Literaturblatt, loc. cit.*,
also states that the printed edition (Venice?) has בן סירטא and not בן סיטרא

and was also believed to have been in Egypt and returned to Palestine, but he was not the only one supposed to have practiced witchcraft. He was also believed as reported in the later Toledot Jeshu to have copied — not charms — but the letters of the holy name for purposes of witchcraft, but he copied them on parchment and hid the parchment in an open wound of his flesh.[134] So this is no reason for identifying Ben Satada (Sarata) with Jesus.

Perhaps, however, the basis for such an identification is to be found in a matter mentioned in connection with the name Ben Satada which occurs in tannaitic statements which we shall now examine. In Tosefta Sanh. 10.11,[135] in connection with the discussion of the procedure in the case of a trial of a מסית "one who beguiles others to idolatry," it s said חוץ מן המסית וכן עשו לבן סטדא (כת״י וויען: לביה סטדא; דפוסים: לאיש אחד) בלוד נימנו (הכמינו) עליו שני תלמידי חכמים וסקלוהו. But even here we have as yet no reason to assume that the Ben Satada mentioned designates Jesus, as we shall see in the discussion of this passage. In p. Sanh. 7.12 (25d) it reads כך עשו לבן סוטר (דפוס ווילנא: לבן סוטרא) בלוד והכמינו לו והביאהו לבי״ד וסקלוהו. Here, בן סוטרא, according to the reading in the Wilna edition, cannot possibly be an allusion to Jesus, although he claimed to be the son and the redeemer סוטרא. Likewise in p. Yeb. 16.6 (15d end) we read: שכן עשו לבן סטרא בלוד שהכמינו ...... והביאוהו לבי״ד וסקלוהו where there is not the least indication that it refers to Jesus. Only in b. Sanh. 67a where it reads: וכן עשו לבן סאדא בלוד ותלאוהו בערב הפסח is there a suggestion that it refers to Jesus who was sentenced and crucified (ותלאוהו?) on the eve of Passover. But as this additional remark ותלאוהו בערב הפסח is found only in the babylonian Talmud, we have reason to regard it as an amoraic comment — which we shall consider when we discuss how the Amoraim understood the name Ben Satada — and not as part of the

---

as given by Zuckermandel in the variants. Reifman, however, seems still to have believed that בן סרטא was a designation of Jesus because he, Jesus, tatooed the charms on his body. In this R. is wrong as there is no reason why it should refer to Jesus and not to any other tatooer or magician.

[134] See above p. 506, and Krauss, *op. cit.*, 40.
[135] Zuckermandel, 431.

original text of the Baraita. Thus, even though we identify the Ben Satada in Tos. Sanhedrin and parallels with the one in Tos. Shabbat and assume that they both refer to one person, we can still maintain that the מסית in Sanhedrin and the מכשף in Shabbat have reference, not to Jesus[136] but to another person whom we shall soon identify.

That Jesus is not referred to in these tannaitic statements can be stated with all certainty. This has been recognized by Derenbourg[137] and he is followed by most modern Jewish scholars.[138] I say most modern scholars recognized that B. Satada is not a designation of Jesus, even though some Jewish teachers, following the amoraic comments in the b. Talmud, understood it as such. But there are some exceptions even among modern scholars. Thus Paulus Cassel in his *Aus Literatur und Geschichte*[139] still maintains that even in the tannaitic sources Ben Satada is a designation of Jesus, but he assumes בן סטדא is a corrupt form of בן סטרא.[140] He explains the name to be like בר כוכבא a designation

---

[136] I cannot refrain from quoting here the ingenious but nonetheless incorrect remark of A. S. Kaminetski in *Hatekufah* XVIII, (Warsaw, 1923), 511 ff., where, assuming that Ben Satada refers to Jesus who was killed by Pontius Pilate, he merely seeks to explain how Ben Satada could be a corrupted form of the designation Christ and hence a name for Jesus. He says: אולם בן סטדא (=ברסטדא) הוא באמת כנוי לישו ונשתבש או נסתרס בכונה (על דרך "בית כריה" במקום "בית גליה" וכדומה) מהשם כרסטוס (או "כריסטא" בתמונת הקריאה כמו גם "ישו"=בקריאה) והמלה "בלוד" נכחבה בטעות השמיעה במקום "פלט" ובכן הנוסח העקרי היה "וכן עשה לכרסטא (על שמו) פלט" (מפני שהנציב הרומי פלט קים את פסק הדין נקרא על שמו). Even if it were absolutely certain that Jesus is referred to in this fanatic statement, such an interpretation בן סטרא or בלוד would not be plausible. One can certainly not base the identification of Jesus with Ben Satada on such an interpretation involving a series of mistakes and mispronunciations.

[137] *Essai sur l'histoire etc.*, 468. In the Hebrew translation of this work, this passage has been omitted. Long before Derenbourg, R. Jeḥiel of Paris in his disputation in 1240 declared — and it was not merely for apologetic purposes — that the passage in Sanhedrin about Ben Satada does not refer to Jesus. See ויכוח רבינו יחיאל, ed. Samuel Grünbaum, (Thorn, 1873), 4–5, and ed. R. Margulies, (Lemberg) 18. Cf. Rahmer's *Literaturblatt* II, No. 10, p. 40 and also *MGWJ*, (1869), 195, the remark by Lewin.

[138] See M. Joel, *Blicke* II, (Breslau, 1883), 55 ff. Exception are Kohut in *Aruk completum*, s. v., and Jacob Levy in his *Wörterbuch*. See their remarks.

[139] (Berlin-Leipzig, 1885), 338, 340–41.

[140] See the variants mentioned above p. 517 and note 133.

for the Messiah. "Im Orient, in Persien mag Christus, weil die Magier daher kamen, zumal diesen Namen wie Bar Kochba getragen haben."[141] "Die Talmudisten welche Ben Satada erwähnen, kennen, wie bei Panther nicht mehr den Grund[142] sonst würden sie solche Erklärungen nicht gebildet haben, wie die dass darin der Name Maria enthalten sei."[143] All this is far-fetched, for there is no warrant for identifying Ben Satada with Jesus.

The tannaitic statements taken by themselves do not justify an identification of Jesus with Ben Satada, and do not contain any indication pointing to Jesus. From these statements we learn only that a certain man, considered a misleader of the people, מסית and a magician מכשף, who came from Egypt, was executed in Lud — not in Jerusalem. Hence, as R. Jeḥiel already pointed out it could not refer to Jesus who was executed in Jerusalem. Suppose we read with the Palestinian Talmud: וכן עשו לבן סטדא בלוד הביאוהו לבי״ד וסקלוהו and interpret it in a forced manner to mean: So did they to B. Satada in Lud, i. e., "they apprehended him in Lud, by hiding witnesses and thus laying a trap for him." Only this much was done in Lud. Subsequently they brought him to court in Jerusalem where they stoned him. I say, even if we could accept such a forced interpretation of the statement in the version of the p. Talmud, we could not identify this Ben Satada with Jesus. For, as far as we know, Jesus is never mentioned as being in Lud, and the sources state that he was apprehended in Jerusalem. So the statement of the Baraita itself speaks against any identification of Jesus with Ben Satada. The additional remark in the Babli ותלאוהו בערב הפסח is due to the misunderstanding of the Amoraim, who, as we shall see, apparently felt they had enough reasons for identifying B. Satada with Jesus.[144]

[141] He is apparently referring either to the Messianic interpretation of the verse דרך כוכב מיעקב (Num. 24.17) or to the son whose coming was heralded by the star which the magi saw.

[142] I. e., that it means בן אסטרא, בר כוכבא, משיח.

[143] Ibid., 341, as to Papus being a shorter form from Josephus, as the modern Italians have Pepi.

[144] Or rejecting a late dating for this phrase, we can make the not impossible assumption that the otherwise unknown Ben Satada actually was executed on the eve of the Passover.

Possibly the reading בן סוטרא, "savior" or "redeemer," suggested to the Amoraim that the passage refers to one, who wanted to be or was called by others, the Son and the savior. There were many features, as we shall see, in the story of this anonymous B. Satada, that could have caused this misunderstanding on the part of the Amoraim. But no matter how we may explain the manner in which the mistake on the part of the Amoraim came about, the mistake remains a mistake, and the fact remains that Ben Satada was not Jesus.

Acknowledging this latter fact, some scholars apparently unable to rid themselves of the suggestion of the Amoraim, still try to find in Ben Satada a designation, if not for Jesus himself, then of a person connected with Jesus. Thus one scholar[145] thought that Ben Satada referred to or designated Jacobus, the brother of Jesus who,[146] according to Josephus,[147] was sentenced to death by the High-Priest Ananus. This Jacobus, a brother of Jesus, could also be called בן סטדא for he and Jesus had one and the same mother, though not the same father. This theory, of course, would indirectly preserve the identification of Jesus with Ben Satada, or Mary with Sata-Da,[148] as understood by the Amoraim. But the theory is false. The same considerations which speak against the identification of Jesus with B. Satada, force us to reject the identification of the brother of Jesus, Jacobus, with Ben Satada, or with the man tried and executed — or merely trapped and apprehended — in Lud. For Jacobus likewise was sentenced and executed — not in Lud, we have no record that he ever was in Lud,— but in Jerusalem during the absence of the Roman governor; Festus was dead and his appointed successor Albinus was on the way to Jerusalem but not yet arrived.

Furthermore, Ananus the High-Priest was a Sadducee and, as Josephus tells us, the law-abiding citizens, especially the Pharisees, were outraged by this unlawful act of Ananus and demanded his removal from office. It is therefore unlikely that the Rabbis should cite this unlawful act of a Sadducean

---

[145] Löwy in Rahmer's *Literaturblatt* VII, No. 4, (1878), 15.
[146] Matth. 13.55.
[147] *Antiquities* XX, 9.1.   [148] See below p. 529.

High Priest as a precedent, or an illustration, for the legal procedure to be followed in the case of a beguiler מסית and to refer to this highhanded act of Ananus as the act of a legal court הביאוהו לבית דין.[149]

Having lost one Jacobus whom he tried to identify with Ben Satada, the same scholar might claim that possibly another Jacobus could play the role of Ben Satada. This other Jacobus (called *major*) or James the brother of John[150] was killed with the sword by King Herod.[151] It appears from the context in Acts that this happened shortly before the Passover, or during "the days of unleavened bread." For we are told that when Agrippa saw that it pleased the Jews he also seized Peter during the Passover festival. Agrippa was a pious king and his action may not have been so condemned as the act of Ananus, hence the later Rabbis might have regarded an act of his as a precedent. But we have no express record that the act of killing Jacobus was done in Jerusalem — though from the context in Acts it would seem that the seizure of Peter during the Passover festival was in Jerusalem — hence it could have happened in Lud. Yet, with all these possibilities, this Jacobus cannot be identified with the Ben Satada of the Talmud. For this Jacobus was killed with the sword — when it says killed by Agrippa it may mean by order of Agrippa through a court process — not stoned or hanged and the death of a מסית is by stoning not by the sword. How then could the Rabbis cite this execution of a man by the sword as a precedent for their law in regard to a מסית who must be killed by stoning only?

Now, there is still left another, or a third, Jacobus, *viz.*, Jacobus Alpheus[152] also called Jacobus *minor*,[153] the lesser. Hence, if we read בן זוטרא בן סוטרא = the younger, or the little one, instead of בן סטרא, the designation could refer to Jacobus minor. But we have no record elsewhere of this younger one having been killed. Löwy[154] made the mistake of imagining that this

---

[149] Cf. Grünbaum, in Rahmer's *Literaturblatt*, No. 8, 20.
[150] Acts 12.2.
[151] Agrippa, grandson of Herod the Great.
[152] Matth. 10.3; Mark 3.18; Luke 6.15; Acts 1.13.
[153] Mark 15.40.   [154] *Loc. cit.*

JESUS IN THE TALMUD 523

Jacobus minor — and not James the brother of Jesus — was executed by the High Priest Ananus. Grünebaum[155] therefore suggests that an *unknown person* — not Jesus! — whom they called Ben Satada, is referred to in b. Sanhedrin. The reason why they called him so was — so Grünebaum imagines — because that unknown person was a מסית and a מכשף and the Rabbis would not believe that such a bad man could have been the son of a good, decent mother. And on the principle מדחציף כולי האי ש"מ ממזר הוא, "his impudence proclaims him a bastard," they assumed that he must have been the son of a bad woman סטא דא . . .[156] One can see that Grünebaum, though he has some good ideas and was on the track of discovering who this Ben Satada was, could not entirely free himself from the idea suggested by the later Amoraim that the designation סטדא was meant to refer to the mother.

He does not, however, follow the Amoraim in assuming that it refers to the mother of Jesus but explains that from the bad character of the son the Rabbis concluded that the mother must have been a bad woman, a סוטה. But not every bad man is a בן סוטה.

Thus far we had only negative results. We have found that Ben Satada was not Jesus nor any of the followers of Jesus by the name of Jacobus, and, we may add, not even that "unknown man" who was so designated merely on the presumption that a bad man must have had a bad mother. Considering the fact that the very reading of this strange designation is doubtful and it is found in different forms in the various readings of the texts, such as סטר, סטדא, סירטא, סוטרא, סוטר[157] we must ask: why limit our efforts to identify the man so designated by accepting just one form of the name סטדא and concentrate our search upon the explanation of the meaning of this one form of the name merely because the Amoraim had this reading and in a fanciful manner sought to explain its significance? We have found

[155] *Loc. cit.*

[156] See below the discussion of the amoraic comment. Grünbaum does not discuss the question whether Ben Satada in Tosefta Shabbat was identical with the one mentioned in Sanhedrin.

[157] R. in *HaLebanon, loc. cit.*, etc.

above, that judging from the context of the Baraita in the Tosefta Shabbath, the reading סרטא gives a better sense and explains the significance of this designation satisfactorily. On the basis of this reading and understanding of the name we can seek with some hope of finding the identity of the person so designated or characterized, and we may even be able to find the causes that led the Amoraim to the mistake which they made in the identification of the person so named. We must approach this question without prejudice and independent of the amoraic comments, and seek to find a 'person believed to be both a מסית and a מכשף who came from Egypt and could properly and befittingly have been described or designaged as בן סרטא as I prefer to read this name, and who might have been caught and entrapped in Lud and perhaps even executed there. *We indeed find such a person.* H. P. Chayes[158] suggests the following. Josephus in *Antiquities* XX, 8.6 reports an incident which happened in Jerusalem during the time of the Roman Procurator Felix, i. e., between 52 and 60 C. E. as follows: "Moreover there came *out of Egypt* about this time to Jerusalem *one who said he was a prophet and advised* the multitude of the people to go along with him to the mount of Olives. He said further that he would show them from hence how at his command *the walls of Jerusalem would fall* down ... But the Egyptian himself escaped out of the fight [with Felix's soldiers] and did not appear again." In *Wars* II, 13.5 Josephus again mentions this false prophet, as follows: "But there was an *Egyptian false prophet* that did the Jews more mischief than the former; for he was a *cheat* and pretended to be a prophet ... But Felix prevented his attempt ... The Egyptian ran away." Mention of this Egyptian is also made in Acts where we learn that the Jews to whom he caused so much harm did not give up hope of catching him, and when they caught one whom they believed to be that Egyptian they sought to harm him and take revenge on him. For in Acts 21.27–38 we read: "The Captain said to Paul: 'Art thou not then the Egyptian who before these days stirred up to sedition?'" This was also during the time

---

[158] *HaGoren* IV, 33–37; also Herford, *op. cit.*, 345.

of Felix's procuratorship.[159] We see then that the Jews, seeking to harm Paul, did so because they believed him to be that Egyptian. They were mistaken this time and suspected the wrong person. But, we may safely assume, they continued to be on the lookout and did not relax their search for him. It may have happened that this Egyptian, who had misled the multitude and hence was a מסית and who was believed to have been a מכשף who had brought witchcraft tattooed on his flesh from Egypt, and hence was called בן סטרא, may have at some later time turned up again in Lud, Josephus' statement that "he appeared no more" nothwithstanding. Or, at least, some people in Lud became suspicious of a person whom they believed to be that Egyptian, and entrapped him by hiding witnesses and by getting him to repeat the seductive speeches whereby they identified him as indeed being that Egyptian; they brought him to court, where the witnesses who listened to him in hiding testified against him and thus he was sentenced to death and executed, and if the reading in the Babylonian Talmud is accepted, this could have happened around the Passover time or even on the eve of the Passover. The saying of the teachers in answer to R. Eliezer[160] מפני שוטה אחד אנו מאבדין פקחין הרבה then has reference to this Egyptian whom Josephus describes as a "madman" from Egypt who was the cause of the death of many sane people who followed him and were killed by the soldiers of Felix. It is not an argument against R. Eliezer as would appear from the Babli version: שוטה היה ואין מביאין ראיה מן השוטה, but, is a sad comment at the mere mention by R. Eliezer of this בן סטרא, the "madman," on the great harm caused by him: "Yes, because of one madman we lost many sane people."

Now let us consider the mistake of the Amoraim and attempt to find out what led them to identify this Ben Satada with Jesus. In the story about Jesus as known among the Jews in Babylon in later amoraic times, both according to reports from the Gospels which reached them in some form and according to other legends that were current among them, there are many

---

[159] See Acts 23.24.
[160] Tosefta, *loc. cit.*

features which resemble the story about the Egyptian false prophet, or "madman," as told by Josephus.

1) Like the Egyptian, Jesus was considered a beguiler of people and a magician. This is mentioned in the Gospels: "The Pharisees said, 'By the prince of the demons [i. e., by Beelzebub] casteth he out demons'"[161] i. e., he is a magician. This report of the Gospels about the opinion of the Pharisees reached the Amoraim in Babylon. Further, in the legend about Jesus having gone with Joshua b. Peraḥyah to Egypt[162] — and come back from Egypt, he is referred to as שכשף והסית והדיח, "one who does magic, entices and misleads."

2) Like the Egyptian, a man who "came out of Egypt," as Josephus describes him, Jesus also came out from Egypt as a child, according to the Gospels,[163] to fulfill the word, "Out of Egypt did I call my son," and according to the Jewish legend in Sanhedrin discussed previously, as a grown up man, a disciple of Joshua b. Peraḥyah.

3) Jesus was believed to have learned the arts of magic or witchcraft in Egypt. Thus in מעשה דאותו ואת בנו Chapter XI[164] it is said: והלך למצרים וישב שם הרבה ימים ולמד שם הרבה כשפים ואח"כ חזר לירושלים. And while this is found only in a later source, it no doubt echoes an older legend which must have already been current in amoraic times.

4) Later Jewish legends, which may echo an older legend, make Jesus also a sort of a שורט, or מסרט, or סרטא. He is supposed to have cut in the letters of the holy name, by means of which he performed his miracles, on his thigh. Thus we read in מעשה דאותו ואת בנו, Chapter V[165] הזכיר האותיות על יריכו וקרע אותה בלי כאב. The text is not quite clear, and while it describes the act as consisting of hiding the parchment with the letters in his open wound, it originally may have read simply וקרע האותיות על יריכו, "he tattooed the letters on his thigh." The verb וקרע like ושרט can mean cutting the letters into his flesh, for in p. Shab. 12.4

---

[161] Matth. 12.24; also Matth. 9.34.
[162] See above pp. 481 *et seq.*
[163] Matth. 2.15–23.
[164] Krauss, 78.
[165] Krauss, 68.

JESUS IN THE TALMUD   527

(13d) the phrase הקורע על העור is used in the sense of השורט
על בשרו. Although this legend reports that Jesus learned the
letters of the holy name שם המפורש and not magic formulae, the
idea is the same. Some Jewish people would not admit that
with magic formulae one could perform miracles, so they reported
his having used for this purpose the letters of the שם המפורש
which were guarded in the Temple and could not be brought
out..... just as the magic formulae were guarded in the
temples or museum of Egypt. We must remember that these
whispering rumors or legends are not reported clearly nor
accurately; they are given in hints and confused indications.
It is significant, however, the the Tosefta Shabbat[166] does not
specify כשפים or מצרים but merely says cryptically לא למד אלא
בכך which may mean "he learned the means by which he could
perform miracles only in this manner" which might thus echo
or have given rise to the later legend that Jesus learned in this
manner the letters of the holy name by which he performed his
tricks or miracles. Other people were less hesitant to admit that
with כשפים, which in the words of Sanh. 67b שמכחישין פמליא של
מעלה, "lessened the powers of the Divine agencies," one could
perform miracles. Knowing that Egypt was the land of witchcraft
and magic, they reported accurately הוציא כשפים ממצרים. Even
after the identification of Ben Satada with Jesus, they still
preferred to say that Jesus, who as they knew from other legends
and reports went to Egypt, learned in Egypt the magic arts by
which he performed his miracles rather than to say that he did
them by means of the שם המפורש.

In the latter case God is made to be rather helpless in the
hands of him who knows the trick of using the holy name.
Against His will He must help Jesus, who got control of His
name, to do whatever Jesus wanted Him to do.

5) The Egyptian is reported to have led the people to the
Mount of Olives and there to have boasted that by his command
he could cause the walls of Jerusalem to fall. We are not told
what the significance of this boast was. It could not have meant
that he could thus be able to enter Jerusalem, for we have not

---

[166] *Loc. cit.*

heard, and it does not seem likely that he was prevented from entering the city. It probably meant that he could by his command also raise other, stronger, or fiery walls. Now Jesus, likewise, is reported to have sat *on the Mount of Olives* when he said: "Verily I say unto you there shall not be left here one stone upon another,"[167] which probably meant that he could bring it about by his command. For he was accused of having said: "I am able to destroy the Temple of God and to build it in three days,"[168] or: "I will destroy this Temple made with hands and in three days I will build another made without hands."[169] While Jesus is reported to have made this boast in regard to the Temple and the Egyptian made his about the walls of Jerusalem, both reports may have been understood by some people at a later time, especially in Babylon, as referring to the same thing. At any rate in both cases the boast is of the same nature and could well have been confused with one another or mistaken one for another.

Thus we see that there are or were sufficient resemblances between the story about this Egyptian false prophet and the legend current among the Jews about Jesus. And the Amoraim in Babylon, in time and place far removed from these supposed or real events, and not sufficiently interested to examine critically the exact facts underlying these reports, could well have confused these two reports with one another and mistaken the report about the otherwise unknown Egyptian false prophet as referring to Jesus who in their opinion was also a false prophet and not better than the other. But once they identified Jesus with the Egyptian madman, they soon realized that there are some difficulties inherent in this identification. For, again by hearsay and inaccurately, they got other information or rumors about Jesus and his family which seemed to be in conflict with his identification with the man designated as Ben Satada. So they set about in their fashion to smooth out these difficulties and to harmonize various conflicting reports about Jesus and Ben

---

[167] Matth. 24.2–3; Mark 13.1–4; Luke 21.5–7.
[168] Matth. 26.61.
[169] Mark 14.58.

Satada, and to explain the meaning of the different designations used for him in these different reports. These harmonizing efforts at explaining away the difficulties in the conflicting designations or descriptions are expressed in the amoraic comment to the Baraita in Sanh. 67b and Shab. 104b which reads as follows:

בן סטדא (בתמיה) (והלא) בן פנדירא הוא? אמר רב חסדא בעל סטדא בועל בן פנדירא בעל פפוס בן יהודה הוא אמו סטדא אמו מרים מגדלא שער נשיא היא כדאמרינן בפומבדיתא סטת דא מבעלה.

The Gemara finds the identification difficult. How could Jesus be called Ben Satada when in another Baraita[170] he is called בן פנדירא which indicates that his father's name was Pandera and not Satada? Rab Hisda (an Amora of the third generation, died about 309) then tries to solve this difficulty by assuming that Satada was the name of the legal husband, the man to whom the mother had been betrothed or married, and Jesus was sometimes called after the name of his mother's husband,[171] since not all people knew that her husband was not the father of her child. The real father, however, was the paramour of the mother, a man by the name of Pandera, and people who knew this called Jesus by the name of his real father, Ben Pandera. But against this assumption of Rab Hisda an objection is raised. The Amoraim had heard a report that the name of Mary's legal husband was Pappos (which is probably a short form of Josephus),[172] whom they confused with Pappos ben Jehudah (who lived in the time of Akiba, first half of the second Christian century.) Hence, they argued, his name could not have been Satada. So they tried to argue, perhaps the name of the mother was Satada, but this too they found incorrect, for they heard that his mother's name was Miriam, whom they designated מרים מגדלא שער נשיא.[173] They finally came to the conclusion that Satada indeed designates the mother although it was not her proper name. It was merely a characterization of her conduct, indicating that she had committed adultery סטת דא מבעלה.[174] That

---

[170] Tosefta, Ḥul. 2.20–24; to be discussed below.
[171] See Rashi, *ad loc.*, ונקרא על שם בעל אמו אעפ"י שהוא ממזר.
[172] See Cassel, *op. cit.*, 341.
[173] See below.
[174] They were correct in their suggestion that סטדא is not a proper name but

the Gemara here was mistaken and confused in the identification of all these names — Josephus, Pappos and Miriam, was recognized by medieval rabbinic authorities. Thus, Tosafot to Shab. 104b *s. v.* בן סטדא objects to the identification of Ben Satada with Jesus and מרים מגדלא שער נשיא with Mary the mother of Jesus. They quote Rabbenu Tam (1100–1171) as follows: אומר רבינו תם דאין זה ישו הנוצרי דהא בן סטדא אמרינן הכא דהוה בימי פפוס בן יהודה דהוה בימי רבי עקיבא... וישו היה בימי יהושע בן פרחיה. Then again *s. v.* אמו מרים Tosafot remarks: והוא קאמר בפ"ק דחגיגה רב ביבי הוה שכיח גביה מלאך המות כו' אמר ליה לשלוחיה זיל אייתי לי מרים מגדלה נשיא משמע שהיתה בימי רב ביבי מרים מגדלא נשיא אחרת היתה אי נמי מלאך המות היה מספר לרב ביב מעשה שאירע כבר מזמן גדול.[175] Tossafot's objection to those identifications are mainly on the basis of the chronological discrepancies. But Tosafot assumes that as is stated in the question of the Gemara in Shab. 104, Miriam Magdala or Megadla was the mother of Jesus. For in b. Ḥag. 4b *s. v.* הוה שכיח גביה Tosafot remarks: מספר מה שאירע לו כבר דהאי עובדא דמרים מגדלא נשייא בבית שני היה דהיתה אמו של פלוני.

Let us now consider here the question whether this identification is correct, i. e., whether מרים מגדלא שער נשיא was the mother of Jesus.[176] From the amoraic discussion here it is evident that there was current a legend among the Jews that Mary the mother of Jesus was מגדלת שער נשיא, a dresser of women's hair.[177] This legend is also found in the later *Toledot Jeshu*. This legend that Mary the mother of Jesus was a hair dresser or *Haarflechterin* was also current in Christian circles.[178] But the understanding of מגדלא שער נשיא to mean "dresser of woman's hair"[179] or "Frauen-

---

a characterization; however, they did not know to whom it referred and what it originally meant.

[175] See these quotations in קבוצת ההשמטות (Krakau, 1893), 3, and cf. R. Jeḥiel in his ויכוח ed. R. Margulies (Lemberg), 16–17, referred to above.

[176] Strictly speaking this should come later in the section discussing the relatives and followers of Jesus.

[177] See Krauss, 186 and note 9 on p. 274. והיא היתה מרים קודם שנשאת מגדלת שער נשיא.

[178] See Lagarde, *Mittheilung* III, 257–260; but cf. Dalman, *Grammatik des Jüd.-pal. Aramäisch*, 141, note 7 and Krauss, *ibid.*, 275.

[179] Herford, 33.

haarflechterin"[180] is in itself not correct. For why should there be specified "a dresser of woman's hair," why not simply a hairdresser? It seems to me that there was in the mind of the Rabbis, who had heard of only one Mary in connection with Jesus,[181] a confusion not alone with Mary Magdalene, as assumed by Laible and by Winer[182] but also with Mary the sister of Martha and Lazarus who anointed the Lord with ointment and wiped his feet with her hair.[183] She must have had long hair, since she could conveniently reach the feet of Jesus with it. They identified this Mary with Mary Magdalene, understanding it to mean not the Mary of Magdala, but the Mary who had especially long hair, and they further identified her with the mother. This would explain the reference in the *Toledot* קודם שנשאת, "before she was married" she had long hair, for after she had been married she could not be expected to show her hair and no one could see whether it was long or short. Had the reference been to hairdresser, the remark קודם שנשאת would not make good sense, for a woman could follow this profession even after she was married.[184]

Having once confused this Mary with the mother of Jesus, they may have thought that the legend of the woman by that name who escaped death merely by the stupidity of the agent of the angel of death (as reported in the legend)[185] referred to the mother of Jesus who, as an adulteress אשת איש שזינתה, deserved and was sentenced to death, though the sentence was not executed. And they also heard that the name of the husband of that Mary was Joseph, shortened or corrupted into Pappos.[186]

---

[180] Laible, 28 and 18–19.
[181] Laible, 18.
[182] See Krauss, 275. It is assumed by some scholars that there is a confusion between Mary, the mother, and Mary Magdalene. In the name Magdalene some saw an allusion to the bad reputation with regard to sexual morality which the town of Magdala had — מגדלא מפני הזנות (Midrash Lam. r. II). It may be that women hair dressers did not have such a good reputation. (See R. Ḥananel in Tosafot, Ḳid. 49a, *s. v.*, מאי מגודלת) and the name was given to Mary to reflect on her character.
[183] John 11.2.
[184] See the remark of R. Ḥananel in Tosafot, Ḳid., *loc. cit.*
[185] Ḥagigah, cited in Tosafot, *supra*.
[186] See Cassel, *loc. cit.*, and also Krauss, 187, reference to קשת ומגן.

Looking around for such a man, they found Pappos b. Jehudah who lived in the time of R. Akiba and who was so jealous of his wife that whenever he left his home he would lock her up, but here is the humor — to no avail, for "There is no guardian against unchastity," אין אפטרופוס לעריות. The legend told in the later *Toledot*, of how Mary was deceived by — or received — the paramour, after her husband or betrothed, ארוס, had left the house, may well have been current and so they decided it must have referred to the same Pappos or Joseph, who was deceived by his wife, no matter how he guarded her. That he lived more than a hundred years later than the husband of Mary did not bother them, as chronology was not their strong point. We thus find that the amoraic identification of Jesus with Ben Satada is based upon confusion of similar reports and on a mistaken identification of different persons by the same name, and there is really no connection whatever between Jesus and Ben Satada.

The other name בן פנדירא mentioned here by the Amoraim in connection with Jesus seems actually to have been a designation for Jesus, though its meaning has not been correctly understood and not sufficiently explained. This name occurs already in tannaitic sources and in different spellings. In Tosefta Ḥul. 2.22 and 24[187] we read: מעשה בר׳ אלעזר בן דמה שנשכו נחש ובא יעקב איש כפר סמא לרפאותו משום ישוע בן פנטירא ולא הניחו ר׳ ישמעאל אמרו לו אי אתה ראש בן דמה אמר לו אני אביא לך ראיה שירפאני ולא הספיק להביא ראיה עד שמת.... מעשה בר׳ אליעזר שנתפס על דברי מינות והעלו אותו לבמה לדון אמר לו אותו הגמון זקן כמותך יעסוק בדברים הללו אמר לו נאמן דיין עלי כסבור אותו הגמון שלא אמר אלא לו ולא נתכוין אלא נגד אביו שבשמים אמר לו הועיל והאמנתי עליך אף אני כך אמרתי אפשר שהסיבו הללו טועים בדברים הללו דימוס הרי אתה פטור וכשנפטר מן הבמה היה מצטער שנתפס על דברי מינות נכנסו תלמידיו לנחמו ולא קבל נכנס ר׳ עקיבה ואמר לו ר׳ אומר לפיכך דבר שמא אין אתה מיצר אמר לו אמור אמר לו שמא אחד מן המינין אמר לך דבר של מינות והנאך אמר השמים הזכרתני פעם אחת הייתי מהלך באיסתרטיא של צפורי מצאתי יעקב איש כפר סכנין ואמר דבר של מינות משום ישוע בן פנטירי והנאני ונתפסתי על דברי מינות שעברתי על דברי תורה הרחק מעליה דרכך ואל תקרב אל פתח ביתה כי רבים חללים הפילה

[187] Zuckermandel, 503.

ונו' שהיה ר' אליעזר אומר לעולם יהא אדם בורח מן הכיעור ומן הדומה לכיעור.[188]

First we must take notice of the fact that the reading is not certain. Tosefta already has two forms of the name פנטירא (22) and פנטירי (24). In the later works, the *Toledot Jeshu*, and in fragments, there are different forms and also different persons, owners or bearers of the name. There occurs ישו בן פנדירה[189] and ישו בן פנדרא.[190] Also יוסף בן פנדירא the paramour of Mary — and father of Jesus,[191] while the husband's name is given as Joḥanan, and contrariwise יוסף בן פנדירא is given as the name of the husband, while the name of the lover, and hence the real father of Jesus, is given as Joḥanan.[192] So Pandera, or Pantera, was either the name of Jesus' father, or of Joseph's father, hence the grandfather of Jesus or of Mary's husband's father and no relation at all to Jesus, or it may be a family name and not the name of any one person in particular.

Now, as to the meaning of this designation, if it was not simply the proper name of a person in which case it need not have special meaning. One interpretation is that פנתירי is corrupted from παρθένος which means the virgin, or young woman. Now, of course, the Jews did not believe Jesus to have been the son of a virgin. But, according to this interpretation of the word פנתירי[193] the Jews, already in very early times, sought to make fun of the claim that Jesus was the son of a virgin and therefore twisted the name to בן פנטרא, the son of the lustful panther. The panther was the animal sacred to Bacchus and also was believed to be descended from the lioness.[194] The Jews then meant by this designation to describe him as the son of the animal devoted to Bacchus, i. e., the result of heathenism ... and also the illegitimate son of the unchaste panther or leopard. The church which also knew the name בן פנתירי for Jesus, did not

---

[188] Cf. b. 'Ab. Zarah 16b–17a and 27b.
[189] Krauss, 144.
[190] *Ibid.*, 146, 147.
[191] *Ibid.*, 38, 40, 118, 131, 140.
[192] *Ibid.*, 64.
[193] Cassel, *op. cit.*, 334 ff.
[194] See Cassel, *ibid.*, 337, note 19.

understand the insult and mockery intended by the Jews with this name, and hence adopted the name, but they first legitimatized, as it were, the panther. The panther is compared with Mary.[195] Perles, in *Die Namen Jesus im Talmud*[196] rejects this interpretation of P. Cassel on the ground that he (Perles) did not find an allusion in Jewish literature to the belief that the panther is the type of unchastity.... In this Perles is wrong, as pointed out by Goldfahn[197] who says: "Dr. Perles hat b. Kiddushin 70a vergessen, wo R. Abbahu die Stelle in Nehemiah 7.61: אמר אדון ואמר כרוב אדון ששמו... עצמו כנמר deutet, wozu Raschi bemerkt: כחיה זו שאינו מקפדת בזוג חברתה. Das von Cassel (*loc. cit.*, S. 337, Anm. 191) erwähnte mittelalterliche zoologische Märchen, dass die Parden von dem unkeuschen Gelüste der Löwinen ableitet, kennt auch die rabbinische Literatur. R. Simon b. Zemaḥ Duran, der es in seinem Commentar מגן אבות zu Abot 5.20 (ed. Leipzig, 1855, S. 91a) mittheilt, macht aber keinen Unterschied zwischen Parden und Panther und sagt der נמר sei ein Mischling בן חזיר היער und בן לביאה. Dieses zoologische Märchen dürfte vielleicht auch einen geschichtlichen Sinn haben. Jecheskel 19.2 ist לביא Symbol des Judenthums, vgl. Sotah folio 11b; חזיר היער ist nach der Deutung der Midraschim zu Ps. 80.14 (vgl. Midrasch z. Ps. *loc. cit.*, ed. Buber § 6 nebst Parall.) Symbol Roms. Aus der Vermischung Roms mit dem Judenthume entspringt der "נמר" der kühne Panther, des Christentum, welches das Judentum u. seinen Gesetzgeber, Gott, schmäht (vgl. Pesikte dr. Kahana, ed. Buber, pagina 41a) אריה ist Symbol Gottes (vgl. Chullin 59b und Pesikta dr. Kahana, ed. Buber, pagina 116a, zu Amos 3.8). Auch der Midrasch zu den Psalmen 78.45 (ed. Buber § 11) sagt: Der Panther (פנתירין) sei ein Mischling (ערוב)." While all this, ingenious though it is, may be correct and Perles' ground for rejecting Cassel's interpretation not sufficient, it does not make the interpretation correct. It is very unlikely that at such an early time, in the days of R. Eliezer, i. e., in the second half of the first Christian century, the Jews wanted to designate Jesus by a name

---

[195] See Cassel, *ibid.*, *loc. cit.*, note 20.
[196] In *Magyar Zsido Szemle*, (1889), 193–200.
[197] In Rahmer's *Literaturblatt* XX, (1891), No. 39, p. 151.

expressive of their appraisal of him, and that they would use such a complicated allusion referring to the legendary nature of the panther. Especially is it unlikely that the church should not have recognized the intended insult, and that the Amoraim too did not recognize its meaning and considered instead Pantera as the name of the father אבי פנדירא הוה. So this interpretation of Pantera is not acceptable. No more acceptable is the interpretation given by Perles[198] that Pandera is like ὕπανδρος.[199]

Another fanciful interpretation of this strange designation is given by A. S. Kamenetzki in ספר יובל של הדואר[200] which reads as follows: מוצא שם בן פנדירא: לדעתי נתחלף אז ליהודים ישו זה בישוע בן סירא[201] והשם בן פנדירא הוא שם המשובש מ„בן סירא" ואפשר גם שאחרי שנעשה החלוף הזה מצאו המחרפים עוד סימן מיוחד בשם בן תירא לאמור בן החיה (תירא=חיה בלשון יוני) בנגוד לכנוי בן אלהים שהמציאו מכבדי הנוצרי. וככה הלך השם הלוך והשתבש עד שהיה לפנתירא (=נמר, חיה רעה) ולבסוף לפנדירא לפטירי ואולי גם ל(ס)טרא שנשתבש אחר כך לסטדא (בן סירא במקום בן סטדא). Previously Kamenetzki in Hatekufah[202] had said quite differently: .... (פנתרי) „בן פנטירי" או „בן פנדירא" השם הוא לדעתי שמסרס בכוונה משם בן אנתרופי בן האדם „מענשענזאהן" שהשתמש בו ישו הרבה לפי דברי האונגליונים. And in the same article[203] he also says אפשר שבן פטירי (נ"א פטורי) הנזכר בתלמוד (ב"מ) הוא בן פנטירי. In the latter point, the writer in Rahmer's Literaturblatt, to be discussed below[204] anticipated him. Of course all these fanciful interpretations involving a series of corruptions and misunderstandings are far fetched and far from plausible. I would add to this, the interpretation of Strauss quoted by Hitzig[205] with some modification and improvement of my own. According to this interpretation פנטירי is the Greek πενθερός meaning "son in law" חתן. Herford's argument: "But surely there is nothing distinctive

[198] Ibid., loc. cit.
[199] Consider the full implication of ὕπανδρος! Does it mean "a married woman" and imply "the son of a married woman by a man other than her husband?" — which might fit Mary, or does it mean, as it seemingly is used by Plutarch "ein liederliches Weibsstück" — an unchaste woman?
[200] New York, (1927), 323.
[201] Cf. Brüll, Jahrbücher, V, 201 and VII, 95. See also above, p. 489.
[202] XVIII, (1923), 511–512.
[203] P. 511, note 1.
[204] Pp. 537 f.   [205] See Herford, 39.

in such an epithet to account for its being specially applied to Jesus" may be met in the following wise. The implication of the name is that Jesus was not a bastard, he was the legal and legitimate son of Joseph and Mary who were merely betrothed — which is legally married but not yet married in fact. Mary was an ארוסה but not a נשואה. Thus there was a good reason to apply the name בן החתן not בן הבעל to Jesus, for while this casts a little reflection on Jesus, it does not call him illegitimate. It seems that in Galilee they were more strict than in Judea as regards the relation between the betrothed and it was considered bad taste and the unusual thing for the חתן to have intercourse with the betrothed before the concluding marriage formalities or נשואין took place.[206] In general it was considered improper for the betrothed to live in the house of his father-in-law before marriage. In b. B. B. 98b there is quoted a saying of Ben Sira disparaging the חתן who does so: קל מסובין, חתן הדר בבית חמיו. And in b. Yeb. 52a and in Ḳid. 12b it is said that Rab (Abba Areka) would administer a punishment to a betrothed חתנא who dwelt in the house of his father-in-law: רב מנגיד על חתנא דדייר בבית חמוה.[207] The name בן פנתירי would then designate or point to Jesus as one merely conceived and born before the marriage was perfected (נשואין) but nonetheless legally and legitimately and not a bastard.[208]

I have cited all these fanciful interpretations of the name, although none of them is satisfactory.[209] *Perhaps, however, we need no interpretation beyond the simple interpretation that Panther was just a name or still better a family name.* Origen quoted by Epiphanius[210] says that Jacob the father of Joseph and grand-

---

[206] See Ket. 12a.

[207] Perhaps, however, this may apply in general even to a married son-in-law, because of suspicion about possible, indecent relations with his mother-in-law. Cf. the saying הוי זהיר באשתך מחתנה הראשון, Pes. 113a.

[208] Perhaps the saying in p. Pes. 1 (37b) האוכל מצה בערב פסח כבא על ארוסתו בבית חמיו contains a subtle, veiled allusion to Jesus who, according to the Gospels, had his סדר with מצה etc. in the evening preceding the eve of Passover, or in the night preceding the 14th of Nisan, just as his father had intercourse with his betrothed before the proper time, and it hints that he acted in a manner like his father in doing things too soon!

[209] Cf. Krauss, 276, for the literature on other interpretations.

[210] See Herford, 39, note 2.

father of Jesus was called Panther. This would explain how in some of the later sources of the *Toledot Jeshu*, Joseph is called יוסף בן פנטירא. The Jews and the Christians had the same legend on this point, and when they speak of Jesus the son of Pandera, they either mean the grandson, for בני בנים הרי הם כבנים, "the sons of one's son are like one's sons"[211] or they mean Jesus of the family of Pandera. Furthermore, as Deismann showed[212] Πανθήρα was quite a common Greek proper name, and there were in Judea, Jews with Greek names. If, however, we want to indulge in speculations about possible corruptions and misunderstandings, we should consider also the name בן פטורי mentioned in b. B. M. 62a.

M. S. Rens (of Hamburg)[213] believes that he has found an allusion to Jesus and his teachings in the Baraita B. M. 62a which reads as follows: שנים שהיו מהלכין בדרך וביד אחד מהן קיתון של מים אם שותין שניהם מתים ואם שותה אחד מהן מגיע לישוב דרש בן פטורא מוטב שישתו שניהם וימותו אל יראה אחד מהם במיתתו של חברו עד שבא ר' עקיבא ולימד וחי עמך חייך קודמין. Now Rens claims, though without any justification for his opinion, that the use of the term דרש when the verse expounded or used as the basis of the opinion is not cited, is unusual[214] and could have been used only by one who was not one of the Rabbis. Who, then, was this Ben Patura who employed terms not usually employed by the Rabbis? Rens suggests that Jesus is here designated by this name.[215] Jesus frequently refers to himself as "the son of the father"[216] so his disciples likewise referred to him as "the son of the father" in heaven, "filius patri" or Ben Patri, and quoted in his name

---

[211] b. Yeb. 62b.
[212] See Strack, *op. cit.*, 21.
[213] In Rahmer's *Literaturblatt* XIV, (1885), No. 42, p. 165.
[214] It occurs, however, in Giṭ. 43a; Pes. 42a; cf. also Ket. 49a זה מדרש דרש ראב"ע, and if it should be claimed that the Mishnah there may have omitted the verse which was the basis for the decision of R. Eleazer b. Azariah and which he cited when giving the decision, then one might as well assume that here, likewise, Ben Paturi cited the verse on which he based his decision but when quoting the decision the Baraita omitted the verse.
[215] He might have simply said that Ben Paturi, or as some readings have it, Ben Patiri, is corrupted from Ben Pantiri, just as we have seen above, it could be claimed that Ben Pantiri is a mistake for Ben Patiri.
[216] Matth. 15.13; John 13.17, etc.

this teaching. Although we do not find this teaching or saying in the Gospels, it may have been one of the Agrapha — though Resch does not mention it either — . At any rate it is in keeping with and in the spirit of the sermon on the Mount[217] and may have formed part of it, though subsequently omitted in the Gospel. It may have been preserved by one of his disciples who referred to him as "filius patri," and another, quoting it, misunderstood it to mean the son of a man named Patri, hence he gave it in Hebrew Ben Patri. This would explain the apparent irregularity of using one word — for son — in Hebrew, בן and the other — for father — in Latin, *patri*. And the term דרש which introduced this teaching may indicate that it originally formed part of the sermon — דרשה — on the mount. This is the theory of Rens slightly improved by me to increase the possibility of its being correct. There is one other difficulty in its way which we must and can remove, *viz.*, how could it happen that all the teachers up to the time of Akiba, should have accepted a teaching of Jesus. This difficulty can easily be explained away. It might have been an old Jewish teaching merely emphasized by Jesus, hence cited by some in his name; or, though it was believed to be his teaching, it was not rejected for this reason by the Rabbis, just as they did not cease to declare that "thou shalt love thy neighbour as thyself" is the great commandment of the Torah[218] although Jesus also declared it to be the greatest commandment. Furthermore, we have seen that R. Eliezer accepted or at least was pleased, as he admitted, with a teaching of Jesus quoted to him by Jacob of Kefar Sekarya. In this latter case it may have been made easier for the Rabbis to accept it for they did not recognize Jesus in Ben Patri, but took Patri to be the name of a person. Thus the teaching, even if it had come from Jesus, might have been circulated and accepted by the teachers until Akiba had recognized it as Christian or for other reasons disagreed with it and rejected it. All this is possible, but what reason have we to assume that it was so, especially when we find no difficulty at all in the name

---

[217] Matth. 5.39–40.
[218] p. Ned. 9.3 (41c); Sifra, *Kedoshim* IV, (Weiss, 89b).

Ben Patura or Patera? This whole Baraita here in B. M. is taken from the Sifra, *Behar* VI[219] and there the teaching of Ben Paturi is given together with the verse[220] on which he based it; it reads as follows: וחי אחיך עמך זו דרש בן פטורי שנים שהיו הולכים במדבר ואין ביד אחד אלא קיתון של מים אם שניהם שותהו אחד מגיע ליישוב ואם שותים אותו שנים שניהם מתים דרש בן פטורי ישתו שתיהם וימותו שנאמר וחי אחיך עמך אמר לו ר"ע וחי אחיך עמך חייך קודמים לחיי חבירך. Here, not only is the verse on which it is based cited, so that there is nothing unusual in the usage of the term[221] but Ben Paturi discusses it with R. Akiba, so he was a contemporary of Akiba and could not have been Jesus.[222]

Dr. Sidon[223] further disproves the theory of Rens by calling attention to the fact that Ben Paturi is mentioned elsewhere with his full name Jehudah b.[224] Paturi, as a contemporary of Akiba, even a younger contemporary, in whose name he gives an interpretation דרש ר' יהודה בן פטורי משום ר' עקיבא.[225] It is strange though that R. Joshua quotes him there, but then this Joshua may have been another Joshua, not Joshua b. Ḥananiah. It is most likely that פטירי is a different form of בתירי (ב and פ interchange as in הבקר for הפקר) and this Judah b. Patera is none other than Judah b. Betera, and in B. M. בן פטורא is a corrupt form of בן בתירה who is often mentioned without his first name.

Another designation assumed by some to have been used in the Talmud in referring to Jesus is פלוני "a certain one" or

[219] (Weiss, 109c).

[220] Lev. 25.35.

[221] Which, as we have seen above, occurs elsewhere even without the verse. In addition to the instances cited above see b. Shab. 21b and 88; Beẓah 33a; Shab. 14a and 39a.

[222] Cf. Goldfahn, in Rahmer's, *Literaturblatt* XIV, No. 42, 173 and No. 49, 193, where Rens answers Goldfahn, insisting that דרש without a verse is rarely used and points to the reading פטירא instead of פטורא as found in some editions of the Talmud, in En Jacob and in Yalkuṭ.

[223] *Ibid.*, 204.

[224] Of course one might argue that יהודה is a mistake for ישו and that it came about by a mistaken resolution of the abbreviation ר"י בן פטורי — reading ר' יהודה instead of ר' ישו! But the time element — his being a contemporary of R. Akiba cannot be argued away.

[225] Tosefta Soṭah 5.13 and 6.1 (Zuckermandel, 307).

איש פלוני, "a certain man," but in all instances where this epithet פלוני is used it is very doubtful, to say the least, whether the reference is to Jesus. First among these is the passage in M. Yeb. 4.13 (b. Yeb. 49a,b) where Ben Azzai says מגלת יוחסין מצאו בירושלים וכתוב בה, איש פלוני ממזר מאשת איש, "They found a scroll of genealogies[226] in Jerusalem in which — among other entries — was written: 'a certain man was a bastard, the son of a married woman by a man not her legal husband.'" Of course, if we assume that Jesus was a *mamzer* and that the Rabbis believed him to have been one, then it is not *impossible* that when they cited a certain geneological list in which an entry was found about "a certain man," that he was a bastard, they had reference to the entry about Jesus whom they designated as פלוני "a certain man." But there is absolutely no positive reason for assuming this. Why should the Rabbis in the first half of the second century seek to shield Jesus in not exposing his name but merely referring to him as "a certain man." For this seems to be the original reading and not a substitute reading due to the fear of any censor, since in no MS or older text, or quotation, is there a passage reading ישו instead of פלוני.

In this connection we might discuss the passage in Masseket Kallah[227] about a certain child who passed by the elders with head uncovered, an act considered bold and disrespectful;[228] the teachers, judging by the disrespectful behavior of the child, declared that that child must be a bastard or one conceived by his mother during the period of her menstruation, בן הנדה and R. Akiba said it was both a ממזר ובן הנדה. The passage in מסכת כלה רבתי reads as follows: פעם אחת היו זקנים יושבים עברו לפניהם שני תינוקות, אחד גלה את ראשו ואחד כסה את ראשו, זה שגלה ראשו, ר' אליעזר אומר ממזר, ר' יהושע אומר בן נדה, ר' עקיבא אומר ממזר ובן נדה, אמרו לו, עקיבא, איך מלאך לבך לעבור על דברי רבותיך, אמר להם אני אקיימנו, הלך אצל אמו של אותו תינוק ומצאה שהיא יושבת ומוכרת קטנית בשוק. אמר

---

[226] On this passage and on the question of genealogical books, see my "The Three Books Found in the Temple at Jerusalem." See above note 129.

[227] Ed. Higger, (New York, 1936), 191–192.

[228] Women and children were expected to cover their heads but not grown-up men; see my responsum "Should one cover the Head when participating in Divine Worship?" in *CCAR Yearbook* XXXVIII, (1928).

לה, בתי אם תאמר לי דבר זה שאני שואליך, הריני מביאך לחיי עולם הבא, אמרה לו השבע לי, היה ר' עקיבא נשבע בשפתיו ומבטל לו בלבו. אמר לה בנך זה מה טיבו? אמרה לו כשנכנסתי לחופה נדה הייתי ופירש ממני בעלי ובעלני שושביני ועברתי את זה, נמצא אותו תינוק ממזר ובן נדה. אמרו גדול היה ר' עקיבא שהכחיש את חברו. באותה שעה אמרו ברוך שגלה סודו לעקיבא בן יוסף. This passage has also been understood as referring to Jesus. Thus Ibn Yarḥi in his commentary פרוש מסכת כלה רבתי[229] says: נחלקו חכמים ז"ל על אותו הפריץ יש"ו שהולך לפניהם בקומה זקופה ובגלוי הראש וכו'. The fact that Akiba spoke to the mother of that child precludes the possibility of that child having been Jesus. The mistake of taking that child for Jesus could have been made by later people only on the basis of two other mistakes, *viz.*, the mistaken identification of Pappos b. Jehudah, a contemporary of Akiba, with the husband of Miriam, the women's hairdresser, and the identification of the latter with the mother of Jesus. The story told by the mother of the child of how the friend of the husband or best man שושבין substituted for the husband, resembles the story told in later *Toledot Jeshu* about Mary mistaking her husband's friend for her husband and hence yielding herself to him, and this resemblance in the stories also helped to mislead some people into believing that both deal with the same persons. Incidentally it may be noticed that the Mishnah in Yebamot, citing the passage from מגלת יוחסין in support of the opinion of R. Joshua that only a child conceived in such sin for which the parents were liable to be punished with death by human courts כל שחייבין עליו מיתת בית דין, could be considered a bastard, could not have known the story of the Tractate Kallah nor its interpretation as referring to Jesus, for in the Mishnah, R. Joshua declared the child — presumed by some to be Jesus — to have been merely a בן הנדה but not a ממזר. But there is not the slightest reason for assuming that either of the passages in מגלת יוחסין or in מסכת כלה refer to Jesus.[230]

[229] Ed. Toledano, p. 4. Quoted by Higger, *op. cit.*, Introduction 25.

[230] See also Chwolson, *Das Letzte Pessahmahl*, 100–102. Cf. also Hans Leisegang, *Pneuma Hagion, Der Ursprung des Geistesbegriffs der synoptischen Evangelien aus der Griechischen Mystic* (Leipzig, 1922), p. 18, who probably, on the basis of the misunderstood and misinterpreted passage above which he accepted from secondhand sources says: 'Auch die Stellungnahme zur

In another passage in the Talmud[231] where "a certain man" פלוני is mentioned, some scholars would discover Jesus. The passage reads: שאלו את ר' אליעזר פלוני מהו לעולם הבא, "What about so and so in the future world?" R. Eliezer who was suspected of heresy or leanings toward Christianity and who once enjoyed a teaching of Jesus reported to him by Jacob of Sakanya, is, according to the opinion of some scholars, here asked what his opinion of Jesus was; whether he will have a share in the world to come?[232] But why did neither the questioners nor R. Eliezer in his answers mention ישו by name? What reason was there to shield Jesus, especially since nothing definite was said about him, and the question was not decided in his disfavor. Rashi's explanation that Salomon is meant here and R. Ḥananel's interpretation that Absolom was meant make very good sense.[233] They wanted to spare Solomon or even Absolom the insult of recording that there was serious doubt as to either of them having a share in the future world. Even if it were not Solomon or Absolom but another person אדם אחד, someone whom they

---

Geburtsgeschichte Jesu innerhalb des Talmud, die stets darauf hinausläuft irgendeinen Ehebruch der Maria zu construiren und so die Geburt Jesu auf natürlichem Wege zu erklären, macht das vor allem deutlich." This is not correct, since with the exception of the reference of the Amoraim to בועל בן פנדירא the Talmud does not ("stets") seek to assume an act of adultery on the part of Mary. Leisegang refers to Hennecke, *Apocryphen* (1904) where he says, the passages from the Talmud are given. In the second edition of Hennecke, p. 21, Hennecke does not give the passages but merely refers to the literature. On one point, however, Leisegang is correct, namely: that in Jewish circles the idea or myth of God physically begetting a child could never have been accepted. Hence Mary was said to have conceived, not directly from God but through an agent of God, the Holy Ghost. Since שלוחו של אדם כמותו and the Holy Ghost merely acted as the agent of God, Jesus could still be called the son of God. Later on the Holy Ghost, the agent who impregnated Mary, was made identical with God and in the Trinity Mary was accounted as the third party, Father, Mother and Son, instead of Father, Holy Ghost and Son.

[231] b. Yoma 86b.

[232] Evidently the author of this Baraita or the Gemara here, as referring to Jesus, did not understand the Mishnah in Sanhedrin which included Balaam among the four commoners who were not to have a share in the world to come.

[233] Tosafot, *ad loc.*, *s. v.* פלוני.

wanted to spare the insult, one can understand why they designate him as פלוני. But there was no such reason for so designating Jesus. The other question asked of R. Eliezer[234] about a bastard, whether he can inherit from his father, ממזר מהו לירש, is also understood by some as possibly referring to Jesus.[235] It is argued that it may have been an ironical question. Jesus boasted of having inherited and acquired from his father powers like his own e. g., to forgive sins, etc.; but how could a bastard inherit from his father? For even God has no right to beget a child with a married woman. Or the question was, how could Jesus who claimed to be the Messiah, inherit the messiahship from David when he was not a real descendant from David, since Joseph, the husband of his mother, was not his father? All these interpretations are far-fetched and forced, and have no basis whatever except the wish to find allusions, and disparaging allusions at that, to Jesus in the Talmud.

Some modern scholars are so eager to discover allusions to Jesus, that at an allusion in the Talmud to any person in whose history or character there is the slightest hint or a resemblance to one feature or another in the life story of Jesus, they immediately jump to the conclusion that the person referred to was Jesus presented under some disguise. To this class of misunderstood passages belongs the passage in M. Sanh. 7.5 (b. Sanh. 56a) where it is said that in the case of a trial for blasphemy, to avoid repetition in their testimony of the words of the blasphemy, the witnesses use a circumlocution, כנוי, and do not recite the blasphemy as it was uttered by the accused, but substitute the phrase יכה יוסי את יוסי in which phrase the second יוסי is a substitute for the Tetragrammaton. Now, why use Josi as a substitute for the name of God?[236] It is therefore suggested that Josi

---

[234] *Loc. cit.*

[235] But if פלוני was Jesus, why did they not ask in one question פלוני ממזר מהו לירש חלק עוה"ב. Of course, it could be argued that the one question is the logical sequel to the other. If a man of Jesus's character could merit a share in the world to come, could he as a bastard whose father was said to be, in Christian tradition, God, claim a share in the world to come, which God, the Father, gives as an inheritance to his beloved and are we to derive from this the general rule that a bastard can legally inherit?

[236] One could ask the counter question, why use the name Josi for the

is an allusion to Jesus.[237] But this is far from plausible. The Rabbis would not have substituted the name of Jesus for the name of God even in a blaspheming phrase, for such a substitution might be taken as an indication of a certain similarity between the two, and it would have suggested that Jesus had a somewhat divine character. It is simply a convenient substitute using names which frequently occur, just as when they wish to refer to a case of two people having the same name, they speak of שני יוסף בן שמעון. Perhaps the choice of this substitute was prompted by the desire of using a four-letter name.[238]

Another such forced allusion to Jesus under a disguised name is found by some in the saying of Rab in b. Sanh. 38b, which reads אמר רב אדם הראשון בלשון ארמי סיפר שנאמר ולי מה יקרו רעיך אל.[239] Duschak[240] assumes that אדם הראשון here is a name for Jesus who was called אדם קדמון "der zuerst ausgeflossene Grundquell der Dinge, die aus Gott emanirten, ist der erstgeborene Sohn Gottes ... diesen angeblichen אדם קדמון nennt der Talmud zuweilen אדם ראשון." Hence in the saying of Rab, the reference is to Jesus who spoke Aramaic, for he said אלהי אלהי למא שבקתני[241] instead of the

---

smiter as well as for the smitten? The first Josi then must also stand for something else, unless we assume that the blasphemy consisted in the utterance: May God smite God or Himself?

[237] See Dr. A. Lewin in Rahmer's *Literaturblatt* VIII, (1879), No. 32, 127.

[238] There are many other theories about the meaning of the name יוסי in this phrase which we might as well mention here. M. S. Rens (*ibid.*, No. 39, 157), assumes that it is a somewhat inverted form of Jovis. This inverted form was used in order to avoid the mention of the heathen deity by name, on the ground ושם אלהים אחרים לא תזכירו. Another theory is that Josi here was pronounced as ὀυσια=הויה or היות i. e., a substitute for the שם היה. But there is no reason for attaching any special significance to the choice of a substitute or circumlocution beyond the possible consideration that they may have looked for another four letter name. Cf. also Dr. Sidon, *ibid.*, Nos. 47, 186, who also favors the idea that the consideration was that Josi was a common name, just as in the case of שני יוסף בן שמעון.

[239] The quotation is Ps. 139.17. The entire psalm is supposed to refer to the creation of man — Adam. See Rashi, *ad loc.*

[240] Rahmer's *Literaturblatt* VI, (1877), No. 51, 203.

[241] Mark 15.34.

Hebrew.[242] Likewise the saying in Sanhedrin[243] אדם הראשון מושך בערלתו, might — according to Duschak — fit Jesus, "da er am liebsten mit dem schönen Geschlecht Umgang pflegte."[244] And, of course, the saying אדם הראשון מין הוא and R. Naḥman's saying כופר בעיקר הוה[245] would fit Jesus.[246] The arguments against Duschak's theory might be augmented as follows: First, Paul calls Jesus the *second Adam*, "the second man is the Lord from heaven."[247] Secondly, if this אדם ראשון who has some divine character, as in Zohar עתיקא קדישא אדם קדמון[248] or אדם עילאה[249] or in Philo[250] οὐράνιος ἄνθρωπος had been meant in these passages, the Rabbis would not have applied it to Jesus, since it would have given him divine character and especially since saying "Adam spoke Aramaic" does not contain anything disparaging.

I believe we have exhausted all the passages in the Talmud in which Jesus actually or supposedly is referred to under any name, surname, or disguised designation.

We shall now proceed to consider such passages in which Jesus is, actually or supposedly, alluded to, not by any special name but as one who claims, or is considered by his followers, to be of unique or divine character, or to possess a special authority. The first passage of this kind is the one in b. Sanh. 106b where the verse in Num. 24.23 אוי מי יחיה משומו אל is interpreted by R. Simon b. Laḳish, a Palestinian Amora of the second generation as אוי מי שמחיה עצמו בשם אל. Rashi,[251] explains it to mean עושה עצמו אלוה,

---

[242] One could perhaps support this by the consideration that according to the Rabbis בלשון הקודש העולם נברא (Gen. r., 18.6 and 31.9). Hence the Biblical Adam must have spoken Hebrew and not Aramaic.

[243] *Loc. cit.*

[244] This is rather doubtful. If one accepts the suggestion that the reference is to Jesus, then perhaps מושך בערלתו means the practice of covering up the circumcision and ascribes to Jesus instead of Paul the abolition of מילה.

[245] Sanh., *loc. cit.*

[246] Against Duschak see Friedländer in Rahmer's *Literaturblatt, ibid.*, 208 and the note of the redaction.

[247] I Cor. 15.47.

[248] Idra r. 141b.

[249] Zohar II, 70b; II, 48.

[250] *De Allegoriis Legum* I, XII.   [251] *Ad loc.*

"one who declares himself to be God." Of course, Resh Laḳish's interpretation of the verse may simply mean, one who supports himself or makes a living by using or abusing the name of God, i. e., employing it in incantations and cures. In this sense it might well refer to Jesus, whose healing of people or driving out evil spirits was claimed to have been performed with, or in, the name of God.[252] But more likely Rashi's explanation is correct and it refers to Jesus who declared himself to be like God, or claimed to have arisen from the dead, שההחיה עצמו, as a god over whom death has no power. Of course, we have no proof that Jesus expressly declared himself to be God, though he claimed equal authority with God. He is reported as having said: "I and my father are one"[253] though in the earlier Gospels,[254] Jesus never declares himself to be God, but merely the son of God who is almost like his father. However, in Luke and John,[255] Jesus is referred to in the narrative portions as the Lord. Simon b. Laḳish in the third century may have heard or known that, according to some Gospels or Christian sources, Jesus was considered to have divine powers or to be God; and he assumed that these sources or Gospels had this idea from their master Jesus who himself made this claim. Simon b. Laḳish interpreted this utterance by Balaam as prophetically cursing Jesus for making such claims, for Balaam (so it was believed) was able to foresee Jesus' claims, just as, according to the passage in Yalḳuṭ to be discussed below, he is reported as having predicted the appearance of Jesus with his misleading doctrines. Furthermore, Simon b. Laḳish could have heard of Ignatius (70–150) and Polycarp (also 70–150) and others who considered Jesus as God and he assumed that they could not and would not have done so if Jesus himself had not declared himself as such.

The development of the idea that Jesus was God was a slow process. The origin of this idea may have been in Greek communities; then it was developed by Paul and then came into the younger Gospels. In the older Gospels, Mark and Matthew,

---

[252] See Matth. 12.24–28.
[253] John 10.10.
[254] Matth. 11.25 ff. is the crucial passage.
[255] Luke 6.46; 7.13; John 4.1.

Jesus is merely the Messiah, Christus, and the name Lord referring to Jesus in the sense of deification is rarely found there. The passage in Mark 12.36–37, "David himself called him Lord" is doubtful.[256] All the other passages where Jesus is spoken of as the Lord Κύριος are either doubtful, as Mark 16.19, or the term may be used merely in the sense of master, like רבון, אדון.[257]

In Paul, however, Jesus' title is no longer Christus. Only occasionally Paul uses the term Christus Jesus. Predominantly Paul uses the title Kyrios, the Lord, for Jesus. This title explicitly denotes Jesus' divine nature and identifies him with God.[258] This conception could not have originated in Palestine among the Jews. It originated among Gentile Christians in Hellenistic communities and Paul learned it from them. We find it, therefore, frequently in the younger Gospels, in Luke and especially in John.[259] The apostolic fathers identify Jesus with God. Ignatius in all his epistles and Polycarp in his epistle to the Philippians, and Barnabas not later than Hadrian, teach that Jesus was God; and Second Clement (about 140) opens with the words: "Brethren, we must think of Jesus Christ as of God . . . as of the Judge of the living and the dead."[260] Simon b. Lakish as well as R. Abahu, a Palestinian Amora of the third generation (whose saying will be cited below) both living in Palestine in the third century, knew from Christians of their time that Jesus was considered to have been God and they believed that Jesus himself made this claim, and hence they, Resh Lakish and Abahu, directed their respective sayings against him and his supposed claims. Of course, these are third century polemics and not contemporary reports about Jesus.

[256] See Bousset, *Kyrios Christos*, 2nd Edition (Göttingen, 1921), 78.

[257] See Bousset, *op. cit.*, 79.

[258] Cf. especially Romans 10.13 where he interprets the passage in Joel 3.5, כל אשר יקרא בשם ד' ימלט, as referring to Jesus. See Bousset, *op. cit.*, 99 ff.

[259] See e. g., Luke 2.11, "a saviour who is Christ the Lord;" 5.24, Jesus claims authority on earth to forgive sin (like God); 6.46, "why call ye me Lord and do not the things which I say?" In John there are many such passages, especially 20.28 where Thomas calls Jesus, my Lord, my God, and 21.7, 12 and 15.

[260] Cf. Edgar Hennecke, *Neutestamentliche Apocryphen*, 2nd ed., (Tübingen, 1924).

While thus considering the development of the belief that Jesus was God, we may, in this connection, also consider here the development of the doctrine of the Trinity, which will also help us in the discussion and understanding of some talmudic and midrashic passages. It is commonly assumed that the doctrine of the Trinity was formulated and accepted in Nicea in 325 and was merely confirmed in the Council at Constantinople in 381, though some scholars maintain that the *Holy Ghost* came into — and thus completed — the Trinity at Constantinople.[261] According to this theory, then, there was, up to 381, only a Dualism but not a Trinity. Robert Rainy[262] maintains that the Trinity was already formulated in the Athanasian Creed, or in the original Nicene Creed. At any rate, the Trinity is much later than the Gospels and was definitely accepted only in the fourth century. It is true a suggestion of the doctrine of the Trinity is already found in Matth. 28.18 in the baptism formula: "In the name of the Father and the Son and the Holy Ghost." Likewise, in Paul's words: "The grace of the Lord Jesus Christ and the love of God and the communion of the Holy Spirit be with you all"[263] there is a suggestion of the Trinity, but it was not formulated as a dogma. And in the third century there were many Christians who rejected the belief in the Trinity. Some, like Noetus, taught that the three are merely three aspects of God but not three entities.[264] At any rate, we may safely say that up to the beginning of the fourth century there was in Christianity — as far as generally accepted doctrines are concerned — merely a dualism — God and Jesus — and not a Trinity. If, therefore, we find in Talmud or Midrash an argument against dualism, it may possibly, dependent on other considerations such as content and context, be interpreted as an allusion to or argument against Christianity, and not as an argument against Persian dualism. Such a statement is, to my mind, the saying of Ḥiyya II bar

---

[261] See Reinach, *A Short History of Christianity*, (Putnam, 1922), 54, who decides in favor of this opinion.

[262] *The Ancient Catholic Church*, (Scribners, New York, 1902), 355 ff.

[263] Cor. 13–14.

[264] See M. Friedländer, *Synagoge und Kirche in ihren Anfängen*, (1905), 225 ff.

Abba, a Palestinian Amora of the third generation, contemporary of R. Abahu and pupil of R. Joḥanan.

In Pesiḳta Rabbati xxi (Friedmann, 100b–101a) we read as follows: אמר ר' חייה בר אבא אם יאמר לך ברא דזניתא תרין אלהים אינון (שעל הר סיני) אמר ליה אנא הוא דימא (על ים סוף) אנא הוא דסיני. "If the *son of the harlot* will tell you that there are two gods [and in support of the doctrine point to the two different manifestations of God, on Sinai, as זקן ויושב בישיבה and on the Red Sea as איש מלחמה][265] you should tell him that I am the same God who manifested Himself at Sinai and at the Red Sea." Of course one could argue that there is no allusion here to Jesus' person, since Mary is nowhere else in Palestinian sources referred to as a harlot (even in the later amoraic description as סטת דא מבעלה she is not characterized as a זונה). Heresy or מינות is very often represented as a harlot.[266] Hence ברא דזניתא here is like בן המינות — the heretic. One might interpret the saying of Ḥiyya II b. Abba as being directed against the heretic who argues in favor of dualism — i. e., Persian dualism. This, however, would not be correct. The Persian dualism consists of two *opposing* powers, the god of light and the god of darkness, while the dualism represented or favored by this heretic consists of two gods in harmony with one another, only manifesting themselves differently, as, at Sinai and the Red Sea, or as the father in heaven and Jesus, the son in human form on earth. Hence the heresy here is Christianity and the argument is against Jesus' claim to divinity. For, as we have seen, in the third century, Christianity had only a dualism of the father and the son. It is, however, possible that Ḥiyya II b. Abba, wishing to refer to Jesus who, by claiming to be God, asserted that there are two Gods, purposely chose the ambiguous designation ברא דזניתא which in a figurative sense means heretic and literally the son of an unfaithful wife. Since Ḥiyya knew that the Christians admit that Joseph, the

---

[265] See the Midrashim *ad loc.* and expecially Mekilta, *Shirata* IV (ed. Lauterbach II, 31) and Lauterbach, מביאורי המכילתא in ספר קלוזנר (Tel Aviv, 1937), 181 ff.

[266] See b. 'Ab. Zarah 7a where the passage in Prov. 5.8 referring to the harlot is interpreted זו מינות, as dealing with heresy, figuratively represented as a harlot.

husband of Mary, was not the father of the child, he drew his own conclusions, rejecting the Christian explanation that the child had been conceived of the Holy Ghost. Hence he calls Jesus ברא דזניתא both in a literal and in a figurative sense.[267] Another saying in which Jesus is alluded to as one who claims to be God is found in the passage preserved to us in the Yalkut Shimeoni[268] to Numbers § 765,[269] which reads as follows:[270] דבר אחר מברך רעהו בקול גדול כמה היה קולו של בלעם ר' יוחנן אמר ששים מילין ר' יהושע בן לוי אמר שבעים אומות שמעו קולו של בלעם ר' אלעזר הקפר אומר נתן אלהים כח בקולו והיה עולה (ט. הולך) מסוף העולם ועד סופו בשביל שהיה צופה וראה האומות (ט. את האומות) שמשתחוין לשמש ולירח ולכוכבים ולעץ ולאבן וצפה וראה שיש אדם בן אשה שעתיד לעמוד שמבקש לעשות עצמו אלוה ולהטעות (ט. להטעות) כל העולם כולו לפיכך נתן כח שקולו (ט. בקולו) שישמעו כל אומות העולם וכן היה (ט. הוא) אומר תנו דעתכם שלא לטעות אחרי אותו האיש שנאמר לא איש אל ויכזב ואם אומר (ט. יאמר) שהוא אל מכזב (ט. ועתיד הוא לומר שהוא בן אלהים ואינו אלא בן אדם שנאמר ובן אדם ויתנחם שהוא) והוא עתיד להטעות ולומר שהוא מסתלק ובא לקיצים ההוא אמר ולא יעשה ראה מה כתיב וישא משלו ויאמר אוי מי יחיה משומו אל אמר בלעם אוי מי יחיה מאותה אומה ששמעה אחרי אותו האיש שעשה עצמו אלוה. The source of this saying is not given. But since the passage preceding it in the Yalkut is taken from ילמדנו, it is probable that this other interpretation is from Midrash Yelamdenu as well. In passing it should be noticed that this passage containing a condemnation of Rome or Edom אותו אומה ששמעה "that nation that listened to" and accepted Jesus who declared himself to be God. So the saying as given in this passage dates from the time after Rome became Christian, that is later than the beginning of the fourth century.

But this saying may be an elaboration of an older saying with

[267] Friedländer suggests that this interpretation of Ḥiyya II b. Abba, repeated in Midrash Tehillim 22.16 (ed. Buber) on the verse אלי may have an illusion to Jesus who called on the cross אלי אלי למה שבקתני, as if he would have believed in two Gods and called on both to help him, when there is only one. This is farfetched. I cannot locate the reference to Friedländer, so I cannot examine it more carefully.

[268] Editio princeps, Saloniki, 1526.

[269] In the MS it is § 765. In the later edition, although it is missing, the paragraph in which it should occur is numbered 766.

[270] The variants found in the Oxford MS are indicated in parenthesis.

additions about the nation that followed Jesus. For the same reference to Jesus claiming to be God, or the same interpretation of the verse in Numbers is also found and even more clearly expressed in p. Ta'an.2.1 (65b near bottom). No doubt Yelamdenu took it from the Yerushalmi and enlarged and developed it. The Yerushalmi passage also alludes to Jesus' claim that he would go up to heaven (=Yalḳuṭ שהוא מסתלק) and would come back after a certain period of time. The passage reads as follows אמר רבי אבהו אם יאמר לך אדם אל אני מכזב הוא בן אדם אני סופו לתחום (לתהות? =, לרדת שחת?) בו ויתנחם שאני עולה לשמים ההוא אמר ולא יקימנה, "If he says he is God he is lying. If he calls himself בן אדם [or בר נש in the technical sense], he will regret it."[271]

A reference to Jesus' claim to be the son of God בן אלהים may be that found in p. Shab. 6.9 end (8d). Commenting on the phrase דמי לבר אלהין, "like unto a son of God," in Dan. 3.25 it says: באותו שעה ירד מלאך וסטרו לההוא רשיעה (נבוכדנצר) על פיו אמר ליה תקין מיליך (correct your words!) חזר ובר אית ליה? (נבוכדנצר) ומר בריך אלההון די שדרך מישך ועבד נגו די שלח בריה לית כתיב כאן אלא די שלח מלאכיה ושיזיב לעבדוהי די התרחיצו עלוהי. This is a protest against anyone speaking of God as if he had a son. And the author, while referring the rebuke to Nebuchadnezzar, no doubt had in mind Jesus and his followers.[272] In connection with this Yerushalmi passage, we may also refer to the passage in the Zohar *Vayakhel*:[273] בריך שמיה וכו', which was incorporated in the prayer-book at a late date, and in which the phrase occurs ולא על בר אלהין סמיכנא. This is probably also directed against Christianity, though Aptowitzer, cited by Zimels[274] would understand it to refer to the angel Gabriel or Michael and protesting against mediatorship.[275]

---

[271] This would be the sense of the reading in the Wilna edition לתהות בו which is explained in *Korban Edah* as להתחרט בו. It may, however, be that לתהות is corrupt from לתחית=לתחיה and refers to his claim that he would come to life again. It is also possible that something is missing in our text. Maybe it read לתחית לתחת, meaning "if he claims to come to life, he will go down to hell instead," and a copyist, considering it a dittography, omitted the one word.

[272] Cf. Zimels in *Oẓar ha-Ḥayyim* VI, (1930), 166.

[273] (Lublin, 1872), 411.   [274] *Loc. cit.*

[275] Cf. Anatoli, מלמד התלמידים, section יתרו, 67b, against the prayer מכניסי רחמים.

A similar protest against anyone claiming to be a son of God is to be found in Gen. r. 26.5 in the comment on the passage רשב"י קרא להון בני דיינא ויראו[276] בני אלהים which reads as follows: רשב"י מקלל לכל מאן דקרי להון בני אלהין. R. Simon b. Yoḥai, Tanna of the third generation, living in the middle of the second century knew that the followers of Jesus called him, as indeed he called himself, the son of God and R. Simon directed his attack against them. When, after having explained that בני אלהים means "sons of the judges" he proceeds to curse those who take the words to mean "sons of God," he meant all those who call anybody a son of God, including the Christians. Likewise the passage in Ex. r. 29.4 no doubt is aimed against the Christian claim. The passage reads as follows: אמר ר' אבהו ... אמר הקב"ה אני איני בן אני ראשון שאין לי אב ואני אחרון שאין לי אח ומבלעדי אין אלהים שאין לי בן. Coming from Abahu who had disputes with Christians, this no doubt points to Jesus' claim to be the son of God.

Likewise the passage in Deut. r. 2.33 which reads as follows: "ועם שונים אל תתערב"[277] עם אלו שאומרים יש אלוה שני אל תתערב .... הפיות שאומרים שתי רשויות הן יכרתו ויגועו .... א"ר אחא כעס הקב"ה על שלמה כשאמר הפסוק הזה אמר לו דבר של קידוש שמא (קידוש השם) היות אומרו בלשון נוטריקון[278] ועם שונים אל תתערב? מיד חזר (שלמה) ופירש את הדבר יש אחד ואין שני גם בן ואח אין לו[279] אין לו לא אח ולא בן אלא שמע ישראל ... ה' אחד, is a protest against Christianity, not against Persian dualism as the middle statement הפיות שאומרים שתי רשויות might suggest. For it was just because of this ambiguity in the interpretation of the expression ועם שונים as "those who believe in two Gods" which might refer to Persian dualism as well as to Christianity, that God was angry with Solomon. For it might be understood that only Persian dualism in which the one god, Ahriman, is antagonistic to and an opponent of the other, Hormuzd, is objectionable, but not the Christian dualism in which the second god works in harmony with and claims to be a son of or associate to the One God. Hence Solomon had to expressly state that there is only one God who has no son or

[276] Gen. 6.2.
[277] Prov. 24.21.
[278] I. e., by indirection and not expressly.
[279] Eccl. 4.8.

brother who shares his divinity. This is expressly a reference to Jesus who claimed to be the son of God, sharing the rule with his father.

In this sense we must also understand the passage from Yelamdenu cited in *Or Zarua*[280] which reads as follows: אמרו בילמדנו פ' שמע ישראל רבינו הקדוש כשהיה כותב לאנטונינוס היה כותב לו יהודה עבדך שואל בשלומך הוה ירא את השם ועם שונים אל תתערב מהו עם שונים ר' נתן בשם ר' אחא עם אותם שהם אומרים שהם שני אלהות. Here likewise the reference is to Christianity which at the time of Judah Hanasi had not yet accepted the trinity but believed in a dualism of Jesus and God. Wohlman in *Hatekufah* XIX is mistaken when he assumes that it refers to Gnostics or Judeo-Christians only. Why mix up Gnostics with Christians and limit this belief in dualism to Judeo-Christians only, when Christians in general believed that Jesus was like God, so that they practically believed in two gods.

Perhaps we ought to mention here a possible, though very doubtful, reference to Jesus in Tractate Semaḥot.[281] The passage reads: ראוין היו ישראל ליפול בחרב אילולי עמד בלעם.[282] Brüll[283] commenting on this passage, says: "Es scheint, dass hier eine antichristliche Stelle unterdrückt wurde." And on pages 240–241 Brüll refers to Galatinus who quotes a passage from Tractate Soferim, as follows: ישו הנוצרי נראה משיח ונהרג בבית דין והיה סָבָה שישראל נהרג בחרב. This passage is not found in any of our editions of מסכת סופרים. S. Liberman[284] suggests that סופרים in Galatinus is a mistake for שופטים and the passage is a quotation not from Tractate Soferim but from Maimonides' *Yad*, ספר שופטים, where in Chapter XI of הלכות מלכים the passage is actually found in the Constantinople edition and reads: אף אותו האיש שדמה שיהיה משיח ונהרג בבית דין וכו' וזה גרם לאבד ישראל בחרב.

Perhaps the passage in Mishnah Soṭah 9.15 בעקבות משיחא חוצפא יסגא . . . והמלכות תהפך למינות is a later insertion referring

---

[280] (Zitomir, 1862), p. 7, דף ד' אלפא ביתא 20.
[281] Ed. Higger, (New York, 1931), Chap. VIII, p. 163.
[282] Our text has פלוני hence it has been assumed that בלעם or פלוני is a surname for Jesus. See however above.
[283] *Jahrbücher* I, 53.
[284] In קרית ספר XV (1938), 60.

to the conversion of Constantine to Christianity and the meaning of בעקבות משיחא is: As the result of that *"would be* Messiah," referring to Jesus, who claimed to be the Messiah.

This, to my knowledge, concludes the list of all passages in Talmud and Midrashim where a reference or an allusion to Jesus himself can be found or read into.

We shall now proceed to a consideration of passages in which an express reference or a veiled allusion may be found to the disciples or followers of Jesus, or to Christians in general. The first such passage to be considered is the one cited in the form of a Baraita in b. Sanh. 43a (omitted in our editions but found in חסרונות) which reads as follows:[285] תני רבנן חמשה תלמידים היו לו לישו (מ. לישו הנוצרי) מתאי נקאי (מ. נקי מתי) נצר (מ>) ובונה (מ. בוני) ותודה איתוהי למתי אמר להו מתי יהרג הכתיב (מ. והא כתיב) מתי אבוא ואראה פני אלקים? אמרו לו (מ. ליה) אין מתי יהרג (מ. >) דכתיב מתי ימות ואבד שמו. אתיוהו לנקאי אמר להו נקאי יהרג הכתיב ונקי וצדיק אל תהרוג? אמרו לו אין נקאי יהרג במסתרים יהרג נקי אתיוהו לנצר אמר להו נצר יהרג הכתיב ונצר משרשיו יפרח?[286] אמרו ליה אין נצר יהרג דכתיב ואתה השלכת מקברך כנצר נתעב. אתיוהו לבוני אמר להו בוני יהרג הכתיב בני בכורי ישראל? אמרו ליה אין בוני יהרג (מ. >) דכתיב הנה אנכי הורג את בנך בכורך. אתיוהו לתודה אמר להו תודה יהרג הכתיב מזמור לתודה? אמרו ליה אין תודה יהרג דכתיב זובח תודה יכבדני.

That this whole account, though stated in form of a Baraita is of a later date and peculiarly legendary in character is evident from the artificial meaning assumed for the proper names and from the twisted childish interpretation given to the verse cited by the opposing parties. The first strange feature to be noticed in this legendary account is that it mentions only five names and says that Jesus had five, not twelve disciples.[287] This, however, may be explained by assuming that the author or authors of this legend may not have heard or known of more than five. More likely, however, it is to be assumed that the author mentions only these five because he had clever interpretations of

---

[285] This passage is quoted in Yalkuṭ Makiri to Isa. 11, p. 84, with a few different readings. The variants are indicated here in the text in parenthesis.

[286] מ has only the defense verse of נצר. All the rest referring to him is omitted.

[287] Cf. also Laible, *op. cit.*, 68.

verses, suggesting that people by these names, who claimed special distinctions or privileges because of their significant names, actually should be punished by death. It is also possible that these five disciples were regarded as the most prominent, hence these alone are mentioned without in any way implying that Jesus had only five disciples. In the same manner Ab. 2.8 mentions that Johanan b. Zakkai had five disciples, but this certainly does not mean that he had only these five disciples.[288] These five are mentioned because they were outstanding and because the Mishnah wants to record the characterizing remarks the master made about each one of them.

It may also be that in Jewish circles they would purposely avoid speaking of the twelve apostles or disciples of Jesus, in order not to support the claim made, or at any rate implied, in the N. T. that the number of the disciples of Jesus corresponded to the number of the tribes of Israel, all of whom were expected to be restored by the Messiah. The apostles themselves were very eager to have this number of their group complete.[289] The purpose of having twelve apostles was to make them correspond to and represent the twelve tribes of Israel, each tribe to have one apostle.[290] The idea, no doubt, was that if Jesus was the Messiah he would bring home the lost ten tribes and restore the ancient Kingdom of David.[291] It may also be that the number twelve was chosen to provide a resemblance between Jesus and his twelve disciples and Moses and the twelve princes שנים עשר נשיאים. In the same manner that Moses was commanded by God: "Gather unto me seventy men . . . . . and they shall bear the burden of the people with thee,"[292] Jesus was declared to have

[288] Cf. also the number "five" in the account of the 5 pupils of R. Akiba ordained by Judah b. Baba, (Sanh. 14a).

[289] See Acts 1.26 where it is reported that Matthias was substituted for Judas Iscariot "and he was numbered with the 11 apostles," that is he completed the number 12, of which the apostles should consist.

[290] See Matth. 19.28 "Ye also shall sit upon 12 thrones, judging the 12 tribes of Israel," and likewise Luke 22.30 "that ye may eat and drink at my table in my kingdom and ye shall sit on thrones judging the 12 tribes of Israel."

[291] Cf. also the superscription of the Epistle of James, saying it was addressed "to the twelve tribes which are of the dispersion."

[292] Num. 11.16–17.

had seventy disciples, thus having a Sanhedrin like Moses.[293] The Jews, of course, would not regard Jesus as being in any way like Moses and they would, therefore, not refer to the twelve and the seventy, which would emphasize the parallel to Moses.

Now let us see whether we can identify any or all of the five disciples, mentioned in the Baraita, with some of the disciples or apostles known to us from the N. T. First, we must ascertain the names of the twelve apostles, as given in the N. T. records. According to Matth. 10, they were (1) Peter-Simon; (2) Andrew; (3) James (Jacobus) the son of Zebedee; (4) John, the son of Zebedee; (5) Philip; (6) Bartholomew; (7) Thomas; (8) Matthew the publican; (9) James (Jacobus) the son of Alpheus; (10) Thaddeus; (11) Simon the Cananaean;[294] (12) Judas Iscariot. In Mark 3.17 the two sons of Zebedee, James and John were "surnamed Boanerges which is Sons of Thunder."[295] In Luke 6.16 and Acts 1.13 Thaddeus is called Judas, the son of James. In John 1.42 Simon is called Cephas כיפא meaning "rock" which is the same as Peter.[296] In John 21.2, Thomas is called Didymus, (the twin) and Nathanael of Cana in Galilee is mentioned as the name of the person known in Matthew as Bartholomew. According to Acts 1.26 the twelfth was Matthias who took the place of Judas Iscariot. These are all the names of the Apostles known from the N. T. records. Now of all these names we can definitely recognize and identify among the five mentioned in our Baraita, only two, i. e., Matthew מתי, which may be either Matthew the Publican or Matthias, the successor or substitute of Judas Iscariot, and Thaddeus here called תודה. The other names mentioned in our Baraita are difficult, if not impossible, to identify with any of the names known from the N. T. records,

---

[293] See Luke 10.1: "The Lord appointed 70 others (besides the 12) and sent them two by two before his face." Also "and the 70 returned with joy" (*ibid.*, 17). Cf. also Eusebius, *Church History*, Book I, ch. 28, English translation by C. F. Cruse, (London, 1851), p. 28.

[294] Of Cana? or קנא =Zealot, as in Acts 1.13.

[295] Is there a possibility in "Boni" בוני, an echo of בני רוגז? Our author would hardly have left out an allusion to the second part of the name רוגז!

[296] See John 21.2.

JESUS IN THE TALMUD 557

or in the case of some even with proper names current among the Jews of N. T. times.

Buni or Boni בוני is a name mentioned in b. Ta'an. 19b-20a as having been the proper name of Naḳdimon b. Gorion נקדימון בן גוריון. This latter name is explained as having been a nickname, recalling the miracle that happened to and through him נקדימון שנקדרה לו חמה, "he was called Naḳdimon because the sun broke through on his behalf." This בוני־נקדימון lived around the year 70 C. E. and, considering the high regard in which he was held by the Jews, he cannot be identified with the Boni in our Baraita who was reprted to have been killed for being one of the disciples of Jesus.[297] Of course, as has already been suggested above בוני may be an echo of the name of one of the בני רוגז, a designation of the sons of Zebedee.[298] But it would be strange to assume that a Jewish author, mentioning one of the sons of Zebedee by his surname, Boanerges, should leave out that part of the surname, the word רוגז, which would have lent itself to an exchange of fancifully applied verses advocating his acquittal, e. g., ברוגז רחם תזכור[299] as well as his condemnation, e. g., וברוגז יגמא ארץ[300].

The name נקאי Nakai or Naki or Niki is peculiar and difficult. It may be a shorter form of Nicolaus, Nicodemus, or Nikanor. All these names in their full form occur in N. T. records, though not as a name of one of the apostles. Nicanor and Nicolaus are mentioned in Acts 6.5 as followers of Jesus, having been chosen and ordained (?) by the apostles. Nikai shortened from Nicolaus may be an allusion to the founder or leader of the Nicolaitans.[301] Again, Nikai, a short form of Nicodemus may refer to the Nicodemus in John 3, referred to above, or to another Nicodemus known in Christian circles. There is an Evangelium of Nicodemus

---

[297] Some scholars have indeed identified our Buni with Nicodemus of the Gospel of John, (3.1, 4, 9). See Laible, *op. cit.*, 70.

[298] Klausner, p. 20, assumes indeed that בוני is a corrupted form from יוחנן or יואני, the son of Zebedee. See against him A. S. Kaminetzki in *Hatekufah* XVIII, 512. Might not בוני be a corrupted form of אביוני?

[299] Hab. 3.2.

[300] Job 39.24.

[301] Revelations 2.6 and 15. See Laible, *op. cit.*, 71.

also called *Acta Pilati*.³⁰² This Gospel of Nicodemus is said to have been written originally in Hebrew. The Jews may have heard of this author of a gospel; hence they took him to have been one of the disciples of Jesus and mentioned him by a shortened form of his name, Niki, together with Mattai, another disciple credited with the authorship of a gospel.

Nakai or Niki as a proper name is mentioned in p. Ma'as. Sh. 5.2 (56a). A man by that name, said to have been warden שמש, or scribe and teacher ואית דאמרין ספר הוה in Magdala Zabuaya, is reported to have gone up to the Temple לבית המקדש (in a miraculous way?) on every Friday and to have returned to his home before the beginning of the Sabbath. According to this story, this Nakai lived in Temple times. In Gen. r. 79.6 a teacher by the name of Nakai also of מגדלא דצבועיא is said to have lived in the time of Simon b. Yoḥai, around 150 C. E., so he could not have been the same as the one mentioned in p. Ma'aser Sheni who lived in Temple times. There is something strange and legendary about this man Nakai. Is מגדלא identical with the town or village Magdala and דצבועיא a surname characterizing a certain class of people, either hypocrites צבועים or Baptists צבע? Or is מגדלא merely a "tower," designating the seat of these people, which may have been not far from the Temple and one could easily go from this tower to Temple in a short time, or is it identical with אנשי הר צבועים.³⁰³

Of course, it is also possible, since the letters ל and נ are interchangeable, that Nakai is here read for לקי and Luke is meant.³⁰⁴ Of course, in this case it need not nor can it be a textual mistake, since in the Baraita the verses cited contain the word נקי. It is possible that the writer had heard of a Luke, the author of a Gospel, whom he believed to have been, like Matthew, a disciple of Jesus, and he pronounced his name נקי. It is strange though

---

³⁰² See Hennecke, *N. T. Apocryphen*, 77. It is printed as "The Gospel of Nicodemus" in *Excluded Books of the New Testament*, (New York, 1927), 51 ff.

³⁰³ See Hirschenson, שבע חכמות, 152.

³⁰⁴ Krauss, *op. cit.*, 57, note 3: Klausner, *op. cit.*, 4th ed. (1933), 20; also Grünwald in his "Eine neue Ethymologie des Wortes נצר=Nazaräer" in Rahmer's *Literaturblatt* XXII, (1893), No. 9, 35. Anm. 2, where he says: "Statt נקי wird wohl לקי zu lesen u. Lucas gemeint sein."

JESUS IN THE TALMUD   559

that they did not make a pun on his name Luke, like לוקה, i. e., should receive punishment.

The name נצר is probably merely an allusion to the name Nazarene = Christian, not a corrupted form from Andrew as assumed by Klausner.[305] But it is strange that the verse ונצר משרשיו should be applied to or claimed by a disciple, when it was understood to refer to the Master. Considering that in Makiri the whole passage about נצר is missing and the verse is cited in connection with נקי it is perhaps possible that נצר = Nacar is identical with Nakai, the "c" being pronounced and written as a ק, as in Caesar, קיסר. And the ר at the end is merely an enlarged י. This would remove the difficulty of a disciple being called נצר which designation belongs to Jesus himself, either because he came from Nazareth or because he was believed to have been referred to in the verse ונצר משרשיו יפרח.

It should be added, that according to Laible[306] our Baraita has no reference to the apostles but to some followers of Jesus, i. e., Christians who were persecuted and killed in the time of Akiba and Bar Kochba.[307]

A disciple of Jesus by the name of Jacobus of the village of Sekanya[308] is reported to have had a discussion with R. Eliezer b. Hyrcanus in which he repeated halakic teaching he had learned from his master Jesus. Whether this Jacob of Kefar Sekanya is identical with Jacob of Kefar Sama and whether he was a disciple of Jesus himself or merely a disciple's disciple cannot be definitely decided, though Klausner[309] assumes that Jacob of Sekanya was a disciple of Jesus and is perhaps identical with James, the brother of Jesus.

Disciples or apostles are believed by some scholars to be found mentioned in the Talmud under disguised names. Thus A. S. Weissman[310] would identify the "other person" איניש אחרינא

---

[305] *Loc. cit.* See against him A. S. Kaminetzki in *HaTekufah* XVIII, 512.
[306] *Op. cit.*, 68, 69.
[307] See against this Klausner, *op. cit.*, 20, and cf. Herford, *op. cit.*, 91–95.
[308] b. 'Ab. Zarah 17a, see reading in דקדוקי סופרים; also 27a and Tosefta Ḥul. 2.24. For a fuller discussion of this person see below p. 563.
[309] See below p. 563, note 329.
[310] Rahmer's *Litteraturblatt* VII, (1879), No. 28, 109–110.

mentioned in b. Sanh. 11a as having intruded into the meeting called by R. Gamaliel, with Saul-Paul who, after having changed, was designated as "another person" אינש אחרינא or אחר. But this is a mistake. Saul-Paul was, or claimed to have been, a disciple of R. Gamaliel the elder in the time of the Temple, while the אינש אחרינא mentioned in Sanhedrin intruded into a meeting called by Gamaliel II of Jabneh.

Some scholars would see in the names אחיתופל, גיחזי, דואג mentioned in the Mishnah Sanhedrin 9 (90a) designations, or epithets, for some of the disciples of Jesus. If Balaam mentioned there in the Mishnah refers to Jesus, as assumed by some scholars, then the other three הדיוטות mentioned with him must likewise be assumed to be, not the Biblical persons by these names, but disguised references to associates or disciples of Jesus. Of course, there is no reason for not taking these names as actually designating the Biblical persons. These men, Ahitophel and Gehazi and Doeg were Jews and could well be discussed in the Mishnah as exceptions to the כל ישראל who have a share in the world to come. But the company of Balaam with whom these three men are mentioned caused some scholars to see in them not Biblical persons but associates of Jesus. I shall quote and discuss these theories, incorrect though they may be, and I shall take up these names in the historical order and in the order in which they are mentioned in the Mishnah: (1) Doeg, (2) Ahitophel, (3) Gehazi. These three names are assumed to refer to (1) Peter, (2) James, and (3) John.[311]

1. Doeg. Some people[312] suggest that Doeg is a surname of Peter who was a fisherman and whom Jesus promised to make a "fisher of men."[313] This implies the pronounciation of דואג like דּוָיָג=צייד דגים. To this I could add that perhaps האדומי suggests, not the Edomite but אדם man, thus specifying the "fisher of men." But on the same ground Andrew, the brother of Peter,

---

[311] See Gustav Rösch in *Theologische Studien und Kritiken*, (1878), 516–521, as to the reasons given for these identifications. See also Laible, *op. cit.*, 54.

[312] See Jacob Ezekiel Löwy, *Kritisch-Talmudisches Lexicon*, (Wien, 1863), 112. Perhaps Rosch, *loc. cit.*, has the same reason for identifying Doeg with Peter.

[313] Matth. 4.18–22.

who also was a fisherman and whom Jesus likewise promised to make a "fisher of men"[314] could also be designated as דויג האדומי. And Doeg could also refer to either John or James, the sons of Zebedee who likewise were "fishermen." Herford[315] suggests that Doeg designates Judas Iscariot who betrayed the Messiah Jesus, just as Doeg betrayed David.[316] But the comparison is lame. David escaped the danger involved in the betrayal while Jesus succumbed to or was the victim of the betrayal by Judas. Furthermore, as Herford himself asks, why should Judas have been so strongly condemned by the Rabbis for his act, so as to declare him to be deprived of a share in the world to come. Did the Rabbis of the second century (time of the Mishnah) already feel that the betrayal which caused the death of Jesus and hence subsequently all the accusations against the Jews, entailing so much suffering, was a sin to deprive one of his share in the world to come? We could just as well suggest that Ahitophel who betrayed David and joined his enemy Absalom and later committed suicide[317] designates Judas Iscariot who betrayed Jesus and then committed suicide. The dissimilarity between the two betrayers, however, is that Ahitophel failed and committed suicide because of the failure of his plot while Judas succeeded in his plot and committed suicide out of remorse, not because of failure. Herford[318] also thinks that Doeg may be identical with James who was a fisherman, and Ahitophel designates Peter, because the high position held by Ahitophel resembles the position held by Peter, and Gehazi may be a designation of Paul, the renegade. But Herford concludes that Ahitophel is Peter; Doeg, Judas Iscariot; and Gehazi, Paul.[319]

2. Ahitophel. As already mentioned above, it could be Judas Iscariot who is so designated, though Herford would

---

[314] *Ibid.* [315] *Op. cit.*
[316] I Sam. 22.9.
[317] II Sam. 17.23.
[318] *Ibid.*
[319] On Paul see Gerhard Kittel in *Arbeiten zur Religionsgeschichte des Urchristentums*, Bd. I, Heft 3, (Leipzig, 1920), under the heading "Rabbinica, Paulus im Talmud, etc." Kittel also discusses there the Mishnah 'Ab. 3.2, המפר בריתו..., see also Weiss, *Dor*, I, 232.

identify him with Peter. But Löwy[320] also Rösch[321] who perhaps read Löwy though he does not mention it, takes him to be James, the brother of Jesus. The name Ahitophel is taken to be a composite of אחי "brother" and תופל which is assumed to be *theofilius*, i. e., בן אלהים so that the name means "the brother of [him who calls himself] the son of God." But in the first place why should James be so condemned? Secondly, the Rabbis would not even thus indirectly acknowledge Jesus as the son of God or even refer to him as such. Against this, however, it could be argued that the Rabbis may have taken תופל to be like תיפלה, "frivolity" or "unseemliness," a fault of the false prophets of Samaria[322] or תָּפֵל, "delusion," which the false prophets are accused of having seen,[323] thus referring to James as the brother of the false prophet or of the prophet of delusions. But any such interpretation of the name Ahitophel, though ingenious, is far fetched and incorrect, although Löwy cleverly interprets the Baraita in B. B. 147a as fitting James the brother of Jesus who was the head of the church of Jerusalem.

The Baraita reads as follows: שלשה דברים צוה אחיתופל לבניו אל תהיו במחלוקת ואל תמרדו במלכות בית דוד וכשעצרת ברור זרעו חטים. The meaning according to Löwy is this: he told his spiritual sons, the members of the church, (1) keep united; (2) believe in the Davidic kingdom, i. e., in Jesus' messiahship and that his kingdom is not of this world; (3) when Pentecost is clear sow your seeds ....i. e., accept proselytes or confirmants by baptism on Whitsunday. This would be an allusion to what is recorded in Acts 2.1–12. This would also explain the remark of Mar Zuṭra[324] בלול איתמר which echoes what is recorded in Acts 2.13: "But others mocking said, 'They are filled with new wine.'" That is, the disciples who talked in different tongues were not filled with the spirit, but were plain drunk, full of spirits and confused. All this is clever but most improbable.

3. Gehazi. We have already mentioned above that this name

[320] *Op. cit.*, 112.
[321] *Loc. cit.*
[322] Jer. 23.13.
[323] Lam. 2.14. See Midrash Lam. r. 2.23.
[324] B. B. 147a.

is regarded by some as an allusion to Paul, the renegade, but there is no reason or justification for this identification.

In. b. 'Ab. Zarah 17a and 27b there is mentioned a certain Jacob of the village of Siknin or *Sekanya*.³²⁵ In *Dikduke Soferim* to 'Ab. Zarah 17a and in הגדות התלמוד Constantinople, 1511³²⁶ there are added the words אחד מתלמידי ישו הנוצרי.³²⁷ In הגדות התלמוד, this Jacob quotes his teaching as having received it from Jesus כך לימדני ישו הנוצרי and in En Jacob³²⁸ it reads כך אמר לי ישוע. From this it would seem that Jacob was a disciple of Jesus.³²⁹ But since the encounter of this Jacob with R. Eliezer b. Hyrcanus and also with Ben Doma, the nephew of R. Ishmael must have been around the year 100, this Jacob must have attained an exceptionally old age, if he had been a direct disciple of Jesus. Most likely, however, the words אחד מתלמידי means, one of the followers, not a direct disciple, and the reading in the Tosefta, משום ישוע, suggests that Jacob did not receive the teaching directly from Jesus. The words כך לימדני need not mean "taught me personally." And כך אמר לי is but a later change from כך לימדני.

A follower of Jesus, though by no means a direct disciple is mentioned in p. Shab. 14.4 (14d) and Kohelet r. to 10.5 in the story of the grandchild of Joshua b. Levi who choked on something he had swallowed. According to the story, they brought in one of the followers of Bar Pandera to assist them, אזל ואייתי חד מן אילין דבר פנדירא לאפקא בלעיה. This Christian was probably called in as a physician to pull out what the child had swallowed, but instead he used magic or recited certain verses, which displeased Joshua b. Levi so much that he would have preferred to have the child die rather than have such a verse recited over him, אמר והוה נייח ליה דקבריה ולא הוה אמר עלוי הדין פסוקה. This whole question of performing *cures* by reciting verses or incan-

---

³²⁵ See above.

³²⁶ Cited by Chwolson, *Das Letzte Passahmahl*, 100, note 1.

³²⁷ Probably this disciple or follower is identical with Jacob of Kefar Sekanya mentioned in in Ḥul. 2.22 and p. 'Ab. Zarah 2 (40d).

³²⁸ Ed. Saloniki.

³²⁹ Klausner 30–31 assumes that he is identical with James the brother of Jesus. But James was killed and it is now here mentioned that he reached an exceptionally old age.

tations requires a careful study into which I cannot enter here. But it certainly has some connection with the attitude toward the early Christians who apparently pursued such practices. Thus it may be that the saying in the M. Sanh. 10.1 that הלוחש על המכה ואומר כל המחלה אשר שמתי במצרים לא אשים עליך כי אני יי רופאך[330] is also among those who have no share in the world to come, may have reference to Christians, who may have applied the words "I the Lord am thy healer" to their Lord Jesus in whose name they were performing the alleged cures. The comment of R. Joḥanan[331] וברוקק בה לפי שאין מזכירין שם שמים על הרקיקה may be an allusion to the baptism or "sprinkling," רקיקה being a derogatory or contemptuous circumlocution of זריקה. Such an explanation would remove the conflict with the practice of Joshua b. Levi to recite Ps. 91[332] though he strongly objected to the לוחש על המכה even though it consisted in reciting Scriptural verses[333] and with the saying of R. Joḥanan in b. Shab. 67a permitting the recitation of verses over a fever sickness, since, of course, as R. Joḥanan said, the objection was only to those who combine זריקה or רקיקה with the recitation. People not suspected of Christianity could well have recited verses over sickness.

An allusion to Christians may be found in the Midrash Kohelet r. to 1.8 in the story of Ḥananiah the nephew of R. Joshua b. Ḥananiah who went to Kefar Naḥum where the מינאי = Heretics did something to him and led him openly to violate the Sabbath laws. Then there follows in the Midrash a story of a pupil of R. Jonathan who ran away from his teacher and went to the מינאי and when R. Jonathan went after him to bring him back he found him (or them?) engaged in some evil practice or immoral doings. The passage reads as follows: חנינה בן אחי ר' יהושע אזל להדיה כפר נחום ועבדון ליה מינאי מלה ועלון יתיה רכיב חמרא בשבתא . . . . ר' יונתן. ערק חד מן תלמידיו לגביהון אזל ואשכחיה עבד בן אפטוניות שלחון מיניא שתריה כך אמרין ליה ולא כך כתיב גורלך תפיל בתוכנו כיס אחד יהיה לכולנו והוה פרח ואינון פרחין בתריהון אמרין ליה

[330] This is the continuation of the saying of R. Akiba אף הקורא בספרים החיצונים which suggests that it was directed against heretics or the Christians.
[331] Sanh. 101a.
[332] b. Shebu. 15b.
[333] See p. Sanh. 10.1 (28b)

ר' איתא גמול חסדא להדא כלתא הלך ומצאן עסוקין בריבה אחת אמר לון
כן ארחיהון דיהודאי עבדין. אמרי ליה ולא כן כתיב בתורה גורלך תפיל
בתוכנו כיס וגו' והוה פרח ואינון פרחין בתריה עד דמטא לתרע וטרד באפיהון.
אמרין ר' יונתן אזיל נלוג לאמך דלא הפכת ולא איסתכלת בן דאילו הפכת
ואיסתכלת בן יותר מן מה דהוינן פרחין בתרך הוית פריח בתרן. ר' יהודה
בן נקוסה היו המינים מתעסקים עמו היו שואלים אותו ומשיב שואלין אותו
ומשיב. אמר לון על מגן אתון מגיבין אתון נעביד בינינן דכל בר נש דנצח
חבריה יהא פצע מוחיה דחבריה בקורנס והוא נצח לון ופצע מוחיהון עד
דאתמלאון פיצעין פיצעין. וכיון דאתא אמרין ליה תלמידוי רמי סייעוך מן
השמים ונצחת. אמר לון ועל מגן לכו והתפללו על אותו האיש ועל אותה החמת
שהיתה מלאה אבנים טובות ומרגליות אבל עכשיו מלאה פחמין...

This passage is the subject of much discussion among scholars and the commentators give many different interpretations, some of which I will cite here though none, however, is completely satisfactory. I will cite and consider here some of these.

Graetz[334] identifies these מינאי with the Nicolaitans. He seems to understand the phrase איתא גמול חסדא לחדא כלתא with which these heretics invited R. Jonathan, to mean, that he should make love to the bride, and like them have intercourse with her. And the phrase עסוקין בריבה אחת, then, means they were engaged in immoral practices with a certain girl. The phrase כיס אחד לכולנו possibly would also have an allusion to the fact that this bride or girl was the common possession of all of them.[335] Against Graetz see Chwolson[336] who thinks that it was simply an invitation to perform a charitable deed מצות הכנסת כלה. They sought to deceive R. Jonathan and cause him to come to them, by pretending that they wanted him to help in some wedding ceremonies. The most obscure and difficult expression in this passage is עבד בן אפטוניות. Perles[337] says: "Ich denke an *optio*, ὀπτίων — Leutnant, Verpflegungsofficier."[338] It may also mean, assistant to or vice-general, the one who takes the place of the general commander. The meaning then here might be: He made or recognized the son, עבד בן or a son, as an assistant or associate

---

[334] *Geschichte* IV, 4th ed., (1908), 92.
[335] See also the commentaries מתנת כהנים and יפה תואר, *ad loc.*
[336] *Das Letzte Passahmahl*, 104, note.
[337] *Ethymologische Studien*, 103, *s. v.*, אבטיונא.
[338] Cf. *Aruk*, *s. v.*, אָבְטִיוּנָס.

to God, that is, he believed Jesus to be the son of God, sharing authority with or substituting for the father. But elsewhere Perles[339] gives a different explanation, taking אפטוניות to be like πουτάνα=harlot. Accordingly it would mean, he practiced harlotry with them (בהן=ב הן), or he committed sodomy with them. Possibly the meaning of the passage would be, "he found him worshipping the son of the harlot," עובד (ל)בן אפטוניות. This then would be a reference to Jesus by the name of ברא דזניתא[340] and it would practically result the same as the interpretation of the word as *optio*. I might also suggest that אפטוניות is identical with πιθανός, i. e., persuading, convincing, and the sense would be that R. Jonathan found the pupil among the heretics, and he, Jonathan, then did some arguing, or attempted to persuade them. This would explain why they again tried to entice Jonathan to come to them for at their first meeting he was successful in his arguments with them.

Dr. Adolph Honig[341] explains the phrase עבד בן אפטוניות to mean he practiced with or among them "ophitische Orgien," excesses of the Ophites. Im. Deutsch[342] assumes the word אפטוניות to be like πύθωνες, ventriloquist. He says: "Es ist möglich dass man bei Orgien und wüsten Ausschreitungen zur Tauschung der unschuldingen Opfer, die man anlocken wollte, das verfahren der πύθωνες, Bauchredner einschlug." Goldfahn in Rahmer's *Literaturblatt*,[343] argues against Perles' interpretation of the word אפטוניות as πουτάνα=harlot. He takes the word to be like ἀπείθεια rebellion, disobedience so that עבד בן אפטוניות would mean he becomes υἱὸς τῆς ἀπειθείας i. e., נעשה בן מְרִי or ἀπειθοῦντες rebellious, denying, ungehorsam = מאין = מין, den Gehorsam verweigern בן מְרִי.[344] Kohut[345] identifies it with the Greek ὑπεύθυνος, responsible or accountable and translates our passage "zog ihn zur Rechenschaft," "he made him account for

---

[339] *MGWJ*, (1892), 272.
[340] See above.
[341] *Die Ophiten*, (Berlin, 1899), 79 ff.
[342] Rahmer's *Literaturblatt* XIX, (1890), No. 28.
[343] *Ibid.*, 162.
[344] Cf. also Sachs, *Beiträge*, I, 168 and II, 140.
[345] *Aruk Completum* I, 211, s. v. אַפְּטוּנִיוֹת.

his conduct" (or if we read בהן = בָּן not בָּן made *them* responsible). He also suggests, without quoting Perles, that it may mean πουτάνα (late Greek) = harlot, and he translates it, בן הזונות i. e., he became a רועה זונות.³⁴⁶

We now come to a consideration of the name מין, pl., מינים which in some instances may designate Christians and in some passages may simply refer to heretics of any kind.³⁴⁷ As to the meaning or etymology of the word מין, it may simply mean genus, species or kind, and may designate any group or class of people within the larger group of the people i. e., among the Jews, and would then designate one who belongs to any Jewish sect, or special group of the Jewish people different or separate from כלל ישראל. Hence, in later times, when the whole Jewish people followed the Pharisees, a Saducean was considered as one who did not belong to כלל ישראל, and therefore was designated as a מין. Perhaps the saying in Ḥullin 13b אין מינים באומות originally meant that among non-Jews we cannot distinguish one from the other and cannot designate one small group as being separated or different from the larger group. Since the larger group likewise has no correct beliefs, we cannot characterize one group with different beliefs as heretic. Among the Gentiles those with correct beliefs are rather the exception and are designated as צדיקי (חסידי) אומות העולם. The Gemara in Ḥullin³⁴⁸ however misunderstood the original meaning of this statement.

Some scholars, however, take the word מין to be like מאין, denier, one who refuses to accept the correct beliefs. Others consider the word as shortened from מאמין "believer." Since the heretics called themselves true believers מאמינים the Rabbis shortened the term and referred to them as מינין.³⁴⁹

The name נוצרים occurs in b. Ta'an. 27b where it designates the Christians who observe Sunday.³⁵⁰

---

³⁴⁶ Cf. further Lewy, Jastrow, Krauss' *Lehnwörter*, and Fürst.
³⁴⁷ See especially Graetz, *Geschichte* IV, 4th ed., 400, note 11.
³⁴⁸ *Loc. cit.*
³⁴⁹ Cf. Kohut, in *Aruk Completum* V, 168–169, *s. v.*, מן חסרונות.
³⁵⁰ See Rashi *ad loc.* יום טוב שלהם (יום א'), מפני הנוצרים שעושין אותו, as to the derivation of his name, whether from Nazareth or from נוצר = נוטר = שומר, see above.

Another possible reference to the Christians who keep the Sunday as their Sabbath may be found in b. Ab. Zarah 6a and also 7b in the saying of Samuel: חסרונות) יום נוצרי אמר שמואל בהוצאות שלנו אחד) לדברי ר' ישמעאל לעולם אסור. In the Munich manuscript the word יום is omitted. Perhaps we ought to read עם instead of יום, the meaning being that in the case of Christians who observe the first day of the week, were we to prohibit three additional days before and three after the Holiday, it would always be forbidden to do business with them. Further, the passage may originally have been meant as a question: עם נוצרים לעולם אסור? Is it forbidden to do business with a Christian at any time? That the reference is to Sunday, even with this emendation is evident from the rest of the Gemara והאיכא ארבעה וחמישה דשרי. As a curiosum we may cite here an apologetic etymology of this name, probably intended to fool the censor. Grunwald in his article in Rahmer's *Literaturblatt* referred to above, quotes from a התנצלות contained in an old מחזור printed in Prague in 1680 which explains נוצרים as referring to the followers of Nebuchadnezar i. e., ancient Babylonians. It says: והם אשר נקראים מקדם דרך כלל הנוצרים כי מלכם בראשם נקרא נבוכדנצר ועל שמו נקראו נוצרים.

Probably the philosopher mentioned in b. Shab. 116b as an arbiter between R. Gamaliel and his sister in a dispute about their inheritance was a Christian, since he seems to refer to the New Testament or quotes a passage from one of the original Gospels, for the אורייתא אחריתא no doubt means the new covenant or N. T. even though the passage quoted from that "other law" is not found in our version of the Gospels.[351] The question as to whether a daughter may inherit may have been a veiled attack on Jesus who could trace his descent from David through his mother only. Hence if a daughter cannot inherit, Jesus could not be the heir of David and had no claim to the Messiaship.[352]

A reference to Christians is seen by some scholars in the two

---

[351] See M. Güdeman, *Religionsgeschichtliche Studien*, (Leipzig, 1876), 65 ff.

[352] The N. T. genealogies trace the descent through Joseph, but of course since he was not Jesus's father, Jesus could not claim Davidic descent through him.

names for groups or assemblies of heretics בי אבידן and בי נצרפי mentioned in the Talmud. I quote here these three passages in full. The first passage is the one in b. Shab. 152a which reads as follows: אמר ליה קיסר לר' יהושע בן חנניה מ"ט לא אתית לבי אבידן אמר ליה טור תלג מחרוני גלידין כלבוהי לא נבחין טחנוהי לא טוחנין. This then was about 100 C. E. when the emperor referred to this institution.

When Eleazar b. Perata, a Tanna of the younger group of the second generation, in first half of the second century, was arrested together with Ḥananiah ben Tradyon and charged with disregarding the Roman decreees, one of the questions asked of him or one of the charges against him was that he neglected to attend the meetings at the בי אבידן. The passage reads: אמרו לו ומאי טעמא לא אתית לבי אבידן אמר להו זקן הייתי ומתיירא אני שמא תרמסוני ברגליכם.[353]

The third passage is found in b. Shab. 116a and reads as follows: בעי מיניה יוסף בר חנין מר' אבהו הני ספרי דבי אבידן מצילין אותן מפני הדליקה או אין מצילין אין ולאו ורפיא בידיה רב לא אזיל לבי אבידן וכ"ש לבי נצרפי שמואל לבי נצרפי לא אזיל לבי אבידן אזיל אמרו ליה לרבא מ"ט לא אתית לבי נצרפי אמר להו דיקלא פלניא איכא באורחא וקשי לי ניעקריה דוכתיה קשי לי מר בר יוסף אמר אנא מינייהו אנא ולא מסתפינא מינייהו זימנא חדא אזיל בעו לסכוניה... Here there is mentioned besides the בי אבידן also the בי נצרפי which latter may have been only in Babylon in the time of Rab and Samuel, i. e., the first half of the third century. But the בי אבידן must have been an institution, both in Babylon during first half of the third century as well as in Palestine during the first half of the second century. We must keep this fact in mind, for any explanation of the term must fit an institution that existed in both countries and in the different periods of time from about 100 to 250 C. E.[354] Of all the interpretations only one, that of Löw[355] who takes

---

[353] b. 'Ab. Zarah 17b.

[354] For the various interpretations see among others: S. J. Rappoport in ערך מלים (ed. תכונה, Warsaw, 1914), 6; L. Ginzberg, *MGWJ*, LXXVIII, 28; Scheftelowitz, *Die Entstehung der Manichäischen Religion*, (Giessen, 1922), 3; Kohut, *Aruk Completum*, *s. v.*; B. Geiger in תוספות הערוך השלם (Wien, 1937), 84; *Hamburger Realencyclopädie*, II, 95–96; Israel Horowitz, ארץ ישראל ושכנותיה (Wien, 1923), 111, *s. v.*, בי אבידן, and 112, *s. v.*, בי נצרפי; Krauss, *op. cit.*, 255; Herford, *op. cit.*, 165–166.

[355] *HeḤalutz* II, 100–101.

נצרפי as a corrupt form of נצרני, i. e., Christians and אבידן as a corrupt form of אביון designating the Ebionites, also Christians, brings the discussion of these names within the scope of our study.[356] I personally think that these names are deprecatory or cacophemistic forms, substituting for the real names, so as to indicate that those who frequent them are headed for hell אבדון, or most certainly should perish, or in the case of נצרפי, those who should go to purgatory, or who need to be purged. They may have referred to Christians and also to other heretic groups or sects whom we can no longer identify, as their real names are hidden under these ill-wishing disguised designations.

A reference to the Gospels may be found in b. Shab. 116a according to the reading of Dikduke Soferim[357] רבי מאיר קרי ליה און גליון ר' יוחנן קרי ליה עון גליון, and hence the הגליונין mentioned in the Baraita there and Tosefta Shab. 13.5 together with ספרי צדוקים which stands for ספרי מינין may also refer to the *evangelium*, i. e., Gospel, and other Christian writings. The phrase ועליהם הוא אומר ואחרי הדלת והמזוזה שמת זכרונך[358] may refer to the secret meetings held by the Judeo Christians!

---

[356] Is the reference in B. K. 117a לבי אביוני also a reference to the Ebionites?
[357] See חסרונות, *ad loc.*
[358] *Ibid., loc. cit.*